LOUIS SPOHR'S AUTOBIOGRAPHY.

TRANSLATED FROM THE GERMAN.

COPYRIGHT EDITION.

LONDON:
LONGMAN, GREEN, LONGMAN, ROBERTS, & GREEN.
1865.

Louis Spohr

Autobiography.
Translated from the German.

Facsimile of the Copyright edition.

Published Longman, Green, Longman, Roberts & Green 1865
Republished Travis & Emery 2010.

Louis Spohr. (1784-1859). German violinist, conductor and composer.

He was taught by Franz Eck and later practiced with Beethoven. He later worked in Vienna, Frankfurt and Kassel. Highly rated during his lifetime.

More details available from
- Stanley Sadie: The New Grove Dictionary of Music and Musicians.
- http://en.wikipedia.org/wiki/Louis_Spohr

© Travis & Emery 2010.

Published by
Travis & Emery Music Bookshop
17 Cecil Court, London, WC2N 4EZ, United Kingdom.
(+44) 20 7240 2129
neworders@travis-and-emery.com

Vol. 1 Hardback: 978-1-84955-106-9 Paperback: 978-1-84955-107-6
Vol. 2. Hardback: 978-1-84955-108-3 Paperback: 978-1-84955-109-0
Vols. 1 and 2 together - Hardback: 978-1-84955-110-6 Paperback: 978-1-84955-111-3

LOUIS SPOHR'S AUTOBIOGRAPHY.

LOUIS SPOHR'S AUTOBIOGRAPHY.

TRANSLATED FROM THE GERMAN.

COPYRIGHT EDITION.

LONDON:
LONGMAN, GREEN, LONGMAN, ROBERTS, & GREEN.
1865.

PREFACE.

In publishing an English translation of the unadorned yet highly interesting Autobiography of the celebrated Violinist and great Composer *Louis Spohr*, we consider we are but satisfying a natural desire on the part of his many admirers in this country to become more intimately acquainted with both the public and private life of this great musical genius — this noble, manly character, in whom were combined in so high a degree the qualities of the true artist with those of the really great-minded and thoroughly good man.

Although nearly twelve years have elapsed since *Spohr's* last appearance in England, and during that time numberless foreign artists of distinction have visited us and gathered well-earned laurels and golden opinions in these islands; yet still above all *Spohr* shines out a star of the first magnitude, and there are no doubt thousands yet amongst us who were present at the performance of his oratorios, under his direction, at Norwich, or attended his concerts in London, and to whom this Autobiography will be of interest. We have little to say of it here — it speaks for itself. Simple and truthful throughout, it is a mirror of the mind of him who jotted down the details composing the same. Modest and unassuming at the commencement of his career, *Spohr* continued so till the end, notwithstanding the celebrity he achieved and the high position to which he attained. The praises showered upon him neither turned his brain nor puffed him up with pride; and he has left us an example of high morality, great amiability, and bright domestic virtues, too rare alas! among artists and men of genius.

Spohr was a man devoted to his art, and although far from wealthy, often sacrificed his time — which to him, as to most of us, was money — in giving gratuitous instruction to young men of ability too poor to pay for lessons; and not unfrequently has he unhesitatingly dismissed some rich, well-paying, but dull scholar to make way for a poor but talented pupil, in hopes of thereby benefitting his art — and this was his sole reward.

Another prominent trait in *Spohr's* character was his childlike simplicity, combined with never-failing good-nature and an inability to bear malice. Nor did the many unavoidable trials and vexations of a long life ever permanently disturb his good humour or sour his temper; and even gross injustice failed to do more than temporarily ruffle the calm serenity of his soul. Thus he passed through the world, an active and highly useful member of society, beloved and respected by all who knew him, till in process of time he went down to his grave full of years and honour.

As is explained in the text, the Autobiography comes to an end with the month of June 1838; but the description of the life and doings of the great master from that date till the time of his death was continued from reliable materials furnished by Mrs. *Spohr* and other members of the family; so that the whole forms a true account and lively picture of *Spohr's* earthly career from his cradle to his grave.

With these few remarks we submit the work to the perusal and kind consideration of the gentle reader.

London, October 1864.

THE TRANSLATOR.

Chronological Index

of Contents.

Vol. I.

Page

1784 to 1799. *Spohr's* childhood and youth at Seesen and Brunswick. — Musical proclivities, and the instrument of his choice. — His first instructors on the violin. — First attempts at composition. — Sent by his father to Hamburg to seek his fortune. — Disappointed hopes, and return to Brunswick. — Singular interview with the Duke of Brunswick. — Appointed violinist in the court orchestra of the Duke. — Undertakes the musical education of his brother *Ferdinand*. — His admiration of the music of *Mozart*. — Disturbs the Duchess of Brunswick at her party of "ombre" with his "murderous fiddling." . . 1

1802. *Spohr* proceeds with *Franz Eck* to St. Petersburg. — Revisits Hamburg. — Cultivates at intervals his fondness for drawing and painting in water-colours. — His first love. — Dussek. — *Spohr's* first published work, violin concerto *Op. I.* — Stay at Strelitz. — Romantic adventure. — Second capture of *Spohr's* heart. — Königsberg. — St. Petersburg. — Impressions, and incidents during his stay in that Capital. — Returns by sea to Germany. — Arrival at Brunswick 14

1803. Appointed court musician at Brunswick . . . 62

1804. Musical tour to Leipsic, Dresden and Berlin . . . 67

1805. Appointed Concert-Master at Gotha. — Present with Prince *Louis Ferdinand* at the military manœuvres at Magdeburg 84

1806. Marriage of *Spohr* with *Dorette Scheidler* . . . 95

		Page
1807.	Musical tour to Weimar, Leipsic, Dresden, Prague, Munich, Frankfort, Stuttgard and Heidelberg	101
1808.	Pedestrian tour through the Harz with his pupils	112
	Composes his opera of "Alruna"	115
	Congress at Erfurt	117
1809.	Musical tour to Leipsic, Breslau, Berlin and Hamburg	128
1810.	Musical festival at Frankenhausen	139
	Performance of the opera: "Zweikampf mit der Geliebten," at Hamburg	153
1812.	Performance of the oratorio: "Das jüngste Gericht" at the Musical festival at Erfurt	157
	Musical tour to Leipsic, Prague and Vienna	159
1813.	Appointed director of the orchestra at the theatre An der Wien	168
	Composes his opera of "Faust"	178
1814.	Composes his cantata: "The Liberation of Germany"	182
1815.	Journey to Brünn, Breslau, Carolath. — Third musical festival at Frankenhausen	203
	Musical tour to Wurzburg, Nuremberg and Munich	211
1816.	Frankfort. — Strasbourg, &c.	217
	Visit to Switzerland	234
	Journey to Milan	251
	Journey to Venice	270
	Journey to Bologna, Florence and Rome	283
1817.	Departure from Rome. — Arrival at Naples	325

Vol. II.

1817.	Residence in Naples	1
	Ascends Mount Vesuvius	3
	Departure from Naples to Rome	32
	"Miserere" in the Sistine Chapel	36
	Departure from Rome	41
	Addenda in reference to the Italian journey	47
	Visit to Holland	53
	Appointed director of the orchestra at Frankfort	53
1818.	Composes the opera: "Zemire and Azor"	58
	Journey to the musical festival at Mannheim	59
1819.	Leaves Frankfort	66
	Musical tour to Berlin, Dresden, Leipsic and Cassel	68
	Visit to Brussels	68
1820.	Journey to London	72
	First concert at the Philharmonic Society	82

		Page
	Spohr's concert at the New Argyll Rooms, London	94
	Mr. Logier's Musical Academy	98
	Return to Germany	102
	Musical festival at Quedlinburg	105
	Journey to Paris by way of Frankfort and Heidelberg	105
1821.	Return to Gandersheim	134
	Concerts at Alexisbad and Pyrmont	135
	Removal to Dresden	138
1822.	Appointed director of the orchestra of the court theatre at Cassel	141
1823.	Institutes the Society of St. Cecilia	147
	Composes the opera: "Jessonda" in Cassel, where it is first performed	148
1824.	"Jessonda" performed in Leipsic	153
1825.	"Jessonda" performed in Berlin	157
	Composes the opera of "The Mountain Sprite" in Cassel, where it is first performed	157
1826.	Composes the oratorio of: "Die letzten Dinge" in Cassel, where it is first performed	159
	Musical festival at Düsseldorf	161
1827.	Composes the opera: "Pietro von Abano"	163
1828.	Musical festival at Halberstadt	165
1829.	Musical festival at Nordhausen	166
1830.	Composes the opera: "The Alchymist"	168
1831.	Celebration festival upon the occasion of the grant of a constitution to Hesse	172
	Celebration of *Spohr's* "Silver Wedding"	173
	Terminates his work "The Violin School"	176
1832.	Composes the symphony: "Die Weihe der Töne"	178
	Celebration of the "Golden Wedding" of *Spohr's* parents	180
1833.	Musical festival at Halberstadt	183
1834.	Journey to Marienbad	184
	Death of *Spohr's* first wife	187
1835.	Finishes the oratorio: "Des Heilands letzte Stunden" (Calvary) in Cassel, where it is performed for the first time	188
	Journey to Sandfort in Holland	188
1836.	*Spohr's* second marriage	194
	Journey to Leipsic, Dresden and Saxon Switzerland	195
	Musical festival at Brunswick	197
	Millenium-jubilee at Paderborn	199
1837.	Projected musical festival at Cassel	202
	Journey to Prague	204
	Vienna — Salzburg, &c.	206

		Page
1838.	Death of *Theresa Spohr*	209
	Journey to Carlsbad	209
	Continuation of *Spohr's* Biography by his family	210
1839.	Composes his "Historical Symphony"	215
	Departure to the musical festival at Norwich	215
1840.	Journey to the musical festival at Aix-la-Chapelle	227
	Journey to Lübeck and Hamburg	229
1841.	Journey to Switzerland by way of Stuttgard and Hechingen	232
	Musical festival at Lucerne	235
	Composes his "Double Symphony"	237
	Musical performance in honour of *Mozart* in Cassel	239
1842.	Journey to Carlsbad	240
1843.	Invitation to Prague	244
	Journey to London to direct the "Fall of Babylon"	249
1844.	Composes the opera: "The Crusaders"	257
	Journey to Paris	257
	Journey to the musical festival at Brunswick	260
1845.	His opera of "The Crusaders" performed for the first time, at Cassel	261
	Journey to Oldenburg, Carlsbad and Berlin	262
	Journey to Bonn to the inauguration of the memorial erected to *Beethoven*	270
1846.	Journey to Leipsic and Carlsbad	276
1847.	*Spohr's* twenty-fifth Anniversary as director at Cassel	282
	Spohr's journey to London	287
	Musical performances in commemoration of the death of Mendelssohn	291
1848.	Festivities at Cassel	293
1849.	Journey to Leipsic and Carlsbad	293
1850.	*Spohr's* fall upon the ice	295
	Composes his symphony "The Seasons"	295
	Journey to Leipsic, Breslau and Berlin	296
1851.	Journey to Switzerland and Italy	300
	Journey to Göttingen	300
1852.	Law-suit relative to the fine imposed upon *Spohr* for his absence on a journey without permission	301
	Journey to London to direct the performance of his opera: "Faust"	302
	Appointment of a second director of the orchestra, Mr. *Bott* at Cassel	306
1853.	Journey to London to direct the performance of his opera "Jessonda," &c.	308
1854.	Journey to Switzerland, Munich and Alexandersbad	314

		Page
1855.	Journey to Hannover	316
	Journey to Hamburg and Lübeck	319
1856.	Journey to Dresden, Saxon Switzerland and Prague	321
	Journey to the Harz	321
1857.	Journey to Holland	323
	Spohr pensioned off by the Elector of Hesse	325
	Breaks his arm	327
1858.	Journey to Magdeburg, &c.	327
	Journey to Bremen	329
	Journey to Prague to the jubilee of the conservatory	329
	Visit to Alexandersbad	331
	Journey to Wiesbaden to the musical festival of the Middle-Rhine	331
	Journey to Leipsic	331
	His *Last composition*	334
1859.	Journey to Meiningen. *Spohr* directs an orchestra for the last time	336
	Journey to Detmold	338
	Journey to Alexandersbad and Würzburg	339
	Spohr's last illness and death	341

Alphabetical list

of the most notable persons, adverted to in the two volumes.

	Page
Beethoven	I. 184, 199
Bott, Jean	II. 232, 313, 336
Boucher	II. 68
Catalani	II. 25
Cherubini	II. 133
Clementi	I. 39
Curschmann	II. 158, 161
Dingelstedt	II. 211
Dussek	I. 79, 86
Eck	I. 13
Feska	I. 193, 225
Field	I. 40
Goethe	I. 102, 116
Grabbe	II. 190
Grund, Edward	II. 103, 336
Hauptmann, Moritz	I. 169, II. 137, 241
Hesse, Adolph	II. 196, 209, 299
Hermstedt	I. 123, 140, 156, 159, II. 135
Hiller, Ferdinand	II. 324
Holmes, Alfred and Henry	II. 320
von Humboldt, Alex.	II. 269
Immermann	II. 189
Joachim	II. 278, 289, 317
Kömpel, Augustus	II. 300
Körner, Theodor	I. 177
Kreutzer	I. 250, II. 108, 119
Laube, Heinrich	II. 277
Liszt, Franz	II. 239, 271
Mendelssohn	II. 189, 210, 277, 290
Methfessel	II. 59
Meyerbeer	I. 80, 312, II. 266, 270
Molique	I. 212
Moscheles	II. 294, 313
Müller, Brothers	II. 228
Napoleon	I. 117
Owen, Professor	II. 304
Ole Bull	II. 213
Paganini	I. 279, II. 168
Pott, Augustus	II. 262, 273
Prutz, Robert	II. 278
von Raumer	II. 2
Raupach	II. 184
Ries, Ferdinand	II. 75, 161
Ries, Hubert	II. 269
Rochlitz	I. 75, II. 159, 186
Rode	I. 61, 161
Romberg, Andreas	I. 135, 210
Romberg, Bernard	I. 78
Schmidt, Aloys	I. 159
Schumann, Robert	II. 210, 296
Schwenke	I. 135
Spontini	II. 156
Taylor, Prof., Ed.	II. 216, 249, 253
Tieck, Ludwig	II. 269
Wagner, Richard	II. 245, 276
von Weber, C. Maria	I. 109, 140
Wichmann, Professor	II. 269
Wieland	I. 102, 116
Winter	I. 105

My father, *Carl Heinrich Spohr*, Doctor of Medecine, afterwards Medical Councillor, was the son of a Clergyman at Woltershausen in the district of Hildesheim. He married, November 26, 1782, *Ernestine Henke*, daughter of the Clergyman of the Aegydian church of Brunswick, and at first resided with her parents at the parsonage*). I was the eldest child of this marriage, and was born April 5, 1784. Two years later, my father was transferred as district physician to Seesen. My earliest recollections reach back to that removal; for the impression made upon me by my mother's weeping, after having taken leave of her parents, and our arrival at the simple and somewhat rustic house at Seesen, have remained with me up to the present time. I remember also the smell of the newly whitewashed walls striking me as disagreeable, and even now I still retain an uncommon acuteness and sensibility of the senses.

In Seesen were born my four brothers, and one sister. My parents were musical: my father played the flute, and my mother, a pupil of the Conductor *Schwaneberger* in Brunswick, played on the piano with great ability, and sang the Italian

---

*) The house is still standing, and, as Number 7, forms the corner of the Aegydian churchyard in Monk street. For several years it has been given up to the Military musical institution, since the parish was abolished during the Westphalian times.

bravuras of that time. As they practiced music very often in the evening, a sense and love for the art was early awakened in me. Gifted with a clear soprano voice, I at first began to sing, and already in my fourth or fifth year I was able to sing duets with my mother at our evening music. It was at this time that my father, yielding to my eagerly expressed wish, bought me a violin at the yearly fair, upon which I now played incessantly. At first I tried to pick out the melodies I had been used to sing, and was more than happy when my mother accompanied me.

Soon after, I had lessons from Herr *Riemenschneider*, and I still remember, that, after the first lesson, in which I had learned to play the *G*-sharp accord upon all four strings, in an extasy at the harmony, I hastened into the kitchen to my mother, and arpeggiod the chord to her so incessantly that she was obliged to drive me out. When I had learned the fingering of the violin from notes, I was also allowed to practise music with the others in the evening, as violinist, and there were particularly three trios by *Kalkbrenner*, for piano, flute and violin, which, after being studied, were executed in presence of our circle of friends.

About the year 1790 or 91 a French emigrant, named *Dufour*, came to Seesen. Although an amateur, only, he was an accomplished violinist and violoncellist. He settled there; and being supplied with free board by the more wealthy inhabitants, maintained himself by giving French lessons. The days on which he used to come to my parents, we always practised music, and I still remember having been moved to tears the first time I heard him play. I now gave my parents no rest until I had lessons from him.

Dufour, astonished at my rapid progress, was the first to persuade my parents to devote me entirely to music. My father, who had predestined me for the study of medecine, was from his love of music soon brought to agree to this; but he had a hard struggle with my grandfather, whose idea of a Musician was limited to that of a Tavern-fiddler who played to dancers. Subsequently, after I had been so early appointed *Kammermusicus**) in Brunswick, I had the satisfaction to induce my grandfather, who loved me very much, to adopt a higher opinion respecting my chosen career as a musical *artiste*.

It was while I took lessons from M. *Dufour*, that I made my first attempts at composition, but without yet having had any instruction in harmony. They consisted in duets for two violins, and I executed them with my teacher at our musical soirées; astonishing my parents with them in the highest degree. To this day, I recollect the proud feeling of being already able to appear before the friends of the house as a composer. As a reward, I received from my parents a gala dress, consisting of a red jacket with steel buttons, yellow breeches, and laced boots with tassels; a dress for which I had long prayed in vain. The duets, which my father has carefully preserved, are indeed incorrect and childish, but possess a certain form and a flowing melody.

This first brilliant success in composition, so inspired me, that from this time I devoted nearly every hour which the school allowed me, to similar attempts: I even ventured upon a little opera, the text of which I took from "*Weisse's Kinderfreund.*" It may be mentioned as characteristic, that, I began with the title-page, and first of all painted it very finely with Indian ink; then followed the overture, then a chorus, then an air, and there the work came to a standstill. As I had never yet seen an opera performed, I took the model for these musical pieces from *Hiller's* operas "*Die Jagd*", and "*Lottchen am Hofe*", of which my mother had a pianoforte arrangement, and which she had often sung with me and my father. But I soon felt that I needed both knowledge and experience for such an undertaking, and I therefore set to work at other attempts. In this however, I had a hard struggle with my father, who strongly insisted that every work once begun should be completed before another was commenced; and only

---

*) Musician in the Ducal Orchestra, or Court Musician.

because my father was convinced that I was unequal to so great a task, was an exception made on this occasion; but it was never allowed again. To this severity I owe my perseverance in working, and I have always recollected the paternal precept.

As my father liked to superintend the labours of his son, he allowed me to establish myself in his study, not being at all disturbed by the humming and whistling of the young composer. When I had written down anything wrong, which happened frequently enough, and was obliged to scratch it out, my father heard it at once, and would say half angrily: "Now the stupid boy is making windows again!" — for thus he designated the marks I made across the lines, in scratching out. I was very sensitive to this, and that is perhaps the reason why I acquired early the habit of writing off a clean score without erasing anything.

Since it was now determined, on the advice of *Dufour*, that I should devote myself entirely to music; *Dufour* insisted that I should be sent to Brunswick to enjoy the advantage of better lessons, particularly in theory. This could not take place till I was confirmed. According to a law strictly observed in the Dutchy of Brunswick, confirmation could not take place before the age of fourteen; in order therefore to lose no time, I was sent to my grandfather in the district of Hildesheim, where it was left to the decision of the clergyman as to when the children could be admitted to confirmation. Here, during the winter, I had lessons from my clever grandfather, both in religion, and other things; but music-lessons were not attended to, for neither my grandfather nor my uncles understood anything about it. I was therefore obliged to walk twice a week to Alefeld with my violin, to take lessons from the precentor there. Tedious as were these journeys, owing to the frequent severity of the winter weather, I was always pleased with them, chiefly, indeed, because I felt that I was above my teacher, and often brought him into difficulties by my fluent reading of the notes; and besides,

I had not unfrequently the secret triumph of seeing him brought to a standstill.

Half way to Alefeld, stood a solitary mill. I once entered there during a heavy shower of rain, and gained the good will of the miller's wife to such a degree, that from that time I was obliged to call every day I passed by, and was treated with coffee, cakes and fruit; for which I used to improvise something upon my violin by way of thanks. I still remember having once so completely ravished her by playing *Wranitzky's* variations upon "*Du bist liederlich*", into which all the juggles with which *Paganini* afterwards enchanted the world were introduced, that she would not let me leave her during the whole day.

Soon after returning from Woltershausen, I was sent to Brunswick, where I was received into the house of the rich gingerbread-baker *Michaelis*, as one of his own children, and treated with kindness by all the members of the family; my father had been their physician and had cured *Michaelis'* wife of a dropsy.

I commenced my musical and other studies with eagerness. I received instruction on the Violin from *Kammermusicus Kunisch*, a well grounded and amiable teacher, to whom I owe much. Less friendly was my instructor in harmony and counterpoint, an old organist named *Hartung;* and I still remember how severely he once rebuked me, when, soon after the beginning of the lessons, I showed him a composition of my own. "There is time enough for that," said he, "you must learn something first." But after some months he himself encouraged me to make trials in composition: he corrected me, however, so mercilessly, and scratched out so many ideas which to me appeared sublime, that I lost all desire to show him anything further. Not long afterwards, our lessons were brought to a close by the ill health of the old man; and these were the only lessons in theory, I ever had. I was now obliged to seek for instruction in theoretical works. But the reading of good scores was of special advantage to me; these I obtained from the Theatrical library through the interest of my teacher *Kunisch*. In this manner I soon learned to write harmony correctly; and I now ventured for the first time to appear publicly in Brunswick with a composition for the violin. This took place in the School-concert of the *Katharinen-Schule*, which I attended as a *Secundaner*. These concerts were instituted by the Prefect for the practice of the School-choir; but from several members of the *Hof-Kapelle*, the Town musicians, and accomplished amateurs taking part in them, they became so important, that greater works could always be executed, such as Cantatas, Symphonies, and instrumental Concertos. From this time everything was studied very exactly, and the performances, which were held in the tolerably large saloon of the head class, soon became so celebrated, that it enabled a trifling entrance money to be charged to defray the expenses. At one of these concerts I thus appeared for the first time in my native-town, and achieved so much success that I was invited to assist at the Subscription concerts at the *Deutsches Haus*, and received the usual remuneration. This first payment which I earned as an artist made me very happy, nor have I forgotten the proud feeling with which I announced it to my parents. I now frequently played solos at the subscription concerts, and generally some of my own compositions. I was also allowed to play in the Orchestra of the Theatre for my own practice, and, thereby, became familiar with much good music.

At this time, still possessing my clear, high soprano voice, it gave me much pleasure also to join the School chorus in its perambulations through the town. The leader, who since then has become celebrated as the Bass singer, *Strohmeyer*, gave the soprano solos to me very readily, from my being able to sing them without fault at sight.

My teacher *Kunisch*, who interested himself for me in a paternal manner, now insisted that I should take lessons of the Concert-Director *Maucourt*, the best violinist of the Brunswick orchestra. My father agreed readily, although it was much against his grain to pay the higher charge for this instruction; and the more so, as I had been obliged to leave *Michaelis'* house from his inability to give me up a special apartment, and that it was quite impossible for me to play and compose quietly in the same room with the children of the house. A further consequence of this change of dwelling was, that my father was obliged to arrange with his former aquaintances about my having free board; this was very galling to his ambitious son. Nevertheless I was treated in a friendly way by all these people, and thus the humiliating feeling of my position was soon dissipated. I now, with another *Secundaner*, inhabited a room in the house of the organist *Bürger;* here however I could practise and compose undisturbed, for our landlord, who interested himself in my musical studies, placed his music room and pianoforte at my disposal.

With M. *Maucourt's* instruction, I progressed more and more towards becoming (for my age) an excellent solo player: and after the lapse of about a year, as my father was unable to defray the great expense of my living in Brunswick, on account of the growing up of his other children, he considered me to have made progress enough to enable me to try my luck in the world as a travelling *"Artiste."* He determined therefore to send me first to Hamburgh, where he had acquaintances to whom he could give me letters of recommendation.

Accustomed to obey my father in everything, and well disposed to consider myself a shining light, I had no objection to this. If it appear hazardous in the extreme to send a boy of fourteen into the world, left entirely to himself, and trust everything to fortune, its explanation is to be found in the character and life-experience of my father. Bold and enterprising in the highest degree, he also had already emancipated himself in his sixteenth year. In order to escape punishment at school, he had run away from Hildesheim, and supported himself most precariously in Hamburgh, first as a teacher of languages, and afterwards, by giving lessons in the *Büsching* Commercial school. He then attended several Universities, struggling through great privations by help of his enterprising spirit and unwearying activity; and, at last, without any help from home; after a most adventurous youth, succeeded in establishing himself in practice as a physician in Brunswick. He found it therefore very natural that his son should try the same course, although my mother shook her head thoughtfully at it. Scantily provided with money for the journey, but furnished with much good advice, I was sent by the mail to Hamburgh. Still, filled with the lively impression made upon me by the crowded Commercial City, and the ships, now seen for the first time, I went, full of hope and in high spirits, to Professor *Büsching*, to whom I had a letter of introduction from my father. But how soon were those hopes to be destroyed! The Professor, after he had read the letter with increasing astonishment, exclaimed: "Your father is then still, the same as ever! What madness to send a boy into the world trusting merely to good luck!" He then explained to me, that, in order to arrange a concert in Hamburgh, one must either possess a well known name, or at least, the means to bear the great expenses it would entail. But, that in summer, when all the rich people were at their country seats, such an undertaking would be quite impossible. Completely down cast by this explanation, I could not answer a single word, and was hardly able to repress my tears. I took leave in silence, and hastened to my lodging full of despair, without thinking of delivering the other letters of recommendation. Here, upon thinking over my situation, the certainty that my money would hardly suffice for a couple of days, terrified me to such a degree, that, in thought, I already saw myself in the claws of the crimps of whom my father had drawn a warning picture. I made up my mind at once, packed up my violin and other things again, sent them to Brunswick by the mail, paid my bill, and with the scanty remainder of my money, which might perhaps suffice to my subsistence, I set out on foot, on my return to Brunswick.

Some miles from the town, calmer reflection brought regret for this overhaste; but it was too late; had it not been so, I would have turned back. I said to myself that it was foolish not at least to have delivered the other letters first. They might perhaps have procured for me the aquaintance of some musical person who would have appreciated my talent, and have procured some information how arrangements might have been made for a Concert. To this was added the humiliating thought that my father who had been so enterprising himself, would upbraid me as childish, cowardly and thoughtless Thus, saddened to the depth of my soul, I wandered farther, thinking continually how I might avoid the humiliation of returning to my paternal home without having effected anything whatever.

At last, the idea struck me of addressing myself to the Duke of Brunswick, to solicit from him the means to carry on my studies. I knew that the duke had earlier played the violin himself, and I therefore hoped that he would recognise my talent. When (thought I) he has heard me play but one of my concertos, my fortune is made. With newly awakened courage I now journeyed onward, and got over the rest of the road in the most cheerful disposition of mind.

Scarcely arrived in Brunswick, I concocted a petition to the Duke, in which I laid before him my whole situation, ending with the request either for aid towards improving myself, or, for a situation in the ducal orchestra. As I knew that the Duke was in the habit of walking every morning in the park of the Palace, I sought him there with my petition in my pocket, and had the good fortune to have it accepted by him. After having glanced over it and asked me some questions about my parents and former Instructors, which I fearlessly answered, he enquired who had worded the petition. "Well, who but I myself? I need no help for that," was my reply. half offended at the doubt as to my ability. The Duke smiled and said: "Well, come to the palace to-morrow at eleven; we will then speak further about your request." Who so happy as I! Punctually at eleven I presented myself before the groom of the chambers and requested to be announced to the Duke. "And who may *Er**)* be?" snarled the groom to me in unfriendly tone. "I am no *Er*. I am here by the Duke's command, and *Er* has to announce me", was my indignant reply. The groom went to announce me, and before my excitement had subsided I was introduced. My first word to the Duke was therefore, "Your Serene Highness! your servant calls me "*Er*"; I must earnestly remonstrate against that." The duke laughed aloud, and said: "Come, calm yourself; he will not do it again". Then, after having put several questions to me to which I gave the most unembarrassed answers, he said: "I have enquired about your abilities from your last teacher *Maucourt*, and am now desirous to hear you play one of your own compositions; this can take place at the next concert in the apartments of the Duchess. I will have it intimated to the director *Schwaneberger*."

In most happy mood I left the Palace, hastened to my lodging, and prepared myself for the concert in the most careful manner.

The Court concerts in the apartments of the duchess took place once a week, and were most disagreeable to the musicians of the Ducal Orchestra: for, according to the then prevailing custom, cards were played during the music. In order not to be disturbed, the Duchess had ordered the orchestra, always to play *piano*. The leader therefore left out the trumpets and kettle drums, and insisted strongly that no *forte* should be played in its full strength. As this was not always to be avoided in Symphonies, however softly the band might play, the Duchess ordered a thick carpet to be spread out under the orchestra, in order to deaden the sound. One heard therefore the words "I play", "I stand" and so forth, much louder than the music.

However, the evening on which I played there for the first time, the card tables and carpet had disappeared; the

---

*) *Er*, or he, used in this mode of address, is a contemptuous style of expression in the German language, which has its equivalent only in the English word *fellow,* used in a rude sense.

orchestra, informed that the Duke would be present, had well prepared themselves, and the music went on excellently. As I then still appeared without any timidity, and well knew that my whole future fate depended upon the success of that day, I played with real inspiration; and must have surpassed the expectations of the Duke, for he, even while I was playing, cried repeatedly "bravo". After I had finished, he came to me, patted me on the shoulder, and said, "The talent is there; I will take care of you. Come to me to-morrow." In an extasy of delight I returned to my lodging, wrote immediately to my parents of my good fortune, and could get no sleep for a long time, from excitement and joy.

The next day, the Duke said to me, "there is a place vacant in the orchestra, I will give it to you. Be diligent and behave well. If after some years you have made good progress, I will send you to some great master; for here you have no great model to follow!" This last speech filled me with astonishment, for till then I had considered the playing of my Instructor *Maucourt*, as the utmost that could be attained.

In this manner, in the beginning of my fifteenth year I was appointed *Kammermusicus*. The Rescript of my appointment which was drawn up later, is dated August 2^d, 1799. Although the salary was only 100 thalers, yet by great economy, and with the help of other trifling earnings, it sufficed to me; and I did not now need any further help from home. Nay, I was even happy enough to be enabled to render the education of the other children easier for my parents, by taking my brother *Ferdinand*, who was eight years younger than I, and who showed an inclination and talent for music, to live with me, and give him my assistance to become an artist.

From this time, the young *Kammermusicus* was in full activity. His duties consisted in playing at the Court-concerts and in the Theatre, for which latter, a French operatic and dramatic company had been engaged shortly before. I therefore became earlier acquainted with the French dramatical music than with the German; and this was not without influence upon the tendency of my taste, and upon my compositions of that time. At last, during the two fairs, a German operatic company from Magdeburgh was also engaged, and the grandeur of *Mozart's* operatic music burst upon me. *Mozart* now became for my life time my ideal and model. Even now I well remember the transport and dreamy enchantment with which I heard for the first time, the "*Zauberflöte*" and "*Don Juan*"; and that I had no rest until I had got the scores lent to me, and had brooded over them half the night long.

Neither did I fail to be present at all the other musical parties in the town: I was a member of all the quartetto circles. In one of these which had been formed by two of the singers of the French opera, who played the violin, I heard for the first time the quartettos of *Beethoven*, and from that time raved no less about them than I had before done about those of *Haydn* and *Mozart*. With such constant practice, my playing and taste could not fail to become more and more cultivated. The presence of two foreign violinists who at this time visited Brunswick, produced also a favourable influence upon me. These were *Seidler*, and the boy *Pixis*. The former impressed me by his beautiful tone and his pure playing, the latter by his execution, which for his years, was extraordinary.

I very often played in private parties, with the brothers *Pixis*, and in their second public concert I performed in a double concerto, by Pleyel the violinist. After such encouragement I always studied with redoubled diligence. The duke, who did not lose sight of me, had allowed me to inform him whenever I intended to execute a new composition at the Court concerts, and he was sometimes present, to the great annoyance of the duchess, who was thus disturbed in her party at Ombre. One day when the duke was not there, and for that reason nobody was listening to the music; the prohibition regarding the *forte* being renewed, and the dreadful carpet again spread, I tried a new concerto of my own. I can only call these performances rehearsals, because no preparation was ever made beforehand, excepting on the days upon which we knew that the duke would be present. Engrossed with my work which, I heard for the first time with the orchestra, I quite forgot the prohibition, and played with all the vigour and fire of inspiration; so that I even carried away the orchestra with me. Suddenly, in the middle of the solo, my arm was seized by a lackey, who whispered to me, "Her Highness sends me to tell you that you are not to scrape away so furiously." Enraged at this interruption I played, if possible, yet more loudly; but was afterwards obliged to put up with a rebuke from the Marshal of the Court.

The Duke, to whom I complained the next day; laughed heartily: but on this occasion he at the same time adverted to his former promise, and told me to choose a teacher at once from among the great Violinists of the day. Without hesitation I named *Viotti,* and the duke approved of the choice. He was immediately written to, to London, where he resided at the time. Alas! He refused the request: he wrote word that "he had become a wine merchant," — "occupied himself but seldom with music, and therefore could not receive any pupils"*).

Next to *Viotti, Ferdinand Eck,* in Paris was at that time the most celebrated violinist. He was therefore next applied to. But he also, would take no pupils. A short time before, when engaged in the Court orchestra at Munich, he had eloped with a rich countess; had married her in Switzerland, and now led an affluent life, partly in Paris, and partly upon an estate near Nancy which had been bought with the fortune of the countess. He, however, proposed his younger brother and pupil, *Francis Eck*, as master. As he was at that time travelling through Germany, and had appeared with great success at Berlin, he was written to; and, in case of his accepting the proposition,

---

*) It is related of *Viotti* (the father of Modern Violin-Playing) when thus established in London as a Wine-merchant, that, a Nobleman who had previously been a great admirer and patron of his talent, rebuked him for having abandoned his art to become a dealer in Wine! "My dear Sir" replied *Viotti,* "I have done so, simply because I find that the English like Wine better than Music!"

invited to Brunswick. *Eck* came; played at Court, and pleased the Duke greatly. As however he was about to start for Petersburgh upon an artistic tour, I was sent with him as a pupil for a year; and it was settled that I should bear half the expenses of the journey: and that *Eck*, at the end of the instruction should receive a suitable reward from the Duke. A diary of this journey exists, which from some extracts may perhaps be of interest. It commences a few days before our departure (which took place April 24, 1802), in the following childish manner; nothwithstanding I was already a youth of eighteen.

"The Leave-taking."

„To the most sorrowful hours of life, belong those of leave taking from loving parents, and tried friends. Not even the prospect of an agreeable and profitable journey can brighten them; time only, and the hope of a speedy meeting again, can assuage their pain. From these also do I expect relief on recommencing my musical tour. Farewell, therefore, parents and friends! The remembrance of the many happy hours enjoyed with you will always accompany me."

We first went to Hamburgh, where *Eck* intended giving concerts. I regarded this town again, from which I had fled some years ago so full of despair, with a certain degree of self-satisfaction and content.

After *Eck* had delivered his letters of recommendation, the lessons began. Concerning these, the following is written in my diary:

"This morning, April 30, Herr *Eck* commenced my lessons. But alas! how was I humiliated! I, who imagined myself one of the first virtuosi of Germany, could not play one single bar to his satisfaction; but was obliged to repeat it ten times at least, in order in some degree to gain his approbation. My bow-ing particularly displeased him, to alter which, I now also see is very necessary. At first it will of course be difficult for me; but at last, convinced of the great advantage of the change, I hope to accomplish it."

The diary now describes everything that the travellers saw and heard. Attractive as these were to me, yet I did not neglect my musical studies for them. The forenoon, which in Hamburgh lasts till three o'clock, was devoted entirely to practising what *Eck* gave me. It was not long before he expressed himself favourably as to my progress. Already on May 10, I wrote:

"Herr *Eck* begins to be more satisfied with my playing, and was kind enough to assure me yesterday that I was now able to play the concerto I had studied under him, without fault."

The intervals between practising, I employed in painting. From my earliest youth I had applied myself to drawing and painting in water colours, and had attained some proficiency without ever having had any good instruction. Yes, I had even hesitated for some time, as to which of the two arts, music or painting, I should choose for my profession. I now made my first attempt at portrait painting. The 12th of May I wrote:

"On Sunday I commenced a miniature which I finished this forenoon. I tried to paint myself, and am quite satisfied with the result. This, and playing on the violin have occupied me so fully, that I have not left the house for four days. I sent this picture to my parents, and then commenced painting Herr *Eck*, who was patient enough to sit to me."

It is now time to mention that the young artist, from his earliest youth, was very susceptible to female beauty, and already when a boy fell in love with every beautiful woman. It is therefore not to be wondered at, that, the diary of the youth of eighteen contains many pages of the outpourings of the emotions of his heart. But there is great comicality in the earnestness with which these fleeting inclinations are spoken of.

In Hamburgh it was a Miss *Lütgens*, the daughter of a music master, who particularly won my heart. After a visit paid to the father, I wrote the following:

"His eldest daughter, a girl of thirteen, a very fine, innocent creature, pleased me particularly by her agreable and modest demeanour. She is very beautiful, has hair that curls naturally, very lively brown eyes, and a neck of dazzling whiteness. Her father, whose hobby is counterpoint and harmony, entertained me continually with the resolution and combination of the chords; finding in me the most patient listener to his sermon, while I would much have greatly preferred to speak with his amiable daughter about the combination of hearts and lips."

In order to a more frequent near approach, I asked permission to take her likeness, which was willingly granted. But before the sittings commenced, I was warned by Herr *Eck*, whom oddly enough I had made my confidant, that she was a coquette, and unworthy of my regard. At first I could not believe that a girl of thirteen could already be a coquette, but after the first sitting, I became of the same opinion, and wrote the following remarks:

"Henrietta begged me to take her portrait in the dress which she wore, assuring me that she had chosen it expressly; for her other dresses were not cut low enough, and covered her neck too much. I was astonished at her vanity, and the sight of this charming neck which otherwise would have enchanted me now saddened me; being convinced that she was already infected by the vanity and shamelessness of the Hamburgh ladies. While I painted, she chatted with her cousin, (an ugly but vain girl,) of nothing but the dress she intended wearing at the ball which was to take place on the following evening. Quite vexed, I returned home, and wished that we might now leave as soon as possible, for Hamburgh began to displease me more and more. My sociable heart, which could so willingly attach itself to any one, finds here nobody. In this girl, I thought to have found something on which to set my affections; but I see I am again deceived. I had intended making a copy of this portrait for myself; but I am still too much embittered against her to be able to do so. Neither have I now any wish to go to the ball."

But two days afterwards I wrote, "This forenoon I worked diligently at Miss *Lütgens*' portrait — and began also a copy of it for myself. After dinner I went to her..... Henrietta received me with reproaches for not having been at the ball..... To-day, she was so modestly dressed, and spoke so reasonably, that I occupied myself more with her than with my painting, which was the cause of my not quite finishing it. It is really a thousand pities that this girl with so much talent and good sense, lives in such vulgar society, and is thereby led away into the follies of Hamburgh."

With the presentation of the portrait, and our departure, which took place immediately after; this little romance, that never came to a declaration, terminates.

With respect to the point I had at that time reached in my art, and my views of the latter, my diary shews proofs at every page, of my opinion of what I heard in Hamburgh. Without doubt those judgments are pronounced with the naïve assurance that belongs to youth, and require without a doubt many modifications, if these were possible after the lapse of so long a time. The opinion about Operas, and their performance, may be well passed over, for those works have for the most part, disappeared from the repertoire, and the singers, also, have passed away.

But respecting other matters, as well as those of my Instructor, the following incidents may be mentioned.

"May 5. To-day we were invited to dinner by Herr *Kickhöver*, and there met *Dussek* and some other musicians. This was very agreeable to me, as I had long earnestly wished to hear *Dussek* play. Herr *Kickhöver* and his wife are very kind people, and in their house good taste is combined with splendour. The conversation at table, was almost always in French. As I am not well versed in that language I could take but little part in it. But, I took all the more in the music which followed. Herr *Eck*, began with a quartett of his own composition, and enchanted all the listeners. Then Herr *Dussek* played a sonata for the piano, of his own composition, which however did not seem to please particularly. Now followed a second quartett by Herr *Eck*, which so delighted Herr *Dussek*, that he enthusiastially embraced him. In conclusion,

Herr *Dussek* played a new quintett he had composed in Hamburgh, which was praised to the skies. However, it did not entirely please me; for, despite the numerous modulations, it became tedious towards the end, and the worst was, that it had neither form nor rythm, and the end could quite as well have been made the beginning as not."

At a musical party at M. *Thornton's* country house, I became acquainted with Fräulein *Grund*, at that time the most esteemed singer of Hamburgh. My diary speaks of her with great enthusiasm. Among other remarks:

"At first, the conversation was very vapourous; for the merchants spoke of nothing but the contrary winds that prevented their ships entering the Elbe. By and by however, it became more interesting, particularly when Fräulein *Grund* joined in it. I had already admired her correct and polished language, and her captivating and obliging manners. But when at table, she spoke alternately French with one, and English with another, and that one gentleman informed me she spoke and wrote four languages correctly, I began to envy her, and to be ashamed that I, as a man, was so far behind this girl. She had also attained great proficiency in music, and enchanted us so much yesterday evening by her singing, that Herr *Eck* proposed to her to sing at his Concert, which she also promised to do. My neighbour at dinner, informed me that her father maintained his family by giving Instruction in Music, and spent a great deal upon the education of his children. In this, his eldest daughter assisted him greatly; since she not only instructed her brothers and sisters in music and languages, but also earned a considerable sum by giving lessons in the first houses in Hamburgh. I would gladly have made her acquaintance at once, but she was so surrounded by young men that I could not approach her."

My diary mentions the following with regard to Herr *Eck's* public concert in the *Logensaal* on the *Drehbahn* on the eighteenth of May:

"Herr *Eck* had great reason to be satisfied with the orchestra, for his concerti were admirably accompanied; not so the arias of Fräulein *Grund*, which were somewhat difficult for the wind instruments. At the head of this well drilled orchestra, is *Massoneau*, well known by his charming compositions. The appearance of this man by not means indicates his great talent; for his manner of playing and his bow-ing are so bad, that one might take him for the greatest bungler — and yet he does not direct at all badly."

Our stay at Hamburgh lasted till June 6. Herr *Dussek* who was commissioned to arrange the concert at a festival with which the English living in Hamburgh were about to celebrate the 4th of June, in honour of their king, engaged Herr *Eck* to perform a violin concerto. It was not until the rehearsal which took place on the evening of June 3, at nine o'clock, that Herr *Eck* discovered that the concert was to be given in the open air, which, until then, had never been mentioned. A tent had been erected, in which the orchestra, about one hundred strong, was disposed on a terrace-like platform. Herr *Dussek* first tried a *Cantata*, composed by him for the occasion, and which, had an uncommon effect upon me; for not only was it well written and thoroughly well studied, but from the accompainment of a large organ which had been erected in the back ground of the orchestra and "from its being executed in the silence of night, it partook of so solemn a character that I was quite charmed by it."

After the Cantata, Herr *Eck* was to try his Concerto. But, he fearing that the damp night air would have an unfavourable effect upon his strings, and that his violin, after so powerful a volume of vocal sound, and hemmed in by the linen walls, would tell badly, had resolved not to play at all. He explained this; and at the same time reproached Herr *Dussek* warmly for not having told him at once, that the concert was to take place in the open air. Hereupon a sharp dispute followed, the consequence of which was that *Eck* left the place immediately with me, and we took no part in the festival itself.

We now went to Ludwigslust, where *Eck* wished to play at

Court. But his offer was declined; and he came also to Strelitz at an unfortunate time, for the Court was absent. Nevertheless, as it was soon expected to return, and the pleasant little town with its charming park, bounded by the lake, invited us to make a longer stay; and, as *Eck* foresaw that in the height of summer it would be impossible to do much in Stettin, Dantzic and Konigsberg, he made up his mind to await the return of the Court. We looked out therefore for private lodgings, and made ourselves at home there for some time.

This was the most favourable period for my studies, during the whole journey. *Eck*, who was now at leisure, devoted himself with great zeal to the instruction of his pupil, and initiated me in all the secrets of his art. I, for my part, urged on by youthful ambition, was indefatigable. I rose very early and practised until exhaustion obliged me to cease. But, after a short rest I began again, and in this way, sometimes brought it to ten hour's practising a day, including the time that *Eck* devoted to me. In a letter from Brunswick, I had been informed that those who did not wish me well had loudly expressed themselves, that I should distinguish myself as little as all the other youths whom the duke had hitherto assisted in their studies. In order to controvert this opinion, I was determined to do my utmost, and even when my zeal sometimes flagged, the thought of my first appearance in Brunswick upon my return, animated me directly to fresh exertion.

In this manner I succeeded after a short time in acquiring such dexterity and firmness in the management of my instrument, that none of the then known Concerto-music was too difficult for me. In these exertions I was supported by sound health, and a Herculean frame.

Between whiles, I composed, painted, wrote and read; and in the later hours of the afternoons we used to make excursions into the neighbourhood. A favourite amusement of the travellers was to row across the lake, and to take supper at a farm house, situated on the opposite shore. As I was already at that time an accomplished swimmer, I often undressed during these trips, and swam a while alongside the boat. The relation in which I stood to *Eck*, which was more that of one comrade to another than of pupil to teacher, admitted of such priviledges.

At this time, I finished a violin concerto I had begun in Hamburgh, and which afterwards appeared as Op. 1 at *Breitkopf & Härtel's* in Leipsic; and wrote the three violin duets Op. 3 published at *Kühnel's* in the same town. While practising these duets with *Eck*, I became first aware that my teacher, like many violinists of the French school, was no thoroughly finished artist; for however excellently he executed his concertos, and some other compositions studied with his brother, yet he knew but little how to enter into the spirit of the works of others. A change of characters would have been very possible while playing these duets, for the scholar could have taught the master how they ought to have been executed. I became also aware from an attempt at composition made by *Eck*, that it was impossible for him to have composed the violin concertos and quartetts he had given out as his own productions. At a later period, also, the concertos appeared with the name of the elder *Eck* affixed to them, and the quartetts with that of *Danzi*, the leader of the Orchestra at Stutgard. Thus the four weeks, during which we waited for the arrival of the Court, passed in a very uniform way, but not fruitlessly for me, when Herr *Eck* fell seriously ill, and being obliged to keep his room for the first four weeks of his indisposition, I took my evening walks alone. During these walks another love affair sprang up, which is related in the diary with great earnestness and minuteness. On the eighth of July, is written:

"This afternoon, impelled by ennui, I entered a circulating library, where I selected *Lafontaine's* well known novel "*Quinctius Heymerom von Flaming*." I took it with me, and, leaving the town, looked for a sequestered and shady place on the shore of the lake, where I lay down and began to read. I became deeply engrossed in the story; grieved with *Lissow* about his *Jacobine*, and compared her to a lady then living, and an acquaintance of mine. Suddenly I heard footsteps near me, I looked up, and two girls stood before me; one with blue eyes, fair curls, and beautiful as an angel, the other with black hair and eyes, less beautiful indeed than her companion, but still not plain. I sprang up, bowed respectfully and gazed after them for a long time. Myrrha, Herr *Eck's* dog which I had taken with me, followed them, fawning upon the fair haired one incessantly, so that it did not heed my calling. I therefore followed to bring back the dog, and if possible to make the acquaintance of the girls. The fair one came to meet me, begging pardon for having kept back the dog, and asked me to promise that I would not punish it for its disobedience. With her sweet silvery voice she might have exacted yet greater promises from me; I therefore gave the desired one with pleasure. The conversation was now commenced; I continued it, and accompanied the girls on their walk. I found that the fair one was very well educated and polite. The dark one spoke too little to allow of judging of her education. We came at length to a meadow separated from our path by a broad ditch, which although shallow, was yet too wet for ladies to cross. As they expressed a desire to walk in the meadow, I offered to carry them over. At first they would not consent, but at last they allowed themselves to be persuaded. I took the fair one first, and an incomprehensible pleasure seized me when thus carrying the beautiful girl in my arms. When I had reached the most dangerous part of the ditch with her, one of her fair curls fell upon my face. This so disturbed me, that I nearly fell with my lovely burthen into the ditch. Nevertheless, I brought her happily over. She thanked me so heartily and gazed so into my face with her large blue eyes that I almost forgot to fetch the other. We now walked on across the meadow, and, at the end, to my great disappointment, found a little bridge which led us back over the ditch. This envious bridge robbed me of the pleasure of carrying once more the sweet burthen. I escorted the girls as far as the town, and then parted from them very unwillingly. — I will immediately enquire their names and station."

Already the next day I again met my fair one. The diary relates this with comical ingenuousness:

"This evening, urged by God knows what impulse, I took the same walk as yesterday, and again laid myself down in the very place where I had been so agreeably disturbed by the girls. I began to read; but, although I was at an interesting part, yet when I had run through some pages, I had not the least idea of the contents. I now confessed to myself that I had not come here to read, but in the hope of again meeting my new acquaintance. I pocketed my book and gazed with longing looks towards the place where I had first seen them yesterday. But; after waiting in vain for two hours, I arose, vexed, and returned towards the town. Just before reaching it, at a place where two roads meet, I encountered some cows, on their way home from the meadow, which blocked up my path and obliged me to wait. But I had not stood there long, before I saw at some distance, a female figure, dressed in white, coming towards me, and which had exactly the same fine form and high bearing of her whom I had waited for with such earnest longing. As she drew nearer, I was more convinced that it must be her, and I went to meet her. I had not deceived myself — it was her! She greeted me with her graceful friendliness, enquired how I was, and told me that her friend had taken cold the evening before, and was obliged to keep her bed. I said I was sorry to hear it, and that I feared I had been the cause of the illness of her friend, in having delayed them too long in their walk. She assured me however of the contrary, and laid all the blame upon her friend herself, who had clad herself too lightly."

During this time the herd had passed by, and we separated. In this second conversation I have again remarked in her so much polish of manner, and so much tender feminine delicacy that I could not but infer that she had been exceedingly well educated. — But, as yet I know not who she is; though from her conversation, I am of opinion she must belong to the bourgoisie."

These meetings were now repeated almost every evening without prior agreement, and I felt very unhappy when on one occasion I did not find my friend. I became more and more confidential with her; spoke of my parents; of my patron who provided me with the means to accompany my eminent Instructor on his travels; mentioned my works, and plans for the future; and felt myself drawn nearer to her by her friendly interest for me. I saw in her the sum of all womanly perfections, and imagined to have met *her* who could make the happiness of my life. When wandering hand in hand in the little wood by the lake side, I was more than once upon the point of declaring my love to her; but a timidity I could not conquer always prevented me. Respecting her own circumstances, she was very reserved, and hence I was still ignorant as to who she was. On the 24 of July I however wrote:

"At last I have learned the name of my fair one; but the enquiries made, have cost me dear! Herr *Eck*, who is now almost recovered and who has already taken some short walks, sent for a hair dresser. Of him, I made enquiries. He told me her name was ***, and, that she was the daughter of a groom of the chambers to the former Duke, who had died some years ago. Her mother, with whom she lived, had a small pension. To my question as to how that could enable her to dress so elegantly? his reply was: they were probably presents from Herr von *** who was very fond of her and visited her frequently. On hearing this, my agony was so great, that I nearly let fall my violin, — and scarcely had the courage to ask, whether her virtue was doubtfully spoken of. He assured me nevertheless to the contrary, and was of opinion, that Herr von ***, who had only come of age two months ago, had the intention of marrying her. He was now travelling, and would return in some weeks. I had made the acquaintance of this Herr von *** at the Inn where we dined, before his departure, and must admit that he seemed to me the most well bred young nobleman we met there. The less therefore do I understand his making her presents and she accepting them; for she can hardly permit herself to hope that he will marry her. And, if so, how as a prudent girl, could she venture during his absence to take lonely walks with a young man, and sit with him in the evening before the door of the house? The affair is a riddle to me, and I am doubtful whether I shall go to her this evening or not."

The girl's character however did not long remain a riddle to me; for scarcely had *Eck*, who now again shared the evening walks, made her acquaintance, than she received his attentions in a much more friendly and forward manner than she had done mine. *Eck*, gallant and liberal, arranged excursion-parties to please her, into the neighbourhood; to Rheinsberg, Hohenzirze, and other places. For this, she rewarded him with the most marked attention, and had eyes for him only. I felt deeply wounded; the diary contains passionate outbursts of jealousy. Fortunately they were confined to writing, and the good understanding with my Instructor remained unshaken. The contempt I now felt for the girl helped me to conquer my passion, and I turned to my studies with renewed zeal. My diary states:

"I never remark the progress I have made in playing, more than when, from time to time, I take up some old theme and remember how I used to execute it. To-day for instance I took the Concerto I had studied in Hamburgh and found, that I now executed with the greatest ease those passages which I then could not play without a break."

My Instructor also, did not leave me without encouragement; and when, on the 16 of August, I had played my new Concerto; to my great delight, Herr *Eck* said: "If every three months you progress as you have done in these, you will return to Brunswick a perfect virtuoso."

Two days later, Aug. 18., I remained almost the whole day at home, and composed a new Adagio to my Concerto; for although I had already written three, yet none of them seemed to suit well to the other parts.

As evincing my youthful pride as a Composer, the following may here be cited:

"I was told of a popular festival which was to be arranged at Hohenzirze, August 27. the birthday of the hereditary Prince. To this festival the peasants of the neighbouring villages are invited to a dance and supper. There is also to be dancing at the castle. In answer to my question, as to where so many musicians would be found, I learned that the *Janitscharen*-music would play for the peasants, and the Orchestra — imagine my astonishment — for the *dancing* at Court! I would not believe it at first, until repeated assurances of it were made to me. But, I asked: how is it possible, that the Duke can require such a thing from the members of his Orchestra, and that they have so little feeling of honour and artistic pride as not to refuse it? The reply was: the Duke does not consider it improper for his Orchestra to play to dancers, and the majority of the members dare not disobey his commands, for if discharged from here, poor bunglers as they are, they would find it difficult to obtain places in other orchestras."

As after the end of my unhappy love affair, my residence in Strelitz had become unbearable, I longed greatly for our departure. This however, was still delayed, for the doctor could not pronounce Herr *Eck* fully restored until the end of September. The unpleasantness of my position was still further heightened by the friend of my faithless one, whom at our first meeting I had named the "dark one", turning her affection most unmistakeably towards me; an affection, which, although the girl was very pretty, I could not return. I withdrew myself from their society as much as possible; but, out of regard to my Instructor, I could not entirely refuse to share in the pleasure parties and excursions which he constantly arranged; and at these I could not avoid being the escort of the dark beauty. There are naive complaints in my diary of the embarrassments which her tenderness caused me, and more than once I wished the moment of our departure to arrive, which would free me from such trials.

On the 27th Sept., came at length the moment, when we were to say farewell to our fair ones. Sophy (the dark one) had affected, or perhaps really felt, an uncommon sadness for the last three days. To-day she spoke not a word, only sighed sometimes, and, when the others in the room did not observe it, threw herself passionately upon my neck. About eight o'clock in the evening, Herr *Eck* and Miss *** left the room. Now for the first time the real outbreak of her tenderness took place; for after she had also sent away her brothers and sisters, she hardly let me out of her arms. I was obliged to bear with it until ten o'clock; then we took leave. The poor girl shed so many tears, that I was ashamed of my own dry eyes, and, in order not to appear quite heartless, I kissed her warmly. Sophy accompanied me to the door of the house, and pressed a paper into my hand, with the request that I would keep it as a remembrance. I hastened home, opened it, and found a letter with a gold ring containing some hair. The letter ran as follows: "Noble friend, pardon a girl whose importunity must certainly have been obvious to you. I knew that sometimes I did more than was befitting my sex. But God knows, when in your company, which was so dear to me, I could not control myself. Now also I force upon you a small token, trifling indeed, but given with the most openhearted impulse. My only wish and prayer is that you will wear it, and remember me. Ah! could this paper but tell you how highly I value having made your acquaintance, and how deeply I regret your going so far away from us! I must conclude, and in the firm hope of seeing you, my best friend, once more, I already rejoice at the day which will restore you to us again. Farewell, and may you live as well and happily as is the wish of your friend Sophy ***"

This unmerited and tender inclination may not have remained without thankful acknowledgement; for the resolution to answer the letter in a most friendly manner from Stettin, is expressed in the diary. But there is nothing mentioned respecting the execution of that resolve.

We went to Danzic, via Stettin, arriving there October 2. As *Eck* had to deliver many letters of introduction, and had to arrange a Concert; the lessons, which till now had been given regularly, came rather to a standstill. Meanwhile, I thought, "that I made progress by only hearing Herr *Eck* practise." We were constantly invited out to dinner, and for the evening; among other invitations was one to the country seat of Herr *Saurmann*, where from a hill behind the house, we could overlook the Baltic and a great part of the town. The view of the sea and the vessels upon it made an indiscribable impression upon me. As the day was somewhat overcast, the ships appeared to hang in the clouds, and to move slowly along with them. I could with difficulty tear myself away from the magnificent sight.

At another dinner, in Mr. *Simpson's* garden, I had the honour to sit beside the hostess. She induced me to relate to her many things of my early life, namely: how I had been at first destined for the study of medecine, and then, from a passionate inclination for music, had been led to devote myself entirely to the art. She listened to me with a benevolent interest, but at the end wounded my feelings by asking whether I should not have done better to follow the profession of my father. Wholly penetrated with the dignity of my artistic career, I replied angrily: "As high as the soul is above the body, so high is he who devotes himself to the ennobling of the mind, above him who only attends to the mortal frame."

Almost everytime that an opera was given, I went to the theatre, and did not fail to note down my remarks upon the performance, in which singers, chorus and orchestra were sharply handled.

To my great joy, Ariadne in Naxos, the celebrated melodrama of *Brade*, which I did not yet know, was also given. But it offended my taste, that in the comedy which followed,

"The peasants and lawyers", Theseus appeared again in the character of a lawyer, and Ariadne as a humble peasant girl. "The music enchanted me although it was very badly performed. But how could it be otherwise, the score having only arrived in the morning from Königsberg, and the first and only rehearsal having been held at noon! Madame *Bochmann*, who played Ariadne, declaimed indeed very well, but was too ugly for the part." A young Englishman, who sat next to me, said, that, he did not think Theseus to blame for forsaking such an Ariadne. And upon this, he related to me the following anecdote. At an amateur theatre in England, Ariadne was also given. A rather elderly and anything but beautiful lady played the part of Ariadne so excellently, that the audience broke out into applause at the end of the piece. She modestly disclaimed the applause, saying: "In order to represent Ariadne well, it was necessary to be both young and handsome." A young man, who wished to say something clever to her, cried out: "O, Madam, you prove the contrary!"

Herr *Eck's* concert on October 16. at the Theatre, went off brilliantly. As I knew the pieces that my Instructor performed, very accurately, I undertook to lead them on the first violin. The musicians, who soon discovered how firm the young Conductor was, followed me willingly, thereby rendering the performance of the Solo player much easier; which he also thankfully acknowledged. Besides the three pieces played by Herr *Eck*, there was also a Symphony by *Haydn*, an Overture by *Mozart*, a pianoforte Concerto by *Danzi*, played by Herr *Reichel*, and two Arias of *Cimarosa* and *Mozart* sung by Fräulein *Wotruba* and Herr *Ciliax*. "The success of Herr *Eck's* performances was great, and the applause enthusiastic and reiterated. I also, had never before heard him play so well in public."

On the 20th Oct. we went on to Königsberg and remained there till Nov. 18. *Eck* gave two concerts which were very well attended. Being introduced into many of the first houses by letters of introduction, we were constantly invited to dinner as well as to musical parties. In the house of the "Surgeon-General" *Gerlach*, I often practised music with Fräulein *Gerlach*, who was a thoroughly cultivated dilettante, and an excellent pianiste; and who also sang my new songs. Whether these had any artistic worth is now not to be ascertained, for they have been lost. I sometimes played quartetts with two Messrs. *Friedländer*. It was not however these quartett parties alone that attracted me to their house; Fräul. *Rebecca Oppenheim*, the younger sister of Madame *Friedländer*, had again inflamed my too susceptible heart. She was a Jewess, and the society that frequented the house consisted almost entirely of Jews only; but they were all polite and educated people. The day on which I took leave, I found Madame *Friedländer* and Fräul. *Rebecca* alone. The latter was overflowing with wit and humour, and we never ceased laughing, and jesting, although this but ill suited the purport of my visit. „It is fortunate," says my diary, "that we leave to-morrow, for Rebecca is a dangerous girl! He who loves his freedom and his peace must fly from her, and the sooner the better."

Before Herr *Eck* gave his first concert, the family *Pixis* arrived at Königsberg upon their return from St. Petersburgh. I immediately renewed our acquaintance. The eldest brother had in the mean time grown very tall, and his soprano voice had changed to a deep bass. But he still dressed "à l'enfant with a turn-down collar and no necktie". They were much dissatisfied with their journey to Russia, and the father even affirmed that he was a thousand rubles out of pocket during their stay in St. Petersburgh, although he had taken with him two hundred letters of introduction.

We met at a musical party at Count *Calnheim's*, where the youngest played first of all some variations on the piano with great execution and taste. The eldest then played a quartett by *Krommer*. But neither the composition, nor his playing pleased me. "His tones", says a remark in my diary, "are without power, and his execution without expression. Added to this, he handled his bow so badly, that, if he does not alter this, he will never become a perfect virtuoso. He holds the bow a hand's breadth from the nut, and raises the right arm much too high. In this manner, all strength fails him in the stroke, and the shades of *piano* and *forte* vanish altogether in his playing." After him, Herr *Eck* also played a quartett by *Krommer*. "But Heavens! what a difference was there! The transitions from *forte* to *piano* in his tones, the clearness of the passages, the tasteful *fioriture* by which he knew how to enhance the most common place composition, lent an irresistable charm to his playing. He gained also, the most undivided applause. *Pixis* then played a quartett by *Tietz*, the celebrated crazy violinist of St. Petersburgh, but had just as little success with it as with his former one. At last, he begged Herr *Eck* to play a duet by *Viotti* with him, in order that he might be able to say that he had played with all the great violinists of the day; for *Viotti, Rode, Kreutzer, Iwanovichi, Tietz, Durand* and others, had all done him that honour. In this request all the company joined, and Herr *Eck* was obliged to consent. *Pixis* played this duet best of all, although he did not bring out *one* of the passages as well as Herr *Eck*, who was not at all prepared for it."

In the Concert also, which the brothers gave, the eldest had no success, "the passages were flat and without expression: he even played very false, and at times scraped so much as to inflict pain on the ears of the audience..... According to my idea, three years ago when I heard him for the first time in Brunswick, he played the easy Concertos of *Iwanovichi* and others, better than the difficult ones with which he now came forward." Yes, I even doubted whether he ever could become a great violinist, "unless he soon got a good master, who, of all things, could give him a good style of bow-ing."

Upon these doubtless too severe criticisms my Instructor who was a very stern judge, may certainly have had some influence. When, ten years later, I again met *Pixis* in Vienna, he had become a distinguished virtuoso, and as Professor at the Conservatory in Prague, he proved himself also an able teacher of the violin.

In Königsberg, I began again to paint. I made the acquaintance of a miniature painter, named *Seidel,* who gave me some lessons, and sat to me. The picture was very like. My diary speaks also of composing. From a remark about the polishing down of a Concerto, it is evident that at that time, I did not understand how to work of a piece; in which I afterwards succeeded so well, that, the rough draught, seldom suffered even from slight changes, and, once written in score, it was never altered afterwards.

For our journey to Memel, "we chose the road along the shore, being twelve miles (German) shorter than that across the country. In winter also, when the sand is hard frozen, it is better to drive on than the latter. Three miles from Königsberg, the road runs close to the sea, and does not leave it until you reach Memel. We travelled the whole night, and suffered much from the cold and cutting sea air. Between the fourth and fifth station we had the misfortune to have a wheel come off. We were now obliged to quit the carriage, to right it by our united strength, and secure the wheel temporarily with ropes. All this may have lasted a full half hour, and I feared I had got my fingers frostbitten; but this I happily found to be groundless. At nine o'clock we reached Memel, but were obliged to wait three whole hours until we could be carried across the harbour, because the boatmen had first to be collected from all parts of the town. Four miles farther we reached the frontiers."

We arrived at Mittau with a large addition to our number; for Myrrha, without our remarking it, had brought forth nine pups, six living and three dead. "All, excepting two, were taken away from the poor mother."

In the families to whom Herr *Eck* was recommended, we found the most hospitable welcome. We were invited to dinners, suppers, musical parties and balls; and everything was done to render our stay agreeable. In the house of a "Collegiate-Assessor", *von Berner,* I played for the first time in the place and in the presence of my teacher. It happened thus; Herr *Eck*, after having played some quartetts with great applause, was solicited to accompany a young Pianiste of 16 years of age, a Miss *Brandt*, who was possessed of a surprising skill, in a Sonata of *Beethoven's*; but he excused himself on the plea of great fatigue. As I well knew that *Eck* did not dare to play any piece *at sight*, that he did not know, I offered to play in his stead. It is true, the Sonata was wholly unknown to me, but I trusted to my readiness in reading. I was sucessful; and the young Artist, in whom probably but little confidence had been felt, was overwhelmed with praise.

At the subsequent musical parties, I was now always solicited to play something; and I remember that Herr *von Berner* on my taking leave of him, said to me with fatherly kindness: "My young friend, you are on the right road — only keep in it! Herr *Eck* as a Virtuoso is certainly still above you; but you are a much better musician than he is."

In the Governor's house I heard a Violinist of the name of *Sogeneff*, who at that time was very celebrated in Russia, and a serf of Prince *Subow*. "He played variations of his own composition, which were immensely difficult. The composition pleased me right well, but his play, although skilful, was very raw, and offensive to the ear. Herr *Eck* played immediately after him, so that the difference between the two Players was very distinctly perceptible. The play of the Russian, was wild and without transition from *forte* to *piano*; that of Herr *Eck* firm, powerful, and still, always harmonious. We heard there, also, some Russian military singers. They were six private soldiers, some of whom sang soprano parts. They shrieked fearfully, so much so that one was almost obliged to stop ones ears. They are practised in singing by a non commissioned Officer, cane in hand. In some songs they accompanied themselves on sort of Schalmey of so piercing a tone, that I expected the ladies would have fainted away. The Melodies of the songs were not bad, but accompanied by a great deal of false harmonics."

At a club in the house in which we lived, I was invited

to a card party "with three Excellencies, but was obliged to pay dearly for the great honour, for I lost more than three thalers in a few hours."

Our departure for Riga was put off until December the second, on account of Herr *Eck* recurring indisposition. I spent my evenings at the houses of Herr *von Berner* and *von Korf*, in turn, and constantly practised with Fräulein *Brandt*. We played through the whole store of sonatas with violin accompaniment, and many of the masterpieces of *Mozart* and *Beethoven* were thus brought under my notice for the first time. After supper we chatted for an hour, or Frau *von Korf* played at chess with me, a game which from my childhood, I had been passionately fond off.

Herr *von Berner*, who had become attached to me, invited me to pass some months with him in the country, upon my return from Petersburgh; and then to give some Concerts about midsummer, a season in which all the Courland nobility are assembled at Mitau. It gave me great satisfaction to hear that I was considered far enough advanced to appear in public as a virtuoso. I gladly consented.

It is odd that there is nothing mentioned in my diary about the children of Herr *Berner;* for one of his daughters who afterwards became a pupil of *Rode*, and distinguished herself as a violin player, must already then have been very nearly grown up.

At last the hour of our departure came, and with a moved and grateful heard I took leave of the families who had so kindly welcomed me.

In Riga, I found a letter from Brunswick, that gave me much pleasure. I had asked permission of the Duke to dedicate my new Concerto, as my first published work, to him; and the answer written by the Lord Chamberlain *von Münchhausen*, brought the consent to my request. Full of impatience to see my work appear, I begged Herr *Eck* to write to *Breitkopf & Härtel* in Leipsic, with whom he was in correspondance, to propose the publishing of the concerto. The reply soon arrived, but was very discouraging to me.

For the consolation of the young Composer who can find no publisher for his first work, the conditions upon which the above named firm consented to undertake its publication, may be mentioned. I had myself given up all claim to payment, and only stipulated for some free copies. The firm required however that I should buy one hundred copies at half the selling-price! At first my youthful Artist-pride rebelled against such dishonourable conditions, as I deemed them. But the wish to see the publication of the concerto so expedited, that, upon our return to Brunswick, I might be able to present the Duke with a printed copy; joined to the hope that he would make me a present, assisted me to conquer my sensitiveness, and agree to the conditions. The concerto was finished in time, and when I returned, was lying ready at a Music-seller's in Brunswick; but the package was not delivered to me before I had paid for the hundred copies.

In Riga, Herr *Eck* had a quarrel with the Society of Musical Dilettanti there. Being in possession of the Concert room; they required from him, as from all foreign artists, that he should first perform in their concert, for which they were ready to give him up the room and orchestra, for his own concert afterwards. Herr *Eck* refused to comply with these conditions and would rather give up his own concert altogether. This made the company more compliant; and they declared themselves satisfied, if he would agree to play in no other concert than theirs, after his own. He consented to this, on the condition that they would be silent about it beforehand: because he had been told that the subscribers to the dilettanti concerts would be unwilling to pay for an extra-concert, if they were sure of hearing the foreign Artist in the former. Silence, however, was not kept, and the consequence was that Herr *Eck's* concert was badly attended. Angry at this, he now demanded the sum of fifty ducats for his appearance in their concert, as a remuneration for the loss which their gossiping had caused him. The gentlemen directors, feeling in some degree that they had been wrong; after long debating, agreed to pay thirty ducats. Herr *Eck*, however, stood by his first demand. The gentlemen now threatened to make the police compel him to appear; and he was actually summoned before the Chief of the police. But he succeeded in winning him over to his cause, and the gentlemen directors were dismissed, with their charge. At last, upon the day of the concert, after the bills parading forth the name of Herr *Eck*, had been posted up at the corners of the streets, they vouchsafed to grant the required demand; but they were not a little surprised at the declaration of Herr *Eck*, that, now, after having been summoned before the police he would not play at all, not even for double the sum demanded. All their threatning and storming was of no avail; they were obliged to give their concert without him. "I was there," says the diary, "and much enjoyed the fermentation that prevailed among the dilettanti. Nothing but Herr *Eck* and his refusal were spoken of; but nobody said one single word in his favour; all were too much annoyed at their disappointed expectations. The concert went off badly. A virtuoso on the flute, from Stockholm, who first played an old fashioned concerto by *Devienne* in place of Herr *Eck*, pleased as little as a dilettante from St. Petersburgh, who executed a concerto for the piano by *Mozart*, in a most schoolboy-like manner."

Eck, had however won the good will of the Director of the police, by having offered to give a concert for the benefit of the Nikolai Asylum for the poor. *Meirer*, the Director of the Theatre, gave the house gratis, und Messeurs *Arnold* and *Ohmann*, as well as the ladies *Werther* and *Bauser* gave their vocal services. The Musical Society did all they could to put a stop to it; but in vain. "Immediately upon his appearance Herr *Eck* was received with the liveliest applause, which was still more increased after he had played. The proceeds, after deducting the expenses, amounted to more than a hundred ducats, which were handed over to the cashier of the Asylum;

but a gift of one hundred ducats from the nobility present was also made to Herr *Eck*, and the next morning, fifty more followed from several rich merchants, who did not wish to be behindhand in generosity."

Among the many invitations, one is also mentioned in the diary, to the house of the rich sugar baker *Klein*, who "kept no less than three tutors for his children" — a German, a Frenchman and a Russian.

On the seventeenth of December we quitted Riga. In Narwa the governor, a great lover of music, who had seen from the *Paderoschna*, which we were obliged to deliver up at the gate of the town, to be examined, what a celebrated *Artist* was passing through, invited us immediately for the evening. "Our excuse, that we could not appear in our travelling clothes, was not accepted. The governor sent his state carriage, and we were carried off half by force. The embarrassment at finding ourselves all at once in the midst of a brilliant society, clad in travelling costume, very soon wore off after the friendly welcome and obliging politeness of those present, and we passed a pleasant evening. At one o'clock when the party broke up, we found our carriage with post-horses ready before the door, and set out immediately."

But, between Narwa and St. Petersburgh, one misfortune after the other occured to us. Two stations on this side of St. Petersburgh, we were persuaded to place our carriage upon a sledge. But hardly had we driven half an hour in it, when the cords with which it was fastened, broke, and we could get on no farther. The postillion was obliged to get some peasants from the neighbouring village to help us. After the job was done, they made us understand by signs that we were to pay them five rubles. Very angry at this shameful demand, we refused to give so much, but as they shewed the intention of cutting the cords with which they had bound the wheels, with their axes; and as we saw that we could not contend against the crowd of wild looking fellows who by degrees had surrounded our carriage, we were obliged to comply with the demand."

"After a halt of more than an hour we were at last enabled to proceed; but it was not long before we stuck fast in the snow, and it was only by the help of several peasants whom we called to assist us, that we were able to extricate ourselves. We now found that in the deep snow, the sledge hindered more than it served us, and we had the carriage taken off. After this was done, and paid for, we were enabled to proceed; but again seven times did we stick fast, so that no less than sixteen hours were necessary to accomplish this post of three miles. As we came nearer to St. Petersburgh we found the roads better, and were also driven faster. At last, Wednesday the 22. at nine in the evening, we arrived; after being six days and five nights upon the road. The last part of the journey from Narwa to St. Petersburgh is dreadfully uniform and tiresome. The perfectly straight road cut through the fir forests, with the party coloured Werst-stones, each exactly like the other, are enough to weary the most patient! Seldom only does the endless forest open, to disclose a few buildings, or a miserable village. The houses, or rather the huts of these villages, have for the most part, one room only, with a window a foot square. In this room, men and animals live together quite peaceably. The walls consist of unhewn beams laid upon each-other, the crevices being filled up with moss. It cannot certainly be very warm in these holes; but the inhabitants do not seem to care for that; for I saw children and grown up people running about in their shirts, and barefoot in the snow. The poorer and more wretched the objects appear during the journey, the more surprising is the magnificent St. Petersburgh and its palaces. . . . . We descended at the *Hôtel de Londres*, and immediately engaged a guide, without whom one cannot be here even for one day; for as soon as the stranger is shown his room, not a soul troubles himself about him any farther."

In St. Petersburgh, I was at first quite left to myself.

This would therefore have been the most favorable opportunity for me to look round that splendid city. But the extreme cold, which already exceeded twenty degrees, would not permit of this. I therefore continued to work with my usual diligence, and indeed with increased zeal, for the period of Herr *Eck's* instruction was more than half elapsed. — Through a member of the Imperial orchestra we were introduced into the "Citizen Club," and there made the acquaintance of almost all the celebrated *artistes* and scholars then in St. Petersburgh. Among others, my diary mentions *Clementi*, his pupil *Field*, the violinist *Hartmann*, the first violin of the Imperial orchestra, *Remi*, also a member of the orchestra, *Leveque*, the son of the leader in Hanover, and director of an orchestra of serfs belonging the senator *Teplow*, *Bärwald* from Stockholm, the hornist *Bornaus*, and others.

Clementi, "a man in his best years, of an extremely lively disposition, and very engaging manners," liked much to converse with me "(in French, which from my great practice in St. Petersburgh I soon spoke pretty fluently)" and often invited me after dinner to play at billiards. In the evening, I sometimes accompanied him to his large pianoforte warehouse, where *Field* was often obliged to play for hours, to display the instruments to the best advantage to the purchasers. The diary speaks with great satisfaction of the technical perfection and the "dreamy melancholy" of that young artist's execution. I have still in recollection the figure of the pale, overgrown youth, whom I have never since seen. When *Field*, who had outgrown his clothes, placed himself at the piano, stretched out his arms over the keyboard, so that the sleeves shrunk up nearly to his elbows, his whole figure appeared awkward and stiff in the highest degree; but as soon as his touching instrumentation began, everything else was forgotten, and one became all ear. Unhappily, I could not express my emotion and thankfulness to the young man otherwise than by a silent pressure of the hand, for he spoke no other language, but his mother tongue.

Even at that time, many anecdotes of the remarkable avarice of the rich *Clementi* were related, which had greatly increased in latter years when I again met him in London. It was generally reported that *Field* was kept on very short allowance by his master, and was obliged to pay for the good fortune of having his instruction, with many privations. I myself experienced a little sample of *Clementi's* true Italian parsimony, for one day I found teacher and pupil with up turned sleeves, engaged at the washtub, washing their stockings and other linen. They did not suffer themselves to be disturbed, and *Clementi* advised me to do the same, as washing in St. Petersburgh was not only very expensive, but the linen suffered greatly from the method used in washing it.

Of all the acquaintances I made in the Citizen's Club, none were dearer to my than my young friend *Remi*. The diary speaks of him immediately after our first meeting, as a "polite and charming young Frenchman." The same enthusiasm for art, the same studies and the same inclinations bound us yet closer to each-other. We met every day at dinner at the Citizen's Club, when I was not invited out with my Instructor; and when in the evening there was no Opera or Concert in which *Remi* was engaged, we played duets, of which *Remi* possessed a great collection, till late in the night. There were many evenings in that cold winter on which the Theatre was closed; for by an *ukas* of the benevolent Emperor *Alexander*, all public amusements were forbidden when the cold should exceed seventeen degrees, in order that the coachmen and servants might not be exposed to the danger of being frozen to death. And during that winter, the cold often remained at above seventeen degrees for a fortnight together. That was a dull, monotonous time for foreigners. But foreign *artistes*, were still worse off, for they were unable to give their concerts. When the cold fell below seventeen degrees there were notices innumerable; but they were often obliged to be recalled on the following day. Herr *Eck's* public concert was also postponed till March 6. O. S. after having been announced more than once. In the mean time however, he played twice at Court at the private Concerts of the Empress, and pleased so much, particularly the second time, that the Empress had him engaged as solo player in the Imperial Orchestra at a salary of 3500 rubles.

The less frequently operas and concerts took place in the cold months of January and February, the more diligently I attended them, in order to become more nearly acquainted with the native and foreign talent. I also saw and heard *Tietz* the celebrated crazy violin player. He was a man of about forty years of age, with a ruddy complexion, and pleasing exterior. His appearance in no wise showed his insanity. We therefore were the more astonished when he addressed every one with the question, "My most gracious monarch, how are you?" He then related to us a long affair in which was but little evidence of sanity; complained bitterly about a malicious sorcerer, who, jealous of his violin playing had so bewitched the middle finger of his left hand that he could no longer play; but at last expressed the hope that he would still be able to conquer the spell — and so forth. On taking leave of us he fell upon his knees before Herr *Eck*, kissed his hand, before the latter could prevent it, and said, "My most gracious Monarch, I must do homage to thee and thine art, upon my knees!"

Four months later, in the beginning of May 1803, all St. Petersburgh rang with the sudden news that *Tietz*, whom the Russians in their blind patriotism regarded as the first violinist in the world, and who on account of his madness had not played for six months, had suddenly commenced again. *Leveque* related the nearer particulars to me. *Tietz* had been invited to a musical party at the Senator *Teplow's*, but had refused to play in spite of all entreaty; Herr *Teplow*, much annoyed, sent away the orchestra saying, "Then I also will never again hear music!" This made so deep an impression upon *Tietz* that he said, "most gracious Monarch, have the orchestra recalled; I will play a symphony to their accompaniment." This took place, and having once began, he played quartets until two o'clock in the morning. The next day the amateurs assembled in his house and he played again. This gave me the hope of hearing him also, and on that account I hastened to him on May the second (20. April). Many amateurs were once more assembled there, who again beseiged him with requests to play; this time however in vain. He was not to be moved, and I afterwards heard that some one had been of the party whom he did not like.

On the eighteenth of May I took my new duet and my violin, and went again to Herr *Tietz*, whom I this time found alone. It did not require much to persuade him to play the duet; but he would not take the primo. We had hardly ended, when Herr *Hirschfeld*, hornist in the Imperial orchestra, and others with whom I was unacquainted, came in. Herr *Tietz* begged me to repeat the duet, and it appeared to please not him alone, but also the others. Herr *Tietz* now opened a quartet by *Haydn*, and required me to take the first violin. He himself took the violoncello part. As the quartet was known to me, I did not refuse. It was pretty well executed, and Herr *Tietz*, as well as the others present, owerwhelmed me with praises. *Tietz* played the secondo of my duet, which is not easy, without faltering and perfectly clean, executing the cantabile passages with taste and feeling. The passages which, according to the old method, he played with rebounding bow, pleased me less.

On the 23th May, we met *Tietz* at the weekly evening concert of the Senator *Teplow*, where a pianiste named Madame *Meier* appeared, and played a piano concerto of her own composition, which was not bad. Then *Eck* and I followed with a concerto of his brother's, which we had been closely practising for the previous fortnight. At the beginning, I was nervous, and played the first solo not so well as at home; but it soon went on better, particularly in the last parts.

Herr *Tietz* now produced a concerto of his own composition, the Allegro and Rondo of which he played twice, possibly because the first time did not please him. As he never had practised since his madness, it may be readily conceived that technical firmness was wanting in his play. The difficult passages also, were executed very much better the second time. Into all the three parts, he introduced cadences in the old style, improvising them; they were in themselves very pretty, but sounded quite different the second time."

The diary closes with the remark, "though *Tietz* indeed is not a great violinist, much less the greatest in the world as his admirers maintain, he is undoubtedly a musisal genius as his compositions prove."

The best violinist then in St. Petersburgh was, without doubt, *Fränzel* junior. He had just come from Moscow where he had been engaged for six concerts at three thousand rubles. His attitude in playing displeased me. The diary says:

"He holds the violin still in the old manner, on the right side of the tail piece, and must therefore play with his head bent...... To this must be added that, he raised the right arm very high, and has the bad habit of elevating his eyebrows at the expressive passages. If this is not unpleasant to the majority of the listeners it is still very disagreeable for a violinist to see...... His playing is pure and clean. In the Adagio parts, he executes many runs, shakes, and other fioriture, with a rare clearness and delicacy. As soon however as he played loud, his tone is rough and unpleasant, because he draws his bow too slowly and too near to the bridge, and leans it too much to one side. He executed the passages clearly and purely, but always with the middle of the bow, and consequently without distinction of piano and forte."

I heard another celebrated violinist, Herr *Bärwald*, afterwards leader in Stockholm. As he came forward to play the concerto of *Viotti* (A-sharp) he was already applauded, before he had sounded a note.

This, together with his good bearing and his excellent manner of managing his bow, raised my expectation very high, and it was with the greatest impatience that I awaited the end of the *Tutti*. But who was I disappointed on hearing the solo! His playing was indeed clean and accomplished, but still so sleeply and monotonous, the passages so flat and drawn out, that I would have much preferred the false but still fiery playing of *Pixis*. He introduced, and played an Adagio of his father's composition, something better, and thus somewhat reconciled me again. After him, one Herr *Palzow*, a man celebrated for his theoretical knowledge, played a concerto of his own composition, on a piano with a flute attachment. Well and scientifically as the concerto was worked out, it pleased neither me nor the others listeners, on account of its length and monotony. The tones also of the strings and of the flute had together a very bad effect.

I also wrote my opinion of *Fodor*, the then celebrated violinist and composer. I heard him in the concert of the "Nobility's, or Musical club," where however everything was very unmusical; for the elite assembled there, "not to listen, but to chat and walk about in the saloon." At first a fine symphony by *Romberg*, (*C*-sharp) was extremely well executed. Then Signor *Pasco*, first tenorist of the Italian theatre, sang an aria so charmingly, tastefully and tenderly, that it actually became somewhat more quiet in the saloon. Herr *Fodor* now followed with a concerto of his own composition, which however appeared to me worse than those I already knew. His playing also did not please me. He played indeed in a pure and rather accomplished manner, but without warmth and taste. In the passages he also played with rebounding bow, which soon became unbearable. Madame *Canarassi*, prima donna of the Italian opera who before had not pleased me on the stage, sung this time so beautifully, that I must confess to having wronged her.

During Lent, the Greek church allowing no theatrical representations, the Intendancy of the Court theatre gave two grand concerts weekly in the Steiner theatre, in which, only virtuosi of the Imperial orchestra performed, among whom Herr *Eck* was now reckoned. The best whom I had the opportunity of hearing there were the violinist *Hartmann, Jerchow* and

Remi, the violinist *Delphino*, the hautboyist *Scherwenka*, and the hornist *Hirschfeld*.

In the first concert, the orchestra consisted of thirty six violins, twenty bass and double set wind instruments. Besides these the choruses were supported by forty hornists from the Imperial orchestra, each of whom had only one single note to blow. They served in place of an organ, and gave the chorus, the notes of which were divided among them, great firmness and strength. In several short soli, their effect was ravishing. Before the orchestra, were the Court singers, men and boys, about fifty in number, all in red uniform embroidered with gold. After the first part of *Sarti's* oratorio, *Remi* played a violin concerto by *Alday* with much success. "After the concert as we drove home, he asked me for my opinion of his playing. As truth alone should be spoken between friends I did not withold from him that: clean and pure as his playing was, I had yet missed the shades of forte and piano, expression in the cantabile, and a sufficiency of vigour in the passages. He thanked me for my candour and declared that he had been particularly embarrassed that day, at having to appear in Herr *Eck's* place, the latter having previously been advertised for this concerto." — After the second part of the oratorio, Signor *Delphino* played a violin concerto. As his playing was much extolled I had expected more from him. "He played without taste, and not once perfectly clean."

The Italian singers appeared in the second concert, and the French in the third. Among the first, Signor *Pasco* and Madame *Canarassi*, already mentioned, distinguished themselves. Among the French there were only two, *M. St. Leon* and the celebrated *Phyllis Andrieux*, who could lay claim to be called singers; they had charmed all Petersburgh by their correct and pleasing singing, their skilful and graceful acting, and their personal beauty. There was especially a Polonaise with which the latter fascinated everybody, and which was always encored. The beginning of its found in my diary as follows:

Between the first and second part of this concert, the Imperial hornists executed an ouverture by *Gluck*, and with a rapidity and exactness which would have been difficult for stringed intruments, how much the more so then for hornists, each of whom blew only one tone! It is hardly to be believed that they performed the most rapid passages with the greatest precision, and I could not have conceived it possible, had I not heard it with my own ears. But as may be imagined, the Adagio of the ouverture made a greater effect than the Allegro; for it always remains somewhat unnatural to execute such quick passages with these living organ pipes, and one could not help thinking of the thrashings which must have been inflicted.

These concerts, with the exception of one in which Herr *Eck* played and Mademoiselle *Phyllis* sang, were but little frequented; for which reason the managers soon discontinued them.

On the other hand a performance of *Haydn's* "Seasons" which was given for the benefit of a widow's fund, (also during Lent,) was very well attended. Baron *Rall*, one of the projectors invited me also to take part. I therefore shared in all the orchestra rehearsals, and in these, as well as in the performance, played with M. *Leveque*, the same part. The orchestra was larger than any I had yet heard. It consisted of seventy violins, thirty bass, and double set wind instruments. The whole therefore was something very grand, and my diary mentions it with delight; as also of the work itself, which I then heard for the first time, although I estimated the "Creation" *yet higher!*

My playing thus with *Leveque*, had increased our friendship, and I learned from him that, during the summer he intended to visit his parents in Hanover. We therefore agreed to make the voyage to Lübeck in the same vessel.

As my new friend now visited me oftener, I played my new violin concerto to him, and expressed my wish, to hear it with the orchestra before I sent it to the publisher. *Leveque* immediately offered to study it with his orchestra, took the parts with him, and invited me to a rehearsal some days later.

"I was in great agitation now that I was about to hear my own composition with full orchestra for the first time. The Tutti were well studied, and from this I could calculate how, in every part, the effect I intended would be brought out. The most of them satisfied me, some even surpassed my expectation...... But I was the less pleased with my own play. All my attention being fixed on the accompaniment, I played much worse than I did at home. I therefore begged permission of Mr. *Leveque* to try the concerto once more at the end of eight or ten days, when I should have received the copy; this permission he readily granted."

The following appears later: "I got the copy of my concerto yesterday, for which I was obliged to pay eight silver rubles. I could have had six concertos copied for a like sum in Germany."

The work was again tried from the new-copied parts. I was much calmer than the first time, and played therefore much better. It was also better accompanied than before, and therefore more effective. *Leveque* declared himself very well satisfied. "I therefore hastened home, packed up my concerto and took it, together with a letter, to the post. I there heard to my great amazement, that there was no parcel's post in Russia by which one can send things out of the country, and that if I would send it as a letter I should have to pay at least fifty rubles." I therefore took it back in order to send it by sea by the next opportunity.

I have mentioned the Imperial hornband, each member of which had only one note to play. On the twelvth of January, the Russian Newyear, upon which day the Emperor, as usual, gave a grand masquerade in the Winterpalace, for which twelve thousand tickets were issued, I found the said band joined with the usual Ball-orchestra, and I heard a music such as till then I had no idea of." The accompaniment of this hornband gave a fullness and harmony to the orchestra such as I have never heard. Several Horn-Soli, produced a most enchanting effect. It was long before I could tear myself away from this place."

In another saloon opposite the Throne-room, the Imperial family, surrounded by the Court, were dancing. But as this part of the saloon was cut off from the rest by a wall of gigantic grenadiers with high bearskin caps, and as I, inspite of my fair allowance of inches, could not even peep over the shoulders of these giants, I was unable to see much of the Imperial state, and of the diamonds of the ladies. I therefore passed on, and entered the third and most beautiful of the saloons. It is entirely of polished marbles, the walls white, the pillars violet, and the window frames blue. The lights mirrored themselves a thousandfold in the polished stone. The whole building was lighted by twenty thousand wax tapers.

"After wandering several times through the apartments, and having gazed at all the magnificence, I tried to find Herr *Eck* again, he having been separated from me in the beginning of the evening. Among the twelve thousand present this was however a vain attempt. I now guessed that he had gone direct home, and not finding our servant in the place where he had been desired to wait, confirmed me still more in this idea. I therefore thought it best to proceed home, also, and hoped, thoroughly warmed as I was, to be able to go the short distance to our hotel without a cloak, although the cold had increased to twenty four degrees. But hardly had I reached the square before the Winterpalace, on the opposite side of which was our hotel, then I felt my nose and ears stiffen, and should certainly have had them frozen, although I rubbed them unceasingly, had I not been able to warm myself at a large fire in the middle of the square which had been lighted for the coachmen; before I attempted the other half of the way. Unluckily, however, Herr *Eck* had not yet come home, and as he had the key to our apartment, and the coffeeroom was already locked, I resolved to return again. Arrived there I managed to press forward to a buffet, and warm myself with a glass of punch. While I was observing the rich gold and silver plate with which the room was decorated, Herr *Eck* also came to the buffet. Arm in arm we wandered through the magnificient rooms once more, and then our servant with our cloaks having once more turned up, drove off together. My friend *Remi*, to whom I related my adventure, blamed me much for my want of precaution."

On the 27. Feb. the so called "mad week" came to an end. It has its name from the circumstance of the Russians allowing themselves the most boundless extravagancies as a sort of indemnification for the ensuing fast. "Not being allowed to taste either meat, milk, or butter for six weeks, they cram themselves well for the last time, and give themselves so diligently to the brandy bottle, that they do not recover their sobriety, and in this state allow themselves every possible liberty, thinking to atone fully for all in the following fast. — In all parts of the town, booths are erected, in which fruit, liquors, and comfits are sold. In others, Polichinelli, trained dogs, juggler's tricks and other things of the kind are exhibited. The chief delight of the Russians during this week is sliding down the ice-mountains, most likely because it is such a break-neck sport. Upon the Newa, and in various other places, high scaffoldings are erected, having on one side a flight of steps by which to ascend to the top, and on the other an incline descending gradually to the ground. This incline is laid down with large slabs of ice, which are joined together in the closest manner by water poured between the interstices. Down this glass-like surface of ice, the descent is then made in little sledges shod with steel, and these are guided by means of a short staff held in each hand. Great skill is required in order to keep the middle of the incline during the extreme velocity of the descent, so as not to fall over the sides which are protected by a slight barrier only. Four drunken Russians, who had scarcely started, having come in contact with each other's sledges and being thereby brought too near the barrier, paid dearly for their awkwardness. They fell over; two were killed upon the spot and the others were carried away with broken limbs. But this did not in the least disturb the enjoyment of the people, who pressed forward anew in crowds to the steps. On the 26, the Court drove out to the scene, and remained for a long time spectators of the neck-breaking amusement. At an evening party at *Baron Rall's*, I met also the Governor of Narva, who upon our passing through that town, had had us fetched almost forcibly to his house. He enquired in a friendly manner after my health; and added "on your return through Narva you will find the Petersburgh gate open, but the opposite one closed, and then you must remain my prisoner for eight days without mercy."

"This evening, *Field* played as well as Herr *Eck*, and in truth wonderfully. At two o'clock, the company sat down to supper, and we did not arrive home till past four o'clock."

On the 5. April, my birth-day; Herr *Eck* invited me to dine at the Hôtel de Londres. Previous to this, availing ourselves of the fine weather we took a walk on the Newa, the granite-faced bank of which was the resort of the *beau monde*. The breaking up of the ice was impatiently looked for, and heavy bets were made respecting the day on which this would take place. — In the evening I had a great and unexpected pleasure.

"*Remi* had again invited me to play duetts with him, and to day I was able to bring him a new one of my composition. After we had played this through for the second time, he embraced me and said: You must change violins with me, so that we may both possess a souvenir of each other! I was overcome with surprise and joy; for his violin had long pleased me better than my own. But as it was a genuine *Guarneri*, and at least worth as much again as mine, I felt obliged to decline his offer. He, however, would hear of no refusal and said: Your violin pleases me because I have heard you play on it so frequently, and though mine is really a better one; yet you must accept it from me as a birth-day present! I could now no longer refuse, and overjoyed carried my new treasure home with me. Here I would have liked but too well to play on it all night, and feast my ears with its heavenly tones; but as Herr *Eck* was already gone to bed, I was obliged to let it lie quietly in its case. Sleep, however, I could not!" On the 12. April, *Herr Leveque* came for me to take a walk down to the Newa. "We there found half St. Petersburgh assembled, awaiting the breaking up of the ice. At length, a cannon shot from the fortress announced the long desired moment. This was also the signal for the sailors to break up the long bridge of boats which connects Wasiliostrow with this part of the city. This was effected in a few minutes. The ice could now float down unimpeded, and in a short time boats were being rowed up and down. The first of these brought over the Governor of the fortress, who accompanied by a numerous suite and by the band of the regiment, brings over a glass of the water of the Newa to the Emperor in his Palace, and receives for it a present of 1000 roubles. After this, the serf-seamen of the Crown in red uniforms row all comers to and fro across, without charge, until the communication by the bridge of boats is re-established between both sides of the town. After we had looked on all this with great interest, walking up and down for some hours, we returned home."

On Easter-Eve, Sunday, 17. April, I was awakened by the firing of cannon, which announced the commencement of the Festival. As the night was very calm, every shot was heard in long repeated echoes, until another fell upon the ear. — On Easter Sunday the Russian greets his acquaintances with the words: "Christ is risen!" upon which the person saluted is obliged to kiss the other. One need only go to the window, to see people on all sides embracing and kissing each other. It was related to me that, "the Empress Catherine was walking on the bank of the Newa one Easter Sunday accompanied by all her Court, when a dirty fellow, probably somewhat drunk, threw himself in her way with the salutation: "Christ is risen" upon which in order not to violate the holy custom, she was obliged to kiss him. But, upon a sign given by her, he was immediately seized, and had ample time afterwards in Siberia to repent of his boldness!"

A few weeks afterwards, I received a commission from *Breitkopf & Härtel* of Leipsic to write an article upon the state of Music in St. Petersburgh for their Journal, which was published in the course of 1803.

On the 13. May, a most original popular Festival took place. Every body who possesses either a carriage, a horse, or a sound pair of legs, betakes himself on this day through the Riga gate to the Katharinen Hof; where they stare at each other for a couple of hours and then return home. I went there with *Leveque*, and must confess, that the sight of the handsome equipages, of which there may have been at least two thousand, together with their fashionably dressed occupants, afforded me much amusement. Katharinen Hof is a small wood, which considering the climate looks tolerably green. From here one has a fine view of the sea. In the middle of the wood stands the Summer-Palace of Peter the Great, which together with its antique furniture is still kept up in exactly the same condition as when he lived there. It is a very poor looking place, and more like the house of a citizen than the Palace of a mighty Emperor. We returned home by another road, and saw numerons fine Villas and gardens, of which there are a great number outside this gate."

Thus amid various occupations, and short excursions to view the magnificent City, the time of our departure drew nigh. We agreed for our passage by sea with a Lubeck captain to whom for the voyage inclusive of board for both of us, we paid 20 ducats. Just before we left, we were present during the celebration of another grand Festival which I have minutely described. It was the Jubilee commemorating the foundation of St. Petersburgh by Peter the Great, one hundred years since.

On the 28. May, the whole garrison assembled on the Isaak Square and was drawn up and commanded by the Emperor in person. In his suite rode the whole of the General Staff, and the Ambassadors from Foreign Courts. At ten o'clock the Empress made her appearance with the Court, occupying some twenty magnificent carriages. The State Carriage in which the Empress mother sat by the side of the Empress, was covered with gilding and richly inlaid with precious stones. On the top of the carriage was a crown of brilliants, fixed upon a purple cushion. This state carriage was drawn by eight cream coloured horses in silver harness, ornamented also with precious stones. The other Court carriages which were also very handsome, were each drawn by six horses. The Emperor rode a magnificent horse richly caparisoned, but was otherwise dressed in a very plain uniform. In his suite was a Turkish Prince who attracted the attention of all by the splendour of his dress. The hilt of his sabre was covered with diamonds, and his stirrups and spurs were of massive gold. When the cortège had arrived in front of the Isaak's Church, the Emperor dismounted and led the Empress into the edifice, where the *Te-Deum laudamus* was immediately chaunted by the Singers of the Court. Unfortunately we were not successful in our effort to get into the Church, as the doors were closed immediately after the entrance of the Court. But it is very probable that even in the interior of the building little of the Music could be heard, for not only were all the bells set ringing, but salvos of artillery were fired from the fortress, and by the ships of war lying in the Newa. The Military drawn up on the Square before the Church increased the noise yet more by the fire of musketry, and the populace were not at all backward in shouting, so in this manner not a single note of the Music reached us on the square. After the Service was ended, the Court proceeded on foot through two lines of soldiers to the Senate House. What ceremonies took place there, I was unable to ascertain. After the space of about half an hour, the Court resumed their places in the carriages, and the cortège returned in the same order to the palace. In the evening the City was brilliantly illuminated, and more so than I had ever yet seen. At nine o'clock, *Leveque* came to fetch me, and took me first of all to the Summer Garden. Dark clouds hung in the sky, and threatened to extinguish the lamps which had been but just lighted, with a heavy shower. With the now clear nights, when it keeps so light till midnight that one can read and write without a candle, this black sky was most welcome, for otherwise the illumination would have been less effective. The Garden was very brilliantly lit up. On both sides of the alleys a wooden frame work had been raised which was thickly hung with glass lamps of different colours. At the end of the Alleys, were seen brilliantly illuminated triumphal arches, in the centre of which shone the capital letters P (Peter) and A (Alexander). The whole of the Pavillions throughout the garden were also lit up in a splendid and tasteful manner.

But the Fortress presented a truly magic sight, as on leaving the Garden we came on the bank of the Newa. It swam in a very sea of fire! The granite masonry of the walls was hung with white lamps, the pillars and the cornice of the entrance gate with red, and the sentry boxes on the top of the ramparts with blue. The graceful tower of the fortress was lit up to its topmost point, and as there was no wind, there was not even one lamp that did not burn. From the place where we stood, the whole fairy like scene was again seen reflected in the Newa at our feet! It was indeed an enchanting sight! But the sky grew constantly darker and more threatening; we were therefore obliged to make haste, in order to see other parts of the city." "Near the bridge, which was also brilliantly illuminated, we saw a large ship hung with lamps up to the very tops of the masts, between which countless streamers were waving.

The streets which radiate from the Admiralty in the form of a fan, many of which are above two miles in length, were lit up as light as day, and presented a magnificent sight, with the merry crowds streaming through them in their gayest attire. Among the Public Buildings which were richly decorated with transparencies and devices, the Admiralty was especially conspicuous. Some private houses also, exhibited transparencies, among others that of the Grand Chamberlain *Narischkin*; in which, Mars, accompanied by the allegorical figures of Wisdom and Justice, crowned the letters P. and A., the first of which had beneath it the Inscription: *Gloire du premier Siècle*, and the last: *Gloire du second Siècle!* — We now followed the stream of the multitude, which pressed forward to the Summer Garden where a display of Fire Works was to take place. But we had scarcely reached the Arcades of the Winter Palace, when a sudden torrent of rain put an end at once to the splendour of the scene, and St. Petersburgh but a few minutes before brilliant as with the light of day, was shrouded in Egyptian darkness! Under the Arcades of the Square where we had taken shelter, was the only place that remained illuminated. This circumstance procured for us a curious and amusing spectacle. The mass of people all dressed in their various coloured Sunday attire, who were flying home out of the Summer Garden, were obliged to pass in review before the place where we stood, and dripping with rain they presented a comical sight enough. Some women had drawn their dresses over their heads in place of umbrellas; others, trusting to the darkness, had even taken off their shoes and stockings to save them, and waded by barefooted, not a little discomposed at being obliged to pass by a place lit up so brightly, and filled with laughing spectators. At length after about an hour, the rain ceased, and we now could also return to our homes. On the 1. June, (20. May) I packed up my last things and then went to take leave of my friends and acquaintances. The parting from my kind friend *Remi*, was very painful, and cost us both many tears. He promised in a few years to pay me a visit in Germany. My leave taking from my Instructor to whom I owed so much, was a very sad one, and the more so, that for some time past he had again been very unwell, and I therefore feared I should never see him again!

This fear was but too well grounded; we never saw each other more! Respecting his subsequent and in part highly romantic fate, I have learned the following, but cannot pledge myself for its entire truth, since I derived it for the most part from hearsay.

At the time I left St. Petersburgh, *Eck* had entered upon a love affair with a daughter of a Member of the Imperial Orchestra, but without the least notion of marrying the girl. Shocked at such levity, I thought it my duty to caution the parents. I did so; but my warning was received with coldness and disbelief. Some months afterwards, when the visits of Herr *Eck* had suddenly ceased, the daughter confessed with tears that she had been seduced by him, and that she already felt the consequences of it. Her mother, a resolute woman, succeeded in obtaining an audience of the Emperor; threw herself at his feet, and implored the restitution of her daughter's honour. The Emperor consented. In true Russo-Imperial style he offered Herr *Eck* the choice: either to marry his sweetheart within twenty four hours, on prepare for a promenade to Siberia. Herr *Eck* naturally chose the former. That a marriage sprung out of such circumstances would soon become a hell upon earth, may easily be imagined. *Eck*, whose health had been already greatly shattered by his former excesses, could not long endure the effects of the daily recurring matrimonial discords. He lost his senses, and soon became so furious, that the mother in law was again obliged to entreat the Emperor's assistance. He granted a dissolution of the marriage; gave the wife a pension, and ordered the husband to be sent under proper care to his brother, at Nancy. The selection of the man to whom the unfortunate sufferer and the sum granted by the Emperor for the journey were entrusted, was however, a very unluckly one, and failed in its object; for scarcely had he arrived in Berlin with the invalid, than he declared to the Russian Ambassor there, that the money was expended, and therefore he could accompany his charge no farther. At the same time he laid before the Ambassor an account of his expenses, according to which indeed, the sum given by the Emperor was exhausted. There were however some very extraordinary items in the account; among others, a dinner of one hundred covers, which the lunatic had ordered without the knowledge of his guardian, in one of the first Hotels in Riga, and which the latter had been obliged to pay. Whether the Ambassador remained satisfied with this account, was never known; but the Guardian disappeared all of a sudden!

In the meantime, the lunatic finding that he was no longer watched, was seized with the desire to escape. One evening, half dressed only, he succeeded in slipping out of his room unperceived; and as there was a heavy fall of snow at the time, he effected his escape unperceived through the city gate. He had already got some miles from Berlin when he was seized by some peasants, and as they believed him to be an escaped convict they brought him back bound to the city. At the Police Office, the poor half frozen fugitive was soon discovered to be a lunatic, and handed over to the Asylum for the insane. Some members of the Court Orchestra who a few years before had known and admired the unfortunate man in the height of his artistic career, became interested for him. They set on foot a subscription among their colleagues and some wealthy amateurs of the Art, and with the proceeds they sent him under the care of a trustworthy man to his brother at Nancy. The latter procured for him a becoming treatment in the Asylum at Strasbourg, where he remained for several years. His misfortune then reached the ears of his former patroness the Dowager Electress of Bavaria, who sent him to a clergyman of Offenbach or somewhere near that place, who devoted himself to the cure of the insane. There, it is said, if not quite cured, he became much more composed, so that a violin could again be placed in his hands, from which it is said he drew the most touching melodies. After the death of the Electress he was then placed in the Asylum for the insane at Bamberg, where, either in 1809 or 1810, he died.

On the 2. June (21. May) at 9 in the morning, we sailed from St. Petersburgh.

"On passing a guard ship at the mouth of the Newa we were compelled to show our passports, these were returned to us without charge, which from our previous experience astonished us greatly. As the wind was against us, the sailors were obliged to row continually, this made the progress slow and at length very tedious; so that we were very glad when at last we arrived at 2 o'clock at Cronstadt. We there put up at the German eating house, the master of which had been recommended to us for his honesty. But with all that, he retained also the thorough bluntness, not to say rudeness of his class, for when we returned at 9 in the evening from a walk, and asked for supper, he replied with a true north-German accent: now is no time for eating, people go to bed now! And with that he turned his back upon us. Dumbstruck, we went up stairs, and had already made up our minds that we must go hungry to bed, when he at length had us called down to supper. At first we were much inclined to refuse it; but our hunger got the better of our sensitiveness. We went down, found a right good repast, and the host who waited upon us himself, sought to make amends for his previous rudeness by the most friendly behaviour."

It was not until after some days that the wind became fair for the farther voyage; but very soon, and for a very long time, the "Saturn" — so our ship was called — was obliged to tack about, and on the 14 June "we were still not far distant from the high land, which we had already reached on the first day." On the second day the sea rose very high, and the passengers therefore, three women and nine men, became all sea-sick one after the other. With me it began with a head ache. "I felt my courage so depressed, that I bitterly repented to have come by sea." But on the fourth day I got better, and in a short time, although the sea was still very rough, I felt as well as on land. It was not so with all, for the ladies and also some of the gentlemen were for a long time sick and invisible. *Leveque* and I amused ourselves meanwhile very well. We played duetts, read, wrote, and made sketches; walked up and down the deck and ate and drank with real appetite. In this way passed day after day. But like the others, we longed for a fair wind, "for this eternal tacking, with which one makes but little progress, is quite unbearable!"

On the 15 June, the wind grew fair; on the 16, it fell almost calm, and on the 20, we had a storm. This was so violent that the ship cracked in every timber. "I crept ill as I was, upon deck, to see the terribly grand spectacle. I got thoroughly drenched it is true, for the waves broke every moment over the deck, nor could I long endure above the piercing wind and cold. But it was worth the effort, to see how the waves like mountains, came rolling on, threatening to submerge us, how they then suddenly seized us, lifted us high in air, and then again as quickly let us plunge into a deep abyss! Although I had become somewhat accustomed to this sight by the previously experienced high sea, yet every time we made a plunge, I felt my back run cold, and should have thought we were in great danger, had I not read the contrary in the calm face of the captain. He gave his orders always with the same coolness. But it was nevertheless fearful to behold how the seamen clambered to the top of the masts, and then out upon the yards to reef the sails. Only those who have grown up amid such perils can brave unmoved the wild rage of the elements."

On the 26 June, we arrived off Bornholm, a Danish island, on which we could perceive two small towns, several villages, and a carefully cultivated country. "The sight of the green cornfields which I had not beheld for so long a time was particularly cheering to me." From a small neighbouring island "some peasants put off to us in a boat with some fresh meat, vegetables and milk. I was particularly pleased with the latter, for I could not at all relish the black coffee."

"On one or two evenings, with a clear sky and calm weather, we had a sight, such as one never sees in the same grandeur upon land, namely, the sun set. It is impossible to describe the splendour of the ever changing colours, with those also of the clouds scattered over the heavens, and which were again reflected in a sea as smooth as glass; but the impression made by this heavenly sight in the solemn stillness of the evening, upon the whole ship-company assembled on the deck, will never be forgotten by me. I saw the most callous among them moved by it."

At length on the 28 June, after a voyage of one and twenty days, the "Saturn" cast anchor in the roads of Travemünde, and on the 5. July, 1803, I was once more in my native town Brunswick, which after my long absence was now doubly dear to me. We arrived at 2 o'clock in the morning.

"I alighted at the Petri Gate, crossed the Ocker in a boat, and hastened to my grandmother's garden. But arrived there, I found both the house and garden doors locked, and as my knocking was not heard, I clambered over the garden wall, and laid myself down on the ground in an open summer house at the bottom of the garden. Fatigued by the journey I immediately fell asleep, and notwithstanding the hardness of my couch, would probably have slept on for a long time, had not my aunts in their morning walk in the garden, discovered me in my retreat. Greatly allarmed, they turned back, and told my grandmother that a strange man was lying in the summerhouse. Returning all three together, they had courage to approach nearer, recognised me, and I was now awakened with joyous exclamations, embraces and kisses. For some time I could not recollect where I was; at length I recognised my dear relations, and was overjoyed to find myself among them once more, and in the home of my childhood. They had been very anxious about me, as owing to our tediously long sea passage they had received no intelligence of us for six weeks.

The first pleasing news that I heard, was, that the celebrated *Rode* was there, and would shortly play at Court. I therefore immediately announced my return to the Duke, in order to be permitted to attend the Court-concert.

I immediately closed my oft cited Diary, with the wish that "it might often afford me a pleasing remembrance of the agreable journey. I was received by my Patron with the same benevolent kindness as formerly, which was manifested also, by his gift of the remainder of the sum furnished for my travelling expenses, which was by no means inconsiderable, and which upon my handing in the account and the balance, was presented to me by the Grand Chamberlain. For the dedication of my Concerto, which I had handed to the Duke on my first interview, I also received twenty Friedrichsd'or.*

I now burned with the desire, to appear with this Concerto before the Duke, in public, as a Violinist and Composer; to exhibit proofs of my industry, and the progress I had made. But this was not to be effected so readily, for *Rode* had already announced a Concert to be given in the Theatre. The idea of making my appearance so soon after that celebrated Violinist was also a source of some anxiety to me. For the more I heard him play, the more was I captivated with his playing. Yes! I had no hesitation to place *Rode's* style of play (then still reflecting all the brilliancy of that of his great master *Viotti*,) above that of my Instructor *Eck*, and to apply myself sedulously to acquire it as much as possible by a careful practice of *Rode's* compositions.

* One Fredericks d'or (single) = 16^s 6^d English.

In this I succeeded also, by no means ill, and up to the time when I had by degrees formed a style of playing of my own, I had become the most faithful imitator of *Rode* among all the young violinists of that day. I succeeded more especially in executing in his style the eighth Concerto, the three first Quartetts, and the world famed Variations in G-Major; in these, both in Brunswick, and afterwards on my first grand artistic tour, I achieved great success.

Shortly after *Rode's* departure, the day I had so ardently wished for arrived, on which in a Concert given by me at the Theatre, I was to exhibit the first proofs of the artistic skill I had acquired on my travels. Curiosity had assembled a numerous audience. From the ready surety with which I could play not only my own Concerti, but the other music I had practised under *Eck's* direction, I might have been expected to feel no embarrassment upon my appearance. Nevertheless, I could not wholly overcome it, when I thought, that, but shortly before, in the very place where I stood, so great a Violinist had played before the same audience. But I had now to put to shame my invidious detractors, who on my setting out upon my journey had loudly asserted that the Duke would again throw away his money upon one who would prove incapable and ungrateful. I therefore summoned all my resolution, and already during the Tutti of my Concerto, I succeeded in banishing from my mind all and every thing around me, and gave myself up to my play with my whole soul. The result, also, was a success beyond all expectation; for already after the first Solo, a general applause broke forth, which increased with every succeeding one, and at the end of the Concert seemed as though it would never cease. The Duke, also, who during the intervening pause sent for the young *artiste* to his box, expressed to him his full satisfaction. That day, therefore, is still borne in my remembrance as one of the happiest of my life.

I was now appointed First Violin, in the place of a recently deceased "*Kammermusicus*" and received the additional salary accruing to that post, of 200 thalers. But as on account of the three months grace allowed to his widow, this salary could not immediately commence, I was compensated by another present of twenty Friedrichsd'or.

With my salary of three hundred thalers, and my additional evenings I could at that time live quite respectably and free from care. I therefore, again took my brother Ferdinand to live with me, and devoted myself assiduously to his improvement. As I had not yet seen my parents and brothers and sister, I went to Seesen to fetch him. While there I received a visit from my fellow traveller *Leveque*, who was about to return to St. Petersburgh. During the eight days we were together, we played diligently, and my parents and musical friends of the little town were especially delighted with the performance of my Duetts, which we had so perfectly studied during the sea voyage.

On my return to Brunswick, I began anew my labours in composition. I first of all completed a Violin-Concerto in E-Minor, which I had commenced on the journey, but which remained unpublished, because it no longer pleased me after I had adopted *Rode's* style of execution. Nevertheless I played it several times with great applause in the Winter-Concerts. At that time also, at the wish of the Violoncellist *Beneke*, whom I frequently met at Quartett parties, I wrote a Concertante for Violin and Violoncello with orchestral accompaniment. Neither was this work ever published, and not even included in the list of my compositions, as at the time I began to make that, I did not lay my hand on it, and indeed had wholly forgotten it. Nevertheless there must be some copy of it in existence, for I heard it once in 1817 or 1818, at a concert in Mayence given by the brothers *Gans*, afterwards members of the Royal Orchestra at Berlin, who played it without at the same time acknowledging it as my composition. It is true, the piece of music seemed known to me, just as though I had heard it before; but not until I had asked my neighbour for the programme of the concert, and seen my name affixed to the piece, did the recollection of that production of my youth recur to my mind. I now recollect nothing more of it, than that it consisted of an *Adagio* and *Rondo*, and the last written in $^6/_8$ time. But I can no longer remember the key.

The practise of this Concertante with *Beneke* may probably have given rise to the resolution we formed to make an artistic tour together, and to Paris; where I had long desired to go. The permission for this journey was readily obtained through the favour in which I stood with the Duke, and so we set out upon it in January, 1804, with the most pleasing anticipations.

We first spent some few days with my parents at Seesen, from whence we announced our coming to Göttingen, to give our first concert there. For the journey thither, we hired a carriage. Shortly before my leaving Brunswick I had had a case made more worthy of the splendid Violin I had brought from Russia, i. e. a very elegant one, and in order to protect this from all injury, I had packed it in my trunk between my linen and clothes. I therefore took care that this, which contained my whole estate, should be carefully fastened behind the carriage with cords. But, notwithstanding, I thought it necessary to look out round at it, frequently, particularly as the driver told me that but recently between Nordheim and Göttingen, several trunks had been cut down from behind carriages. As the carriage had no window at the back, this continual looking out behind was a very troublesome business, and I was therefore very glad, when towards evening we arrived between the gardens of Göttingen, and I had convinced myself for a last time that the trunk was still in its place. Delighted, that I had brought it so far in safety, I remarked to my fellow-traveller: my first care shall now be to procure a good strong chain and padlock for the better security of the trunk.

In this manner we arrived at the town gate, just as they were lighting the lamps. The carriage drew up before the guardhouse. While *Beneke* gave our names to the sergeant, I anxiously asked one of the soldiers who stood round the carriage: is the trunk still well secured?

"There is no trunk there!" was the reply. With one bound I was out of the carriage, and rushed out through the gate with a drawn hunting knife. Had I with more reflection listened awhile, I might perhaps have been fortunate enough to hear and overtake the thieves running off by some side path. But in my blind rage, I had far overshot the place where I had last seen the trunk, and only discovered my overhaste when I found myself in the open field. Inconsolable for my loss, I turned back. While my fellow-traveller looked for the Inn, I hastened to the Police Office, and requested that an immediate search might be made in the gardenhouses outside the gate. With astonishment and vexation I was informed that the jurisdiction outside the gate belonged to Weende, and that I must address my request there. As Weende was half a league from Göttingen, I was compelled to abandon for that evening all further steps for the recovery of my things. That these would prove fruitless on the following morning, I now also felt assured; and I passed a sleepless night, in a state of mind such as in my hitherto fortunate career had been wholly unknown to me. Had I not have lost my splendid Guarneri-violin, the exponent of all the artistic excellence I had till then attained, I could have lightly borne the loss of the rest. A moderate success during the tour would soon replace them. But in this manner, without a violin, I should be compelled not only to give up the journey, but in a certain degree recommence my study anew from the very beginning.

On the following morning the Police sent to inform me that an empty trunk and a violin-case had been found in the fields behind the gardens. Full of joy I hastened thither, in the hope that the thieves might have left the violin in the case, as an object of no value to them, and as likely to lead to their discovery. But unfortunately it did not prove so. The bow of the violin, only, a genuine *Tourté*, secured in the lid of the case, had remained undiscovered; everything else, inclusive also of a sum in gold for the expenses of the journey, had been carried off. The Music had been considered unworthy of the thieves' notice. It was found strewed all over the field. As my manuscripts were among it, of which I had no copies, I was glad to have recovered these at least.

Without money, without clothes and linen, I was now first of all obliged to procure on credit what was most necessary, before I could give with my fellow-traveller the concert which we had already announced. In the meantime, I practised diligently upon a very good violin by *Stainer* which I borrowed of a student from Hanover, and thus prepared, I made my first appearance out of Brunswick as an artiste. The concert was unusually well attended. Perhaps the account of my loss had contributed to it. The Solo performances of the two artistes, as also together, in my Concertante, were received with enthusiastic applause.

This it is true was very encouraging for a further prosecution of the journey; but anxiously concerned for my reputation, I could not make up my mind to appear publicly, before I had procured a good violin of my own, and had carefully practised myself upon it.

As *Beneke* was unwilling to proceed further on the journey without me, we therefore returned to Brunswick. The intelligence of my loss had already become generally known there. The Duke, also, had heard of it, and in order to facilitate my purchase of a new instrument sent me again a handsome present. With the aid of that, I purchased from a *Herr von Hantelmann*, a distinguished amateur, the best violin in Brunswick at that time, but I soon felt, that it could not fully replace the one which I had lost.

In order to prepare myself well for a future journey, I again applied myself diligently to composition. Thus I wrote the Concerto in D-Minor which was published by *Kühnel* of Leipsic as (Op. 2), a Potpourri upon chosen themes (published also by the same, as Op. 5.) and a Concerto in A-Major which has remained in manuscript. In these, as also, in some subsequent compositions, *Rode's* style is predominant, from which at a later period only, my own style and peculiar mode of execution develloped themselves.

In this manner passed the summer of 1804. In the autumn, fully prepared for a fresh Musical tour, I felt disposed to repair first to the German Capitals. I much desired also to appear once in Leipsic, which through the excellently conducted Musical Journal of *Rochlitz* had risen to be the Centre of Musical criticism. I therefore set out upon my second Artistic tour on the 18. October, through Leipsic and Dresden, to Berlin.

Of this journey also, a Diary exists, but which extends only to the 9. December, and then suddenly breaks off. The cause of this will be related hereafter.

I made my first stay at Halberstadt, where I gave a public Concert, and on the following day played at the house of Count *Wernigerode*. Among the Musical amateurs who received me in a particularly kind manner I must mention the Vicar of the Cathedral, *Augustin*, and the Auditor *Ziegler*. With the latter, who was an accomplished connoisseur of Music and an excellent pianist, I remained on terms of intimacy until his death. I received also great attention and assistance in getting up my Concert, from the there resident Musicians, the brother Organists *Müller* and *Holzmärker*, the Violinist *Glöckner*, with whom I played my Duetts, the Bassonist *Barnbeck,* and *Clase,* the Secretary and Musical Director of Count *Wernigerode*. I therefore passed many pleasant days in Halberstadt.

One afternoon, "I took a walk with Herr *Holzmärker* and one of his friends outside the gate of the town. We visited the Klus, a mountain on the top of which rise several isolated steep rocks, the inside of which is excavated, and which according to the legend was the work of robbers, who in former times took up their abode there. I could not resist the desire to ascend one of these rocks, hazardous as was the attempt, and earnestly as my companions dissuaded me from it. I succeeded in reaching the summit without accident, and besides the pleasure I felt at having effected what few had the courage to attempt, I had that of an extensive and magnificent view. So far all went well. But when at length I wished to descend, and looked down the declivity, a sudden giddiness overcame me, and I was instantly obliged to sit down to save myself from falling over the precipice. Full ten minutes elapsed before I could summon the necessary composure to make the descent, and it is doubtful whether I should have effected it in safety, if the gentlemen below had not shouted to me, where to set my feet, which I could not see to do, having my face turned towards the rock. Trembling from the exertion and the convulsive clinging to the rock, as well as thoroughly ashamed at having disregarded the warning of the two gentlemen, I reached them at length, and returned with them to the town not a little glad to have escasped uninjured from so eminent a danger."

On the 22. October, I gave my Concert. At the rehearsal, my Concerto in D-Minor had made a great sensation.

"Messrs. *Ziegler*, *Müller* and others declared to my great satisfaction, that they had never heard a finer Violin Concerto."

"The Concert itself began at five o'clock. The Theatre was very empty, but the audience was composed of persons possessed of a high intelligence of Art, as I could readily see by the deep silence and sympathy with which my play was listened to." Among other things, the following were executed: A Symphony by *Haydn;* my Concerto in D-Minor; a Concerto in D-Major by *Kreutzer;* a Polonaise by *Rode* from the Quartett in Es-Major. After the Concert, Count *Wernigerode* expressed his satisfaction to me, and invited me to a Concert at his house on the following day, in which the third Count assisted as Clarionetist in the orchestra. I played *Rode's* Concerto in A-Major and his Quartett in Es-Major.

"After the Concert was over, the company surrounded

me and overwhelmed me with expressions of praise. I was obliged to relate to the ladies a great deal about St. Petersburgh."

In Magdeburg, as artiste I also met with the most friendly reception. Captain *von Cornberg*, Major *von Witzleben*, Regimental Quartermaster *Türpen*, and Privy Counsellor *Schäfer*, to whom I was recommended, exerted themselves to the utmost, both to procure a numerous audience for me, and to make my stay as agreeable as possible. Already at my first Concert on the 3. November, the audience was very numerous. I played my D-Minor-Concerto, the A-Minor-Concerto of *Rode*, and the G-Major-variations.

"I succeeded right well in all, and the people seemed to be quite carried away by my play."

At this time I occupied myself with the remodelling of my last Concerto but one, in E-Minor. I wrote an entirely new Adagio for it.

At a Musical party at the house of the Secretary to the Board of Finance, *Feska*, I heard his son play in a Quartett of his own composition.

"The Quartett," says the Diary, "is very well worked out and evinces great talent. As a Player he pleased me less. He is certainly not wanting in mechanical skill, but in a finished and well regulated handling of the bow, and therefore in a good tone, and in clearness of the passages. Neither was his intonation always pure. Were he to study under a good master, he might become something great."

I went frequently to parties at the houses of the Merchants *Hildebrandt* and *Schmager*, of the Criminal-Counsellor *Sukrow*, and the Privy Counsellor *Schäfer*, and "everywhere pleased much."

"I was also invited by *Türpen* to an interesting Musical Soirée. I found assembled there a small but a very select company of the most zealous friends of Music in Magdeburg. I played Quartetts by *Haydn*, *Beethoven*, *Mozart*, and in conclusion the Es-Major-Quartett of *Rode*. I was accompanied very well in all of them, so I that could give myself entirely up to my feelings. The company seemed enchanted. Herr *Türpen* affirmed that I understood better than any one how to render the peculiar style of each Composer. As finale, our host played a Trio by *Mozart*, right well, on a very good pianoforte by *Blum* of Brunswick. But he has the bad habit of drawing out the "Canto" too much, by which he rather injures the expression than improves it."

On the 10. November, I gave my second Concert, which was not quite so numerously attended as the first, and in which I executed a Symphony by *Haydn* and my Violin-Concerto in E-Minor, I also played a Concertante by *Eck*, with *Feska*. The remodelled E-Minor-Concerto went well. The new Adagio appeared to please very much.

Of the other circumstances that occurred while I was in Magdeburg, I will only mention a theatrical representation, the Author of the Piece having made himself a name in the theatrical world by his piquante notice "Musical Ollapodrida from Paris." It was the first representation of "The Female Aballino" by *Sievers*.

"Never have I read or seen enacted a more wretched piece. It is a sorry imitation of the well known "Great Bandit," but has neither the exciting scenes nor the clever dialogue which made that piece a favorite of the public. The chief personage Rosa Salviatti, who in order to protect her lover from a conspiracy of his uncle's, resorts to the most romantic and absurd means, explains the reasons of her conduct in a speech that lasts at least a quarter of an hour. The public, which had already previously manifested signs of impatience, became so noisy during this discourse, that the play could scarcely be concluded. At length when the curtain fell, a general hissing and whistling broke forth. The unfortunate Author, unappreciated as he considered he had been in Brunswick, and who thought to achieve a triumph here, is said to have been present in the Theatre, but made a hasty retreat before the end of the piece."

Respecting my stay in Halle, whither I next went, the Diary gives but very scanty information. The more I was drawn into society by an increased circle of acquaintances, the less pleasure I took as it would appear, in the previous frequent freedom of style in my remarks upon it. I may also not have had the time, as I was very careful in preparing myself for every performance whether public or private, and was constantly engaged in composing.

My two Concerts on the 21. and 23. November, were very well attended. Besides my own works, I played a Concerto of *Rode,* A-Minor and the G-Major variations.

"My play met with an enthusiastic reception." The persons, who took a particular interest in me, and whom I have to thank for many pleasant hours, were the Family *Garrigues,* consisting of the father, mother, daughter and two sons, all of them very charming, polite people; *Lafontaine* and his fascinating adopted daughter; *Chodowiecki, Niemeier* and *Loder.* Among the students I made the acquaintance of some clever amateurs. One Herr *Schneider* played well on the piano; another, Herr *Müller* right well on the violin. Herr *Gründler,* from Trebnitz near Breslau, immediately took instruction from me on the violin.

I yet remember also the following incident: Among those who were also of assistance to me in the arrangements for my Concert was the celebrated Counterpointist *Türk.* He directed the Academical Concerts, one of which took place during my stay in Halle. The Opera "*Titus*" was given as Concert-Music. The public had been already assembled for the space of half an hour; the Orchestra had finished tuning and awaited the signal to begin. Among the Student part of the audience, great dissatisfaction had begun to shew itself at the delay in the appearance of the Singer; but when he at length made his appearance, in very unseemly dress for the occasion, in an overcoat and with dirty boots, the general disapprobation was shewn by hissing and a shuffling of the feet. The Singer, into whose hands the impatient Director had already thrust the notes, stepped forward and said with a contemptuous look: "If I do not please you as I am, why then I can go away again!" Hereupon he threw the notes at the feet of the Director and rushed out of the place. They ran after him to bring him back; but all in vain! I now expected that the Concert would be postponed, or at least that all those "Numbers" in which Titus has to sing, would be omitted. Nothing of the kind! The conscientious Director did not allow his auditory to go short of a single bar of the music; he knew how to help himself!

He played upon his Grand-Piano the whole Part of Titus, Recitative, Airs, and Concerted-pieces from the first note to the last! I was astounded, and knew not whether to be vexed, or to laugh at the singularly naive expedient. But it was made quite clear to me that evening, that a man may be a learned Counterpointist and yet not possess an atom of good taste!

After my arrival in Leipsic on 29. November, the Diary gives two short notices and then remains wholly silent. The first concerns a representation of the Opera by *Paer*: "Die Wegelagerer" (The Way-layer); the second relates to a visit to the Drapers-Hall-Concerts.

"These Concerts", it says, "are got up by a Society of shopkeepers. But they are not Amateur-concerts; for the orchestra is alone composed of professional musicians, and is both numerous and excellent. For the Vocal part a foreign female singer is always engaged, as the Director of the Theatre does not allow his singers to appear in concerts. This year it is a Signora *Alberghi* from Dresden, the daughter of a Church-singer of that City. She is still very young, but has already a very good method, and a clear, melodious voice. She sang two arias with great applause. Besides that, I heard the Concert Master of the society, Herr *Campagnoli*, play a Concerto by *Kreutzer*, extremely well. His method, it is true, is of the old school; but his play is pure and finished. The Room in which these Concerts are given is exceedingly handsome, and particularly favorable to the effect of the music."

I had many difficulties to overcome for the arrangements of my concert. Engrossed in the business pursuits of this commercial city, people did not come forward to assist me with the readiness I had been hitherto accustomed to meet, and I had much to do before every obstacle was overcome. It annoyed me also that the wealthy merchants to whom I was recommended appeared as yet to know nothing of my artistic reputation, and that though politely, they received me coldly. I was therefore exceedingly desirous to be invited to some musical party, in order to attract notice to my capabilities. This wish was gratified; I received an invitation to a large evening party, with the request to perform something. I selected for the occasion, one of the finest of *Beethoven's* six new Quartetts, with my performance of which I had so frequently charmed my audience in Brunswick. But already after a few bars, I remarked that those who accompanied me were as yet unacquainted with this music, and therefore unable to enter into the spirit of it. If this already annoyed me, my dissatisfaction was much more increased when I remarked that the company soon paid no more attention to my play. For by degrees, a conversation began, that soon became so general and so loud that it almost overpowered the music. I therefore rose up in the midst of my playing, before even the first Theme was concluded, and without uttering a word, hastened to replace my violin in its case. This excited a great sensation among the company, and the master of the house advanced towards me with an enquiring look. I went forward to meet him, and said aloud, so as to be heard by the company: "I have hitherto been accustomed to find my play listened to with attention. As that has not been so here, I of course thought the company would prefer that I discontinued." The Master of the house knew not what reply to make, and retired much embarrassed. But when, after having apologised to the Musicians for breaking off so suddenly,

I shewed the intention to take my leave of the company, the host returned and said in a friendly tone: "If you could be persuaded to play something else for the company more adapted to their taste and capacity you will find a very attentive and grateful auditory." I, who had already clearly comprehended, that I was most to blame for what had occurred, from my misapprehension in the choice of music for *such* an auditory, was glad of the opportunity to conciliate matters. I therefore willingly resumed my violin and played *Rode's* Quartett in *Es*, which the Musicians knew and therefore well accompanied. A breathless silence now reigned, and the interest shewn in my play increased with every passage. On the conclusion of the Quartett so many flattering things were said to me of my play, that I was induced now to parade my hobby-horse the G-Major-Variations of *Rode*. With this I so enchanted the company that I became the object of the most flattering attention for the remainder of the evening.

This incident became the subject of conversation for many days, and was probably the cause, that the musical-amateurs whose attention had been thereby directed to me, came even to the rehearsal of my Concert in considerable number. At this, I succeeded so well in winning them over to me, by the execution of my D-Minor-Concerto, that before the evening on which my Concert was to take place they had spread a favourable account of my performances throughout the City, and thereby a more numerous audience was attracted than I had dared to hope. The élite of the musical amateurs of Leipsic and a very sympathetic public were present. I now succeeded also in awakening such an enthusiasm in my auditory, that at the conclusion of the concert I was vehemently solicited to give a second. This took place a week later, and was one of the most numerously attended that had ever been given by a foreign artiste in Leipsic. In the meanwhile, I was frequently invited to Quartett parties, at which, after I had previously practised them with those who were to accompany me, I obtained more particularly a hearing for my favorites the six first of *Beethoven's* Quartetts. I was the first, who played them in Leipsic, and I succeeded in obtaining a full appreciation of their excellence by my style of execution. At these Quartett parties I also first made the acquaintance of the Editor of the Musical-Journal, Councellor *Rochlitz*, and from that time till his death maintained the most friendly relations with him. *Rochlitz* wrote a notice of my concert in his paper.

As that Notice first established my reputation in Germany, and had an influence upon my career in life, it may serve as apology for my verbal citation of it in this place:

"On the 10. December, 1804, Herr *Spohr* gave a Concert in Leipsic, and at the solicitation of many, a second, on the 17. in both of which he afforded us a treat such as, so far as we can remember, no Violinist with the exception of *Rode* ever gave us. *Herr Spohr* may without doubt take rank among the most eminent violinists of the present day, and one would be astonished at his powers, more especially when his youth is considered, were it possible to pass from a sense of real delight to cold astonishment. He gave us a grand Concerto of his own composition (D-Minor), which was called for a second time, and another, also from his own pen (E-Minor). His Concerti, rank with the finest existing, and in particular, we know of no Violin Concerto, which can take precedence of that in D-Minor, whether as regards conception, soul and charm, or also, in respect of precision and firmness. His peculiarity inclines mostly to the grand and to a soft dreamy melancholy. And so it is with his brilliant play. Herr *Spohr* can execute everything; but he charms most by the former. As regards, in the first place, correctness of play in the broadest sense, it is here, as may be presupposed, as sure fundamental principle; a perfect purety, surety and precision, the most remarkable execution; every manner of bow-ing, every variety of violin-tone, the most unembarrassed ease in the management of all these, even in the most difficult passages; these constitute him one of the most accomplished virtuosi.

But the soul which he breathes into his play, the flights of fancy, the fire, the tenderness, the intensity of feeling, the fine taste, and lastly his insight into the spirit of the most different Compositions, and his art of rendering each in its own peculiar spirit make him a real Artiste. This last faculty we have never seen possessed in so remarkable a degree as by Herr *Spohr*, and more especially in his Quartett-playing. It is therefore not surprising that he should please everywhere, and scarcely leaves any other sentiment behind, than the wish to detain and to hear him always."

I felt exceedingly happy that moment! But it was not alone the recognition of my merits as an artiste that infused a new life into my whole being: it was another, a more tender feeling. I loved and was beloved.

The day after I saw and heard *Rosa Alberghi* for the first time at the Draper's Hall Concert, I paid her a visit, to invite her to take part at my concert. Both mother and daughter received me in a very friendly manner. The former, although a resident in Germany for many years, had not acquired one word of our language. As she also shook her head on my addressing her in French, I was obliged to make my wishes known to the daughter, who, educated in Dresden, spoke German fluently. She very willingly assented to my request, and forthwith chatted with me a child-like ingenousness, as though we had long known each other. On my taking leave, *Rosa* asked me to come again soon. I had already gazed too deeply into her brilliant dark eyes, to let her wait long for me. And as the mother soon made me cordially welcome, I passed all my hours of leisure at their house. I accompanied *Rosa* in her singing practice on the piano, to the best of my ability; assisted her in the study of the Music sent to her by the Directors of the Concerts, and embellished her Arias with new ornaments, at which she always evinced a really child-like pleasure. In this manner, without our perceiving it, our relations became constantly more tender. The notes in my Diary on this subject had however come to a stop, nor were they afterwards resumed. *Rosa* now sang in my second Concert, and as her engagement in Leipsic was drawing to a close, and that she was about to return to Dresden, she offered also to sing in my concerts there.

I now therefore, left for Dresden, furnished with high recommendations. A letter from *Rosa* introduced me to her father, who received me in the most friendly manner. He, with some members of the Dresden Royal Orchestra, namely the brothers *Röthe* assisted me in the arrangements for my concert, and thereby made an always unpleasant business much lighter for me.

Rosa returned to Dresden a few days before the concert, and sang in it with her father. The success which my play and compositions met with, was even more brilliant than in Leipsic. As there, also, I was invited on all sides to give a second concert. While I was making arrangements for this, I was advised to announce myself also at Court, as from the sensation which my Play had made, there could be no doubt of a favourable result.

But, when I was informed, that the Court-Concerts took place during Dinner and that no exception to the rule was made in favour of foreign artistes, my youthful Artistic pride kindled with indignation at the idea that my Play would be accompanied by the clatter of plates; so that I immediately declined the honour, of playing at Court.

My second Concert was extremely well attended, and the applause almost greater than at the first.

I now thought of my departure for Berlin, but could not make up my mind to it; for the parting from my beloved *Rosa* seemed too painful to think of. When, on a sudden, her father surprised me with a proposal which still further delayed the dreaded parting. He said, that he had long wished his daughter should appear in Berlin, and if I had no objection to give some concerts there together with her, as he was himself unable to obtain leave of absence, his wife should accompany her on the journey.

To this proposal with joy I acceded and immediately began to make every preparation for our departure. As the journey by Coach, was considered too fatiguing for the ladies, we hired a carriage together. I sat opposite to my beloved one, and complained neither of the slowness of our progress nor the length of the journey. Arrived in Berlin, we found apartments all ready for us in the same house, which my former Instructor *Kunisch*, now a member of the Berlin Royal Orchester, had provided for us upon receipt of a letter from me announcing our coming. The latter, not a little proud to introduce the young Artiste as his former Pupil, procured for me the acquaintance of the most distinguished artistes of Berlin, and was also of great assistance to me in making arrangements for a concert, which nevertheless owing to the great number of persons then giving concerts, was obliged to be postponed for some time.

Meanwhile I delivered my letters of recommendation, and thereupon was invited to some Music parties. I first played at *Prince Radziwill's*, himself well known as a distinguished Violoncellist, and talented Composer. I there met *Bernhard Romberg, Möser, Seidler, Semmler*, and other distinguished artistes. *Romberg,* then in the zenith of his fame as a Virtuoso, played one of his Quartetts with Violoncello obligato. I had never yet heard him, and I was charmed with his play. Being now solicited to play something myself, I thought that to such Artistes and Connoisseurs I could offer nothing more worthy than my favorite Quartetts of *Beethoven*. But again I soon remarked that, as at Leipsic, I had committed an error; for the musicians of Berlin knew as little of those Quartetts as the Leipsickers, and therefore could neither play now appreciate them. When I had finished, they praised my play, it is true, but spoke very disparagingly of what I had performed. *Romberg,* even, said very bluntly: "But dear *Spohr*, how can you play such stuff as that?" I was now quite doubtful of my own taste, when I heard one of the most famous artistes of the day express such an opinion of my favorites. Later in the evening when again asked to play, I selected as I had done in Leipsic, *Rode's* Es-Major-Quartett, and was gratified by a similar favourable result in this instance.

The second Music-party, to which also my fellow-travellers were invited, was at Prince Louis Ferdinand's of Prussia. We drove there together, and were received by the host in the most courteous manner. We there found a brilliant circle of decorated gentlemen and fashionably dressed ladies, as also the principal artistes of Berlin. I met there, also, a former acquaintance of Hamburgh, the celebrated Pianist-Virtuoso and Composer *Dussek*, who was now Instructor to the Prince, and resided in his house. The music commenced with a Piano-Quartett, which was executed by him with real artistic brilliancy. It was now my turn. Made wise by my recent experience, I only selected such compositions, as I could shine in as Violinist, namely: a Quartett, and the G-Major-Variations of *Rode*. My play met with the most enthusiastic applause, and *Dussek* in particular, seemed delighted with it. My loved *Rosa*, also won general admiration by her execution of an aria, in which she was accompained by *Dussek* on the piano.

After the conclusion of the music, the Prince offered his arm to one of the Ladies present, and led the company who at a sign from him had done the same, to the dining room, where a splendid supper had been laid out. Each gentleman without ceremony took his place by the side of his lady; and I by the side of my dear fellow-traveller. At first the conversation though free and unembarrassed was yet marked with decorum. But when the champagne began to circulate, many things were heard not suited for the chaste ears of an innocent girl. As soon therefore as my observation had led me to infer that the supposed distinguished ladies did not belong to the Court as I had believed, but more probably to the Ballet, I began to think of withdrawing unperceived from the company, with my fellow-traveller. I succeeded also, without being remarked or prevented, in making good our retreat; and reaching my carriage, I returned with *Rosa* to her expecting mother. The next day I was told that the Prince's Music-parties generally ended in similar orgies.

I still remember an other Music-party — it was at the house of the Banker *Beer* — where I heard for the first time, the now so celebrated *Meyerbeer*, play in his paternal house, then but a boy of thirteen years of age. The talented lad already then excited so much attention by his accomplished execution on the piano-forte, that his relatives and admirers regarded him with the greatest pride. It is related, that, one of these on returning from a Lecture on popular Astronomy exclaimed full of joy to the boy's parents "Only think! our *Beer* has been already placed among the Constellations! The Professor shewed us a constellation, which in honour of him is called "the little *Beer!*"*

I conceived the shrewd idea of inviting the young virtuoso to perform a Solo in my Concert, this was willingly assented to by the family. As it was the boy's first appearance in public, it drew a crowd of his admirers, and I may chiefly thank that circumstance for my concert having been one of the most numerously attended of a period that teemed with Musical performances. After overcoming numerous obstacles it eventually took place in the theatre. My playing, and the singing of my fair fellow traveller were received here as at Leipsic with great applause. Not so favorable however was the criticism that appeared in the new Musical Journal then but recently published by *Reichard* the Musical conductor of the Royal Orchestra. He aminadverted in his own peculiar offensive manner chiefly upon my easy *abandon* in respect to Time.

Although I felt hurt by such an imputation, to which I

---

* This pun on the *idem sonans* of the word "Beer" with "Bär" anglice "Bear", being almost as obvious in the English as the German, will be readily understood by the reader.

was not yet accustomed, I was obliged to confess that yielding to my depth of feeling, I had kept back in the Cantabile, perhaps, too much, and in the Passages and more impassioned parts carried away by my youthful fire, I had precipitated them too much. I therefore determined to correct such blemishes in my execution without diminishing its force of expression, and by unremitting attention I succeeded.

After several unavailing attempts to give a second concert in Berlin, I was compelled to abandon the idea. I therefore divided the not unconsiderable receipts of the first, with my fellow-traveller, and began to think of my return to Brunswick, as the period of my leave of absence was drawing to a close. *Rosa's* mother also made preparations to return home, having failed in an endeavour to procure an engagement for her daughter at the Italian Opera in Berlin.

Rosa had daily evinced an increasing attraction towards me, and manifested her partiality without disguise. I, on the contrary, on a nearer acquaintance, was obliged to confess to myself that she was not suited for a partner in life for me, and I therefore carefully avoided being betrayed into any declaration. She was it is true, an amiable, unspoiled girl, and richly endowed by nature; but her education, apart from the polish of social forms, had been greatly neglected, and what was more especially displeasing to me, was her bigotted piety, which had once even led her to attempt the conversion of the Lutheran heretic to the only true Church of salvation. I bore the parting with tolerable self-controul; but *Rosa* burst into tears, and with the last embrace pressed into my hand a card with the letter *R*, worked upon it with her beautiful black hair, as a souvenir.

Upon my return to Brunswick, I devoted myself with renewed zeal to Composition. I wrote my H-Minor-Concerto, which was subsequently published by *Simrock* as Fourth Violin-Concerto. For the first time, a foreign pupil was sent to me, one Herr *Grünewald* from Dresden. During my stay in Brunswick, I also gave lessons to a Miss *Mayer*, a talented young lady of sixteen, who as Violiniste gave several concerts at Brunswick with much applause; under my direction she studied my concerto in D-Minor. This pupil, after a lapse of five and twenty years, during which time I had heard nothing more of her, suddenly excited a general interest, as much on account of her fate, as of her accomplished execution on the violin.

On one of her earlier artistic-tours, when in Poland, she had there married a landed-proprietor of considerable fortune. Although then in affluent circumstances, she never neglected the further cultivation of her great talent, though only as amateur. This enabled her, after her husband had lost his whole fortune in the Polish revolution, and had become a refugee, to support herself and her daughter. As Madame *Filipowicz*, she again made her appearance as an artiste, in Dresden, and played there the same D-Minor-Concerto she had studied under me five and twenty years before. As she considered that she was chiefly indebted for her now increasing success to her rendering of that Concerto, she felt impelled to express her thanks to her former Instructor in a letter. It was thus I became acquainted with the above circumstances. After her artistic-tour through Germany, she settled in Paris, and at a later period in London. From both places I received several letters from her. Upon my last journey but one to London, when I had hoped to have seen her again, I was informed that she had died a few days before my arrival, and I only made the acquaintance of her daughter, and of her husband, who was a Doctor, and also a Polish refugee.

But to return to the year 1805. In the spring, I received a letter from *Rosa*, in which with her ingenuous simplicity she said, that, so great had her longing become to see me again, that she had prevailed on her father to make an artistic tour to Brunswick; that she would arrive in a few days, and begged me to make the preliminary arrangements for a concert. I was not best pleased with this intelligence, and foresaw that great embarrassments might arise from it. I now perceived with regret that *Rosa's* inclination towards me was much more earnest than I had beleived, and I reproached myself bitterly for my conduct towards her. It was also evident to me, that her father had only undertaken this journey to bring me to some declaration in respect to his daughter. I therefore looked forward to their arrival with great anxiety. But everything passed off much better than I had anticipated. *Rosa's* heartfelt joy, to see me again, her lively unsuspecting simplicity, which did not permit her to feel the least doubt of a reciprocity of her feelings, assisted me to the avoidance of any explanation. Thus, after a fortnight's stay, they left Brunswick and returned to Dresden, very satisfied with their visit, and the brilliant Concert which my assistance obtained for them; and it was arranged that I should visit them after my projected journey to Vienna, in the autumn.

As they wished to return by way of Göttingen, I gave them a letter of introduction to my parents. During a stay of several days with my parents, *Rosa* so won their hearts by her amiability, that with unhesitating confidence she confessed her love for their son. Concluding from this, that I returned her affection, my parents had embraced her as my betrothed. I was greatly allarmed when I learned this in a letter from my father; protested against this engagement, and assigned as ground for my refusal, *Rosa's* want of education, and the difference in our religious faith. My father would not see the matter in this light, and repeatedly declared that I was a fool, to refuse so charming a girl.

In June 1805, I received a letter from *Bärwolf,* a Musician of the Ducal Orchestra at Gotha, who was unknown to me, that greatly influenced my destiny. Herr *Bärwolf* wrote to inform me of a vacancy that had taken place in the Orchestra there, by the death of the Director *Ernst,* and that the Intendant, Baron *von Leibnitz,* who had read so favorable a notice of my performances in the Leipsic Musical-Journal, was very desirous to recommend me to that post, if I would make immediate application for it. But, for this, it was required that I should repair personally to Gotha. He therefore invited me to come and play at the Concert that was to take place at Court on the 11. July, in celebration of the birth-day of the dutchess.

Extremely pleased at this, I hastened to the Duke, to request his consent to my journey. I received it, and immediately anounced this at Gotha. Arrived there, Herr *Bärwolf* introduced me to the Intendant. The latter appeared astonished to see before him so young a man, and said with a thoughtful expression of countenance, that I appeared to him almost too young to place at the head of so many men, all older than myself. But after I had conducted two Overtures at the rehearsal, and executed my Concerto in D-Minor, the Herr Intendant, had quite changed his mind, for he requested me to conceal my real age, and to give myself out as four or five years older. I was therefore introduced to the Court as a competitor for the situation, of twenty fours years of age. But the resort to such a deceit was indeed scarcely requisite to obtain it, for on my first appearance at the Court-Concert I won the favour of the Dutchess so completely, that the other competitors were all obliged to retire. By a Decree of the 5. August. 1805, I was installed as Concert-Director to the Ducal Court of Gotha, with a salary of nearly five hundred thalers, inclusive of allowances, my service duties to commence on the 1. October.

As my leave of absence was not quite expired, by the advice of Herr *Bärwolf*, before returning to Brunswick, I made a little excursion to Wilhelmsthal near Eisenach, the family seat of the Court of Weimar. With the recommendation of the Dutchess of Gotha it was easy for me to obtain a hearing. I played, pleased greatly, and on leaving, received a handsome present. On my return to Gotha, I gave in haste, a Concert that had been meanwhile arranged for there, which was also attended by the Court, and then set out on my return to my native town highly gratified with the result of my journey.

I went by way of Seesen, and was joyfully congratulated by my parents and the friends of my family upon the new dignity conferred upon me. In order to make the rest of the journey more pleasant for me, my father lent me his saddle-horse, and thus conduced to give my hitherto prosperous journey a tragical end; for a few leagues from Brunswick, while riding homewards at a sharp trot, absorbed in deep thought upon the future, and paying but little attention to the road, the horse fell, his foot having caught in a deep rut, and threw his rider rudely to the ground. I fell over the horse's head with my face upon a small heap of broken road-stones, before I could spread out my hands sufficiently to break my fall; my face was therefore cut in such a manner by the sharp stones, that the blood flowed profusely. In a few minutes also, the wounds became so swollen as almost to close my eyes. Half blind, and wholly unable to help myself, I stood in the road, until at length some foot-passengers came to my assistance. After they had caught my horse, they led me to the nearest village. They there procured for me a four wheeled peasant's-cart, with straw spread out in it, upon which I was brought in the most deplorable condition to my lodgings at a late hour in the evening. A Doctor having been sent for, he ordered my face to be bathed and bound with linen-rags steeped in Goulard water, which being continued throughout the night, the swelling had so much subsided by the morning, that I could again open my eyes. After the Doctor had carefully examined my face, and allayed my anxiety respecting all further results from my fall; I soon recovered my cheerfulness of mood, and alone lamented that I could not immediately wait upon my noble Patron to solicit his permission to accept the situation of the Directorship. But as meanwhile I was not without some anxiety, lest my benefactor, to whom I was so greatly indebted, might take it ill that I could thus leave his service, I was rather pleased that my accident furnished me with an excuse to address a letter to the duke. But I had judged him wrongfully; for on the following day I received the solicited permission in his own handwriting. I have carefully preserved that letter as a cherished Memorial, and cannot deny myself the pleasure of quoting it here, as follows:

My dear Herr *Spohr*.

I have read with much interest the successful result of your performance at Wilhelmsthal and Gotha. The advantageous offer made to you at Gotha is such as your talents well merit, and as I have always taken great interest in your fortune and success, I can but congratulate you on your appointment to a position where you will undoubtedly find more opportunity for the exercice of your talent.

I remain very respectfully
your well wisher
Carl W. Ferd.

Releived now of my last anxiety, I was truly happy. But it occurred to me, that in this letter, the Duke addressed me for the first time "*You*", while hitherto he had always honoured me with the benevolent, fatherly "*Thou*". I nevertheless consoled myself readily with the reflexion, that the Duke might have thought it more becoming so to address a person leaving his service.

In about a fortnight or three weeks, my face was so far healed, that I could again announce myself ready to resume my orchestral duties.

Before I had done so, I received a letter from *Dussek*, who wrote to say that his master, Prince *Louis Ferdinand*, was about to proceed to the grand military manoeuvres at Magdeburg, and wished that I should be his guest during that time, in order to give my assistance at the projected Music-parties there. The Prince would himself write to the Duke to solicit the leave of absence for me. This was immediately granted. I therefore proceeded to Magdeburg, and found in the house which the Prince had taken for himself and his suite, a room also, for me. I now led an extraordinary, wild and active life, which nevertheless suited my youthful taste right well for a short time. Frequently at six o'clock in the morning, were *Dussek* and I roused from our beds and conducted in dressing-gown and slippers to the Reception-saloon, where the Prince was already seated at the pianoforte in yet lighter costume, the heat being then very great, and indeed, generally in his shirt and drawers only. Now began the practice and rehearsal of the music that was intended to be played in the evening circles, and from the Prince's zeal, this lasted frequently so long, that in the meantime the saloon was filled with Officers decorated, and bestarred. The costume of the Musicians contrasted then somewhat strangely with the brilliant uniforms of those who had come to pay their court to the Prince. But this did not trouble his Royal Highness in the least, neither would he leave off until everything had been practised to his satisfaction. Then we finished our toilet in all haste, snatched as hasty a breakfast, and rode off to the review. I had a horse appropriated to me from the Prince's stud, and was permitted to ride with his suite. In this manner for a time to my great amusement, I took part in all the warlike evolutions. But, one day I found myself jammed in close to a battery, where I was obliged to endure for more than an hour a truly hellish-noise, and when in the evening at the Music party I found that I could not hear so distinctly as before, I held back from the warlike spectacle and from that time spent those hours in which the Prince did not require me, with my former acquaintances in Magdeburg. In the house of the Privy Counsellor *Schäfer* I met with a most friendly welcome. His daughter *Jettchen*, who, previously, while residing in Brunswick, in the house of her brother-in-law the Conductor *Le Gaye*, had been an object of my admiration, was now returned to her paternal home, and here also performed the part of a kind and attentive hostess to me.

Soon, however, the Prince was recalled from his exile to Magdeburg, and dismissed by him with friendly thanks, I could now return to Brunswick. *Dussek* on taking leave of me, told me that the Prince had intended to have made me a present, but that his purse was at so low an ebb, he must postpone it to a later and more favorable time. But that time never came; for the Prince found an early death in the following year in an action near Saalfeld. In the beginning of October, after an honourable discharge from the Duke's service had been duly made out for me, I left my native town. On my taking leave, the Duke said to me with truly paternal benevolence, as he extended his hand to me: "should you dear *Spohr* find your new place unpleasant to you, you can re-enter my service at any time."

I parted with my benefactor, deeply moved; and alas! never saw him more, — for as is well known he fell mortally wounded at the unfortunate battle of Jena, and died a fugitive in a foreign land. I mourned for him, as for a father.

Arrived in Gotha, I was introduced to the members of the Ducal Orchestra by the Intendant Baron *von Leibnitz*, as Concert-Director, and made acquainted with my sphere of duties. This consisted, both in winter and summer, in the arrangement of a concert at Court every week, and in practising and rehearsing the orchestra in the music chosen for the occasion. As the orchestra had no other duties beyond these concerts, I was enabled to have three or four rehearsals of each, and to practise all that was to be performed at these with the greatest precision. By my zeal, and the good-will of the members, I soon succeeded in attaining an exceeding accuracy of *ensemble* which was recognised by the Dutchess and some of the Musical-connoisseurs in the Court-circle, and elicited much praise.

The orchestra consisted in part of musicians of the Ducal Chamber, and in part of Court-hautboyists. It was the duty of the latter to play also during the repasts, and at Court-balls. Among the musicians of the Chamber, there was a whole bevy of solo-players. The chief were: on the violin, Madame *Schlick* and Messrs. *Preissing* and *Bärwolf*; on the violoncello, Messrs. *Schlick*, *Preissing jun.* and *Rohde*; on the clarionet, bassoon and harp, Herr *Backhofen;* on the hautboy, Herr *Hofmann;* and Herr *Walch* on the horn.

For the vocal parts at the Court-Concerts two Court-singers Mesdames *Scheidler* and *Reinhard* were engaged. The husband of the latter accompained the vocalists on the pianoforte. Being the oldest member of the orchestra, he had warmly competed for the vacant post of Conductor; and as the Duke's musical instructor, some regard was due to him; he also, therefore, had the title of Concert-Master conferred upon him on my appointment, and his rescript was even of anterior date to mine. For this reason he at first made some weak attempts, to assume the direction of the vocal performances. But I knew so well how to overawe him by my decisive bearing as first Violin, that he soon succumbed as willingly to my lead at the pianoforte, as at the viol, on which he performed in the instrumental music. I was also soon enabled to overcome the opposition of the *Schlick* family who relied on the favour of Prince *Augustus*, the Duke's uncle, and then undisturbedly maintained my directorial-position.

In the introductory visits I made to the members of the orchestra I was received most cordially by the Court-singer Madame *Scheidler*. She introduced me to her daughter *Dorette*, of the age of eighteen, of whose skill upon the harp and pianoforte I had already heard much. In this charming *blondine* I recognised the girl whom I had seen on my first visit to Gotha, and whose pleasing form had since then frequently recurred to my memory. At the Concert which I then gave in that town, she had sat in the first row of the auditory, by the side of a female friend, who upon my appearance, astonished at so tall a figure, exclaimed rather louder than she had intended: "Just look, *Dorette,* what a long hop-pole!" Upon hearing this exclamation, my eye fell upon the girls, and I saw *Dorette* blush with embarrassment. With a similar graceful blush she now again stood before me, probably recollecting that circumstance. To put an end therefore to a situation so painful to me, I entreated her to play something on the harp. Without the least affectation she complied with my wish.

When a boy, I had myself once made an attempt to learn the harp, and took lessons of one Herr *Hasenbalg* in Brunswick, when I soon got so far as to be able to accompany my songs. But after my voice had broken, and that for a considerable time I remained without any voice at all, the harp was neglected, and at length wholly laid aside. My predilection for that instrument had nevertheless remained the same; and I had given my attention to it sufficiently long, to know, how difficult it is, if one would play more than mere accompaniments upon it. My astonishment and delight may therefore be imagined, when I heard so young a girl execute a difficult "Fantasia" of her instructor *Backofen*, with the greatest confidence, and with the finest shades of expression. I was so deeply moved, that I could scarce restrain my tears. Bowing in silence, I took my leave; — but my heart remained behind! Irresistibly impelled, my visits now became frequent, and my reception more friendly every time.

I accompanied the daughter on the piano, which she played with the same excellence as the harp, assisted the mother in the practise of her songs for the Court-Concerts, and so made myself more and more necessary to the family. The first piece that I composed in Gotha, was a grand "Vocal Scena" for a soprano voice, which I dedicated to *Dorette's* mother, and which she sang with great applause at one of the Court-Concerts. For myself and the daughter, I then wrote a Concerted Sonata for violin and harp, which I practised with her in the most careful manner. They were happy hours!

Thus, after my arrival, had a month passed away for me in the most agreable manner, when the Court set out for the session of Parliament at Altenburg and took the orchestra with it. *Dorette* also accompanied her mother thither. I offered myself to them as a travelling-companion, but unfortunately made my application too late, for they had already arranged to travel in company with Messrs. *Preissling*, the brothers of Madame *Scheidler*. I was therefore obliged to seek other travelling-companions; but at every place where we stopped to take refreshment I did not fail to join immediately the *Scheidler* family, and always contrived to get possession of the place at table next to *Dorette*. These meetings after a separation of four or five hours, gave a peculiar charm to the otherwise long and tedious journey, so much so indeed, that when at length on the evening of the third day we entered the gates of Altenburg, it seemed too short to me. I was lodged in the house of Secretary *Brummer* who as a great lover of music had begged that I might become his guest. I met with the most friendly reception and a well furnished table. But I had previously arranged to dine always at Madame *Scheidler's*, who like an active housewife had immediately established a kitchen of her own, for herself and brothers. Henceforth, treated almost like a member of the family, I had full opportunity to become more nearly acquainted with my beloved *Dorette*. Her father, an excellent musician, and a man of scientific attainments, had, up to his death, which had taken place two years before, devoted himself entirely to the education and improvement of this daughter. With an almost extreme severity he had compelled her not only from her earliest childhood to pursue the study of Music, but also, instructed her, in part personally, and partly through the medium of other able teachers in every branch of education suitable to a young female. She therefore spoke Italian and French with the greatest fluency and wrote her mother tongue with ease and correctness. But her brilliant execution both on the harp and pianoforte was already then despite her youth, truly remarkable! Yes, even upon the violin on which instrument her uncle *Preissing* gave her instruction, she had acquired so much skill, that she could play *Viotti's* Duetts with me. But as I advised her to discontinue the practise of that instrument so unbecoming for females, and to devote rather her undivided study to the two others, she adopted my advice and from that moment gave it up.

Meanwhile the Court-concerts had commenced. They took place in a large saloon in the Palace, very favourable for music, and together with the Court were attended by the parliamentary Deputies and by the dignitaries of the town. The orchestra, as well as the performances both of myself and the other soloplayers met with great applause. *Dorette's* Soli's on the harp and piano made also a great sensation. In this manner the concert-days were soon looked forward to by the Altenburgers as real festival days, and the auditory encreased so much in number each time, that at length there was scarcely room for their accommodation. There were also many private Music-parties, at which I and the members of the *Scheidler* family never failed to be invited. One day, however, I was invited with *Dorette*, but without her mother, to a Fête given by the Minister *von Thümmel*, to the Court and its immediate circle. We were requested to reproduce my Sonata for the harp und violin, which we had already played with great success at the Court-concerts. With some timidity I ventured to ask whether I might fetch *Dorette* in the carriage, and felt delighted beyond measure, when her mother without hesitation gave her consent. Thus alone for the first time with the beloved girl, I felt the impulse to make a full confession of my feelings towards her; but my courage failed me, and the carriage drew up, before I had been able to utter a syllable. As I held out my hand to her to alight, I felt by the tremor of hers, how great had also been her emotion. This gave me new courage, and I had almost plumped out with my declaration of love upon the very stairs, had not the door of the Reception-saloon been thrown open at the same moment.

That evening we played with an inspiration and a sympathy of feeling that not alone carried us wholly away, but so electrified the company also, that all rose spontaneously, and gathering round us, overwhelmed us with praise. The Dutchess whispered some words in *Dorette's* ear, which brought blushes to her cheek.

I interpreted them as favorable to me, and now on the drive home I at length found courage to say: "Shall we thus play together for life?" Bursting into tears, she sank into my arms; the compact for life was sealed! I led her to her mother, who joined our hands and gave us her blessing.

The next morning I announced my happiness to my parents. But before I could enjoy it without alloy, I felt compelled to write another letter, and one which was to me a most disagreable task. I felt the injustice of my conduct towards *Rosa*, and the necessity to ask her forgiveness. I had it is true, never made a declaration of my love to her; but it had been but too apparent in the earlier period of our acquaintance. To that was added moreover, the circumstance that, my parents had greeted her in Seesen as my betrothed. What the arguments were that I resorted to in exulpation of my injustice, I no longer remember at this distance of time. Probably I may have again adverted to the difference of religion, which could alone serve me as excuse for my withdrawal. The letter was at length finished; and with a lightened heart I took it to the post. I anxiously expected an answer; but none came. At a later period I learned that *Rosa* had returned to Italy with her parents who had acquired some fortune in Germany. Some years afterwards, I was told when in Dresden, that *Rosa*, led by her devotional turn of mind, had retired to a convent, and after the year's novitiate had taken the veil. I never could think of that charming maiden without sentiments of the deepest sorrow!

At the dinner-table on the following day all appeared in full dress; it was to celebrate our betrothal. The news of this had soon spread through the town, and not only the members of the Ducal orchestra, but also many of the inhabitants of the place came to felicitate the engaged couple. At the next concert the same took place on the part of the Dutchess and the Court.

With the end of the year, the session of Parliament drew also to a close, and the return of the Court to Gotha was already spoken of, when I solicited an eight day's leave of absence to go to Leipsic in order to give a concert there. Preparatory to that, I had already made enquiries of my friends of the foregoing year, and received from them the most favorable assurances. My bride, and her mother accompanied me, to appear also in the same concert. This therefore offered a diversity of attraction to the public, and consequently the attendance was very numerous. I played a new Violin-Concerto in C-Major (published by *Kühnel* as the third) which I had begun in Gotha and finished at Altenburg. Both my playing and composition found as warm a reception as in the previous year. My bride also met with the most enthusiastic applause. She played *Backhofen's* Fantasia, and with me the new Sonata. On this occasion, it was again our combined play that was considered the most brilliant performance of the evening. The mother, a singer possessed of a powerful, pleasing tone, and of a good school, executed, accompanied by her daughter, the aria of *Mozart* with Pianoforte obligato, as also, my new vocal-Scena, with great success.

Highly satisfied with the result of our undertaking, we returned to Altenburg, and shortly afterwards with the Court to Gotha.

Madame *Scheidler* resided there in a very roomy and well furnished house, of which without feeling in the least inconvenienced, she could readily give up to me an apartment or two. As she offered to take my brother *Ferdinand* who as my pupil lived with me, together with ourselves as boarders, nothing therefore stood in the way of my immediate marriage. The wedding was accordingly fixed for the 2. February, 1806. I hastened therefore, to procure the documents, requisite for the occasion, my certificate of baptism, and the consent of my parents. To my regret, they were unable to bring this to me in person, as my father dare not leave his patients, some of whom were dangerously ill, but they sent my brother *William** to be a witness to my happiness.

---

* Afterwards architect to the Court of Brunswick, and father of the well known harpiste *Rosalie Spohr*.

It created no little astonishment when I produced my certificate of baptism, that instead of growing older in Gotha, I had become several years younger! But as I had already sufficiently established my authority as Concert-Director I experienced no subsequent prejudice from this discovery.

The ardently desired 2. February, dawned at length. At the request of the Dutchess who wished to be present, the marriage took place in the Palace-chapel. Upon the conclusion of the ceremony the newly married pair received the felicitations and wedding-presents of their illustrious Patroness. At home, we found assembled as wedding-guests, the two uncles *Preissing* and several other of the most intimate friends among the members of the Ducal orchestra, as also Cantor *Schade*, an old friend of the *Scheidler* family. After dinner many others came. Among these the playmates and schoolfellows of *Dorette*. All brought with them their friendly gifts. Neither was she wanting who had compared me to a hop-pole, and as punishment for the unbecoming comparison, she was frequently obliged to endure a little raillery. As the weather was too unfavourable for an excursion, or promenade, music was kept up till a late hour in the evening.

In the midst of Music also, the happy pair passed the honeymoon. I began forthwith a diligent study of the harp, in order to ascertain thoroughly what was best adapted to the character of the instrument. As I was prone to a richness of modulation in my compositions, it was therefore requisite to make myself especially well acquainted with the pedals of the harp, so as to write nothing that would be impracticable for them. This could not readily occur, on account of the great accuracy with which my wife had already then mastered the whole Technics of the instrument. I therefore gave free play to my fancy, and soon succeeded in obtaining wholly new effects from the instrument.

As the Harp sounded most advantageously in combination with the singing tones of my Violin, I wrote more especially Concerted compositions for both instruments alone. At a later period, it is true, I made trial, also, of two Concertanti with Orchestral accompaniment, and of a Trio for Harp, Violin and Violoncello; but as I found that every Accompaniment only disturbed our mutual and deeply felt harmony of action, I soon abandoned it.

Another attempt to obtain a greater effect, had however, a more successful result. I conceived the idea of pitching the harp half a tone lower than the violin. By so doing I gained in two ways. For, as the violin sounds most brilliantly in the cross or sharp notes, but the harp best in the B-tones or flat notes, when the fewest pedals possible are moved; I thereby obtained for both instruments the most favourable and most effective key-notes: for the violin namely, D and G; for the harp E and A-flat. A second advantage was, that, from the lower tuning of the harp, a string would less frequently break, which in public performances in very warm rooms so frequently happens to the harpist, and mars the enjoyment of the hearers. From this time therefore, I wrote all my Compositions for harp and violin in that difference of the keys.

Dorette, forcibly attracted by these new Compositions, devoted at that time her attention exclusively to the study of the harp, and soon obtained such a brilliant execution, that I felt an eager desire to exhibit this before a larger public than that of the Court-concerts of Gotha. As I beleived also, to have now perfected my own Play in a manner such as no other could readily surpass, I resolved to set out on an Artistic tour with my wife in the ensuing autumn. I had already stipulated for such a leave of absence upon receiving my appointment, and it had been acceded to in consideration of my then small salary.

Meanwhile as the autumn drew near, a twofold obstacle presented itself to the execution of my cherished projects. The war between Prussia and France threatened to break out. The Prussian army prepared for the struggle, was already assembled in the neighbourhood of Gotha, and the inhabitants of the Dutchy had much to endure from the billeting, and overbearing insolence of the Prussians.

Even though I might have been able to take my journey in a direction that would have carried us from the tumult of war, yet when my home was in danger of becoming the scene of conflict, I could not well leave it in such an extremity. Then, one day, with blushing cheek and beaming eyes, my little wife imparted to me that towards the end of winter she looked forward to a mother's joys. Now, therefore, indeed it was no longer possible to think of undertaking a journey, and all hesitation on the subject was set at rest. I therefore bethought me of some engrossing work that would distract my attention as much as possible from all the anxieties of the times. I had long wished to try my hand at a Dramatic composition; but I had never yet found a favourable opportunity. Neither, indeed, did that present itself now, for Gotha possessed no Theatre. Yet, I thought; if the opera were once written, some opportunity to hear it might yet present itself. Just at that time, I received a visit from a companion of my youth *Edward Henke* my mother's youngest brother, afterwards Professor of Jurisprudence at the university of Halle, who had already met with some success in lyrical compositions. I persuaded him to write the words of an opera for me. We cogitated together the subject-matter, and the scenes, of a one act Opera, to which we gave the Name of "Die Prüfung" (The Trial). *Edward* began forthwith the composition of the Song-parts and finished them wholly before his departure. He promised to supply the dialogue afterwards.

But before I could begin my work, the storm of war broke loose. The battle of Jena had been fought; and with that, the fate of Prussia decided. The Prussians who had lain in and around Gotha, and who but shortly before had been so-overbearing in their demeanour were now seen flying in the greatest confusion. The disorganisation of their troops was so complete, that their arms were to be found in thousands strewn over the fields near Gotha. In a walk I took a few days afterwards, I found as a further gleaning, a ramrod, which I took home with me as a reminiscence of that fatal day. Suspended from a thread it gave with a clear sound the note *B*, once struck, and served me for many years instead of a tuning-fork when tuning the harp.

Although after the advance of the French army in pursuit, the theatre of war was soon removed farther and farther from Gotha; yet the quartering of troops upon the inhabitants was no less continuous. Fresh reinforcements of French and South-German troops were constantly moved forward in support; and a greater part of the Prussian prisoners taken at Jena, was brought through Gotha. These came in bodies of from 3 to 4000 men of all arms, frequently escorted by 40 or 50 voltigeurs, only, and were shut up in the great Church on the market place, opposite to our dwelling, with merely a few sentries mounting guard over them before the closed doors. As the nights were already very cold, the men in their thin uniforms must indeed have been nearly frozen. For that reason also they kept up a continual noise and outcry. The inhabitants of the houses in the neighbourhood, in constant dread that the prisoners from their greatly superior numbers would liberate themselves, were obliged to keep continually on the watch, and for many nights together could not retire to rest.

This, therefore, was by no means the most propitious time for me to attempt a style of composition that was quite new to me. But as my study was situated near the garden, at a distance from the noise in the streets, I soon succeeded in forgetting every thing around me, and gave myself up heart and soul to my work. In this manner, before half the winter had passed, I completed the composition of the 8 "Numbers" of the Opera, together with the Overture. The four Song-parts in these, permitted of being well rendered by the Female Court-singers and two Dillettanti whose assistance I had already obtained for the Court-concerts. I therefore had the opera written out with all despatch, practised it carefully, and then played it as Concert-Music at one of the Court-concerts.

Great as at first was my satisfaction with the new work, I nevertheless soon became sensible of its deficiencies, and weak points. With every successive rehearsal these were made more clear to me, and even before its production in public took place, the Opera (with the exception of the Overture and one aria for a tenor-voice) had become distateful to me. Even the great applause it had met with from those who executed it, and those who heard it, could not reconcile me the more to it; so that I laid it aside, and with the exception of the two "Numbers" mentioned, I never played any thing more of it in public. But with this feeling of dissatisfaction with my work I was truly unhappy; for I now thought to perceive that I had no talent for Operatic compositions. There were, however, two things which I had forgotten duly to consider; first, that I had assumed a much too elevated style, for I had put my Opera upon a par with those of *Mozart*, and secondly, that I was wholly wanting in the practice and experience requisite for this kind of composition. This did not occur to me till some years afterwards, and encouraged me then to make another attempt at dramatic composition.

For the present, I again devoted myself wholly to Instrumental composition; wrote the already mentioned Concertanti for Harp and Violin with full orchestra; a Fantasia (op. 35) and Variations (op. 36) for Harp-Solo; and, for myself, my Fifth Violin Concerto (op. 17. published by *Nägeli* of Zurich) and the Pot-Pourri (op. 22, at *André's* in Offenbach).

As *Dorette* anticipated her confinement in the spring, it was impossible we could remain longer in the limited accommodation of her mother's house, and we were now obliged to furnish a house of our own. This took place at Easter 1807.

Shortly after, on the 27. May, we were gladdened by the birth of a little daughter. I now had to invite the Duke as Godfather to the new-born, he having already previously offered himself for that post of honour. On the day of the

Christening, he made his appearance, in the full splendour of his Ducal rank, accompanied by the dignitaries of his Court and followed by the idlers of the town, who attracted by the grandeur of the rarely used state carriage and its occupants, stared with astonishment to see it draw up before my house, at the door of which I received him, and conducted him to the apartment decorated with garlands of flowers. The ceremony began, and the new-born was christened *Emilie*, after the Duke's second Name, Emilius.

To my great regret, my parents could not take part in this delightful family festival. And yet, in the previous summer, when on a visit at Seesen, I had introduced my dear wife to them, and had the gratification to see not only that they soon evinced much affection for her, but the satisfaction also, that my father was obliged to admit I might not have been so happy with *Rosa*, even had my love for her been more lasting.

As soon as *Dorette* had fully regained her strength, she began anew to practise the recently finished compositions for the Harp, in order to prepare herself for our projected artistic tour. But while thus engaged, she became more and more convinced of the defects of the instrument she had hitherto used, a Strasburg pedal-harp, which she had received as a present from the Dutchess. It was therefore decided in a family consultation, to apply a small capital appertaining to her as inheritance, to the purchase of another, and a better harp. Herr *Backofen*, had such an instrument, a very superior one, by *Nadermann* of Paris, and was disposed to part with it to his pupil for a moderate price. This, therefore, was purchased. Of *Dorette's* small inheritance there yet remained a few hundred thalers, to expend in the acquisition of an indispensible convenience for travelling, namely a travelling-carriage, constructed at the same time for the transport of the harp. For a considerable time I turned over in my mind the form of build best adapted to this purpose. There were two things that required especial consideration; first, that it should not be too expensive, and secondly that it should be sufficiently light for one pair of post-horses. At length I hit upon the right plan. I ordered a long, but not too heavy Basket-carriage to be built, with a chaise compartment behind for the travellers. In front of this between the basket-sides, lay the box for the harp, slung by leather straps, and covered with a leather apron, which fastened by means of a bar of iron hooking into the chaise-seat in front of the occupants. Under this was a seat-box to hold the violin-case, and behind it a larger one to contain a trunk adapted to the space, in which all the other travelling requisites could be packed. In front, above the harp-box, was the raised seat for the driver. A trial trip, for which the carriage was completely packed, shewed that it fully answered the object proposed. Thus, therefore, every thing was in readiness for our artistic tour.

After a painful leave-taking of our child, of whom my mother-in-law undertook the care, we set out on our journey, in the middle of October. As I unfortunately kept no diary upon this and our subsequent journey from Gotha, I am left wholly to my somewhat faint recollections of that period, which have been but sparingly refreshed by a few notices in the Leipsic Musical-Journal. Of a diary kept by my wife at that period, but which she never let me see, I have neither been able to find anything since her death. Probably, it was destroyed by her in after years.

On the very first day, our journey began in a very ominous manner, by the overturning of our carriage at a place between Erfurt and Weimar, where there was at that time no paved high-road. Fortunately, however, neither the travellers nor their instruments were injured, we therefore considered ourselves very fortunate to have escaped with the fright only. No such accident re-occurred to us on any of our numerous journeys. In Weimar, whither we took letters of introduction from the Dutchess of Gotha, we played at Court with great applause, and received a munificent present from the Heriditary Grand Dutchess, the Princess *Maria*. Among the auditory at the Court-Concert were the two Poet-heros *Goethe* and *Wieland*. The latter seemed quite charmed with the play of the artiste-couple, and evinced it in his own animated and friendly manner. *Goethe*, also, addressed a few words of praise to us with a dignified coldness of mien.

In Leipsic, as I perceive from a notice in the Musical-Journal, we gave a concert on the 27. October. The opinion therein expressed of the compositions I played on that occasion, namely the Overture to the "Prüfung", the Violin-Concerto in E s, the first Concertante for Harp and Violin, the Potpourri in B, and the Fantasia for the Harp, was very favorable. As regards our play, it says:

"Respecting the play of Herr *Spohr*, and his wife, we have already spoken in detail, and here alone add, that he has entirely corrected himself of many of the too arbitrary mannerisms (in Time, and the like) which he had acquired, and of which we had now and then complained; and, without a doubt, as regards Tone and Expression, Surety and Skill, both in *Allegro* and in *Adagio* (in the latter more especially, in our opinion) he now takes rank among the foremost of all living Violinists: and Madame *Spohr*, by her great skill, neatness and feeling in her play, is certain to meet with the most distinguished reception."

Of Dresden, where we also gave a Concert and also, if I do not mistake this occasion for a later one — played at Court (though certainly not during dinner, to which neither of us would have consented) I recollect nothing more particular. But I well remember many circumstances of our stay at Prague. My fame had not yet reached there, and at first I had many difficulties to contend with. These, however, were forthwith overcome when I and my wife had played at a Soirée given by the Princess Hohenzollern, and when that lady declared herself our Patroness. We now immediately became the fashion, and the *beau-monde* came in crowds to the two concerts we gave in the City so famed for its cultivation of

Art. We had therefore full reason to be satisfied with our stay there. This is also confirmed by a notice in the Musical-Journal beginning as follows: "Among the strangers who have given concerts, the third was Herr *Spohr*, the celebrated Director of Concerts to the Duke of Saxe-Gotha. Herr *Spohr* performed on the Violin, as did his wife on the Pedal-Harp. It will be long before another artiste will have such reason to be satisfied with the reception he met here as Herr *Spohr*, and of a certainty every friend of Art, will acknowledge that he well deserved that distinction."

But in the course of his notice, the Editor animadverts on several points in my Play, though this opinion would seem to have been a somewhat isolated one, as in his notice of the concert given by the brothers *Pixis* which immediately followed mine, he says: "his place has been assigned to him far below *Spohr*," and then continues: "as but a few days before people were so charmed by the Play of the latter, and the opinion was expressed from that point of view, it may not be considered altogether fair."

Among the friends of Art in Prague, I then made the acquaintance of a man with whom up to the time of his death I constantly remained on terms of the closest friendship. This was Herr *Kleinwächter*, the head of the commercial firm of *Ballabene*. At his house, every Sunday forenoon, a small but select circle of Professionals and lovers of Art met to play and listen to Quartett-music. Every foreign artiste sought to be introduced there, and whether violinist or violoncellist took an active part in them. I took a pleasure in playing there; for my execution and my endeavours to give each composition in its appropriate style were fully appreciated. One Sunday morning I was playing a Solo-quartett of mine (D-Minor, op. 11. published by *Simrock)* when the master of the house was suddenly called away; but returning after some time, announced to the company, that during the playing of the Quartett a son had been born to him! Among the congratulations of those present the wish was also expressed that this harmonious greeting of the new citizen of the world, would be of the most happy augery for his future life, and above all things might endow him with a taste for Music! With the latter, he was indeed gifted in a high degree. *Louis Kleinwächter*, (in compliment to me he was christened after me) though only as an amateur (his profession was the law) became a distinguished musician, as his compositions many of which have been published, sufficiently attest. Whether it was that he had been told he was born during the performance of one of *Spohr's* compositions, and that, that had awakened his predeliction for them, or whether it was his diligent study of them, there never was a more enthusiastic admirer of my music than he. Whenever in the Musical Reunions of Prague, a choice was mooted of the Compositions which were to be played, he always strove for those of *Spohr*, and never rested until he had carried his point. For that reason, also, he soon acquired the general cognomen of "the mad Spohrist."

It is to be regretted that this young man of whom mention will frequently be made in these pages, was snatched from his family by an early death; he died several years before his father.

From Prague, the Artiste-couple proceeded to Munich, via Ratisbonne. I no longer recollect whether I succeeded in getting up a Concert in the latter town. I could find no notice of it. And respecting Munich, in a summary notice of the Musical-Journal on the winter-season of that year, it was curtly remarked "Herr *Spohr*, from Gotha, gave a Concert and met here also with a warm approval." Of our stay there I have nevertheless a tolerable clear recollection. Before we gave our concert in the City, we played at Court. When we came forward to play our Concertante for Harp and Violin, there was no stool for *Dorette*. King Maximilian who sat beside his Consort in the front row of the audience, observed it, and immediately brought his own gilded arm-chair surmounted with the Royal Crown, before an attendant could procure one. In his own friendly good-tempered manner he insisted upon *Dorette* seating herself in it, and only when I explained to him that the arms of the chair would impede her playing, he consented to her taking the seat brought by the servant.

When the Concert was over, he presented us to the Queen and her Ladies of the Court, who discoursed with us in the most friendly manner. On the following day the Royal Gifts were presented to us; to me a diamond ring, to *Dorette* a tiara of brilliants; both of great value.

At our Public Concert, we were supported by the members of the Royal orchestra with the greatest good will. Herr *Winter*, the Director, led. I was delighted with the precision and spirited execution of my compositions, and thought it very natural that they should please, played in such a manner. But it was a special satisfaction to me that the Composer of the "Opferfest" (the Festival of the Sacrifice) assured me also in his candid and straight forward way, of his full approval. I went frequently to *Winter's* house, and was greatly amused with his original character, which united the most singular contradictions. Of a colossal build, and gifted with the strength of a giant, *Winter* was withal as timid as a hare. Readily excited to the most violent rage, he nevertheless allowed himself to be led like a child. His housekeeper had soon observed this, and tyrannised over him in a cruel manner. As an example of this, he took great pleasure in dressing up the little images for the Christmas tree, on the Eve of that Festival, and would amuse himself in this way, by the hour. But ill befel him if the housekeeper caught him at it. She would then immediately drive him away from them, and call out: "Must you then be eternally at play?! Sit down directly to the Pianoforte, and get your song ready!"

The junior members of the Royal orchestra, whom he took great pleasure in having about him, and sometimes invited to dinner, teazed him in return, unceasingly. They had soon discovered that he had a great fear of Ghosts, and invented all manner of tales of apparitions and ghostly narratives to frighten him. In the summer time he frequently went to a public garden outside the town, but as he was timerous in the dark, he always returned before night-fall. One day, the mischievous young folks contrived by various means to delay his return longer than usual, and it was already quite dark when he set out on his way home. As the other guests still remained quietly seated, he found the road which lay between two gloomy hedge-rows fearfully lonely. Seized with a sudden terror, he unconsciously began to run. Scarcely had he commenced, than he felt a heavy load upon his back, and he beleived that it could be nothing also but a Hobgoblin that had sprung down upon him. Hearing other footsteps behind as though running after him, he thought the Devil and all his Imps were in full chase, and he now ran still faster. Reeking with perspiration and panting for breath he at length reached the city gates; when the goblin sprung down from his back, and said in a voice that he knew: "Thank you Herr Kapellmeister, for carrying me, for I was very tired!" This speech was followed by a general titter, and he whom they had so befooled, burst into an uncontrolable rage.

From Munich, we continued our journey to Stuttgard, where we took letters of introduction to the Court. I presented these to the Court-Chamberlain, and on the following day received from him the assurance that we should be permitted to play at Court. But in the meantime I had been informed that here also cards were played during the Concerts at Court, and that little attention was paid to the Music. At Brunswick I had been already sufficiently disgusted with such a degradation of the Art, that I took the liberty to declare to the Court-Chamberlain, that I and my wife could alone appear, if the King would be graciously pleased to cease card-playing during our performance. Quite horrified at so bold a request, the Court-Chamberlain made one step backward, and exclaimed: "What? You would prescribe conditions to my gracious Master? Never should I dare make such a proposal to him!" "Then must I renounce the honour of playing at Court", was my simple reply. And on this, I took my leave.

How the Court-Chamberlain betook himself to lay so unheard of a proposition before his Sovereign, and how the latter prevailed upon himself to yield to it, I never learned. But the result was, that the Court-Chamberlain sent to inform me: "His Majesty would be graciously pleased to grant my wish; but on the condition, that the musical pieces which I and my wife would play, should follow in quick succession, so that His Majesty would not be too frequently inconvenienced."

And so it occurred. After the Court had taken their seats at the card-table, the Concert began with an Overture, which was followed by an aria. During this, the lacqueys moved to and fro with much noise, to offer refreshments, and the card-players called out: "I play, I pass" so loud, that one could hear nothing connectedly of the music and the singing. The Court-Chamberlain now came to inform me that I should hold myself ready. Upon this, he announced to the King, that the strangers would begin their performances. Presently, His Majesty rose from his chair, and with him all the company. The servants placed two rows of stools in front of the orchestra, upon which the Court seated themselves. Our play was listened to in the greatest silence, and with interest; but no one dared utter a syllable of approval, as the King had not given the lead. The interest he took in the performances was shewn only at the close of each by a gracious nod of the head, and scarcely were they over, than all hastened back to the card-tables, and the former noise began anew.

During the remainder of the Concert, I had leisure to look about me. My attention was particulary directed to the King's card-table, in which in order to accommodate itself better to his Majesty's obesity, a semi-circular place had been cut out, into which the King's belly fitted closely. The great size of the latter, and the little extent of the Kingdom, gave rise as is well known to the smart caricature in which the King in his Coronation-robes, with the map of his Kingdom fastened to the button of his knee breeches, is represented as uttering the words: "I cannot see over all my States!"

As soon as the King had finished his game, and moved back his stool, the Concert was broken off in the middle of an aria by Madame *Graff,* so that the last notes of a cadence actually stuck in her throat. The musicians accustomed to this vandalism, packed their instruments quietly in their cases; but I was deeply exasperated at such an insult to the Art.

At that time, Würtemberg groaned under a despotism such as indeed the rest of Germany had never known. To cite only a few examples of this, it suffices to say: that rain or snow, every one who entered the Palace-Court at Stuttgard was compelled to walk hat in hand from the irongates to the portal of the palace, because his Majesty's apartments were on that side. Every civilian was furthermore obliged by the most imperative order to take off his hat before the sentry, who was not required to salute him in return. In the theatre, it was strictly forbidden by notices to that effect, to applaud with the hands before the King had commenced. But his Majesty on account of the extreme cold of the winter sat with his hands buried in a large muff, and only took them out when his Royalty was graciously pleased to feel the want of a pinch of snuff. When that was done, it little mattered what was going on upon the stage, he then clapped his hands. Upon this the Chamberlain who stood behind the King, immediately joined in, and thereby gave notice to the loyal people, that they might also give vent to their approbation. In this manner the most interesting scenes and the best pieces of music of the opera were almost always disturbed, and interrupted by a horrid noise.

As the citizens of Stuttgard had long learned to accommodate themselves to the Royal humours, they were not a little astonished at what I had stipulated for before my appearance at the Court-concert, and had actually granted to me. This made me the object of public attention, and the result was, that my concert in the town was attended by an unusually numerous auditory. The Royal orchestra gave me their support in the most friendly manner, and the Director *Danzi* endeavoured to facilitate the whole arrangements for me in every possible way.

Danzi was a most amiable artiste, and I felt the more inclined towards him, from finding he had the same admiration for *Mozart*, that I was so deeply impressed with. *Mozart*, and his works, were the inexhaustible subjects of our conversation, and I still possess a most cherished memorial of that time, a four-handed arrangement of *Mozart's* Symphony in G-Minor, composed by *Danzi*, and in his own handwriting.

In Stuttgard I also first made the acquaintance of the since so greatly famed *Carl Maria von Weber,* with whom up to the time of his death I was always on the most friendly terms. *Weber* was then Secretary to one of the Princes of Würtemberg and cultivated the Art as an amateur only. This however, did not hinder him from composing with great assiduity, and I still well remember hearing at his house, as a sample of *Weber's* works some "Numbers" from the Opera "*Der Beherrscher der Geister.*" (The Ruler of the Spirits.) But these, from being always accustomed to take *Mozart* as the type and rule by which to measure all dramatic works, appeared to me so unimportant and amateur-like, that I had not the most distant idea *Weber* would ever succeed in attracting notice with any opera.

Of the Concerts which we gave besides, in Heidelberg and Frankfort on the Mayne, before our return home, I can now speak but imperfectly from memory — I therefore give a few extracts from the notices of the Musical-Journal.

First of all speaking of Heidelberg, it says: "*Eisenmenger's* violin would still have been unforgotten, had not the Heidelbergers had the pleasure in the last Concert to hear *Louis Spohr* play in his *Rode*-like style of firm, sustained and skillful bow-stroke. His wife played the harp, in a way one seldom hears in Germany — with a tenderness, lightness and grace, with a confidence, strength, and expression, that are quite captivating."

To me it seems very strange, that even at this time my play was still designated as a *Rode*-like style, for at that period at least I thought to have wholly laid aside his manner. Perhaps it arose merely, from the circumstance, that, on account of the easier accompaniment, I had selected a Concerto of *Rode's* for execution.

Respecting the Concert in Frankfort on the 28. March, the remarks were also very eulogistic. The Frankfort Journal spoke of the "wellmerited, and distinguished applause" that we met with, and reverted to a "in many respects similar Pair, who five and twenty or thirty years before made much sensation in Mannheim, and afterwards in London — to *Wilhelm Kramer*, the great Violinist and his wife, the splendid Harpiste".

On my return to Gotha I was met at some miles from the town by my pupils, some of whom had remained there during my absence, and others but shortly returned, and escorted by them as in triumph to my tastefully decorated dwelling. We there found *Dorette's* parents and relatives all assembled to welcome us, and also our dear child, who under her grandmother's excellent care was in blooming health. As on our tour we had not only earned a rich harvest of applause, but had saved a sum of money which for our circumstances was considerable, we now felt on our return to our domestic hearth right happy and free from care.

As soon as I had resumed the Direction of the Court-concerts, I felt impelled so set to work at new compositions. I first wrote a Potpourri for the violin with orchestral accompaniment (Op. 23, published by *André* of Offenbach) which had already suggested itself to me during the journey, and for the most part in the carriage. I was very desirous to see on paper what I there thought a very artistic combination of two Themes in one and the same; but still more desirous to hear it executed by an orchestra. This Potpourri begins with a lively, and for the solo, brilliant *Allegro* in G-Major, connected with and passing into the Theme from the *"Entführung"*: *"Wer ein Liebchen hat gefunden"* in G-Minor. After this has been varied five times alternately in the Minor and Major, it is taken up in sixth Variation by the wind-instruments, and for a time carried out in free-fugued Entries. On the return into the pricipal key, the first horn takes up the melody of the song in the Major and carries it out completely to the end. This is then succeeded anew in a very startling manner by the introductory *Allegro* of the primo, blending with it as it were in the style of a Fantasia, though it previously appeared as an independant piece of Music.

With the working of this combination at the Rehearsal, I was very satisfied; but when the Potpourri was executed at the Court-Concert, I was doomed to see my ingenious combination of the two themes was noticed by a few musicians only, and was totally lost upon the rest of the hearers.

The next that I wrote, was the Concertante for two Violins (Op. 48, published by *Peters* in Leipsic). I was prompted to this chiefly by the artistic genius of one of my pupils one Herr *Hildebrandt* of Rathenow, with whom I was very fond of playing. This young man had made so much progress under my guidance in twelve months, that he promised to become one of the first violinists of Germany. Unfortunately, at a later period, by what mischance I now no longer remember, a wound which he received in his left hand became a bar to the full development of his talent, so that he did not become so known in the Musical world, as was previously to have been expected. This pupil had acquired to such a degree his instructor's method of execution in all its shadings, that he might have been considered a true copy of him. Our play blended therefore so intimately, that, without looking at us, no one could tell by the ear which of us played the upper or which the lower key. In this manner we had practised the new Concertante, before we executed it at the Court-concert. We achieved, also, such success with it, that the

Dutchess requested its repetition in the next concert, and afterwards, insisted, also, as long as *Hildebrandt* remained in Gotha to have it put in the programme when strangers were on visit at Court.

As my pupils at that time were of much the same age as myself, and were young people of good breeding and inspired with a love of their Art; I liked to have them about me, and took great pleasure in permitting them to accompany me in my walks and little excursions in the neighbourhood. I used then to join in all their amusements, played at ball and other games with them, and taught them to swim. Yes, perhaps I was even somewhat more *en camerade* with them than beseemed the dignity of the Instructor with his pupils. But my authority suffered no diminution on that account; for I knew not only how to maintain a strict discipline during the hours of tuition, but also at other times, a becoming behaviour.

In this manner, I had already made a longer excursion in the spring, to Liebenstein, and up the Inselsberg, and returned from that journey so pleased, that I longed once more to make a similar excursion to the Harz, which I so loved. Quite unexpectedly, a temporary absence of the Dutchess, through which some Court-concerts were suspended, furnished the necessary leave of absence. I therefore, immediately, proposed to my pupils, a pedestrian journey to the Harz, which they welcomed with the most joyful assent. As our absence would of a necessity extend to a fortnight, the lessons could not be suspended for so long a time without great prejudice to the pupils, and I therefore determined to continue them on the journey. For this purpose I took two violins with me, with which the orchestra-servant *Schramm*, yet a young man, and greatly attached to me was loaded, while we carried all the other necessaries distributed in two knapsacks, each in his turn. Before our caravan could set out, I had yet to console my wife, who could not make up her mind to so long a separation, the first since our marriage, and who shed, indeed, a torrent of tears. Not until I had promised to write to her every other day, could she be somewhat pacified, and it was long before she let me from her arms. To me, also, this first separation was no less extremely painful!

How far we went the first day and where we stopped the following night, I no longer remember; but I still know well, that at every rest after dinner, I gave two of my pupils regular instruction, and required of them a punctual alternate practise of the lesson in the evening, as soon as we reached our quarters for the night. In this way, on the third or fourth day, (the heat was intense,) we arrived about a league from Nordhausen, and very tired sat down to rest ourselves under the shade of an oak by the side of a large pond, when by an unlucky accident one of our knapsacks rolled down the steep bank and fell into the water — and so far from the bank, also, that we could not reach it with our walking sticks. As the water was deep, I was soon obliged as the only practised swimmer of the party, to make up my mind to jump in and fetch it out. But before I could get my clothes off, the knapsack had taken in so much water, that it began to sink. I was therefore obliged to dive at the place where it had disappeared until I succeeded in recovering it. When I brought it to the bank, and it was opened, I found its contents so saturated with water, that we were obliged to spread them on the grass in the sun to dry them. As it was to be anticipated this would be an operation of several hours, and noon was drawing near with its attendant hunger, I resolved to take our customary dinner-rest in this place, and to send to Nordhausen to procure the necessary provisions. The purchase of these fell by lot to one of the pupils, and *Schramm* accompanied him to carry them. Meanwhile, I gave my two lessons unter the great oak, and those pupils who were not engaged therein, bathed themselves at a more shallow part of the pond. After the lapse of two hours, our foragers returned heavily laden, and under the shadow of the dear oak, which served us with equal hospitality as a Dining- or Concert-room, a capital-dinner was soon spread and despatched in the merriest humour, and with the best appetite. Then resounded in joyous harmony the tones of four male-voices, in choice four-part glees of which we carried with us a good collection, and had also well-practised them. After this, our properties which were once more dry, were packed up, and our troop set itself again in motion.

After this merry fashion we visited every remarkable spot of the lower Harz, and then climbed the "Brocken." When we got to the top, that which occurs to nine tenths of all travellers, befel us also; we found it envelloped in mist, and waited in vain until noon, in the hope that it would clear off and enable us to enjoy the view from the summit. We endeavoured to dispel as much of our disappointment as we could by singing, playing and looking through the pages of the many tomed "Book of the Brocken"; indeed, one of the party put our Jeremiade on this misfortune into really decent rhyme, which I immediately converted into a Canon for three voices. This was diligently practised, sung both within the "Brockenhause" and outside in the mist, and then written together with our names in the Brocken-Book, in the hope that at length the weather would clear up.* But in vain! We were obliged to make up our minds to continue our journey.

We now took the direction of Clausthal, and when we reached the plain, we had the mortification to see the summit of the Brocken, after we had left it about one hour, lit up with the brightest sunshine! — Arrived at Clausthal; our first care was to get rid of the unseemly growth of beard that had accrued to all during our journey, so as to reassume a somewhat more civilized appearance. We sent, therefore, for a barber, and submitted ourselves one after the other to his razor. A somewhat comical incident arose out of this operation. We had all of us more or less, a sore place under the chin from holding the violin, and I who first sat down,

* This Canon was found among *Spohr's* manuscripts, and a fac-simile is appended to this volume.

directed the barber's attention to this, and begged him to go over it very lightly with his razor. As the barber found a similar sore place under the chin of each that followed, his countenance assumed more and more the grotesque expression exhibited in the disposition to whistle and smile at one and the same time, murmuring every now and then something, inwardly. Upon being asked the reason, he replied with a grave look: "Gentlemen, I see very clearly that you all belong to a secret Society, and you all carry the sign. You are Freemasons, probably, and I am right glad that I know at last how that is to be discovered!" As upon this we all broke out into a loud peal of laughter, he was at first very much disconcerted, but, nevertheless, not to be shaken in his belief.

After we had descended into a mine, and visited the smelting-huts and stamping-works, we continued our journey to Seesen, by way of Wildemann. There, we were joyfully welcomed by my parents and brothers and sister as well as by the musical friends of the little town. We had music now from morning to night, and even got up a Public concert, in which all exhibited our skill to the utmost in playing and singing. The proceeds of the concert, we presented to the School for the Poor, for the purchase of new schoolbooks.

Highly pleased with our journey we returned through Göttingen and Mühlhausen to Gotha. I yet think with emotion on the intense pleasure, with which my dear little wife welcomed me home, and never did I feel more acutely, the happiness of being loved!

At this period, a young Poet, a Candidate in Theology, who was awaiting his appointment in Gotha, offered to me an Opera he had written, to set to music, and I seized this opportunity with pleasure, to try my hand, and as I hoped with more success, in dramatic composition. The Name of the Opera was "Alruna, *die Eulenkönigin*" (the Owlet-Queen) it was founded on a popular tradition, and in matter had much resemblance to the "*Donauweibchen*", (the Danube Water-Nymph) which at that time excited general admiration.

I immediately commenced my work with great zeal, and finished the three Acts of the Opera before the end of the year. As some of the "Numbers" which I played at the Court-concerts found great favour, I was encouraged by this to offer my work for representation at the Court-Theatre in Weimar. I went thither in person to obtain a favourable reception of it from Herr *von Goethe*, the Intendant of the Theatre, and Frau *von Heigendorf*, the prima Donna and the mistress of the Duke. To the former I handed the Libretto, to the latter the Music of the Opera. As she found some brilliant parts for herself and her favorite *Stromeyer*, she promised to interest herself in getting the Opera accepted, and as I knew that this depended solely upon her, I returned to Gotha with the most sanguine hopes. Yet it required many reminiscences from me, and month after month passed away, until at length the study of the Opera was commenced. As this had now gone so far that a grand orchestral rehearsal could be effected, Frau *von Heigendorf* invited me to direct it. I therefore proceeded to Weimar a second time, and now in company with the author.

As I had written all manner of new things after I had completed the Opera, it had somewhat faded from my recollection, and I therefore thought I should be the better able to judge of it without partiality. Accordingly I was greatly preoccupied with the impression that it would make upon me. — The Rehearsal took place in a Saloon at the house of Frau *von Heigendorf*. Among the assembled Auditory, besides the Intendant Herr *von Goethe*, and the Musical Amateurs of the Town. *Wieland* was also present. The Singers had well studied their parts; and as the orchestra had already had one rehearsal, the Opera was right well executed under my direction. It gave general satisfaction, and the Composer was overwhelmed with congratulations. Herr *von Goethe*, also spoke in praise of it. The Author did not come off so well. *Goethe* found all manner of defects in the Libretto, and especially required that the dialogue which was written in Iambics should first be put into simple prose, and considerably curtailed before the Opera was performed. This requisition was particularly painful to the Author, as he prided himself not a little on his metrical dialogue. He nevertheless declared to me his readiness to undertake the required alteration, but on account of other pressing work, he could not set about it immediately. This was not displeasing to me, for with the exception of a few of the "Numbers", my Music at the rehearsal in Weimar had not satisfied me, greatly as it had pleased there, and I was again tortured with the thought, that I had no talent for Dramatic music. For this reason the Opera became more and mort indifferent to me, and I was glad to see that its representation would be delayed. At length the thought of seeing it represented and thus made public was so distasteful to me, that I withdrew the parts and score. Hence with the exception of the Overture which was published as Op. 21 by *André* in Offenbach, nothing else of it was engraved. But on the other hand, I was unjust towards this work; for it shews, compared with the first Opera, an unmistakably great progress in dramatic style.

In the year 1808, took place the celebrated Congress of Sovereigns, on which occasion, *Napoleon* entertained his friend the Emperor *Alexander*, and the Kings and Princes of Germany his Allies. The lovers of sights and the curious of the whole country round, poured in to behold the magnificence which was there displayed. In the company of some of my pupils I also made a pedestrian excursion to Erfurt, less to see the Great Ones of the earth, than to see and admire the great ones of the French Stage, *Talma*, and *Mars*. The Emperor had sent to Paris for his tragic performers, and every evening one of the classic works of *Corneille* or *Racine* was played. I and my companions had hoped to have been permitted to see one such representation, but unfortunately, I was informed that they took place for the Sovereigns and their suite only, and that every body else was excluded from them. I now hoped, with the assistance of the musicians, to obtain places in the orchestra; but in this I also failed, for they had been strictly forbidden to take any person in with them. At length it occurred to me, that I and my three pupils, by taking the places of the same number of musicians who played between the acts, might then be enabled to remain during the performance. As we were willing to pay handsomely, and the musicians knew that their substitutes would fill their places in a satisfactory manner, they gave their consent. But, now a new difficulty presented itself: three of us only could be introduced for the violins and the bass-viol; and as neither of us played any other orchestral-instrument but those, one of us of a necessity must remain excluded. The thought then struck me, to try whether I could learn sufficient of the horn, by the evening, so as to be able to undertake the part of the second hornist. I immediately prevailed upon him whose place I wished to take, to yield his horn to me; and began my studies. At first I produced the most terrific tones from it; but after about an hour, I succeeded in bringing out the natural notes of the instrument. After dinner, while my pupils went to walk, I recommenced my studies in the house of the "Stadt-Musicus"* and although my lips pained me very much, yet I did not rest until I could play my horn-part, perfectly, in the certainly. very easy overture and "between acts" which were to be played in the evening.

Thus prepared, I and my pupils joined the other Musicians, and as each carried his instrument under his arm, we reached our places without opposition. We found the saloon in which the theatre had been erected, already brilliantly lit up, and filled with the numerous suite of the Sovereigns. The seats for Napoleon and his guests were close behind the orchestra. Shortly after the most able of my pupils to whom I had assigned the direction of the music, and under whose leadership I placed myself as a new fledged hornist, had tuned up the orchestra; the high personages made their appearance, and the overture began. The orchestra with their faces turned towards the stage, stood in a long row, and

* Musician to the Corporation.

each was strictly forbidden to turn round and look with curiosity at the Sovereigns. As I had received notice of this beforehand, I had provided myself secretly with a small looking-glass, by the help of which as soon as the music was ended, I was enabled to obtain in succession a good view of those who directed the destinies of Europe. Nevertheless, I was soon so entirely engrossed with the magnificent acting of the tragic artistes, that I abandoned my looking-glass to my pupils, and directed my whole attention to the stage. — But at every succeeding "entre-acte", the pain of my lips increased, and at the close of the performance they had become so much swollen and so blistered, that in the evening, I could scarcely eat any supper. Even the next day, on my return to Gotha, they had a very negro-like appearance, and my young wife was not a little alarmed when she saw me; but she was yet more nettled, when in a jesting tone I said: that it was from kissing to such excess the pretty Erfurt-women! When, however, I had related to her the history of my studies on the horn, she laughed heartily at my expense.

About that time, though I do not exactly remember whether it was on that journey to Erfurt, or upon a previous one, the Emperor Napoleon slept also once in the palace at Gotha, and on that account a Court-concert had been commanded the previous evening. I and my wife had the honour to play before the allpowerful man, and he addressed a few words to us. On the following evening also, we received our share of the "Gold Napoleons" which he had left as a present to the Court-orchestra.

The Duke of Gotha was at that time high in his favour, and therefrom great advantages were expected for the Duchy. But he must have lost it afterwards by some neglect; for when the Emperor passed through on a subsequent journey, a scene occurred that filled the inhabitants of Gotha with bitter rage against the tyrant. The Emperor was expected about 11 o'clock. A breakfast had therefore been prepared in the palace at Friedrichsthal, the summer-residence of the

Court, and the whole Court-circle was assembled in state-costume. The posthorses ready harnessed were waiting in the palace-square, to take the Emperor immediately after breakfast upon his farther journey. — At length, the first gun of the salute resounded above on the Friedenstein, from whence every time the Emperor passed through, 101 guns were fired. Shortly afterwards, his carriage drove up. The Duke, surrounded by his Court, already stood with uncovered head at the iron gates, approached the carriage with humble demeanour, and begged that his Imperial Majesty would deign to take breakfast. An abrupt *non!* and the order to his Mamelucks to put to the horses, was the reply. Without condescending any further word or look to the Duke, he leaned back in the carriage and left the Prince standing at the closed door in the most painful perplexity. The Duke turned pale with inward rage to see himself so insulted in the presence of his Court and People, and yet, had not the courage to return immediately to the palace. Thus passed in a dead silence, five or six fearfully long minutes, until the horses were put to. At the first forward movement they made, the Emperor's head was once more visible, and with a cold nod, he drove off. The Duke, as though annihilated, returned to the palace, and the citizens loudly expressed their rage, that the overbearing Corsican should have so insulted their Prince.

On the 6. November, 1808, my wife presented me with a second daughter, who was named *Ida*, after my wife's stepsister Madame *Hildt*, who held her over the font. Her confinement passed over as lightly and happily as the former one, and during the first days the health of the invalid was excellent. This, however, induced her to leave her bed too soon, whereby she caught cold, and the sad consequences were, that she was seized with a violent nervous fever. For several days her life was in imminent danger. I left her neither by day nor night, for she would receive attention from no one but me. What I suffered at the side of her sick-bed is indiscribable! Alarmed by her fits of delirium, by the grave countenance of the physician, who shunned my interrogatories, and tortured with self-reproaches for not having taken more care of her, I had not a moment's rest during *Dorette's* illness. At length the more cheerful expression of the physician's face betokened that the danger was passed, and I, who during the last days, first became really sensible of all I possessed in my wife, and of the intense love I bore her, now felt unspeakably happy. Her recovery progressed rapidly. Yet there was great weakness still remaining, from which *Dorette* was not wholly releived until the spring, when by the recommendation of the Doctor I hired a house in the country with garden attached, and by that means procured her the continual enjoyment of fresh air. Strengthened by this, she then gradually began her musical studies, which for almost six months she had been obliged to discontinue. In the Catalogue of the whole of my works, which I began shortly after my appointment in Gotha and continued up to the present time, besides those Compositions already named, dating from 1808, the following are specified: Two Duetts for violin (op. 9) and one for violin and viola (op. 13). Variations for the harp and two Quartetts for stringed instruments. In Quartetts, certainly the most difficult of all compositions, I had already made a trial the year before. But with them I succeeded no better than with Song-compositions. Shortly after their completion they no longer pleased me; and for that reason I should not have published them had not my Leipsic publisher, Herr *Kühnel*, at whose house I played them in the autumn of 1807, retained them almost by force, and shortly afterwards published them (as op. 4). The new Quartett (op. 15) also brought out by *Kühnel*, pleased me it is true somewhat longer; but at a later period when I had learned to produce a better style of Quartett-composition I regretted also that I had published them. The two first Quartetts I dedicated to the Duke of Gotha, but only at his personal request; for though I felt a pleasure in dedicating my works to *Artistes* and amateurs of music, as a token of my respect and friendship, yet my artistic pride would never permit me to dedicate them to Princes for profit's sake, though even at their express desire.

At the time when the Duke invited me to dedicate my Compositions to him, he frequently used to send for me to converse with him upon his tastes in Art. As is well known, in spite of his peculiarities, he was a man of mind, and cultivated taste, which his published Poems and his Correspondance with *Jean Paul* sufficiently prove. But with the affairs of Government he did not in the least trouble himself, and left them entirely to the Privy-Counsellor *von Frankenberg*, who, therefore, was virtually the Regent of the land. Obliged *pro forma* to be present at the sittings of the Privy-Council, he invariably got tired of the subjects of discussion, and endeavoured to make them as short as possible, himself frequently, saying, in derision of his own want of interest "will not the Gentlemen of the Privy-Council soon be pleased to command what I am to command?"

At that time, perhaps incited by my Compositions for the voice, he was seized with the desire to have one of his longer poems, a kind of Cantata, set to music. He did me the honour to consult me on the subject. But as the Duke probably could not prevail on himself to let me see his limited knowledge of music, he applied to his old music-master, the Concert-Director *Reinhard*, to carry it out. From him at a later period, in an unguarded and confiding moment, I heard how the composition of the Cantata was brought about. The Duke, read to his master seated at the piano, a passage of the text, and explained to him his ideas respecting the style in which it should be composed. When the Duke had once heard or read the characteristics of the different tones, *Reinhard* was then obliged to strike several of them in sequent accords, so that he might find the right one for his text. If this was cheerful, a Major-Key was chosen, if it was mournful, a Minor-Key was selected. It happened one day that the Duke took the Major too sprightly, and the Minor was too mournful, upon this he required poor *Reinhard* to sound the Key in *half* Minor. When they had agreed upon this point, the melody suited to the text was next sought for. The Duke then whistled every melody that came into his head, and left his master to choose the most suitable to the character of the words. When in this manner a few lines of the poem had been disposed of, they passed on to the next. As *Reinhard* could not compose, or at least not arrange the instrumentation, the plan of the Cantata thus sketched out in the Duke's leisure-hours was handed over to the "Kammer-Musicus" *Buckofen* to complete with score. The latter, as may readily be imagined, could make but little use of the materials given to him, and was therefore obliged to recompose as it were the Cantata anew. Possessing considerable talent for composition, he accordingly put out of hand a piece of music such as could well be listened to. The work thus completed, was now written out, carefully practised under my direction, and then produced at a Court-Concert. The Duke, though he may well have been somewhat astonished that his music sounded so well, received the congratulations and praises of the Court with a satisfied mien, praised me for having so well entered into his ideas in practising it with the orchestra, and privately sent his two fellow-workmen their gratuity. In this manner all parties were satisfied.

In the winter of 1808—9, I arranged some Subscription-Concerts in the town for the benefit of the Court-Orchestra. But as these could present nothing better than was heard at the Court-Concerts, and those were much frequented by the amateurs of music of the town, for whom a large space behind the orchestra in the Concert-saloon was set apart, these Subscription concerts met with but little support. The product therefore was so small after the deduction of the expenses, that it was not considered worth while repeating the undertaking.

At one of these Concerts, Herr *Hermstedt*, Director of the "Harmonic-music" to Prince Sondershausen, appeared as Clarinet player, and attracted much attention by his admirable performance. He had come to Gotha to request me to write a Clarinet-concerto for him, for which the Prince upon the condition that *Hermstedt* should be put in possession of the manuscript, offered to pay a handsome gratuity. To this proposal I gladly assented, as from the immense execution, together with the brilliancy of tone, and purity of intonation possessed by *Hermstedt*, I felt at full liberty to give the reins to my fancy. After, that with *Hermstedt's* assistance I had made myself somewhat acquainted with the technics of the instrument, I went zealously to work, and completed it in a few weeks. Thus originated the Concerto in E-minor, published a few years afterwards by *Kühnel* as op. 26, with which *Hermstedt* achieved so much success in his artistic tours, that it may be affirmed he is chiefly indebted to that for his fame. I took it over to him myself to Sondershausen, at the end of January, and initiated him in the way to execute it. On this occasion, I appeared also as Violinist at a concert given by *Hermstedt*, and played for the first time, my Concerto in G-Minor (op. 28) which I had just finished a few days before, and, also, a new Pot-pourri (op. 24).

Secretary *Gerber*, the author of the "Musical Lexicon", speaks of these not only in that work, under the article "*Spohr*" but also in a spirited notice in the Musical-Journal, a reprint of which is to be found in number 26. of the eleventh volume. The third part of this Concerto is a Spanish *Rondo*, the melodies of which are not mine but genuine Spanish. I heard them from a Spanish soldier who was quartered in my house, and who sang to the guitar. I noted down what pleased me, and wove it into my *Rondo*. In order to give this a more Spanish character, I copied the guitar-accompaniments as I had heard them from the Spaniard, into the orchestral part. At the beginning of the same winter, I had also a visit from *Reichardt*, Director of the orchestra at Cassel, and then first made his personal acquaintance. *Reichardt* told me he was going to Vienna by the command of his Court, to engage singers for a German theatre that was about to be opened at Cassel. This, proved afterwards to be false; for *Reichardt* was at that very time no longer in the Westphalian service. I had felt at first much annoyed by a sharp criticism of *Reichardt's* upon my play, on my first appearance at Berlin; but as I soon found that it contained many truths and well founded strictures, and that it had prompted me to correct the faults it pointed out in my execution, a sentiment of gratitude had long taken the place of my former resentment. I therefore welcomed my guest with great cordiality, and immediately arranged a musical party at my house in his honour, at which I let him hear my two new and just finished Violin-Quartetts.

As at that time I knew none of *Reichardt's* compositions beyond a couple of successful songs, and looked upon the famous author of the "Confidential letter from Paris" and the dreaded Critic, as a great Composer, I set much value upon his opinion, and awaited it with a feeling of acute expectancy. I therefore again felt somewhat chafed when *Reichardt* had various objections to make, and expressed them *sans gène*. But it was perhaps more the self sufficient look of infallibility with which he pronounced his judgement, that wounded me; for some time after, I was again obliged to admit to myself, that *Reichardt's* observations were in many respects just. There was *one* remark, which I frequently called to mind in my subsequent studies. For instance, in an *Adagio*, from the beginning to the end, I had carried out a figure after the style of *Mozart*, now in one Key, and then in the other, and in my delight at this scientific interweaving, had not remarked that it at last became monotonous. But although *Reichardt* praised the manner in which I had carried it through, he spoke unsparingly against it, and added more over, maliciously, "You could not rest until you had worried your motive to death!"

* * *

In the spring of 1809, from the unusual expenses attendant upon my wife's confinement and subsequent illness, as well as those incurred by the necessary removal to another house outside the town, I found myself in such straightened circumstances, that I earnestly desired to see realised the promise of an increase of salary that had been made to me on my appointment. I therefore addressed a petition to the Duke, which as he never troubled himself with administrative matters, was without effect, and probably, was laid aside unread. I was therefore advised by the Intendant, Baron *von Reibnitz* to make a personal application to the Privy-Counsellor *von Frankenberg* and deliver to him my petition for the desired increase of salary. I followed this advice, and in the afternoon of a fine spring-day, walked over to the seat of the Privy-Counsellor, distant about two miles from Gotha, on the road to Erfurt. I found him in his garden, sitting under a large lime tree, playing chess with his daughter. As I had been familiar with this game from my early youth, played it often, and was passionately fond of it; after a short salutation of the players, I immediately directed my whole attention to the game as it stood. The Privy-Counsellor observing this, had a chair placed for me close to the table, and quietly played on. When I first arrived, the game looked very threatening for the daughter, and it was not long before she was checkmated by her father. I had taken particular notice of the position of the pieces, and in so doing, a move had suggested itself to me by which the checkmate could have been prevented. I represented this, and was immediately challenged by the Privy-Counsellor, who thought himself sure of the victory, to try it. The pieces were again replaced in the position they stood when I arrived, and I now took the daughter's game. After a few well combined moves I succeeded in extricating my King from all danger, and I then played against my opponent with such success, that he was soon obliged to confess himself beaten. The Privy-Counsellor, though somewhat nettled at his defeat, was nevertheless much struck with the unexpected issue of the game. He held out his hand to me in a friendly manner and said: "You are a capital Chess-player, and must often do me the pleasure of playing with me." This I did; and as I was world-wise enough not to win too many games, I soon got in great favour with my new patron; the result was, that a rescript, for an additional two hundred thalers to my salary was soon made out.

*   *   *

Towards the middle of the summer, from the constant enjoyment of fresh air, and frequent walks which were extended by degrees to little excursions into the neighbourhood; *Dorette* had regained her former strength and health, and again devoted herself with renewed assiduity to the study of her instrument, in order to prepare herself thoroughly for our projected second artistic-tour. As I also now became more and more acquainted with the properties of the harp, with its effects, and what my wife in particular was capable of performing with it, I at that time wrote another grand Sonata for harp and violin (op. 115 published by *Schuberth* in Hamburg), and took great pains to introduce into it the result of my experience. I was completely successful; the part for the harp in this Sonata was easier to play, and at the same time more brilliant than in the previous ones. *Dorette* therefore, practised it with special predeliction and soon played this new work with the same precision as the others.

Thus once more prepared for an Artistic tour, we began to consider in which direction it would be most advantageous to go. I had learned from a traveller just returned from Russia, that my Musical fame and that of my wife had already reached there, and that in the previous winter a visit from us had been expected. As I had reason to hope, moreover, that I should receive powerful letters of recommendation from the Court of Weimar to the Imperial Court of St. Petersburgh, the journey to Russia appeared to me to hold out the most advantages. But, *Dorette* would not consent to so distant a journey from home, as she beleived herself unable to bear so long a separation from her children. Yet, when I represented to her, that if at any time it was our intention to go to Russia, the present was the most favourable moment, in which our children under the assiduous care of their grandmother, would miss us less than at a later period, she at length, though with a bleeding heart, consented to it. As I had foreseen that the Dutchess, also, would not consent to so long an absence as would be required for a journey to Russia, I kept secret for the present the real aim of our journey, and named Breslau as its object, for which I asked and obtained a three-month's leave. From there, I intended to apply for an extension of leave, to proceed farther.

We set out on our journey in October, 1809; played first at Weimar, and received from the Grand-Dutchess the desired introduction to her brother, the Emperor Alexander, as also to other Russian Magnates. We then gave a Concert in Leipsic, of which the Musical-Journal contains the following short notice: "Herr Concertmeister *Spohr* and his wife afforded us the pleasure to hear for a whole evening, several of his newest Compositions, and himself on the Violin; as, also, his wife on the Harp. Respecting this *true* artiste and his talented wife we have already spoken fully and decidedly, we shall here therefore be succinct. Since we last heard them, both have made a surprising progress, not alone in their mastery and ready command of all the resources of their Art, but in their skilful application of them to the best and most effective purposes: — And if the former Compositions of this Master found both here and everywhere else the most unanimous applause, his later Compositions which we have now heard, will much less fail to do so."

Of our Concerts in Dresden, and Bautzen, having sought in vain for a notice of them, I am unable to say more than that they took place on the 1. and 7. November, as I perceive from a memorandum of the receipts on this journey, which has by chance been preserved. But of the three Concerts we gave in Breslau, on the 18. November, and the 2. and 9. December there is a notice in the Musical-Journal, which speaks in great praise of our Play, though it finds some fault with the Compositions. It says: "The opinion of our musical friends of Herr *Spohr* as a Composer, agrees fully with that which they previously pronounced respecting him. He is in truth a Musician of high merit. He has nevertheless a peculiarity, and one which by degrees perhaps, will lead him to uniformity in style; namely, his latest compositions, so far as we are acquainted with them are *one and all of a melancholy character*. Even the Pot-Pourri which he played at the close of the Concert, partook somewhat of it."

This remark upon the melancholy character of my Compositions, which is here made for the first time, and so often repeated at a later period in criticisms upon my works, as to become regularly stereotyped, has always been a riddle for me; for, to me, my Compositions appear for the most part quite as cheerful as those of any other Composer. Those in particular which I then played in Breslau, with the exception of two subjects, were all of so lively a character, that I am still unable to understand the above remark. The two first Allegro's alone of the Concertante in H- and G-Minor are serious, the former perhaps even somewhat mournful, but the other subjects are all of them, lively. The same may be said from beginning to end of the Concertante for two violins in A-Major, which I played with Herr *Luge*, and more than that, the third Thesis is even saucily playful. Neither does the Composition for the harp, nor the Overture to "Alruna" bear any trace of melancholy; how then does the Reviewer come by his remark? — Nevertheless, as something similar has been maintained respecting my Compositions even up to the present time, so that people who have not known me personally, have considered me a misanthrope, or an hypochondriac, though I am happy to say I am always of a cheerful tone of mind; there must be something in it, and I think it is, that people have taken the prevailing dreaminess and sentimental character of my Compositions, and my predeliction for the Minor Keys, as outbursts of melancholy. If it is so, I am content to bear with it, though at first it always annoyed me. Of the Overture to "Alruna", the same Breslauer critic says: "It is not free from reminiscences." He might have said right out, it is an exact imitation of the Overture to the "Zauberflöte"; for that was the object I had in view. In my admiration of *Mozart*, and the feeling of wonder with which I regarded that Overture, an imitation of it seemed to me something very natural and praiseworthy, and at the time when I sought to develope my talent for Composition I had made many similar imitations of *Mozart's* master pieces, and among others that of the aria full of love-complaints in Alruna, imitated from the beautiful aria of Pamina: "*Ach, ich fühl's, es ist verschwunden.*" Although shortly after that time, I became sensible that a Composer should endeavour to be original both in the form of his musical pieces, and in the development of his musical ideas, yet I retained even up to a later period, a predeliction for that imitation of the Overture to the "*Zauberflöte*", and still consider it as one of my best and most effective Instrumental-compositions. Neither is it so slavish an imitation as to contain nothing of my own invention; for instance, the striking modulations in the introductory *Adagio*, and the second Fugue-theme with which the second half of the *Allegro* begins, and, which then is so happily connected with the chief theme. The instrumentation, also, though quite in the *Mozart* style has nevertheless, some original characteristics.

In Breslau we met an old acquaintance from Gotha, Baron *von Reibnitz*, who hitherto had been Intendant of the Orchestra, but had resigned, and retired to his estate in Silesia. He was then in town for the winter months, and acquainted with all in Breslau who were fond of music, and who played, he introduced me into the Musical Circles there, and was of great assistance to me in making arrangements for my concerts. In Breslau, from olden time one of the most musical Towns of Germany, there was at that moment such a succession of Concerts, that one took place almost every day in the week. As the Theatre, was open also every evening, it was therefore very difficult to fix upon a day favourable for an Extra-Concert, and almost more difficult to get together a good and numerous orchestra. The kindness of *Schnabel* the Leader of the Cathedral-Choir enabled me nevertheless to overcome this difficulty, for he not only procured for me a good Orchestra for each of my three Concerts, but each time undertook to conduct it. The experienced Director evinced a particular interest in my compositions, which he soon transferred to the Composer, who returned it in the most hearty manner. We became much attached to each other, and until *Schnabel's* early death remained on the most intimate terms of friendship.

Shortly after my arrival in Breslau, just as I was about to write to Gotha for an extension of my leave to proceed to Russia, I received through Baron *von Reibnitz* a letter from the Court-Chamberlain Count *Salisch* in Gotha, to the following effect:

The Dutchess has with great regret received the information from Weimar, that I had the intention of proceeding to Russia and did not contemplate returning before the expiration of the year. As she would be extremely unwilling to miss my services and those of my wife at the Court-Concerts for so long a period, she therefore offered, if I would give up the journey to Russia, and return speedily to Gotha, to indemnify my wife, by procuring for her the appointment of Solo-player at the Court-Concerts, and Teacher of Music to the Princess.* — Scarcely had I communicated to my wife the contents of this letter, than I saw how the hope of sooner rebeholding her children brought tears of joy into her eyes.

* The Step-daughter of the Dutchess, afterwards married to the Duke of Coburg, and mother of the present reigning Duke and of His R. H. the late Prince Albert, Consort of the Queen of England.

This moved me so deeply, that I at once resolved to give up the journey. I therefore immediately put myself in communication with Count *Salisch,* the new Intendant of the Gotha Orchestra, and when he had definitively arranged the appointment of my wife with a suitable salary to commence from the 1. January 1810, I agreed on my side to return to Gotha as soon as possible. We therefore hastened our departure from Breslau to Berlin, and proceeded through Liegnitz to Glogau, where we gave two Concerts on the 13. and 18. December, that had been previously arranged for by our musical friends there, and which were very numerously attended.

Of the Concert at Glogau, I still remember a very ludicrous incident. It took place in a building which was perhaps unique of its kind; for on the basement were the Butcher's shambles, on the first floor the Concert-Saloon, and above that the Theatre of the town. As the Saloon was very low and much overcrowded, it soon became insufferably hot. The public, therefore, soon demanded that a trap-door in the ceiling of the Saloon should be opened, which could be effected from the Pit of the Theatre overhead. Now, however, the key of the Theatre was nowhere to be found, the latter not having been used during the whole of the winter; a long pole was therefore brought with which to push up the door. At first, it would not move; but upon several men combining their strength, it sprung suddenly, open, and at the same moment let down upon the ladies sitting underneath such a shower of dust, cherry-stones, apple-peel and the like, the accumulation of years, in the pit, that not only were they completely covered, but the whole orchestra and audience envelloped in such a cloud of dust, that at first nobody could make out what it really was. When it had cleared off again, the ladies endeavoured as well as they could to free their necks and dresses from the dirt; the Musicians cleaned their instruments, and the Concert was continued.

We found Berlin very full of strangers, and in a state of festive excitement in expectation of the return of the Court, which ever since the unfortunate battle of Jena had continued to reside in Königsberg. The moment was favourable for giving Concerts, and even before the arrival of the Court we had a numerous audience at our first. Of our performances, the Editor of the Musical Journal says: "Yesterday, the 4. January, the Director of Concerts in Gotha, Herr *Spohr*, gave a Concert at the Theatre. Of his own Compositions he played a Violin-Concerto in G-Minor, with a Spanish *Rondo*, a Pot-Pourri for the Violin, and with his wife an accomplished and most expressive player, a Sonata for pedal-Harp and Violin, also of his composition. The Musical Journal has already frequently spoken in praise of this talented Virtuoso, and recently also adverted to this composition. In the present instance, also, both his Compositions and his Play were highly commended. Particularly admired were the double chords, the distances, and the shakes which Herr *Spohr* executed with the greatest skill, and by the impassioned expression of his play, especially in the *Adagio*, he won every heart. We hope, to hear this estimable Artiste-Couple again next week."

On the 10. took place the Public Entry of the returning Court. It was indeed an affecting scene, when the King seated by the side of his Wife in an open carriage, drove slowly through the crowded streets, greeted by the acclamations of thousands and by the waving of handkerchiefs from every window. The Queen seemed deeply affected; for tear after tear was seen to steal from her beautiful eyes. In the evening the City was splendidly illuminated.

On the following day, we gave our second Concert. Early in the morning we were beseiged with questions, whether the Court would be there. We could as yet afford no information on the subject; but when about noon, the Queen sent for tickets, the news of it spread through the City like wildfire, and the auditory now came in such crowds that the spacious Saloon could scarcely hold them. I played, as I see by the notice in the Musical Journal, my third Concerto in C-Major; and with my pupil *Hildebrandt* who was on a visit to a relation in Berlin, my Concertante in A-Major. The precision of our Duo-playing was the same as usual, and here, as in Gotha gained for us the most lively applause. But the critic, nevertheless does not appear to have been wholly of the same opinion, since he expresses himself as follows: "Both Players in the Concertante played not only together, but as *one*; and though this merits on the one hand praise and even elicits astonishment, yet on the other, it is somewhat uniform and monotonous; one missed and regretfully, that charm which derives from the union of things different in themselves, when through that very unison the difference is still observable — instead of being a union of accord, it was one and the same thing." — This sounds very sensible, and yet has very little sense in it! The two Solo-voices of this Concertante are written in such a manner that their full effect is only to be attained by the closest union of play. But to achieve that in the highest degree, is possible only when both players are of the same school and have the same style of execution. In fact, it is even necessary that their Instruments should possess a like power, and as much as possible the same qualities of tone. These were all combined in my Pupil and me; hence the great effect of our Duo-playing. At a subsequent period in my travels both in Germany and abroad, I have played that Concertante with several of the most celebrated Violinists of the day, who as Virtuosi stood higher than my pupil *Hildebrandt*, but with them I never could attain the same effect as in my play with him, their school and mode of execution being too dissimilar from mine.

It was at first my intention to return to Gotha direct from Berlin, in order to keep my promise. But being informed by a musical friend in Hamburgh that it was then a most favourable time of the year to give Concerts, I wrote to Gotha requesting a few weeks more extension of leave, to visit Hamburgh before my return. It was granted to me.

Hamburgh was at that time in the possession of the French, who had laid a severe interdict upon all commerce with England. The then even very rich merchants had therefore little to do, and the more leisure to occupy themselves with Music and Concerts. As we were now preceeded by a good artistic reputation, our first Concert, which we gave on the 8. February in the Apollo-Saloon was exceedingly well attended, and brought in at the high admission-price of one Hamburgh Species, nearly 400 thalers. Our play in that Concert having made a great sensation, the receipts increased at the second, on 21. February, to the large sum of 1015 Thalers. Between those two Concerts we gave one also at Lubeck on the 14. which we had been invited to do by the Musical amateurs of that place, and, lastly, played also at Altona in the Museum, for a moderate remuneration.

Highly gratified with the business we had done, we were now on the point of leaving; when the Secretary to the French Governor called upon us, and invited us in his name to give a third Concert, as he and his Circle had missed the opportunity of hearing us. Under the apprehension that a third would not be well attended, as I hesitated in my reply, the gentleman added, that he was charged to take two hundred tickets for the Governor and his friends. All hesitation on my part was now dismissed, and on the 3. March we gave a third Concert, which again brought a receipt of 510 thalers.

At that time, in Hamburgh, I first became personally acquaintained with *Andreas Romberg* and the Director of Music *Schwenke*. Both those celebrated Artistes received me in the most friendly manner, and rendered me every possible assistance in my concerts. *Romberg* took care to provide a good Orchestra and directed it himself, and *Schwenke*, the dreaded critic, undertook to announce the Concerts in the newspapers. As his opinion was considered the highest authority, the favourable manner in which he introduced the Artiste-Pair to the notice of the Public, and afterwards pronounced upon our performance, and upon my compositions, contributed not a little to the great success we met with in Hamburgh. Both those Artistes lived amid an agreable family circle and were much pleased when I and my wife looked in upon them at tea-time. We then chatted on nothing but Music, and many were the entertaining and instructive discussions that arose. *Romberg* took great pleasure in reverting to his former residence in Paris, and related many piquante incidents of the musical celebrities there. *Schwenke* amused us highly with his witty but biting criticism, which scarcely spared any one. I might therefore well be proud that my Compositions and Play were favourably spoken of by him. The specialities touched upon by *Schwenke* in these discussions were very instructive for me, and I was therefore always delighted when I met him at these Music-Parties. At this time, Quartetts were much played in Hamburgh, and *Romberg* had studied his Quartett admirably, in which the execution of the Violincellist *Prell* formed a most attractive feature. It was therefore a pleasure to join them. *Romberg* only played particular Quartetts, and though no great Virtuoso on his instrument, executed them with skill and taste. But he only grew right warm with the subject, when he could smoke his pipe at his ease while Quartett-playing*. I played his favorites among the Quartetts of *Mozart* and *Beethoven* and in this instance, also, excited much sensation by my truthful rendering of the distinctive characters of each. *Schwenke* expressed himself thereon in the most eloquent terms. At his desire, also, I was obliged to play two of my own Quartetts. I did it unwillingly, as they no longer came up to the standard I now prescribed to myself in that kind of composition. This I expressed also without reserve; but they pleased nevertheless, and found grace even from *Schwenke's* sharp criticism. *Romberg* was of a different opinion. He said to me with ingenuous openheartedness: „Your Quartetts will not do yet; they are far behind your Orchestral pieces!" Much as I agreed with him, yet it wounded me to hear another express that opinion. When therefore, a few

---

* *Bernhard Romberg*, also, constantly smoked while playing, and I once heard him in his house at Gotha, executed his most difficult Concerto in F-Minor, without taking the pipe from his mouth.

years afterwards I wrote some Quartetts in Vienna, which seemed to me more worthy of my other Compositions, I dedicated them to *Romberg*, in order to shew him that I could now write Quartetts, "which would do."

At one of the Musical Parties where I and my wife were present, a comical misunderstanding arose which excited much laughter.

A rich Jew banker, who had heard my Quartett-playing much praised, was desirous to give his Circle a treat, and so he invited me to his house. Although, I knew that I should meet an auditory there but little able to appreciate such high class Music, I could not well refuse, as the wealthy man had taken forty tickets for each of my concerts. I therefore accepted the invitation, but on the condition that the best Artistes of Hamburgh should be invited to accompany me. This was promised, and upon my entering the brillant company I not only found *Romberg* was present, but saw another distinguished violinist. Just as the Quartett-playing was about to begin a fourth Violinist made his appearance with his instrument, and we now saw with astonishment that the master of the house had invited Violinists only. As a good Accountant, he knew that to play a Quartett, *four* persons were necessary, but not that a Violist and Violincellist should be among them. To extricate him from his perplexity, he was advised to send quickly for Herr *Prell* at the Theatre. But as the performances were already over there, in spite of every endeavour, neither he nor any other Violincellist could be found, and the company would have been obliged to separate without any music, had not I and my wife played one of our sonatas. If the musical knowledge of this Macenas of Art was but little, his delicacy was still less. For when I took leave of him that evening, he went to his writing table and taking out 40 Species, said as he held them out to me: "I hear, you are going to give a third Concert; send me forty more tickets; I have still, it is true, almost all the others, but will take new ones, nevertheless." Indignant at the meanness of the rich Jew, I declined to take his money, and said:

"The former tickets, certainly, do not admit to the next Concert; but yours shall. You will not therefore require any new ones." And so I left him standing embarrassed and ashamed before his company, and turned my back upon him. On the day of the Concert, nevertheless, one of the servants of the Hebrew Cresus came for the forty tickets.

Before I left Hamburgh, another offer was made to me that gave me much pleasure. The celebrated Theatrical-Manager, Actor, and Play-writer *Schröder*, who for nearly ten years had lived in retirement, and had then let his Theatre to other speculators, was suddenly seized with the desire to resume the management after the expiration of their lease. The Play-going public of Hamburgh were rejoiced at this, for they looked forward to see their Stage reassume the distinguished rank to which it had formerly attained under *Schröder's* direction. The new management was to commence with the year 1811, and open at first with several new Plays and Operas. *Schröder* himself had already written a number of Plays and Comedies, for the occasion, and had procured the librettos of four Operas, for which the music was now to be composed. Three of these were already in the hands of *Winter* of Munich, of *Andreas Romberg* and *Clasing* the teacher of music in Hamburgh; but the fourth "*Der Zweikampf mit der Geliebten*" of *Schink* was offered to me for composition. The negotiator in this matter, was a former acquaintance of mine, *Schmidt*, the actor, previously on the Magdeburgh but now on the Hamburgh stage.

Little satisfied as I had hitherto been with my Dramatic labours, the desire to make another trial was by no means diminished. I therefore accepted the offer without much preliminary enquiry about the conditions, and without submitting the libretto destined for me to any proof. The conditions were nevertheless very fair. A written agreement was drawn up in which these were stipulated and signed by both parties. I undertook to deliver my composition in the spring of 1811, and to go to Hamburgh in the course of the summer, to direct the three first representations of the opera.

With the prospect of a pleasant task before me, I now gladly returned to the quiet of Gotha. But I was somewhat anxious lest the Dutchess might have felt offense at our protracted absence, and I was the more confirmed in that fear when upon paying our visit of return, to the Dutchess, we were not received. We saw her therefore for the first time again at the Court-Concert. As I well knew that the surest way to make our peace with her, was to appear in this at once, I played one of my Sonatas with my wife, and afterwards the Dutchess's favorite Variations of *Rode* in G-Major. This had the desired effect; for at the end of the Concert, the Dutchess advanced towards us, greeted us in the most friendly manner, and would not permit us to finish our apologies. With our mind at rest, we could now fully enjoy the happiness of being once more united to our children.

As soon as we again felt at home, I longed to commence the composition of the Opera I had brought with me. I now first saw, upon a nearer examination of the libretto, that I had not drawn a very great prize. The subject though in itself not uninteresting, had been worked out in a manner that little suited me. I felt the necessity for some alterations, and therefore applied first to Herr *Schröder* for permission to make them. This was readily conceded, and with the assistance of a young Poet in Gotha, I altered what did not please me, but saw later on its representation, that I ought also to have erased many other things. I was then, however, still too little experienced in Dramatic-writing.

Scarcely had I begun the Composition of the first acts of the Opera, than I was called away from it by another task. In the spring, *Bischoff*, the Leader of the choir at Frankenhausen, came to Gotha, and offered me the Direction of a Musical Festival, which he purposed to give in the church of his town, in the course of the summer. He had already secured the assistance of the most celebrated Singers, as well as of the most distinguished members of the Court-Orchestras of the neighbouring Thuringian Capitals, and therefore had no doubt of the most brilliant success. As the junior Director of these Court-Orchestras, I felt not a little flattered at having the Leadership offered to me, and accepted it with pleasure, although I had never yet directed so large an Orchestra and Chorus company as would be there assembled. I was now obliged to lay aside for some time the work I had begun, for *Hermstedt* urgently besought me to write another new Clarinet-Concerto for him, to play at the Festival. Although sorry to be disturbed in my studies, I allowed myself to be persuaded, and finished it in sufficient time for *Hermstedt* to practise it well under my direction. This first Musical Festival at Frankenhausen, which at that time attracted great attention in the Musical World, and gave rise both on the Elbe, the Rhine, in North-Germany and Switzerland, to the institution of similar Musical Festivals, found in Herr *Gerber,* the author of the Musical-Lexicon, so eloquent a Commentator, that I think I cannot do better than quote in part here his notice, in the 12. Annual-Volume Nr. 47 of the Musical Journal:

"On the 20. and 21. of June, a Musical-Festival was celebrated in Frankenhausen, a Town in the Schwarzburg-Rudolstadt Circle, four leagues from Sondershausen; at which *Haydn's "Creation"* was performed, and a Grand Concert; a Festival as remarkable for the successful manner in which the numerous difficulties attending the arrangement of the whole had been overcome, as for the high degree of excellence exhibited in the presence of thousands, who had gathered to hear it from a distance of twenty leagues round. When it is considered that we are here speaking of a country town in Thuringia, in which the Musical-*personel* consisted alone of the "Stadt-Musicus" and his assistants, with the vocalists of the Choir, the possibility of accomplishing such an undertaking must excite the greatest surprise . . . .

"The Precentor Herr *Bischoff* of Frankenhausen, a young,

active man, and an enthusiast in his love for Music, who already in 1804, with the assistance of his neighbours and a few members of the Ducal Orchestra of Gotha, under the leadership of Concert-Director *Fischer* of Erfurt, and *Ernst* of Gotha, performed "The Creation" in the principal church of that place with about eighty Singers and Instrumentalists to the great satisfaction of the hearers; felt thereby encouraged to reproduce once more that great master-piece, according to the idea of its great Composer with *two hundred* Singers and Instrumentalists. His purpose was long hindered by the passage to and fro of foreign troops. At length in the present apparent calm in Germany, he undertook to carry it out. With that view he had some time previously visited Weimar, Rudolstadt, Gotha and Erfurt; to several towns he sent written invitations, and as these were everywhere favourably received, early on the 19. June, 101 Singers and 106 Instrumentalists, for the most part of Thuringia, had assembled for the rehearsal, and among these, twenty Artistes from Gotha with their celebrated Director, Concert-Master *Spohr*.

"The Assistants were partly graduated Musicians, and Members of Orchestra, partly Dilletanti and Virtuosi of first rank, each with his own instrument, and most of them already familiar with the "Creation". . . .

"Of this assemblage, the following Orchestra was formed: Director, Concert-Master *Spohr*; Soprano-Solo, Madame *Scheidler* from Gotha; Tenor-Solo, "Kammer-Singer" *Methfessel* from Rudolstadt; Bass-Solo, "Kammer-Singer" *Strohmeyer* of Weimar; Organ, Director *Fischer* and Professor *Scheibner*, both of Erfurt; Pianiste, Director *Krille* from Stollberg; Director of the Chorus, Precentor *Bischoff* of Frankenhausen; Chorists, Soprani 28, Alti 20, Tenori 20, Bassi 30."

Here follow the names of all the Musicians, and a description of the arrangement of the Orchestra. The notice then continues:

„This appropriate and excellent arrangement, by which each had sufficient room, and the Director constantly in view, contributed without doubt not a little after one rehearsal only to the successful execution of so great a work of art, new to many, and exceedingly difficult, as was in particular produced on the second day:

"1) A grand new Overture for full Orchestra (with bassoons also) by *Spohr*. 2) A grand Italian Scena for Bass by *Righini*, sung by *Strohmeyer*. 3) A grand new Clarinet Concerto, written expressly for this Festival by *Spohr*, and played by Director *Hermstedt*. After which 4) Concert-Master *Fischer* played upon the full Organ an artistic Introduction to the last Chorus from *Haydn's* "Seasons". This was followed 5) by a Double-Concert for two Violins (also of *Spohr's* original-Composition) played by himself and *Matthäi*. 6) A grand *Rondo* from a Concerto in D-Major by *Bernard Romberg*, artistically played by *Dotzauer*, and lastly, Beethoven's C-Major Symphony. . . .

"Herr *Spohr's* leading with a roll of paper, without the least noise, and without the slightest contortion of countenance, might be called a *graceful Leading* if that word were sufficient to express the precision and influence impressed by his movements upon the whole mass, strange both to him and to itself. To this happy talent in Herr *Spohr* I ascribe in great part the excellence and precision — the imposing power, as well as the soft blending of this numerous Orchestra with the voices of the Singers in the execution of "The Creation."

"The full toned yet flexible voice of Madame *Scheidler*, so well adapted to a large church, the expressive execution of the Art-experienced Herr *Methfessel*, the magnificent bass-voice of Herr *Strohmeyer*, indisputably the finest I ever heard, reaching from Contra D to G *on the second line*, ... these three Solo-Singers, in unison with so many distinguished Virtuosi leading every Voice, where each sang or played voluntarily and with pleasure, justify me in affirming that this execution of "The Creation" was the most powerful, most expressive and in a word the most successful that I had ever heard. . . . .

"The Overture with which the Concert began on the

following day, belongs properly considered to the *Master-pieces in modulation*. Almost with every new bar, one *Inganno* succeeds the other, so that it may be looked upon as a connected series of studies in modulation. Probably, this restlessness, this vacillation, has reference to the character of the "Alruna" for which drama this was written. Great, however as the effect of this Overture may certainly be in a Theatre, yet as Concert-Music it did not appear to make the impression that might have been expected from its execution by so good and numerous an orchestra. This result can be explained in no other way than, in as much as continuously disappointed hopes depress the spirits and make the mind uneasy, so a music which to the end disappoints the expectations of the ear, never satisfies. A profusion of crooked and sometimes rough passages, leading to no object, to no repose, and to no further enjoyment, in which the Composer merely keeps the mind of the hearer in suspense become at length wearisome. The music of our forefathers 200 years ago, consisted of just such a profusion of crooked passages, without resting place — of numberless modulations and sustained terminals. But our worthy ancestors were as yet wanting in the flowers wherewith to embellish and make a little resting place interesting, that is: they were yet wanting in figures of Melody to entertain their hearers agreably in one Tone. But how easy would this have been to the admirable *Spohr*, who has so many of the beautiful flowers! The so called contrast in great Musical works is by no means to be despised; and least of all, the more it is grounded upon human perception and feeling.

"Of the effect of Herr *Strohmeyer's* execution of the grand Scena of *Righini*, it is here unnecessary to say any thing further, since his splendid delivery has had full justice done to it above. *Righini's* charming Song, and admirable instrumentation are sufficiently known. The Scena kindled the enthusiasm of the whole audience.

"*Spohr's* Clarinet-Concerto in E-Minor, played by *Hermstedt*, is indisputably one of the *most perfect Artistic Works of the kind*. A grand and brilliant handling of the concerted instruments, combined with a most original accompaniment for the Orchestra, in which as it were each instrument even the kettle-drum, is *obligato,* and which for that reason requires a more than usually practised and attentive Orchestra, entitles it to be so considered. The third, Polonaise-like theme, is particularly remarkable, in which one knows not whether to admire most the brilliancy of the artistic Soli's or the admirably elaborated Tutti's — in the latter of which, the wind instruments seem actually to engage each other in a Thematic struggle. This artistic work is moreover conspicuous for the cheerful spirit that pervades it throughout. The admirable execution of this Concerto did great honour to the Composer, the Player and the whole Orchestra; and set thousands of hands among the audience in lively and continuous motion.

"Hereupon, Concert-Master *Fischer* surprised the Orchestra as well as the audience not a little, by falling in with the full Organ, in order to introduce the now ensuing chorus of the Finale, in C-Major. This novel kind of Music, of which nothing had been heard at the rehearsal, its artistic connecting of the Voices, its harmonious turns and masterly modulations made every member of the Orchestra doubly attentive. For some minutes he may have entertained the audience in this manner, when, he dwellt upon the dominant, and to keep the expectation yet more alive for the entry of the Chorus, by means of a sort of Organ-Point, formed a close at this interval. This was no sooner observed by Herr *Spohr*, than he lifted his roll of paper, and scarcely had the last organ-tone ceased, when the whole Orchestra fell in with the first single chord C of the Chorus; which C, the trumpets had then to sustain alone to the end of the bar. This was executed with the greatest punctuality. One of the trumpeters, only, preoccupied with the Organ play, had forgotten to change his mouth piece and so blew on in E-Minor. In an instant Herr *Spohr* made a motion, and nothing more of the second bar was heard from the Orchestra. Upon this Herr *Fischer* instantly fell in again with the Organ, continued his Prelude, and this time closed in form with the dominant C-Major — just as if that occurrence had been intentionally introduced.

"As no pause whatever in the music took place, so that, except by the Orchestra, it would have been difficult for any one to have remarked this oversight, it might have been wholly concealed, were it not to be feared, that experienced Musicians might laugh at my here repeated assurances of nothing but faultless and successful performances by an Orchestra collected from twenty leagues round, after one rehearsal only, in the same manner as our present newspaper political reports are frequently ridiculed.

"After a pause of about a quarter of an hour, Herr *Spohr* resumed his Violin, Herr *Matthäi* drew nearer to him, and now those two admirable Artistes, by their perfect execution of a double Concerto of Herr *Spohr* afforded us the most lively enjoyment of alternating admiration, astonishment and pleasure. They seemed frequently in open feud for superority in artistic execution, then became as it were reconciled and poured forth together the most harmonious roulades upon the listeners. The precision, and the rapidity with which they took up and combined their respective tones, was worthy of admiration. The quite original *Adagio* of this masterly work which now followed, commenced with a Trio for two Violincellos, impressively performed by Herren *Preissing* and *Müller*, and for a Contra-Bass, by Herr *Wach* of Leipsic. When these three had ended their soft melodious play, a *Quadro* in long drawn and tied chords, as though from a Harmonica, but somewhat deeper, was heard. It had a thrilling, and sweet effect. Everybody looked round to the Bassi and Violi, from which this heavenly harmony seemed to have in part proceeded, but every arm was still, and the bows of Herren *Spohr* and *Matthäi* moved alone. It was they alone, also, who had played that *Quadro* — and with a purity, that upon the taking up of the Con-sonants after releasing the ties, the ear was frequently moved with a singularly deep felt charm. After a second similar Violincello-trio, the Quadro of the two Concerto-voices recommenced, and proceeded to the close. The last Thesis accorded fully with the science and beauty of the first.

"Upon this, Herr *Dotzauer* advanced to the front music-desk, and played, owing probably to the shortness of the remaining time, a *Rondo*, but a Rondo of masterly elaboration and very difficult, from a Violincello-Concerto in D-Major by *Bernard Romberg*, with an execution, roundness and force in the sustained passages, and with a lightness, purity, expression, and silvery tone in the melodic parts of the higher octaves, that in his performance of this *Rondo* alone, he displayed in the most admirable manner his great mastery of his instrument.

"*Beethoven's* Symphony in C-Major; indisputably his most pleasing and popular one, formed the conclusion. It could not have been executed with more grace, fire and precision. The Chorus of wind instruments in the *Trio* of the Minuett afforded particular enjoyment. One imagined to hear the tones of an exceedingly pure harmonica. A general and long continued applause evinced the thanks and satisfaction of the audience with the choice of the masterly compositions performed, and with the manner inwhich they had been executed by the assembled artists.

"Though we commenced by adverting to the difficulties which had been surmounted by the gentleman who carried out this undertaking, both in the arrangements for the mental and bodily recreation of his numerous guests, we feel it a duty to add yet something in respect to the latter, a by no means easy thing to effect in so small a town.

"The hundred Chorists were distributed among the different Inns, where they found both bed and board. "The whole of the Virtuosi, Singers and Dilettanti were on the other hand received into respectable private houses. But in order to render the stay of the kind lovers of Music who had met together from such distant places, as agreable to them as possible, Herr *Bischoff* had made a sacrifice of the flower garden immediately behind his house, and converted it into a Dining-room. The Saloon erected for this purpose was decorated with green branches the pleasing freshness of whose verdure seemed a friendly welcome to the company.

"In this Saloon, the tables were laid out, and the repasts served. It was a pleasure to behold so many worthy Artists and Lovers of Art assembled here for one and the same purpose, proceeding thence to their labour of Love, and returning therefrom to meet here anew for cheerful enjoyment, and to pay unanimous and hearty tribute to the great father *Haydn*, the excellent *Spohr* and many other first rate Artists in brimming glasses. The hilarity of the supper table was generally heightened by lively and well sung songs. Fine voices joined, and sang Quartetts and Canons; Herr *Methfessel* taking his guitar would entertain the company with pleasing Ballads, and touching Romances of his own Composition; by way of change, he then sang a Comic Song, or two, and exhibited his liveliness of fancy, his richness of invention, wit, and humour of expression, as well as his intimate knowledge of tone and harmony. Herr *Hachmeister*, the Assessor of mines from Clausthal taking then the guitar from him in turn, charmed the company with National Songs in the Thuringian dialect, replete with such wit and humour as compelled the hearer despite himself, to laugh at the cares of life."

I and my wife, made many agreable acquaintances among the artistes and friends of Art then assembled in Frankenhausen, among others, that of Amtsrath *Lüder* of Catlenburg, who up to the present time has remained one of my most intimated friends. *Lüder* then resided in the neighbourhood of Bremen and was upon a journey of business to Berlin. On arriving at the foot of the Hartz mountains, his postillion informed him of the approaching Musical Festival in Frankenhausen and pictured to him in so attractive a shape the Musical treat that was to be expected there, that *Lüder* immediately made him diverge from the road, and take the direction of Frankenhausen. Arrived there, his first care was to enquire for me, to ask permission to be present at all the rehearsals. This was not only very readily granted, but I also invited my new acquaintance whose enthusiasm for Art greatly pleased me, to join our meetings under the tent at dinner and supper. Here in the hours intervening between the rehearsals and the performances, amid artistic enjoyments seasoned with lively sallies of wit and good humour, a social intercourse sprang up so delightful, that all who shared in it will assuredly have looked back upon it with the greatest satisfaction. A small circle of similarly minded enthusiasts for Art had especially gathered round me, and we soon became so mutually attached, that after the close of the Festival it became difficult to separate, and an excursion together to the Kyffhäuser was determined upon. On this mountain-excursion which was favoured by the most beautiful weather, it was the Singer *Methfessel* from Rudolstadt, who more particularly kept the company in the merriest mood by his inexhaustible humour. I still remember with great pleasure an improvised Capucin-sermon which he preached from the chancel of a ruined cloister, in which he interwove in a half serious, half comical manner the chief incidents of the Musical-festival. From the summit of the Kyffhäuser, he sang also the praise of the Emperor Barbarossa, and urged him to a speedy resurrection for the final enfranchisement of Germany.*

* According to the ancient legend, the belief in which was once popular throughout Germany; *Frederick Barbarossa*, seated at a stone table in the vaulted tower of the Imperial Castle of the Kyffhäuser, awaits since 600 years the hour of Germany's regeneration, in order to reappear once more in the vigour of life, prepared for new works and achievements for the glory and well being of a united Germany. The red beard of the Emperor grows round the table of stone in front of him, and so soon as it has wholly grown round it for the third time, *Frederick* will awake. His first act will then produce a symbol of his further mission. He will hang his shield upon a withered tree, which will then suddenly shoot out its buds and leaves again, till it is covered anew with verdant life and beauty! Such is the legend, the origin of which dates far back into

Arrived again at the foot of the mountain, the new friends were reluctantly obliged to part, and each returned to his home highly gratified.

I immediately resumed the composition of my Opera, and finished it in the course of the winter of 1810—1811. Besides this, in my catalogue appears the following Works at this period: A Violin-concerto afterwards published by *Peters*, a Sonata for Harp and Violin (Op, 114, by *Schuberth*) and an Italian aria, *alla Polacca*, with Violin Obligato, which was never engraved. I wrote the latter at the request of Prince Frederick von Gotha, brother of the Duke, who gifted with a pleasing tenor voice, frequently sang in the Court-concerts, and much wished to have an Air with Violin accompaniment of my composition. It was frequently sung, particularly when visitors were at court.

The Prince was an amiable well meaning man, who interested himself in Music much more than his brother, and who, with the Dutchess, kept alive the interest for the Court-concerts. Unfortunately he was subject to an incurable complaint, epilepsy, with which he was seized every fourteen days, (in later years, still more frequently) which kept him down from 12 to 15 hours at a time. He was then deprived of the use of all his limbs, and the organs of speech and the muscles of his face were the only parts that remained unaffected. During these dreadful attacks he would lie in bed as motionless as a corpse; but was always pleased when any one visited him, and entertained him with conversation. From the continual recurrence of these attacks he had become so accustomed to his condition, that he could be quite cheerful during their duration. His physicians considered that a milder climate

---

the middle ages, and must be considered as a long subsisting expression of that yearning of the popular mind in Germany which under long enduring circumstances of political oppression looked towards the future with hopes of enfranchisement and relief, and which associated those hopes and aspirations with the memory of an honoured name.

(Note of Translator.)

would be most likely to cure him, and for that reason sent him to Italy. I met him in Rome during my tour in Italy in 1816; and mention will therefore be frequently made of him at that part of my narrative.

In the spring of 1811, the Precentor *Bischoff* again paid me a visit, and invited me to conduct a second grand Musical Festival which he intended giving in Frankenhausen. He also begged me to play a Violin-Concerto on the second day of the Concert, and to write a grand Symphony for the opening. Although I had not yet attempted that kind of Musical composition, I acceded with pleasure to his request.

In this manner the opportunity presented itself for another interesting task, and I immediately set about it with spirit. Although hitherto it had been usual with me to lose after a time all taste for my first essays in a new style of Composition, this Symphony was an exception to the rule, for it has pleased me even in after years. As I had previously practised it very carefully with my Orchestra, which was composed of the *élite* of the Frankenhausen Orchestra, although we could have but one rehearsal of it, it was nevertheless executed in an admirable manner at the Festival, and met, particularly from those who took part in it, with an enthusiastic reception. I felt highly gratified at this, more even than at the applause I gained as Solo-player. In Leipsic also, where the Symphony was executed in the Drapers'-House-Concert, it met with great approbation, as is shewn in a notice of the Musical Journal, which says: "*Spohr's* new and yet unpublished Symphony excited the interest and admiration of all real lovers of music. Both in invention and elaboration, we consider it not only to surpass all that we know of the Orchestral-Music of this Master, but confess also, that for many years we have scarcely heard a new work of this kind, which possesses so much novelty and originality, without singularity and affection; so much richness and science, without artifice and bombast. We may therefore confidently predict, that when published, it will become a favorite piece with every great and skilled Orchestra, and with all serious and cultivated Auditories; but it requires both."

Besides this Symphony, I had also written for the Musical Festival at *Hermstedt's* earnest solicitation, Variations for the Clarinet, with Orchestral accompaniment, upon themes from the *"Opferfest"* which he performed with his usual skill. This Composition, (published by *Schlesinger* in Berlin as Op. 80) which carries out those themes with a more artistic Fantasia-like freedom, than as Variations, were greatly admired by Musicians and connoisseurs.

On the afternoon of the second day, the Musical Festival was followed by a family fête in the house of the projector. A few weeks before, a son had been born to him, who was now christened. He had invited the whole of the assistants to be godfathers, who now in holiday attire ranged themselves round the altar at the church. I held the infant son over the baptismal font, and gave him my name "Louis". When the clergyman put the question to me and the other godfathers, whether we would take care that the child should receive a Christian education, a solemn "Yes" from full three hundred voices echoed through the church. A Chorus executed by the singers, with Organ accompaniment, terminated the holy ceremony.

At this second Festival my gratification was still more enhanced by the presence of my parents among the auditory, and that they took a lively part in the social gaieties under the tent. The projector was no less satisfied with his speculation, and thus this Festival terminated like that of the previous year, to the satisfaction of all.

Shortly after my return, I received intelligence from Hamburgh that my Opera, which I had sent in in the spring, had been at length distributed and that its representation would take place in the first days of November. I therefore applied for a month's leave of absence for myself and wife, and set out with her, in the middle of October, via Hanover, where I intended giving a concert. As this was the first Opera of mine that was to be represented, I was in a state of great anxiety. The shock I felt may therefore be readily imagined, upon receiving a letter in Hanover from the manager *Schröder*, informing me that the Opera would not be produced, because the *Prima Donna* Madame *Becker* refused to take the part assigned to her, and that according to the theatrical laws she was perfectly justified in doing so.

The matter was in this wise: Previous to beginning my work, I had certainly taken pains to inquire of Herr *Schwenke* respecting the range of voice and the capabilities of the Hamburgh singers, and in accordance therewith, I had constructed the chief parts of the opera. But as I was without all experience in these things, I had neglected to ascertain the personal appearance of the singers, so that, for Madame *Becker*, a small, delicate figure, I had written the part of Donna Isabella, who seeks for her faithless lover at the Court of Princess Matilda disguised in man's clothes, and at last challenges him to mortal combat armed cap-à-pied as a knight. So long as Madame *Becker*, knew no more about the Opera than her part, she was highly satisfied and began to practice with great zeal. But as soon as she had read the libretto, she declared, that she could not undertake the part, as she would make herself perfectly ridiculous. Exceedingly annoyed at my mistake I set off for Hamburgh, to remedy it wherever possible, and to induce the representation of the opera. I found old *Schröder* in very low spirits, and exceedingly dissatisfied with his theatrical untertaking. But he had every reason to be so. Several of the performers had failed to make their appearance, others came too late, and some had not answered the expectations entertained of them; his new Plays and Comedies had not been very successful, and empty houses had been the result. Of the four Operas which he had Music written for, two were already laid aside, because they had displeased. The one composed by *Winter*: "*Die Pantoffeln*" had lived through some few thinly attended representations; that of *Clasing*: "*Welcher ist der Rechte?*" had been withdrawn from the *Re-*

pertoire immediately after the first night, for in spite of the strenuous efforts of *Clasing's* numerous friends it was a complete failure.

With such disappointments, it was not to be wondered that the old grumbler should be mistrustful of my Opera also, and the more so since the most favorite singer of his theatre would not lend her aid. But when he offered me payment of the sum agreed for it, and at the same time laid it aside without having given it a trial, I was much hurt and protested against it in the most positive manner. At length after much entreaty, I obtained *Schröder's* consent that I should make a trial of it with another singer, who hitherto had played only in secondary characters, and practise her in the rôle refused by Madame *Becker*. In this singer, a Madame *Lichtenheld*, I found great willingness and natural capacity, and when I had simplified the most difficult bravura passages of the part to her powers of execution, I succeeded well with her. Thus at length the rehearsals could be commenced, and when *Schröder* had heard one, and had become convinced that Madame *Lichtenheld* would fill the part satisfactorily, the first representation was announced for the 15. November. My former musical acquaintances one and all, including *Romberg* and *Prell*, offered their services to me in the two representations in which I was to lead the orchestra. *Hermstedt*, also, who had come to Hamburgh to give a Concert with my support, joined them, and undertook the First Clarinet part, for which there were some telling Soli's and a concerted accompaniment or a Soprano-air. With the aid of these distinguished artists the Orchestra was considerably strengthened, and as the Singers and the Chorus were likewise well practised, I was already greatly pleased with the precision with which my music was performed in the rehearsals, and therefore entertained the most lively hopes that the Opera would please. Nevertheless on the evening of the representation, it was not without fresh anxiety that I took my place at my desk, for it had come to my ears that, *Clasing's* friends would evince an inimical feeling towards me in revenge for the failure of his opera. But when the music had begun, I thought of that alone, and forgot every thing else around me. The applause with which the Overture was received, shewed me, nevertheless, that the unfriendly party would not make any demonstration; and so it proved. Almost every piece was applauded, and the approbation increased yet more towards the end of the opera. Upon the fall of the curtain a long sustained storm of applause was given to the composer.

I ought now to have been very happy, but was by no means so. Already at the first rehearsal some things in my music had displeased me. At every fresh rehearsal these were increased by something new, and before the actual representation, the half of my Opera had become distasteful to me. I now thought I well knew how I could have made it better, and was greatly annoyed that I had not discovered it before. Yes, indeed, had my work appeared to me in that light on my arrival at Hamburgh, I should have made no opposition to *Schröder's* intention to lay it aside unperformed. But my musical friends were of a different opinion; they were exceedingly pleased with this work, and wished me every further success. *Schwenke* wrote a full and very laudatory criticism of the Opera, wherein he adroitly combated the well founded opinion of its opponents, that it contained many reminiscences of the Operas of *Mozart*, and while admitting that the form of the musical pieces as well as the whole design recalled *Mozart*, he assigned that, as a recommendatory feature and proof of its excellence. By this, made watchful of myself, I became sensible of the necessity to break myself of it, and think that I already fully effected it in "Faust" my next Dramatic work.

With my permission, *Schwenke* had some time before made a Piano-forte arrangement from the Opera, which was now published by *Böhm* in Hamburgh, and soon found an extensive circulation.

Of the Concert which I then gave in Hamburgh with my wife and *Hermstedt*, I recollect but little more than that the latter created a great sensation by his highly cultivated skill. But I have a clearer recollection of another Concert in Altona, at which we and several of our Hamburgh friends assisted, and in which all manner of little misfortunes befell us, which afterwards afforded matter for much merriment.

This Concert was given by a rich Musical-amateur of Altona, who invited the assistants from Hamburgh to a luxurious dinner. After the company had been at table for two hours, and addressed themselves diligently to the champaign, they became so merry and forgetful, that nobody gave a thought to the Concert that was to follow. The terror therefore was general, when a Messenger suddenly appeared, and announced that the numerous Audience which had assembled was become impatient and demanded the opening of the concert. All now hurried to the Concert saloon; although in reality no one was any longer in a fit state to make a public appearance. It was especially remarkable that, those who were usually the most timid had now become the most courageous. The Altona dilettanti-Orchestra, who were to serve as nucleus and support to the Hamburgh Artists, were already in their places, and the Concert immediately began with an Overture by *Romberg* who conducted it himself. He, who was unjustly accused of taking the *tempi* of his Compositions too slow, hurried the *Allegro* of his Overture this time so much, that the poor Dilettanti could not keep up with him. Little therefore was wanting for the whole thing to break down from the very overture. My wife and I were then to follow with a Sonata for harp and violin, which as usual we were about to play without notes. Just as we had seated ourselves, and I was about to begin, my wife, who at all other times was self-possession itself, whispered anxiously to me: "For Heaven's sake, *Louis*, I cannot remember which Sonata we are to play, nor how it begins!" I hummed softly in her ear the commencement of it, and restored to her the necessary calmness and self-possession. Our Play now proceeded without mishap to the end, and was received with great applause.

It was now Madame *Becker's* turn to sing an Air, and *Romberg* had just led her forward to the raised platform of the Orchestra, when to the great astonishment of the public, she all at once ran off, and disappeared in the room adjoining. *Dorette,* allarmed lest she should have been taken suddenly ill, hastened after her. But, both shortly reappeared, and I now ascertained from my wife, that Madame *Becker* had found her breath too short from the effects of the dinner, and was therefore obliged to have her clothes loosened before she could sing.

Hermstedt, now followed with a difficult composition of mine. He, who always when appearing in public, went to work with the most nervous precision in every thing, emboldened now to rashness by the fumes of the champaign, had screwed on a new and untried plate to the mouthpiece of his Clarinet, and even spoke vauntingly of it to me as I mounted the platform of the orchestra. I immediately anticipated no good from it. The Solo of my composition began with a long sustained note, which *Hermstedt* pitched almost inaudibly, and by degrees encreased to an enormous power, with which he always produced a great sensation. This time he began also in the same way, and the public listened to the increasing volume of tone with wrapt expectancy. But just as he was about to encrease it to the highest power, the plate twisted, and gave out a mis-tone, resembling the shrill cry of a goose. The public laughed, and the now suddenly sobered Virtuoso turned deadly pale with horror. He nevertheless soon recovered himself, and executed the remainder with his usual brilliancy, so that there was no want of enthusiastic applause at the end.

But with poor *Schwenke* it fared worse than all. The waist-buckle of his pantaloons had given way during the dinner, without his being aware of it. When therefore he had mounted into the orchestra to take the Viol-part in a Pot-Pourri with Quartett-accompaniment which I played at the close of the Concert, shortly after he had begun to play, he felt his pantaloons begin to slip with every movement he made in bow-ing. Much too conscientious a Musician, to omit a note of his part, he patiently waited for the pauses, to pull up his nethergarment again. His predicament did not long escape the notice of the public, and occasioned considerable merriment. But towards the close of the Pot-Pourri, when a $^1/_{16}$ movement shook him so roughly, that the downward tentency of his pantaloons made serious progress, and threatened to exceed the limits of propriety, the public could no longer restrain itself, and broke out into a general titter. By this untoward interruption of the execution of my Solo, I was thus dragged also, into the general calamity of the day.

On my return to Gotha, I found a letter from *Bischoff*, in which he informed me that he had been commanded by the Governor of Erfurt to make arrangements for a grand Musical Festival there, in the ensuing summer, in celebration of the birthday of Napoleon, August 15. He had already agreed with him as to the terms, and now asked me to untertake its direction, and to write a new Oratorio for the first day. I had long desired to try for once, something in the Oratorio-style, also, and readily consented to the proposal. A young poet in Erfurt had already offered me the text of an Oratorio, in which I had found several grand passages for composition. It was called: "The last Judgement."

I sent for the libretto, and set to work at once. But I soon felt that for the Oratorio-style I was yet too deficient in Counter-point and in Fugeing; I therefore suspended my work, in order to make the preliminary studies requisite for the subject. From one of my pupils I borrowed *Marpurg's* "Art of Fuge writing" and was soon deeply and continuously engaged in the study of that work. After I had written half a dozen Fugues according to its instructions, the last of which seemed to me very successful; I resumed the composition of my Oratorio, and completed it without allowing any thing else to intervene. According to a memorandum I made, it was begun in January 1812, and finished in June. There would not therefore have been sufficient time to write it out and practise it before the performance, had I not sent the two first parts of the work to *Bischoff*, immediately after their completion. By that means, not only could the Choruses be carefully practised in it, but I had also sufficient time to study the Orchestral-parts with my own orchestra, which was again to form the nucleus of the great Erfurt orchestra. In this manner, although the work is a very difficult one, I was enabled after one general rehearsal only, to effect a tolerably successful performance of it. One of the Solo-singers, alone, who sang the part of Satan, did not give me satisfaction. This part which was written with a powerful instrumentation, I gave by the advice of *Bischoff* to a village schoolmaster in the neighbourhood of Gotha, who was celebrated throughout the whole district for his colossal bass-voice. In power of voice he had indeed quite sufficient to outroar a whole Orchestra, but in science, and in Music, he could by no means execute the part in a satisfactory manner. I taught and practised him in the part myself, and took great pains to assist him a little, but without much success. For when the day of public trial came, he had totally forgotten every instruction, and admonition, and gave such loose to his barbarian voice, that he first of all frightened the auditory, and then set them in a roar of laughter.

From overstraining his voice, he moreover almost always intonated too high, and by that spoiled several of the most effective parts of the oratorio. I suffered intensely from this, and my pleasure in my composition was greatly embittered. Nevertheless it gave general satisfaction, and was most favourably spoken of in a detailed notice of the Musical Festival in one of the Thuringian newspapers. Another criticism which appeared in a South-German (if I am not mistaken a Francfort Journal) found on the other hand much to cavil with in the work, and was altogether written in a bitter and malevolent tone. For many years I suspected this malicious criticism was written by Counsellor *André* of Offenbach, as he was present at the Festival with two of his pupils, *Arnold* and *Aloys Schmidt*. What induced me to suspect him of it, although *André* had expressed himself to me personally in praise of the work, I now no longer remember; and in later years when I questioned him on the subject, he assured me that he was not the author. I, myself, not only considered the work the best I had written up to that time, but I thought I had never heard any thing finer. Even to this day I like so much some of the choruses and Fuges, as well as the part of Satan, that I could almost pronounce them to be the most grand of all I ever wrote. Not so, however, with the other themes particularly with the Soli-parts of Jesus and Mary. These are wholly written in the Cantata style of that day and overladen with bravoura and ornamental passages. Shortly afterwards, also, I felt the impropriety of this style, and in later years frequently resolved to re-write those Soli parts. But when about to begin, it seemed to me as though I could no longer enter into the spirit of the subject, and so it remained undone. To publish the work as it was I could not make up my mind. Thus in later years it has lain by with out any use being made of it.

As the above mentioned Festival in honour of Napoleon's birth-day was the last that took place in Erfurt and in Germany just before the Russian Campaign, it was considered to have been ominous, that the principal Musical piece then performed should have been "the last Judgement".

*   *   *

In the Autumn of 1812 I again applied for a leave of absence for myself and wife, which after some reluctance on the part of the Dutchess was granted. We this time directed our journey to Vienna as the least disturbed by the war, and the passage of troops. Our first stay was at Leipsic, where we assisted at a Concert given by *Hermstedt*, and where I afterwards performed my new oratorio. Of this the Musical Journal speaks in the following manner:

"Herr *Hermstedt's* Concert as regards the Compositions executed, was one of the most attractive that could be heard. With the exception of *Mozart's* Overture, and the Scena by *Righini*, all the pieces were of the composition of Concert-Master *Spohr*, and with the exception of the Clarinet-Concerto, all newly written. This Concerto, the first in C-Minor, and, as a Composition, the most brilliant of all Concerti for that instrument, was again listened to with great satisfaction. A grand Sonata for Violin and Harp, played by Herr and Madame *Spohr*, the leading theme of which must be pronounced masterly in conception and elaboration, and the second, consisting of a delightful Pot-Pourri of happily combined and most pleasingly handled melodies from the "*Zauberflöte*", — this as well as each of the other pieces were received with the warmest approbation. We heard besides another Violin-Concerto* played by Herr *Spohr* and a Pot-Pourri for the Clarinet with Orchestral accompaniment. In the former, the first *Allegro*, as regards composition and execution pleased us least. Here and there, it seemed to us both tricky and overladen with ornament, and considering its contents, much too long; neither was the execution of the Virtuoso every where sufficiently distinct and clear. But the *Adagio*, as regards composition and execution is one of the finest we ever heard on this instrument, we may even say the very finest that was ever produced by any Virtuoso."

Of the Oratorio, also, it speaks upon the whole, favourably. It contains not only "many details that are original and attractive, some even that are really charming, but which, also, too closely crowd upon and obliterate each other." Every hearer whether he agrees or not with *Spohr* in his idea of an Oratorio, that is, whether he may be disposed or not to tolerate its combination of almost every kind of treatment and style, or rather, to see them replace each other in turn — yet every hearer must be impressed with a lively interest in

---

* This must have been the 6. (Op. 28).

this work, and experience a real pleasure not unmingled with astonishment at several of its principal parts."

According to a notice in the Musical Journal of the 8. November, I do not appear to have made any stay at Dresden, upon this journey. But in Prague I gave a Concert on the 12. November, and eight days after, my Oratorio at the Theatre. A very favourable notice of the former appears in the Musical Journal, which adverts especially to the "enchanting unity" of execution, from which the most perfect harmonic marriage of the two admirable artistes was to be recognised.

Of the performance of the Oratorio I alone remember that Fräulein *Müller* afterwards Madame *Grünbaum*, sang exquisitely in it, and that the work was right well received by the public.

I now hastened towards the chief object of my journey. Vienna was at that time indisputably the Capital of the Musical world. The two greatest Composers and Reformers of Musical taste, *Haydn* and *Mozart* had lived there, and there produced their Master-pieces. The generation still lived, which had seen them arise, and formed their taste in Art from them. The worthy successor of those Art-heroes, *Beethoven*, still resided there, and was now in the zenith of his fame, and in the full strength of his creative power. In Vienna therefore the highest standard for Art creations was set up, and to please there — was to prove one's self a Master.

I felt my heart beat as we drove over the Danube-bridge, and thought of my approaching début. My anxiety was yet more increased by the reflexion that I should have to compete with the greatest Violinist of the day; for in Prague I had learnt that *Rode* had just returned from Russia, and was expected in Vienna. I still vividly recalled to mind the overpowering impression which *Rode's* play had made upon me ten years before in Brunswick, and how I had striven for years to acquire his method and execution. I was now therefore anxious in the highest degree to hear him again, in order thereby to measure my own progress. My first question therefore on alighting from the carriage was whether *Rode* had arrived, and had announced a concert. This was answered in the negative, but with the assurance that he had long been expected.

It was now therefore a matter of importance to me to be heard before *Rode*, and I hastened as much as possible the announcement of my concert. I succeeded also in appearing first; but *Rode* had arrived meanwhile, and was present at the concert. To my great surprise I felt less intimidated than inspired by that circumstance, and played as well as I could have desired. The Musical Journal spoke of my appearance before "a crowded house" in the following manner:

"On the 17. December we had the pleasure to hear and admire Herr *Louis Spohr* and his wife at a concert. We subscribe gladly to the favourable opinions expressed of this worthy Artiste-pair and can only add that here also every one was charmed by their masterly play. Herr *Spohr* played a Violin-Concerto with a Spanish *Rondo* and at the end a Pot-Pourri, both of his composition; with his wife, he executed one of his published Sonatas for harp and violin. The composition both of the Concerto and this Sonata are excellent, and contrasted not a little with the watery, patchwork productions with which so many practising Musicians without talent or genius for composition, make their appearance here."

By the advice of some kind friends I relinquished my intention of giving my Oratorio at my own expense, as I had projected doing in a second Concert; since the great expenditure which a large Orchestra and a numerous Chorus would have superadded to that of an usual Concert, forbade the hope to realise any profit from the undertaking. Yet as I was very desirous to have this work heard in Vienna, for I still considered it one of the grandest of its kind, I offered to perform it for the benefit of "the Widow's and Orphan's Society" on the condition only, that for its production, the society would provide a well appointed orchestra supported by the most distinguished Singers and Instrumentalists in Vienna. This condition was accepted, and fully carried out by the society, which provided a *personel* of three hundred assistants from among the best artistes in the city. The work was carefully studied in two grand rehearsals, and on its production, was performed better than I had yet heard it. I became anew enraptured with my creation, and with me several of the assistant Musicians, among whom more especially Herr *Clement* the Director of the Orchestra of the "Theatre an der Wien".

He, had so thoroughly imbibed the spirit and substance of the work, that the day after its performance he was enabled to play to me on the Piano several entire parts, note for note, with all the harmonies and orchestral figures, without ever having seen the score. But *Clement* possessed a musical memory such perhaps as no other artiste ever possessed. It was at that time related of him in Vienna, that after he had heard several times "the Creation" of *Haydn*, he had learned it so thoroughly, that with the help of the text book he was able to write a full Pianoforte arrangement of it. He shewed this to old *Haydn*, who was not a little alarmed at it, thinking at first that his score had either been stolen or surreptitiously copied. Upon a nearer inspection he found the Pianoforte arrangement so correct, that after *Clement* had looked through the original score, he adopted it for publication.

Before my Oratorio was performed, I had a quarrel with the Censorship, which nearly subverted the whole untertaking. They would not suffer the names of *Mary* and *Jesus* to be used in the list of the Dramatis-Personae of the Text-Book, nor above the words which they had to sing. But after long negotiation, upon the omission of these, the text was allowed to be printed. I could readily accede to this omission, since from the context it was easy to understand who the persons were.

Greatly as the work pleased the Musicians, and increased their opinion of my talent for composition, yet its reception by the Public was not nearly so brilliant as that which my play and my Concerted compositions had met with. It is true there was no want this time also of marked applause, but it was not so general as to attract a numerous audience to the second performance which took place three days afterwards. This second representation in Vienna was the last the work ever had; for in later years I saw too well its weak points and deficiencies ever to persuade myself to give it again in public. Of the first representation in Vienna on the 21. January the Musical Journal spoke tolerably well.

Salieri the Leader of the Imperial Orchestra had undertaken the direction of the whole; Herr *Umlauf* presided at the Piano, and I led the violins. The principal parts were sung by Demoiselle *Klieber*, Madame *Auenheim*, Demoiselle *Flamm*, Messrs. *Anders*, *Wild*, and *Pfeiffer*. "It is difficult" says the notice "here in Vienna to bring out an Oratorio, so as either to awaken attention to it, or to procure for the work a permanent name — here where such grand, successful masterpieces of the kind first made their appearance, which are familiar to every body and which have procured for their creators a lasting fame in the musical world. Herr *Eibler* already attempted to set the "Four last Things" . . . to music. But his work was only twice publickly performed, because he failed in a thoroughly even and original style, and his composition would not bear comparison with the works of his great predecessors of this kind. The same may be said also of Herr *Spohr's* "Last Judgement" although the composer of that work is infinitely superior in severe passages to the writer of te "Four last things." All the chorusses and fugues in the severe style, with which one can find fault in some secondary parts only, have a real artistic merit; are worked out with great industry, and were received also with loud and general enthusiasm. The Airs, Duetts and single Song passages, depart however too much from the real Oratorio style, are too frequently repeated in the text, and approach more or less to the Italian Operatic style. Some too striking reminiscences of the "Creation" and particularly of the "Zauberflöte" lessen the merit of the work in respect of originality. The Chorus of Devils at the end of the first part would be more admissably in its place if introduced in a ballet. Herr *August Arnold* the author of the text, has also, certainly not produced a work such as might satisfy the composer for musical treatment .... The Theatre was scarcely half full. On the 24., this Oratorio was repeated before scarcely two hundred auditors. But a work of this kind should not have been brought out in such a pleasure loving City in Carnival time!" —

A fortnight after my first appearance, *Rode's* Concert came in turn. Relying on his European reputation he had chosen the most spacious Concert-room in Vienna, the great "Redouten-Saal" and he found it completely filled. With almost feverish excitement I awaited the commencement of *Rode's* play, which ten years before had served as my highest model. But, already, after the first Solo, it seemed to me that *Rode* had lost ground in that time. I now found his play cold, and full of mannerism. I missed his former boldness in conquering great difficulties, and felt particularly dissatisfied with his execution of the Cantabile. The composition as well of the new Concerto, appeared to me far behind that of the seventh in A-Minor. In his execution of the Variations in E-Major, which I had heard him play ten years before, convinced me fully, that he had greatly lost in technical precision, for he had not only simplified for himself many of the most difficult passages, but he produced also those modified passages with timidity and a degree of uncertainty. Neither did the public seem satisfied; at least he failed to rouse them to any enthusiasm. The Reviewer in the Musical Journal says, also, that *Rode* had "not *quite*" satisfied the expectation of the public. "His bow-stroke" continues the Reviewer, "is long, grand and forcible, his tone full and strong — indeed, almost too strong, cutting; he has a correct, pure intonation and is always sure in his rebounds up to the very highest notes; his double notes although occurring but seldom, are good, and in *Allegro* he conquers great difficulties with ease: on the other hand he is wanting in that which electrifies and carries away all hearts — fire, and that winning grace which is not otherwise to be defined, that witchery of charm that ravishes the ear and inspires the soul. In *Adagio*, the sharpness of his tones was still more perceptible than in *Allegro;* the result therefore was cold. Neither did the composition awaken much interest; it was thought far fetched and mannered. It is probable the vast size of the great "Redouten-Saal" may have induced Herr *Rode* to bring out his tones so sharply, and thus they lost much of their sweetness."

Eight days after *Rode's* Concert I gave my second, in the small "Redouten Saal." The Musical Journal speaks of it as follows: "*Spohr* shewed himself to be a great Master of violin-play. He produced a new composition in A-Major (published as the tenth), which was solemnly and slowly preceded by an introduction in A-Minor. The *Adagio* was in D-Major. A most charming *Rondo* concluded it. In the pleasing, and the tender, *Spohr* is indisputably the nightingale, of all living, at least, to us known, Violinplayers. It is scarcely possible to execute an *Adagio* with more tenderness and yet so clearly, combined with the purest good taste; added to this, he overcomes the most difficult passages in quick-time measure, and effects the greatest possible stretches with wonderful ease, to which certainly the large size of his hand may be of some advantage to him. This evening he again received a general and unanimous applause, and was repeatedly called forward, an honour — which so far as we remember, — was conferred only upon Herr *Polledro*. With his wife, Herr *Spohr* played an *Allegro* which she performed upon the harp, with great execution, taste and expression. We think, of all the Virtuosi whom we have heard upon that instrument none possesses so much school, and such intensity of feeling in expression, as Madame *Spohr;* though Demoiselle *Longhi* may have more power, and Demoiselle *Simonin-Pollet* more equality in their play."

Speaking of *Rode's* second Concert, the Musical Review says: that "with a very crowded saloon he met with much more applause than before; but in the Cantabile this time, also, he did not sufficiently satisfy the expectations of the public."

On the 28. January I played with *Seidler* of Berlin in his Concert, and as a notice of it says "bore away the palm although Herr *Seidler's* play was worthy of praise."

I could thus be very satisfied with the reception I had met with in Vienna as an Artiste; for the public newspapers also awarded the palm to me. At private Parties where as the rule, I not only met the above named Violinist, but also the most distinguished of the native Violinists Herr *Mayseder*, and had to compete with all these, my performances met also with special acknowledgment and attention. On these occasions there was at first always a dispute who should begin, for each desired to be the last, in order to eclipse his predecessor. But, I, who always prefered playing a well combined Quartett to a Solo piece, never refused to make the beginning, and invariable succeeded in gaining the attention and sympathy of the company by my own peculiar style of reading and executing the classical quartetts. Then when the others had each paraded his hobby-horse, and I observed that the company had more liking for that sort of thing than for classical music, I brought out one of my difficult and brilliant Pot-Pourri's, and invariably succeeded in eclipsing the success of my predecessors.

In the frequent opportunities of hearing *Rode* I became more and more convinced that he was no longer the perfect Violinist of earlier days. By the constant repetition of the same compositions, a mannerism had crept by degrees into his execution, that now bordered on caricature. I had the rudeness, to remark this to him, and asked him if he no longer remembered the way in which he played his compositions ten years ago. Yes! I carried my impertinence so far, as to lay the variations in G-Major before him, and said, that I would play them exactly as I had heard him play them so frequently ten years before. After I had finished playing, the company broke out into a rupturous applause, and *Rode*, for decency's sake was obliged to add a "bravo"; but one could plainly see that he felt offended by my indelicacy. And with good reason. I was soon ashamed of it, and advert to the circumstance now, only, to show how high an opinion I then had of myself as a Violinist.

Satisfied in the highest degree with Vienna, I now thought of proceeding farther, when quite unexpectedly I received from Count *Palffy* the then Proprietor of the Theatre "an der Wien" the offer of an engagement there for three years, as Leader and Director of the Orchestra. As I could not make up my mind to give up my and my wife's permanent life engagements, I at first decidedly declined it. But when Herr *Treitschke*, who was the agent in the matter, offered me more than three times the salary which I and my wife together had received in Gotha; when he informed me that the Theatre "an der Wien" would soon become the first in Germany, that the Count had suceeded in engaging for it the best singers of the day, and that he now contemplated to entrust to me the formation of the Orchestra from among the first artists of Vienna, and further represented to me that in such an excellent Theatre I should have the first opportunity to cultivate my abilities and distinghuish myself as a Dramatic Composer: I could no longer withstand the temptation; requested a short delay in order to consult with my wife, and promised to give a definite answer in a few days.

Of the large salary that was offered to me, and which much exceeded those of the two Leaders of the Imperial Orchestra *Salieri* and *Weigl*, I might hope to economise a third or perhaps the half. I might furthermore, from the reputation I had acquired in Vienna as an Artiste, safely reckon upon earning something considerable by Concerts, Compositions and Tuition. Besides, I was secured as regarded the future, even in case the proffered appointment should terminate at the expiration of the three years, and could then carry out a favorite plan conceived from my earliest youth, of a journey to Italy, in company with my wife and children.

More than all these, however, I was disposed by my reawakened desire to write for the stage, to accept the Count's proposal. So, after *Dorette* had given her consent, although with sorrow at the now necessary separation from her mother and family, the written Contract was drawn up and signed under the direction of a Notary, a friend of ours. I bound myself therein as Director of the Orchestra to play in all grand Operas, to undertake the Violin Soli's in Operas and Ballets, and as Conductor, to lead from the score when the other leader should be prevented doing so. From small Operas, Ballets, and the music in Plays, I was exempted. I now, conjointly with Count Palffy and my new colleague, conductor *von Seifried* proceeded to remodel the constitution of the orchestra. The Count wat not niggardly in regard to the salaries; so I soon succeeded in procuring the services of the most talented young artistes, and to establish an *ensemble* that made my Orchestra not only the best in Vienna, but raised it to one of the first in all Germany.

Among the new appointed members was my brother *Ferdinand*, and one of the most gifted of my other pupils, *Moritz Hauptmann* of Dresden. He had just arrived in Vienna and desired to establish himself there. But my brother did not arrive till the spring.

I had stipulated at the same time for a month's leave of absence in the spring, to arrange my affairs in Gotha and to fetch my children. But before that, it was necessary for me to make arrangements for another domicile, so that on my return I could commence my own housekeeping. At this time a circumstance took place that not only greatly influenced this business, but, also, my artistic labours in Vienna. Scarcely had it become known in the City that I was to remain there, when one morning a stranger of gentlemanly exterior called on me, who introduced himself as Herr *von Tost*, a proprietor of manufactories and a passionate lover of music. In excuse for the intrusiveness of his visit he pleaded his desire to make a proposition to me. After he had seated himself, and I full of expectation had taken a chair opposite to him, he first expressed his admiration of my talent as a Composer, and then the wish that I would assign over to him for a proportionate pecuniary consideration all that I might compose or had already written in Vienna, for the term of three years, to be his sole property during that time; to give him the original scores, and to keep myself, even, no copy of them. After the lapse of three years he would return the manuscripts to me, and I should then be at liberty either to publish or to sell them. After I had pondered a moment over this strange and enigmatical proposition, I first of all asked him whether the compositions were not to be played during those three years? Hereupon, Herr *von Tost* replied: oh! "yes, as often as possible, but each time on my lending them for that purpose, and only in my presence." He would not, he added prescribe the kind of compositions they should be; but he more particularly wished they should be such as would permit of being produced in Private Circles, therefore, Quartetts and Quintetts for stringed instruments and Sextetts, Octetts and Nonettes for stringed and wind instruments. I was to consider upon his proposal and fix the sum for each kind of composition. Upon this he presented me with his card and took leave of me.

My wife and I vainly endeavoured to discover the object Herr *von Tost* could have in making such a proposal; and I therefore resolved to ask him the question plump and plain. Before doing this I made enquiries about him, and ascertained that he was a wealthy man, the proprietor of large cloth manufactories near Znaim, was passionately fond of music, and never missed being present at every public concert. This sounded well, and I resolved to accede to the proposal. As compensation for the three years cession of my manuscripts, I fixed the amount for a Quartett at thirty Ducats, for a Quintett five and thirty, and so on progressively higher for the other kinds. When I now wished to know what Herr *von Tost* intended doing with the works during the three years; he at first would not satisfy me, and said, that as soon as he had bound himself by writing not to publish my compositions, it could not in the least concern me: but when he perceived, that I had still some misgivings, he added: "I have two objects in view. First, I desire to be invited to the music Parties in which you will execute your compositions, and for that I must have them in my keeping; secondly, possessing such treasures of art, I hope upon my business journeys to make an extensive acquaintance among the lovers of music, which may then serve me also in my manufacturing interests!"

Although unable to understand thoroughly Herr *von Tost*'s speculation, I was obliged mentally to confess, that at any rate he had an exalted idea of the worth of my compositions. This was very flattering to me, and suppressed all further hesitation. As Herr *von Tost* had now also, nothing to object to in the price demanded, nor to the requisition for payment upon delivery of the manuscripts, the business was soon concluded by a written agreement in form.

I had brought with me to Vienna one manuscript, a Solo-Quartett for Violin, which I had finished on the journey. I was just then also engaged upon a second. I determined to finish that before leaving for Gotha, and then deliver both to Herr *von Tost*.

Meanwhile I had been so fortunate as to find convenient apartments in the immediate neighbourhood of the Theatre "an der Wien" on the first floor of the house of a cabinet maker. As they had been somewhat disfigured by their last occupants I had them newly painted and decorated, and was just on the point of furnishing them. I therefore delivered my two Quartetts to Herr *von Tost*, and demanded their price of sixty ducats, remarking at the same time that I required the money for the furnishing of my new domicile. "I will provide you with that, complete in every respect" was his reply, "and much cheaper also than if you were to buy them yourself; for I have business transactions with all those with whom you will have to deal, and therefore can obtain them on lower terms than you. It will give me moreover an opportunity to collect some outstanding debts. Appoint therefore a day when I shall call for you and your wife in order that we may choose the things together."

And so the thing was done. We first drove to the new apartments, where Herr *von Tost* with great tact and business knowledge sketched an estimate of all we should require. We then went from one shop and warehouse to the other, and my wife and I had continually to guard against his choosing too much, and frequently the most costly and beautiful articles. We could not however prevent him from ordering for the best room, a suite of mahagony furniture with silk coverings and curtains to match; and for the kitchen, a mass of cooking utensils, crockery and a table service more befitting a capitalist than an unpretending artiste. It was in vain that *Dorette* represented we should give no parties, and therefore did not require so large a table service. But he was not be persuaded, and when I expressed the fear that the whole arrangements would be too expensive for my circumstances, he replied: "Make yourself easy, it will not cost you too much; neither shall I ask for any cash payment. By degrees you will soon square all accounts with your manuscripts."

Nothing more was to be said against this and thus we found ourselves in possession of apartments fitted up in a style so handsome and yet tasteful, as for certain no other artist-family in the City could shew.

I now got every thing ready for my journey. My wife was invited to reside with a lady of her acquaintance, the sister of the Advocate *Zizius*, a great lover of music, in whose house we had frequently played, so that during my absence I could leave her without any uneasiness.

I had been informed, that a Leipsic merchant about to return home in his own carriage with extra-post-horses was desirous of meeting with a fellow-traveller; I hastened therefore to offer my company, and soon agreed with him upon the terms. I now no longer recollect his name, but, that he was a well informed and agreable companion, from whom I parted in the most friendly manner. We journeyed without stopping to Prague, but remained there a whole day to rest ourselves. I spent that day very pleasantly at the house of my friend *Kleinwächter*. On leaving Prague we were obliged to leave the high road to Dresden, as the armies of the belligerent powers were drawn up there opposite to each other, and the bridge over the Elbe had been made impassable, the French having blown up several arches. We were therefore obliged to find a way over the Erzgebirge, where we also met with detachments of troops, by which however, we were neither stopped nor turned back. We arrived therefore without further adventure at Chemnitz. But here something befell me that filled me with such terror, that I fainted away, a circumstance which with my strong frame of body, never occured to me before or since.

We arrived at Chemnitz at noon, just as a numerous company at the hotel were about to sit down to dinner. We joined them, and I took a seat between my fellow-traveller and the hostess. While the latter was helping the soup, I like the rest of the guests proceeded to cut a slice from a large brown loaf that lay before me. I applied the knife to the loaf, but it would make no incision, from having (as afterwards appeared) come in contact with a small stone baked into the crust. This induced me to think the knife was blunt, and to increase the force of the pressure. Upon this it suddenly slipped off and glancing on to the ball of my left fore finger cut off a considerable piece of the flesh, which fell upon the plate before me. A stream of blood followed. The sight of this, or rather the thought, that now there would be an end to my violin playing, and that I should no longer be able to support myself and family, filled me with such horror that I fell insensible from my chair. When after the lapse of about ten minutes I recovered my senses, I saw the whole company in commotion and occupied with me. My first look fell upon my finger, which I found wrapped round with a large piece of English plaister that the kind hostess had brought. It adhered closely in the hollow of the wound, and to my comfort I could now see that the whole ball of the finger had not been cut off, as I had at first imagined. Nevertheless almost the half of it, together with a large piece of the nail were gone. As I scarcely experienced any pain, I left the strapping undisturbed, and first applied to a surgeon on arriving at Leipsic, who also let the plaister remain, and only advised me to be careful of all ungentle contact with my finger.

Thus somewhat consoled I arrived home in Gotha. I found the Court very much annoyed about my contemplated removal to Vienna; the Dutchess was so angry that I had much difficulty to soothe her, and the more so, as I was now unable to play once more as she had so much wished, at a parting Court-Concert. My mother-in-law was also greatly grieved. I hastened therefore as much as possible to get away from all these unpleasant circumstances. A few weeks before, I had commissioned my old friend *Bärwolf* to dispose of the furniture and things which I did not purpose taking with me. In this he had been successful. I had therefore the reserved articles packed up, consisting chiefly of beds, looking glasses, music, clothes, linen etc., and dispatched beforehand as freight to Ratisbonne for water carriage. Eight days afterwards I followed with my brother *Ferdinand*, my two children and a young girl, an orphan, whom my mother-in-law had taken charge of, and brought up, and now gave to me as nursemaid for the children.

The parting with my relations and dear Gotha, was a very sorrowful one; but favoured with the most delightful weather, we soon cheered up again, and I was highly amused with the artless remarks of the children upon the numerous objects now seen by them for the first time. So we arrived very tired it is true, but very happy, in Ratisbonne. There we stopped some days, during which I made every preparation for the voyage down the Danube to Vienna. I hired at a moderate price a boat to myself, and had my packages which had already arrived as freight, put on board. The beds were unpacked, and spread out under the little wooden house on board the boat, for our repose at night. The trunks and boxes served as seats. As we purposed continuing our voyage day and night without stopping anywhere, provisions for four or five days were laid in. The boat's company consisted besides me and mine, of the skipper, his wife who undertook the cooking, the boatman, and three trades-apprentices to to whom I gave a free passage and food, for which they had agreed to lend a diligent hand at the oars.

We were in the month of May, the moon was full, and the deep blue sky was outspread over the charming country round. Spring had just decked all nature in her first dress of tender green, and the fruit trees were still laden with their beautiful blossom. The bushy banks of the majestic stream were the resort of numerous nightingales, which in bright calm nights particularly, poured forth an unceasing melody. It was indeed a delightful voyage, and I have striven continually, during my whole long life, to make it again under similar favourable circumstances; but alas! in vain.

While we were passing the celebrated *Rapids* and the *Whirlpool*, which at that time could not be effected wholly free from danger, our skipper who till then had been very jovial became all at once serious, and impressively cautioned the rowers to obey his orders with the greatest punctuality. The moment the downward rushing stream seized upon our boat, he turned pale, his wife threw herself upon her knees and howled more than spoke a prayer to the Holy Virgin. Hereupon I cautioned my brother who like me was a skillful swimmer, should any accident occur, to stand by me in saving the children. But we descended safely the shooting rapids and steered clear of the whirlpool, which is only dangerous for very small boats.

Upon the rock, which stands in the middle of the stream at the end of the rapids, and which by its throwing back the waves with violence occasions the whirlpool, dwellt then an old hermit, who subsisted upon the charitable gifts of the passing travellers. He put off and rowed over to us in his little skiff, to the great delight of the children, who had never before seen a hermit, and when alongside of us he received the customary donation.

On the fourth day of our voyage we arrived towards evening at Vienna, and from afar could see *Dorette* in company with her hostess, awaiting our arrival at the landing place. That was a happy meeting! The luggage was taken to our new domicile the same evening, whither we moved the following day.

By the time I had arrived in Vienna, my wound was almost healed. To my surprise, and to that of the surgeon to whom I related it, under the English sticking plaister which still enveloped my finger, a new flesh had grown in the place of that which had been cut away, and had by degrees assumed the previous form and size of the ball of the finger. The piece cut out of the nail had also grown again, though but imperfectly joined to the rest of the nail, so that there yet remained a gap, which is even still visible, and shews plainly the extent of the excision. With the help of a leather finger stall I could use my finger again, and though I could not yet play a Solo, yet I could perform my duties in the orchestra.

I now led a very active and a very happy life in the enjoyment of the society of my family. The early dawn found me at the piano, or at the writing table, and every other moment of the day which my orchestral duties or the tuition of my pupils permitted was devoted to composition. Yes, my head was at that time so continually at work, that on my way to my pupils and when taking a walk I was constantly composing, and by that means acquired a readiness in working out mentally, not only long periods, but whole pieces of music so completely, that without any further labour they could be at once written off. As soon as this was done, they were as though effaced from my mind, and then I had room again for new combinations. *Dorette* frequently chid me in our walks for this perpetual thinking, and was delighted when the prattle of the children diverted me from it. When this had once been done, I gladly gave myself up to external impressions; but I was not to be permitted to relapse into my thoughtful mood again, and *Dorette* with great skill knew how to prevent it.

In the first summer of our residence in Vienna, we already made ourselves well acquainted with the beautiful environs of the City, and almost every fine evening, when I was not engaged at the Theatre, we spent in the open air. Then, accompanied by the nursemaid carrying our simple evening-repast in a small basket, we used to seek out some spot from whence we could have a fine view of the country, and see the sun go down. On Sunday, also, we used to hire a fly at the "Linie", and make farther excursions to Leopoldsberg, or to the Brühl or to Laxenburg and Baden.

But the favorite walk of the children was always to Schönbrunn to see the menagery, or to the "Dörfl" in the Prater, where they ever beheld with new transport the puppet and dog shows, and other diverting wonders. I and my wife, half children too in disposition, shared intensely in all the pleasure of our little pets. It was a lovely, joyous time! so free from care!

After my return from Gotha, my first work was the composition of "Faust." Before my journey thither, I had had another subject in view, which *Theodor Körner* was to have worked out for me as an Opera. I had made the young poet's acquaintance soon after my first arrival in Vienna; he was then already as much admired for his amiable manners as for the success of his theatrical pieces. I met him at almost every party where I played, and as *Körner* was very fond of music we soon took to each other. When it was decided that I should remain in Vienna, I asked *Körner* to write an Opera for me and proposed for subject the legend of the "Rübezahl".

Körner, who had been present at both performances of the "Last Judgement", and who had a good opinion of my talent for composition acquiesced without hesitation, and went to work with zest upon the materials proposed. But, suddenly it was reported that *Körner* was about to join *Lützow's* light horse, and fight for the freedom of Germany. I hastened to him and endeavoured like many other of my friends to dissuade him from that intention; but without success. We soon saw him depart. It became afterwards known, that it was not alone his enthusiasm for the war of German independance, but an unfortunate and unrequited love for the handsome actress *Adamberger* that drove him from Vienna, and to an early death.

I thus saw my hope of an Opera-libretto from the pen of the youthful and gifted poet, destroyed, and was now obliged to look elsewhere for another. It was therefore very opportune that Herr *Bernhard* had offered me his version of "Faust" for composition, and we were soon agreed upon the terms. Some alterations that I had wished to have made, were completed by the author during my journey to Gotha, so that I could begin upon it immediately after my return. From the list of my Compositions, I find that I wrote that Opera in less than four months, from the end of May to the middle of September. I still remember with what enthusiasm and perseverance I worked upon it. As soon as I had completed some of the parts I hastened with them to *Meyerbeer*, who then resided in Vienna, and begged him to play them to me from the score, a thing in which he greatly excelled. I then undertook the Vocal parts and executed them in their different characters and voices with great enthusiasm. When my voice was not sufficiently flexible for the purpose, I helped myself by whistling, in which I was well practised. *Meyerbeer* took great interest in this work, which appears to have kept its ground up to the present time, as he during his direction of the Opera at Berlin put "Faust" again upon the stage, and had it studied with the greatest care.

Pixis the younger, also, who then resided with his parents in Vienna, as well as *Hummel* and *Seyfried*, shewed a great predeliction for this Opera, so that I offered it for representation at the Theatre "an der Wien" with the fairest hopes of a brilliant success. Count *Palffy*, with whom I was then still on good terms, accepted it immediately, and promised to distribute the characters as soon as possible and to bring it out. While engaged on the work, it is true, I had the personnel of my Theatre in my eye; and wrote the Faust for *Forti*, the Mephistopheles for *Weinmüller*, Hugo for *Wild*, Franz for *Gottdank*, Cunigunda for Madame *Campi*, and Rosa for Demoiselle *Teiner;* but nevertheless, (apart from the circumstance that I at that time especially did not yet understand how to keep myself within the bounds of the natural compass of the voice) all manner of things had escaped my pen that did not suit the above named singers, as, for instance: the long ornamental passages in the air of Hugo, for *Wild*, who at that time had but a limited power of execution. This at a later period was urged by the Count, when I had a disagreement with him, as an excuse for withdrawing his consent, and actually the opera was never produced while I was in Vienna. Some years afterwards, it was brought out with great success, and in more recent times was put upon the stage again with increased approbation. I, who had always felt an interest in my compositions so long only as I was engaged on them, and so to say, full of them; bore with great equanimity of mind the banishment of my score to the shelves of the library of the Theatre, and immediately set to work on new subjects. Even the pianoforte-arrangement of the opera that *Pixis* had taken great pleasure in preparing, I did not publish till many years afterwards at *Peter's* in Leipsic.

After having finished Faust, I thought it my duty to proceed to the fulfillment of my agreement with Herr *von Tost*. I therefore enquired of him, what kind of composition he would now prefer. My Art-Mæcenas, reflected a while, and then said: a Nonet, concerted for the four stringed instruments, Violin, Viol, Violincello, and Double-Bass; and the five principal wind-Instruments, Flute. Oboë. Clarinet, Horn and Bassoon, written in such a manner that the character of each of those instruments should be properly brought out, might be both an interesting and grateful theme; and as he did not in the least doubt that I should successfully accomplish it, he would suggest that to me as the next subject to choose. I felt attracted by the difficulty of the task, consented to it with pleasure, and commenced the work at once. This was the origin of the well known Nonet., published by *Steiner* in Vienna as op. 31, and which up to the present time is the only work of its kind. I completed it in a short time and delivered the score to Herr *von Tost*. He had it written out, and then invited the first artists in Vienna to his house, in order to study it under my direction. It was then performed at one of the first musical parties in the beginning of the winter, and met with such unanimous applause, that its repetition was frequently called for during the season. Herr *von Tost* would then appear each time with a music-portfolio under his arm, lay the different instrumental parts upon the music-stands himself, and when the performance was ended, lock them up again. He felt as happy at the success of the work as if he himself had been the composer. I played, also, very frequently at musical parties, the two Quartetts of which he possessed the manuscripts, and thus his desire to be invited to numerous musical parties was fully accomplished. Indeed, wherever I played, people soon became so accustomed to see Herr *von Tost*, also, with his portefolio of music, that he used to be invited even when I did not play any of his manuscripts.

Before the end of the year 1813, I wrote another *Rondo* for harp and violin for my wife and self, and a Quartett for stringed instruments for Herr *von Tost*. It is the one in G-Major, Op. 33 which from an oversight the publisher has marked as Nr. 2. It was nevertheless, written six months before the one in E-Major.

This Quartett was the occasion of my becoming entangled in a literary feud, which was the first and also the last that I ever engaged in about my compositions. It had met with a particularly favourable reception among the Artists and lovers of art in Vienna, and I considered it, also, and with reason, as the best I had written up to that time. It was therefore the more mortifying to me that the reviewer in a Viennese Art-journal of the day could find nothing good whatever in it. I was more particularly hurt by the malicious manner in which he spoke of the theoretical handling of the first theme, of which I was proud; and which had excited the admiration of connoisseurs. Even now, after so long a period I recollect the words, which were nearly as follow: "This eternal rechewing of the theme in every voice and key, is to me just as if one had given an order to a stupid servant, that he cannot understand, and which one is obliged to repeat to him over and over again in every possible shape of expression. The composer appears to have considered his auditors in the same light as the stupid servant.

I soon ascertained that the anonymous reviewer was Herr *von Mosel*, the composer of a lyric tragedy called "Salem", of which I certainly had said very openly: "I never heard any thing so wearisome in all my life." This opinion had unluckily reached the ears of the writer, and had excited his gall to this degree. Herr *von Tost* who was more proud of my compositions, particularly those he had in his portefolio than the composer himself, would not rest until I had written a replication to the criticism. What I said in reply, particularly in defence of the treatment of my theme, I now no longer remember, but I recollect, I was prodigal in sidethrusts at "Salem". This was pouring oil on the fire, and so a disputation ensued, which would have been continued much longer, had not the censorship put a stop to it by forbidding the Editor of the journal to insert any thing more on the subject. As such quarrels were exceedingly unpleasant to me, I was very glad to be able to return to my harmless occupation of composing.

In the autumn of 1813, *Dorette* presented me with a son. Our joy at this increase to our family was unfortunately of short duration; for the boy soon became sickly and died, before he was three months old. His poor mother sought and found relief in her harp; she practised with me the new *Rondo* for my benefit-concert that was to take place in December. According to the musical journal, this concert took place in the small "Redouten-Saal", and my brother *Ferdinand* made his début in a Violin Duet with me.

In the meantime, the great battle of Leipsic had been fought. The allied armies had crossed the Rhine, and it was hoped they would soon enter Paris. In Vienna great preparations were made to celebrate that entry, and the return of the Emperor and his victorious army. All the Theatres, had had incidental commemorative pieces written and composed, and the newly instituted *Society of the friends of music of the Austrian Empire* under the patronage of the Archduke *Rudolph* made preparations for a monster performance of *Handel's* "Samson" in the Imperial Riding-school; for which Herr *von Mosel* increased the instrumentation. Other Societies undertook similar performances. This gave Herr *von Tost* the idea of making arrangements for a grand musical performance on the return of the Emperor, and he asked me if I would write a Cantata for the occasion, the subject of which should be the liberation of Germany. I willingly consented, but with the observation, that this subject in itself offered but few favourable passages to the composer, and that in order to obtain such, the text should be written by a *good* poet.

"Oh! there shall be no want of that" was the reply. "I will immediately go to Frau *von Pichler*, and have no doubt, that she will undertake to furnish you with the text." And so she did. I consulted with the authoress upon the form and contents, and she then handed me a text-book, which in rich variety of domestic and warlike scenes presented a succession of favourable materials for composition.

I immediately set to work upon it, and finished this Cantata, which takes two hours to perform, in less than three months, from January to the middle of March 1814, in the midst of all my other numerous occupations.

Meanwhile Herr *von Tost*, had engaged the four best singers in Vienna for the soli-parts, viz Mesdames *Buchwieser* and *Milder*, and Messrs. *Wild* and *Weinmüller*, and for the choruses he purposed to combine the whole of the church-choirs and the chorus-singers of the theatre. The vocal parts were written and distributed, and I had already gone several times to Madame *Milder*, to assist her in practising her part; when, one morning Herr *von Tost* rushed into my room and exclaimed in despair: "I have just now had the great Redouten-Saal refused to me for our performance, under the idle pretence that it cannot be spared on account of the preparation for the Court-festivals! It is from sheer jealousy alone of the Musical Society, who will not allow any other grand performance in the Riding-school but their own. What is to be done? Since the destruction of the Apollo Saloon, there is no locale in Vienna except the "Great Redouten-Saal" fit for such a musical performance."

At the moment, the thought occured to me of the Circus of Herr *de Bach* in the Prater. We immediately drove out there, to see whether the Riding-ring in the centre of the building would afford sufficient room to hold our orchestra and the personnel of the theatre. I thought it would, and promised myself an immense effect from the disposing of the body of assistants in the centre of the building. But unfortunately, this locale also, for some reason which I no longer recollect, was not to be had, and so the whole undertaking failed, to the great grief of Herr *von Tost*.

This Cantata shared the same fate as "Faust." It was first produced long after I had left Vienna. I heard it for the first time in 1815 at the musical Festival at Frankenhausen, on the anniversary of the battle of Leipsic.

As with me, so it fared with *Beethoven* in a similar Festive composition; neither, also, was his performed at that period. It was called "Der glorreiche Augenblick"* and was published later with altered text by *Haslinger* in Vienna.

While mentioning *Beethoven*, it occurs to me, that I have not yet adverted to my friendly relations with that great artist, and I therefore hasten to supply the deficiency.

Upon my arrival in Vienna I immediately paid a visit to *Beethoven*; I did not find him at home, and therefore left my card. I now hoped to meet him at some of the musical parties, to which he was frequently invited, but was soon informed that, *Beethoven* since his deafness had so much increased that he could no longer hear music connectedly, had withdrawn himself from all musical parties, and had become very shy of all society. I made trial therefore of another visit; but again without success. At length I met him quite unexpectedly at the eating-house where I was in the habit of going with my wife every day at the dinner hour. I had already now given concerts, and twice performed my oratorio. The Vienna papers had noticed them favourably. *Beethoven* had therefore heard of me when I introduced myself to him, and he received me with an unusual friendliness of manner. We sat down at the same table, and *Beethoven* became very chatty, which much surprised the company, as he was generally taciturn, and sat gazing listlessly before him. But it was an unpleasant task to make him hear me, and I was obliged to speak so loud as to be heard in the third room off. *Beethoven* now came frequently to these dining rooms, and visited me also at my house. We thus soon became well acquainted: *Beethoven* was a little blunt, not to say uncouth; but a truthful eye beamed from under his bushy eyebrows. After my return from Gotha I met him now and then at the

---

* "The glorious moment."

theatre "an der Wien", close behind the orchestra, where Count *Palffy* had given him a free seat. After the opera he generally accompanied me to my house, and passed the rest of the evening with me. He could then be very friendly with *Dorette* and the children. He spoke of music but very seldom. When he did, his opinions were very sternly expressed, and so decided as would admit of no contradiction whatever. In the works of others, he took not the least interest; I therefore had not the courage to shew him mine. His favorite topic of conversation at that time was a sharp criticism of the management of both theatres by *Prince Lobkowitz* and Count *Palffy*. He frequently abused the latter in so loud a tone of voice, while we were yet even within the walls of his theatre, that not only the public leaving it, but the Count himself could hear it in his office. This used to embarrass me greatly, and I then always endeavoured to turn the conversation upon some other subject.

Beethoven's rough and even repulsive manners at that time, arose partly from his deafness, which he had not learned to bear with resignation, and partly from the dilapidated condition of his pecuniary circumstances. He was a bad housekeeper, and had besides the misfortune to be plundered by those about him. He was thus frequently in want of common necessaries. In the early part of our acquaintance, I once asked him, after he had absented himself for several days from the dining rooms: "You were not ill, I hope?" — "My boot was, and as I have only one pair, I had house-arrest", was his reply.

But some time afterwards he was extricated from this depressing position by the exertions of his friends. The proceeding was as follows:

Beethoven's "Fidelio", which in 1804 (or 1805) under very unfavourable circumstances, (during the occupation of Vienna by the French), had met with very little success, was now brought forward again by the director of the Kärnthnerthor-Theatre and performed for his benefit. *Beethoven* had allowed himself to be persuaded to write a new overture for it (in E), a song for the jailor, and the grand air for Fidelio (with horns-obligati) as also to make some alterations. In this new form the Opera had now great success, and kept its place during a long succession of crowded performances. On the first night, the composer was called forward several times, and now became again the object of general attention. His friends availed themselves of this favorable opportunity to make arrangements for a concert in his behalf in the great "Redouten Saal" at which the most recent compositions of *Beethoven* were to be performed. All who could fiddle, blow, or sing were invited to assist, and not one of the most celebrated artists of Vienna failed to appear. I and my orchestra had of course also joined, and for the first time I saw *Beethoven*, direct. Although I had heard much of his leading, yet it surprised me in a high degree. *Beethoven* had accustomed himself to give the signs of expression to his orchestra by all manner of extraordinary motions of his body. So often as a *Sforzando* occured, he tore his arms which he had previously crossed upon his breast, with great vehemence asunder. At a *piano*, he bent himself down, and the lower, the softer he wished to have it. Then when a *crescendo* came, he raised himself again by degrees, and upon the commencement of the *forte*, sprang bolt upright. To increase the forte yet more, he would sometimes, also, join in with a shout to the orchestra, without being aware of it.

Upon my expressing my astonishment to *Seyfried*, at this extraordinary method of directing, he related to me a tragi-comical circumstance that had occurred at *Beethoven's* last concert at the Theatre "an der Wien."

Beethoven was playing a new Pianoforte-Concerto of his, but forgot at the first *tutti*, that he was a Soloplayer, and springing up, began to direct in his usual way. At the first *sforzando* he threw out his arms so wide asunder, that he knocked both the lights off the piano upon the ground. The audience laughed, and *Beethoven* was so incensed at this disturbance, that he made the orchestra cease playing, and begin anew. *Seyfried*, fearing, that a repetition of the accident would occur at the same passage, bade two boys of the chorus place themselves on either side of *Beethoven*, and hold the lights in their hands. One of the boys innocently approached nearer, and was reading also in the notes of the piano-part. When therefore the fatal *sforzando* came, he received from *Beethoven's* out thrown right hand so smart a blow on the mouth, that the poor boy let fall the light from terror. The other boy, more cautious, had followed with anxious eyes every motion of *Beethoven*, and by stooping suddenly at the eventful moment he avoided the slap on the mouth. If the public were unable to restrain their laughter before, they could now much less, and broke out into a regular bacchanalian roar. *Beethoven* got into such a rage, that at the first chords of the solo, half a dozen strings broke. Every endeavour of the real lovers of music to restore calm and attention were for the moment fruitless. The first *allegro* of the Concerto was therefore lost to the public. From that fatal evening *Beethoven* would not give another concert.

But the one got up by his friends, was attended with the most brilliant success. The new compositions of *Beethoven* pleased extremely, particularly the symphony in A-Major (the seventh); the wonderful second theme was *encored*; and made upon me also, a deep and lasting impression. The execution was a complete masterpiece, inspite of the uncertain and frequently laughable direction of *Beethoven*.

It was easy to see that, the poor deaf *Maestro* of the Piano, could no longer hear his own music. This was particularly remarkable in a passage in the second part of the first *allegro* of the symphony. At that part there are two pauses in quick succession, the second of which, is *pianissimo*. This, *Beethoven* had probably overlooked, for he again began to give the time before the orchestra had executed this second pause. Without knowing it therefore, he was already from ten to twelve bars in advance of the orchestra when it began the *pianissimo*. *Beethoven*, to signify this in his own way, had crept completely under the desk. Upon the now ensuing *crescendo*, he again made his appearance, raised himself continually more and more, and then sprang up high from the ground, when according to his calculation the moment for the *forte* should begin. As this did not take place, he looked around him in affright, stared with astonishment at the orchestra, that it should still be playing pianissimo, and only recovered himself, when at length the long expected *forte* began, and was audible to himself.

Fortunately this scene did not take place at the public performance, otherwise the audience would certainly have laughed again.

As the saloon was crowded to overflowing and the applause enthusiastic, the friends of *Beethoven* made arrangements for a repetition of the concert, which brought in an almost equally large amount. For some time therefore *Beethoven* was extricated from his pecuniary difficulties; but, arising from the same causes, these reoccurred to him more than once before his death.

Up to this period, there was no visible falling off in *Beethoven's* creative powers. But as from this time, owing to his constantly increasing deafness, he could no longer hear any music, that of a necessity must have had a prejudicial influence upon his fancy. His constant endeavour to be original and to open new paths, could no longer as formerly, be preserved from error by the guidance of the ear. Was it then to be wondered at that his works became more and more eccentric, unconnected, and incomprehensible? It is true there are people, who imagine they can understand them, and in their pleasure at that, rank them far above his earlier masterpieces. But I am not of the number, and freely confess that, I have never been able to relish the last works of *Beethoven*. Yes! I must even reckon the much admired Ninth Symphony among them, the three first themes of which, inspite of some solitary flashes of genius, are to me worse than all of the eight previous Symphonies, the fourth theme of which is in my opinion so monstrous and tasteless, and in its grasp of *Schiller's* Ode so trivial, that I cannot even now understand how a genius like *Beethoven's* could have written it. I find in it another proof of what I already remarked in Vienna, that *Beethoven* was wanting in æsthetical feeling and in a sense of the beautiful.

As at the time I made *Beethoven's* acquaintance, he had already discontinued playing both in public, and at private parties; I had therefore but one opportunity to hear him, when I casually came to the rehearsal of a new Trio (D-Major ³/₄ time) at *Beethoven's* house. It was by no means an enjoyment; for in the first place the pianoforte was woefully out of tune, which however little troubled *Beethoven*, since he could hear nothing of it, and, secondly, of the former so admired excellence of the virtuoso, scarely any thing was left, in consequence of his total deafness. In the *forte*, the poor deaf man hammered in such a way upon the keys, that entire groups of notes were inaudible, so that one lost all intelligence of the subject unless the eye followed the score at the same time. I felt moved with the deepest sorrow at so hard a destiny. It is a sad misfortune for any one to be deaf; how then should a musician endure it without despair? *Beethoven's* almost continual melancholy was no longer a riddle to me now.

The next thing I wrote after finishing the Cantata, was a Violin-quartett (the tenth, op. 30 published by *Mechetti* in Vienna.) Being very brilliant for the first violin, it was soon my hobby-horse, and I played it times innumerable at private parties. Then followed the Octett, in which by Herr *von Tost's* wish, who then contemplated a journey to England, I took up a theme from *Handel*, varied, and carried it out thematically, as he was of opinion it would on that account excite great interest in that country. I also played this composition very frequently, in which besides myself the clarinetist *Friedlowsky* and the hornist *Herbst*, and another whose name I now forget, found especial opportunity to distinguish themselves.

In the autumn of 1814, the crowned heads of Europe and their Ministers assembled in Vienna, and that famed Congress began, from which the German nations expected to see the fulfilment of all the promises made to them for their self devotion. A swarm of idlers and curious poured from all parts into Vienna, to be present at the splendid festivities, with which the Emperor was to entertain his guests. Before the Emperor's return to Vienna several had already taken place, which from their magnificence yet more increased the expectation of what was to follow. At one of these I had also assisted. It was a grand serenade in the Court-Yard of the Burg Palace, and was given either to the Emperor or to Prince *Schwarzenberg*, I now no longer recollect which. In the centre of that not very large square, surrounded by lofty buildings a raised platform was erected for the numerous personnel of the orchestra and choruses. Upon a balcony opposite the singers, the Court and State officials were assembled. The remaining space was filled by a numerous public, to whom free admission had been allowed.

When I saw the locality, and the assembled crowd which had increased to thousands, I felt alarmed, for I had promised to perform a violin-concerto, and now feared, that my tones would be unheard, and lost in the wide surrounding space. But to withdraw now, was no longer possible, so I resigned myself to my fate. But every thing went off better than I had expected. Already during the overture I remarked that the high buildings threw back the sounds right well, and I then came forward with renewed courage. The very first tones of my solo allayed all my anxiety that the damp night air would affect my strings, for my violin sounded clear and powerful as usual. As the public also, during my play, maintained the most perfect silence, even the finest shades of my instrumentation were every where distinctly heard. The effect, therefore, was a very favorable one, and was acknowledged by loud and long applause. I have never played before a more numerous nor a more sympathetic public.

Among the many strangers attracted by the Congress were several artists, who thought the opportunity a most favourable one to give concerts in Vienna. In this they very much deceived themselves. For as all the native artists gave concerts, these became so numerous and close upon each other, that it was impossible for all to be well attended! One that I and my wife gave on the 11. December was an exception to this, for it attracted a numerous and brilliant audience. I gave the overture to "Faust," and it was received with great approbation. The reviewer of the Musical-journal says: "it increased our desire to see this opera, which has now been ready a twelvemonth, brought out at last." Several lovers of art among the ambassadors and foreign diplomatists who had heard me play for the first time at my concert, paid me a visit, and expressed the wish to hear me in a quartett. This was the cause of my giving several music-parties during the Congress, and in which I played to those lovers of art the new compositions I had written for Herr *von Tost*. I still recollect with great satisfaction the general delight with which those productions were received. Certainly, I was supported also, upon those occasions by the first artists in Vienna, so that as regards execution nothing more could be desired. I generally began with a Quartett, then followed with a quintett, and concluded with my octett, or nonett.

Others also besides me, gave music parties to the visitors to the Congress, among these my friend *Zizius* particularly distinguished himself. All the foreign artists had been introduced at his house, and at his music parties therefore, there arose frequently a spirit of rivalry between the native and foreign virtuosi. I there for the first time heard *Hummel* play his beautiful Septett, as well as several other of his compositions of that period. But I was mostly charmed by his improvisations in which no other Pianoforte-Virtuoso has ever yet approached him. I especially remember with great pleasure one evening when he improvised in so splendid a manner as I never since heard him whether in public or in private. The company were about to break up, when some ladies, who thought it too early, entreated *Hummel* to play a few more walzes for them. Obliging and galant as he was to the ladies, he seated himself at the piano, and played the wished for walzes, to which the young folks in the adjoining room began to dance. I, and some other artists, attracted by his play, grouped ourselves round the instrument with our hats already in our hands, and listened attentively. *Hummel* no sooner observed this, than he converted his play into a free phantasia of improvisation, but which constantly preserved the walz-rhythm, so that the dancers were not disturbed. He then took from me and others who had executed their own compositions during the evening a few easily combined themes and figures, which he interwove into his walzes and varied them at every recurrence with a constantly increasing richness and piquancy of expression. Indeed, at length, he even made them serve as fuge-themes, and let loose all his science in counterpoint without disturbing the walzers in their pleasures. Then he returned to the galant style, and in conclusion passed into a bravoura, such as from him even has seldom been heard. In this finale, the themes taken up were still constantly heard, so that the whole rounded off and terminated in real artistic style. The hearers were enraptured, and praised the young ladies' love of dancing, that had conduced to so rich a feast of artistic excellence.

Among the foreign artists who came to Vienna before and during the Congress, were also, three of my former acquaintances, *Carl Maria von Weber*, *Hermstedt* and *Feska*. *Weber* played with great success and then left for Prague, whither he was summoned to direct the opera. *Hermstedt* came at a time, when the concerts were so numerous, that he could not give one of his own. He played, however, with immense applause at a concert of the flutist *Dressler*, in which he accompanied the air with clarinet obligato in "Titus", accompanied and played a pot-pourri of mine which I wrote for him for the occasion, after a new composition for harp and violin, that had particularly pleased *Hermstedt*. Both compositions were afterwards published; that for the clarinet with quartett-accompaniment as op. 81 at *Schlesinger's* in Berlin, and that for harp and violin as op. 118 by *Schuberth* in Hamburgh.

Feska, who since I had known him in Magdeburgh, had become member of the Westphalian orchestra in Cassel, and now after its dissolution had been made Concert master at Carlsruhe, had made great progress both as violinist and composer. His quartetts and quintetts, which he executed in a pure, accomplished, and tasteful manner, took greatly in Vienna, and found a ready sale among the publishers there. One of them began in one of its themes with the notes, which form the composer's name:

This the auditors thought very pretty, and joked the other composers present, *Hummel, Pixis*, and me, on account of our unmusical names. This suggested the idea to me of making something musical out of my name, with the assistance of the abbreviation formerly used of the *piano* into *po*, and of a quarter rest, which when written looks like an r. It was in this form:

and I immediately took it as a theme for a new violin-quartett, which is the first of the three quartetts published in Vienna by *Mechetti* as op. 29 and dedicated to *Andreas Romberg*. When I first played it at my friend's *Zizius*, it met with great applause, and the originality of the theme, with its descending, diminished *Quarte*, was especially praised.

I now called together those who had previously quizzed me for my unmusical name and *shewed* them, (for naturally they had not *heard* it) the famous thema formed out of my name. They laughed heartily at my artistic trick, and now quizzed the more both *Hummel* and *Pixis*, who with all their skill could make nothing musical out of their names.

*   *   *

Meanwhile many things had changed in my position at the theatre and in respect to its proprietor. I had openly broken with Count *Palffy*. It was brought about by the following circumstance: One evening, when I entered the orchestra I saw Herr *Buchwieser*, the father of the prima donna, and third orchestra director, had taken *Seyfried's* seat. I observed to him that I alone was charged with the direction of the orchestra, when *Seyfried* was prevented coming, and I therefore requested him to leave it. This he refused to do, with the remark, that the Count himself had ordered him to direct the opera, and at the express wish of his daughter, who preferred singing under his direction. As all my expostulations were unavailing, and I considered it beneath my dignity to play the first violin under so obscure a director, I quitted the orchestra, and returned home. The next morning I sent in a written remonstrance to the Count respecting this invasion of right that had been secured to me in my engagement, and requested, that I might be exposed to no further repetition of it.

The Count, incited by the *Prima Donna*, who was very incensed because I would not lead under the direction of her father, answered me with rudeness instead of with the apologies I had reason to expect, and which I replied to in yet stronger terms. From that moment, the Count and his creatures studied to annoy me in every possible manner that my position exposed me to. Added to this, since *Palffy* had been so fortunate as to become lessee of the two Court Theatres, he put his own theatre greatly in the back-ground.

He took away from it the best singers, and the best part of the chorus, to incorporate them with the personnel of the Kärnthnerthor-Theatre; so that "an der Wien", from that time, *Spectacle-pieces*, and low class popular operas alone, were given. As I was not bound to assist at these, I had scarcely any thing more to do at the theatre. I could therefore clearly see, that I should be discharged after the termination of my engagement.

As now, after Napoleon was vanquished and banished to Elba, a general European peace seemed in perspective, and that I greatly desired to set out as soon as possible on my long projected artistic tour through all Europe; I made a proposition to the Count to cancel our agreement on the expiration of the second year, and demanded as compensation the half of my salary for the third year, paid down in *one* sum. He readily consented to it, and so we parted in peace. I now hastened to make every preparation in order to be enabled to commence my journey in the spring. I contemplated first, to travel through Germany and Switzerland to Italy, whither I had long ardently desired to go. As I purposed taking my children with me, foreseeing that their mother would not be able to separate from them for so long a time without pining to death; I was first of all obliged to provide myself with a larger travelling carriage to hold us all, with the instruments. The difficulty was to build one for this purpose, sufficiently light of draught for three posthorses. I conferred upon this therefore with Herr *Langhans*, the clever machinist at the theatre "an der Wien", and afterwards director of public buildings in Berlin, who made a drawing of the design suggested in our conference, according to which the carriage should be built. It had a solid roof, upon which were packed the leather covered harp-case, and a trunk for linen. The violin-case was stowed in a boot under the coachman's seat, so that the whole space in the interior of the vehicle remained for the travellers.

In my relations with Herr *von Tost*, also, a serious

alteration had taken place. After the settlement of our earlier account, which was effected by the delivery of the Cantata "Das befreite Deutschland" I had delivered again, four manuscripts, the octett, two quartetts and a second quintett, without receiving the agreed price. At first I had argued no ill of this delay in settlement. But when it became suddenly reported in the city, that the wealthy Herr *von Tost* had sustained severe losses, and was on the point of bankruptcy; that he no longer called upon me, and even failed to appear at a musical-party where I played one of his manuscripts, but sent the portfolio instead of coming; the matter looked dubious. I therefore took back to him the portfolio myself, in order if possible, to come to a clear understanding with him at the same time. I found the otherwise so jovial man very much depressed in spirits. He confessed to me his position without reserve. It was, he said, extremely painful to him, to be unable to fulfil his engagements with me; but as his plans for the future were unsettled if not quite destroyed, he would forthwith return all my manuscripts to me before the expiration of the stipulated time, so that I might sell them as soon as possible to a publisher. For the loss I might thereby sustain, he was willing to indemnify me with a bill for one hundred ducats, which as soon as his affairs had assumed a more favourable aspect, he would honourably meet. Upon this he fetched the whole of the manuscripts and handed them to me. I, who considered that Herr *von Tost* had amply compensated me for the short time he had them in his possession, by the costly furniture he had bought for me, and reckoned at so low an estimate, was quite satisfied with the return of my manuscripts and refused all further indemnification. However, as I perceived that Herr *von Tost* felt hurt by this arrangement, I took the bill, well knowing that from my contemplated departure from Vienna its early liquidation was not to be thought of.

I now sold the whole of the returned manuscripts to

two Vienna publishers, and from their having acquired a great celebrity by their frequent performance, I received a considerable sum for them.

At the commencement of the year 1815, I wrote another Quartett, in C-major (No. 2 of the op. 29) and a new violin Concerto (the seventh, op. 38) as also Variations, which remained unpublished, for use upon the coming journey; the two last of these compositions I played at my farewell-Concert on the 19. February 1815. Respecting this last concert I gave in Vienna, the Musical journal spoke very favourably. Of the newest violin concerto (E-minor. C-major. E-major) it says: "Very difficult for the solo player as well as for those who accompany. A splendid, perfect composition; a fine flowing cantabile; striking modulations, replete with bold canonic imitations, an ever new, charming and happily calculated instrumentation. The melting *adagio* is especially captivating." In conclusion it says: "As to the merits of this masterly artist, both here and throughout Germany there is but *one* opinion. We yet remember with lively satisfaction the triumph, which he achieved two years ago over his rival, the great *Rode*. He is now about to leave us upon a grand artistic tour. He first proceeds to Prague, where his new opera "Faust" is now being studied .... May he, who by his talent and his open, manly character has left an honourable memorial of his worth in our hearts, meet always, and every where with success!"

I at that time really had the intention of going first to Prague, to be present at the production of my opera, which was being studied under *Carl Maria von Weber*. But I afterwards abandoned that plan. I had in fact received a letter from my former Intendant Baron *von Reibnitz* at Breslau, wherein in the name of a family of his acquaintance that of Prince *von Carolath*, he asked me if I would feel disposed to pass the summer months with them at their seat, *Carolath*, in Silesia? The Princess was very desirous, that her two daughters, one of whom played the harp, the other the pianoforte, should receive instruction in music from my wife. They would endeavour to make the stay of myself and family at their charming castle as agreable as possible. He, the Baron had been invited also, and would be extremely pleased if I would accept the invitation, so that he might again pass some time with me.

As the spring and summer were any way but little favourable seasons of the year to give concerts, and that *Dorette* and the children anticipated much pleasure from the stay at Carolath, I readily assented. I therefore hastened the preparations for our journey, in order to avail ourselves of the opportunity to give a few concerts at Breslau and in its neighbourhood, before the fine season had set in. The next thing was to effect the sale of our furniture and household chattels, which was very speedily done, for immediately upon the announcement of the sale, a host of purchasers presented themselves. As our furniture was very elegant, and withal nearly new, the purchasers bid warmly against each other, and we therefore realised a sum far beyond our expectation. This as well as my Vienna savings, which were still in paper currency, I now took to a banker's and changed for gold. Scarcely had I done this when all Vienna was alarmed by the intelligence that Napoleon had escaped from Elba, landed in France, and been hailed with the greatest joy. The rate of exchange fell suddenly so low, that if I had delayed the conversion of my paper into specie but *one* day more, I should have suffered a loss of more than fifty ducats.

When first contemplating my grand tour through Europe, the idea struck me, also, of commencing an album, in which I purposed making a collection of the compositions of all the artists whose acquaintance I might make. I began immediately with the Viennese, and received from all the resident composers of my acquaintance, short, autographic works written for the most part expressly for my album. The most valuable contribution to me, is that of *Beethoven*. It is a Canon for three voices to the words from *Schiller's* "Jungfrau von

Orleans": "Kurz ist der Schmerz, und ewig währt die Freude." It is worthy of remark, in the first place, that *Beethoven* whose handwriting, notes as well as text, were usually almost illegible, must have written this page with particular patience; for it is unblotted from beginning to end, which is the more remarkable, since he even drew the lines without the aid of a ruler; secondly, that after the falling in of the third voice a bar is wanting, which I was obliged to complete. The pages concluded with the wish:

May you dear *Spohr* where ever you find real art, and real artists, think with pleasure of me, Your friend.

Ludwig van Beethoven.

Vienna March 3. 1815.

Upon all my subsequent travels I received contributions to this album, and possess therefore a highly interesting collection of short compositions from German, Italian, French, English and Dutch artists.*

* * *

On the eve of taking leave of Vienna, I yet think I must recall some further incidents of my stay there, which hitherto I have had no opportunity of relating. First, in respect of my orchestral duties. These were sometimes very onerous for me; the same piece being frequently represented twenty or thirty nights in succession. This happened not only with two of *Mozart's* operas "Don Juan" and the "Zauberflöte", which during my engagement were brought out with a new distribution of characters and with a very brilliant *mise en scene*; but, also, with a ballet, which during the Congress was repeated an innumerable number of times, and in which I had to play violin soli's. What its name was, I no longer recollect, but that the celebrated dancers *Duport*, and mesdames *Bigottini* and *Petit Aimée*, whom Count *Palffy* had sent for from Paris, danced in it. It is true, I did not play

---

* A selection from the pages of this album will be found in the appendix.

those soli's unwillingly, upon their own account, for the audience always listened with the greatest attention, and were profuse in their applause of me; but it annoyed me that I was obliged to measure my *tempi*, by the steps of the dancers and that I could not lengthen at pleasure my closes and cadences, as the dancers were unable to sustain themselves so long in their groupings. This gave rise therefore to many bickerings with the ballet master, until at length I learned compliance. I endeavoured to sweeten the monotony of my duties in some degree by always enriching and ornamenting my soli performances. This I did especially with the troubadour in "John of Paris" for whom a *pas de trois* was introduced in that ballet. As in the opera of that name, there were three strophes, the first of which had to be executed by the horn, the second by the violincello, and the third by the violin. I at first ornamented my strophe in a very vocal style. But as I remarked, that the *Prima Donna*, demoiselle *Buchwieser* at the next representation had borne them well in mind, sang them, and obtained great applause for them, this so annoyed me, as I could not bear the singer, that I thenceforth ornamented them in a style she could not imitate with her voice.

Besides the two above mentioned operas of *Mozart*, I experienced a third ordeal in a new popular-opera, with music by *Hummel*, which by a singular chance such as will assuredly never occur again, went through a long succession of nightly representations. It was called "Princess Eselshaut" and as far as the author's text, was so wretched a piece of patchwork, that in spite of the pretty music of which five or six of the Numbers were received with great applause, it was at the conclusion unanimously hissed. This according to Vienna custom at once consigned it to the tomb. *Hummel* who conducted, had, already, quite resignedly expressed himself to me, who in honour of him led as first violin. "Another pure labour in vain!" But on the following evening when another piece was to have been announced, it could not be given, owing to the illness of several of the performers in the opera and play, and the manager was therefore obliged to repeat the condemned opera though at the risk of exciting an uproar in the theatre. On that evening nevertheless, just on account of the anticipated tumult, the theatre was crammed to excess, and the piece was hissed at the end of each act, and again at the conclusion. But the musical pieces met with more applause than on the first night, and at the fall of the curtain when the hissing had ceased, the composer was even called for, and greeted with vehement applause. As the indisposition of the invalids still continued, a third trial of it was obliged to be made, which went off nearly like the former one. Yet was the opposition against the piece much less, and the music obtained more friends than ever. Thus it could be continued with confidence, and on the succeeding nights it again found new friends in sufficient number. At length it became the fashion to go and hiss the piece, and praise the music. *Hummel* took speedy advantage of this, and published a piano-forte arrangement of the most favorite Numbers, which had a rapid sale. So it was no "labour in vain" after all, as he had feared on the first evening!

Pixis, was not so fortunate with his opera, the "Zauberspruch". That was swamped by the badness of the libretto, nor could the music keep it above water, although it had, also, many successful "numbers." It was the occasion for the display of a bit of real Viennese wit. A friend of the composer, not having been able to see the first representation of it, enquired of another who had been present "Well what do you think of the opera of *Pixis*. — "Nix is!" was the reply.

I may here relate another of my Vienna recollections, since it is one of those which make a deep impression and therefore do not so easily fade from the memory. It was an unusually great inundation, such as occurs once only in every century, occasioned by the overflowing of the little river "die Wien" on the banks of which my house was situated. On that occasion it was so great from the simultaneous overflowing of the Danube, which would not allow the waters of the "Wien" an outlet. I had not observed the commencement of the inundation, being engaged at a rehearsal at the theatre. After it was over, I found the street leading to my house already flooded, and I saw that I must use all haste to be enabled even to wade through it.

Nevertheless I first fetched my violin-case out of the orchestra, as I foresaw that, also, would be laid under water. By this time the flood had risen so high that in some places the water reached above my knees. I found my family in the greatest consternation and the other inmates of the house still more so. My landlord, the cabinet-maker, with his family, were already hurrying up past my floor to the top of the house, and endeavouring to secure a dry stowage for their effects, in the loft. He had need to hasten; for the water rose so fast, that in a few hours it almost reached to the first floor. The terrified inhabitants of the suburb had now a scene before them such as they had never before beheld. The rushing waters swept by, bearing along with them articles of every description commingled in the strangest confusion. Implements of husbandry, carts laden with hay or wood, the wreck of stalls and stabling, dead cattle, and even a cradle containing a screaming infant, which, however, was happily rescued by a boat. The owners of the houses, furnished with long poles, were exerting themselves to keep off the objects as they floated by, so that they might not damage the walls of the houses, others on the other hand provided with boat hooks, endeavoured to lay hold of the furniture and other household chattels in order to save them, and pull them up into the windows for security. Some hours afterwards, when such like articles had ceased to float past, boats made their appearance laden with provisions, which were readily bought up by the inhabitants of the flooded streets. Other boats towards evening brought the employés and men of business from the city to their dwellings, and anxiously expecting families. As the rain also poured down in torrents, the inundation still continued at the same height, and even at night fall there was no perceptible decrease of the waters. So long as it remained light, the scene afforded great diversity of interest, but when night came it was fearful to behold. The roar of the waters, and the howling of the storm forbade all thought of repose; nor was it advisable to retire to rest, as no one knew what might yet occur. I therefore laid my children near me on my sofa with their clothes on, and as *Dorette* had soon fallen asleep beside them, I sat down to my work, a new song-composition, in order to resist sleep more effectually. In this I succeeded. But my zeal at composition led me several times to the piano, which the family of my landlord who passed half the night in the floor above me upon their knees in prayer, took in very great dudgeon; for on the following morning the nurse-maid informed me, that the wife had bitterly exclaimed: "That Lutheran heretic will bring yet greater misfortune upon us with his unchristian singing and playing." But the night passed without further misfortune, and by day-break the water had greatly decreased. Nevertheless, it was evening before it had sufficiently subsided to admit of again traversing the streets on foot. But the "Theatre an der Wien" remained closed for eight days, for it required that time before all traces of the inundation could be removed.

* * *

After a sorrowful parting from dear Vienna, where we had passed so many happy days, I set out with my family upon our great journey on the 18. March, 1815. My brother *Ferdinand* whose engagement at the "Theatre an der Wien" was to last for another year, remained alone behind. After its expiration, he obtained an appointment in the Royal Orchestra of Berlin.

Our first resting place was at Brünn, where we gave a concert. How it succeeded, I no longer remember, but I well recollect, that I was very dissatisfied with the orchestral-accompaniment. In respect to that, of course my excellent orchestra in Vienna had accustomed me to a very different style of performance.

From Brünn we went to Breslau, where in April we also gave two concerts; but they were not well attended. The unsettled state of the public mind arising from the recommencement of hostilities and from the great sacrifices entailed upon each individual by the contributions required of them, was in truth then so general, that a more unfavourable time to give concerts could not well have presented itself. But in so musical a city as Breslau, even in that period of warlike commotion, there was no dearth of zealous musical amateurs, to whom music was a necessary of life. I was therefore frequently invited to private circles, in which I had an opportunity to perform my Vienna compositions of Herr *von Tost's* portfolio. They met with a brilliant reception, particularly the two Quintetts, which I was frequently obliged to repeat. At the earnest wish of my friend *Schnabel*, director of the Cathedral-orchestra, I wrote an Offertorium for a Solo-soprano voice and chorus, with violin obligato and orchestra, which, as is shewn by the catalogue of my compositions was performed in the Cathedral on 16. April, and where I took the violin-part. As I left behind me there the original score, and have never seen it since that time, I am unable to say whether the composition has any merit. Probably it is still to be found in the library of the cathedral.

* * *

On a fine evening in the spring, I arrived with my family at Carolath. As we had to pass over a small river near the castle, in a ferry-boat, our arrival was perceived before hand. We therefore found upon driving into the Castle-court, the whole of the Prince's family assembled at the foot of the steps, and were welcomed by them in the most friendly manner. The prince himself led us to the apartments assigned to us. After we had changed our dress we were summoned to the supper-table. The Prince, a somewhat ceremonious but friendly and well meaning man from fifty eight to sixty years of age received us at the entrance of the dining-room, and introduced us to the other guests. They consisted of the Princess his second wife, her sister, a lady passionately fond of poetry and music, his two daughters by his first marriage, amiable maidens of fifteen and seventeen years of age, and their tutor, Herr *Kartscher*, a young man of polished manners. The conversation at table was with the exception of the somewhat antiquated formality of the Prince, both free from restraint and lively, and convinced me that I was in a high bred circle having a sympathy for all that was beautiful. *Dorette* was also very pleased with the conversation of her neighbours the Prince and his sister-in-law, and the children in whom the young ladies had interested themselves in the most friendly manner, were also extremely happy. Our whole family looked forward therefore to a pleasant residence at the castle.

On the following day, the regulations were forthwith adopted for the subjects and hours of study, which with few exceptions remained unchanged during the whole time of our stay. In the forenoon, while *Dorette* gave instruction to the Princesses, the eldest on the harp, the youngest on the piano, I also gave the first music lessons to my children. Afterwards they were permitted to participate in the lessons given to the Princesses by their tutor, and he was so good as to adapt his instruction as much as possible to the capacities of the children. Meanwhile, my wife and I occupied ourselves with our own musical-studies, or I composed. As the members of the Prince's family were very fond of singing, this was inducement sufficient to me to write two small books of songs, the text of which was furnished by the sister of the Princess from her large collection of poetical pieces. Among these were also some poems of Herr *Kartscher*. Both volumes were published by *Peters* of Leipsic as op. 37, and 41. When the studies of the forenoon were terminated, a careful toilette was made by all, to appear at the dinner-table, as it was always the custom with the Prince's family to dine *en parure*, or full dress. The remainder of the day was devoted to social intercourse and amusements. When the weather was fine, coffee was served in the castle garden, and towards evening an excursion-drive was made into the neighbouring environs. A farm belonging to the Prince was a frequent object of our visit, and either there or in the woods around it we frequently partook of a rustic supper. At other times when the weather was overcast, or that visitors came from neighbouring parts, we had music in the evening. As soon, however, as Herr *von Reibnitz* arrived as guest at the Castle, an attempt at Quartett music was made. The old valet of the Prince who in his younger days had played the violincello, was then summoned to produce his instrument, the schoolmaster of the village his viol, and Herr *von Reibnitz* took the second violin. Unfortunately I had no other Quartetts with me, than my own, which were certainly never written for *such* performers. The first attempt therefore was very discouraging. But as the others evinced much zeal, I was not wanting in patience and endurance; and by dint of several rehearsals I succeeded so far as to enable me to let the company hear two of my quartetts. They were not so well accustomed to enjoyments in art as not to receive their performance with great approbation. A polonaise also, which I then wrote (op. 40, published by *Peters*) pleased greatly, and soon became a frequently requested and favorite piece with the company, perhaps, merely, because they had seen it composed. After I and my family had passed the first two months of our residence in Carolath in this sufficiently pleasant though somewhat uniform manner, the Prince announced one day at dinner with some solemnity, that he would be obliged to leave his dear guests for one day, as it was his custom every year on the 24. June to proceed to Glogau, to be present at the Freemason's festival of St. John. This induced me upon rising from table to make myself known to him as a brother Mason, which so agreably surprised the Prince that he immediately invited me to accompany him on the journey. I have forgotten to relate that I had already become a freemason in Gotha, had there received after the expiration of a year the second degree of the order, and a year later on a journey to Berlin, the third, of master-mason. But as in Austria, freemasonry was prohibited, and that for two years and a half I had frequented no lodge, I longed to assist once more at a meeting of the brothers. The Prince's invitation to accompany him to Glogau came therefore very opportunely. Grand preparations were forthwith made. The great travelling carriage emblazoned with the Prince's armorial bearings was drawn out of the coach-house, and cleansed from dust; a Jäger, and another servant had squeezed himself into the state livery, and the Prince himself made his appearance for the first time in state-uniform, with his star upon his breast. We set out early on the morning of the 24. Arrived at the lodge, the Prince was received and welcomed by a deputation, and his guest, also, after having testified his prerogative, was greeted as a brother in the most friendly manner. After the meeting of the work-lodge, a splendid dinner-lodge followed, in which I joined the musical brethren, directed their singing, and myself, sang with my powerful bass voice some mason's songs and the "Heiligen Hallen" from the "Zauberflöte." Among the musical brothers I found several acquaintances of my earlier travels through Silesia, who eagerly sought to honour me with their attentions.

The chairman, also, welcomed the „renowned craftsman" to the circle of brothers, and thanked the Prince for having introduced him. The Prince seemed greatly pleased to find the honours paid to his guest, redound to his own, for on his return to Carolath he redoubled his already great attentions towards me and my family, so that we were even frequently embarrassed by them.

After a further highly agreable stay of from six to eight weeks, we resumed our journey through Dresden and Leipzic to Gotha. Returned thither after an absence of nearly three years from her home, *Dorette* felt so happy, that I could not think of leaving it for some time. I therefore settled down quietly for a few months, and only made a few short excursions in the neighbourhood. The first was to my parents at Gandersheim, where my father had in the meanwhile been transferred as District-Physician, and from thence to Hanover, where I gave a concert. The second was to Frankenhausen, where *Bischoff* got up another musical festival.

Here begins one of my diaries which I continued without any break off up to my return from Italy. The title is "Passing Remarks, during a Musical-tour" and the work begins:

Frankenhausen, Oct. 19. 1815.

...... " In Hanover we made the interesting acquaintance of the *Violinist*, and the highly uninteresting one of the *Man*, *Kiesewetter*. As violinist he is distinguished for a powerful very pure, and even feeling style of play, without however as it seems to me, a true feeling for the beauties of art; as a man, he is the most inflated wind-bag, that I ever met! He conducted in our concert on the 11. October, but without certainty and foresight.

"After a pause of three years, the musicians of Thuringia have again assembled here, for the purpose of celebrating after the speedily terminated war, the now complete emancipation of Germany, upon the anniversary of the Leipsic "Battle of the Nations", in a manner worthy of the musical science. This day, the first of the musical festival, the performance of my Cantata "Das befreite Deutschland" and the "Te Deum" of Gottfried *Weber*, took place. As it would not beseem me as composer to express an opinion of my own work, we will here alone speak of its performance. The solo-parts were throughout not well distributed, for which reason the arias and *ensemble* parts produced the least effects. But the chorus and the orchestra were excellent, and therefore the overture and collective choruses produced a great sensation. The double chorus of the flying French and that of the pursuing Russians followed by the Prayer of thanks of the German peoples, and the concluding chorus with the fuge, pleased the most. I again experienced that in a spacious locality, and with a numerous orchestra and chorus, the most simple subjects when written in a worthy and noble style produce the greatest effects; that on the other hand, a richness of figures in the instrumentation, and a rapidly changing sequence of harmony are, there, by no means in their proper place. The *Te Deum* of *Gottfried Weber* which had been greatly extolled in favourable reviews of it in the public journals, did not quite fulfil my expectations. It betrays too much that, it was not the production of a moment of inspiration, but rather of cold speculation. The very commencement is a straining after effect, and as introduction to a *Te Deum*, certainly very unsuited. To what purpose the long roll of the kettle-drums that sounds like a passing peal of thunder? And then, above all, the ensuing flourish of four trumpets and sackbuts, like that with which cavalry draws up on parade?"

October, 20.

"On the second day, a miscellaneous Concert took place in the following order: A Symphony of *Mozart* (C-Major) executed with spirit and precision, its effect was ravishing! To-day I became convinced that in a spacious *locale,* and with a powerfully oppointed orchestra, the four themes of the concluding fuge, at the part where they combine to form the finale, can be right well understood by a practised ear. If, hitherto, this part appeared to me more scientific than effective, I was this day convinced of my error. 2dly a violin-Concerto (E-Minor) my own. To-day, I again became convinced, that, the masses are far more taken with the skilful and brilliant execution of the virtuoso, than by the merit of the composition. All were delighted with my play, and but few adverted as well to the composition. 3dly an Italian air with chorus, by *Paer*, sung by Herr *Strohmeyer*. This aria from an Oratorio called *"La Religione"* is written in so unecclesiastical a style, that with a change of the text it might be converted into a right good *Opera buffa*. During the time that the impersonation of Religion (who certainly might with much more propriety, sing soprano, instead of bass) executes the most common place operatic melodies, shakes and throat-tearing bounds, the chorus screams now and then *unisono*, and *fortissime*, *Santa! Santa!* between; just as a robber-band would call out to travellers the "Stand! your money or your life!" As this aria gave Herr *Strohmeyer* an opportunity to display his fine and powerful voice as well as his skill in its management, it was received with great applause. 4thly an *Adagio* and Potpourri of mine for the clarinet, played by Herr *Hermstedt*, likewise very favorably received. Yet I found, and several other musicians were of the same opinion, that, though *Hermstedt* constantly made more progress in the technics of his instrument, he did not devellope his taste in the same degree. His execution has somewhat of a mannerism that borders on caricature. 5thly a patriotic song on the melody of "God save the king" with orchestral and organ accompaniment by *Methfessel*. The public to whom the words had been distributed, joined in."

Poor *Bischoff* did not find his account in this third Frankenhausen musical festival. The reason of the deficit in the receipts was doubtless the quartering of Russian troops in the neighbourhood, which kept both the town and country residents from attending the festival. As *Bischoff* was not in a position to cover this deficit from his own means, the musicians who had assisted, agreed, upon my proposition, to defray their own expenses of the journey both ways, and to collect the necessary sum by a concert to be given on their return home. To that effect I also gave one at Gotha on the 28. October, in which *Andreas Romberg* who since two years had been director of concerts there, supported me in the most friendly manner.

Gotha, October, 29.

My intercourse with *Andreas Romberg*, the educated and reflective artiste, afforded me again many hours of rich enjoyment. But I again found that he performs his compositions in an indiscribably cold and dry manner, as though he himself did not feel the beauties they contain! He played several of his Quartetts, which I had long admired, because I had frequently heard them played by others, and have myself played them; but the soul which they so plainly bespeak, and which every violinist by whom I have heard them played till now has rightly seized, seems to have remained unknown to him, for in his execution of them, no trace of it was to be discovered! It struck me as remarkable, also, that his predeliction leaned more especially to those which seemed to me the weakest. But I was yet more astonished that he often takes his tempi, according to my feeling, false, and thereby frequently spoils their effect; for I almost invariably found the Allegro's too slow, and the Adagio's too fast.

Meiningen, October, 31.

We gave a concert here to-day, at which the Dutchess and the whole Court were present. Herr *Wassermann*, one of the cleverest of my former pupils, played my Concertante with me.

Würzburg, Nov., 10.

I made here the acquaintance of two known artistes, that of Herr *Fröhlich*, and of *Witt*. The former, Professor at the University, lectures on æsthetics and is in many respects a highly talented artist, as well as a zealous contributor to the Musical journal. As a critic he appears tolerably conscientious, but I remarked, that he also, like many other reviewers, writes opinions upon works without having the score before him. He that knows how difficult it is even with the aid of the score, to acquire a knowledge of a work from merely reading it, must be greatly astonished that these gentlemen will commit such an oversight, and merely place the separate voices side by side, and alternately cast their eyes on each. In a work of many voices, the perusal of the score is not alone sufficient, to enable a correct judgement to be pronounced; it is necessary also to have heard it, and well performed too! . . . . .

Witt is Concert-master of the formerly grand-ducal Court-orchestra, which as well as the *personnel* of the singers of the Castle-church, after the acquisition of the grand-duchy by Bavaria are still continued in pay as formerly, and have remained up till now at their full complement. It is kept in good play-practice, and accompanied me to my full satisfaction in the concert we gave on the 7. November. I experienced much pleasure also from the performance of one of *Haydn's* masses in the Castle-church, which was excellently executed under *Witt's* direction. Herr *Witt* let me hear on the piano, his oratorio. "Die vier Menschenalter" ("The four ages of man"). As he played badly, and if possible sung still worse, it would be premature in me, from what I heard and read after him of the score, to give an opinion of the effect the work would produce when performed. Yet it seemed to me somewhat common-place, and here and there, almost trivial. Nevertheless, the fuges and some other "Numbers" written in the severe style showed great skill in counterpoint.

Nürnberg, Nov., 16.

Music appears very little cultivated in the ancient Imperial city, for the orchestra here is remarkably bad. At our concert yesterday, there was it is true both a numerous audience and no want of applause of our performance, but every thing accompanied by the orchestra was totally spoiled by it.

To render my diary complete, I must here add that, in Nürnberg, young *Molique*, then about fourteen years of age introduced himself to me, and requested me to give him instruction in music during my stay in Nürnberg; this I readily assented to, for the lad already then gave evidence of very uncommon talent for his years. As *Molique*, since that time, by an assiduous study of my violin-compositions formed himself more and more upon my model in style of play, and therefore called himself *Spohr's* pupil. I have mentioned this circumstance in a supplementary manner.

Munich, Dec., 12. 1815.

Our stay here afforded us much artistic enjoyment. Already on the day after our arrival we were present at an interesting concert, the first of the twelve winter-concerts given every year by the royal orchestra upon their own account. These concerts are very numerously attended, and merit it in a high degree. The orchestra consists of the simple harmony, twelve first, twelve second-violins, eight viols, ten violincelli and six double-basses. The violins and basses are excellent, and the wind instruments, also, up to the horns. At every concert, a *whole* Symphony is performed; (which is the more praiseworthy, from its becoming unfortunately daily more rare, and that the public for that reason are losing more and more the taste for that noble kind of instrumental-music); then an overture, two vocal, and two concert pieces. As the Court-orchestra of Munich still maintains its ancient repute as one of the first in the world, my expectation was greatly on the stretch; yet was it far exceeded by the execuiton of *Beethoven's* Symphony in C-Minor, with which this first concert was opened. It is scarcely possible, that it could have been performed with more spirit, more power, and at the same time with greater delicacy, as also, throughout, with a closer observance of all the shades of forte and piano! It produced therefore a greater effect, also, than I had beleived it capable of, although I had already frequently heard it, and even under the direction of the composer himself in Vienna. Nevertheless, I found no reason to retract my former opinion respecting it. Though with many individual beauties, yet it does not constitute a classical whole. For instance, the introductory theme of the very first passage is wanting in that dignity which according to my feeling the commencement of a Symphony should of a necessity possess. Setting this aside, the short and easily comprehended theme, certainly permits of being carried out very thematically, and is combined also by the composer with the other principal ideas of the first subject in an ingenious and effective manner. The *Adagio* in *as* is in part very fine, yet the same passages and modulations repeat themselves much too frequently, and although always with richer ornamentation, become in the end wearisome. The *Scherzo*, is highly original, and of real romantic colouring, but the *Trio* with the noisy running bass is to my taste much too rough. The concluding passage with its unmeaning noise, is the least satisfactory; nevertheless the return to the *Scherzo* at this part is so happy an idea, that the composer may be envied for it. Its effect is most captivating! But what a pity that this impression is so soon obliterated by the returning noise!

In this first concert we heard also Herr *Rovelli*, a young and but recently engaged violinist, in a Concerto in C-Minor by *Lafond* which is excellent, and was executed to the satisfaction of all. This young artist, a pupil of *Kreutzer*, combines with the chief excellencies of the Parisian school that which is usually wanting with pupils, viz. feeling and peculiar taste. The chief points of excellence in that school consist in a careful study and development of the Technics of the instrument, in which, however, the real cultivation of art is very frequently neglected. This, nevertheless, is not the case with Herr *Rovelli*; for he reads well from the sheet, and knows how to accompany, as I afterwards had an opportunity of proving when playing my quartetts.

Madame *Bamberger* from Würzburg, of whose fine second-tenor voice and good school, I had there already heard spoken of in such praise, sang in the concert, but appeared nervous, which was probably the reason why she took breath so frequently, and rendered the tones so imperfectly.

In the second subscription-concert, we heard Herr *Flad*, who performed an hautboy-concerto in a very brilliant manner. He has a very fine tone, and a very tasteful execution. Herr *Legrand*, on the other hand, who played *Romberg's* violincello-concerto in E-Minor, seems to me to be already going down hill, for his play is wanting both in power of endurance, and in sure, and pure intonation. An overture from the Romeo and Juliet by *Steibelt*, does not reach beyond common-place.

In the third subscription-concert, my Symphony in E-Major was exceedingly well performed under the spirited yet circumspect direction of Herr Concertmaster *Maralt*, and made more effect here than in Frankenhausen, where I had heard it for the first time four years ago. Herr *Franzl* director of music, played his old violin-concerto in C-Major with Turkish-music. Its composition is in the namby-pamby taste of *Pleyel's* time, and will never suit the taste of the present day. His play is just as antiquated, and retains of its former excellence nothing but its vigour, but which now carries him frequently away into an indistinctness and want of purity in intonation. Although this was the case to-day, also, yet he was applauded like mad. This might have impressed a stranger with an unfavourable opinion of the taste of the people of Munich, had it not been evident, how well a small party of his personal friends knew to carry away the public by an uproarious clapping of hands, and a vigorous shouting of bravo. Though it certainly may be conceded to an artist who excelled in former times, that he should still meet with applause in later years, yet this may readily mislead him to overstep the period when he should cease to appear in public.

In the fourth subscription-concert, I played with Herr *Rovelli*, my Concertante, in satisfaction of the expectation that every foreign artist who desires to be supported in his own concerts by the royal orchestra, is in duty bound to play in one of the subscription-concerts. I never heard my Concertante to better advantage. Herr *Rovelli* had practised his part with the greatest attention and played in a masterly manner. The accompaniment was equally good. The *Adagio* with the three violincelli-obligati had a particularly fine effect.

Vogler's celebrated overture to "Castor and Pollux" did not come up with my expectations. It begins in a spirited and powerful manner it is true, but becomes lame towards the end, and the commencement itself derives its effect only from the noise of the brass instruments.

On the third of December, we played before the Queen in her private apartments, where besides herself and the King, a few only of the élite of the Court were present. Both Sovereigns appeared to take great interest in our play, for they loaded us with civilities. Besides ourselves, Madame *Dulcken*, a distinguished artiste played also, with her daughter and pupil, a *Rondeau* by *Steibelt* for two piano-forti.

On the sixth, our public concert took place in the Redouten-saloon, which the Queen also honoured with her presence, a mark of distinction, that for many years had been shewn to no foreign artists. I derived a great satisfaction from hearing my compositions again performed with so much brilliancy.

In the Museum, I found the Musical-journal, and therein a notice of the last musical-festival at Frankenhausen, which also contains an opinion upon my Cantata: "The emancipation of Germany." The writer adduced so many shallow and false objections to that work, that I was greatly inclined to reply to it, had I not come to the resolution since my paper-war with *Mosel,* never again to write an anti-criticism.

Würzburg, Dec., 26.

On our journey thither from Munich, we have given in ten days, in four different towns, four flying concerts, that we had previously made arrangements for, which were numerously attended, and returned a rich harvest; viz, on the 16. in Nuremberg, on the 18. in Erlangen, on the 22. in Bamberg, and yesterday, the first day after Christmasday, here. It was nevertheless an arduous exertion, particularly for *Dorette;* the continual packing up and unpacking, rehearsing and concert-giving! We will now give ourselves a little rest. — The day before yesterday, I let Herr Professor *Fröhlich* hear my two Vienna Quartetts, dedicated to *Romberg,* chiefly with the view that he might notice them in the musical-journal.

They went off well, and therefore did not fail to make a favourable impression upon the hearers.

Frankfurt on the Mayne, January, 14. 1816.

Our stay here was but very poor in art-enjoyments. During the whole time, not a single concert besides our own, not one musical party! While eight years ago, on our first coming here we scarcely could find time to satisfy all the invitations to musical-soireés, now, not one of the Frankfurt musical amateurs (if indeed there are any left) takes it into his head to make a single demand upon our talents.

Even the theatre offered nothing very attractive, and only one, (for us new) opera, viz, "Carlo Fioras" by *Fränzl*, was performed. — Madame *Graff* in this opera, and as the countess, in the "Marriage of Figaro" proved herself a singer of an excellent school, gifted with feeling and taste. The remaining *personnel* of vocalists is of no importance, but the orchestra excellent, and worthy of its ancient repute.

On the twelfth, we gave a concert at the Red-House. Madame *Graff* sang brilliantly the grand scena from "Faust." The orchestra accompanied with predeliction, and the greatest precision.

We passed a day rich in music at the house of *André*, in Offenbach. I found him mounted upon a new hobby, which he rode with yet greater self satisfaction than his former ones. It was called "declamation!" He is firmly convinced, and affirms it also with honest openheartedness, that with the exception of himself, no composer, from *Mozart* to *Bornhard* has understood how to declaim a song properly, and to set it to music as it ought to be. He has therefore taken compassion of that neglected art-orphan, and written a number of pattern-songs! He had heard of my new songs and urged me to sing them. But already at the second, he found a reason to return to his own. Fräulein *von Goldner* his pupil, sang them, and really in a most charming manner. It is not to be denied, that she declaims correctly, and has given a reading to several of them both new and interesting in its kind. When executed besides in so masterly a manner as they are by Fräulein *von Goldner*, the effect is certainly very great. I readily admitted this. but did not conceal from him at the same time what I thought objectionable therein: which is principally, that he has frequently sacrificed both form, rhythm, and melody to the right declamation. In order to avoid the fault of many song-composers. who restrict themselves too stringently to the rhythm of the poem, he has fallen into the opposite extreme. In order to give every syllable its proper duration and accent. he frequently changes the time in many of these songs, and thereby destroys the rhythm as well as the melody. Thus, the hearer cannot follow. and feels dissatisfied. I had further to object, that, the piano accompaniment to most of these songs is too much obligato. and distracts the attention from the song. Some sound like independant piano-fantasia's, to which the song has been adapted. The selfsatisfaction with which *André* gave us these songs to hear, was quite unbearable. For instance, he took an old song of *Schulze*: "O selig. wer liebt" sang it burlesqued to make it appear ridiculous. and then requested Fraulein *von Goldner* to execute his own on the same text. "Aha!" said every one of the company. "You shew us the shadow first, that the light may have the greater effect afterwards!" This ill treatment of an old meritorious composer annoyed me so much, that I could not refrain from saying:

"Dear *André,* you seem to forget. that it does not redound to the credit of your song. that it should require a piece of buffoonery to introduce it; that this song of *Schulze* was composed upwards of five and twenty years ago. when the notions of song-composition were very different from what they now are; that the melody. which appears antiquated to us. was new at that time. and that you in the end have made no happy selection for your purpose. since this song with all its simplicity of form and melody is nevertheless correctly declaimed, and in the repetition of the: "O selig. wer liebt" at the end of every strophe. has some depth of feeling in it.

whereas it is very problematical whether our songs will impart so much pleasure after a lapse of five and twenty years. as this song is still capable of doing when it is *well* sung."

André seemed somewhat ashamed, and from that moment evinced much more discretion. I was now desirous to gratify his wish to hear some of my Vienna Quartetts and Quintetts; but the accompaniment was so bad, that I soon relinquished it. and gave no more than the first.

After dinner, Herr *Aloys Schmitt* gave us a Fantasia upon the piano "A sea voyage with a storm". Although this trivial style of thing first introduced by *Wölffl*, was not bad, yet from so clever a virtuoso on the piano I should have expected to hear something more refined and solid.

In the evening. *André* took us to Herr *Ewald*, a great lover of music, at whose house the Offenbach Singing-academy had assembled to let him hear three compositions which they had practised with great care. It was called "Die drei Worte" (The three Words) of *Schiller*, set to music by *Aloys Schmitt*, a patriotic chorus by *André*, and "Die Bürgschaft" (The pledge) by *Schiller*, also composed by *Aloys Schmitt*, all with pianoforte accompaniment. The chorus numbered about forty eight voices, and the performance succeeded well. The only regret was. that the locality was not more spacious. The music to the "Drei Worte" pleased me very much. It evinced a great talent for that kind of lyrical composition. The poem is also right well adapted to it. The second; "Die Bürgschaft" is less so. In this, the composer distributes the persons represented as speaking. among the several solo-voices; but it sounds very strange to hear these sing what the poet relates. The chorus has its share in the text distributed in the same arbitrary manner. It is nevertheless not to be denied. that several of their *entreés* have an extraordinary effect. as for instance, where it says: "Und unendlicher Regen giesset herab". "And neverceasing rain pours down", and later. where the exhausted wanderer hears the murmering of a spring of water. The whole poem throughout is conceived and rendered with much fancy, yet the music suffers from a want of form through the frequent change of the tempi and measure. The repetition of *single* words which of themselves express no meaning is very much to be reprehended, and sometimes sounds truly comical. The four handed piano-forte-accompaniment is so rich in ornamentation, passages and modulations, that with very little modification it would not require to be rewritten for the orchestra. *André's* chorus was not distinguished by any thing remarkable. At the conclusion, Herr *Hasemann* of the Frankfurt orchestra, who as violincellist accompanied me in my Quartett in the morning much better than any of the others, astonished us with his skill on the bass-sackbut! He played variations on the well known song: "Mich fliehen alle Freuden" (All pleasures depart from me). But it makes an unpleasant impression upon a hearer of taste, when an instrument is constrained to produce what is neither natural to, nor consistant with its character.

Darmstadt, 9. Febr.

Constrained to nearly a month's stay by the illness of my good *Dorette*, I have had ample time to inform myself on the state of music here. Little satisfactory can be said of it. The Grand-Duke is certainly very fond of music, and spends considerable sums of money upon it; but this love of it is one sided, egotistical, and is limited solely to Theatrical music. He takes a pleasure for instance in enacting the Director of music, and Manager, in the Opera-rehearsals; he therefore not only directs the orchestra from a desk in the theatre, but directs also every thing upon the stage. As he considers himself incapable of error in both capacities, nor will allow either the director of the orchestra, or the stage manager to gainsay his regulations in the least, as a matter of course many mistakes occur. For, although of all Grand-Dukes he may be the best director of an opera, that does not make him *a good one!* He clearly proves this in his selection of the works which he allows to be performed in his theatre. As he has so liberally endowed the theatre that the management has no need to study the taste of the public for the sake of the receipts, they might therefore procure a Repertoire of really good and meritorious works, if he would only allow them the choice. But this he reserves to himself, and therefore not only much of what is given is of mediocrity merely, but many excellent works are wholly excluded, such as the operas of *Cherubini*, because the Grand-Duke cannot bear them. He may by chance let "Den Wasserträger," (the Watercarrier) pass, but only the first act of it. Neither do the operas of *Mozart* seem to please him any better; for when a few days ago the turn came again for "Don Juan", after nothing else had been given for thirty consecutive nights but *Poissl's* "Athalia", and that the orchestra relieved from the distressing wearisomeness with which that opera had overcome them, executed the first finale with great spirit, the Grand-Duke turning to the director of the orchestra, said: "After *Poissl's* opera there's no relishing "Don Juan!"

Considering the large salaries paid by the Grand-Duke, the *personnel* of solo-singers might be a much better one, with a few exceptions, than it really is; but it is maintained, that he only wishes for middling talents, so that they may yield more willingly to his regulations. The chorus (thirty females and thirty men) is very excellent. The orchestra is also very numerous, and comprises several very good artists among its members; but there is also a good deal of ordinary talent among them. The Grand-Duke may claim some credit for their *ensemble*, and particularly in the *pianissimo*; but as regards pure intonation, and clearness of expression, there is yet much to be desired. No orchestra in the world is so harrassed as this is; for the whole of the members without exception, must attend every blessed evening in the theatre, from 6 to 9 or 10 o'clock. Every Sunday, there is opera; on two other days in each week a play; and on the four remaining days the Grand-Duke has his opera-rehearsals. These never fail unless he is prevented by illness. Then no operas are given. A short time ago he was obliged to keep his room for several weeks with a bad leg; during this time no rehearsal dare be held, nor any opera performed. He seemed to beleive, or wished others to beleive that without him, nothing could be studied.

It is a singular sight, to see the old gentleman already grown quite crooked, seated at the desk in uniform with his star on his breast, giving the time; ordering the chorus and the "statists" to recollect this thing or the other, or calling out *piano* or *forte* to the orchestra. If he but understood all this, there would be no better director of an opera; for he has not only great zeal and perseverance, but from his station also, as Grand-Duke, the necessary authority. But his knowledge of scores extends no farther than at most to enable him to read after the violin-voice, and as he once played the violin when a young man, he continually harrasses the poor violinists with his reminiscenses, without making things any better! On the other hand, the singers may sing as false or with as little taste as they choose, or the wind-instruments may be one beat before or behind, — and he does not observe it!

It is just the same with his arrangements on the stage; but there the manager can yet come in unobserved to the rescue, while the director of the orchestra is not permitted the slighest reproval of any error that may occur. That the operas, therefore, despite the numerous rehearsals should come off badly, and invariably worse the more rehearsals that have been held, is sufficiently accounted for above, so that in the end both singers and orchestra become incapable of more attention from sheer exhaustion and disgust. This was the case with the opera "Athalie" of *Poissl*, which during our stay was rehearsed every evening when no performance took place, and in which on its representation at last, after thirty stage-rehearsals, faults still occured, both on the stage and in the orchestra. Of the music of this opera but little can be said in praise. It is too common-place, and the same kind of thing too frequently heard before. Several of the musical pieces are imitations of the most admired pieces of *Mozart* and *Cherubini*, yet without producing any other effect than recalling them to mind: so for instance, the procession of Priests, with its single strokes of the kettle-drum, is exactly like that in the "Zauberflöte (the Magic Flute) during the "fire and water ordeal." In the same manner also, the concluding Allegro of the first act, which contains striking reminiscences from the finale of "Don Juan," and so forth. The first act is besides extremely tedious, from the circumstance that so many slow tempi and prayers succeed each other so closely, so that in point of fact, the opera has neither life nor action.

The Grand-Duke, who considers the music of this opera very fine, perhaps merely, because it was written by a Baron, had the vexation to find that the public considered it very wearisome, which was even loudly expressed close to the box of the Grand-duke. This so much enraged him, that he said in a loud voice: "All those who do not comprehend this splendid opera should have the doors of the theatre closed against them!" If what people say here, is true, that he compels the servants of his Court and officers, to frequent the theatre, by deducting without any ceremony the amount of the subscription for the *entrée* to the theatre from their salaries, he might readily carry out his threat by releasing them from this soccage!

As the Grand-Duke refused to us the assistance of the orchestra for a public concert, because as he expressed in his reply to my request, he could not spare it from the theatre on any evening, we were on the point of leaving without having played in Darmstadt, when the directors of the Cassino proposed to us to appear in their *locale*, for which they offered us a sum of twenty carolins.* This offer we accepted. I played with *Dorette* a sonata, and two concert-pieces with pianoforte accompaniment; and *Dorette* concluded

---

* One Carolin = 20 s, 4 d English.

with the Fantasia in C-Minor. We met with a very sympathising audience. The violinists of the orchestra, who much desired to hear me, and Herr *Backhofen* the former instructor of my wife who would have been greatly interested in her present artistic skill, were however, not permitted to be of the auditory; for the Grand-Duke had said on the previous evening in the theatre: "Let me find nobody absent himself to-morrow evening!"

Heidelberg, February, 11.

Notwithstanding the extreme cold that set in last night, we this afternoon climbed the castle-hill, to behold once more the magnificent ruins of the castle. I was pleased to find that since the last eight years it has not been allowed to fall into further decay, and that much more care is taken to preserve the ruins in their present condition. The view over the town towards Mannheim, and into the valley of the Neckar, is even in winter, beautiful in the extreme!

Carlsruhe, February, 26.

Our stay here was made very agreable, from our meeting with old acquaintances. It afforded us also some art-enjoyments. It is true we did not hear any good orchestral-music; for the orchestra here, although latterly several distinguished artists have been engaged, is still very middling. A few good members cannot cloak the weak points of the rest. On the other hand, we heard two good female singers, Demoiselle *Bahrenfels* and Madame *Gervais*. On the 21., when we played in the private apartments of the Grand-Dutchess, the former sang an aria; and a few days before, the soprano-soli in *Romberg's* "Glocke" (the "Bell") which was right well performed by a society of dilettanti in the museum. Demoiselle *Bahrenfels* has a fine voice, good taste and great ease of execution, but overloads her singing too much with ornamentation. Madame *Gervais*, who is also a distinguished actress, I heard in *Weigl's* pretty opera: "Adrian van Ostade" in which she sang a Cavatina in a very brilliant manner. We then heard her sing in our concert on the 24. the grand scena from "Faust" with universal applause. She has also a fine voice, is of a good school, has feeling, and great execution, but embellishes also too much at the wrong place, and now and then sings out of tune ....

I frequently played my Quartetts and Quintetts; twice at Herr *von Eichthal's* and once at Messrs. *Freidorf's* and *Brandl's*. I was excellently accompanied in them by Messrs. *Fesca*, *Viala*, *Bönlein*, and *von Dusch*. *Fesca* played also a new Quintett of his composition, which had many new and beautiful points in it. In the last passage there was nevertheless something far-fetched.

Strasburg, March, 6.

I must first speak of that which strikes the eye of the traveller even before he has crossed the Rhine, — I mean the Cathedral! Far beyond Kehl we saw its colossal and yet graceful form towering high into the air. It has been so often and so well described (and poetically also in Baggesen's travels) that I shall not attempt it. But I must say, that nothing I had ever seen before, awakened in me so much the sentiment of the sublime, and the holy, as that wonderful structure! What stateliness of form, what elegance, what richness of decoration, and what imposing grandeur are here united! All that the Iconaclausts damaged during the time of the revolution has again been restored, and the new statues that have been placed in the room of those which were destroyed have more artistic merit than such of the old ones as were then spared. The building is very carefully kept in repair throughout, and 20,000 francs annually are set apart for the external repairs alone. Such care is nevertheless doubly necessary with this structure, on account of its delicacy of ornamentation, as the slightest damage would readily entail a greater and more dangerous one; for the gigantic tower has no foundation wall running round its base but is built upon piles, between which deep in the ground below flows a navigable canal. Half way up, where the structure seperates into two halves, one of which unfortunately, is finished only, every part throughout is so, aërial, so elegant, and permits the eye to see through it so completely, that here, where when one pillar is the support of the other, the least damage, if not immediately re-established, might readily entail the falling in of the whole tower.

After we had sufficiently satisfied our feeling of admiration of the bold, gigantic structure; the telegraph which extends its arms upon the roof of the Cathedral attracted our attention. At that moment the telegraph was being worked, and we were greatly amused with the ease and rapidity of its movements. As we were desirous to understand the mechanism, we ascended to it, but only reached it just as it had ceased, and we alone saw the Despatch about to be transmitted, in the curious characters still standing wet upon the paper. I was desirous to know whether these characters of which there might be about twenty four at the utmost, represented the letters of the alphabet, or separate words, or whole sentences, and I put a few questions to the telegraphist upon the subject. He, however, gave me but little information, either because he durst not, or did not know himself, which is the most probable, as the director alone is allowed to possess the key to the characters. According to him, each sign or character expresses a word. But this is very improbable, as it would be impossible to communicate with sufficient clearness with four and twenty words, even supposing the intervening missing words might be for the most part guessed at. On the other hand, that the meaning of one or more of the signs must have been known to him, was evident from the circumstance, that in order to shew us the mechanism, he gave the *signe d'attention*, by which was asked, whether in the course of the day another Despatch was to be expected, and if each telegraphist was to remain at his post. This sign was immediately taken up by the next telegraph, as we could see through the telescope affixed to the wall, and then also by the next one, although it could be seen less distinctly. After a lapse of 7 or 8 minutes the reply came back from

Paris: "Every body must remain at his post." This sign was immediately taken up also by our telegraph, and then all were again at rest. The mechanism is very simple. Three large wheels in the telegrapher's room, over which run cords of twisted copperwire set the three limbs of the telegraph in motion. Smaller wheels, affixed to the larger ones set in motion a smaller telegraph in the interior of the room, by which the mechanist sees whether the signs have been correctly made above, on the roof. A third moderately sized telegraph outside of the room, directed towards the residence of the director, serves to impart to him the signs coming from Paris. The whole contrivance is very ingenious and does credit to man's creative mind. The telegraphists have a very onerous duty. From the first dawn of day-light to night fall, they must be at their posts. The slighest negligence is immediately punished with dismissal from the service.

In Strasburg I made the acquaintance of three distinguished *artiste*s and of several passionate lovers of music. The former were: Herr *Spindler*, director of the Cathedral Orchestra, the successor of *Pleyel*, who previously held that appointment, Herr *Berg*, *pianiste* and composer, and Herr *Kuttner* also a pianiste and a singer. Of *Spindler's* Ecclesiastical-compositions a Requiem is very much praised; of his dramatic works an Opera: "The Orphan Asylum." Spindler sent the score and the libretto of this opera, which was also his property to the directors of the Vienna Court-theatre. It was not accepted and returned under the pretence, that the song-parts would not suit the operatic-personnel there. But a copy was thievishly taken of the libretto, and *Weigl* then composed music for it also. As shortly before, his "Schweizerfamilie" had been very successful, this new work soon became popular at all the theatres in Germany, while *Spindler's* composition up to the present time has only been heard in Strasburg. For this dishonest transaction he nevertheless obtained some slight satisfaction, for when *Weigl's* composition was given here last year by a German operatic-company, it pleased infinitely less than his. *Spindler* is a well educated and extremely modest artiste. Among the ardent lovers of music the Advocate *Lobstein* ranks first. He is Director of a well assorted Amateur-Concert-society; the numerous Orchestra of which consists for the most part of dilettanti, and they do not give badly such compositions, as are not too difficult and which they have sufficiently rehearsed. As in France since the Revolution a law is still enforced, which requires that every person who gives a Concert, if he publicly announces it by bills, and takes money, shall pay over one fifth of the receipts to the Directors of the Theatre of the town; Herr *Lobstein* made the proposal to me to give a Concert in the same place and on the same day as the Amateur-Concert-Society, by which means I avoided the impost. The Concert was announced privately only, but was nevertheless so well attended that above one hundred persons were unable to find further room in the by no means small saloon. This as well as the enthusiastic reception that our play met with, induced me to give a second and a public Concert after having come to an understanding with the manager of the theatre to pay over a fixed impost of eighty francs; but it was not so numerously attended as the first, probably owing to the price of admission being raised to three francs. The Orchestra was the same in both, half composed of dilettanti and half of skilled musicians; the string-instruments tolerably good, the wind-instruments for the most part bad. As the latter have a good deal to do in my compositions, they therefore got sadly mishandled. My Quartetts and Quintetts which I frequently played at private parties, were on the other hand very well accompanied. Upon these occasions Messrs. *Baxmann* (first Violincellist of the theatrical Orchestra) and *Nani* (Violinist) especially distinguished themselves. Although the Strasburghers are much behind the inhabitants of the larger towns of Germany in the cultivation of music, and know little or nothing of our newest music and its spirit, they yet appear to relish well my compositions. My stay here therefore served to make my compositions in demand, few of which only were known here, and they were now frequently written for to the music sellers.

While we were in Strasburg Messrs. *Berg* and *Kuttner* gave together a public Concert, in which both shewed themselves good pianistes, and Herr *Berg* a talented composer. He gave on Overture, a Pianoforte Concerto and variations for two Piano's. The allegro of the overture pleased me especially, an account of its natural flow and the manner in which the theme is carried out. But Herr *Berg* is not free from the complaint common to all modern composers, who are always striving after effects, and in so doing miss the carrying out of their ideas.

We went a few times to the theatre, and with the exception of the Prima Donna Madame *Dufay*, found the Opera very bad, but the Comedy and Vaudeville excellent. I became again convinced, how greatly the French excel the Germans in the two last kinds of entertainment. The company here, which is generally considered but very middling, perform nevertheless their Comedies with roundness, and life like truth, such as is seldom seen on the stage of the best theatres in Germany.

Münster, near Colmar, March. 26.

For the last fortnight nearly we are here in a small manufacturing town in the Vosges mountains, on a visit to a wealthy manufacturer *Jacques Hartmann*. Our host, who is an ardent lover of music, was informed by Herr Kapellmeister *Brandt* of Carlsruhe, that we should pass through Colmar on our journey. He had ascertained from Strasburg the day on which we should pass through; he therefore way laid us and with friendly force compelled us to follow him to his house at Münster. Arrived there at nightfall, we were welcomed by his family in the most hearty manner, and conducted immediately through the garden to a brilliantly lighted Concert-Room, which was decorated all round with the names of our great Composers, among which probably from to-day mine also has found a humble place. The Orchestra of Herr *Hart-*

mann was already in their places and received us upon our entry with a by no means ill executed Overture. The Orchestra consists of Herr *Hartmann's* family, and in part of some of the employés, musicians and workmen employed in his Cotton-manufactury. As he as much as possible engages those only who are musical, he has succeeded in getting together an almost completely appointed Orchestra, which executes in a very decent manner compositions that are not too difficult and which it has diligently practised.* Herr *Hartmann* himself is a virtuoso on the bassoon and has a fine tone and much skill. His sister and his daughter play the pianoforte. The latter a child, eight years of age is the star of this Dilettanti orchestra. She already plays very difficult compositions with wonderful facility and precision. But more than this, her fine musical ear surprised me, with which (though at a distance from the Piano) she distinguishes the intervals of the most complicated discordant accords that can be struck for her, and will name consecutively the tones of which they consist. Of this child for a certainty if properly guided will one day be made a distinguished artiste.† After the family

---

* From the leader of the Orchestra an employé in the manufactory, I than made the acquisition of a Violin by *Lupot* of Paris. I was so much struck with the full and powerful tone of this Instrument, which was then only thirty years old, that I immediately proposed an exchange for an Italian Violin, which I had purchased in Brunswick, and played upon in my first journey; the possessor of the *Lupot* willingly acceded to my desire. I soon got so fond of this Violin, that I preferred it to my hitherto Concert-Violin, an old german by *Buchstetter*, and from this time I played on it in all my travels. — — — — —

It was not till the year 1822, when my artistic tours as Violinist had ceased, that I bought of Madame *Schlick* in Gotha my present instrument, a *Stradivari*, and yielded to Concert-master *Matthaei* of Leipsic at his urgent entreaty this Violin of *Lupot*, which in the course of years had become very good and had acquired a great reputation. *Matthaei* played on it till his death, when it came into the possession of Concertmaster *Ulrich*.

† Unhappily she died young and before her full development.

had exhibited their capabilities, we let them hear one of our Duetts and found a very grateful and enthusiastic auditory.

Herr *Hartmann* does not readily permit a Musician of note to pass through Alsace without calling on him and therefore has already seen many of them under his roof; among others, *Rudolpho*, *Kreutzer*, *Durand*, *Turner*, *Bärmann* and the brothers *Schunke*. And for a certainty all must have been as satisfied with their stay in his house as we were; for a more agreable host, and one more desirous to please than Herr *Hartmann* could not readily be found. Of the two first mentioned artistes he related the following, which is sufficiently characteristic. *Kreutzer* gave a Concert at the theatre in Strasburg, which was very fully attended. After the first part, he went and took the receipts, and lost them at Roulette in the refreshment room to the last *sous*. He was now called for the second part of the Concert, and was obliged to earn wherewith to supply what he had already lost. *Durand* did still worse! Herr *Hartmann* had got up a Concert for him at Mühlhausen and accompanied him thither. *Durand* immediately forgot himself in a beerhouse, and it was a difficult matter to get him away from it to hold the rehearsal. At this he missed his bow, which he had forgotten at Colmar. He declared that he must fetch it, otherwise he would not be able to play in the evening. Herr *Hartmann* gave him his carriage and urged him to return as soon as possible. The hour of the Concert was fast approaching, but *Durand* had not yet come back. The public had assembled, the Musicians were tuning up, — but the Concert-giver was still wanting! After waiting for half an hour, as the auditory had become very restless, Herr *Hartmann* had the Overture played. But as *Durand* had not yet made his appearance, he was obliged to come forward and explain the absence of the Concert-giver. Exceedingly displeased at this, the public left the Concert-room. Late in the evening the coachman returned without the vainly expected musician, and informed his master that he had sought for him for several hours in all the Coffee-houses and taverns at Colmar but in vain, and that at length he had found him in a beerhouse where in company with other jovial guests he had totally forgotten the concert.

Three days ago, we gave a Concert in Colmar which was very fully attended, and which Herr *Hartmann* had previously solicited his there resident musical friends to make arrangements for. As the Orchestra which was almost wholly composed of dilettanti was very bad; I was compelled to renounce playing any of my own compositions and chose some of easier accompaniment by *Rode* and *Kreutzer*. After the Sonata which I played with my wife, a crown of laurel was thrown to us from a box to which was attached the following poem:

> Couple savant dans l'art heureux
> Qui fit placer au rang des Dieux
> L'antique Chantre de la Grèce.
> D'un instrument melodieux,
> Et de la harpe enchanteresse
> Quand les accords delicieux.
> Nous causent une double ivresse,
> Faut-il, que les tristes apprêts
> D'un depart qui nous désespère,
> Mêlent d'inutiles regrets
> Aux charmes que votre Art opère!
> Ah! près de nous il faut rester!
> Quelle raison pour s'en défendre?
> A nos voeux, si *Spohr* veut se rendre,
> Il pourra, j'ose l'attester,
> Se lasser de nous enchanter,
> Jamais nous lasser de l'entendre.
> Par E. C. (outerèt), habitant de Colmar.

In the second part of the Concert Herr *Hartmann* played also some variations for the bassoon by *Brandt*. He seemed very nervous, but played nevertheless right well. The receipts were very considerable for so small a town. The day after the Concert we dined at General *Frimont's*, Commander of the Austrian troops in Alsace. We found our host an extremely amiable and jovial man. By his love of justice, his strict discipline and agreable manners, he has acquired in a high degree the esteem of the inhabitants of Colmar. — In the evening we returned here.

Yesterday I received information from the Director of music *Tollmann*, in Basel, to whom Herr *Hartmann* had previously announced our arrival, that he had made arrangements for a Concert for us on next Sunday the 31. We must therefore take leave of our kind host and his family. But we have been obliged to promise to come once again if possible during the summer.

Herr *Hartmann* conducted us several times over the Cotton factory. It is very extensive and produces goods which in respect of taste in the designs greatly excel the English. It gives employment to upwards of one thousand persons, and among these to artists of great talent as Draughtsmen and Engravers on copper. Cotton prints of all kinds are made, common ones by hand-press, the finer sorts by Roll-press, with furniture prints as well as carpets ornamented with large and small designs. The latter are chiefly made for the East Indian and China markets. On the copper-plates for these kinds, artists often work for several years together. The designs are for the most part copies of celebrated pictures. The mechanism by which the copper-plates are printed off upon stuffs is a secret in the possesion of the *Hartmann*-manufactory, which is not shewn to strangers. We were made an exception to the rule. An ingenious machine for rubbing colours was also invented here, and is as yet the only one of the kind. Alsace which is so rich in manufactories, is very discontented with the new government, which does nothing for the encouragement of industry as did the exiled Emperor, to whom the people are devotedly attached. This may be readily imagined when we consider, that in the palmy days of the Empire, the manufactories in this part were in an extremely flourishing condition, which arose in a great measure from the exclusion of English manufactures from the Continent by the celebrated Berlin decrees. But now again when the whole of Europe is inundated with English goods, the facto-ries here are obliged to restrict their labours considerably. People express here without reserve their discontent with the present government, and say quite openly, that the favourable opportunity is only waited for to shake off the present yoke once more. It is true, also, that many things that tended greatly to the public good, such as canal and road making, the distribution of prizes for encouragement of Industry, Art-institutions etc. such for example as the Conservatory of Music in Paris, have been in part suppressed or greatly limited, as hateful reminiscences of the Revolution and of the Empire. All this had made much bad blood, and rendered the new Government extremely hated. People will therefore be by no means displeased, should the report be verified, that Alsace is to be ceded to Austria.

Basel, April, 2.

Herr *Tollmann*, a good Violinist and Director and at the same time the most obliging man and most willing to render a service I ever met, had already with the assistance of the Union-society of Music here, prepared every thing for our concert. Nothing remained to be done but to obtain the permission of the Head Burgomaster to raise the price of admission to half a laub-thaler. This was immediately granted. Herr *Tollmann* introduced me to the Directors of the society, whom I found both agreable and well bred people. They completely disproved in their persons the report which prevails in Alsace, that the Baseler is cold and uncourteous, and usually cuts short the visits of strangers at the street door. I was received with politeness by all whom I visited, and even with distinction. As the Orchestra, with the exception of four or five artistes was composed of Dilettanti merely, the accompaniment of my Solo-pieces, particularly by the wind-instruments was fearful. How poor *Tollmann* is to be pitied, to be obliged to hear such music all the year round! And yet, he says, the Orchestras in the other towns of Switzerland are still worse. If that is the case, then indeed Music is in a more pitiable condition in Switzerland than in Alsace. The good folks here are enraptured still with compositions such as in Germany even in *Pleyel's* time were considered intolerable. *Mozart, Haydn* and *Beethoven* are scarcely known by name to the majority. But they are fond of music, and the best of all is, they are easily pleased; for badly executed as all the orchestral passages were in our Concert the people were nevertheless content, and considered that on this occasion the Orchestra had particularly distinguished itself. Even a Bravoura air which was awfully tortured by a Dilettant, they found delicious. The expenses being slight, the receipts were somewhat considerable.

Zürich, April, 10.

On the road from Basel to this place, like all other travellers coming from Germany, we had ample proof that though one travels with more comfort in Switzerland, yet is as expensive again as there. At every inn here, even in the smallest villages, one finds a complete and well dressed dinner or supper, but the price all through Switzerland is half a Laubthaler a head. All other necessaries are equally good, but also very dear. The expense of travelling is almost still worse. With the exception of the short distance from Basel to Zurich, there is no extra-post in all Switzerland, and one is therefore obliged to travel either by the Diligence or with hired horses. Both are very dear. The price for a pair of hired horses per day is three laub-thaler, and their days for return are also charged for.

There is here also an "Union-society of Music." These societies in the Swiss towns are a great boon to the travelling artiste, for they very willingly undertake all the arrangements for his concert. Ours took place already on the fourth day after our arrival. We had nothing more to do but to play. The accompaniment certainly was again very bad, and I suffered the more from it, by allowing myself to be persuaded to select a Concert of my own compositions. At the rehearsal, by dint of innumerable repetitions of the most difficult parts, I at length succeeded in making them sound like music; but in the evening the orchestra got so frightened that it upset every thing again! Fortunately, the auditory did not appear to notice anything of it, for they evinced the greatest satisfaction with every thing they heard.

The receipts were yet greater than at Basel. There are two artistes living here who are also known in Germany. One of them, Herr *Nägeli,* is the proprietor of a music-shop, and the composer of the song sung throughout Germany: "Freut euch des Lebens" (Life let us cherish) he has also since made a name for himself by his Singing Instructions on the *Pestalozzian* system. He may have great merit as a Theorist and musical Composer but in the pratical part of the science of music and in the development of taste, he does not appear to have effected much; for of three of his pupils whom he introduced to us as his best, one sang an Aria, and the other two executed a Duett in our Concert, with a bad method, and without taste.

The other artiste is Herr *Liste,* who is considered here a first rate pianiste and Instructor, he is known by some compositions for the piano. He shewed me some Glees and Quartetts for male voices, which pleased me much for their melody, harmony and induction of the voices.

Zurich is most charmingly situated. From our room, at the Inn "zum Raben" (The Raven) we have a view over great part of the lake. The arrival and departure of boats and other craft give great life to this part of the town.

Bern, April 20.

With most beautiful weather we had an extremely pleasant journey thither. From the summit of a high hill about a league from here, we saw for the first time since we entered Switzerland the whole magnificient chain of the Alps quite distinctly, and in all its grandeur. We hailed the sight with joy! How we long to approach yet nearer to those mountains!

The musical society of Bern undertook also with zeal the preparations for our Concert, and relieved me of all trouble in the matter. The attendance here likewise, was more numerous than had ever before been known at the Concert of a foreign artist. The receipts however, on account of the here customary low price of admission, were not so great as at Zurich. The Orchestra here is if possible still worse than in Basel and Zurich, and the public with the exception of very few yet more uncultivated. At the head of the Orchestra is a brother of *Carl Maria von Weber*, who, as I am told, is a good theorist. As a Violinist and Director he is very weak. Among the dilettanti and members of the Society of music Professors *Meissner* and *Jahn*, and the Burgomaster *Hermann* are particularly distinguished for their cultivated taste for the science of music. The former is Director of the society, and a very good violinist.

As the season is already too far advanced, to give further Concerts in the other towns of Switzerland, we intend giving up our journey there for the present, and at once set ourselves down to rest in some beautiful part of the Bernese Oberland, of which *Dorette* has such urgent need for the full re-establishment of her health. Our acquaintances here recommend to us a village in the neigbourhood of Thun. Yesterday, accompanied by *Edward** we drove out there, and found every thing so much in accordance with our wishes, that we resolved to remove thither on the next day. The name of the village is Thierachern, and it lies in one of the most beautiful spots that we had yet beheld. At the Inn we hired two rooms, for which together with a coach house for our carriage, and breakfast and dinner daily, we agreed to pay the host two Carolines per week. We are all longing to settle in this paradise, and looking forward to the enjoyment of its rural repose. I think especially to avail myself of it to write some

---

* *Edward Henke*, previously adverted to, my mother's youngest brother, then Professor at the University of Bern; and afterwards of Halle.

new Violin compositions, with very simple and easy accompaniments for Italy, as from all accounts the Orchestras there are worse than those of the provincial towns in France. *Edward* has promised to visit us frequently, and then join us in excursions into the beautiful environs.

Bern, the handsomest of all the towns of Switzerland that we had yet seen, is situated upon an eminence of moderate height in the centre of a somewhat long and narrow valley. The Aar, a rapid, clear mountain stream, flows round three sides of it. The mountains which surround it are not so high as to impede the view of the Alps from the town. From the Platform in particular, a spacious quadrangular bulwark near the principal church, planted with chesnut trees and furnished with benches, the view is extensive, and charmingly beautiful. On leaning over the wall which surrounds this platform on the south side, the foaming Aar is seen deep below rushing between the rocks, above this in the middleground, smiling meadows, hills covered with woods, and villages thickly surrounded with fruit trees, and in the back ground the majestic Alpine chain with its summits covered with eternal snow! The Bernese are not a little proud of this spot; and the first question they put to a stranger is usually: "Have you been on the platform?"

The houses of the town are all of them massively built, and have open Arcades running the length of the street, under which one is able to traverse the whole town dry footed in wet weather. Under these Arcades are the warehouses and shops of the merchants and trades-people.

Thierachern, April, 26.

We have been here three days in our beautiful little village, and are inhaling in full draughts the breath of the first spring days in this indiscribably charming place. We have no thought of work as yet, for early every morning we feel impelled to hasten out into the fresh air. We have already wandered a full mile in different directions round our little village, and always discovered new beauties. The situation of our dwelling is beautiful beyond conception; it stands upon a hill from which one has a view of the country on every side. Our rooms open upon along balcony which extends the whole breadth of the house, and is covered in by the eaves of the main roof. These open galleries, which almost all the houses have, are called „Lauben". * From this laube, where in the hitherto fine weather we breakfast every morning, we have a most extensive view over wood and meadow, as far as Thun, and its ancient castle; then upon the right across the lake as far as the chain of the Alps, with the white peaks of the Jungfrau, the Eiger, and Schreckhorn. Still farther again to the right, the eye rests upon green copse-covered hills, and villages embosomed amid orchards, and beyond these upon the fearful rocky ridges of the Riesen, as far as the Stockhorn. Almost every day these mountains present aspects different from those of the previous one. Sometimes the foremost mountains are covered with dense masses of clouds, and the hinder ones appear majestically above them at an altitude, such as one can scarce believe possible for any thing firm to exist; at others the farmost mountains stand out clear and distinct; and the highest peaks alone are shrouded in clouds. But in the evening, shortly after sun set, the sight of these snow covered mountains is quite entrancing to behold. When the valley is wholly wrapped in gloom, and the lights from Thun are seen reflected upon the lake, the mountain peaks are still resplendent with the most beautiful rosy light, which when the darkness encreases changes into as beautiful a blue. It is a spectacle from which it is difficult to tear one's self away!

May, 16.

We have now begun to divide our time between pleasure and work. In the forenoon, while I compose, *Dorette* gives the children instruction in arithmetic, writing, geography etc.:

* From *Laube,* an arbour, bower.

in the afternoon I teach them the Piano and singing. Then away we sally out into the free air. If the weather permits an extended excursion, we take our frugal evening repast in some "Küher's" (so the shepherds are called here) and do not return till late in the evening. Should the weather be uncertain, we go provided with umbrellas, at least as far as Thun, to enquire after letters from home; procure some amusement for rainy days from the lending library, and purchase our little necessaries. The daily exercise in the beautiful pure balmy air strengthens our bodies, enlivens our spirits and makes us joyous and happy. In such a disposition of mind, one works easily and quickly, and several compositions lie already completed before me, namely a Violin Concerto in the shape of a Vocal-scena and a Duett for two violins.

I must not forget to mention a musical Natural-curiosity which we remarked in our walks. There is a Cuckoo here which does not sing its name like ours in a terza, but adds another "koo" between, and which may be expressed as follows:

Whether this is a different kind from ours, I have not been able to ascertain, but, that every year in this part, such Cuckookoos are heard.

Something also, I have here remarked, which has still more interested me as a musician. The serving boy belonging to our house and some maidens of the neighbourhood who hold their Singing-Academy before our window every Sunday evening, intonate in their songs just like the notes from a tin instrument when unassisted by the stopping of the finger, i, e, the Terza somewhat too high, the Quarta still higher and the little Septime considerably too low. From this it is evident, that this intonation is natural to the human ear, if it is not accustomed from early youth to the attemperated system of tones. These nature-singers would sound as false to our tone-scale, as we to theirs. But it is nevertheless specially remarkable, and *almost disquieting*, that in order to attain our present richness of harmony, we have been obliged to deviate from the Tone-scale given to us by nature. For without our attemperated Tone-system we should be confined to the nearest tones, and obliged to renounce the enharmonical changes which are the *haut goût* of modern harmony. And yet by this deviation from nature, it seems to me that music is alone elevated to a real Science, while all other arts, must be content to copy Nature, and even when they would idealise, still imitate nature in all individualities. The songs of these Nature-singers have a great deal of originality, and when I have learned to understand better the dialect of these parts, which has much resemblance to the Allemanic, I will endeavour to note down some of them.

June, 4.

Yesterday we returned from the first more distant excursion which the fine weather tempted us to undertake, and enjoyed ourselves exceedingly. We went to Kandersteg, a small village high up in the mountains, distant from here between seven or eight leagues. I had hired for this purpose our host's one horse "Rietwägeli" and drove myself. The map was again our guide. Our road lay at first along the right bank of the lake of Thun as far as Spiez. Behind Gwatt we crossed the Kander over a wooden bridge, which in a single arch of most ingenious construction spans high and boldly the broad and rushing stream. About a hundred years ago the course of the Kander was turned into the lake, by which means the beautiful valley from Glutsch to Thierachern which lay waste and uncultivated every spring owing to the inundations, was converted into fine meadows and fruitful fields. But this must have been a giant-labour, for it was found necessary to pierce a high mountain for the purpose. From the centre of the bridge one looks down from a dizzy height upon the foaming Kander in its passage over the rocks, and at the same time upon the lowering banks on either side. From Spiez the road turns to the right round the majestic Riesen, and leads through a fruitful and highly cultivated valley to Frutigen, a cheerful little place. Here a second valley opens, out of which the Kander issues. In this gloomy, fearful rocky vale, which is frequently scarce broad enough for the bed of the river and the road, the ascent now begins. On both sides, rocks of stupendous height, and which in many places hang so much over the road as to make it quite dark, and fearful to behold. Added to that, the roar of the onward rolling Kander over its rocky bed, and the numerous waterfalls which on both sides of the glen precipitate themselves frequently from a height of more than a hundred feet. As we by degrees ascended higher with every step, we receded as it were more and more back into the season of Spring. The cherry trees, which at Thierachern had already bloomed a month ago, were here only in their first bloom. But higher, all fruit trees ceased, and after we had crossed the last steep mountain of the Kandersteg we saw nothing but a few thinly scattered fir trees. The village, consisting of small wooden huts, unsurrounded by gardens and trees, lying wide apart from each other between masses of rock, presents a cheerless aspect. The snow which lies here for nine weary months, was scarcely melted, and the meadows upon which lean looking cattle sought a scanty fodder, still wore the sickly yellow hue of the winter season. Upon all the lofty peaks which tower on either side of the valley of Kandersteg, lay still a deep mantle of snow, from which innumerable small rivulets had their rise, and leaped foaming down. From this part, the road still ascends for three leagues more to Gemmi, and then descends precipitously to the Leuker Baths, whose hot springs are greatly frequented in the autumn. As the made road ceases at Kandersteg, the visitors to the Baths, who are bad pedestrians, are obliged to be carried on there by bearers, or upon mules, and with this arduous occupation the majority of the inhabitants of the little village eke out a scanty subsistance.

We slept at Kandersteg, and returned on the following day. It was an agreable feeling to return by degrees as it were from winter once more into the spring and summer.

July, 1.

A few days ago I sent five new works to Herr *Peters* at Leipsic to be engraved. They were two collections of Songs, three Duetts for two Violins, the seventh Violin Concerto and a grand Polonaise for Violin and Orchestra, work 37—41. The Duetts and one of the Songs are new; the other Songs which I wrote the previous summer at Carolath, I have partly rewritten and newly instrumentated the Polonaise.

After mature consideration we have resolved to make the journey to Italy without our carriage, as one travels there more economically and safely by Vetturino. The chief reason for this decision was the fear that the renewed exertion upon the instrument which so much affects the nerves might again shake the health of my good *Dorette*, and embitter both for her and us the long anticipated enjoyment of the deligthful journey. As therefore we were going to leave the harp and a part of our luggage behind with our host, until our return, we should not require the carriage, and save at the same time the long circuitous route by the highroad to the lake of Geneva, and through the whole length of the valley of the Valais. That *Dorette* however, as artiste, should not wholly sink into inactivity, I shall write several things in part anew, for Violin and Pianoforte, and re-arrange some from former things, which we can then play both in private circles and in public in Italy, where it is even said there is great difficulty in meeting with a good Quartett accompaniment. In the way of preparation for our next winter journey, I may also mention an improvement I have made upon my newly acquired violin. By a variety of experiments with voice and bridge, I have at length so far succeeded as to make it speak as softly with the Quinte which was hitherto hard and brittle, as with the other strings. The change in the instrument has not been without effect on the style of the new Violin-compositions, as also upon my method of execution! So certain it is, that, the instrument exercises an influence upon the method of the player in the same manner as does the voice upon that of the the singer. As one endeavours to conceal the weak points of the instrument, and to bring out its good qualities, one plays more especially what the instruments renders with the most ease, and in this manner the whole method of play becomes by degrees subordinate and appropriate to the peculiarity of the instrument. One may therefore not only recognise the peculiarities of a Virtuoso by his compositions, but those also of his instrument.

August, 1.

We have again made some farther excursions in the neighbourhood. First of all, a fortnight ago we went to Bern, to repay the solicited visit to Professor *Jahn,* who accompained by his wife and *Edward* had several times visited us. We passed a most delightful day with our Bernese friends. For the last month we had been in hopes of settled weather, in order to make an excursion on the lake; but with the wet-cold weather of this summer we have as yet not had three wholly bright days in succession. At length it appeared as though it would be finer! The mountains, which for a long time we had not seen wholly unshrouded, stood out on Friday evening in all their majestic distinctness. On Saturday the horizon remained quite clear. As the height of the barometer now also indicated settled fair weather, we resolved to set out on our journey early the following morning. On our awaking, a bright clear sky filled us with the most agreable expectations, and we got into our Rietwägeli amid the joyous exclamations of the children. At Thun I hired an extra-boat which carried us over the whole length of the lake. This voyage in the beautiful calm Sabbath morning gave us the most inexpressible delight. The sail so over the green, clear bosom of the lake, and along its banks clothed in the richest verdure, the majestic chain of the Alps in the back ground, whose snow covered peaks mirrored themselves in trembling outlines in the fathomless depth of the lake, the solemn tolling of the bells calling to Divine worship, every thing was entrancing, and inspired as with a sense of the purest joy. At Neuhaus, where we landed after a three hour's sail, we were pounced upon immediately by one of the drivers of the carriages plying there for hire. We permitted him drive us to Lauterbrunn. The road leads through the little, poverty stricken town of Untersee, round the base of a projecting mountain into a deep valley, resembling that from Frutigen to Kandersteg, but not quite so wild and barren. Almost at the extremity of this valley, after it has gradually become somewhat higher, lies Lauterbrunn. As soon as we had turned the base of the last projecting wall of rock, the Staubach lay before us in all its grandeur. The water precipitates itself down from an immense height upon a perpendicular wall of rock, and scatters itself so completely into a vapoury spray, that one would almost imagine it a cloud of the finest dust rather than water. Every thing around this wonder of nature is worthy of it. In the back ground of the valley, barriers of rock, over which also, leap numerous small streams of water; above them a glacier of a greenish hue, and near that, stretching far away, the Wengern Alps, above which the Jungfrau towering majestically over all. Upon our arrival, we were so fortunate as to be still enabled to behold the whole grandeur of this sublime scene under favour of the most beautiful weather. But shortly afterwards, to our regret, the sky became obscured, and while we were taking dinner at the inn, hail and rain poured down in torrents. Towards evening it again cleared up a little. We hastened therefore to take a walk through the village in the direction of the waterfall, but found that our previous point of view from the side, was far more favorable than close in front of it. We were exceedingly annoyed by the pertinaceous solicitations of beggars on every kind of plea. One offered small pieces of quartz or minerals, and another cristals for sale. Two grown up maidens had posted themselves on the road and howled a Duett, for which they expected to be remunerated. We were however soon driven back into the inn by the recommencing rain, from the windows of which we enjoyed a third view of the waterfall from another aspect.

August, 12.

We are just returned from Freiburg, where we went to hear the Swiss Musical festival. Herr *Nägeli*, the President of the Swiss Society of Music, had in Zurich previously invited me to it, and offered me its direction, which I willingly accepted. But he had not then bethought him that the statutes of the Society expressly forbid that a foreign and non-member of the Union should direct the concerts. We received therefore from the Director of the Society (who here in Switzerland is not the same who directs the music, but he who conducts the correspondance, provides the locale, superintends the erection of the orchestral platform and the printing of the tickets of admission) a friendly invitation it is true, to be present at the Festival, but not a word was said about the direction of the orchestra. Instead of that, he begged me to assist with the violin. But as I had always replied both by word of mouth and writing in the affirmative, whenever questioned whether I would direct the Musical Festival this year, and that this had been more widely circulated, I could not now well undertake a subordinate *rôle* at the Festival. I therefore excused myself from assisting at it, but wrote to say that we would attend the Festival as hearers. On the 6th, with clear favourable weather we drove to Freiburg in our Rietwägeli. Upon our arrival, although I had declined to assist at the Festival, we were lodged in a private house just the same as the members of the society, and found there tickets for admission to all the rehearsals and performances as also to a dress ball, with text books of the "Schöpfung" (Creation) in French and German, and for myself also an invitation to the sittings of the Society .... As the weather was very fine, we resolved upon a walk with the children to the celebrated Hermitage, three miles distant from Freiburg, situated in a narrow wild rocky valley on the banks of the Saane. This was the habitation of a pious Recluse who many years ago had hewn it in the sandstone rock in this secluded part of the country. It now consists, after having been enlarged by his son and successor, of a Chapel with a bell tower 86 feet in height, hewn out of the rock, five or six rooms, a kitchen with a chimney of the same height as the tower, and several passages of intercommunication. The whole of this space, the architectural proportions of which are very pleasing, is gained by boring and excavating the gigantic perpendicular rock, and has no where not even in the window spaces any supports of masonry. One is filled with wonder not only at the immense patience and perseverance of the two architects, but with admiration also at their skill and sentiment for beauty of proportion.

The chapel is still very prettily decorated, and the bells in the tower are still sometimes rung to summon the pious of the neighbourhood to mass. The remaining apartments were taken possession of by a peasant-family after the death of the last Recluse and therein they possess a commodious and healthy dwelling at all seasons of the year.

We dined at an inn in the immediate neighbourhood and returned to Freiburg in the evening. There we were informed, that during our absence a deputation of the Musical Society had called at our house, to announce to me, that on the following morning at their second sitting, I was to be nominated honorary member. At the same time, the gentlemen had again begged that I would lead with the violin. I was very glad that my absence had exonerated me of the unpleasant obligation to give a refusal. In order not to be taken by storm, I slipped secretly into the Church and concealed behind a pillar, listened to the rehearsal. It went very badly, and I was therefore very pleased that I was not of the party. After the first part was over, I was obliged to retire in order not to be seen.

When I appeared the next morning at the sitting, I was received with applause. The President announced to me, that the members present had unanimously elected me honorary member of the Society, adding thereto many things very flattering to me, and made honourable allusion to our musical Festival at Frankenhausen. I returned thanks to him and the Society in a few words, and then seated myself in the place assigned to me. They were then engaged in the choice of a President and of the other Officials for the next year, and after some debates nominated Zurich as the place of meeting for the next assembly.

At three o'clock in the afternoon the performance of the "Creation" took place. The locale was exceedingly favourable for music, and the orchestra very well placed, but unfortunately, on the opposite side to the Organ, so that of this no use could be made. The assistant *personnel,* which on former occasions was at least estimated at three hundred and fifty persons, amounted this time scarcely to two hundred, and as the larger half formed the chorus, the orchestra was relatively to the strength of the chorus much too weak, so that it was frequently not heard at all. As it was also very bad besides, the Chaos, and the accompanied Recitative in particular, went awfully bad. The Violinists intonated unbearably false, and the wind instrumentalists, particularly the Hornists, and trumpets, brought out tones sometimes which excited general laughter. *Tollmann* directed with firmness and foresight, but unhappily took several *tempi* totally false, almost all the airs too slow and the chorus too fast. His greatest mistake was in the chorus after the Chaos: "Und der Geist Gottes etc." (And the spirit of the Lord etc.) which he gave just like an *Allegro*. The chorus had been well practised and sang powerfully and purely. It consisted chiefly of German singers. Among the Solo-singers there were however two from French Switzerland who sang in their mother tongue which sounded droll enough, particularly in the Duett between Adam and Eve in which the latter replied in French to the tender breathings of her German Adam. To the auditors at Freiburg this appeared however in no wise strange, as their town forms, the frontier boundary of both languages, and on one side of the Saane they preach in French, on the other in German. Hence all the inhabitants understand and speak both languages. — The part of Eve was sung by Madame *Segni* from Lausanne, who has a very fine voice, but unhappily also for a German ear, an unbearable style of execution. Among the German singers were also good voices. The assembled public applauded the music in a very lukewarm manner, and there was not a spark of the enthusiasm that inspired us so much in Frankenhausen.

On the 9th, the reheasal for the Concert took place. As it had been previously the intention to give it in a smaller saloon, but it was found insufficient for the accomodation of the audience present, there was a want of written voices for the whole of the orchestra. It was therefore much less numerously appointed than the day before, and its want of purety, and stupidity were still more obvious to the ear. But how could it be otherwise with an Orchestra composed wholly of dilettanti and particularly of *Swiss dilettanti?* The easiest passages were obliged to be repeated from six to eight times before they went even tolerably. I was astonished all along with the indefatigable patience of the worthy *Tollmann*, but who nevertheless, it must be confessed, was born with every qualification for the Director of an Orchestra of Swiss dilettanti. — At three o'clock this remarkable concert began at once in an ear-rending manner with the Overture to *Gluck's* "Iphigenia." The trumpets were pitched a quarter of a tone too high, and notwithstanding the weakness of the orchestra were blown with the utmost strength of lungs. Had the Overture only lasted a little longer the greater part of the auditory would now already have run out of the church. Then followed a long succession of dilettanti, partly Singers, partly Instrumentalists with their Solo-pieces. Some of them were very good, for instance a gentleman from Iverdun distinguished himself by the ease and good taste with which he executed a Harp-concerto by *Bochsa*. Madame *Segni* also, the „Eve" of the day before, sang this time in Italian and right well. A gentleman, whose name is as little known to me as those of the other performers, for no programme was distributed, played variations upon a clarinet, in tone and form similar to the Basset-horn, with much skill and beauty of tone. In the second part of the Concert, which we did not stop to hear, for we were now satiated to nausea, we were informed that a Clergyman of Lucern and the worthy *Tollmann* executed a Violin-Rondo in a very effective manner. We regretted that we were not aware that the latter was going to play, otherwise we would have remained to the end. Such were the productions of the Swiss Society of Music so highly spoken of in Germany. Director *Conradin Kreutzer* of Stuttgard and his wife, a native of Zürich, whose acquaintance we made here, sat near us during the performances, and we were pleased to be enabled to interchange our opinions upon what we heard. But we were obliged to keep a constant guard upon our looks and gestures, fore we were continually watched by those sitting round us, who sought to read in our faces the impression their music made upon us. When we were asked also for our opinion, which was not unfrequently, and always with a sentiment of national pride, we carefully kept in the mean between truth and flattery, and by that means successfully extricated ourselves without giving offence.

Kreutzer told me in confidence that, he would not return to Stuttgard because the despotism there had become thoroughly insufferable.* My former Viennese acquaintance *Romberg* and *Kraft* were just in the same position; they also longed to get away and made application for other appointments. — We passed the greater part of the time while at Freiburg in the society of *Kreutzer* and his wife. We dined and supped

* *Mozart* has recorded his hatred of the "insolent Aristocracies of Germany" towards whom *Haydn* demeaned himself with more courtly subserviency than became the great Master of Sound.

together, and during the continous fine weather made frequent promenades into the charming surrounding country. It is true the Society had a place of meeting at the "Schützenhouse", where most of the members dined; but as women were not admitted, because there were several unmarried Clergymen in the society, we did not pay a single visit to that place. But I heard that there was a total absence of that sociability and cheerfulness which gave such a zest to our meals at Frankenhausen. — The ball which took place in the same locality, had neither any attraction for us, as none of us danced. We sat therefore meanwhile, in confidential discourse at the tea-table, and amused ourselves with the relation of past incidents of our lives and experience. *Kreutzer* in reality had come with the sole view to give a concert upon his own account at the conclusion of the musical festival, as he had been told in Zurich that this year the Society would only give one performance. He seemed to think that I had the same intention, for he proposed that we should make common cause and give one together. But I had never thought of giving a concert here, and had not even brought my violin. His concert however never took place, for the Society gave a second, and thus we had no opportunity of hearing the play and compositions of this famous artist.

On the 10. early in the morning we left Freiburg, spent the afternoon and evening very pleasantly in Bern in the society of *Edward* and *Jahn*, and returned here at 11 in the forenoon.

Journey to Milan.

In *Edward's* company, who was desirous to avail himself of his vacation to make a little excursion into North-Italy, we set out upon our journey on Sunday the 2ᵈ September. At one o'clock we arrived at Kandersteg, where I immediatly hired four horses with as many guides, to carry us over the Gemmi. On three of them, rode *Dorette*, *Emilie* and *Ida*, the fourth carried our luggage. *Edward* and I preferred to do it on foot. Three quarters of a league on this side of Kandersteg, the ascent begins and continues tolerably steep for a good $2\frac{1}{2}$ leagues. The road then leads round the Gemmihorn for some distance upon a level, till at a distance of $3/4$ of a league from Schwaribach it ascends again. — The weather had up till now been very favorable; but here a hail storm over took us which soon changed to rain and wetted us completely through. As it was already tolerably late besides, and we had still the greatest and most difficult part of the way before us, the guides easily persuaded us to put up for the night in Schwaribach. The inn here is a mere rude blockhouse, and has nothing in common with the hotels in the Swiss vallies, that one should be made to pay here equally their exorbitant overcharges. But as one of the two habitable rooms was wholly given up to us, and that besides a bundle of clean straw for us men, we found there a large bed for *Dorette* and the children, we passed the night nevertheless in tolerable comfort. We could certainly not help feeling a shudder of horror when we called to mind previous to going to sleep, that the midnight murder in *Werner's* "Twenty fourth of February" was enacted here.*

During the night, snow had fallen, and it was bitter cold upon our setting out next morning. I therefore sent back three of the horses, and let *Dorette* and the children walk also, more especially as the descent to the Leuker Bad cannot be made on horseback. At Schwaribach all vegetation ceases, and even the beautiful Alpine rose is not to be found. The road has again a very steep ascent as far as the Daubensee (then half covered with ice) along which it runs for the disstance of half a league through a barren valley, in which

* At this inn in 1807, two Italians murdered the daughter of the Innkeeper, and this circumstance suggested to *Zach. Werner* the Tragedy adverted to.

seemed to reign the stillness of the grave; to the last ascent, which as it leads through snow and icefields was the most toilsome ascent of all. Arrived at the top, to our disappointment we were favoured with one look alone into the abyss opening beneath us; for in a few minutes we were envelloped in a mist, which scarcely permitted us to see a few paces before us. We were now compelled to follow blindly the packhorse and its guide, and to keep quite close together. The road led precipitously down between fissures in the rocks and sometimes even between perpendicular walls of rock in which a small path had been cleared by blasting. At the part where it runs, the horse's neck projects over the abyss, and the guide is obliged to hold him up by a rope secured to the load on his back, or even by holding on to his tail with all his might. At this place the view down into the depth which had been concealed from us by the thick fog, makes the head so giddy, that many invalids who wish to go to the Leuker Bad have not the courage to make the descent, and prefer, after having had the object of their journey under their very eyes, to take the immensely circuitous route of nearly twenty leagues by way of Bern, Freiburg, Lausanne and through the Valais.

After we had continued descending for more than an hour without finding any other vegetation than here and there a violet blooming in the clefts of the rocks, we came suddenly to a region where the mist ceased, and we were now favoured with a most unexpected and charming view far away down upon the Leuker Bad beneath us. At this place we rested ourselves for a moment, to recover a little from the highly fatiguing exertions of the steep descent. But it required many such resting places before we reached the bath, at 11 o'clock. The children only, were not fatigued, and were always in advance of us.

While we refreshed ourselves in the large and well appointed inn, I sent for fresh horses, and at 2 o'clock in the afternoon, animated with new spirits we continued our journey, *Edward* and I on foot, *Dorette* and the children on horseback.

Previous to leaving, we inspected the sulphur-spring which rises out of the earth at boiling heat, in front of the inn.

At Leuk it was not possible to procure any vehicle for the farther journey. We were therefore obliged to pass the night in the miserable inn to which our guides brought us. On Friday the 4th, at an early hour in the morning, we continued our journey to Brieg in two one- horse vehicles, and arrived there at noon. The valley of the Valais is very narrow and little cultivated. We saw numerous marshy meadows, and but few maize and potatoe fields. At Brieg commences *Napoleon's* famed Simplon-road, a gigantic work, which cannot be enough admired. We here hired a two-horse vehicle to take us to Domo d'Ossola. The road is so ingeniously carried in and out of the mountain ravines, that it never rises more than five inches in six feet, so that heavy loaded waggons can descend without using the drag-shoe. Especially remarkable are several colossal bridges, which are thrown across deep glens and clefts in the rocks, and those parts of the road which have been bored through the rocks by blasting, and resemble subterraneous galleries. One of these is so long, that it is but imperfectly lighted by the light admitted on both sides. At the distance of every league, one finds a house to afford shelter on the sudden coming on of stormy weather. In the third of these houses is the post-house, the sixth the custom-house, where we were obliged to pay a few laubthaler for roadway duty. Considerable as this tax is, it is still insufficient to keep the road in good repair, and it is greatly feared that it will by degrees fall into ruin. Nevertheless what one hears of this decay in foreign countries is without foundation, for with the exception of some of the barriers which had been carried away by avalanches and not yet reconstructed, we found it in good condition. Upon the highest part of it, the construction of a gigantic house has been begun, in which if it were finished, a corps of 4000 troops would be able to pass the night. But since the fall of *Napoleon*, its construction has been stayed, and it will now soon fall into decay. The Simplon pass is certainly not so high as that over the Gemmi, but here also all vegetation ceases, and even in the village of Simpeln where we slept, we found it very wintery.

Wednesday the 5th, September 1816, was the happy day on which the realisation of the wish of my early childhood, to behold the land "where the citrons bloom" was at length to be fulfilled. After we had travelled for two leagues more in continual descent, we came to the frontier of Lombardy and soon found ourselves transported into the midst of the South. Now we beheld woods of the sweet chesnut, and in gardens, figs, almonds and magnificent festoons of the vine, trained from one tree to another, and pendant with masses of the finest grapes. At every step as we descended, the warmth increased; at first agreably, but. soon quite oppressively. At noon we arrived at Domo d'Ossola, a small but pretty town. Here in the Hotel of the *Capello verde* we were for the first time imposed upon in real Italian style, and impressed with the necessity of the caution. to agree always before hand with the hotelkeeper on the charges for the accommodation. After dinner we travelled as far as Laveno, which lies close to the shore of the beautiful Lago Maggiore, and opposite to its celebrated islands. Here although we had agreed before hand on the charges for our nights accommodation, we paid as we were afterwards informed too much by half. On the 6th, early in the morning, we visited the so oft-times enthusiastially described Borromean islands, Isola Madre and Isola bella. Like many others whose expectations have been unduly raised by the too lavish praises of enthusiastic travellers of particular localities, they did not come up with our too sanguine expectations. We were most pleased with the Isola Madre, where for the first time we beheld with admiration the vigorous vegetation of the South, in the ancient and majestic laurel, citron, pomgranite and fig-trees, with other shrubs and plants of southern growth. Though of necessity these plants must here also, as with us be protected in winter, to secure them from the frost, yet their growth is so much more vigorous, and the fruits are much larger and more juicy than those of our greenhouses. On Isola Bella, there is a large but as yet not wholly finishedpalace, which contains some fine apartments, in which are several fine pictures, but the building is already going to decay. The remaining space on the island comprises the celebrated garden, which rises in ten terraces from the shore of the lake. The inside is supported by masonry which rises in progressively higher arches from terrace to terrace. The plan of the garden is gigantic, but in a bad old french style. The numerous wretched statues in the alleys and on the steps of the terraces are particularly repulsive and offensive to the eye. The terraces are oramented with beds of flowers and numerous yet more southern products, which in the winter time are put under cover under the arches. All were in most beautiful flower, and diffused unknown sweets around us. From the summit of the garden site, a most charming view is obtained of the opposite side of the lake, towards Palanza, Intra, Laveno, and the beautiful outline of mountains which bound the sight. Far as the eye could reach, all was canopied by a sky of the purest and deepest blue, and lit up with such a flood of sun light that the most distant objects could be clearly distinguished. This, and the mild balsamic air made us especially feel that we had entered a southern climate. Before we left the Islands, the gardener conducted us to an historical curiosity, to the name of *Napoleon* cut by himself in the bark of a laurel tree, shortly before the battle of Marengo.

The same boat that brought us to the Islands, took us six leagues farther to the little town of Sesto Calende, at the extremity of the lake. On this excursion we again had many a fine view of the beautiful banks of the lake. Belgirate, Arona, and the colossal statue of *St. Carlo Borromeo*, were seen to great advantage. At Sesto Calende, we already found the dirt and smell peculiar to Italian towns, and that of an Oil-boilery, so offensive to a German palate. On the 7th we performed the last days journey to Milan in the vehicle of a

Milanese driver, through a flat and uninteresting country, and put up at a *Pensione Suizzera* which was recommended to us for its German cleanliness.

Milan, Sept. 9.

The first of the remarkable things in Milan which we visited yesterday, was the cathedral. This beautiful building upon which the labour of nearly five centuries has been almost uninterruptedly devoted, and which nevertheless is as yet unfinished, approaches most nearly in style and architecture to the cathedral of Strasburg, but in form is nevertheless very different from the latter. It is in the form of a lengthened cross; at the place where the two lines meet, stands the high-altar, and above that, the span of the majestic dome, upon which the pretty tower in the form of a pyramid is built, the top of which is surmounted by the colossal statue in bronze of the holy Virgin. Innumerable other pierced gothic pyramids ornamented with niches and statues rest in part upon the pillars of the external walls, and in part on the marble-slabbed roof, increasing in height more and more the nearer they approach to the tower. On the pinnacle of each stands the statue of some Saint. The whole structure, from the ground to the highest point, is of white, polished marble, quarried at Baveno on the Lago Maggiore, and brought thither by the Ticino-Canal. During *Napoleon's* rule, the work was prosecuted with great zeal and not only was the *façade* of the chief entrance completed (which had been carried out only to the top of the door) but all the pyramids also, upon the external walls. At first sight, and seen from below, the building now seems finished; but upon ascending the roof, and the tower, one sees how much yet remains to be done.

The pillars and niches are in the Gothic, the doors and windows in the Roman style, and the statues are clothed after the Greek manner. All the sculptured works, of which in small and large statues, in high- and low-reliefs, in arabesques and other ornaments there are an immense quantity in this splendid building are from the chisel of celebrated masters, and it seems to me that, the modern works excel even the ancient in beauty and correctness.

The Interior of the church is by reason of the painted windows somewhat dark, but on that account and from the imposing grandeur and height, is the more fitted to raise religious feelings. Among the numerous statues in the interior of the cathedral, that of *Carlo Borromeo* is the most esteemed. Its great merit as a work of art is considered to lie in the anatomical correctness displayed by the sculptor in the deliniation of all the muscles, tendons, veins and prominent joints. From the gallery of the tower one has an extensive view, bounded on the north by the Swiss Alps, and on the south by the Apenines.

In the evening we went to the theatre *della Scala*, where was given "*la statua di bronza*", a *semiseria*-opera by *Soliva*, a young composer and pupil of the conservatory here. Upon our entrance, we were surprised at the size and beauty of the house. It is built after the model of the *St. Carlo*-theatre at Naples, the largest in Italy, and contains a spacious pit and six tiers of boxes one above the other, but will not hold much over 3000 people, so much space having been wasted in the manner of its distribution. The price of admission is the same to every part of the house, viz, two *Lire di Milano*. The orchestra is very numerous; four and twenty violins, eight counterbasses, the same number of violincellos, all the customary wind instruments, trumpets, bass-horn, turkish music etc. and yet with all, not numerous enough for the size of the locale. The performance very much surpassed my expectation; it was pure, vigorous, precise, and withall very calm. Signor *Rolla* an *artiste* known also in foreign countries by his compositions, directed as first violin. There is no other directing whether at the piano, or from the desk with the baton, than his, but merely a prompter with the score before him, who gives the text to the singers, and if necessary, the time to the choruses. The composition of the opera is more in the German than the Italian style, and one could hear very plainly that the young artist had taken our German composers, particularly *Mozart*, much more for his models, than his own countrymen. The orchestral parts are not so subdued as is usual in Italian operas, but are rendered in a very prominent manner, and sometimes even so much so as to cloak the singing. It is therefore astonishing that this opera has pleased so much, as this *genre* is never much liked. The well studied *pièces d'ensemble* and the finale have certainly not been the reasons for the success of the opera, but a few little unimportant cantabili's which were well executed by the singers. These *alone* also, were the points listened to with attention. During the powerful overture, several very expressive accompanied recitatives, and all the *pièces d'ensemble,* the audience made so much noise that one could scarcely hear the music. In most of the boxes, the occupants played at cards, and all over the house, people conversed aloud. Nothing more insufferable can be imagined for a stranger who is desirous to listen with attention, than this vile noise. On the other hand, from such persons as have perhaps seen the same opera thirty or forty times, and who come to the theatre only for the sake of the society, no attention is to be expected, and it is a great condescension if they only listen quietly to some "numbers". At the same time, I can imagine no task more ungrateful than to write for such a public, and one is surprised that good composers will submit to it. After the first act of the opera, a grand serious ballet was given, which from the skill of several of the dancers male and female, and the splendour of the decorations and costumes, presented a very imposing dramatic spectacle. As it lasted nearly an hour, the auditory had forgotten the first half of the opera. After the second act of the opera, another, but a comic-ballet, not much shorter, was produced, so that the whole of the performances lasted from eight o'clock to midnight. What work for the poor musicians!

September, 14.

Last evening we went to a concert, given by *Ferlendis* of Venice, a *Professore di Oboa*. His composition and play were alike pitiable. It is impossible to imagine a worse Tone and a greater want of Taste in the execution of the passages and of the cantabile, than this Professor *di Oboa* displayed. In Germany he would most certainly have been hissed off; here of a necessity, he was applauded as a matter of course by the Free-tickets. In the second part, *Luigi Beloli* played a Horn-Concerto of his own composition. This it is true did not exceed the line of mediocrity, but the execution was very superior. *Beloni* has a very beautiful tone, much skill and a cultivated taste. In order that the horrid Oboe should not obliterate the last more pleasing impression, we would not stop to hear the remainder of the concert.

September, 16.

That the Italians are a very musical nation may be judged from the fact that their beggars always solicit alms either singing or playing. Here are parties of four or five such musicians, who play of an evening in front of the Cafés, a by no means intolerable music, usually accompanied by a finely dressed female vocalist, who afterwards collects the money; sometimes they consist of three singers who with guitar accompaniment execute Trios and short Canons very efficiently; at others, blind fiddlers, flute players or singers who either without accompaniment, or who accompany themselves on the tambourine, seek their fortune singly; and even those who hawk things about for sale, offer their wares singing. Yesterday we came upon a comical fellow of this kind. He had manufactured for himself a remarkable instrument out of a whip-handle, from one end of which to the other he had stretched a single string. On the top, this cord was passed through a ball of paste, from the aperture of which rose a large bouquet of artificial flowers by way of ornament. In the right hand he carried a violin-bow, with which he produced the single tone which his instrument was capable of. The remarkable talent of this artist consisted there-in, that on a constantly repeated melody, for the fundamental tone of which his instrument furnished the Quinte, and which therefore never concluded in the Tonica, but always in the dominant, he improvisated the politest compliments to all who passed, or who sat before their doors; for these, the persons flattered, seldom refused a gift of money, which he collected in his hat, but without interrupting his song. In this style of recitative singing, in which his instrument fulfilled the duty of the orchestra, he would now praise the shape, now the dress of the passers by, and one could see by the self-satisfied smiles and generosity of the persons bepraised, that he well knew how to touch them on the weak side.

This afternoon we went to another concert, given by the *Società del Giardino*. The two Mesdames *Marcolini* and *Fabré* sang a duett of *Rossini's*. The former is celebrated throughout Italy as an contralto, her voice is fine, and she has great execution; but she almost always sings too low, by which in my opinion her singing was much injured. Signora *Fabré* is the *Prima donna* of the great theatre whose high notes are particularly fine, and her method of execution cultivated. Although both singers stand equally high in regard to voice and skill, yet here also the soprano bore away the palm from the contralto, just as a bass-viol can never please by the side of a violin. In the second part were sung also, a duett of *Paccini*, a Cavatina by *Bonfichi*, and a *Rondo* by *Paer*. All alike, the humorous or the serious, were sung in the same manner and with the same ornamental trimmings which have been heard a thousand times. The compositions were almost all insipid and without intimate connection, and the singing frequently disturbed or cloaked by meaningless figures of instrumentation.

September, 17.

We have just seen the Mosaic-Manufactory here. The most important work is a copy in mosaic of *Leonardo da Vinci's* "Last supper" on which the artist has been uninterruptedly engaged for twelve years; it is of the same size as the original, (the figures of the size of life). It is divided into twelve pieces, each of which is about three ells in length and of the same breadth. All the pieces are now finished, but only some have as yet been polished, these (from the ceiling part only) have a bright polish, those containing the figures were somewhat matt in the colours, at least as compared to the good copy of the picture from which it had been worked; but perhaps it will gain yet more life when the polishing has been completed. *Bonaparte* had given the order for this work, which will now be finished at the expense of the Emperor of Austria. As eight ducats a day are paid to the workmen, it already costs in wages for labour 34,960 ducats. Besides this herculean labour we saw several mosaics in the establishment, of exceeding beauty, exhibited for sale.

September, 17.

To-day we were present at the concert at the Conservatory of music, for which Count *Saurau* had presented us with tickets.

What I could ascertain respecting the interior administration of the Conservatory is as follows: The Professors, of whom four teach singing, one the violin, one the violincello, one counterbass, and some others the wind instruments, are appointed by and receive their salaries from the government, which pays also for the board and lodging of twelve pupils, six boys and six girls. All the other pupils some of whom live at the Conservatory, and some attend only at the hours of tuition, are required to pay for every thing. The Milanese are said to be very much opposed to the Institution; at the present time also, there are scarcely thirty pupils.

September, 22.

To-day I paid a momentary visit to a kind of Practising-Concert, where the dilettanti of this place, perform Symphonies under *Rolla's* direction, and in particular of the German masters. The string-instruments are chiefly played by dilettanti, the wind instruments by players from the *della Scala* theatre. When I arrived, they had already given the old symphony in D major of *Mozart,* and some overtures by Italian masters, and were just then engaged practising one of the grand Symphonies of *Haydn* (B major). It was played with tolerable accuracy, but without *piano* and *forte,* and for the most part crude. Nevertheless, the Institution which is moreover the only one of the kind in Italy, is a very praiseworthy one, since it enables the lovers of music here to become acquainted with our magnificent Instrumental-compositions. If I do not mistake, this weekly Practice-Concert takes place in the house of Signor *Motto,* who is said to have a fine collection of first class violins. But there are a great many fine violins here. A Signor *Caroli* has two very fine Stradivari's; *Rolla* has one also of great beauty; a Count *Gozio de Solence* has in his numerous collection of fine violins among several others by *Amati, Guarneri* and *Guardagnini,* four Stradivari's also, which have never been played upon, and which although very old look as though they had only just been made. Two of these violins are the production of the last year of that artist, 1773, when he was an old man of ninety three years of age. But it is immediately perceptible on the violin that it was cut by the tremulous hands of an infirm old man; the other two are however of the best days of the artist, from 1743 and 1744, and of great beauty. The tone is full and strong, but still new and woody, and to become fine, they must be played upon for ten years at least.

September, 28.

Last evening we gave our concert in the *della Scala* theatre. The orchestra kept its usual place, but the female singers, and *Dorette* and I, for our performances, took our places under the Proscenium, between the curtain which remained down, and the orchestra. The house although favourable for music, requires nevertheless on account of its immense size, a very powerful tone, and a grand but simple style of play. It is also very difficult *in a place* where people are always accustomed to hear voices only, to satisfy the ear with the tone of a violin. This consideration, and the uncertainty whether my method of play and my compositions would please the Italians, made me somewhat nervous on this my first *début* in a country where I was as yet unknown; but as I soon observed after the first few bars, that my play was listened to with attention, this fear soon left me, and I then played without any embarrassment. I had also the satisfaction to see that in the new concerto I had written in Switzerland, which was in the form of a *Vocal-Scena*, I had very happily hit upon the taste of the Italians, and that all the cantabile parts in particular were received with great enthusiasm. Gratifying and encouraging as this noisy approbation may be to the Solo-player, it is nevertheless exceedingly annoying to the composer. By it, all connexion is completely disturbed, the *tutti* so industriously worked out, are wholly unheeded, and people hears the Solo-player begin again in another tone without any one knowing how the orchestra has modulated with it. — Besides the Concerto, I played with *Dorette* the new Pot-pourris for piano and violin, and another with orchestral accompaniment. The latter, at the general request, I was obliged to repeat. The orchestra, the same that played in the opera, accompanied me with great attention and interest. *Rolla*, in particular, took great pains. My overture to "Alruna" was played at the beginning of the second part with great power it is true, but not without fault. The orchestra is accustomed to too many rehearsals, to be able to execute any thing free from fault after one rehearsal only. Madame *Castiglioni*, a Contre-Altiste engaged as a supplementary vocalist at the next carnival in Venice, sang an aria in the second part, with a fine voice and a good school, and was rewarded with a general applause. It had cost me infinite trouble to procure these two song-pieces; for the singers of the great theatre some of whom would have been very pleased to sing, could not get permission from the Impressario, and all the other singers of note who lived here, had already either signed engagements, or did not dare to appear at the Scala. The Impressario at first demanded the fifth part of the receipts for the grant of the theatre, but by the intercession of the governor Count *Saurau,* this tax was remitted in my favour.

After the concert, I was solicited on all sides to give another; but as next Friday, the only free day in each week, is the Emperor's Name-day, on which the governor gives a grand fête, and we have no desire to prolong our stay another fortnight, I shall rather defer this second concert till my return, and proceed forthwith to Venice. The first concert moreover, has but little more than paid the expenses, which amounted to fifty ducats.

A few days ago we visited the Picture Gallery in the Arena; the locale is the finest we ever beheld. It consists of three large saloons, which receive the light from above, of a long gallery, and two cabinets. In the gallery are the pictures *al fresco* collected from the churches in Milan, from the walls of which they have been taken with the plaster on which they were painted, and here let into the walls again. Among them are some of high artistic worth, of which copies and engravings have already been made. In the saloons, the paintings are chronologically arranged, and the name of the master given under each. In the first saloon are those of the earlier period, in the middle are those of the later, and in the third those of the modern school. Yet as far as I know there are no works of any living artists hung up. In the Cabinets, the smaller paintings are exhibited. The most precious of all, a *Raphael*, which although of his earlier days when he still painted in the style of his master, is nevertheless of infinite beauty. It is the betrothal of the Holy Virgin with *Joseph*. In the centre stands the Rabbi who in a grave and dignified posture pronounces his blessing; on his left is *Joseph*, a manly figure with dark hair and beard, placing with a kindly expression the ring upon the finger of the Virgin, who upon the right, softly blushes in all the graceful sweetness of maiden modesty. Among the other figures, a youth is also conspicuous, who breaks a stick against his knee. Artists admire greatly the foreshortening of the inclined posture. At first sight the sharp outline of the figures strikes one as unpleasing; but after one has become somewhat used to it by a longer contemplation, one is irresistibly fascinated with the elevated expression both of countenance and position. In this as in all *Raphael's* pictures the hands and feet are of exceeding beauty.

Venice, October, 5.

On Monday the 30th September we set out upon our journey thither in company with two amiable Polish Counts, whose acquaintance we had made in Milan, and of a painter who had just returned from a tour in Sicily. For myself and family I had hired a Vetturino as far as Padua, for seven louisd'or, for which price it was also agreed he was to pay for our supper and beds. . . .

The road to Brescia presents very little variety. Brescia is an ancient town, in which there is very little worth seeing; but it is situated in a charming locality on the slope of a mountain covered with vineyards and countryhouses. We took a walk trough the town, in which we saw nothing remarkable except a vine that covered the fronts of five houses up to their roofs, and was every where loaded with clusters of the finest grapes. One of the Poles, Count *Zozymola*, had meanwhile paid a visit to Signora *Mulonatti*, one of the most celebrated Contre-Altistes of the day, whose acquaintance he had made in Florence, where a few months previously she had sung. She is now reposing from the fatigues of the last months in the society of her *Cavaliere servente*, a Count *Secchi* who has a fine house in Brescia, and a still finer estate in the neighbourhood. During the Carnival she will again make here appearance here in Venice, at a salary of 10,000 francs and a benefit. Her admirer, a man of large fortune and extensive knowledge bas devoted his whole life to his *Donna*, while his two elder brothers have greatly distinguished themselves as Generals in the French Army. For the last ten years he has accompanied her every where she has sung, manages her affairs, and devotes himself to all her caprices. His sole somewhat earnest occupation is to write her memoirs i, e, her triumphs over other singers, and her love adventures. Once a year she furnishes him with the written data for the latter, which are the originals of the love-letters received, and although he is very jealous, she nevertheless prevails on the good natured fool to copy those letters himself, and introduce them with their respective explanations in her history. She has a husband as well, and two children by him, of whom she is said to be very fond. This husband plays a thoroughly pitiful part; he always keeps a certain distance, and awaits every look and beck of his ruling mistress. Up to the present time Count *Secchi* has seen neither Rome nor Naples, because his lady has not yet sung in those Cities, and she would not readily grant him permission to go there without her.

Between Brescia and Verona, the road passes along the Lago de Garda, whose beautiful wooded shores studded with country seats and enclosed by mountains, present the most beautiful views, which richly repaid us for the uniformity of the previous days journies. At the farthest end of the lake and half in the water, lies Peschiera, a small mean-looking town containing but few houses, but with extensive fortifications. From thence to Verona, the road is again very uninteresting. Upon our arrival, we learned that a female Pianiste and Harpiste of note from Naples was to give a Concert in the theatre, and we proposed to ourselves to go there. Through the slowness of the waiters who brought our supper an hour later than we had ordered it, we were however prevented going. We went nevertheless, at eleven o'clock at night by a beautiful moonlight to see the Coliseum, of all the monuments of Roman greatness, the one which is in the best state of preservation. . . . We ascended to the topmost benches, which equal in height the loftiest buildings of the town; from thence we had a splendid view over the whole colossal structure. We pictured to ourselves the immense mass of stone filled with the Romans of old — how they cheered the victors in the Arena beneath, — and then lost ourselves in the contemplation of the perishableness of all human greatness, and in comparisons between that vigorous people of yore and the present inhabitants of this beautiful land.

On one side of the Oval, the prisons are still to be seen where the malefactors were confined who were to be thrown to the wild beasts. The arrangement is still existing also, by means of which in a few minutes the circus could be laid under water for naval fights and boat races. During the visit of the Austrian Emperor, the people were treated with a resuscitation of the ancient horse and foot races. We had seen something similar in Milan of which I had forgotten to speak.

Napoleon has erected in the *Foro Buonoparte*, a Circus in the Roman Style, whose exterior consists also of a wall having passages for ascent; but the benches in the interior are of turf only. Of these there are about twelve, but from 25- to 30,000 people find nevertheless room sufficient. On one side of the breadth, stands a handsome building with a fine colonnade looking into the interior, from which stone benches run the whole breadth of the building down to the circus. In this modern Arena, which can also be laid under water, the people were treated at the time of the coronation of *Napoleon*, as king of Italy, with a free admission to a *rechauffé* of the ancient Roman games. A third but smaller edition, on payment, took place the day before our departure.

First of all, eighteen runners in Roman costume made their appearance, who upon a signal from the trumpets ran forward in a seemingly encumbered manner to the goal. The victor received a flag, from the top of which was suspended a wreath of laurel. The two next best after him, were also presented with tokens of triumph. Twelve horsemen now advanced to compete in speed. Several fell from their horses at the first start, and all of them rode so badly that they excited nothing but laughter and compassion. After the winners had been again rewarded, came the Chariot Race, which however presented both a new and interesting sight. The six charioteers were mounted on small two-wheeled Roman chariots such as one sees upon old coins, and on a given signal to start, lashed their horses, of which there were two to every chariot into a full gallop; at the extremity of the course, one of them in turning fell twice, horses and all, but without taking any harm. The others drove round the course three times, and the victors were again presented with their rewards. Now commenced the grand Triumphal-procession. From thirty to forty Hautboyists in the *Roman* costume with *Turkish* music! — playing a March from the Opera "John of Paris" opened the spectacle. Then came the Runners carrying spears; and at length a large Roman triumphal chariot drawn by four oxen, with the whole of the victors. The handsomely decorated oxen had been harnessed in pairs in the Roman manner; but the poor animals had not been accustomed to that sort of thing, and they would not move an inch; so that it was at length found necessary to yoke them in the same manner as they were used to, in their dung carts, and when this was done they went off in style. Behind them came the unsuccessful riders and charioteers who closed the procession.

The costume of all these people and animals was well chosen, and had one not seen round the Circus the modern *beau monde*, with now and then among the runners a three cornered hat, the wearer of which kept order in the games, and, not have heard the Turkish music playing the march from "Aline", one might indeed for a moment have fancied, to see beneath one the old Romans of yore. But these soldiers and hackney carriage drivers were so sparing of their miserable horses, and at the same time so clumsy, that they soon dissipated every deception.

On the 3rd early in the morning we parted from our agreable fellow travellers, who now proceeded on their farther journey by another road through the Tyrol to Munich. We slept in Vicenza, a filthy dirty place. Our windows looked out upon a lonely street, in which heaps of dirt of the most disgusting kind infected the air in an unbearable manner. But one meets with the same kind of thing here even in the largest Cities, and in the most magnificent squares. If one ascends a retired flight of steps, often of the finest marble, at the grandest palaces, it behoves one to keep in the centre, to avoid contamination, and even the Cathedral of Milan is unapproachable on many sides for the high heaps of filth. This exceeding dirtiness, in which the Italians surpass almost all other nations, prevails also in most of the apartments and kitchens. I thought to myself that a Dutchman would go out of his senses here!

On the 4th at noon, we arrived at the ancient, unsightly Padua, where we stopped till eight o'clock in the evening. We then continued our journey by water in the Canal-Diligence. On getting into the bark, deceived by the uncertain moonlight I missed my footing, and fell into the water; but in my fall I fortunately caught hold of the gunwale of the bark, and was immediately pulled on board again. With the exception of the fright and the trouble of changing my clothes I experienced no unpleasant consequences from this fall. The bark is very conveniently fitted up for the accommodation of from twenty four to thirty persons, and towed by a horse at full trot, goes very fast. The last half of the Canal is thickly dotted on both sides with beautiful country seats and gardens, which at this period are inhabited by the wealthy Venetians. The Palace of the former Viceroy, in which the governor Count *Goes* resides during the fine season, is particularly remarkable. We much regretted passing this beautiful part of the country in the night, but even by moonlight the view presented is magnificent. At five o'clock in the morning, when all Venice was yet asleep, we arrived, and alighted at the *Albergo della Scala*.

Venice, October, 10.

Little as Venice upon the whole, has come up with my expectations, yet I was the more surprised by the beauty of some parts of the city. The Piazza San Marco, is particularly imposing. The thousand-year old church of St. Mark, built in the oriental style, with its five cupolas, its innumerable statues and magnificent mosaic-pictures with their resplendent gold ground; the colossal Bell tower with its pyramid which serves as a beacon to the mariner far away on the Adriatic sea, the three grand buildings almost in the same style of architecture which enclose the square upon three sides; the busy life under the Arcades, the rich shops of the traders and the tastefully decorated coffee-houses, in and in front of which from eight o'clock in the morning till far into the night the fashionable idle world of both sexes may be seen collected: the mingled vociferations of the numerous vendors of refreshments, and of the criers who read aloud the proclamations of the government, or announce the pieces to be performed in the evening at the different Theatres — all these together form so varied a picture, that a stranger finds subject therein for a whole week's entertainment.

If one then proceeds to the second square which abuts on the first near the church, enclosed on the east side by the former palace of the Doges, and on the west by the prolongation of one of the three large buildings adverted to; a new spectacle quite different from the former one presents itself. Before you, the harbour dotted with gondolas, barks and trading ships of all sizes; on the left the quay bordered with magnificent buildings and churches extending as far as the *giardino publico*. Opposite, situated upon a small island, a monastery in whose handsome church the last Pope was elected, and to the right on the other side of the grand canal the church of *San Giorgia maggiore* with its majestic dome, surrounded by other beautiful buildings. When the eye has feasted itself on these objects, it is attracted by the nearer surroundings; by the moltey crowd of human beings upon the high-arched stone bridges leading over the numerous canals which from this spot intersect the City; by the loading and unloading of the larger ships, the embarking of the fashionable and unfashionable world in gondolas and barks for pleasure-excursions, or journeys of business; by the singular forms of the fish and shell-fish exposed here for sale, and the other numerous striking objects peculiar to a sea-port. Having seen all this, one returns gladly to the square of St. Mark, and there finds new subjects for admiration. Upon contemplating the church more attentively, the four gigantic bronze horses over the chief entry first attract the eye, less by their artistic worth, for they are not of the finest proportions, than on account of their antiquity and their various fortunes. Carried off by the Venetians on the taking of Constantinople, they were placed as war-trophies over the chief entrance of the church of St. Mark, and there remained undisturbed until the French after the conquest of Italy took them to Paris. From thence with all the other treasures of art carried from Italy, they were again brought back after the capture of Paris by the allies, and reinstated in their old place amid the exultations of all Venice. Besides these horses, there are many other memorials of the triumphs of the Venetians in the church of St. Mark. Statues, bas-reliefs, arabesques, columns and capitals from Greece, Egypt and the Barbary States, and it is subject of astonishment in this building, that, though comprising so many objects executed in the most different styles of Art, it presents nevertheless a whole of such harmonious beauty. In front of the church, stand three lofty red painted masts, which on Festival days are decorated with long silken streamers reaching to the ground, and their cast bronze foot-sockets are ornamented with fine bas-reliefs.

On the second square, close to the water, stand two colossal pillars of Egyptian granite, each pillar hewn in one single block. One supports a winged lion in brass, which was also carried to Paris, the other, the patron Saint, the holy Theodorus upon a crocodile.

The interior of the church of St. Mark, is not less beautiful than the exterior. Walls, niches, and domes are entirely covered with Mosaic-pictures, among which it is true some are of little artistic worth; but in the most of them, the composition, drawing, and colouring are very fine, and all have a pure gold ground which in spite of its great age still shines as though it were new. Here, however, one is soon surrounded by whole rows of mendicants, who plead hunger so piteously and look so disgusting, that one is glad to make one's escape from them with the sacrifice of a few copper coins. In fact one cannot pass through any part of the city at any time without being addressed by beggars, and it is said as many as 25,000 here suffer from hunger. At this period, it is true, the poor subsist very cheaply on cooked, or rather roasted, pumpkins, which are sold at the corner of every street, and of which a piece as big as the hand costs but a centisimo.

On leaving the Square, one finds but little to divert attention, for in Venice people neither ride nor drive, the streets being so narrow that frequently two persons cannot walk side by side. In the busiest part of the city not far from the *Ponte Rialto*, the crowd is so great that one has a difficulty to work one's way through it. From the dirty habits of the Italians, who throw every sort of refuse into the canals, and from the pestilential smell of half-putrid fish and muscles, together with the disagreeable effluvia from the workshops of most of the artizans, it is very natural to suppose that in these narrow streets, the whole year long, one cannot once breathe a pure air.

Here gondolas take the place of vehicles, and are to be had at a very cheap rate. They all have an awning of black cloth, which gives them a mournful appearance. At the time of the Republic such luxury prevailed in the decoration of the gondolas, that the government found it necessary to establish the present mode of covering. The gondoliers are very expert in rowing and steering, and however great may be the throng on the canals, they pass each other with great swiftness, without coming in collision. When one hires two of them, the speed is equal to that of a horse in full trot. As the houses have, besides the front entry towards the water, a side door or exit upon the street, one can go, it is true, everywhere by land; but on account of the bridges one is obliged to make so many turnings, that one can get to the required place as quickly again by water.

October 12.

By the most beautiful weather we to-day enjoyed the singularly splendid view from the tower of St. Mark, which is ascended very conveniently by a spiral ascent without steps. The view is truly enchanting! On one side one sees over the extensive mass of houses to the mainland, in the distance the snow-covered mountains of the Friaul; on the other side the harbour with its varied and busy life, the Islands covered with handsome churches and buildings; and in the back-ground the open sea. I do not remember having ever seen so beautiful a view from any tower, not even from that of St. Michael's at Hamburg.

At 4 o'clock we visited the church of the Foundling, where a mass was being performed by the female foundlings. The orchestra and choir were composed entirely of young girls; an old instructress of music gave the time, another accompanied on the organ. There was more to be seen than to be heard, for the composition and execution were execrable. The girls playing the violin, flute, and horns, looked strange enough; the contra-bassist was eunfortunately not to be seen, being hidden behind the trellis. There were some good voices among them, and one quite remarkable, which sang up to g on the fourth leger line (g^3); but the style of singing of all was horrid.

We have made the acquaintance of several lovers of music, the two Counts *Tomasini*, and Signors *Contin*, *Filigran*, and several others whose names I do not know. The two former are assisting me greatly in making arrangements for my Concert, and if at the present bad time of the year for business, when every body of note is in the country, I should have a tolerable Concert, I shall have them to thank for it.

To-day we had a visit from a German musician, Herr *Aiblinger*, from Munich, and a pupil of *Winter*, who has been residing in Venice for the last sixteen years. He is a pianist and composer, and seems to possess much real taste for his art. At least he complained to us, with a most piteous face, that in this country it was impossible for him to keep pace with his German brothers in art, because he had scarcely ever the good fortune to hear a German work of any note, and that with his enthusiasm for music, his heart was fit to break; that his circumstances bound him to a city where, for sixteen years, he had heard every year the same things over again, while the Germans, in the meantime, had witnessed the production of so many classic works. I afterwards saw some of his productions, and it is much to be regretted that he has been confined in this Siberia of art. In order to give me an idea how little art and artists were esteemed, even by gentlemen who wished to pass for Mæcenas's, he related to me an anecdote of what occurred to *Bärmann* of Munich, who was here last winter with Demoiselle *Harles*. Count *Herizo*, a very rich nobleman, who, during the winter, gives a concert at his house every week, to which he frequently invites as many as two hundred persons, besought *Bärmann*, through a third party, to play at one of them. The latter had himself already announced a public concert, and presuming that it would be greatly to his disadvantage if he played elsewhere before, he declined the invitation, but promised to play *after* his own concert. On the same day, however, Count *Herizo* gave one of his customary grand concerts in which "the Creation" was performed, I believe for the first time in Venice; and *Bärmann* had so thin an attendance, that to cover the expenses of the concert he was obliged to add forty francs from his own pocket. Nevertheless a week afterwards, Count *Herizo* repeated his invitation to *Bärmann*, who now, however, demanded a gratification of twelve Louisd'or. After much debate this was at length agreed to. But *Bärmann* shortly after was apprised that it was intended to play off a hoax upon him. To avoid this he wrote anew to decline the invitation, and went on a pleasure excursion with *Harles* to the mainland. Upon his return, a friend of Count *Herizo's* came to inquire of him the reason why he would not play, and on being told, he assured him upon his honour that nothing of the kind was intended, and that *Bärmann* had not the least to fear; upon which the latter gave his promise to appear at the next concert. He was very politely received by Count *Herizo*, and the music began. After the space of an hour, when six pieces had been performed, *Bärmann* was curious to know when his turn would come; he therefore asked the loan of a programme from his neighbour, and found at the end of the whole of the pieces of music, which at least would last two hours more, the following words: "If time will permit, Herr *Bärmann* will also perform a concerto on the clarinet." His rage may be imagined. Count *Herizo* is reported then to have said to him at the end of the concert, in a loud tone of voice: "We have no time to hear you this evening, but we shall perhaps another time!" and in this manner he was cheated of his pecuniary gratification. *Bärmann* immediately slunk out, but in so doing was so unfortunate as to mistake the way, and instead of taking the passage leading out upon the street, plumped right into the canal. Fortunately the gondoliers plying near the spot came to his assistance, and soon pulled him out. Half-perished with cold, and highly exasperated, he returned home. Next morning he was summoned before the police by Count *Herizo*. The director of police, after the matter had been explained to him by *Bärmann*, had nevertheless courage sufficient to justify *Bärmann*, and to point out to Count *Herizo* the rudeness of his conduct. Under such circumstances, however, *Bärmann* thought it advisable to hasten his departure, especially as a suspicious-looking fellow had been making inquiries about the hours of his going out of evenings. Fräulein *Harles*, also, came badly off. In the first opera she gave tolerable satisfaction, and fault was found only with her bad accent; but on the first representation of the second opera, she was so disconcerted, in her very first scene, by the loud talking, coughing, and laughing of the audience, that she ran off the stage in the middle of her aria, and fell down behind the scenes like one dead. She was seized with an inflammation of the throat, and, during the whole winter, was unable to sing any thing else but the speaking recitatives. All *pièces d'ensemble* and both finales were sung without her, and yet, as she could find no substitute, she was obliged to appear before the public every evening. The managers deserve praise, for they played her no underhand tricks, but paid her according to the agreement made.

October 15.

There are two kinds of dilettanti-concerts given here. One takes place every fortnight at the *Fenice* theatre, under the direction of Count *Tomasini*. At the one at which I was present *Teresa Sessi*, who was formerly engaged at Vienna, sang two airs, a duet, and a quartet, with much applause, in her old style, which is neither better nor worse. Besides her, a dilettante attracted the attention of the auditory by singing several buffo things in the genuine Italian caricature style. All the rest, particularly the composition and execution of the ouvertures, was, as is usual in Italy, exceedingly bad.

The other is a sort of practice concerts, and takes place once a week, under the direction of Signor *Contin*. With the exception of some of the wind instruments and of the bass-viols, the orchestra is wholly composed of dilettanti, and the pieces performed consist mostly of symphonies and overtures by German masters. But a proper study of these works is quite out of the question, and it is considered matter of gratulation if they are got through without coming to a stillstand. On the day I was present, a very old symphony of *Krommer's* was performed first, which was followed by the one in E flat major by *Andrew Romberg*.

For the finale I was solicited to direct *Beethoven's* second symphony in D major, which I could not refuse. But I had a rare job with the orchestra, for they were accustomed to quite other *tempi* than I took, and seemed not at all to understand that there are shades of *forte* and *piano* in music, for all worked with bow and breath as hard and incessantly as they could, and my ears rang the whole night with the infernal noise. But these practice concerts are nevertheless so far good that they afford the lovers of music in Venice the opportunity of hearing several of our classical instrumental compositions, such as the overtures to "Don Juan" and the "Zauberflöte," which they had not hitherto been acquainted with; and, though but imperfectly, they learn to feel that the Germans are immensely superior to them in that kind of composition. Indeed they say so themselves, but they do not thoroughly believe it, and only acknowledge it, in order to be enabled to boast with more freedom of their superiority in song and vocal compositions (!!). The self-satisfaction of the Italians, despite their poverty of fancy is in fact unbearable; whenever I executed in their presence any of my things, they thought they could pay me no higher compliment than when they assured me they were quite Italian in taste and style.

October 16.

To-day in the forenoon, in company with three Silesians, we went to the ancient palace of the Doges. The so-called golden stair case was the first thing that attracted our attention. It is outside the building as far as the first floor, is of the finest marble, and ornamented with colossal statues of beautiful proportions. Up to the second and third stories it is in the interior of the building, and there is richly decorated on the sides with marble bas-reliefs, on the ceiling with gilt mouldings and small fresco-paintings, and with very fine statues in the niches. We then saw an extensive suite of salons and apartments, which were truly grand in decoration, the walls and the ceilings are painted in oil by the best masters, and here and there at intervals are the richest and most beautiful sculptured ornaments I ever beheld. The subjects of these pictures are almost exclusively incidents in the history of Venice; Doges returning thanks to the Holy Virgin for victories achieved, or the surrender of the keys of some one of the fortresses besieged by the Venetians, etc. etc. Despite the want of good taste in the bringing together, in the sepaintings, of heavenly and earthly personages, the execution and grouping of each, particularly in those by *Paul Veronese,* is exceedingly fine. Altogether in my opinion, there is no kind of decoration so befitting and worthy of a princely palace as this, in which the deeds of the nation are immortalized at the same time with the name of the most skilful national artist. In the present day how little feeling exists for this kind of patriotism! Where up to the present day is there to be seen any painting illustrating the modern deeds of heroism of the Germans, executed by the order of a Sovereign? And yet how greatly the artists of the present day are in want of such encouragement and support! And I am here speaking of painters and sculptors only; poets and musicians ought also to have been invited to immortalize the deeds of the German people.

We came at last to the great library, which contains also a perfect treasure of paintings and antique statues. From the gallery of this hall one has a charming view of the harbour. — In order to be enabled to make a comparison between the style of decorating palaces in former time with the modern method, we visited the apartments in the government building fitted up by order of the former Viceroy. We found them pretty and convenient, it is true; but what a difference between the earnest splendour of that ancient palace and the tasteless ornamentation of the new! Instead of the marble bas-reliefs and the rich gilt mouldings and ornaments of the latter, here we found slovenly painted arabesques by the hands of unknown daubers, and the walls hung with silk tapestry or figured paper instead of the pictures of famous masters.

October 17.

Yesterday *Paganini* returned here again from Trieste, and therefore, as it would appear, has at once abandoned his project of going to Vienna. He called on me this morning, and so I have at length made the personal acquaintance of this wonderful man, of whom since I have been in Italy I have heard some story or other every day. No instrumentalist ever charmed the Italians so much as he, and although they are not very fond of instrumental concerts, yet he gave more than a dozen concerts in Milan and five here. On making nearer enquiry, what it is that he in reality fascinates his auditory with, one hears from the non-musical portion the most exaggerated encomiums — that he is a complete wizard, and brings tones from his violin which were never heard before from that instrument. Connoisseurs, on the other hand, say that it cannot be denied he certainly possesses a great dexterity with the left hand, in double-chords and in passages of every kind, but that the very thing by which he fascinates the crowd debases him to a mere charlatan, and does not compensate for that in which he is utterly wanting — a grand tone, a long bow-stroke, and a tasteful execution. But that by which he captivates the Italian public and which has acquired for him the name of the "Inimitable," which is even placed under his portraits, consists, on a nearer enquiry, in a succession of feats which, in the dark times of good taste, the once so famous *Scheller* performed in the small towns and some capitals of Germany, and which at that time equally excited the admiration of our countrymen, viz, in the flageolet tones; in variations upon one string, in which for the purpose of imposing more upon the audience, he takes off the other three strings of the violin; in a peculiar kind of *pizzicato*, produced with the left hand without the help of the right or of the bow; and in many tones quite unnatural to the violin, such as the bassoon tone, the voice of an old woman, etc. etc. — As I never heard the wonderful *Scheller*, whose saying was: *"One God! one Scheller!"* I should much like to hear *Paganini* play in his peculiar manner, and the more so, because I presume that so admired an artist must possess some more real merits than those adverted to.

The origin of his present skill as a virtuoso is said to have been a four years incarceration, to which he was condemned for strangling his wife in a fit of violent rage. Such, at least, is the public report in Milan and here also. As from a wholly neglected education he could amuse himself neither with writing nor reading, he cheered the *ennui* of the tedious hours of his existence in the invention and practise of all the tricks of art with which he now astonishes all Italy. By his disobliging and rude behaviour he has made enemies of several of the lovers of music here, and they, after I have played any thing before them at my lodgings, extol me upon every opportuuity at *Paganini's* expense, in order to annoy him, which is not only very unjust, since between two artists of such entirely different style no parallel can be drawn; but is also disadvantageous to me, because it makes all *Paganini's* admirers and partizans my enemies. His opponents have inserted a letter in the journals, in which they say that my play recalls to them the style of their veteran violinists, *Pugnani* and *Tartini*, whose grand and dignified manner of handling the violin has become wholly lost in Italy, and had been compelled to make room for the petty and childish manner of their virtuosi of the present day; while the Germans and French had understood how to adapt that noble and simple method of play to the taste of modern times. This letter, which appeared in to-day's paper without my knowledge, will certainly do me rather harm than good with the public, for the Venetians are firmly persuaded that it is impossible to come up to *Paganini*, much less to surpass him.

October 19.

Our concert took place yesterday, and was better attended than I had expected, since all who have the means to go into the country, or who are not tied to the city by very urgent business, are away, and of all my letters of recommendation the only one I have been yet able to deliver is the one to the governor Count *Goes*. Neither is it worth the trouble, to bring letters of introduction to Italians, for they are of no manner of use. A cold offer of their services, which they do not intend to give, is all that one gets from them. But I must return to the concert. It took place in the St. Luca theatre, which, next to the Fenice, is the largest and handsomest in

Venice. The proprietor, Signor *Vendremi,* let me have it on the condition that I should relinquish to him two-thirds of the sale of the boxes which were not private property. There exists, namely, a curious custom in Italy, which is, that certain boxes are sold to private individuals for as long as the house stands, whereby the proprietor of the house abandons all right to them. But these proprietors of boxes must pay the price for admission at the entrance the same as everybody else. This is the same for every part of the house, and always a very low one; with the boxes which remain in the hands of the proprietor of the theatre rare bargains are sometimes driven, and on the performance of very attractive pieces they are frequently paid as high as several carolini. Yesterday very little was taken for the boxes, so that signor *Vendremi* did not profit much. From the coldness of the public at the commencement of my play, I immediately observed that there was a prejudice against me; but by degrees it subsided, and towards the close of the concert the applause was so unanimous, that I was twice called for. All that I afterwards played now found a much more ready reception, and the clapping of hands was as boisterous as in Milan.

To-day there has also appeared in the paper a very favorable report upon yesterday's concert, in which it says, in reference to the letter adverted to, that it is unjust and partial to endeavour to praise one style at the expense of another, and that there should be no monopoly of any one genre in art: in which report, however, it also says of me, among other things, "that I unite the Italian sweetness with all the depth of study peculiar to our nation, and that I must be acknowledged to take rank among the first of living violinists — encomiums therefore, such as might content the vainest artist.

October 20.

Paganini called upon me early this morning to compliment me upon the concert. I very urgently solicited him to play something, and several musical friends who were at my place united their entreaties to mine. But he very bluntly refused, and excused himself on account of a fall, the effects of which he still felt in the arms. Afterwards, when we were alone, and I again besought him, he said, his style of play was calculated for the great public only, and with them never failed in its effect; and that if he was to play anything to me, he must play in a *different* manner, and for that he was at the moment by no means in the humour; but that we should probably meet in Rome or Naples, and then he would not put me off with a refusal. I shall therefore leave this place in all probability without hearing the wonderful man.

This morning, on going out, we had the wholly unexpected pleasure of meeting *Meyerbeer* and all his family. He is now returned from a tour through Sicily to meet his parents here, who have not seen him for five years: he will then turn back through Florence and Rome to Naples, to be present at the opening of the new theatre of *St. Carlo*. It was a real enjoyment to me to be able once more to converse with a well-educated German artist on subjects of art. His brother gave me the gratifying information that my opera "Faust" had been performed in Prague. On their journey through they were present at a rehearsal of it. I now look forward with hope to more detailed information respecting its representation.

At the theatre St. Moise we were present at the first performance of the old opera "Don Papirio," which had been studied with great attention by the vocalists and the orchestra. The prima donna, Madame *Marchesini*, already somewhat *passée*, distinguished herself greatly on that evening by good execution and clever acting. The buffo singer, whose name I do not remember, was also very excellent.

Bologna, October 25.

Late on Monday evening we left Venice by the "mail boat." As the wind was very favorable, we performed the first part of the journey by water, as far as where the canal falls into the Lagunes, very quickly. Twice, for a short distance, we crossed a part of the open sea, that is the great and lesser harbour of Chiozza, where the motion of our bark was so violent from the roughness of the sea, that *Dorette* and the children were regularly sea-sick. I only escaped this affliction by seating myself on the deck in the fresh air. When we had run into the canal, and afterwards into the Po, where the boat was towed by horses, it went slowly and quietly enough, so that I soon went to fetch up the patients. As I am told here, that the rich people of the town are still in the country, and that even at the most favorable season of the year concerts scarcely cover their expenses, we shall abandon the idea of giving one here, and continue our journey to Florence tomorrow morning by vetturino.

Florence, October 28.

The journey here over the Apennines, with very fine weather, was exceedingly pleasant. The mountains, though of a considerable height, are wooded almost to their summits, and the trees and bushes, were now rich with the most beautiful colours of their autumnal garb. The valley in which Florence lies presents a highly charming prospect. When one looks down upon the beautiful gardens and country seats, one seems to be entering a very Paradise.

November 2.

Florence does not quite come up to the expectations one forms of it from the description of over-enthusiastic travellers. Dresden is called the German Florence, but is not much honoured by the parallel. The situation of Dresden, as well as the city itself, are incomparably finer. The Arno is a dirty, mean-looking river, and is not in the least to be compared with the majestic Elbe. The four bridges which lead over it and connect the two parts of the town are certainly good and substantial, but not so long or so elegant as that of Dresden. Neither has Florence such fine buildings nor such handsome squares as Dresden, and excels it alone in its treasures of art of every kind. Of these there are so many here, that one can scarcely find time to see them all. On the square in front of the ancient palace stand several groups of colossal statues in marble and bronze of the most celebrated of the old masters, which make of this square, otherwise so irregular and unattractive, one of the most interesting in the world for connoisseurs in art. A group in marble, representing the rape of a Sabine, especially charmed us. From this square it is not far to the cathedral, a gigantic building with a cupola, which in circumference and height is said to be little inferior to St. Peter's at Rome. The exterior is somewhat too party-coloured and not very tasteful; the walls are inlaid with tables of marble of different colours, which present a variety of patterns. Near the church stands a very lofty square clock-tower, which is ornamented in the same manner. Belonging thereto, although isolated from it, is also a christening chapel built in the same style, and also with a tolerably high dome. Here are the celebrated gates of bronze, of which *Michael Angelo* said they were worthy to stand at the entrance to the abode of the blessed, as they were too beautiful for any earthly building. There are three of them, two of which are executed and ornamented in the same style. But the single one is by far the handsomest and has far larger bas-reliefs than the other two. In the whole world is not to be seen any thing more beautiful in the grouping, drawing, perspective, softness and purity of the work than these bas-reliefs.

In another church we saw a succession of tombs, among which those of *Michael Angelo, Nardini,* and *Alfieri* interested us greatly. On the tomb of the former is his bust, executed with his own hand, and three female figures (by one of his pupils) personifying the three arts in which he excelled: architecture, painting, and sculpture, mourning for his loss. What however does it not confer upon the arstists who merited such memorials of their worth, and upon their contemporaries also who raised them to them! Where can one find anything of the kind in Germany? Where have *Mozart* and *Haydn* the memorials to their honour? In Vienna no one even knows where they are buried.

November 5.

On the day we arrived, and almost every evening since, we have been to the theatre in the *Via della Pergola*. They are now giving an opera of *Rossini*'s, "L'Italiana in Algeri," and a grand ballet. *Rossini* is now the favorite composer of the Italians, and several of his operas, "Tancredi," "Il Turco in Italia," and the above-named, are performed with great applause in almost every town in Italy. I was therefore glad, after having heard his compositions so frequently and highly praised in Milan and Venice, to hear something of his myself. This opera has, however, not wholly satisfied my expectations; in the first place it is wanting, like all Italian music, in purity of style, characteristic proprieties in the personages, and judicious calculation of the length or shortness of the music for the scene. These indispensable qualities of an opera to which we would give the appellation classic, I had however not expected, as we do not at all miss them in an Italian opera. One is accustomed to have the same person sing alternately in the tragic and comic style, and to hear from a peasant girl the same pompous vocal ornamentation as from a queen or a heroine, and to hear one of the persons performing sing alone, for a quarter of an hour at a time, in situations of the most impassioned kind, while the others walk about in the back-ground, or partly behind the scenes, and chat and laugh with their acquaintances. But I did indeed expect qualities which should distinguish *Rossini's* work above that of his colleagues — novelty of ideas, for instance; purity of harmony, etc.; but of all these I found but little. What the Italians consider new in *Rossini's* operas is not new to us; for they consist of ideas and modulations for the most part long since known in Germany; for instance the appoggiatura in the bass at the beginning of the much-admired duett in the first act:

which the musicians in Florence boasted of to me as something quite new, and discovered by *Rossini*. In Milan, where I heard the same duet at a concert, it was probably found too hard, and the fifth and sixth measures were thus changed:

Or the following modulation, also, at the finale of the first act:

Purity of harmony is not to be found in him any more than in any other modern Italian composer; and I have heard many sequences of quints like the following:

But in attention to the rhythm and in the complete use he makes of the orchestra, he distinguishes himself above his countrymen.

The instrumentation, however, as compared with ours, first introduced by *Mozart*, is still very meagre, and the Italians in that still cling too much to the old. The viols and bassoons almost always go through the whole opera *col Basso,* and the clarinets and hautboys in *Unisono*. As in most Italian operas with from six to eight contra-basses there is only one violincello, and usually not even a good one, they as yet know nothing here of the (since *Mozart's* day) frequent use of the violincello for middle voices, which, skilfully brought in, has such a splendid effect; and they are far behind the Germans in the knowledge of how to get the best effect from the wind instruments. But what surprised me most, was to hear sometimes in these operas a very uneven cantabile, while a flowing and for the voice grateful and well arranged cantabile is the only praise-worthy quality of the modern Italian operatic music, and must compensate for all the deficiencies and faults. The two following passages struck me most; the first in an aria of the prima donna, the second, in the first finale, where it frequently recurs:

2.

[musical notation: Poco adagio.]

Both these passages are not only unsingable but exceedingly insipid, and the second especially, from the somewhat slow movement and its frequent recurrence, is wholly unbearable.

Among the singers in this opera, Madame *Georgi*, the prima donna, is the only remarkable one. She has a full, powerful voice of rare compass, from  to . Her part is written for a contralto, and she can therefore exhibit her high notes in the *fioriturí* only; if she possesses equal power in the low notes a deep soprano part would suit her much better. Like almost every singer we have yet heard in Italy she has the vice of ornamenting too much, and does not know how to derive all the advantage she might from her splendid voice. One hears very plainly, moreover, that she does not draw in the least upon her own spontaneous feeling and taste, but everything has been studied; so that her *fioriturí*, which are repeated every evening, note for note, become so wearisome that one cannot hear her again without repugnance. She was formerly a dillettante, and only now sings in the third theatre; but nevertheless she is already an excellent actress.

The ballet, which is given every evening between the two

acts of the opera, is the most splendid of any I have ever yet seen. I think it is called "The Destruction of the Western Empire," and is especially remarkable for the constant introduction of great masses of persons on the stage in full activity who form the boldest and most surprising groups. It has been studied with extraordinary correctness, and is performed every evening with the same precision. At the end a cavalry engagement was represented, which however always looks somewhat stiff and awkward.

November, 8.

Last evening our concert took place in the theatre *della Pergola*. The Grand-duke, to whom I brought a letter from his brother *Rudolph*, and who has received me several times very graciously at his residence, honoured it with his presence, accompanied by his whole family. The small though select auditory was very animated, and after having greeted the Grand-duke with the usual recognitions, were not restrained from a loud expression of applause of my performances. The music had a very good effect in the spacious and sonorous theatre; but the accompaniment was not of the best. — To-day I have received a great number of invitations to give a second concert next week, from which I am promised a better result. I shall make the venture, although the Grand-duke, who goes to-morrow to Pisa to meet his brother *Rainer*, will not be here. Yesterday's concert, exclusive of the Archduke's present to me, did not bring in more than the evening's expenses, which were, as they always are, very considerable; the price of admission being only three paoli, and all disposition over the sale of a single box being again denied me. A very favorable notice of my concert appeared this afternoon in the newspaper.

November, 12.

As we have now been several times to the picture-gallery, and attentively observed all that it contains, I will commit to paper a few words, not upon the truly splendid works of art which it contains, for they have already been frequently and well described, but also the expression of the impression which they made upon me. I must first of all give due praise to the admirable custom, one by no means usual in Italy, of admitting the public to the gallery free. At the entrance one finds a notice in four or five languages, that the guardians of the gallery are forbidden under the penalty of the loss of their situation, to take the smallest present. Though perhaps they may not altogether adhere too strictly to this injunction, one is at least fully secured from the importunate begging, with which one is everywhere pursued in Italy, and in this place, made sacred by art, gives oneself peacefully up to the enjoyment.

To assist my memory hereafter I have sketched a plan of the gallery and marked the position where the works of art stand which made the greatest impression upon me. As I never make use either of a guide or a book to find the objects worthy of observation in a city (I am averse to all dictation as what I should admire, and never permit myself to be deprived of the pleasure of finding for myself the works of art in a gallery which are known to me by reputation), therefore it is very possible that I have erred in many instances. On the first day I looked for a long time and with attention at the works of art which are in the gallery proper, before the apartments were opened in which the *most choice* are situated. I am even now glad I did so, as afterwards, when I had seen the most perfect specimens of art, I could never again remain for any length of time with the works exhibited in the gallery. One exception to this was the *group of the Laocoon*, which I always contemplated with renewed admiration. When the sanctuary of art was thrown open we first beheld the celebrated *Medicean Venus*, whose perfect and surpassingly beautiful form is yet more thrown out by the large curtain of red-velvet suspended behind her. In the same rotunda with her are the greatest master-pieces ever produced

by the chisel and by the brush: the *Apollo del Belvedere**
and *Raphael's St. John*. To contemplate and admire in these
three works of art the highest ideal of human beauty is
an enjoyment quite peculiar in its kind. After reiterated
contemplation and long hesitation I gave the palm for beauty
to the *St. John*. Any thing more charming and at the same
time more noble than the whole form of this Youth cannot
be imagined by the most lively fancy. What may have contributed somewhat to this decision on my part is the circumstance that the *Apollo* as well as the *Venus* are of a three-
quarter-life size, a proportion which seems to be not quite
happily chosen, as the figures being so nearly the real size of
life, always appear to be wanting in something, which, if they
were smaller, would not be the case. The *Apollo* has nevertheless a rather too feminine beauty, which not I alone, but
my wife also and several other persons present remarked. In
this apartment are numerous other master-pieces, among which
a head by *Raphael*, the *Venus* of *Titian*; and a group of gladiators in marble, excited most our admiration. Of the pictures arranged according to the schools in the side apartments,
the head of a female, by *Carlo Dolce*, pleased me most; but
one soon returns again to the gems of the whole collection.
On the other side of the building, in two apartments, is the
collection of Bronzes, among which the celebrated flying *Mercury* excites the most admiration. In another saloon is a collection of *Niobes*, among which are some beautiful works of
art. Besides these we saw innumerable portraits of celebrated
masters, for the most part painted by themselves.

November 13.

Behind the residence of the Grand-duke is a large garden called, I know not why, *Boboli*. It is open to all on Sundays and Fridays. Last Sunday we went there for the second
time, and afterwards heard mass in the Court-chapel. The

---

* This is the *Apollino*. *Spohr* himself corrects this error at a subsequent part of his narrative.

Grand-duke, who has a collection of between three and four-hundred masses of celebrated masters of every period, had given out upon this occasion one of *Michael Haydn's* for performance; it was executed with tolerable precision, but it was found necessary to play a very simple solo for the tenor-trumpet upon the viol. The musicians asked me afterwards whether we had players on the trumpet in Germany who could execute such soli as that!

Upon our way back our hired lacquey pointed out to us the covered passage leading from the Grand-ducal residence to the water side, which passes through several streets at a considerable height, and after being carried across the river Arno over one of the bridges, and through a few more streets, abuts at the government buildings in which the gallery is also situated. This gallery, which is at least a quarter of an hour's walk in length, is used by the Grand-duke when in wet weather he attends the sittings of the privy council.

November 15.

Our concert yesterday was not better attended than the first and therefore brought in nothing. I am now convinced that an instrumental-musician, even under the most favourable circumstances, can earn nothing in Florence; for in the first place the Italians esteem and like instrumental music too little, and in the second the price of admission is much too low in proportion to the considerable expenses. I must here observe, as somewhat worthy of note, that one part of the orchestra, namely, all the violinists, took no payment, which for people who must live from their daily earnings, and for Italians who, wherever possible, extort three times the price of every thing, is certainly very astonishing. For the rest, my play was received with still greater applause yesterday than the first time. Madame *Georgi* sang exceedingly well the admired cavatina (sung everywhere in Italy) in *Rossini's* "Tancredi," with the following theme:

It was again to be deplored, that upon the return to the theme she overwhelmed it with so much ornamentation that one could recognise nothing of the original song. Signor *Sbigoli*, first tenor at the *Pergolo* theatre, who had also given his assistance at the first concert, again sang two airs in a good style, and with much exertion, but with little voice. He, like the singers in Venice and Milan who sang at my concerts, required payment, but was satisfied with the very moderate sum of a carolin for each concert.

This afternoon we, for a last excursion, strolled out to the *Porta Romana*, to see the fresco-painting, so celebrated from the circumstance which gave rise to it, and which adorns a small mean-looking house there. The following is related concerning it: The Medici had sent to Rome for the most famed masters of that time, to paint, I believe, the chapel *al fresco*. The Florentine painters first became informed of this upon the day previous to the arrival of the strangers, and jealous of the preference which they had attained, they resolved at least to shew them, that they were quite as well able to execute the work, which they were sent for to perform. They combined their abilities therefore, and in one night, by the light of torches, painted this large fresco-picture, of which it is true but few traces now remain, but which sufficiently attest the excellence of the work. As the house on which this painting is executed, is so situated that it must attract the immediate attention of all persons entering at this gate, the foreign artists immediately observed the work, which had been completed but a few hours before, and as modesty was not then so rare among artists as it is in the present day, they immediately turned back, and sent word to the Medici, that they could not understand why they had been written for, since Florence produced artists who could execute so admirable a work of art in the space of a single night, as they had beheld. As a matter of course the work was then given to the Florentines for execution.

We have fixed our departure for to-morrow. Some things of note, such for example as the tomb of the Medici, which we have not yet been able to see, we must defer until our return journey.

Rome, November 22.

We arrived at length last night, after a long and tedious journey, in the former capital of the world. The journey was rendered tedious, first by the slowness of our vetturino, the driver of which had taken up, besides ourselves, who had hired the interior of his vehicle for twelve Louisd'or (*inclusive* of night lodgings and supper), three other travellers in the so-called cabriolet, and therefore could only drive at a walking pace, secondly, by reason of the raw weather and the cold, which for Italy was very great, and against which so little shelter is found at the inns where we stopped for the night, where the windows and doors are always open a good hand's breadth, the floors of stone, and the generally very lofty rooms not to be warmed by a chimney fire; thirdly, from the uninteresting and barren country through which the road passes. One has the choice of two roads. The one longer, but more interesting, by way of Perugia, a journey of seven days; the other through Sienna of six days. We took the latter. As far as Sienna it is not without interest, and it is a clean and a pretty town, which has moreover the reputation that the purest Italian is spoken there. But from there the road runs through numerous barren stretches of country. Neither houses nor trees are to be seen, and now and then only the melancholy testimonials of Roman justice, that is, high posts from which are suspended the arms and legs of bandits and murderers. How in a country whose soil yields without manure two harvests, one of corn and the other of maize, men should be compelled by hunger to subsist by robberies, is to me incomprehensible: but so it is. So long as corn is in abundance, all the roads are safe, but when hunger pinches, the sternest severity is unavailing. During the rule of the French knives were forbidden to be carried on the person on pain of the galleys; if any one drew a knife upon an opponent he was treated as a murderer and hung without mercy. By such measures the public security was soon re-established and for a long time one heard of no more assassinations. Now, though certainly those regulations still exist, they are not rigorously carried out: the previous insecurity prevails anew, and it is not safe to venture alone into the more lonely streets of the city.

Before we could drive to an inn, we were obliged to proceed to the custom-house, where our trunks and other luggage were inspected in the closest manner. For my violon, although it is an old one and for my own use, I was obliged to pay a duty of seven Paoli.

December 5.

This is the first music we heard in Rome, and since then have heard it so frequently, that I have been enabled to write it down easily. During the time of Advent, when all public music is forbidden, the theatres closed, and a real deathlike stillness prevails, whole troops of virtuosi on the bagpipe come from the Neapolitan territory, who play first before the pictures of the Virgin and Saints, and then collect in the houses and in the streets a *viaticum*, or travelling penny. They generally go in pairs, one playing the bagpipe and the other the shepherds-pipe. The music of all, with a few unimportant deviations, is the same, and is said to have its origin in a very ancient sacred melody; but from the way in which these people now play it, it sounds profane enough. Heard at a certain distance it nevertheless does not sound badly; the one who plays the bagpipe produces an effect somewhat as though three clarinets were blown, he of the shepherds-pipe a sound like that of a coarse powerful hautboy. The purity of the notes of the bag-pipe and shepherds-pipe is very striking. Wherever one now goes, be the part of the city which it may, one hears the above music.

Last Sunday Prince Frederick of Gotha took me to the famous Sestine Chapel, where I for the first time saw the Pope, surrounded by all the Cardinals in their fullest ecclesiastical splendour, and heard his celebrated singers of the choir. Whether it is that I am differently organized from other travellers, or that my expectations are always too exalted from the perusal of books of travel, neither the music, the place, nor the ecclesiastical ceremony pleased me, or impressed me with awe. The singers of the choir were about thirty in number, who comported themselves in a somewhat off-hand and uncouth manner. The soprani, for the most part old men, frequently sang false, and altogether the intonation was anything but pure. They commenced with melodies for two voices of very ancient date, which were declaimed by the singers rather than sung. Then followed some things for four voices, written in a condensed style, and arranged for the voices to fall in like in a catch. The composition of these seemed to me very dignified. in the genuine old ecclesiastical style, and well calculated for the place. The execution was correct, it is true, but, as we have said, too coarse, and not better than most of our German choristers could have sung the same kind of thing. Three and four-voiced soli interchanged alternately with the choir; sometimes one heard also the *crescendo* effected by the gradual and successive entry of the voices, and the *diminuendo* produced by the inverse process, which in the celebrated *Miserere* on Good Fridays is said to have so charming an effect. It had also a good effect to-day, but this can be equally obtained from any well-practised choir. The place is indeed extremely favorable to simple slow church music, as it is very sonorous and the voices blend well with one another; but I know several churches in Germany — for instance the castle chapel at Würzburg and the catholic church at Dresden — where music sounds even better. I became also, convinced anew, that vocal and instrumental music combined have a much finer effect than vocal music alone, which, after all is always somewhat monotonous, and, on account of its restricted limits, becomes tedious. But in the papal chapel there is never any instrumental music, being contrary to ecclesiastical etiquette. Lastly, as far as regards the ceremonies, which, according to the accounts of travellers, are on Good Friday of so elevating a character, and increase immensely the effects of the music, this was by no means the case on Sunday; on the contrary, many things took place which could not but appear ridiculous to an unprejudiced spectator; for instance, the frequently repeated removal, as though at the word of command, of the little red caps of the cardinals, the clumsy awkwardness of several of their attendants when carrying after them their long violet-coloured trains, and on handing to them and again taking off their caps, etc. I also felt indignant when I saw that the priests who read the mass, and the preacher, before he ascended the pulpit, threw themselves upon their knees before the Pope and kissed his red slipper; and how every time previous thereto two assistants fell upon one knee, spread out his capacious mantel and lifted his sacerdotal frock to enable him to raise his foot for them to kiss. Neither did any of his assistants hand any thing to him, not even his pocket handkerchief, without previously kneeling before him. What is this but a degradation of humanity?

The celebrated "Last Judgement" of *Michael Angelo*, and all the other fresco-paintings which decorate the chapel, have greatly suffered and are much blackened with smoke. But one can still see sufficient of the former, which covers the whole wall behind the altar, to admire the grandeur of the composition and the masterly touch of the artist in the execution.

After the mass the sacrament was presented to the Pope and all the Cardinals in the Pauline Chapel, which, illuminated by innumerable tapers, presented when first seen an imposing spectacle. As we got there first, we heard the chaunt of the choristers who walked at the head of the procession, approach by degrees nearer and nearer, which produced a fine *crescendo*. A silent prayer, during which all present remained kneeling, here closed the ceremony.

In Rome there are two private musical réunions: one, a kind of singing academy, takes place every Thursday at the house of its institutor, *Sirletti*, a teacher of singing and of the piano-forte. From thirty to five-and-thirty singers, mostly dilettanti, meet here, some of whom have very fine voices, as, for example, Madame *Vera* (née *Häser*) and the tenor, Signor *Moncade*. Up till now we have been there twice. The first day, in compliment to us Germans, they gave *Mozart's* Requiem, and that very powerfully and purely;

all the soli and the quartet were especially well sung. Madame *Vera* with her splendid sonorous organ, her firm intonation, and her fine management of the voice, sang her part in an irreproachable manner. The grand and very difficult fugue was in particular sung purely and well. The only disturbing influence upon the execution, which otherwise would have afforded us great enjoyment, was signor *Sirletti's* pianoforte accompaniment from the score. It is true we ought not to have expected better; for where should an *Italian* teacher of singing and pianoforte get a knowledge of harmony sufficient to read and play correctly a score of *Mozart's?* But as his deep (!) knowledge of harmony had been greatly extolled to me previously, I had certainly expected something better. He struck some such barbarous harmonies at times, that, could *Mozart* have heard him, he would have turned round in his grave. After the Requiem they sang a piece of *Händel's* hitherto unknown to me, and, for the finale, the Halleluja; the latter in particular was powerfully and purely sung.

On the previous Thursday they had sung some of *Marcello's* Psalms, for two and three voices. These Psalms, which the Italians consider classic master-pieces, and of which some years since a fine edition was published with long commentaries on the particular beauties of each Psalm, pleased me very well, but I did not find anything so very particular in them; on the contrary, I am persuaded, although I am not very familiar with the German works in this style, that we have compositions of the kind by *Bach* and others which are greatly superior to them. They appear to me, particularly in the form, to have been carelessly constructed, they deviate frequently for a length of time from the chief key, and then close immediately after the return to the tonic in a very unsatisfactory manner. Those for three voices begin generally with soprano and tenor, and the bass first enters with the repeat; but this third voice was never essential, and always sounded like an orchestral fundamental bass; there were however some among them in which the voices took up their parts as in a canon, and these were very remarkable. Nevertheless, on the whole, the part-writing and modulation were very monotonous, and the same intrate and appoggiaturas recurred in all. Signor *Sirletti's* accompaniment was again also very disturbing in these Psalms, and particularly unpleasant to me was an impurity of some of the full chords, which in these simple three-voiced things was still more out of place. With that, like all Italians whom I have yet heard accompany, he has the execrable fashion practice of doubling the bass notes with the right hand, which with some accords, for instance $^6/_5$ accords, sounds quite unbearable with the leading tone. That moreover, by this method octaves must arise in the solution, does not appear to trouble the Signori, nor are their ears offended by it. To me it was also exceedingly displeasing that some Germans who were present seemed so much delighted. What is the meaning of these grimaces? The Italians really might be induced to believe that we have never heard any thing so good in Germany. When will Germans cease to be the blind admirers and the apes of foreigners!

The other private musical réunion takes place every Monday, at the home of Signor *Ruffini*, the proprietor of the great manufactory of strings for instruments. Here operas are executed also by dilettanti as concert music, before an auditory of from 200 to 250 persons. The singers stand upon a slightly raised platform, and the orchestra, consisting of four violins, viol, violincello, double bass, two clarinets, two horns, and a bassoon, is disposed round them in a semi-circle on the level floor. Last Monday, when Prince Frederick took us there, an old *opera buffo* of *Paisiello* was given. The selection was certainly not the best concert music. The music of a comic opera can alone be produced with the desired effect upon the stage, combined with the proper action which belongs to it; but apart from that, this one appeared to me somewhat insipid. The execution both on the part of the singers and the orchestra, was equally bad; Signor *Moncade*, with his splendid tenor voice, was the only one worthy of remark. Between the two acts a dilettante executed the first Allegro of a clarinet concerto with much ability and a tolerably good tone, but without the least taste. He was another illustration of a remark I have already made, that Italian virtuosi and dilettanti direct their whole attention to the acquirement of mechanical skill, but as far as regards a tasteful style of execution, they form themselves very little after the good models which their best singers might be to them; while our German instrumentalists generally possess a very cultivated style and much feeling, which, without taking pattern of any one, they must find in themselves.

December 7.

As Rome, like other Italian cities, offers us no great musical treats (and even less than usual, at the present moment, as all the theatres are closed), we must, like all other travellers, content ourselves with the creations of architecture, painting, and sculpture of the former flourishing period of Italian art. Of these certainly there is a wealth such as is not to be found in any other city in the world. Wherever one goes — in the streets, in the squares, palaces, churches, and gardens — one sees everywhere columns, obelisks, statues, bas-reliefs and paintings. We first strolled through all the streets, in order to familiarise ourselves with the remains of ancient Roman architecture. The venerable Pantheon, the Forum Romanum with its triumphal arches and columns, and particularly the Colosseum, filled us with wonder and admiration. We then ascended the Capitol, saw the Tarpeian rock and a thousand other places and objects made interesting by Roman history.

On the following day we visited the immortal *Michael Angelo's* master-piece, the church of St. Peter. Several travellers whose expectations of this gigantic structure from their point of view had not been satisfied, had much depressed mine, and from that circumstance perhaps it made a powerful impression upon me. The open space before the church, with the semi-circular colonnades, the obelisk and the two stupendous fountains are of themselves of imposing grandeur. But on entering the interior of the church, one is seized with wonder and admiration at the magnificence of the decorations. Without being overloaded, it contains such wealth in mosaic pictures, statues, and bas-reliefs, that it would occupy weeks to examine all the separate works of art. As all these things are in the most harmonious relation and proportion to each other, and are as colossal as the whole structure itself, one is greatly deceived at first in regard to the size of the church. But upon contemplating more nearly the separate objects, one finds, for instance, that the little angels which hold the basins for holy-water, when seen closer, are taller than the tallest Prussian grenadier; and one finds the assertions of the architects who have taken all the dimensions of the building, more creditable, that, for instance, the cathedral of Strasburg could conveniently stand under the dome without the top of the tower reaching higher than into the lantern. But it is necessary to ascend into the interior of the lantern itself to convince oneself of the correctness of the other calculations, viz., that the pen of St. Peter is eight feet long, that four men abreast can conveniently walk round upon the cornice, etc. etc.

From the church we went to the museum of the Vatican. The riches it contains in treasures of art and antiquities, and the size and splendour of the place, surpass even the most exalted expectations. One first enters a long gallery on both sides of which the walls are encrusted with ancient Roman inscriptions and sepulchral stones, which had but little interest for us. We then came into a second gallery, in which are statues, busts, and fragments of sculpture innumerable. We then entered the famed Belvedere, where all round a circular open court, in the centre of which is a fountain, a number of niches, apartments, and saloons contain the most precious works of ancient and modern art. We first saw in one of the niches the celebrated *Apollo of Belvedere*, whose form is still considered the beau ideal of manly vigour and beauty. By a mistake for which I may be readily pardoned, since as I have said I never make use either of a guide or book, I had taken the somewhat feminine figure in the gallery at Florence for the universally admired Apollo of Belvedere. That statue, which is also of extreme artistic beauty, is, as I am now informed called the Apollino. In a second niche we saw the celebrated group of *Laokoon and his sons;* in a third, three master-pieces of *Canova*, a *Perseus* and two Roman gladiators. The *Perseus* is a wonderfully beautiful figure, but evidently imitated from the *Apollo;* for the head as well as the position of the body and of the mantle are strikingly similar. One of the gladiators is said to resemble more an English prize-fighter than a Roman gladiator; at least such is the opinion of the pupils and partisans of *Thorwaldsen,* who cannot forgive *Canova* his certainly very blamable vanity, that he should have placed his work, the only one of a modern in a museum of antiques. Nevertheless, if one judges without reference to persons, it must be admitted that in *Perseus* he has produced a splendid work of art, and that there are hundreds of antiquities in the museum which are not equal to it in artistic beauty.

In one apartment there is a great number of animals, single and in groups, in marble and other yet more costly and rare varieties of stone, of the most perfect execution. I could not give the preference to any one of them without disparaging the others. In other apartments are vases of immense size, of Egyptian granite and porphyry, cups, fountains and sarcophages with bas-reliefs, arabesques and other ornaments, as well as statues of all sizes. A two-wheeled Roman chariot, such as were used in chariot races, with two incomparably beautiful horses, greatly pleased us. The magnificence of the saloons, rotundi, apartments, and staircases exceeds anything we have ever seen. The floor consists almost wholly of ancient mosaics, and the ceilings are decorated with the most splendid fresco-paintings.

From the Belvedere two handsome staircases then lead one story higher up to a long gallery. One then enters an apartment in which the tapestries are hung which were worked after the drawings of *Raphael*. As is natural to suppose, not only the colours are said to be bad, as is usual with all tapestries, but the drawing is also defective, so that connoisseurs in art esteem them but little. In the composition and throughout the grouping, nevertheless, the spirit of *Raphael* is visible.

Now come the celebrated "Stanzi" of *Raphael*, which are considered by painters and connoisseurs in art as the most costly and beautiful, not only in Rome, but in the whole world. One of these apartments he finished entirely himself; in the others only some of the figures are of his execution; the rest were painted by his pupils and friends after his drawings and under his eye. The paintings are in much better preservation than those in the Sixtine chapel and, with the care which is now taken of them, they may for centuries to come attract the admiration of connoisseurs. It is nevertheless a sad reflection that some of the most precious things produced by the genius and pencil of *Raphael* are here adherent to the walls, and must perish with them. It is therefore fortunate that these paintings have been and are so frequently copied and engraved, that something of them will yet remain when the originals shall be no more. But this must not be permitted to be done in the way resorted to by the young Parisian academicians, who stick their tracing paper upon the paintings with wax or even fasten it on with nails, in order to copy the contours, by which proceeding a quantity of the lime cement has already crumbled away from one of the walls. An iron rail is now put up round the apartments, so that one can no longer approach close to the walls. The passages from these apartments lead to the "Logge" of *Raphael*, by which is understood the arched galleries outside the buildings. Those decorated by that master himself are now enclosed by glazed windows to shield them from the destructive effects of the weather, the rest are open. In these "logge" there are but four small paintings from his own hand; all the rest are painted by others after his drawings. In a niche at the end of the gallery stands a bust of *Raphael*, which is said, however, to be but an indifferent likeness of him.

December 9.

On a second visit which we made yesterday to the museum, we saw the room containing the celebrated oil paintings of *Raphael*. The finest of them is without a doubt the Transfiguration, respecting which so much has been written, and disputed. Connoisseurs of art are not agreed as to whether the composition is correct or defective. Some maintain that it consists of two separate groups which do not harmonise with each other in the least; others, on the contrary, say that every part is in the most perfect and beautiful accord. Without troubling ourself with the contentions of the æsthetics, which was renewed by two persons in our presence, we gave ourselves up to the enjoyment of its contemplation. It is extremely interesting to see here three paintings of *Raphael* of different periods of his life in close proximity to each other. The eldest, or that of his youthful days, hangs by the side of one by his master *Perugino,* and is painted wholly in his style, with the same hardness of outline and the same formal, almost symmetrical grouping. The one of the middle period (a Madonna with the child, and some others figures, resembling very much the painting at Dresden in the grouping) evinces his own genius enfranchised from the form of his teacher. In the third, the "Transfiguration," his last important work, we see the fully developed artist.

December 12.

As we live in a couple of rooms which cannot be heated, we have suffered somewhat from cold the last eight days, on account of the *Tramontana,* or north wind, which has not ceased to blow all that time; but although we have had hoar-frost a few times in Rome, we have had no ice yet, neither has it snowed. When we rose this morning, we found that the outside of our window was dim with moisture, and on opening it a warm moist air blew in; while the weathercocks informed us that the *Sirocco* (south wind) was blowing. It now soon became overcast, and this afternoon it is raining. Generally, however, the *Tramontana* brings bright settled weather. As Rome is very damp and dirty, one soon longs for the return of that wind, and is better content with a little cold than with the unwholesome moisture. In the spring of the year especially, when it begins to grow warm, this moisture is said to be quite unbearable, and to engender dangerous fevers, particularly on the other side of the Tiber, in the neighbourhood of the Vatican, where many a stranger, who has taken up his residence there on account of the cheaper rate of the lodging, has found a grave. In the summer months especially Rome must be very unhealthy, the air being charged with the exhalations from the dead bodies, which, according to ancient custom, are here all deposited in the vaults of the churches. Every time one of these vaults is opened, which takes place almost every day, a stench rushes out which penetrates into the interior of the very palaces of the living. At the time of the domination of the French the dead were buried outside the city, but no sooner was the papal rule restored, than that wholesome regulation was discontinued. No corpse is permitted to remain unburied longer than twenty-four hours, and accordingly the body of any one deceased is laid upon a bier, some eight or ten hours only after the breath is out of it, and carried with uncovered head, breast, and feet, in broad daylight, through the street to the church, and set down before the altar, when if the estate is sufficient to pay the expenses, a mass for the dead is read, and the body is thrown uncoffined through one of the openings of the vaults. That many only apparently dead are in this manner buried with the rest, may be readily imagined; and a few years ago such a case actually occured. A poor man, who a few hours after his apparent death had been thrown into the vault, was aroused by the fall and passed two fearful days among the half-decomposed bodies, when fortunately the chief entrance to the vault was opened in order to clear it out, and the poor fellow was rescued and is still living.

In no city in the world, I think, is the contrast so striking between the most luxurious splendour and the most abject misery as here. On the marble steps of the palaces, among the statues for which thousands have been paid, near the altars of the churches which are laden with golden ornaments and utensils — everywhere, in fact, one sees half-starved mendicants lying, who moan for bread, and gnaw the stumps of cabbages or the peel of lemons, which they have picked out of the gutter. At first I thought this a trick merely to excite the compassion of strangers; but I became convinced afterwards that many of the poor must for days subsist on such horrid food, or perish with hunger. The Romans are accustomed to see this misery from their youth, and seldom give alms (except they drop it into the begging-box of some well-fed monk collecting for his monastery), and strangers soon become hardened to pity, when they find that as soon as they have given something to one beggar, they are immediately surrounded by *twenty others*. It is true there are many among them who beg from sheer idleness, but there are many also who are quite unable to work for a livelihood. In this respect also I admire my native country, where every pauper has at least potatoes and bread, and a case of one dying of starvation in the midst of his richer fellowmen is wholly unheard of.

December 19.

Last evening our concert took place. As I had been refused permission to give a public concert in the theatre during Advent, I was obliged to make arrangements to give it at a private house, without any public announcement. Prince *Piombino* granted me an apartment for the purpose in the *Ruspoli* palace, and Count *Apponyi*, the Austrian ambassador, procured for me a considerable number of subscribers; so that this was the first concert in Italy that brought me a somewhat considerable profit. The price of admission was one Piaster (nearly a Laubthaler). The orchestra, composed of the best musicians of Rome, was nevertheless the worst of all that had yet accompanied me in Italy. The ignorance, want of taste, and stupid arrogance of these people beggars all description. Of *nuances* in *piano* and *forte* they know absolutely nothing. One might let that pass, but each individual makes just what ornamentation comes into his head and double strokes with almost every tone, so that the *ensemble* resembles more the noise of an orchestra tuning up than harmonious music. I certainly forbade several times every note which did not stand in the score; but ornamentation has become so much a second nature to them, that they cannot desist from it. The first hornist, for instance, blew once in the *Tutti,* instead of the simple cadence,

The Clarinets blew perhaps at the same time

and now if one imagines the figured passages for the violins, which the composer has prescribed, some conception may be formed of the bewildering noise which such an orchestra gives you for music. With that, the musicians have so little musical taste, and are so unskilled in note-reading, that we nearly broke down twice. Here also, my concerto in the form of a vocal-scene pleased most, and I gained far more applause for the way in which I played the song parts, than for the mastery of very great difficulties. A tenor belonging to the papal orchestra, the permission for whose co-operation I had obtained with great difficulty, sang a duet with Mademoiselle *Funk* of Dresden, and a very beautiful air of *Rossini,* the best of that composer which I had yet heard.

December 20.

Last evening I was present at a small private musical performance at the house of Count *Apponyi*. There was much good vocal music with piano accompaniment. The best were a duet from a "Passione" by *Paisiello*, most charmingly sung by Madame *Häser* and the Countess *Apponyi*; an aria by *Zingarelli* with chorus, written for Madame *Häser* and executed by her in the most finished manner; a duett of *Rossini's*, sung by Countess and Signor *Moncade*. Madame *Häser* sang with a feeling and a purity such as I never heard her display before. Her magnificent sonorous voice, which in a room with much reverberation sounds almost too sharp, particularly in the higher tones, had a fine effect yesterday in an apartment where the tapestry and carpeting deadened the sound. She has at command every nuance of tone, from the most tender breathings to the greatest fullness of power, and she knows how to avail herself of it in a masterly manner. She has lost, it is true, the brilliant fluency of voice which was formerly so much admired in Dresden, but she retains still enough of it to enable her to give every vocal ornamentation with ease and elegance. The only thing I miss in her singing is the shake, which in the present day is so much neglected. *Moncade* is a singer with a fine chest voice, and a tasteful though not a very feeling execution. Besides them, Prince *Frederick of Gotha* sang an air, and a bass singer a couple of Buffi.

I have again been twice to *Sirletti's* music parties. A week ago some parts of the Requiem were repeated and the Halleluja; but the rest of the evening was wholly devoted to *Marcello's* Psalms. With regard to the latter, I find my former opinion still more confirmed. In the fine edition of these Psalms, there is also a biography of *Marcello*, in which the reason is given for his relinquishing theatrical compositions, to which alone he had previously devoted himself, and taking all at once to sacred music. On visiting a church in a retired part of Venice, he had the misfortune to fall through a badly covered opening into one of the subterranean dead-vaults, and remained there a long time before his cries for assistance were heard. This accident induced so serious a tone of mind, that ever after he would write nothing but sacred music.

I have again been to *Ruffini's* music parties also, and heard a tragic opera by a young and early deceased composer, who had much native talent but evinced also a complete deficiency of study. The singer showed to more advantage in this opera than in the one they gave previously; but the orchestra was just as unbearable. I sat next to the formerly so celebrated singer *Crescentini* (but, who is said to have now wholly lost his voice, although he is scarcely fifty years of age), and I had the satisfaction to find that his opinion upon the present state of music in Italy agreed in every respect with mine. His conversation evinced the highly cultivated artiste, free from the trammels of prejudice. He deplored that at the present day the good school of vocal music, the only one in which Italians had distinguished themselves, had become more and more rare every day, and upon his last return to Italy (I think he had been in Paris) he had found so frivolous and bad a taste, that it no longer bore the least trace of the former simple yet noble style of his time. To him, also, who had heard much good music in Germany and France, the insipidity and incorrectness of modern Italian music are abominations.

December 23.

Now that the festival of Christmas is approaching, begging, with which one is plagued here at all times, will be carried on on a large scale. Wherever you go, you are greeted with the cry of "Pleasant holidays!" and you are then expected to pull out your purse. This system of begging occurs, it is true, in Germany at New Year, but is by no means so general as here. For instance, the servants of all the nobility and gentry at whose houses have shewn yourself, if but once, come to beg of you; and indeed at other times as well, foreigners are laid under contribution by them. If you have paid the master a visit, the servant comes the next day and asks you for a present. As one cannot give less than three Paoli, it becomes a dear amusement to deliver many letters of introduction here. The poor devils are certainly very badly paid, and must resort to such a system of begging if they would not starve.

Yesterday *Meyerbeer* and his mother arrived here. He received a letter in Florence from *Carl M. von Weber*, and read to me from it the gratifying intelligence that my Opera "Faust" had already been twice performed at Prague with marked approbation.

December 25.

Last evening we were present at a service in the Sixtine chapel preparatory to the approaching high festival. I had anticipated something very effective but I found myself very much mistaken. The illumination was by no means effective, for the chapel was soon so filled with the smoke of the tapers that you could not see distinctly ten paces before you. Instead of the four-voice Psalmody which I had hoped for, the singers of the choir recited merely a rather long Litany of prayers in *unisono,* without any melody, something as the following:

To listen to this for almost half an hour without interruption was the greatest musical penitence that I ever endured. At length, in the midst of a silent prayer, we were refreshed by a four-voiced solo, in which the splendid soprano-voice before alluded to was again remarkable. But immediately after this, the monotonous chaunt was again resumed, and now we thought it preferable to work our way through the compact crowd at the expense of great exertion rather than to endure it any longer.

This morning early we at length saw the head of the catholic church in the highest ecclesiastical pomp perform mass in the church of St. Peter. The high altar under the dome, divested of its habitual covering, was radiant with gold and precious stones; the clergy and cardinals, habited in their richest gold-embroidered stuffs, the body-guard in their splendid uniform, the Swiss guard in their bright polished old German armour, in a word all converted with the pope contributed to render this service the most splendid spectacle ever performed in a church. For more than a theatrical spectacle it was not to the surrounding crowd: not a sign of emotion or spiritual elevation was to be seen among the many thousand spectators! The appearance of a spectacle got up for amusement was more especially given to it by the circumstance that for the accommodation of the high personages who were present — the king of Spain, the queen of Etruria, the princes of Prussia, Gotha and others — a sumptuously decorated box had been erected, and, that upon the amphitheatre the fashionable world of Rome was present in full dress. A singular contrast with this splendour was presented by the rags and dirt of the riff-raff of the Roman populace who had pressed to the very step of the high altar. As the "service" became tediously long, and what the singers sang was neither very interesting, nor could be heard distinctly for the noise in the church, we preferred to take a walk, as the weather was so mild and bright, but returned in sufficient time to the church to see the procession, which forms the close to the whole performance.

In front moved a detachment of the body-guard, behind these the Cardinal's hat was carried upon a sword; then came the Cardinals, and lastly the Pope seated upon a richly decorated sedan or throne borne by eight priests; on either side of him two large fans of white ostrich feathers; then all the clergy, and lastly the remainder of the body-guard and Swiss guards. During the procession, the Pope, a venerable old man of 75, on whose pale and interesting face the exhausting influence of frequent fast and of the long fatiguing service were very distinctly visible, bestowed with a feeble motion of the hand his blessing upon the people. But the latter shewed during this no sign of devotion; not a knee was bent; there was laughing and loud talking during the whole service. The procession passed out through a side chapel into the Vatican. The immense size of the church could be first rightly seen to-day, from the mass of human beings which it held. It was full half an hour before they could make their exit through three large doors.

December 27.

Yesterday, at last the theatres were once more opened, after being closed six months. At the *Argentino* theatre, the largest and handsomest, *Rossini's* "Tancredi" was performed, at the theatre *Valle*, a new *Opera buffa* by Signor *Pietro Romano*, called "Il Quiproquo." As "Tancredi" is an old opera, the first night of which is not more interesting than the succeeding ones, *Meyerbeer* easily persuaded me to go with him to the *Valle* theatre, while my wife and the children, with Madame *Beer*, went to the *Argentino* theatre. Before the opera a farce in prose was given, imitated from our German "Proberollen." Then came the first act of the opera, the text of which we soon recognised as an adaptation of the *"Nouveau Seigneur de Village."* The subject, though spun out somewhat too much, was neither so stupid nor so wearisome as those of most Italian operas. But so much the more insipid and common-place is the music. Signor *Romano* has taken the now so much admired *Rossini* as his model, and so closely imitated him, or rather copied him outright, that the pit called out every moment *"Bravo Rossini!"* With that his music is so incorrect, that an ear accustomed to a pure harmony cannot hear it without disgust. Nevertheless that was no injury to it here, but much more so its want of fire and noise, the last of which the Italians are as fond of as the French and Germans. Once only, after a duet, the pit called out the encouraging and joyful *"Bravo Maestro!"* for which he immediately made a most profound bow. All the rest was listened to with coldness, and at the conclusion of the opera neither approval nor displeasure was expressed. The singers were by no means sure of their parts, and were continually making mistakes. Madame *Georgi*, the *prima donna*, who in the previous carnival had been the favorite of the public, did not please much yesterday, and had the annoyance of seeing the *seconda donna*, who certainly did not sing badly, called forward after her aria in the second act, an honour which had not fallen to her lot all the evening. She shewed her displeasure at this by singing the rest of her part with the utmost indifference and and with half-voice only, by which however she injured the last finale very much, and was perhaps the cause of the opera's going off so coldly, and of the report which prevails in the town to-day, that she had not given satisfaction. The orchestra, composed for the most part of the professors (!) who had played at my concert, played crudely, incorrectly and without any sort of difference between piano and forte.

This morning there was another private music party at Count *Apponyi's*. Nothing else scarcely was sung but things from *Rossini's* operas, of which a terzette, from "Elisabetha," if I am not mistaken, pleased me most, on account of the excellent treatment of the voices. The more I hear of *Rossini's* compositions, the more I am disposed to join *in part* with the general opinion, which pronounces him the most distinguished of modern Italian composers, and as a reformer of the taste in operatic style. *Mayer* may nevertheless with propriety be excepted, who has, if not so much imagination as *Rossini*, yet, certainly, more knowledge and æsthetic feeling. That the latter is wanting in knowledge of harmony, delineation of character, sense of the difference between the serious and comic style, and of propriety. I observed already in Florence, after hearing the "Italiana in Algeria." *Rossini*, however, has devised *some quite new things*, although they are not necessarily good because they are new: for instance his "flowery song," as *Meyerbeer* very characteristically calls it, which in reality is nothing more than that the passages hitherto sung on one vowel are sung with a series of syllables, as in an aria in the "Italiana":

or in a duet between a tenor and a bass in the same opera, where the part for the second voice is very unsingable and more like an orchestral bass than a singing bass: *

Every time such little tricky passages occur, and are well executed by the singers, as to-day by *Moncade* especially, the auditory breaks out into an ecstasy of applause which causes Italian music to degenerate more and more into a mere tickling of the ears and both singers and composer; become every day less capable in use of working upon the feelings; so that I may say without exaggeration, that of all the compositions we have yet heard in Italy, I have not experienced the least emotion, with the exception of one or two passages in the "Testa di bronzo"; and of all the singers we have yet heard,

---

*) As I do not know the text, I have appended dots for the syllables.

Madame *Häser* alone, in a duet from the old "Passione" of *Paisiello* moved me for a few seconds.

Likewise new, and first introduced by *Rossini,* is the way in which the speaking passages in the *Opera buffa,* hitherto usually written in one tone, or at least at very close intervals only, and formerly always given *legato,* are provided with syllables, as for instance in the beginning of the above duet:

Well known as this commencement is (it resembles the beginning of a finale in a quartett of *Haydn* in E flat-major):

yet his method of giving it with the different syllables of the text in this manner is quite new; but whether good or not, is still the question; to me it always sounded as though travestied, as if, for instance, a song which admits of a feeling execution were executed upon a singing instrument and for fun's sake so caricatured that it excited laughter instead of emotion. At any rate no instrumentalist of taste would play the above song *staccato*.

The following and similar *crescendo* passages are also peculiar *to Rossini,* they appear in almost all his musical pieces, and the Italian public are thrown into ecstasies by them; for instance, in the overture to the "Italiana."

In this manner it continues for a while, until at length at the strongest *forte*, the public break out into a furious clapping of hands and shouts of "Bravo!" In fact it can so little resist such a *crescendo*, that even the luckless imitators of *Rossini*, like Signor *Romano* in the opera last night, understood how to draw down a storm of applause by it. That such passages are frequently very incorrect and offensive from the passing notes occurring in them, it is not necessary for me to remark; even in the celebrated cavatina from "Tancredi," so enthusiastically admired throughout Italy, and which was also sung to-day, there are in the very first bars the most hideous-sounding octaves, between the bass and the second hautboy, that I ever heard.

The first result of my judgment of *Rossini* is, therefore, that he is by no means wanting in invention and genius and with those qualifications had he been scientifically educated, and led to the only right way by *Mozart's* classical masterpieces, he might readily have become one of the most distinguished composers of vocal-music of our day, but, as he now writes, he will not raise Italian music, but much rather lower it. In order to be new, *Rossini* departs more and more from the simple and grand style of song of former days, and does not reflect that in so doing he wholly robs the voice of its charm and advantages, and actually debases it, when he farces it to execute passages and fioritures, which every petty instrumentalist can produce much purer, and especially much *more connected,* because he has no need to express a syllable every time on the third or fourth note. With his "flowery song," however much it may please, he is therefore in a fair way to make a clearance of all *real* song which is already now very scarce in Italy, and in which the despicable horde of Imitators, who here as well as in Germany pursue their pitiful calling, are doing their best to assist him.

December 29.

Last evening I went with *Meyerbeer* to hear "Tancredi" at the *Argentino* theatre. I never wetnessed a more wretched performance. The singers, with the exception of *Paris* the elder, are very *mediocre;* the *prima donna,* the younger *Paris,* is yet quite a beginner, the *basso* was frightful, the orchestra worse than in the smallest provincial town in Germany, and in a word, it is an assemblage of folks such as had all Italy been ransacked for the purpose, it would have been difficult to find worse. God help the composer whose work falls into such hands! They disfigured it in such a manner that one can no longer recognise it. The only one person who distinguished herself, was the elder *Paris*, who, in the part of "Tancredi," displayed a powerful, healthy contralto voice and a cultivated execution. It would be unjust after such a representation to pass judgment upon the opera, and the more so, as several passages were omitted and others substituted. The ballet which was given between the acts, was quite of a piece with the rest: a serious ballet executed by a number of grotesque dancers! But among these were some men, who made themselves remarkable by the power, and agitity and by springs of all kinds.

During the last week we have again seen many interesting things; the museum of the Capitol, in which the dying gladiator and several Egyptian statues pleased me most — the latter less remarkable for artistic beauty than for singularity; the picture gallery in the *Doria* palace, which contains among many other remarkable pictures, four beautiful handscapes by *Claude Lorrain;* another gallery in the *Colonna* palace, in which hangs an extremely beautiful head of *Raphael;* the handsome and richly decorated churches of *Santa Maria Maggiore* and *St. Giovanni in Laterano,* &c. From the portal of the latter one has an extensive view in the direction of Albano, which with the ancient aqueducts, which the eye can follow for miles, and other remains of ancient Roman architecture, possesses much romantic interest.

On Sunday evening, the weather being very clear, we asscended the dome of St. Peter's church. The ascent is at first by a footway of a spiral form without steps as far as the roof of the church. Arrived there once fancies one'sself again in the streets of a town, for the ground is paved, and a number of houses, some of which are inhabited, together with numerous small and large cupolas, prevent a view into the distance. But if you walk up to the gigantic statues over the portal of the church, you then see at how great a height you are standing. The pavement of the square in front of the church looks like a minute mosaic, and the people little puppets creeping about upon it. On looking up to the dome from here, it looks like an enormous isolated building; from the first interior gallery one has also to mount to a considerable height before one arrives at the second, where the first swell of the dome begins. The view from these galleries, particularly from the second, down into the church is quite *sui generis*, and makes one positively shudder. The hundred lamps which burn right under the dome at the entrance of the subterranean chapel, seem to mingle as in one flame, and the human beings below appear like moving black spots. From the second gallery one then ascends between the inner and exterior dome by wooden steps up to the lantern, from which one has again a view down into the church that makes the head turn. From here a flight of winding stone steps once more leads up into a tolerably large chamber situated in the top of the lantern, and thence at length ascending an iron ladder, one passes through the shaft to the ball, which is large enough to contain from twelve to sixteen persons.

The foolhardy can ascend yet higher, by a ladder outside the ball, up into the cross, but we were quite satisfied with having been as high as the ball. The view from the external galleries is magnificent and varied beyond description. Below, proud Rome with its innumerable palaces, ruins, columns and obelisks; around it the villas.

In the distance the mountain near Tivoli and Albano, above which are seen the peaks of snow-covered mountains, and far away on the west the Mediterranean, which at the time of the day we ascended the dome looked like a fiery stripe in the distant sky. After we had long enjoyed this entrancing view, we descended and found that two hours had passed very rapidly in the ascent of the dome.

We also went up the high column on the *Piazza Colonna*, and from its summit, which rises high above all the houses, enjoyed one of the finest views of Rome and its immediate environs.

December 30.

I have acquired the conviction that the Italians, even in modern times, are not wanting in natural abilities for the study of the fine arts, and indeed, that on the whole they surpass therein the northern nations. Almost all their singers have a happy ear for intonation, and the faculty of immediately seizing and repeating a melody once heard; although but very few of them, even among the theatrical singers possess *what we call music*, and most of them scarcely even know their notes. At the last musical party at *Apponyi's* there was a Canon of *Cherubini's* to be sung, in which *Moncade* who, as I had been told, is one of the singers who cannot read music, although formerly a theatrical singer, was solicited to take a part. As he willingly assented to sing something that he did not know, I immediately thought that in his case at least what I had heard was untrue. The Countess first sang the slow melody consisting of eight bars and *Moncade* repeated it note for note with all the little ornaments which she had added. But when his part began, he could get no farther: nevertheless, he did not permit himself to be disconcerted, but sang away by ear, which certainly sometimes did not sound much like music by *Cherubini*. When, however, the third singer, who also had no music before him, began, after his first simple entry in the second part, also to compose, such confusion and discord arose that they were obliged to leave off. Both singers declared very ingenuously that they had hoped, they would have accomplished it; like the Englishman who, when he was asked if he played the violin, replied: "It is possible, but I have never yet tried."

Among the lower uneducated classes of the people, a remarkable genius for painting is by no means rare here, which is awakened by the early contemplation of the public works of art. In this manner the attention of the painters here has been attracted for the last year and more by the extraordinary artistic talent of a lad in the streets. This boy, without ever having had the least instruction, draws large historical sketches in charcoal upon the white walls of the houses, and there is scarcely a street in which some of his artistic work is not to be seen.

Sometimes he chooses for his subject a Madonna, or some legend, at others a Roman triumph. But in no one instance has he ever copied from any existing subject, or even repeated himself; his fancy constantly creates something new. Some of these sketches excite the greatest astonishment by the richness of the composition, comprising frequently more than thirty or forty figures, and by the correctness of the drawing. The most remarkable to me is the certainty with which he throws off and depicts his ideas. You see no double stroke in the contours — nothing wiped out — everything stands there at once clear and prominent. When he draws he is always surrounded by a crowd of people, who look on with gratification at the skill he displays; but he is so deeply engrossed with his work, that he heeds neither the surrounding spectators nor their remarks. I have been told that *Canova* took this lad, with the view of developing his talent; but that regular kind of life did not all please him, and he soon ran away.

January 1. 1817.

The new year has begun very unpleasantly for us. This morning *Emily* was taken suddenly ill. The doctor thinks she will have the scarlet fever; should that be the case, we shall be obliged to postpone our departure for Naples, which we had fixed for the 7th, for at least a fortnight. Added to the annoyance of remaining here yet longer without any object and in anxiety, is that of being compelled to see our fellow-countrymen with whom we had contemplated making the journey together depart alone, and that also of missing the opening of the St. Carlo theatre at Naples, which is to take place on the 12th. To console ourselves for the latter we shall meanwhile hear the new opera of *Rossini*, which he is writing for the

Valle theatre, and the début of Madame *Schönberger* at the *Argentino*.

January 3.

Not only *Emily*, but *Ida* also has caught the scarlet fever, and now for a certainty we shall not be able to leave before the 20th. Both children were very ill for some days, and my good *Dorette* has been extremely alarmed and anxious. I have kept up my spirits und amused myself in inventing some puzzle-canons and have now began to write a new solo-quartett.

I should so much have liked to make *Rossini's* acquaintance; but before he has finished his opera this is quite out of the question. The impressario, in whose house he lives, neither permits him to go out nor to receive visits, so that he may not neglect his work. Should his opera not be brought out before our departure, I shall probably not be able to see him.

January 18.

The children have recovered sooner than we had anticipated, and we have fixed to leave for Naples the day after to-morrow.

Last Thursday I went again to *Sirletti's*, and yesterday to the morning concert at Count *Apponyi's*; at neither place, however, was any thing played worth particular notice, with the exception of a fine quartett by *Mayer* and a duet from a comic opera of *Fioravanti*. *Mayer* is remarkable for scrupulously correct harmony, regularity of rhythm and a good treatment of the voices in part compositions, and surpasses therein all modern Italians. The duet out of *Fioravanti* more particularly interested me from the circumstance that it is also adorned with the modern so-called "flowery song," from which I find that *Rossini* is neither the first nor only one who makes use of it. I begin moreover to judge him more favourably, as long as he does not venture beyond the limits of *comic* opera, and when his music is as gracefully executed as by the Countess *Apponyi* and *Moncade*.

* * *

On the 20th January we left Rome. The *Campagna di Roma* is as little cultivated on this side as on the other; the road as far as Albano derives nevertheless much interest from the many antiquities seen on the way. The numerous remains of three or four old Roman acqueducts give a particularly romantic aspect to the country round. One of the acqueducts, which was less injured, has been repared in later times, and still serves to supply Rome with water upon this side.

While our *vetturino* was baiting his horses at Albano, I ascended the mountain upon which the lake of Albano is situated. The view across it towards Rome is exceedingly beautiful. Below at one's feet is seen the lake with its high precipitous banks thickly covered with trees and underwood; upon the right a long building, the use of which I do not know; to the left, upon the high steep bank, Castel Gandolfo, and in the extreme distance the mass of houses of Rome. The form of the lake and of its high precipitous banks indicates plainly that it has been formed by the falling in of a burnt-out crater.

The road from Albano to the little dirty town of Velletri, where we took up our first night-quarters, presents a great variety of scenery.

On the second day we crossed the Pontine marshes, which extend from Velletri to Terracina, a distance of four and twenty Italian miles. We did not find them so desolate and barren as we expected, for one has always a sight of the mountains on the left, and here and there of even a few patches of cultivated land. The numerous herds of oxen, buffaloes, swine, and in the dry parts, of sheep also, give some life to the uniformity of the level. But houses are of rare occurrence, and the inhabitants have always a pale unhealthy appearance. In the heat of summer the exhalations from the marshes are very dangerous, even to travellers who do but cross them, particularly if they abandon themselves to sleep, to which one is greatly induced by the uniformity of the road. Only last summer a young lady who could not resist the disposition to sleep inhaled death here, and was carried off by a malignant fever three days after her arrival in Naples. Such cases are not unfrequent in summer.

At *Torre a tri ponti*, a solitary hostelry, all the inmates of which looked as if they had just risen from their graves, we dined, and had very excellent meat, and roast ducks and geese, of which there are swarms in the uncultivated parts of the marshes.

Terracina, where we arrived at night-fall is most charmingly situated. The town stands upon a wild rocky eminence, but we stopped below at a very excellent inn close to the sea. From our windows we had a view of the sea, and on the following morning enjoyed the magnificent sight of the rising sun. Close below our windows, the waves broke with considerable noise, although during the previous day the wind had not been high. The air was as mild as after a warm summer's day in Germany, and in the evening late we saw the fishermen launch their barks through the surf by moonlight, to cast their nets.

On the next morning we had to pass through the most dangerous part of the whole journey, from being the most infested with banditti. This part is between Terracina and Fondi, where the road lies through a thinly inhabited country and almost always between masses of low bushes in which the scoundrels easily conceal themselves, and can shoot down travellers and their escort from an ambuscade without being perceived. It is here where the most robberies are perpetrated, and but recently only some travellers were again attacked. But the government has at length taken earnest measures to suppress this. We found several hundred peasants employed in cutting down all the bushes on both sides of the road and burning them; and we met several strong detachments of soldiers, sent out to hunt up the banditti in their fastnesses. From twenty to thirty have already been brought in and hung up with little ceremony. On this side of the Neapolitan frontiers we met a picquet of soldiers at intervals of every quarter of an hour, which bivouacked on the side of the road and sent out patrols during the night.

At Fondi, a poor dirty looking hole, where we were almost torn to pieces by beggars, we saw the first gardens of lemons, pomegranates and oranges. We took a walk through the town and were delighted with the sight of the splendid trees, which were loaded with the finest fruit. In the gardens and in the market we saw fine fresh vegetables, such as cauliflowers, savoy-cabbages, carrots, &c. But at noon the heat was so great, that we were obliged to seek the shade.

We passed the night at Molo di Gaëta, also a small town situate close to the sea. From the windows of our inn in the evening we saw the fishermen put out to sea by torchlight to fish. Between Molo and Santa Agata we saw a great number of evergreen shrubs and plants, which do not grow even in the north of Italy, and upon the rocks several kinds of aloes, such as we grow in greenhouses. Several other shrubs which are also indigenous with us were already in their first leaf. On the road-side the air was perfumed by the violets, and the fields with the blossoms of the beans.

Capua, where we passed the last night of our journey, is a handsome town with fine buildings. We supped in the evening with two Austrian officers, who told us among other things, that they did not bury people in Capua, but threw them down a hole about a mile from the town, which was unfathomly deep, but was believed to have a communication with the sea, as after some lapse of time one could hear the bodies of those who where thrown down fall into the water.

The road from Capua to Naples is the most uninteresting of the whole journey. Nothing else is to be seen on either side of the road but high mulberry trees and pendant vines, both now without leaves. At two o'clock in the afternoon we at length arrived at the long-wished for Naples, and found a lodging which had been already engaged and prepared for us by one of our fellow-countrymen.

END OF THE FIRST VOLUME.

Naples, January 1.

Naples, although not remarkable for beautiful architecture, is, from its situation and many peculiarities, one of the most beautiful cities of the world. On coming from Rome, one certainly misses the grander taste in architecture and other works of decorative art formed upon and refined by the study of the antique, which for ages has rendered that city the most interesting of all others to the architect, the sculptor and the painter; but one is compensated for that in Naples by other advantages that Rome has not. To an inhabitant of northern lands, the city presents from its amphitheatrical position a most imposing spectacle, and with its flat roofs covered with party-coloured and lacquered tiles, its cupolas and towers, it has a very novel and oriental appearance. It is moreover one of the most lively cities of the world, at least one of the most noisy; for although Vienna and Hamburg, the two most populous cities that I have yet seen, may have proportionately as many inhabitants as Naples, yet the latter, partly from its southern liveliness, and partly from the circumstance that here all classes idle away more time in the streets than they work at home, is much more animated than those cities. The noise in the streets is positively great beyond description, and until one has become somewhat accustomed to it, one is completely deafened by it. All the mechanics pursue their calling in the streets: blacksmiths, locksmiths, copper-smiths, carpenters, tailors and shoemakers — all alike sit in front of their houses variously intermingled, and work. Added to that the rattling of the carts and vehicles, which in the principal streets almost always move on two lines, the wild cries of itinerant vendors, always endeavouring to undersell each other, and lastly the animated language and gestures of those who meet, or converse in the streets, who to a German seem as though they were in violent dispute, although they are perhaps merely talking of the weather or some unimportant piece of news or town gossip. But more striking than in any other city of the world is the contrast between the luxury in the equipages and dress of the higher classes, and the dirt and nakedness of the lower ones, particularly of the so-called Lazzaroni. Of these whole families are to be seen lying in the streets in the midst of the *beau monde*, looking for vermin upon their half-naked bodies. A more disgusting sight I never beheld! And yet before *Murat's* time, who made soldiers of all the able-bodied Lazzaroni, these vagabonds were far more numerous.

February 3.

Yesterday we made our first excursion. In company with our Silesian fellow-countrymen, Herren *von Raumer, von Luttorf, Hagen* and *Kruse*, we first drove out to Portici to see the museum. Here, in a suite of apartments, are preserved the paintings and interior-decorations found in Herculaneum and Pompeii, from whence they have been taken from the walls with the plaster, and are here hung up in frames with glass doors. Of the greater part of them the colours are in excellent preservation, especially a very fine red. The room or interior decorations, consisting of arabesques, small landscapes, and the figures of animals, are almost all well painted. The larger historical paintings taken from temples and public buildings have great artistic merit, and are remarkable both for drawing and colour. Some of these are in a wonderful state of preservation, and appear as though they had been painted but recently. Besides these paintings, there is in another room a collection of a variety of metal utensils, a helmet, and some vases in pottery, with different kinds of grain, partly burnt by the glowing ashes, such as wheat, barley, Indian corn, beans, &c. &c. These different kinds of grain are readily recognised, and we found them quite similar to our own in size and form. All the other antiquities which were formerly preserved here have been transferred to Naples, and it is intended to transfer the paintings there also.

As the weather was extremely fine, we felt a great disposition to make the ascent of mount Vesuvius without loss of time. But as it was almost impossible for women and children to climb the last steep ascent, *Dorette* and the children returned to Naples, accompanied by Herr *Kruse*. We others hired some asses for the journey and return, at the extremely low charge of four Carlini (about 15 $\frac{1}{2}$d.), and set out at 12 o'clock at noon. At first the road lies through vineyards for about the distance of an hour and a half's journey, and with but a gentle ascent only; but the road begins already to be difficult, being very uneven and stony. We saw several vineyards enclosed with large bush-aloes instead of hedges. After the lapse of an hour and a half we came to a plain which spread away before us like a desolate waste, as far as the proper base of the volcano. Not a vestige of vegetation met the eye; on every side nothing but masses of lava piled upon each other! Our path now turned leftward across the plain towards a mountain ridge, which rises like an island out of the midst of this fearful wilderness. On this stands the so-called hermitage, a building of two stories high, where we refreshed ourselves with bread, wine, cheese and fruits, and enjoyed the fine and now tolerably extensive view. After a short rest, in company with ten Englishmen whom we met here, we resumed the road, which still continues to run over the summit of the ridge as far as the crater. This part of the way is the least difficult, leading for some distance through bushes of sweet chesnuts, the plain covered with black lava stretching away before the eye. After half an hour's progress we reached the steepest part of the ridge, at the foot of which we were obliged to leave the asses. Now began the difficult part of our work. Treading upon deep ashes without solid bottom, at every footstep one slips back so far, that one has often scarcely advanced an inch; and the mountain is here so steep, that one is obliged to use the hands as well for progression. Fortunately a ridge of solid lava extends downwards almost from the whole height, and rises like a ridge of rock from out of the ashes. When one has reached this, the toil is less, as the ground beneath has again become firm. But were one obliged, as at first, to wade always through the ashes, it would require a whole day to make the ascent of this height alone. Nevertheless it took a good hour to accomplish it, although we set out from our resting place with recruited strength, and with the hope of soon reaching the summit. On reaching the top, we saw again a small plain before us, from which in several places between the lava-rocks a white sulphurous steam ascended. The ground here was more or less hot and our footsteps produced a hollow sound. After we had passed rapidly over this we had to climb another though a lower height, and then beheld at a moderate distance before us the two craters, which were now vomiting fire. We sat down upon the ground between the lava-rocks and found ourselves as though sitting in a heated stove, for a great heat rose from the earth, which was nevertheless very agreeable to us. After we had rested here some time, some one of the company asked whether one could not ascend between the two cones close to the brink of the crater? All the guides replied in the negative, and assured us it was very dangerous to approach it nearer. We saw sufficiently well ourselves that it would be impossible to ascend direct from the place were we stood, as we should have run the risk of being stifled with the smoke of the crater upon our left. But it seemed to us that a way might possibly be found round the left side of one crater, from which we could ascend on the windward side of the other; so we immediately proceeded to make the trial together; after some objections our guides followed also. We had scarcely proceeded a distance of two hundred paces, when one of the craters with a fearful report threw out a quantity of red-hot stones, some of which fell at no great distance from us. This soon brought the whole party to a standstill; but after some little hesitation the foremost proceeded onward and the rest of us followed. In this manner, after a toilsome passage, we reached the rear of the left-hand crater, and then began to ascend the cone. But this was the most laborious task of the whole day, for we had now to climb a very steep incline up to our knees in ashes. Nevertheless, after great exertion we reached the summit and stood on the narrow edge of the crater, which, in the form of a funnel, is about two hundred feet in diameter at the upper part of the opening. After we had taken breath here awhile, and contemplated the eruptions of the other crater, which lay before us to leeward, the one closeto which we were standing, became suddenly quite clear of smoke, and we could look down into the awful abyss. We there saw large cavernous fissures between the masses of rock forming the neck of the funnel, out of which flames burst at intervals; but as these were immediately followed by smoke, this sight was of short continuance only. One of the Englishmen of our party took it into his head, at a moment when the smoke of the crater upon the brink of which we were standing was somewhat less, to run across even to the other, in order to look down into it. But scarcely had he reached the brink, when an eruption, though fortunately not a very strong one, took place, from which he had barely time to save himself, and rush back again to us. At the same moment a third crater behind us began to make a noise, and it was now indeed high time that we should make our retreat. Though it was ashes merely that it threw up, yet by the timely fear with which it filled us, it was our saviour from utter destruction; for scarcely had we reached our old halting-place than the hitherto very quiet crater on the brink of which we had stood, threw out such a mass of red hot stones, exactly in the direction of the place where we had stood, that we should all have been struck down and overwhelmed by them had we stopped there five minutes longer. After our daring party had recovered from the terror which had seized upon all, we were compelled to avow our extreme rashness in having ventured to ascend so high despite the warnings of our guides.

We now once more bivouaked upon our warm place, and recruited our spirits with the provisions we had brought with us. But with night drawing on, far away from every living creature, and surrounded on all sides by desolation, it was a fearful reflexion to think that we sat here suspended as it were over a sea of fire, upon a perhaps not very thick crust, which sooner or later might give way beneath us. Several of our party made the observation, that it was indeed a mad piece of folly to have risked life upon chances so eminently possible, for the mere gratification of an idle curiosity. But these reflexions nevertheless did not prevent us from enjoying with much relish the eggs our guides had brought with them and cooked in the hot ashes, and which we washed down with a draught of delicious *Lacrymæ Christi*.

We here awaited the approach of night; saw the sun sink below the sea, and the full moon rise behind the craters, her yellow light forming a beautiful contrast with the red flames that issued from them. On our right we saw at the same time the reflexion from the burning lava which poured from an opening in the side of the mountain, which however it was impossible to approach without the greatest danger.

About seven o'clock we set out upon our return, which at first, from our being obliged to descend on the shaded side of the mountain was on account of the darkness both very difficult and dangerous. But when we arrived at the precipitous places, our guides led back us by another way, where we slid down with giant steps over deep ashes. Below we found our asses, upon which we rode to Portici by a magnificent moonlight. At ten o'clock at night we arrived once more at Naples, highly gratified with the extremely interesting day's adventures.

February 7.

During the constant fine spring weather we daily take a walk to see the immediate environs of the city. The favorite walk of the children is to the quay, on which is the lighthouse, partly because the busy life in the port itself, as well as the sight of the different kinds of vessels, from the ship of war mounting a hundred guns down to the fisherman's boat, affords them immense pleasure, and partly because the way leading to it presents the most lively picture of the habits and occupations of the lower classes. From the St. Carlo theatre to the harbour there is, next to the Toledo-street, always the greatest crowd; at a short distance from which are all the small hole-and-corner theatres, where performances take place all the day long and where, upon a platform outside, a couple of fiddlers and a merry-Andrew constantly invite the passers-by to enter. Between these are the booths of the itinerant vendors, who, perched upon a table, recommend their medicaments to their numerous listeners and purchasers. Upon the quay, where there is no noise from the carts and carriages, the puppet-show players pitch their portative theatres, and the *Improvisatori* entertain the Neapolitans with the heroic feats of their ancestors. Sometimes one of these reads aloud to his auditory and then explains what he has been reading. But here also swarm the most impudent and disgusting beggars, and the most expert pick-pockets; so that one cannot be too careful how one gets mixed up with them. On my first walks into that quarter I lost my pocket handkerchief each time. If one waits here till the evening the Vesuvius, with its red fire, presents a singular and magnificent contrast with the white lights of the Pharos.

The Royal garden on the Chiaja is also another very interesting walk. It extends for a considerable length close to the sea, and consists of three very broad alleys with small flower-beds laid out in the English style. It is ornamented with several fine statues and groups in marble; in the centre stands the celebrated Farnesian Bull, a splendid antique by a Greek master; on both sides are several fine copies of ancient works of art, such as that of the Apollo of Belvedere, the rape of the Sabines, &c. &c. From eleven in the forenoon on fine days, the *beau monde* assembles here to look and to be looked at. If one proceeds still farther along the Chiaja, one soon comes to the road that leads through the Grotto of Pausilippo to Puzzuoli. This long gallery, extending at least for a thousand paces right through a mountain of considerable height, is very remarkable of its kind, for the galleries cut through the rocks in the road over the Simplon are but child's play compared to this work. The entrance on this side between towering rocks is exceedingly romantic; at a great distance off the noise of the carriages driving through resembles thunder, and it is said that at night, when all is quiet here, the sound of the vehicles in the streets of Naples, is echoed through this rocky gallery like that of distant thunder. The interior is lighted day and night with numerous lamps. At the entrance and in the middle are little chapels, at which the passengers are solicited for alms. Above the entrance high up on the rocks, a small grotto is pointed out, where the immortal poet Virgil lies buried.

A few days ago we visited also Fort St. Elmo, from which one has an extensive view over the whole city and of the expansive bay.

February 12.

Last evening we returned from a delightful excursion to the islands. On Sunday at noon, in company with our three Silesian countryman, we went across to Ischia in a hired boat. We were at first obliged to sail round the promontary of Pausilippo: Nisida and Procida lay quite close to us, Cape Micen somewhat in the background, and Ischia at a greater distance, in a direct line before us. These islands and promontories with their steep, and towering rocks close to the sea, and the rich fertility of their interior, present every moment and on every side on which they are beheld new aspects of varying interest, now of a beautiful and now of a bolder and grander character. Procida, in particular, one of the most populated spots of the whole world, presents a magnificent view from the sea, the whole island having the appearance of a large city. As the wind blew tolerably fresh and against us, night came on before we could reach Ischia. But the beauty of the evening would not permit us to regret our having been delayed. The stars shone with a brightness such as in Germany at least they are never seen to shine with; and Venus in particular was resplendent with so clear a light that its beams were reflected in the sea like those of the moon, and one could plainly discern a shadow from any intervening object. The sea, also, at every stroke of the oar shone as with the light of myriads of glowworms. About eight o'clock we at length landed at the north shore of the island and found a comfortable night-lodging in the handsome house of a clergyman.

On the next morning we soon set out upon our way to see the interior of the island and to ascend the Epomeo. As at Ischia there are neither vehicles nor roads to travel on, we all mounted upon asses, which carried us more conveniently and safely over the rocky and uneven ground. After passing through several level tracts in the highest cultivation we came to the small but lively town of Ischia, on the sea-shore, and onward to the foot of the Epomeo between vineyards to the opposite side of the mountain, where it is more convenient to climb. After we had ascended about half-way by very bad roads, we halted for an hour to rest and refresh the animals, and then completed the other still more toilsome part of the ascent. Meanwhile the sky had unfortunately become overcast with clouds, and upon reaching the summit of the mountain we were enveloped in a thick mist. We then entered a a hermitage of some size, consisting of several rooms and passages, and of a chapel. It resembles that at Freiburg in Switzerland, and like that also is hewn out of the solid rock, by two industrians recluses. We waited here some time in the hope that the weather would clear up, and several times also we had a glimpse between the clouds over the level parts of the island, which lay like a map outspread in the distance before us; but Naples, Capri, and Sorrento were veiled from our sight. We were at length obliged to set out on our way once more, without having had the pleasure of enjoying the fine view from here, which is perhaps one of the finest in the world, and had already considered our toilsome journey as a labour in vain, when on a sudden, after we had descended somewhat lower and stood under the stratum of clouds, the magnificent view of the whole of the islands, promontories and bay, with Vesuvius smoking in the background, displayed itself to our enraptured eyes. Long we stood lost in admiration of the singular beauty of the scene, and at length, when the setting sun gave token of departure, we returned by the shortest but steepest road, where we could make no use of the asses, to our quarter of the previous night. The Epomeo, which 450 years ago was a volcano, exhibits on this side, which is much more wild and barren than the other, numerous traces of former eruptions. The road led now almost continually over weather-worn lava. Upon the rocks we saw at very frequent intervals the stock-gilliflower in bloom, which here and in the neighbourhood of Naples grows wild. On the wayside violets and other plants, several of which are not indigenous with us, were in full flower, and in the gardens, the almond tree. At length we came to a place where there are warm baths, which in summer are much frequented by the Neapolitans. At the house of our host we found a plentifully spread table awaiting us, which after all the fatigue of the day was exceedingly acceptable. A fiery white Ischian wine of the year 1811 we found especially agreeable to the palate.

We re-embarked the next morning at eight o'clock and landed first at Cape Micenus, where we visited the large subterranean reservoirs of soft water from which the Roman fleets were supplied, and the *cento camere* of Nero, which were probably prisons for the detention of prisoners of war. We then sailed right across the bay to Puzzuoli, and there made another pilgrimage to some antiquities. On running into the harbour we sailed past the still standing piers and arches of the bridge of *Caligula*, which that Emperor designed throwing across the bay. Although built of bricks merely, such is the excellence of the cement used in their construction, that their remains, after the lapse of so many centuries, still bid defiance to the unceasing action of the waves.

Our cicerone led us first to the Solfatara, a round level field-like space enclosed on all sides with rocks, apparently a crater which at some remote period had fallen in. The subterranean fire still burns beneath, nevertheless, for in many places smoke issues out of the earth, and as on Mount Vesuvius, deposits sulphur. At those places the ground is burning hot, and the foot-tread sounds hollow. Our guide flung a large stone upon the ground, which made it vibrate for a considerable distance round us, and produced a very loud, hollow sound. Thence we proceeded to another subterranean reservoir of water similar to that at Cape Micenus; inspected the ruins of an amphitheatre and several temples, and at last reached the most interesting antiquity in the whole neighbourhood — the ruins of the temple of Serapis, close to the sea-shore. So much has been written respecting all these antiquities, that it would be superfluous to dwell upon them here, but the remains of the temple of Serapis are so remarkable, and afford such evidence of its former size and grandeur that to see them alone amply repays a journey here. Towards the evening we drove back to Naples through the grotto of Pausilippo.

February 15.

As I have now been several times to the St. Carlo theatre, I can with confidence put my judgment to paper respecting it. On the first visit I experienced the same feeling as in the church of St. Peter: it did not appear to me so large as it really is, and it was not until I had been frequently told that it is four feet wider and I know not how many longer than the theatre at Milan, that I could believe it. But when the curtain drew up and I could compare the size of the human beings with the painted objects of the decorations, I readily observed that here also I had been deceived by the correct proportions of each gigantic object. Here for the first time the horses introduced on the stage did not appear out of proportion with the rest, and the people one saw at the extreme depth of the theatre, were still in just proportion with objects which surrounded them. For ballet and pantomine I know of no better adapted locality, and military evolutions of infantry and cavalry, battles, storms at sea, and such things can be produced without falling into the ridiculous and the paltry; but for operas the house is too large. Although the singers, Madame *Colbran* and Signori *Nozzari*, *Benedetti*, and others, have very powerful voices, yet one hears only the highest notes given out with the full strain of the voice; but all tender pathos in song is wholly lost. This is said not to have been the case before the fire, and the theatre was then quite as sonorous as *Della Scala* at Milan. This prejudicial change is ascribed to three causes first, the proscenium has been widened by several feet; secondly, the ceiling is not so concave as formerly; and thirdly, the high projecting decorations in stucco obstruct the sound and do not send it back. If the house was in reality so sonorous formerly, then they have greatly deadened that faculty in the new building, and they would do very wisely to eject (the sooner the better) all the unnecessary trumpery of ornament and gildings, which besides is exceedingly heavy and not in the best taste, and so regain the former advantages.

The first opera I saw was "*Gabriele de Vergi*," by Count *Caraffa*, who formerly was a dilettant merely, but now as a younger son without means, is become an artiste, and as such strives to earn a subsistence. The opera pleased me very much, but without being altogether particularly attractive for me. The style is even and dignified, but the orchestra is too much overladen, and the voice parts are too much obscured. The execution was very precise, both on the part of the singers and of the orchestra. The latter, under the correct and spirited but somewhat too loud direction of Signor *Festa*, had studied it well, but were somewhat wanting in *nuances* of *piano* and *forte*; the wind instruments in particular are always too loud in the *piano*. Of the singers nothing further can be said than that they have good and powerful voices. Whether they have a good execution cannot be ascertained in this theatre; for one hears them either singing at the top of their voices, or one cannot hear them at all. After the opera *Duport's* ballet of "Cinderella" was given, the decorations, costumes, &c., of which were of a very expensive character. Besides *Duport* and his wife, the dancer *Vestris* attracted much notice. The music was nearly the same as that we heard in Vienna in that ballet; a polonaise newly introduced by Count *Gallenberg*, the ballet-composer here, pleased greatly from its originality and sweetness.

Another opera, also by a dilettant, Signor *Carlo Saccenti*, was given a week ago, after a three months' study and rehearsal. The king, who is a great patron of the composer, had fixed on it for the opening of the San Carlo theatre, and *Mayer*, who had been sent for here by the impresario, to write a new opera for the occasion, was obliged to keep his back. But as it was afterwards found that it would be impossible to be perfect in it by the day appointed for the opening, *Mayer* was permitted to write a Cantata in all haste, with which on the 12th January the theatre was at length opened. This cantata, through written with great despatch, is said nevertheless, according to the opinion of connoisseurs to contain a good deal of fine music; but as the text or subject was the burning of the theatre, one little calculated for composition, it could not well have been other than a somewhat tame production. Nor could it be expected, with the little attention given to it by the public, more occupied with the brilliant illumination of the house and the splendour and Spanish etiquette which the court displayed at the opening of the theatre, that the reception given by the public to the cantata should have been other than a very cold one. Nevertheless, it was not properly speaking a failure. After this had been brought out, the study of *Saccenti's* opera was again resumed. All that reached the public concerning these rehearsals was very unfavourable. His friends said he had composed a work which from its originality and excellence would produce a complete reform in operatic compositions: the singers and musicians, on the other hand, said that in all their lives they had never sung or played anything more villanous, tedious and incorrect than that unfortunate opera. The impartial conjectured that, as is usual with such conflicting opinions, the truth would lie in the mean; but I soon satisfied myself, after a few rehearsals which I attended, that the musicians were perfectly right in the judgment they had formed of it. It would indeed be scarcely possible to put together a more outrageous piece of music, even if one strove expressly, and with the greatest industry to act contrary to all the most approved rules of rhythm, structure of the periods, harmony and instrumentation. There was no trace of song or sensible carrying out of an idea; every third bar was something else, with the most incorrect modulations. In the very beginning of the introduction three ugly quints follow each other in quick succession. One of the musicians from recollection said that the composer justified it very ingeniously with the example of the English sailor who was brought before a magistrate for having married three wives, but whom the law could not reach as it forbade bigamy only, and made no mention of trigamy; in the same manner, said the composer, it is forbidden to have *two* quints in succession, but by having *three* the penalty contemplated by the law was evaded.

After rehearsals innumerable, the representation took place in the presence of the court and with a crowded house. Notwithstanding the here prevailing formal Spanish etiquette, which commands that the curtain shall be drawn up immediately the king enters the box and which constrains the poor singers to exhibit themselves on the stage during the whole duration of the overture, without being able to move in the spirit of the characters they impersonate; and which moreover forbids every demonstration of applause or of disapprobation; despite this constraint, which impedes free judgment, the opera was hissed in *optima forma*. On the following night it had the same fate, without a single friend of the composer's daring to clap a hand. With this second representation, at which I was present, the opera was for ever consigned to the tomb. It is called "Aganadeca;" its author is Signor *Vincenzio de Ritis*. The subject, from *Ossian,* is said not to be without merit, and it is regretted that it did not fall into the hands of a better composer. The latter, however is not sensible of his own defiency; he ascribes its failure to the little musical judgment of the Neapolitan public, and intends sending his work to Germany. May Apollo and the muses bestow their blessings upon it!

February 20.

The Carneval came to a close yesterday, and the fasts have begun. After the noise of the last day of the carneval, the quiet which has now succeeded does one really good, although the evenings are somewhat dull, as all the theatres are closed for four days. At the St. Carlo theatre instead of the customary oratorios this year operas will be given as usual, but without ballets, which are wholly forbidden at this season. At the *Fiorentino* theatre we saw an opera of *Guglielmi* (son), "Paolo e Virgina," which met with some success. But the music of the third act is quite Italian for insipidity, in which *Paul,* during a storm at sea, sings an air in the usual form, and with the usual insipid intermediate acting, exhausting himself in shakes and passages, when he would act much more sensibly if he hastened to the assistance of his loved one. This sea-storm without an appropriate music was therefore the most ridiculous thing I ever saw at a theatre, and solicited no sympathy for the whole affair from the spectators. It is true the machinery also at this theatre was most mean and childish.

Among the singers Mesdames *Chabran* and *Canonici* distinguished themselves greatly. The former has a fine soprano voice, great ease of execution and a good school; the latter the same qualifications with a powerful contralto voice. They had particularly well studied their duets. In this theatre we found for the first time in Italy, with a full house and a frequently repeated performance, a quiet and sympathetic audience. The house is roomy and prettily decorated, but the stage very small and narrow.

I had expected the end of the carneval to have been far more gay than I found it. The whole amusement consisted in the crowding together of half Naples, masked and unmasked, in vehicles and on foot in the street of Toledo, where they moved up and down and pelted each other with little balls of gypsum. The masks of the carriages were provided for the purpose with whole baskets full of these little bullets, and with shovels, so as to enable them to throw them up to the balconies. They carried tin shields on the left arm, with which to ward off the missiles of other maskers. As these were frequently of a tolerable size and were thrown with full force, the fun frequently proved somewhat rough for those persons who were not masked, and many a lady must doubtless have taken home with her a few blue marks on her neck and arm. Nevertheless all was borne with good humour and without dispute, as the liberty conferred by the mask serves to excuse all impoliteness. The masqued balls at the San Carlo theatre are said to have been somewhat wearisome affairs; although there was no want of masks in character, yet there was very little wit and ability to personate the characters in accordance with the costume and manners of the period.

February 26.

I have been twice to the conservatory of music. The first time I was present at a practice concert of the pupils, in which several overtures, or first themes of symphony composed by one of them, who at the same is first violin also, were tried.

They were not devoid of fancy, but in form and instrumentation complete imitations of the overtures of *Rossini*, which certainly are not calculated to serve as models. The execution was but tolerable; the young folks, particularly the violinists, have no school at all; they know neither how they should hold the violin nor the bow, and play neither purely nor distinctly. Nor can it be otherwise with the bad instruction they receive. *Festa*, the only violinist here of a good school, is not employed in the conservatory of music. It is highly reprehensible that the young people are permitted to give their practise-concerts without the superintendence and guidance of their instructors; their first violin and director, who is himself still a pupil, is wholly wanting in self possession and judgment. He bungles the allegro tempi in such a manner that all distinctness is out of the question. Among the wind instruments, a hornist, a lad of eleven years of age, is very remarkable. On the occasion of the second concert at which I was present, two singers made their appearance, who had neither good voices nor a good method. All that I have yet heard, is far inferior to what the Milan musical students can perform. Signor *Zingarelli*, director of the conservatory here, and teacher of the theory of music and singing may possess many qualifications as a composer of operas; but it is generally said that since his appointment the conservatory has very much declined. That he at least does not know how an orchestra should be conducted or a symphony executed, he proves by allowing so quietly these things to take place in his presence. Of the merits of our German composers he has some very erroneous notions. One day, when I paid him a visit, he spoke for a long time of *Haydn* and other of our composers with great respect, but without even once mentioning *Mozart*; I therefore turned the conversation upon the latter, upon which he said: "Yes, he also was not deficient in talent, but he lived too short a time to cultivate it in a proper manner; if he could only have continued to study ten years longer, he would then have been able to write something good."!

March 3.

An opera has been again put on the stage written by *Mayer* several years ago. It is called "*Cora*" and is founded on the same subject as *Kotzebue's* "Sonnenjungfrau" (Virgin of the Sun). There are certainly some fine passages in the music, but taken as a whole it has not satisfied my expectations of *Mayer's* music. He is after all deeply tinctured with the Italian manner and almost wholly an apostate from the German. His method of carrying out the vocalisation and his instrumentation are thoroughly Italian. This certainly is not to be wondered at, for since the age of fourteen he has lived in Italy, and never wrote for any other than Italian audiences. I think, that apart from his natural talent, he has raised himself above the others alone by having always endeavoured to procure all the best German works, which he studied, and made use of, the latter indeed sometimes a little too much. Throughout Italy, and here in particular, he is very much admired and liked: he merits it also in very respect, and as a man is ever the upright, smooth-smoken unassuming German. He is much attached to his fatherland, and seems only to regret that it was not his fate to pursue his career as a composer in Germany. In Bergamo, where he is director of the orchestra, he now only desires to live in retirement, and write solely for his church. He assured me that nothing but the honour of writing for the reopening of the San Carlo theatre could have induced him to leave his retreat once more, but that the opera "La vendetta di Junone," which he had now completed, should certainly be his last work for the theatre. In "Cora" the favorite piece with the public is the finale, consisting of a theme in three variations in the old style of *Pleyel*; one of the singers sings the theme, *Davide* the first variation in quavers, then *Nozzari* the second in triplets, and in conclusion la *Colbran* the third in semiquavers. At it is well sung, it greatly pleases the public, and critics therefore must be silent.

March 6.

Last evening Signor *Pio Chianchettino* gave a concert in the *Fondo* theatre. He is a nephew and pupil of *Dussek*, and played two concertos of that master in his manner. Although his play was pure, distinct and even full of expression, yet here again, as every-where else, the piano-forte as concert-instrument proved itself insufficient to awaken the enthusiasm of an audience; and the more so is this the greater the size of the place. For that reason also upon this occasion, the song-pieces pleased far more than the concertos, although no one could find fault with his play. I myself felt this also; for although I am very fond of the piano, when a composer rich in ideas improvises upon it, yet as concert-instrument I am wholly unmoved by it; and a piano-forte-concerto in my opinion is only effective when written like those of *Mozart*, in which the piano is not much more thought of than any other orchestral instrument. The singers, Madame *Chabran* and the Signori *Davide*, *Nozzari* and *Benedetti*, all distinguished themselves, and were loudly applauded. One becomes more sensible of their merits when one hears them in a smaller place than the San Carlo theatre. *Davide* and *Nozzari* may be called almost perfect singers, they both have very fine voices; the former a very high tenor, the latter a high baritone, remarkable fluency of execution and much true expression. *Benedetti* has a very fine bass voice, but sings rather coldly.

March 7.

We have again taken some rather more distant and highly interesting walks. The object of one was the Camaldula convent, which is situated upon a hill above two hours' drive from the centre of the city. We rode as far as the foot of the mountain, where as the carriage road terminated, we were obliged to make the ascent on foot. The view from the convent garden is perhaps one of the most extensive and beautiful in the world. On one side are seen Ischia, Capri, Procida, Nisida and the promontories which we had visited in our previous excursion, accompanied by the blue mirror of the sea; on the opposite side Capua, Caserta, and in the back-ground the snow-covered mountains; on the side of Naples a part of the city itself, the whole bay with the opposite coast, and on the left the smoke-emitting Vesuvius; lastly, on the fourth side, the shores and salient promontories near Gaëta, as far as Terracina. As the weather was very propitious for us, this was one of the most magnificent days we ever passed in the enjoyment of the beauties of nature. The monks, some of whom we caught sight of, did not appear in the same humour as we were; for they all wore a gloomy aspect.

We took a shorter but not less interesting walk on the new road to Rome, which was begun under *Murat*, but has remained unfinished since his dethronement. It leads over a mountain from which one has the most admirable view of the city, and it is much to be regretted that it is not complete; for then the traveller would be able to form a more worthy conception of the city before his entry into Naples, while now by the old road, which winds through a narrow mountain ravine, he sees nothing of Naples until he has entered the most dirty and least attractive part of the city; which leaves him long in doubt whether he actually is in the world-famed Naples.

We passed a very pleasant day at the villa of the banker *Heigelin*, which is situated also upon a mountain near the *Strada Nuova,* whence one has a beautiful view. Old *Heigelin,* an amiable, open-hearted German, has ornamented this place of his own creation with so many fine things, such as grottoes, ruins, temples, fountains, &c. &c., that it would be actually impossible to crowd any thing more together in so small a space. Although perhaps the whole is somewhat frivolous as regards the manner in which it is laid out, it has nevertheless many individual things worthy of attention. For us Northerns, for instance, the vast number of exotic plants, which were for the most part in full bloom, were objects of great interest.

March 11.

Last evening our concert took place. As the impressario of the court theatres, *Barbaja*, an extremely selfish man, asked me too much money for the hire of the theatres, for the *Fondo* for instance 100 Neapolitan ducats and for the *San Carlo* 200 even, I adopted his proposal rather to give my concert in the assembly-room of the San Carlo theatre, which he offered me lit up for nothing. This apparently disinterested offer was nevertheless calculated also for his advantage, for the assembly-room and the adjoining rooms were the places for the hazard-tables, which he had rented, and to which by means of my concert he hoped to attract the most fashionable and wealthiest company of the city. This use of my concert, which could in no way prejudice me, I could readily allow him. As the saloon is not very spacious, I fixed the price of admission, as at Rome, at one piaster, and although I had not a more numerous, yet I had a more susceptible public than there. Encouraged by this and supported most efficiently by the very accurate accompaniment under *Festa's* direction, as well as by the room itself, which was so advantageous for my instrument, I played better than I had done in many others town in Italy. Besides my compositions a duet by *Mayer* and a terzet of *Cherubini* were sung by Signore *Davide*, *Nozzari* and *Benedetti*. Even during the evening I was solicited on all sides to give a second concert in the theatre.

March 18.

This morning early we visited the "Studii," *i. e.* the building in which the treasures of art from Pompeii and Herculaneum are preserved, together with the collections previously made of statues and paintings. The library is situated also in the same building. As it is impossible to see all in one day, we chose for to-day the statues and the library. Among the former are some very celebrated statues from the Farnese collection, of which numerous excellents casts have been made, and two equestrian statues found in Pompeii, of great artistic worth. In one room are two glazed cases, full of antique bronzes, also from Pompeii and Herculaneum, consisting of lamps, small penates and all kinds of domestic utensils. These things, as well as the statues in marble are in the most perfect preservation, and appear scarcely so many days old as they are years; but every thing of iron is much eaten by rust, as for instance the handles and rings of various vessels of bronze.

The library is contained in a fine handsome and spacious apartment and several adjoining rooms. On the floor of the grand room the line of the meridian is drawn, on which, through a small hole pierced in the wall for that purpose, the sun's rays fall at noon. When a person claps his hands at a particular spot in this apartment, an echo repeats it more than thirty times in rapid succession. This arises probably from the position of the window-recesses, which are high up, near the ceiling.

Lastly we visited the room where the rolls of papyrus are preserved and unrolled. They have all the appearance of charcoal, and one might mistake them for that, were it not that one can easily distinguish the edges of the leaves. A manuscript fully unrolled, mounted upon linen, framed and glazed, hangs against the wall. As the paper is burnt quite black the letters are scarcely to be distinguished, and one cannot but admire the patience. the penetration, and the knowledge of languages of those who have known how to unravel its sense. It is a treatise on music: each side is divided into three columns. In the first is seen an engraved, accurate copy of the unrolled papyrus, with all its defects, and rents; in the second, the contents in modern Greek characters, in which the letters and words that are wanting in the original are filled in with red letters, and in the third, a Latin translation. They are now unrolling another manuscript, but do not appear to be hurrying themselves much, for we found one person only thus occupied. The method pursued is a very simple one. Small strips of fine parchment are stuck with gum close to each other or rather somewhat lapping over each other, upon the charred rolls, after which the paper is gradually and carefully released and removed. The process is of a necessity a slow one, but considerably more might have been unrolled by this time. If these precious remains of ancient learning were in the possession of a German sovereign, they would all have been deciphered long since.

March 22.

As I did not like the trouble of making the arrangement for a second concert, I readily accepted the proposal of the impressario to play twice at the San Carlo theatre between the acts of the opera for the sum of 300 ducats. This I did the evening before last for the first time. I was very much afraid that the violin would not fill the immense house, but I was soon set at rest on that point on being told at the rehearsal that every note was distinctly heard in the most distant parts of the house. But of a necessity nevertheless I was obliged to forego every finer *nuance* in my play. Although the house was very full, yet the greatest silence prevailed whilst I was playing, and after the second piece of music I was called forward.

Last evening I played at the *Casino mobile*, in a very fine saloon, my concerto in the form of a scena, and a pot-pourri with pianoforte accompaniment. As the room is very favourable for music, both of these had a very sensible effect upon the audience. The remainder of the concert, consisting of symphonies and *pièces d'harmonie*, was not of importance.

I forgot to mention a concert given by Signora *Paravicini* at which we were present, at the *Teatro nuovo*, on Wednesday last. She played, between the acts of a comedy, the first violin-concerto of *Rode* in D minor, a pot-pourri by *Kreutzer*, and at the end an *Adagio* and *Rondo* of the same composer. I have been accustomed to hear my instrument ill used by women, but I never saw it used so badly as by Signora *Paravicini*. I was the more surprised at this, as she has acquired some fame, and has a vast deal of pretension; as an instance of this, she told people here that she had heard *Rode* in Vienna, but that he had excited no other sentiment in her than pity. Her turn had now come to excite pity if one can feel it at all for arrogance and unskilfulness. She has a very excellent violin, a *Stradivari*, and in the cantabile draws from it a tolerable tone; but that is her only merit. In other respects she plays in bad taste, with a profusion of meaningless ornamentations, and the passages indistinctly: her intonation is not pure and her bow stroke extremely bungling. The applause was very lukewarm and was elicited only when Prince Leopold her patron began to clap his hands. Much more interesting than *Paravicini's* play, was the comedy, which was capitally performed. Signor *de Marini* played remarkably well, and he is altogether one of the best actors of the day. The theatre, certainly, is smaller than the Fiorentino and Fondo, but quite as pretty.

At private-parties I have played my quartetts and quintetts a few times, which were exceedingly well accompanied by Messieurs *Dauner* and son, the young and talented violinist *Onario*, whom I have practised in some of my things, and by the accomplished violoncellist *Fenzi*, who lived formerly in Cassel. They afforded great pleasure, and *Mayer* assured me he had never enjoyed a greater musical treat. On the second occasion we played them at the house of Lady *Douglas*, who herself plays the piano very well and is said to have sung exceedingly well some years ago. She and her husband are the first English in whom I have found a real taste for music.

March 23.

On looking through this diary I observe that I have forgotten to mention the performance of two masses given at the expense of Prince *Esterhazy* of Vienna. The first by old *Umlauf* of Vienna, was remarkable for nothing in particular; but the second by *Haydn*, in D minor, which was performed with great solemnity and military pomp on the emperor's birthday, afforded much gratification. Mesdames *Chabran* and *Canonici*, and Signori *Nozzari* and *Benedetti* sang the solo parts very beautifully; the chorus and orchestra were also admirable.

Unfortunately, at the express desire of the Prince, almost all the *tempi* were taken too quick, and thereby much spoiled.

Milan, April 22.

Prevented from writing by the great press of business in the last days of our residence in Naples, and the hurry of our return journey, which was almost unbroken by a day of rest, I have got greatly in arrears, and have therefore much to fetch up, even respecting Naples.

Mayer's new opera was at length brought out a fortnight before Easter, after it had been once more re-christened, but it was a total failure, so that it lived through two and a half representations only, and probably is for ever at rest. On the third evening, in fact, the first act alone was given, with one act of *Paer's* "Sargino." Both the subject and the music of *Mayer's* opera are equally uninteresting and tedious. The latter especially is wanting in life and spirit; it is so common-place and so spun out, that one can hardly hear it without falling asleep. This actually occurred to me, to Count *Gallenberg,* and to several others, at the grand rehearsal. *Mayer* seems to have exhausted himself, which is no wonder with the enormous quantity of operas which he has written. It is certainly high time for him to retire as a composer of operas, that he may not entirely forfeit the repute he had acquired, and he would have done well if he had not accepted the last invitation to Naples. The evening after the first representation of his opera he set out on his return to Bergamo.

About this time the arrival of Madame *Catalani* set all the lovers of music in Naples in great commotion. She immediately took advantage of this enthusiasm and announced a few days afterwards a concert in the Fiorentino theatre, the prices of admission being seven-fold the usual ones. On the day before the concert, it was with difficulty that I got two pit tickets, and that because I had previously bespoken them, at 22 Carlini each. Never perhaps were the expectations of an audience at a higher pitch of tension, than were those of the Neapolitan public on that evening. My wife and I, who for years had longed to hear this celebrated singer, could scarcely repress our impatience for the moment of her appearance. At length she did appear, and a deathlike silence pervaded the whole house. She came forward with a cold and pretentious air, and saluted neither the Court nor the public, which created an obvious unpleasant sensation. Perhaps she had expected to have been received with a burst of applause, which however is not the custom in Naples, and this perhaps put her out of humour. But when after her first song she was greeted with a storm of applause, she became more friendly, and remained so for the rest of the evening. She sang four times, two airs by *Pucitta, Ombra adorata* of *Zingarelli* (or, as the Neapolitans insist, of *Crescentini*, whose name also was down on the bills) and variations on the thousand times varied "*Nel cor non più mi sento.*" The airs by *Pucitta* were extremely poor; the famed *Ombra adorata* can only be considered fine, when all thoughts of the text are banished from the mind; the variations were common place, but become piquante from her manner of execution. She pleased us greatly, by the constantly pure intonation and the perfect finish with which she executes every kind of vocal ornamentation and of passages, and by her quite peculiar and characteristic style of singing; but she does not come up to that ideal of a perfectly accomplished singer, which we had expected to find her. Her voice which has the extensive range of  to is both full and powerful in the low and midle notes, but the transition to the *voce di testa* at 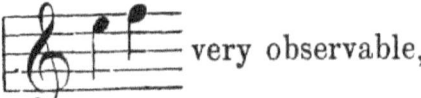 very observable, and from three to four notes in that region are much weaker, than the deeper and highest; for which reason she gives all passages which occur in those notes, with half-voice, only in order to conceal the inequality. Her voice is wanting also in the youthful freshness, which, however, in a female singer of forty years of age, is not to be wondered at. Her shake is wonderfully beautiful; and equally pure whether in the half or whole notes. A peculiar style of run through the half notes, properly speaking the enharmonic scales, since every note was produced twice, is greatly admired as something quite her own. To me, nevertheless, it was more remarkable than beautiful; for it sounded to me like the howling of the storm in the chimney. Another kind of vocal ornamentation, which in itself is common enough, she gives, however, in a manner that imparts great charm to it. It would be expressed in notes somewhat in this manner:

but at the same time it must be observed, that she took breath at every sixteenth-pause, which gave to this part a very impassioned character. Among the variations was one with syncopated notes, which from her peculiar style of execution derives also a very characteristic and interesting charm; and another in triplets *legato* she gives in perfection. But what I most missed in her singing, was *soul*. She sings recitative without expression — I might say with carelessness, and in *Adagio* she remains cold. Neither were we even *once* deeply moved, but experienced merely that sense of pleasure one always feels when one sees and hears mechanical difficulties overcome with ease. This, also, was the sentiment of all those who sat in our immediate neighbourhood. Some unpleasant and prejudicial habits, which she is not likely now to correct, I must yet advert to. To these belong firstly, that in certain passages, particularly those which she gives with force, every note is delivered with a sort of see-saw movement of the lower jaw, as in mastication, so that a dumb person, if he *saw her sing*, would have no great difficulty in distinguishing crochets from quavers and up and down running passages from one another. In the shake, more especially, the movement of the lower jaw by which every note might be counted, is very striking and disfiguring. Secondly, in impassioned passages her whole body partakes of a southern but highly unbecoming mobility, from which a deaf man would likewise of a certainty easily guess the subject.

A few days afterwards we heard her again in the rehearsal to her second concert, in which she sang five times, and exhibited the same qualifications, but also impressed no one at any time by a show of feeling in her execution. She seemed to me much less pretentious here and more amiable; and she was very polite to the orchestra and the persons who had gathered to hear her, so that I can readily believe what I was told — that her pretentious air when appearing in public, arose more from embarrassement than pride, and was assumed by her to conceal her fears. A young man who stood behind the side-scenes during her concert assured me, that upon first stepping forward on the stage she trembled in every limb, and could scarcely breath for nervousness. It is said that here in Milan she did not give general satisfaction; and her last concerts were much less numerously attended than the first. One part of the public was in favour of *Grassini*, whom we have now heard here also, but of whom I shall speak later. The admirers of the latter had played *Catalani* a malicious trick by distributing for sale at the entrance of the theatre at her first concert an Italian translation of the unfavourable opinions respecting her that had appeared in the Hamburg and Leipsic musical journals. *Catalani*, herself, expecting to find in it a sonnet or something of the kind in her praise, purchased a copy.

The day after *Catalani's* first concert in Naples took place, *Rossini's* "Elisabetta" was given at the San Carlo theatre, in which *Colbran* played the first part. As every body knew that it was her intention to compete with *Catalani*, the house was more than usually crowded, both by partizans and antagonists of *Colbran*. The latter on the previous evening called *Catalani's* concert the exequies of *Colbran*, and people were therefore extremely curious to learn what would be the result of the evening. Immediately upon her appearance she was received with a concert of hisses, but simultaneously also with vehement applause. As, however, this time she really sang and played exceedingly well, the applauders increased in number and the hissers grew less, so that at last she was called forward almost unanimously by the audience. She is far behind *Catalani* in voice and every mechanical point of excellence, but she sings with true feeling and plays with considerable passion. The composition of this opera is one of *Rossini's* best, but with all the merits, it has also all the weak points of the others. — In the theatre, a ridiculous trait of pretentious magnanimity on the part of *Catalani* furnished subject of amusement. A few evenings before, when she first went to the theatre, she sent her secretary behind the scenes to express to *Colbran* and the other singers that "she was perfectly satisfied with their performances."

Freiburg in Breisgau, June 20. 1817.

Previous to our leaving Naples, we devoted one whole day more to a visit to Pompeii. We were so fortunate as to have a clear and tolerably warm day, a real wonder throughout the whole of the month of March! While from the middle of January to the end of February the weather was almost without interruption the most beautiful spring weather, with the beginning of March winter suddenly returned. A cold and stormy rain fell in the vallies, and snow in the mountains to such a depth, that they were no longer accessible. On Vesuvius it was said to be from three to four feet deep. But March is generally very cold and the real winter month of the Neapolitans.

The ruins of Pompeii, which from having lain covered for nearly 2000 years with a light crust of dry ashes, are in far better preservation than all the remains of that period which have been exposed to the air, made a deep and really solemn impression upon us. The ruins of the Colosseum and other ancient buildings in Rome, impress one with an idea of the artistic taste, the wealth, and love of grandeur of the ancients; but here the sight of simple small private dwelling-houses, which are as entire as on the day of the fearful catastrophe, makes one acquainted with the habits and ways of their civic life, and, by ocular evidence, with many customs unknown to our mode of living, and described to us by ancient writers.

On entering one of these houses, which may have belonged to a well-to-do individual in the middle class of society, one finds a row of small, neat rooms all painted *al fresco*, like the paintings cut out of the walls from Herculaneum, which are preserved at Portici. These chambers have rarely any window, and but one door to admit light and air, which opens upon a court yard, round which runs a covered gallery. In the centre of the court is a fountain, near this a circular marble table round which stand marble benches to recline upon at meal time, furnished with a somewhat higher projection to support the elbows; and on one side of the court is one or more tastefully decorated baths. All these houses had but one floor or story and were much smaller than our dwelling houses. It is greatly to be regretted that the domestic utensils which were found there could not be left in their place! One would then have had a perfect conception of the habits and mode of life of the former inhabitants of this remarkable city. The pavement of the streets is still in the same condition as it then was, and the impression of the wheels of the vehicles as also of the feet of the foot-passengers are still to be seen in the streets. Over the shops one still sees expressed in Greek characters painted on walls, the wares which were sold in each, and at the corner of a street an advertisement of that period. In the shops where oil was sold huge earthen-ware jars, let into the masonry of the front wall, are still to be seen, from which that article was dipped out for sale. In many cellars in good preservation, similar tall jars, but with very narrow necks are to be seen, in which wine was kept. In one of these cellars the skeleton of a woman was found, and so completely imbedded in the ashes, that the form of her body could be distinguished as in a mould. A part of this form in which the impress of her breast is left, is preserved at Portici. In her hand was found a large leathern bag with coins in it.

The street which is in the best preservation is the street of the tombs, in which on both sides scarcely any thing is to be seen but tombs, some of which are built in the Egyptian pyramidal-form, and others in the Roman style. In these tombs, urns have been found in which the ashes and bones of the burned dead were preserved. The inscriptions upon these tombs are sometimes Greek, sometimes Latin, and begin very frequently with the exclamation: *"Siste viator!"* "Stop passer-by!" &c., which mode of arresting the attention of the way farer here in a frequented and busy street was much more in place than it is in our generally very retired churchyards, in which it has been imitated in a somewhat inappropriate manner.

The public buildings, theatres, temples, &c., which attract attention in Pompeii, are certainly neither so vast nor so grand and beautiful as those of Rome, Puzzuoli and other places; but they nevertheless exceed in importance everything that a modern provincial town can offer to the visitor. Where, for instance, would one find in any of these, a vast circus for public games, and two large theatres! Of the latter, one was roofed over, and served probably for the performance of comedies; the other, with a stage, an orchestra, and a circular, very lofty amphitheatre gives us an idea of the sort of place in which the Roman actors, provided with a mask to increase the volume of sound, performed their tragedies before an audience of from 10,000 to 15,000 spectators. But the temples also, the finest of which is now being dug out of the ashes, afford ocular demonstration of the love of grandeur and of the good taste of the ancients in architecture.

The vineyards and cultivated land which lie above the yet unexcavated part of the city, have been already long purchased by the former king of Naples; hence if the work had been carried on with energy, which, however, is not to be expected from the present government, which prosecutes all such things very indolently, the whole of this highly interesting city would be laid bare in a few years, and from the high ground which surrounds it might all be surveyed at one glance. At present the different parts which have been excavated are still separated from each other by long strips of land under cultivation, which one is obliged to ascend like so many hills; and one is greatly surprised after having traversed one of this sort of fields to see beneath one another part of the city, which contrasts so strangely with the vines, trees, fields and peasant's huts upon the high ground.

The day before our departure from Naples we once more paid a visit to the Studii, and inspected the large collection of Etrurian vases of every imaginable form. We were greatly pleased also, with the fine collection of paintings, among which the pictures by *Raphael* recently brought back from Sicily were special objects of our admiration.

On the 29th March we set out on our return journey to Rome. The morning of our leaving was very stormy and unpleasant for me; for in the first place I had a dispute with the vetturino, who wanted to thrust a fifth person into the interior of the vehicle, in the shape of a dirty and ill-smelling Capucin friar, till at length after much desultory disputation we consented to his being accommodated in the cabriolet, and as a further incident of annoyance, my family was at first not permitted to pass out of the gate, because they had not been mentioned in the new Neapolitan passports which it is requisite to take upon leaving the country. It was in vain that I shewed my old passport, in which my wife and children were mentioned; and it was not until I had pledged my word to go back and procure another passport that I was allowed to move from the spot. I therefore went back to the minister, while my wife and children proceeded without further hindrance on their way. Arrived at the minister's, I there found all still buried in sleep; but with fair words and that which with Italians is far more effectual, money, I at length succeeded in procuring a new passport. Furnished with this I jumped into a hired carriage, and drove with all speed to overtake my family, which I did about half-way to Capua and thus relieved them of a great anxiety respecting me. Among the annoyances with which travellers in Italy are almost worried to death, is the excessive strictness in regard to passports, which is frequently carried to a ridiculous extreme. We subsequently saw an instance in which a traveller who had already got beyond Parma on the Lombard frontier was sent all the way back to Leghorn because his passport had not been signed by the Austrian consul at that place.

In a second vehicle which accompanied us travelled an Englishman, who was possessed of an extraordinary skill in taking the fine views in a few minutes. For this purpose he made use of a machine which transmitted the landscape on a reduced scale to the paper. Between Velletri and Albano, where we went part of the way on foot in order better to enjoy the magnificent landscape and the mild air, we saw the whole method of his proceeding, which afforded infinite pleasure to the children. He shewed us afterwards his collection of views, of which he had upwards of two hundred of Naples and its neighbourhood alone. He gave me his address: Major *Cockburn*, Woolwich, nine miles from London.

Our re-entry into Rome filled us anew with wonder and admiration of the remains of the old Roman architecture, which we had not seen for three months. We were much amused also with the simple remarks of the Capucin friar, whose first visit this was to the mainland, and who was totally inexperienced in every thing. Apart from his dirt, he was really a good-tempered, simple sort of man, and quite endurable. He was full of restless impatience to see the pope officiate. How various are the wishes and inclinations of men! He perhaps felt as we did the day before the concert given by the celebrated *Catalani!* I wish with all my heart that he may return to his convent, better satisfied then we returned home from that concert.

With great difficulty we procured a miserable apartment in a private house, for which nevertheless we were obliged to pay half a piaster per diem. Strangers from every part of Italy had poured into Rome to be present during the Holy Week, in addition to whom also, pilgrims, and the devout gathered together from all parts of the world, were now here to receive remission of their sins. The streets were thronged to that degree that we were frequently obliged to pull up as we drove through.

Our apartments had a look-out upon the Tiber from a wooden balcony; from here we could follow the course of the Tiber from the Porta Romana to the bridge in front of the castle of St. Angelo. The stillness of the quarter of the city beyond the Tiber, lit up by the ruddy evening sky and the moonlight, contrasted in a remarkable manner with the dense throng which poured to and fro across the bridge and then disappeared in the streets leading from the castle of St. Angelo to the church of St. Peter. High above all the houses and palaces which lay between us and the church of St. Peter, rose the latter, proudly and majestically, filling us with wonder and admiration of its gigantic proportions. Tired as we were, it was long before we could tear ourselves away from this magnificent sight, and we remained till a late hour in the mild evening air upon our balcony. When we at length lay down to rest, we called to each other once more: "To-morrow, to-morrow, then we shall hear the famous Miserere!"

Aix la Chapelle, Aug. 10. 1817.

Here at length, I find once more a few moments leisure to continue my narrative of our return journey from Italy.

On the 3rd April we at last heard the-long-wished-for Miserere in the Sixtine chapel. We had been told that females were admitted by tickets, and that men were required to appear in shoes. But a ticket for *Dorette* was now not to be had, and I was therefore obliged to make up my mind to go alone. But when I recognised among the Swiss guard at the entrance of the church one whom I knew and whose good will I had won upon a former occasion by a present for accompanying us up to the dome of St. Peter's church; I enquired of him whether he could not assist to procure me an admission into the chapel for my wife without a ticket; and upon his assurance that he would do his best, I hastened home to fetch her. After some discussion with the other Swiss guards we were so fortunate as to be admitted, although several English ladies of rank who came unprovided with tickets were refused admittance and turned back. The Swiss cannot bear the English nor the French, and favour the Germans upon such occasions much more, particularly if one can talk to then in a few words of *"Schwizerdütsch."*

We yet arrived in good time, and only regretted that we were not allowed to remain together, so as to interchange at the moment the impression which the music would make upon us.

Before the commencement of the singing, nineteen psalms were chaunted alternately by high and low voices, in the same manner *unisono*, and in the form of prayer, as we had already found so tedious at Christmas; and we had to bear with the last eight or nine of these: after every one, which lasted for five long minutes, one of the tapers is extinguished that burns upon a gigantic pyramidal-shaped candelabra in front of the high altar. How one wishes that the last of them also was extinguished! At length the wished-for moment comes, and by degrees a silence ensues which not a little increases the expectation of that which now follows. To this sentiment

of expectation, the solemn twilight which now prevails in the
church faintly illumined with the last gleam of the rosy tints
of evening, and the repose felt at length by the ear after the
hoarse bellowing of the psalms may be ascribed the delicious
impression that I experienced from the first long-drawn chord
of *C flat*, and which seemed to me like music from another
world. But one was too soon reminded that it was an earthly
music that fell upon the ear, and one indeed sung by Italians;
for immediately after the second bar, the ear was rent by a
horrid succession of quints! The theme was doubtless after
this manner:

but was given by the singers in the following barbarous manner:

I could not have believed even my own ears, much more those
of others, that they sing *in such wise* in the Sixtine chapel, had
I not heard it subsequently repeated. Is this perhaps the mysterious method of executing these old compositions, of which it
is related that it is known alone to this choir, and has been
handed down traditionally? Impossible! *Modern* Italians only
can sing in so barbarous a style, who may perhaps possess a
feeling for melody, but who in all that is called harmony are
grossly ignorant.

When however this first Miserere had been endured, I was soon attracted by something else. These simple sequences of harmony, consisting almost wholly of triads, this mixing and sustaining of the voices, at one time increasing to the most tumultuous *forte*, at another dying away into the softest *pianissimo*; the continual and lengthened sustaining of single tones to a degree attainable only by the lungs of a castrated person, and then especially the soft introduction of a chord, while that of other voices is still faintly sustained, give to this music, in spite of all its deficiencies, something so peculiar, that one feels irresistibly attracted by it. I can now therefore readily understand that in former times, when the choir was much better, this must have made an immense impression upon foreigners who had never heard pure vocal music and the voices of castrated persons. It might even now be made most charmingly effective, if the singers of the choir had only a director of more extensive knowledge. But as it is, they do not generally sing even with purity.

On this first day, two compositions of *Allegri* and *Baini* were given, and each of them repeated once. Between each of these ten not very long divisions a prayer was recited in a low tone by the cardinals, bishops, and other clergy, which from its resemblance to the roll of distant thunder had a good effect. At the conclusion of the ceremony however, the servants, scraping and treading upon the foot-boards, made a very unpleasant noise for musical ears, which greatly disturbed and then obliterated the impression made by the music, to which one would willingly have abandoned oneself a little longer. This noise they tell me is to represent an earthquake!

On the second evening I managed things in such a manner as to arrive at the chapel just at the commencement of the real singing, and on the extinguishing of the last taper. The crowd was so great, that I was obliged to remain standing some time at the entrance surrounded by Englishmen, who during the whole time of the music spoke to each other in a very loud tone of voice, and would not even allow themselves to be restrained from it by any signs to keep silence. Besides this, the singers sang much more carelessly than the day before, and frequently very false, so that I was very glad when the earthquake came to put an end to the ceremony. Three new compositions were added to the two of yesterday, for which reason each required to be sung but once. In other respects everything was exactly the same as the first time.

At a later period I had an opportunity of seeing the Miserere collection published by *Kühnel* of Leipsic, but did not find a single one of those which we heard in Rome. The library of the Sixtine chapel must however be so rich in such compositions, that they are enabled to select different ones for many years in succession.

Both evenings after the Miserere we saw the illumination of the cross in the church of St. Peter. Upon entering by the grand entrance, whence one sees the illuminated cross at the farthest distance, it makes an imposing impression, but so soon as one approaches nearer, it loses greatly. The effect would be far greater if all the other lights in the church were extinguished. But as it is, not only hundreds of lamps burn round the entrance to the subterranean chapel, but innumerable other lights besides in every part of the church. The brilliant illumination in the cross casts therefore no prominent shadow. The Pantheon was also illuminated this evening, which must have had a magnificent effect. Unfortunately we arrived just as the lights were being extinguished.

On the previous evening prince *Frederick* took me to a party, at which the fiftieth psalm, or the Miserere of *Marcello*, was exceedingly well sung by dilettanti. But as the orchestral accompaniment was, as is usual in Rome, very bad, and the composition throughout monotonous, I soon got tired of it and was glad when it came to an end.

On Saturday forenoon we took a long walk to St. Paul to see the magnificent ancient pillars in that otherwise very ugly church. On our way back, we saw the pyramid of *Cestius* and he so-called mount of pot-sherds. At noon we met at the eating-house at the sign of "The Ermine" a German drawer, Herr *Rösel*, who easily persuaded us to take another walk in his company. He first pointed out to us an arched, old Roman subterranean canal, the *Cloaca maxima*, I think; we then went to a small, insignificant church, but which contains many fine antiquities, in order to see the divine service of the Greek church, which is celebrated on this day only; but the crowd was so great, that we could not obtain an entrance. Upon this we went to see the temple of Vesta, and lastly ascended the mount Aventino, where our companion led us before the door of a garden and shewed us through the key-hole one of the most startling sights imaginable. Through a long arched gallery overgrown with wild strubs and verdure the dome of the church of St. Peters is seen magnificently lit up and gilded by the rays of the setting sun. We had then the door of the garden opened for us, in order to admire closely, a very large and beautiful palm tree which was just then in full bloom.

On the following morning the ringing of bells and salves of artillery from the castle of St. Angelo reminded us that it was Easter Sunday, and of the necessity of a speedy toilet if we would not lose the sight of the great ceremony in the church of St. Peter's. But the fearful crush of the crowd upon the bridge almost compelled us to turn back. Completely carried along by the throng, we at length arrived on the other side of the Tiber, and then hastened to get into a less crowded side street, which also led to the grand square in front of the church. We there found many thousand persons assembled, and among them many pilgrims, with their hats ornamented with shells collected from every quarter of the world, who were impatiently awaiting the moment when the Holy father should give his benediction from the balcony. But some time was to elapse before that would take place, and we therefore first took a turn through the church, where we found every part decorated just the same as at Christmas, and as we could hope to see very little of the ceremony, we preferred taking a walk in the open air as the weather was so fine. We got back again about 12 o'clock, and found the populace still in a state of acute suspense. The balcony over the grand entrance to the church was decorated with crimson velvet, and to shield it from the rays of the sun a gigantic tent was stretched over it. In the gallery above the pillars on the left-hand side a box had been erected for the accommodation of the most distinguished foreign visitors. A number of pages bearing tapers first made their appearance on the balcony, then followed the cardinals, and lastly the Pope, borne upon a sedan, and having on each side of him the white fans of ostrich feathers. As soon as he appeared, all the people fell upon their knees and a solemn stillness took the place of the wild tumult which had previously prevailed. There was something exceedingly imposing in the reverential awe impressed by this moment upon the feelings. The pale old man then arose, and with a slow and dignified movement of the hands, blessed the assembled multitude. In the mean-time, two folded papers were thrown down from the balcony, one of which, as I was told, contained the damnation of all heretics, and the other the papal indulgence for all good believers then present. The damnatory-bull did not however reach the ground, but flew driven by the wind into a window that stood open, while the bull of indulgence was caught by the people who struggled for its possession.

On our way to the eating-house, we were joined by Herr *Kelle* of Stuttgard, whose acquaintance we had previously made in Dresden. He asked us among other things whether we were satisfied with our tour in Italy and with what we had seen. Upon which I complained that we had found many things which did not realise the expectation that had been raised in our minds by previous travellers. He found that very natural, and considered that it arose from the circumstance that not one of the travellers upon his return would confess, that he also had been made an April-fool of by his predecessors. It reminds me, he continued, of the well-known anecdote of a man who advertised that he had a horse in his stable which had its head where other horses had their tails. But the curious who went to see it found nothing more than a horse fastened to the crib by the tail, yet took good care to conceal it from the others who were waiting outside the door — because they were ashamed. The application of the story is easy!

After dinner we took another walk in the villa Borghese, and then made our preparations for our departure, which was fixed for the next morning.

In company of two persons from Stuttgard and one from Munich, with whom we had collectively hired a vetturino, we this time performed the far more interesting return-journey by the way of Perugia to Florence, in six days. On the evening of the second day we arrived at Terni, and hastened before the sun had set, to visit the celebrated waterfall, about two hours' walk from that place. We proceeded as far as the foot of the mountain and then hired some asses already saddled for the purpose in the very romantically situated village, to which half Terni attracted by the mildness of the Sunday evening had repaired as a pleasant promenade. These soon and safely carried us up the ascent to the waterfall. The view from the mountain, before one turns into the valley into which the waterfall precipitates itself, is very varied and charming. The scene then, as one approaches nearer to it, becomes more and more wild and romantic. As the sun was now about to set, we did not tarry long but made all possible haste to reach the waterfall before nightfall, in part to see the imposing spectacle in a proper light, and partly for security's sake, as the country hereabouts has not a very good reputation. With the last declining rays of the sun we reached the rock which rises out of the dark foaming abyss opposite the fall, and where for the convenience of visitors a pavillon furnished with benches has been erected. The view of the majestic spectacle from this point of sight is beyond the power of language to describe. We were all riveted as it were to the spot with admiration and wonder. Certainly at no former period of my life did any of the beauties of nature, not even the first sight of the Alps, make so deep an impression upon me. After we had stood here for full ten minutes and fully feasted our eyes with the magnificent sight, we returned to Terni without accident, on one of the mildest and finest evenings of spring, exceedingly delighted with our charming excursion.

On the fourth day of the journey it became suddenly very cold, so much so that towards evening snow even began to fall, and lay upon the ground till the morning. But when we entered the deep valley in which Florence lies, we found everything in bloom.

We remained one day only in Florence, which we nevertheless turned to good account. In the forenoon we visited the cathedral, the baptistery and the Boboli gardens. Unfortunately, as it was a holiday, we could not get admittance to see the tomb of the Medici and the Pitti Palace. In the afternoon we took a walk to the Cascini.

Next morning, the 14th April, we resumed our journey, to Bologna without our previous companions, who remained some time longer in Florence. We found a great deal of snow in the Apennines, and once more got into complete winter. In dismal Bologna we stopped one day only. The host of the "Pellegrino" had made out a somewhat shamefully long bill against us, in abatement of which I resorted to a means I had frequently put in practice; that is, I deducted a third from the account, which after some discursive wrangling, he was obliged to submit to. Subsequently I always resorted to this expedient, and found it answer better than the previous plan of pre-arrangement, which I had hitherto followed, but in which after all I always found that I was cheated.

We now proceeded by way of Modena, Reggio, Parma and Piacenza, to Milan. As we did not stop long any where, I can say nothing more of those cities than that we everywhere found similar crowds of ragged beggars, the same system of cheating among the hotel keepers, and the same dirt. On the market place of Piacenza, we saw the two gigantic bronze statues. Whether they have any artistic merit, I cannot take upon me to say, as we saw them only in the evening twilight.

In Milan we put up at the *Pension Suisse,* which I recommend to all travellers for cleanliness and cheapness. We were again struck on our first going out by the magnificence and beauty of the exterior of the cathedral. It is without doubt the finest building that we ever saw, more noble and richer than the *façade* of the church of St. Peter's.

The celebrated *Grassini,* to the imitation of whose singing *Rode* is said to be indebted for his peculiar method of play, which differs from the school of *Viotti,* had announced six representations in the theatre *della Scala.* As they were however but thinly attended, three only took place, at the last of which we were present. It consisted of unconnected scenas from "the Horatii and Curatii" of *Cimarosa,* and some other airs, among which also *Ombra adorata. Grassini,* who in the flower of her age was without doubt a distinguished vocalist, is now somewhat *passée.* In that however which time could not steal from her she still stands alone; that is, she has a good style, and plays and sings with much intensity of feeling — in truth with far more feeling and expression than *Catalani,* but she is nevertheless greatly behind the latter in brilliancy of execution and as regards voice. — Hence whenever the production of a brilliant effect alone, was the desideratum, she did not altogether give satisfaction, but in impassioned recitative she charmed the audience by her truthful force of expression.

I found this time also, the della Scala theatre admirably adapted to give effect to music. I know of no place in which the voices as well as the orchestra sound so grandly, and so distinctly at the same time; it is therefore immeasurably preferable in an acoustic point of view to the San Carlo theatre.

As upon our first appearance at the theatre our speculation had been so unprofitable, we tried this time the music hall of the conservatorium, fixed the price of entrance at three francs, and on account of the theatre gave our concert in the forenoon. Whether attributable to the unusual hour or to the already too advanced season of the year — suffice to say, it was again very thinly attended, and did not return much more than the expenses.

In the company of two Englishmen, the younger of whom was tolerably amiable, we set out from Milan on the 2nd of May, slept in Arona, and on the following morning were anew enraptured by the heavenly scenery round the *Lago maggiore*, which we now again found in the garb of spring, and arrived towards evening at the village of Simplon, at the foot of the Simplon pass. Here, upon taking leave of Italy, we were again cheated in real Italian style, being compelled, for instance, to pay two francs for each cup of coffee.

The next morning we commenced the at this season of the year somewhat difficult journey over the mountain pass, and reached the snow region one hour after leaving Simplon. Here it was necessary to take the carriage to pieces; the body was placed upon one sledge, the wheels upon another, and our luggage upon a third; and in this manner the caravan proceeded with several additional horses at a slow rate. In the higher regions of the pass, where the snow remained hard, there were not many stoppages, but further down, where the warmth was already considerable, and the snow not very deep, we came every moment to a standstill. Sometimes the horses sank in up to their bellies, at others the carriage would get jammed fast between walls of snow as high as a house, when it became necessary to clear a passage for it; and then again the road had to be cleared of the fallen avalanches that encumbered it and obstructed our progress. We therefore went on before, and arrived two hours earlier at the fourth refuge station, wet through up to the knees, it is true. At this place the snow had disappeared, and here we refreshed ourselves with a simple breakfast, and rested from the fatigues of our toilsome promenade. We heard many avalanches come thundering down, and were in constant fear that it might fare with us as with some travellers who had passed the day before. These, arrived near to one of the galleries pierced through the rock, saw a fearful avalanche sweeping down upon them, and had but just time sufficient to take refuge in the gallery. To their horror, however, they found both exits had been blocked up by the snow, so that for three fearfully anxious hours they were shut in, until the inspector of the road had worked his way through to them.

When at length the carriage arrived, we drove on to Brieg, where we passed the third night, and for the first time again heard our mother-tongue spoken, which sounded right welcome to our ears. Our fourth day's journey brought us to Sion, where French is spoken. In the Valais we found the spring much less forward than on the other side. Here, the cherry-trees were scarcely in bloom, while in Lombardy and on the *Lago maggiore* they had long passed their bloom. We thus once more found ourselves in spring, in which we had constantly been since the beginning of February.

On our fifth day's journey we came to the celebrated Pissevache, which is close to the road. But our expectations were not altogether satisfied; for in comparison with the waterfall at Terni, this looked very insignificant in our eyes. We slept at Bex, a charmingly situated little village, which the inhabitants call not without reason *un paradis terrestre*. The inn here may compete with the largest hotels of many capitals.

On the sixth day we travelled continuously along the lake of Geneva through Vevay to Lausanne. This place, so much lauded, and also much resorted to in summer by the English, is not so beautiful as I expected. The views on the lake of Thun, and still more on the lake of Zurich, are far more varied; but all the Swiss lakes are in my opinion far behind the *Lago maggiore*. On the seventh day we arrived at length at Geneva.

* * *

In consequence of a severe cold I was confined for some days to my bed. During this time Herr *Dupont* and the Rev. Pastor *Gerlach*, with some other musical friends, took some pains to make arrangements for a concert. But it was easy to see beforehand that it would not be a very brilliant affair, for in part the prevailing distress and dearness of provision were still too great; and partly because several concerts had taken place shortly before for the benefit of the poor. The season was also too far advanced, and the majority of the wealthy families had already retired to their country-seats. In fact it did not much more than cover the expenses. We also permitted ourselves to be persuaded to play at Herr *Piclet Rochemont's* and Herr *Dupont's* private parties; and the very numerous company assembled at both their tea-parties then thought it no longer worth while coming to our concert. The brothers *Bohrer*, who had been there a month before we came, did not meet with better success. Taken as a whole the Genevese have very little taste for art, and are always speculating how they can best squeeze the numerous foreigners who reside there summer and winter. At any rate they know very little of *German art* and *German artists*, and do not know our classical composors even by name. The foreign language, and the long French rule to which they were subjected, explains all this sufficiently.

Of all towns of Switzerland Geneva may boast the greatest number of distinguished artists, but who here, as almost everywhere else, are split into two or more parties, and live a regular cat-and-dog life among themselves. Of these the brothers *Hensel* and *Wolf* and Herr *Berger* (properly *Münzberger*) are the most prominent. I was so fortunate as to bring these gentlemen together at my concert, who otherwise never played together, and had thus for a Swiss town a really good orchestra. The Rev. Pastor *Gerlach* received us in the most friendly manner, and rendered us even many obliging services; he even gave up to us the Lutheran church for our concert, in which music has a very good effect. Without that we should been compelled to give it in the dark and cheerless theatre, which would have occasioned considerable expense (300 Francs).

In Geneva I had the unexpected pleasure of meeting once

more my old teacher *Kunisch* of Brunswick. This worthy man had experienced every possible caprice of fortune. When a young man he was a first-rate hornist, but from its inducing at last a spitting of blood, he was obliged to abandon that instrument to save his life. By the most untiring application he then in three years attained to a considerable skill on the violin, and subsequently procured an apointment as first violin at the national theatre in Berlin. When after the battle of Jena the Prussian court was obliged to fly from Berlin and the royal orchestra was dispersed, he was driven from Berlin by the intrigues of Herr *Schick*, who much wanted to obtain his place. He then first went to Switzerland, when already advanced in years he learned the French language, and, afterwards went to Lyons, where he again procured an appointment as first violin at the theatre. Well pleased with his situation here, he had just begun to feel comfortably settled down, when by an unluckly fall he dislocated his left hand, which soon became perfectly rigid, so that he could no longer play the violin, and consequently was obliged to give up his situation. He was now for a third time compelled to learn another instrument, and thenceforth earned a scanty subsistence as a teacher of the piano-forte. He was exceedingly pleased to meet me again, and seemed very proud to be able to call me his pupil.

* * *

Upon perusing the here intercalated diary of the Italian journey I miss some incidents which even now (in 1847) are so vividly impressed on my memory that I cannot forbear appending them here in continuation.

Mention has already been made of the circumstance that I had alone to thank the exertions of the Austrian ambassador Count *Apponyi* for being enabled to give a concert in Rome during Advent, at which time all public music is forbidden. Count *Apponyi* undertook to represent my request for permission to the governor of Rome, but advised me nevertheless not to wait for the reply, but to make arrangements as quickly as possible for the concert, while he would procure for me the necessary subscribers. I went to work immediately, but found my efforts impeded by very considerable difficulties. The salon in the Ruspoli Palace, which Count *Apponyi* had procured for me, was like every other part of that fine uninhabited building, in a very ruinous condition. It was necessary to re-glaze the windows in many places, to fill up the holes in the marble pavement with bricks, and to hire the necessary furniture, chandeliers, seats, music desks, &c. &c. But it was first of all especially necessary to cleanse the palace, from the entrance to the saloon, from the filth with which the esplanade and the handsome flight of marble steps ornamented with statues were filled in such a manner, that whole cart-loads of it required to be carried away. I was also first obliged to find one by one singers and musicians in the immense city, and to engage them for my concert, all of which occupied a great deal of time. Until the day of the concert, and even on that itself till the evening, I was in continual anxiety lest a refusal of my request should arrive and overthrow every thing I had done. But the police were so humane, that they did not forward this to me till the day *after* the concert when I had already in hand a satisfactory return in the shape of receipts. I was hereby relieved of great uneasiness and one which until then had greatly embittered my stay in Rome. My travelling funds had come to so low an ebb, from the hitherto scanty receipts from my concerts in Italy, that I saw with alarm they would in no manner suffice for an extension of our journey to Naples, and scarcely even for a direct return to Germany. To be so near to Naples, the most desired object of the whole journey, and now to turn back — that was a reflexion too fearful for me to bear with calmness! I therefore conceived the idea of applying to the *Beer* family, which had meanwhile arrived from Venice, for a loan. Intimate as was my friendship with the son *Meyer Beer* (afterwards *Meyerbeer*) I could nevertheless not overcome my reluctance to express my wish on the subject, and applied therefore in preference to a rich friend of mine in Alsace, who however, as it frequently happens with such applications, paid no attention to it. But now, thanks to the handsome receipts which my concert had brought in, all prospect of pecuniary want was dissipated, and I could venture upon the further journey to Naples without anxiety. This was nevertheless delayed by the illness of my children till the latter end of January; and as *Dorette,* wholly occupied with attending to them, could now no longer accompany me in my excursions, I kept frequent company with the *Beer* family, and they having arrived later, I could now serve them as Cicerone. Of an evening, when the light no longer permitted anything more to be seen (for the theatres were still closed during Advent), the three sons accompanied me sometimes to my lodgings, and we then shortened the long evenings with a game at whist. As it was at that time, however, very cold in Rome, and there was no means of heating my room, we used to set ourselves down in my enormous bed with our backs turned to the four cardinal points, with the leaf of a table between us, and in that manner played our rubber in comfortable warmth and in the best humour.

Of my stay in Naples, the following incident is to be added.

On the day of my first concert, I received in the green-room of the San Carlo theatre, a visit from the celebrated singer *Crescentini,* whom I had already become acquainted with in Rome. After he had said many very complimentary things relative to my play and my compositions, he made the following proposition to me. The present director, *Zingarelli,* who, with his religious turn of mind, was very unremitting in praying with his pupils, but who practised them in music very little, was to be pensioned off, and he, *Crescentini* was applying for the appointment. But as he understood nothing of instrumental music, the Neapolitan minister contemplated appointing a second director for that, and had thought of me, as my play and my compositions had quite enchanted him at my concert on the previous day. If therefore I felt disposed to make an application for the place, I was to accompany him immediately to the minister, where further proposals would be made to me. This took place. I returned to *Dorette* highly satisfied with the propositions of the minister, and we were not a little pleased at the thoughts of taking up our home in such a paradise as Naples. But week after week passed away, without any further communication from the minister, and we learned from *Crescentini* that the whole project had been abandoned by reason of the expense it would entail. We dared not therefore delay any longer the period of our departure, for I again found that my treasury was so decreased by our numerous excursions in the environs of Naples, which we had made in the company of our Silesian friends, and of which I was always obliged to bear half the expenses, that my means would scarcely suffice for the return journey to Switzerland.

This calculation proved indeed but too correct; for on our arrival at Geneva, my funds were completely exhausted. As my concert there also brought in but very little, and I knew beforehand that with the then (in the spring of 1817) prevailing famine in Switzerland, but very little was to be earned in the other Swiss towns. I for the first time in my life experienced the bitter anxiety arising from a want of the means of subsistence. It is true we possessed some valuables which had been presented to us at several courts; but the bare thought of being obliged to sell or to pledge these, was still much too painful to our feelings. Necessity, however, compelled us to do so. I was just on the point of looking for a place where money was advanced upon pledges, when *Dorette* suggested that it would be preferable to reveal our position to the most friendly of all our acquaintances there, the Pastor *Gerlach,* and offered to go to him herself, as I had not the courage to do so. She took with her her handsomest ornament, a diadem of brilliants, a present from the Queen of Bavaria, and proceeded to the reverend gentleman's house. Never in all my life did I pass such painful moments as those which elapsed during her absence. At length, after a seemingly never-ending half hour, she returned, and brought back the pledge — but with it the sum necessary for the prosecution of our further journey. She was still in a state of excitement from a fright she had experienced there. While, with the greatest embarrassment and with faltering lips, she disclosed to the Pastor our momentary necessities, and made a request for a loan upon the pledge she proferred, he had suddenly burst into a loud fit of laughter and vanished into an adjoining room. But before she had time to reflect upon the meaning of this outburst of hilarity, which seemed to her so greatly out of place, he returned bringing the required sum, and said to her in the kindest manner: "I am delighted that the worthy pair of artists have afforded me so great a pleasure as to render them a service; but how could you think that a clergyman would lend upon pledges like a jew?"

Thus, then, our immediate wants were relieved and we could resume our journey. We now first went to Thierachern to fetch our carriage and the harp, which we had left there the previous autumn. As *Dorette* required a little time to get her hand again into play upon her instrument, and we did not moreover require to hurry, as the favorable period for concert-giving was passed, we stayed there a fortnight, practised again each forenoon our duets for harp and violin, and in the afternoons, favoured by the most beautiful spring weather, visited once more all our former favorite spots. At length, however, we were obliged to make up our minds to leave the paradise of Thierachern and proceed further upon our artistic tour. In Switzerland we met with very little success, for the permission to give public concerts was everywhere refused on account of the prevailing famine, and it was permitted in Zurich only because we there offered to hand over a part of the proceeds to the poor. I there played for the first time since my return to Germany my vocal *scena* and a solo-quartet (Op. 43) that I had begun in Italy and finished in Thierachern; both compositions were received with very great applause. But with that I was obliged to content myself; for the receipts from this concert were far below those of the previous year. I could not therefore keep my promise as to time, in the repayment of the sum borrowed in Geneva, which gave me much uneasiness. But the Pastor *Gerlach,* upon my communicating to him the reason, in excuse for my failure, returned the most satisfactory reply, and I could thus proceed on my journey with a mind more at ease.

But even in Germany also, where we gave concerts in Freiburg, Carlsruhe, Wiesbaden, Ems, and Aix-la-Chapelle, the receipts were but middling, on account of the generally prevailing distress, so that they scarcely covered our travelling expenses; and not until we reached the last-named town, where our play produced a great sensation and enabled us to give three very numerously attended concerts, did sufficient remain to enable us to liquidate my debt to *Gerlach.*

From Naples to Aix-la-chapelle we had now travelled for four months continually in the direction from south to north, without stopping very long anywhere. We had therefore found everywhere beyond and on this side of the Alps, the trees in bloom, and thus enjoyed an extension of the spring season in a degree such as it has never since been our lot to know. At Aix-la-Chapelle we arrived in the height of summer, and in the middle of the bathing season. For our farther journey to Holland this was the most unfavourable time for concert-giving, and I therefore resolved to stop some weeks in Aix-la-Chapelle. We had there become acquainted with several zealous musical amateurs, at whose houses music parties were frequently given. I had also found some good quartet-accompaniers with whom I practised my Vienna quartets and quintets; and as they were greatly admired by all who heard them, I gave them frequently.

We thus passed the time of our stay in Aix-la-Chapelle in a very pleasant manner, equally divided between work and pleasure. The instruction of the children, which indeed had never entirely ceased during the whole journey, for we used to give them instruction even in the carriage as we travelled along, was now resumed with more earnestness and regularity.

I also began to compose again, and wrote there the first number of my four-voice songs for men's voices (Op. 44) of which *Gœthe's* "Dem Schnee, dem Regen" became afterwards a favorite table song.

Towards autumn we continued our journey to Holland, and on our way thither first gave some concerts at Cologne and Dusseldorf which were very well attended. Thence we proceeded to Cleves, where we made the acquaintance of the notary, Mr. *Thomae*, a zealous friend of art and a distinguished dilettante, who played several instruments. In his house we had music very frequently, and the two families, inclusive of the children, soon became so attached that they formed a life-enduring friendship. Through this circumstance our stay in Cleves became so attractive that we took leave of the friendly little town and its charming environs with much reluctance.

The fame of the *Spohr* artist-couple had however not yet reached Holland, and we were therefore first obliged to break ground there. In this however we soon succeeded. In that wealthy land, favourably disposed towards German art and German artists, we made a great sensation, and consequent thereon also a flourishing business. We had already played at Rotterdam and the Hague, and had just arrived at Amsterdam, where we had also already made our appearance in *Felix meritis* and had afterwards given a concert upon our own account, when I received a letter from Mr. *Ihlée*, director of the theatre at Frankfort on the Main, in which, on the part of the shareholders of that theatre, he offered me the appointment of director of the opera and music, and in case of my acceptance thereof, added the request that I would enter upon it with all possible despatch. The terms, it is true, were not so brilliant as those of my Vienna appointment, but sufficient nevertheless to maintain a family. Certainly I should have liked to have continued my artistic tour, in which I took great pleasure, at least till the spring; but they were very pressing in Frankfort, and *Dorette* longed once more for domestic repose. I therefore consented without further hesitation and set out immediately upon the return journey. At Cleves, where we alighted at the friendly house of the *Thomae* family, we were forced, despite the pressing urgency to accelerate our journey, to stop a few days. Although it was now mid-winter, every thing was again done to make our stay agreeable. Music parties, sledge excursions and other amusements succeeded each other alternately. On the evening before our departure, as we sat at the supper-table, cracking nuts and thinking regretfully of the approaching parting, my friend *Thomae* made the proposal that the *Spohr* family, as a memorial of their presence there, should plant one of the nuts in the garden. This proposition was received with general acclamation. Upon a spade being brought, both families, wrapped in warm cloaks, repaired in procession to the garden, in the very centre of which, after I had cleared away the snow, I dug a hole, in which the children planted the nut. In the following spring the appearance of the germ above ground was announced to us at Frankfort. This, carefully protected by a circular fence, grew by degrees to a fine tree, and even now (1852) the *Thomae* family, as one of the sons not long since informed me, thinks with pleasurable feelings of that evening and the absent friends.

In Frankfort I was received by the shareholders of the theatre and by the whole company of the theatre and orchestra in the most friendly manner. A dinner was given in my honour in the the saloon of the "*Weidenbusch,*" at which the usual toasts were given and speeches made in due form. The orchestra, which, under the able direction of its previous leader Mr. *Schmitt,* had acquired the reputation of being one of the best in Germany, I found somewhat deteriorated, from his long illness. But as a ready disposition was shewn by all to meet my wishes and arrangements, and as they soon accustomed themselves to my method of directing, the former *ensemble* was soon re-established. My predecessor had led with the violin, and by the wish of the singers I began also in the asme manner, indicating the time with the bow, and keeping the violin ready at hand, in order to assist with that when necessary. But I soon accustomed them to so precise a practise of their parts that such assistance as that was soon no longer necessary. I now laid the violin aside and directed in the French style, with the bâton.

The routine of business on the Frankfort stage was at that time as follows: the managers chosen by the shareholders, met every week the technical directors (Mr. *Ihlée* for the drama and I for the opera) at a sitting at which the programme for the week was agreed upon and everything concerning the management arranged. The *præses*, or *senior* of this directory, was a merchant of the name of *Leers*, who liked the office and therefore always managed to be re-elected. In the course of time he had acquired a certain tact in the routine of managing the theatre, and spoke usually therefore in a very decided tone. His whole endeavour was directed to economy, in order to diminish the yearly recurring deficit of from 14 to 17,000 florins, which the shareholders were obliged to cover. He liked best the singers, performers and musicians, who engaged at the lowest salaries, and in the choice of the operas and plays which were to be given he always decided upon those which would entail the least expense. *Ihlée* and I had also an especial interest in getting rid of the deficit, as we had a share in any overplus secured to us by agreement; but we thought this would be much more surely attained if an endeavour was made to raise the character of the theatre by engaging distinguished talent and the representation of classical works. We were therefore frequently in opposition to Mr. *Leers* and his colleagues, and one of them only, Mr. *Clement Brentano*, entertained the same opinion as ourselves. But he seldom succeeded in obtaining the victory for it, as it was always his custom to defend it merely with light sallies of wit and sarcasm. The animosity which sprung out of this difference of opinion between Mr. *Leers* and myself was not perceptible, however, till a later period, for at first we agreed very well. It was therefore not very difficult for me to obtain the consent of the managers to bring out my opera "Faust." I was very desirous of at length hearing this work, which I had written five years before at Vienna, and I hastened all the preparations as much as possible. As there was no baritone among the singers of the theatre who could satisfactorily take the part of Faust, I was obliged to give it to the tenor, Mr. *Schelble*, afterwards the founder and director of the society of St. Cecilia, who possessed in his *mezzo-tenore*, the necessary compass as also the requisite skill in execution. After the rehearsals had commenced, *Schelble* expressed the wish that I would write another air for him which would shew his voice off to more advantage than those which were in the opera. As I found a suitable place for its introduction immediately after the duet at the commencement, and Mr. *George Döring* (hautboy of the orchestra and subsequently a much admired romance writer) furnished me with appropriate words for it, I was very pleased to be enabled to satisfy *Schelble's* wish. This air: "Liebe ist die zarte Blüthe" (Love is the tender blossom), which was afterwards so frequently sung at concerts, and innumerable times in London by *Pischek*, is therefore the first thing I composed in Frankfort. Meanwhile the study of the opera had proceeded so well that it could be announced and performed for the first time in March (1818). At first, it is true, it pleased the great majority less than the connoisseurs, but with each representation gained more admirers; so that from that time it has remained almost constantly in the repertorium of the Frankfort stage, and has been studied anew after short intervals.

This success encouraged me to new dramatic compositions. I therefore looked about me for the materials for a work of the kind, and found one that suited me in *Appel's* book of ghost stories, in the tale called "Der schwarze Jäger" (the black huntsman). *Döring*, with whom I spoke upon the subject, offered to work it out as an opera. We devised together a plot which differed chiefly from *Kind's* text-book (which was at that time as yet unknown to us) in this, that we retained the tragical conclusion of the story. As soon as *Döring* had written the first scenes, I immediately set about the composition. The introduction was already for the most part sketched out, when the celebrated tragedian Madame *Schröder*, and her daughter, the afterwards more celebrated *Schröder-Devrient*, came to Frankfort, and during her visit saw the work I was engaged upon on the piano. They then informed that *C. M. von Weber* was composing music for the same subject as an opera, and had already finished the first act. This induced me to lay my work aside, as I had reason to fear *Weber* would come forward with his opera much earlier than I. As it afterwards proved, however, such was not the case; for the "Freischütz" appeared first in 1820, and my opera "Zelmira and Azor," which I began almost a year later, was already given on the 4th April 1819. Nevertheless I have not regretted that I abandoned the materials of *Appel's* story, for with my music, which is not adapted to please the multitude and excite the popular enthusiasm, I should never have met with the unexampled success that the "Freischütz" met with.

As I was now again obliged to look about me for a libretto, I began meanwhile to write quartets. The chief reason for this was the solicitation of some lovers of that kind of music to institute public-quartet performances, which had not hitherto been given in Frankfort. At these I wished also to be enabled to bring forward some new compositions, and for that purpose I wrote in the course of the summer the three quartets (Op. 45). When I played the first of these at a musical soirée at *Schelble's*, *Jean Paul* was one of the audience. He appeared to interest himself very much for this new composition and ascribed to it a highly poetical signification, of which while composing it I certainly never thought, but which recurred in a very striking manner to my mind at every subsequent performance of the quartet.

On the 29th July 1818 my family was again increased by the birth of a little daughter, who was christened by the name of Theresa after her godmother Mrs. *Thomae* of Cleves, and was held over the font by my friend *Speyer*. *Dorette* now felt very happy at having a permanent-dwelling place, so as to be able to devote herself wholly to the care of the new visitor.

In the autumn began the first set of the public quartets in the little saloon of the "Rothes Haus." The assistants were: second violin the concertmaster Mr. *Hofmann*, viol Mr. *Bayer*, violoncello Mr. *Hasemann*, at that time bass-trumpet of the orchestra, and afterwards first violincellist of the Cassel orchestra. I brought forward some quartets of *Haydn*, *Mozart*, *Beethoven*, and some of my own, which we had practised in the most careful manner in two rehearsals. They made therefore a great sensation by the precision of their execution, and were so well received that in the course of the winter another set could be given.

In September 1818 I began also the composition of the new opera. Mr. *Ihlée* had proposed as subject the text of the formerly very much admired opera *"La Belle et la Bête,"* by *Gretry*. As this at that time had wholly disappeared from the German repertory, and was wholly unknown to the younger generation, I readily assented to the proposition; for from my earliest youth I had a predeliction for this tale, and even remembered an air of *Gretry's* opera, that namely of *Zelmira* with the echo, which as a boy I had frequently heard my mother sing, and also sung myself. Herr *Ihlée* offered to alter the text to the style of the modern opera, which, as he well understood stage business, he did greatly to my satisfaction. — At that time *Rossini's* music became then first known in Germany, and "Tancred" in particular brought down a very storm of applause in Frankfort. Almost at every sitting of the theatre I was obliged to hear from Mr. *Leers* the words: "That is an opera that pleases and attracts the public, you must bring out more of that kind!" — Little as I was an admirer of *Rossini's* music, as the severe criticism thereof in the diary of the Italian journey shews, yet the applause which "Tancred" had met with in Frankfort was not wholly without influence on the style of my new opera. I was furthermore induced to this by the considerable power of execution possessed by four singers (Miss *Friedel*, the sisters *Campagnoli*, and Mr. *Schelble*) who were at my command. This explains why the music to "Zelmira and Azor" has so much colouring and vocal ornamentation in the parts sustained by the three sisters, and that of Azor. The opera was studied most attentively by the singers and the orchestra, and met with great success at the very first representation, indeed a more general one than "Faust," which however, at a later period, both in Frankfort and the rest of Germany, reassumed the place in public estimation which its real merits as an opera more properly justified.

During the course of the winter I gave another concert with my wife, for which I had written a new sonata for harp and violin. As, since I had once more a fixed residence, pupils again presented themselves, both native and foreign, I was overburdened with work the whole winter. When spring at length came I was therefore very desirous of a little rest and I was well pleased when four of my earlier musical friends of Rudolstadt, Messrs. *von Holleben, Müller, Sommer* and *Methfessel*, came to Frankfort and urged me to accompany them to Mannheim, where a musical festival was to take place. I managed to get leave of absence for eight days, and joined the party. From Darmstadt, where the charming mountain-road begins, we went on foot to Heidelberg, and carried our necessary luggage in knapsacks, on our backs. Three of the Rudolstädter, *Müller, Sommer* and *von Holleben*, who were first-rate harmonists, had strapped their horns upon their knapsacks, and *Methfessel*, who accompanied our four-part songs with the guitar, carried his instrument slung by a band over his shoulders. In this manner our travelling-party, notwithstanding their respectable exterior, had completely the appearance of an itinerant music-band, and as, in high and jocund spirits, we always entered all the villages and small towns either playing or singing, we had always a long train of jovial listeners, and numerous applications to "strike up," which, to the great regret of the applicants, were of course not complied with. We made short stages, and ascended the ruins of several castles which lay near our road. There we partook of the meal brought with us from the neighbouring inn and seasoned it with horn-music, song and mirthful jest. On the third day we arrived at Heidelberg, where we visited the castle. A flourish of horns soon brought a number of hearers around us, who were highly delighted with our four-part songs and *Methfessel's* comic lyrics. As we had inscribed our names in the visitors' book, it soon became known in the town that I and some musical friends were on our way to the festival at Mannheim, and in the evening a deputation from the Heidelberg musical society made its appearance at our inn with an invitation to make the passage to Mannheim the next morning on board the society's vessel. We consented with very great pleasure.

This voyage was the most brilliant episode in the whole journey. When I and my companions set foot on board the vessel, which was dressed out with festoons of flowers up to the top of the mast, we were welcomed in the most friendly manner by the already assembled male and female singers, with a choral-song. While the boat was passing directly afterwards between high rocky banks on either side, which threw back the echo, the Rudolstädter first returned the compliment with their horns, which had a fine effect there. Then followed our songs, and *Methfessel* again distinguished himself in particular by the execution of his humorous songs, which he accompanied in a masterly manner on the guitar. These put the whole company in the merriest mood. As we drew near the end of our journey we were met and welcomed by the Mannheim musical society on board several boats decorated with flags and flowers. My presence on board the Heidelberg boat was already known. The committee of the festival therefore saluted me and my companions, and presented us with tickets of admission to the rehearsals and performances. To me even apartments were offered in a private house, which I was however obliged to decline, as it would separate me from my companions. As soon as we had landed, therefore, we sought for an inn. Unfortunately, however, we found it already so full of visitors that we were obliged all five to accommodate ourselves in one room, and the next day the crowd of applicants for lodging was so great that we had great difficulty in protecting our room from the invasion of yet more guests. In the evening, since, as may be readily supposed, beds were not to be had, we lay down contented beside each other on some clean straw, nor was our good humour in the least disturbed thereby.

As regards the musical performances, I now only recollect that I and my companions, who, together with me, had assisted at the festival at Frankenhausen, were not so satisfied with the effect of the music here as there, which can alone be accounted for by the circumstance that the performance at Frankenhausen took place in the church, a place sonorous and well adapted on account of its excellent acoustic qualities, while at Mannheim they were given in the theatre.

On the third day we set out upon our return journey. As the road from Mannheim to Mayence would have been too uninteresting to travel on foot, we hired a boat with two vigorous rowers, and went by water. But in this way also the journey was rather tedious. We had, moreover, passed the previous night at a ball, and felt very tired; it was therefore no wonder that we sought to make up for the lost night's rest, and passed the greater part of the time in sleep. On our arrival at Mayence we nevertheless met with a little adventure which put us in the merriest mood during the last hours of our being together. Evening was drawing in when, after our landing, we proceeded to look for the best inn in the town. Just as we were about to enter it, in the already described dress of travelling musicians, the host, who was looking out of the window, called out to us in an angry tone of voice: "Be off with you! we don't take in such people as you!" This style of address amused me amazingly, as I had frequently joked my companions upon their dress, and laughing, I called out to

Mr. *von Holleben:* "High warden of forests, did you hear that? they will not take us in here; we must look for another inn!" But the host, startled at hearing my friend addressed by such a grand title, darted down-stairs in a minute and made his appearance immediately in the street, and with bows innumerable entreated the gentlemen to walk in and graciously pardon his silly mistake!" As we followed him into the house and were all ushered by him into the well-lighted dining room, his embarrassment was ludicrous in the extreme: our highly respectable appearance seemed now to allay all his fears, when the unlucky horns strapped upon the knapsacks, and *Methfessel's* guitar suspended from his neck, excited new doubts as to whether we were guests worthy of entertainement in his house. But when we ordered three rooms with wax lights (which latter I purposely mentioned), five beds and a good supper, all uttered in the curt imperative tone of persons of importance, his last lingering scruples vanished, and his whole demeanour became thenceforth cringingly servile. This specimen of the mean vulgarity of innkeeper-nature amused us long, and was subject of mirth up to the last moment of our being together. The next morning, as my leave of absence was expired, I returned to Frankfort and the Rudolstädter continued their journey down the Rhine, as they had proposed.

As I entered my house, the children ran joyfully to meet me, but my wife, who had been in very low spirits at our parting the week before, was now suffering extremely from the shock sustained from a fright. In order that the reader may understand the cause of this, I must advert to some previous incidents that had occurred while in Frankfort.

In the latter part of the autumn of 1818 *Turner*, a player on the hautboy, came to Frankfort. I had previously known him in Brunswick, where we were both members of the orchestra. Already at that time *Turner* distinguished himself greatly by his skill upon that instrument, as also by his talent for composition. Upon his subsequent travels, particularly while in Vienna, where he lived some time, he had acquired the reputation of being the first of living hautboyists. At the same time, however, many strange stories were current of his residence there; of a *liaison* with a lady of rank, whom he afterwards accused of having given him poison in a cup of coffee. A criminal inquiry was instituted, whereat it was elicited that he had periodical fits of insanity, at which times he was possessed with the fixed idea of being poisoned. These relations concerning him, which passed from mouth to mouth, imparted to him a certain interest, and his concerts were on that account most numerously attended. I found him on his arrival in Frankfort — for he immediately paid me a visit — more earnest and reserved, it is true, than when I was previously acquainted with him in Brunswick, but otherwise remarked nothing whatever peculiar in him. As his play pleased very much, and as I knew moreover that his orchestral skill was very great, and as from *George Döring's* retirement from the orchestra (he had now thought of devoting himself entirely to authorship), a vacancy had occurred for a hautboy player — I proposed at the next sitting of the theatrical committee that *Turner* should be engaged as first hautboy. The salary he asked was not unusually high, and therefore the proposition met with no opposition, even Mr. *Leers* himself making no objection. *Turner* took his place therefore in the orchestra, and proved a real acquisition by the tasteful execution of his soli and by his fine tone. After some time, however, a remarkable melancholy was observed in him, which gradually increased so much, that at length not a word above a whisper was to be got from him. Nevertheless he always performed his orchestral duties with punctuality, so that I hoped these periods of sadness would pass off without further results. Soon however they assumed the character of complete aberration of mind, in which the fixed idea of the Vienna poisoning again evinced itself. It was now full time to remove him from the orchestra, to prevent the possiblity of some unpleasant occurrence. *Döring*, a near relation of *Turner's*, undertook to provide for him and get him cured, and engaged also to temporarily fill his place. The malady now soon increased with such violence, that it was necessary to have him constantly watched by keepers. One evening, nevertheless, he suceeded in escaping from them scarcely half-clothed. During a violent snow-storm he wandered about in the open fields half the night, nor did he return home till towards morning, covered with a thick crust of snow and ice. As he had immediately gone to bed in this condition, the doctor found him in the morning bathed in perspiration and in a violent fever. This perhaps, however, brought about a crisis, for from that day he got better, and he was soon enabled to resume his duties in the orchestra with fully restored sanity of mind. I remarked, nevertheless, that for about eight days in every month, and always with the moon's increase, he was visited by a slight return of his melancholy madness, which announced itself beforehand by a fixed look and a certain feverish restlessness. I then, with *Döring's* assistance, managed to keep him away from the orchestra for a few days, until his more cheerful look bespoke anew his recovery. In this manner *Turner* performed his duties up to the summer and it was hoped that by degrees he would also be cured of these slighter attacks also. In the latter part of this time he again, as formerly, called upon me now and then, and even spent the evening with me, and demeaned himself in a friendly manner towards my wife, and shewed much interest in the children. When therefore I went to Mannheim with my Rudolstädt friends, it did not at first appear at all strange to *Dorette* to see him walk one morning into the room; but as, without any salutation or uttering a word, he sat down opposite to her and gazed upon her with his eyes fixed, she began to feel uneasy, and was at length seized with fear. As she was quite alone with him (the children being at school) she was about to call in a needlewoman, who was sewing in the adjoining room; but scarcely had she risen than he also sprang up and clasped her in his arms. With a shriek of terror she tore herself from his grasp, rushed into the adjoining room, the door of which the sempstress had then just opened, and she succeeded in closing and bolting the door before *Turner* could follow her. There was, however, unfortunately no further issue from this room, and the two terrified women found themselves besieged by the madman. His endeavours to force the lock they met by pressing against the door with their whole weight, and all the strength which terror imparted to them; and succeeded, for after a few vain efforts he abandoned his purpose, ran down the stairs and out of the house. *Dorette* now felt about to faint, was obliged to send for the doctor, and kept her bed for some days. After my return, her pleasure thereat and the assurance of again being under my protection, soon restored her, and thus this circumstance was fortunately attended by no worse results. For the unfortunate young man this last violent outbreak of his malady entailed his discharge by the directors of the theatre. After again recovering, he went to Holland, and at first gave there several concerts in which he was greatly applauded, and which were also very remunerative; but upon a fresh attack was put into a mad house, where he soon afterwards died. The world lost in him a very great musical genius, the full development of which was barred by the sad affliction that befel him.

Meanwhile the acrimony of feeling that existed between Mr. *Leers* and myself became constantly more apparent, and a sitting of the directors seldom passed over without a regular dispute. He asserted that I required too much time for the study and production of new pieces because I was too fastidious in the matter. He expressed the opinion, that a new opera ought to be studied every fortnight, or at least an old one completed in those parts that required to be newly filled up. In vain I represented to him, that it was impossible for an opera that was carelessly studied to go off well, and therefore that it never could give satisfaction; that once brought into discredit, it would draw no audience, and then the time and money expended upon it would be sheer waste. With this self-willed, obstinate man, who, moreover, before my appointment had never met with any opposition in the management, every sensible representation was ineffectual; and as I would not allow any opera to be brought out until it had been studied thoroughly as far as the means and strength of the company allowed, our contest never ceased. This, together with an intimation made by Mr. *Leers* at a general meeting of the shareholders, "that for their theatre they did not require a musical artist of eminence, but merely a good indefatigable workman, who would devote his whole time and energies to the theatre," induced me to give in my resignation at the next meeting of the committee, to date from the end of September (1819). The news of this soon spread through the town, and excited general regret among the lovers of music. *Börne*, in his journal "The Balance" gave expression to his sentiments on the subject, and indeed in a by no means gentle manner towards the theatrical-committee of management. I left Frankfort with a light heart, for my summons to that town had only been an interruption to the gratification of my love of travelling; but my good wife was very grieved at it — she who looked forward to the consequent separation from the children, as these, from requiring now a regular school education, could no longer be taken with us on our artistic tours. But I consoled her nevertheless with the promise that she should always pass the summer months with her children, and only travel with me during a period of from four to five months in the winter. Before my departure from Frankfort I had accepted an engagement from the Philharmonic Society of London for the next season of the sitting of Parliament, which engagement was offered me by *Ferdinand Ries*, the celebrated pianist and composer, in the name of the society. This had been instituted but a few years before by from twelve to sixteen of the most eminent musical artists in London: *Clementi*, the two *Cramers, Moscheles, Ries, Potter, Smart*, and others, with the object of giving every year eight grand concerts during the season. Notwithstanding the very high price of admission, the number of subscribers was so great, that many hundreds of those who had inscribed their names could not obtain seats at the commencement of the season, and could obtain them only by degrees in the course of the summer. The funds of the society were therefore so great, that they could not only engage the first artists and singers in London for the soi in their concerts, but the most reputed musicians on the Continent. — In this manner I was also engaged for the season of 1820, and for a considerable remuneration, which secured to me the expenses of the journey thither and return, and the expenses of a four months' residence in London. I undertook the performance of a fourfold duty. I was required, namely, to direct some of the eight concerts, to play soli in some, to assist in all of them as orchestra violinist, and lastly to leave in the hands of the society as their own property one of my orchestral compositions. At the same time a benefit concert was also insured to me in the rooms of the society, with the joint assistance of the orchestra. Although my wife was not included in this engagement, yet I could not make up my mind to leave her behind me for four long months. It was therefore resolved, on consulting with my family, that my wife should accompany me and make her appearance as artiste in London at least in my own concerts. As the season commenced in the middle of February, and therefore the sea-passage would be made at the roughest time of the year, we resolved, in order to shorten it as much as possible, to go by way of Calais; and in order to be enabled to give concerts on the journey in the Belgian and French towns, to set out six or eight weeks earlier. We first proceeded to Gandersheim to my parents, who had undertaken the care and education of the children during the winter, and then set out upon an artistic tour to Hamburg, where we gave two concerts with very great success. I played there, before highly respectable audiences, my new quartets, which had been previously published there: they were exceedingly well accompanied, and as violinist upon those occasions I made the most sensation with my two solo-quartets. I played likewise a few times the two quintets, and I found the passion for this kind of music to be greater here than anywhere else, except perhaps in Vienna. In the catalogue of my compositions, *Goethe's* ballad "Wenn die Reben blühen" is enumerated as composed by me in Hamburg, but I do not now recollect the reason of its being so designated.

We then proceeded to Berlin, Dresden, Leipsic, Cassel, and other places, in all of which we gave concerts, but respecting all of them I now no longer remember anything particular. Of our performances in Berlin one of the newspapers gave a most favourable notice.

In Brussels we found another travelling artist-couple who, like ourselves, gave performances on the harp and violin. They were Monsieur *Alexandre Boucher* and wife from Paris. I had already heard a good deal about him and was therefore very desirous of making his personal acquaintance. *Boucher* had the reputation of being a distinguished violinist, but a great charlatan also. He bore a striking resemblance to *Napoleon*, both in the features of his face and in his figure, and did his best to turn this resemblance to account. He had acquired by study the deportment of the exiled emperor, his way of wearing his hat, and of taking a pinch of snuff with the greatest possible exactitude. When on his artistic tours he arrived in a town where he was unknown, he immediately presented himself with these acquired arts on the public promenade or in the theatre, in order to attract the notice of the public and to be talked about; he even endeavoured to spread the report that he was persecuted by the present sovereign and driven from France on account of his resemblance to *Napoleon*, because it brought back the recollection of the beloved exile to the mind of the people. In Lille, at least, as I there afterwards learned, he had announced his concert in the following manner: "Une malheureuse ressemblance me force de m'expatrier; je donnerai donc, avant de quitter ma belle patrie, un concert d'adieux," etc. That announcement had contained also some similar charlatanerie, as follows: "Je jouerai ce fameux concerto de *Viotti* en mi-mineur, dont l'éxécution à Paris m'a gagné le surnom: *l'Alexandre* des violons."

I was just on the point of calling upon Monsieur *Boucher,* when he anticipated me by paying me a visit. He offered in a most friendly manner to assist me in the arrangements for my concert, and shewed himself in every respect, deduction made of his self-glorification, a very amiable man. He introduced us to several families who were lovers of music, who then by inviting us to their musical parties, procured for us the opportunity of hearing the *Boucher*-couple. Both shewed in their joint performances great skill; but all the compositions they played were poor and barren, and of those of Monsieur *Boucher* himself I no longer recollect anything. At first Monsieur *Boucher* played a quartet of *Haydn,* but introduced so many irrevalent and tasteless ornaments, that it was impossible for me to feel any pleasure in it. The manner in which *Boucher* allowed himself to be waited upon by his wife on these occasions was remarkable. When he had taken his seat at the quartet desk, she would ask him for the key of the violin-case, open it, bring him his violin, then the bow, which she had previously resined; she then laid the music before him and lastly seated herself near him, to turn over the pages. When we were then invited to play, the whole of this process was inverted; for I not only fetched my own instrument, but took my wife's harp out of the case also, led her to the seat where she was to play and then tuned up, all of which in the previous performance had been the business of Madame *Boucher*. But I took upon me the tuning of the harp upon every appearance in public, not only to save my wife the trouble, but also to bring the instrument to a perfectly pure and tempered pitch, which, as is well known, is not so easy a matter. We played one of our brillant duets, and met with great applause. *Boucher* in particular seemed charmed with my play, and he may perhaps have meant it with some sincerity; for in a letter of recommendation which he gave me to Baron *d'Assignies* in Lille, and which the latter shewed to me as a curiosity, after describing the characteristics of my play; he said: "Enfin, si je suis, comme on le prétend, le *Napoléon* des violons, Mr. *Spohr* est bien le Moreau!"

My concert took place in the new large theatre and met with marked approbation; but the receipts, after deduction of the very considerable expenses, were but small, for our fame had not yet reached Brussels. It is true we were invited by lovers of music and the public journals to give a second concert; but as a favourable day did not immediately offer, and our stay at the chief hotel where we had stopped was very expensive, we preferred setting out immediately on our journey to Lille.

Arrived there, my first visit was to Monsieur *Vogel*, who had been mentioned to me as the best violinist in the town and as director of the dilettanti-concerts. I did not find him at home, but Madame *Vogel*, who received me in a very cordial manner. When I told her my name, her face became animated, and she anxiously inquired whether I was the composer of the nonette, the theme of which she sang to me. As I smiling replied yes, with an outburst of French vivacity she threw her arms round my neck, and exclaimed: "Oh how delighted my husband well be, *car il est fou de votre Nonetto!*" I had scarcely returned to the inn, when Monsieur *Vogel* appeared with a countenance lit up with pleasure, and welcomed me with the warmth of an old friend. In the house of this amiable couple we passed some very happy hours, and gave a concert in the saloon of the dilettanti society, the arrangements for which were made by Monsieur *Vogel*, the whole of the members of the society being desirous to hear the composer of the so frequently performed nonette play in person. The joint play of my wife and self was especially received with such enthusiastic acclamation, that the day was immediately fixed for a second concert. Some lovers of music from the neighbouring town of Douay, who had come over to the concert, invited us in the name of the musical society of that place to give a concert in Douay also, and insured to us the sale of 400 tickets at five francs each. I had therefore the finest prospect of carrying from Lille plenty of money, when an unexpected occurrence quashed all my hopes. The carriage was already packed and we were on the point of starting for Douay, when the report was spread in the town that the telegraph had just announced from Paris the assassination of the Duke *de Berri*. It was not long before placards were posted at the corners of the streets by order of the mayoralty, announcing officially this mournful intelligence to the inhabitants of Lille. As all concert-giving was now necessarily suspended throughout France, but the period of my engagement in London not yet arrived, I was easily induced by Messrs. *Vogel, d'Assignies*, and other lovers of music, to remain yet longer in Lille. Private musical parties now took place almost daily, and I had thus an opportunity of performing all my quartets, quintets, and compositions for the harp to this circle of enthusiastic lovers of music. I found on these occasions a very sympathetic and graceful auditory, and therefore still recall with infinite pleasure the remembrance of those musical soirées. At these many other interesting things were related to me concerning *Boucher*. Among others, upon one occasion, in the midst of his play, when according to his idea something had gone wrong, he suddenly ceased playing, and without paying any regard to those who accompanied him, he again repeated the unlucky passage, addressing himself aloud with the words: "Cela n'a pas réussi; allons, *Boucher*, encore une fois!" The termination of his second and last concert was also of a highly comic character. As his concluding subject he played a rondo of his own composition which had at the end an impromptu cadence. At the rehearsal he had begged the gentlemen dilettanti to fall in right vigorously with their final tutti immediately after the shake of his cadence, and added that he would give them the signal by stamping with his foot. In the evening, when this concluding piece began, it was already very late, and the dilettanti were growing impatient to get home to supper. But when the cadence in which *Boucher* as usual exhibited all his artistic *tours de force* seemed never likely to end, some of the gentlemen put their instruments into their cases and slipped out. This was so infectious, that in a few minutes the whole orchestra had disappeared. *Boucher*, who in the enthusiasm of his play had observed nothing of this, lifted his foot already at the commencement of his concluding shake, in order to draw the attention of the orchestra beforehand to the agreed signal. When he had now concluded the shake he was fully satisfied of what would follow, namely the most vigorous entry of the orchestra and the burst of applause it was to bring down from the enraptured audience. His astonishment may therefore be imagined when all that fell upon his ear was the loud stamp of his own foot. Horrified he stared aghast around him, and beheld all the music desks abandoned. But the public, who had already prepared themselves to see this moment arrive, burst out into an uproarious laughter, in which *Boucher*, with the best stomach he could, was obliged to join.

The time for our departure for London had now arrived. As I was desirous of purchasing in London a new *Erard* harp with the improved *double mouvement* for my wife, we left the old instrument in the care of Monsieur *Vogel*. The family were very pleased at this, as they now reckoned with certainty upon seeing us again on our return journey.

Arrived in Calais, I immediately went to the packet-boat office to take our berth for the passage. Thence I took a walk to the port, to look at the vessel in which we were to sail in the afternoon. As I now, however, remarked that the sea, even in the inside of the harbour, was very rough, and ran so high outside that the waves broke high over the pier head, I lost all inclination to cross with the sea so stormy, and hastened back to the office, to have the berths taken transferred for the following day. In the afternoon while taking a walk in the town I took good care not to take my wife near the sea, so that, dreading the passage as she already did, she might not observe how rough it was. The thoughts of being obliged to cross at so stormy a season of the year with my delicate and nervous wife disturbed my rest throughout the night; as soon as day broke I hastened therefore again down to the harbour to see whether the storm had not abated. It appeared to me to have done so, and I therefore fetched *Dorette*, brought her on board, and advised her to lie down in the cabin. A good-natured German who served as seaman on board this English packet-boat, promised me to take every care of her and bring her all she might require. This enabled me to go upon deck, where in the open air I hoped to be somewhat enabled to resist sea-sickness. Meanwhile the preparations were made for departure, and the vessel was towed out with long ropes close along the left-hand side jetty of the harbour by from sixty to eighty men. Scarcely, however, had she reached this, when a gigantic wave seized her and in a moment hurled her to the opposite side of the harbour, so that she was almost thrown against the extreme point of the right hand-pier. Immediately upon this the waves broke over the deck, and the hatches and cabin doors were obliged to be closed. Of all the passengers I was the only one who remained on deck, and had seated myself on a bench near the mast, round the foot of which was piled a high coil of cable. Here I hoped to be protected from the water that poured in torrents over the deck; but the waves soon broke in over the bows to such a height, that to prevent being completely drenched by them I was compelled to stand up upon the bench. I had not done this many times, before I found my strength fail me to repeat it; and in a short time therefore in spite of my thick cloak I found myself wet through to the skin, which made my already wretched condition but more distressing. In addition to this I was then seized with such violent cramp in the stomach from the straining which follows when the stomach has nothing more to yield, that I thought I should expire under it. Fortunately, however, favoured by the storm, the passage was an unusually quick one. Nevertheless, the three hours of its duration seemed to me an eternity; — at length we arrived at Dover, but another misfortune awaited us here; for on account of the tide being at ebb, we could not enter the harbour, and were constrained to disembark the passengers in in open boats in the offing. For this purpose as soon as we had cast anchor, the boats were lowered, and we were called to get into them to be put on shore in the harbour. I now saw my suffering fellow-passengers come from below, pale and trembling like ghosts from the grave, and it was very evident that they had not fared better in the cabin than I upon deck. At length, supported by the kind sailor, my poor wife appeared also, in a most suffering condition. I was just about to hasten to her, when a young and beautiful girl, whom I had already remarked, it is true, when we came on board, but who then did not think me worthy of a look, suddenly threw her arms round my neck, and without uttering a word, clung close to me. I readily guessed the motive of this extraordinary conduct. The poor, terrified creature had been a joint spectator of the manner in which the first passengers had been put on board the boat, and how when it had been lifted by the still surging waves as high as the deck of the vessel, it then sank as it were into an abyss, and was again lifted up, which was the moment seized by the sailors to thrust another passenger or pitch another object of luggage into it. This rough method of proceeding had so terrified her, that she left the arm of the female who accompanied her, and clung to me, whom she may have considered the strongest of the passengers. There was no time for explanation; I bore her therefore in my arms into the boat, and then hastened back to my wife, to put her also into it. Scarcely had I effected this without accident, when the still terrified fair one clung close to me anew, and indeed so as to excite *Dorette's* extreme surprise. But the danger of the passage was too absorbing to permit of any remark on the subject, and upon landing the young girl had scarcely felt the firm ground under her feet than she left hold of me without a word of thanks, and taking the arm of her companion walked away. That she was some young lady of rank accompanied by her governess, may be readily imagined from this truly English behaviour.

Arrived at the inn, I exchanged my thoroughly wet clothes for dry ones, and having satisfied our re-awakened appetite at the *table d'hôte*, and gained strength for the further journey, we immediately took places in the coach, which was to leave in the afternoon for London. The greater part of this journey was made at night, and when on the following morning we were set down in the yard of the coach-office with our luggage, I found myself in very great difficulty. In spite of every endeavour, I could not succeed in finding any one either there or in the office to whom I could explain myself, for I knew not a word of English, and none of all whom I addressed, understood either German or French. Nothing therefore remained for me but to hunt up some interpreter in the public street while my wife watched the luggage. But it was yet early in the morning, and I saw therefore none but people of the lower class, from whom I could hope nothing. At length a better dressed man approached, whom I first addressed in German, then, as he shook his head, expressed to him my wants in French; but the man shrugged his shoulders and went on his way. A second person, however, who had witnessed this scene, approached me, and asked me in good French what it was I wanted? He was one who hired himself out as day-interpreter, and out-door servant at hotels, and at my request immediately fetched a hackney-coach for me, to drive to Mr. *Ries*, whose address I fortunately remembered. We were now soon taken to the lodgings that had been engaged for us, where we could at length repose from the fatigues of our voyage and night journey.

The next morning, on which a meeting of the directors of the Philharmonic society was to assemble, I was to be introduced to them by Mr. *Ries*. I therefore made a careful toilette, and expressly for the occasion put on a bright red Turkish shawl-pattern waistcoat forming part of my ward-robe, and which was considered on the Continent as a most elegant article and of the newest fashion. Scarcely had I appeared in it in the street than I attracted the general attention of all who passed. The grown-up people contented themselves with gazing at me with looks of surprise, and then passed on their way; but the young urchins of the street, were loud in their remarks, which unfortunately I did not understand, and therefore could not imagine what it was in me that so much displeased them. By degrees, however, they formed a regular tail behind me, which grew constantly louder in speech and more and more unruly. A passer-by addressed me and probably gave me some explanation of its meaning; but as it was in English, I could derive no benefit from it. Fortunately Mr. *Ries'* house was not very distant, and I reached it shortly after. His wife, a young amiable English woman, and who spoke French fluently, now soon solved for me the problem of my adventure. The death of George III. had but recently taken place and a general mourning had been officially ordered, and according to English custom no person durst appear in public otherwise than in a black suit. In all other respects it is true my dress was black, and therefore in accordance with the requisition, but the unfortunate red waistcoat contrasted with it but the more prominently. Mrs. *Ries* observed to me that I had doubtless to thank my imposing height and my earnest expression of countenance for having escaped from the rude licence of the boys in the street, and from their resort to its more open exhibition of pelting me with mud. In order to avoid all further offence, *Ries* then first drove with me to my lodgings, in order to exchange my red waistcoat for a black one.

After I had been welcomed in a friendly manner by the directors of the Philharmonic Society, some of whom spoke German and others French, a council was held respecting the programme of the first concert. At this I was required to play solo twice and to lead as first violin. To this I replied that I was quite ready to perform the first, but must beg that I might be permitted to lead in one of the subsequent concerts, as my solo play would appear to less advantage if both were required of me on one and the same evening. Clear as this was acknowledged to be by some of the gentlemen who were themselves solo-players, yet it gave rise at first to a long and earnest discussion, as it was contrary to the custom of the society, but at length it was complied with. Still greater subject of offence, however, was my request to be permitted on this my first appearance to play my own compositions only. The Philharmonic Society, in order to exclude from their programmes all shallow and worthless virtuosi-concerti, had laid down the law, that with the exception of the pianoforte concerti of *Mozart* and *Beethoven* no similar musical pieces should be played, and that solo players had only to perform that which they should select. Nevertheless, after *Ries* had continued the discussion in English, and therefore unintelligibly to me, and represented to the gentlemen that my violin-concerts in Germany would therefore become excluded by their bann, they at length yielded in this also. I therefore at the first Philharmonic concert, came forward with my cantabile scena, and in the second part with a solo quartet in E major, and met with great and general applause. As a composer it afforded me an especial gratification that the whole of the directors now shared the opinion of Mr. *Ries,* and as a violinist the greatest pleasure, that old *Viotti,* who had always been my pattern, and was to have been my instructor in my youth, was among the auditory and spoke to me in great praise of my play. As I had thus so successfully passed through the ordeal of my first appearance in London, I devoted the next day to the delivery of my letters of recommendation. Not knowing a word of English this was for me by no means a pleasant business, and brought me into frequent perplexity. Not having been told that in London people announced themselves by knocking at the street doors, and gentlemen always by giving a succession of loud rapid knocks; I, in German fashion, rang very gently at the bell, which is done in London only by those who have business with the kitchen, and I could not imagine why the servants who opened the door always looked at me with an expression of astonishment, and could not at all imagine that I wished my name to be announced to their masters. As those also for whom my visit was intended frequently understood as little as their servants either German or French, the most perplexing scenes were of frequent occurrence. I was however exceedingly amused by one at *Rothschild's*, to whom I brought a letter of recommendation from his brother at Frankfort, and a letter of credit from *Speyer*. After *Rothschild* had taken both letters from me and glanced hastily over them, he said to me in a more subdued tone of voice: "I have just read (pointing to the "Times") that you managed your business very efficiently. But I understand nothing of music; this is my music (slapping his purse), they understand that on the exchange!" Upon which, with a nod of the head, he terminated the audience. — But just as I had reached the door, he called after me: "You can come and dine with me, too, out at my country-house!" A few days afterwards also Madame *Rothschild* invited me to dinner; but I did not go, although she repeated the invitation. Nevertheless, the letter of recommendation to *Rothschild* was not wholly useless, for he took a whole box at my benefit concert.

As immediately on our arrival in London I was obliged to prepare for my appearance in public; and my wife was engrossed with our domestic arrangements, we had unfortunately delayed writing to apprise my parents at Gandersheim of our safe arrival, by which the old folks were thrown into a state of alarm from which they did not recover for a long time. The vessel in which we had designed to cross the channel on the day of our arrival in Calais, and for which I had at first paid the passage money, and had the tickets transferred for the next day's packet, on account of the roughness of the weather, had been driven completely down channel and was given up for lost, until it at length turned up again somewhere on the coast of Spain. A French newspaper had cited our names among the passengers on board. What therefore could be natural, than that the French papers should collectively announce: "The artist-couple *Spohr* and wife have perished on the passage to England." This was soon copied into German papers, and to wit into the country paper taken in by my parents. Unfortunately, this first fell into the hands of my mother, who was already in a state of anxiety from the long delay of letters from England. A shriek of anguish and and an immediate fainting of it were the result of this. The whole family was thrown into confusion, and when at length my mother recovered her senses, there began a general outburst of tears and mourning. My sister first recovered some calmness of mind, and urged as subject of hope and consideration how frequently newspaper reports were wholly false. She also entreated that no one should speak on the subject in the presence of my children, who were now seen returning from school, which request was faithfully promised. But my mother could not refrain from embracing those she believed to be now orphans with more than usual tenderness. This circumstance, together with the yet swollen eyes of the mourners, excited no small astonishment in the children, and when no reply was made to the inquiries they made respecting these incidents, and no one would sit down to supper, they also began to weep, without knowing wherefore.

At length the arrival of the postman put an end to this painful scene. All sprang up delighted, with the expectation of a letter from England. But the joy was but of short duration, for when they recognised the "Frankfort" post-mark and *Speyer's* hand writing on the address, they now indeed believed that they were about to read nothing else than the corroboration of the sad newspaper report. No one, therefore, had the courage to open the letter, until at length my sister summoned the resolution. Scarcely had she glanced her eyes over a few words than she exclaimed with joy: "They have arrived safe," and then handed the letter to my father, who read it aloud to them with great emotion. *Speyer* informed them that he had just received the announcement from the house of *Rothschild* in London, that they had there made me a payment of money, and that therefore the newspaper report of the loss of Herr *Spohr* and his wife was unfounded, which he had therewith immediately communicated to allay all their alarm. A general exclamation of joy was now uttered by all, and the previously neglected evening meal was turned into a very feast of delight. Immediately after supper my father seated himself at his writing table, to thank Mr. *Speyer* for his kind attention, and to give the editor of the country paper a sound rating for having thrown a family into such grief by the heedless insertion of an unauthenticated report in his columns.

The following day my letter arrived also from London, and increased yet more by its good intelligence the joy of my family.

At the house of Mr. *Ries* I had made the acquaintance of Mr. *Erard*, the head of the London firm *Erard Brothers*, and accompanied by my wife had already visited his show rooms of finished harps. We could not however immediately make up our minds in the choice of one, as *Dorette* wished first to try which size would suit her best, and in particular whether she could be able to accustom herself to the new mechanism. Mr. *Erard* removed all hesitation from her mind in that respect, by kindly offering to lend her a harp for trial and choice, during our stay in London, which if it did not suit her, she could change for another or wholly return. This offer she thankfully accepted, and began immediately to practise on the new instrument; but at first she could not well succeed upon it. The new harp, though of the smallest pattern, was nevertheless considerably larger, as well as much more strongly strung, than her own, and therefore required a greater exertion of strength, and it was very difficult for her to acquire a mastery of the new mechanism *à double mouvement*, from being accustomed from her childhood to the single movement. She therefore soon felt convinced that it would require several months' practice on this harp before could play upon it in public, and I accordingly resolved to allow her to appear once only, at my benefit-concert, in order that she might give an additional attraction to it. Meanwhile my turn had come to direct one of the Philharmonic concerts, and I had created no less sensation than with my solo play. It was at that time still the custom there that when symphonies and overtures were performed, the pianist had the score before him, not exactly to conduct from it, but only to read after and to play in with the orchestra at pleasure, which when it was heard, had a very bad effect. The real conductor was the first violin, who gave the *tempi*, and now and then when the orchestra began to falter gave the beat with the bow of his violin. So numerous an orchestra, standing so far apart from each other as that of the Philharmonic, could not possibly go exactly together, and in spite of the excellence of the individual members, the *ensemble* was much worse than we are accustomed to in Germany. I had therefore resolved when my turn came to direct, to make an attempt to remedy this defective system. Fortunately at the morning rehearsal on the day when I was to conduct the concert, Mr. *Ries* took the place at the Piano, and he readily assented to give up the score to me and to remain wholly excluded from all participation in the performance. I then took my stand with the score at a separate music desk in front of the orchestra, drew my directing baton from my coat pocket and gave the signal to begin. Quite alarmed at such a novel procedure, some of the directors would have protested against it; but when I besought them to grant me at least one trial, they became pacified. The symphonies and overtures that were to be rehearsed were well known to me, and in Germany I had already directed at their performance. I therefore could not only give the tempi in a very decisive manner, but indicated also to the wind instruments and horns all their entries, which ensured to them a confidence such as hitherto they had not known there. I also took the liberty, when the execution did not satisfy me, to stop, and in a very polite but earnest manner to remark upon the manner of execution, which remarks Mr. *Ries* at my request interpreted to the orchestra. Incited thereby to more than usual attention, and conducted with certainty by the *visible* manner of giving the time, they played with a spirit and a correctness such as till then they had never been heard to play with. Surprised and inspired by this result the orchestra immediately after the first part of the symphony, expressed aloud its collective assent to the new mode of conducting, and thereby overruled all further opposition on the part of the directors. In the vocal pieces also, the conducting of which I assumed at the request of Mr. *Ries*, particularly in the recitative, the leading with the baton, after I had explained the meaning of my movements, was completely successful, and the singers repeatedly expressed to me their satisfaction for the precision with which the orchestra now followed them.

The result in the evening was still more brillant than I could have hoped for. It is true, the audience were at first startled by the novelty, and were seen whispering together; but when the music began and the orchestra executed the well-known symphony with unusual power and precision, the general approbation was shewn immediately on the conclusion of the first part by a long-sustained clapping of hands. The triumph of the baton as a time-giver was decisive, and no one was seen any more seated at the piano during the performance of symphonies and overtures. On this evening also the concert overture which I had composed before I left Frankfort was given for the first time. As it pleased very much the Philharmonic society accepted it as the composition which according to my contract I was to leave in their hands. I kept no copy of it and soon forgot it entirely, so that a few years afterwards when preparing a thematic catalogue of my compositions I could not recal to mind the beginning of it, for which reason the theme of it is wholly wanting in the text.

During the delivery of my letters of introduction in London, as also upon many other occasions, I had so much felt the want of some one to serve me as interpreter that I was continually making inquiries for a person to accompany me who could speak German and English. At length Mr. *Ries* bethought him of an old servant of the deceased *Salomon** of the name of *Johanning*, who would be competent to fill that office. It is true, that he had retired from service, and as heir to his late master had bought a small country-house in the neighbourhood of London. Mr. *Ries* hoped nevertheless that the yet vigorous old man would consent to take the situation, for which purpose he sent for him to town, and the offer on my part was made to him. When he learned that it was to enter the service of a German and a musician, and furthermore of a violinist, as his deceased master had been, he immediately expressed his readiness, and even left it to my option what remuneration I should give him at the close of the season. Thenceforth he came every morning into town, and having first interpreted the wishes of my wife to the landlady respecting the dinner, he then accompanied me on my rounds of business. From his long residence in London, however, he had forgotten a great deal of his German, and his English doubtless was not very classic; for in his interpreting frequent misunderstandings would take place. When I had thus presented the remainder of my letters of introduction with less difficulty than before, I again found time and leisure for new compositions. I first wrote a symphony (the second D flat, Op. 49) and played it for the first time at one of the Philharmonic concerts, which I had to conduct, April 10. 1820. At its rehearsal, it met with very great approbation both from the orchestra and the numerous persons who were present; but in the evening it was received with real enthusiasm. I had in part to thank the numerous and particularly excellent stringed instruments of the

---

* It was this *Salomon*, who, as concert-giver, induced his friend *Haydn* to visit London and compose symphonies for his concerts; and to him therefore the musical world owes the twelve most beautiful symphonies *Haydn* wrote.

orchestra for this brillant success, and in this composition I had given them a special opportunity of exhibiting their skill in playing with purity and precision of *ensemble*. In fact, as regards the stringed instruments, I have never since heard that symphony given with so much effect as on that evening. The next morning all the London newspapers contained reports respecting the new symphony that had been composed in their town, and vied with each other in their praise of it. Similar favourable notices of my play upon every occasion of my appearance soon spread my fame throughout the town, and pupils readily presented themselves to receive instruction from me on the violin, as well as ladies who were desirous of being accompanied on the piano. As all expressed their willingness to pay a guinea for each hour's instruction, I readily accepted their offers, as I considered that I owed it to my family to turn the good fortune I had met with in London as a musician to my pecuniary advantage. In this manner, after having first devoted a few hours to composition at home or to music with my wife, I was running or driving about all day in huge London, and frequently right weary of it; for the greater part of my pupils had neither talent nor application, and took lessons of me merely to be enabled to say that they were pupils of *Spohr*. I nevertheless call to mind with some pleasure several originals who amused me with their singularities, and therewith somewhat relieved the bitter trouble I had with them. One was an old general on half-pay, but who always made his appearance in full uniform, decorated with all his orders, and with the extreme of high military bearing. He, as an exception, came always to my house, but, nevertheless, required to play for three quarters of an hour only, as according to the custom there deduction was made of the quarter of an hour for the drive. He came every morning, Sundays excepted, in his old state carriage, precisely at 12 o'clock, ordered one of his belaced and powdered footmen to bring up his violin-case, and after a dumb greeting sat himself down immediately to his music desk. But previous to that he took out his watch to see at what o'clock the lesson would commence, and then set it down close to him. He would bring easy duets with him, chiefly of *Pleyel*, in which I played second violin. Although there were many things in his play that indicated the unpractised pupil, I soon saw that it would not be wise to point them out to him; I contented myself therefore with accommodating my tones as much as possible to those of the old gentleman, and so we played one duet after the other in the best concord. As soon, however, as we had played the three quarters of an hour, the general would stop, though in the middle of the piece, take from his waistcoat pocket a one-pound note in which a shilling was wrapped up, and put it upon the table. He would then take up his watch, and take leave in the same taciturn manner as he had entered.

The other original was an old lady whom I accompanied on the piano. She was a passionate admirer of *Beethoven*, against which I had nothing to say, but she had the whim, moreover, never to play any other music than that of her favorite. She had all *Beethoven's* pianoforte-compositions, as also his orchestral works arranged for the piano. Her apartment was also hung with every portrait of him that she had been able to procure. As many of these differed greatly in resemblance to each other, she urged me to inform her which most resembled him of the whole. She possessed also some relics of him which had been brought to her from Vienna by English travellers, among others a button of his dressing-gown and a piece of music paper with some note marks and inkblots from his hand. When I apprized her that I had lived for some time on terms of great intimacy with him, I rose greatly in her estimation, and she had then so much to ask that on some days we never played at all. She spoke French with tolerably fluency, and could even bring out a few words of German. Her pianoforte play was not at all bad, so that I was rather pleased to play the sonatas for piano and violin. But when she subsequently produced the trios also, and played with me *without* violoncello, and then even the piano concertos, in which, with the exception of first orchestral-violin, which I played, all else was wanting, it became very clear to me that her enthusiasm for *Beethoven* was nothing but affectation, and that she had not the least perception of the excellence of his compositions.

I became acquainted with a third singular character in the following manner. One morning a servant in livery brought a letter to me, which my old *Johanning* translated in the following manner: "Mr. *Spohr* is requested to call at the house of the undersigned, at 4 o'clock precisely." As I did not know the name appended to the note, nor could ascertan from the servant the purpose for which my attendance was requested, I replied thereto in an equally laconic manner: "At the hour indicated I am engaged and cannot come." The next morning the servant reappeared with a second much more polite note: "Mr. *Spohr* is requested to honour the undersigned with a visit, and to appoint the time himself." At the same time the servant had been ordered to offer his master's carriage, and as I had been meanwhile informed that the writer was a celebrated physician, who frequently attended concerts, and interested himself especially in violin music, I no longer hesitated to go, but indicated the appointed hour to the servant and was duly fetched in the doctor's carriage. An amiable old gentlemen with snow white hair received me at the foot of the stairs, but we now discovered to our mutual regret that we could not make ourselves intelligible to each other, for he spoke neither German nor French. We stood opposite to each other in great embarassment, until he took me by the arm and led me into a spacious room on the walls of which a number of violins were hung. Others had been taken from their cases and placed upon tables. The doctor handed a bow to me and pointed to the instruments. I now comprehended that I was to give my opinion of the respective merits of the violins, and immediately began to try them and to arrange them in order according to their worth. This was no easy work to do; for there were a great number of them, and the old gentleman brought them all in succession, without omitting one. When at length, after the lapse of about an hour, I had found the best six of them, and still played on these alternately to discover the very best of them, I observed that the doctor eyed one of them with looks of particular fondness, and his face lit up with pleasure every time I struck the strings. I therefore readily gave the kind old gentleman the satisfaction of indicating that instrument as the matador of the whole collection. Quite delighted with this announcement, he now brought a *viola d'amour*, and began to play a fantasia on this long-unused instrument. I listened to him with pleasure, as I had not heard the instrument before and the doctor played by no means ill. Thus terminated the interview to the satisfaction of both, and I had taken up my hat, to take my leave of him when the old gentleman, with a kindly expression of countenance and several low bows, handed to me a five-pound note. Astonished at this, I looked at the note and the donor, and at first knew not what he meant; when it struck me that he intended it as a remuneration for my testing his violins, and shaking my head with a smile, I laid the note on the table, pressed the doctor's hand with warmth, and hastened down stairs. He followed me out into the street, assisted me into the carriage and then spoke some words with evident emotion to his coachman. This had made so much impression on the coachman, that he immediately told it to old *Johanning,* who had come with the carriage, to open the door. He had said to him: "You are driving there a German who is a perfect gentleman; and I expect you will take him home to his house with the greatest care." — A few months afterwards, when I gave my benefit concert, the doctor sent for a ticket and forwarded to me at the same time a ten-pound note.

Meanwhile my wife had by unflagging industry acquired great proficiency on the new harp, but in doing so — on account of the greater stretch of arm it required and the stronger tension of the strings — she had exerted herself over much and now suffered greatly from the exhaustion it had induced. From former experience I had learned that nothing so quickly imparted fresh strength to her nerves as the frequent enjoyment of fresh air. I therefore availed myself of every moment of sunshine in the first days of spring to take gentle walks into Regent's Park, which was very near to our dwelling in Charlotte Street. On Sundays, when all music ceases in London, and when even without fear of giving offence we could not play in our own apartments, we used to make more distant excursions to Hampstead, and to the other parks. Our companion and guide was alternately the younger *Ries* and an old amiable man of the name of *Stumpf*, an instrument maker. I soon had the gratification of seeing my wife regain fresh strength and spirits from the mild influence of the English spring, but I adhered strictly to my previous resolution that she should appear once only at my own concert, and declined with firmness several offers that were made to her. But as for myself, I played at all concerts where they were willing to pay the price I asked, and as this according to English notions was not excessively high, I was in frequent requisition, and saw my name announced on almost all the concert-programmes of the season. But I never could make up my mind to play for renumeration at private parties, for the manner in which musicians were then treated there, was to me most unbecoming and degrading. They were not admitted to join the company, but were shewn into an adjoining room, where they had to wait until the moment arrived when they were summoned to the apartments where the company was assembled before whom they were to play; their performance over, they had to leave the room again immediately. My wife and I were ourselves once eyewitnesses of this contemptuous treatment of the first and most·eminent artists in London. We had received letters of introduction to the king's brothers the Dukes of *Sussex* and *Clarence,* and as the latter was married to a German, a Princess of Meiningen, I paid them a visit accompanied by my wife. The Ducal couple received us in a very kind manner and invited us to a musical party they were to give in a few days and at which we were also asked to assist. I then thought in what way I could best extricate myself from this disgusting exclusion from the company, and resolved if I could not succeed to return home immediately. When therefore we entered the palace, and a lacquey was on the point of opening the door of the room where the other musicians were assembled, I told *Johanning* to deliver my violin case to him, and with my wife on my arm, immediately ascended the staircase before the lacquey had time to recover from his astonishment. Arrived at the door of the apartments where the company were assembled, I announced my name to the footman in waiting, and as he hesitated to open the door I evinced an intention of opening it myself. Upon this the lacquey instantly threw open the door and called out the names of the new-comers. The Duchess, alive to German usages, rose immediately from her seat, advanced a few steps to meet my wife, and led her into the circle of ladies. The Duke welcomed me also with a few frendly words and introduced me to the gentlemen around him. I now thought I had successfully achieved all; but I soon observed that the servants notwithstanding not did consider me as properly belonging to the company, for they always passed me by with the tea-tray and other refreshments, without offering me any. At length the Duke may also have remarked this; for I saw him whisper a few words in the ear of the steward of the household. After this the refreshments were also presented to me. When the concert was to commence the steward of the household sent a servant to summon the invited artists in the order in which their names appeared on the programme. They hereupon entered the apartment with their sheet of music or instrument in hand, saluted the company with a profound bow, and began their performances. They were the *élite* of the most distinguished singers and musicians in London, and the execution of their respective pieces was almost without exception charmingly beautiful. This, however, did not appear to be felt by the noble and fashionable auditory; for they did not cease their conversation one moment. Once only when a very favorite female singer entered the room they became somewhat more silent, and a few subdued *bravas* were heard, for which she immediately returned thanks with profound curtsies. I was exceedingly annoyed by this derogation of art and still more so with the artists who submitted to be so treated, and I had a great mind not to play at all. When the turn came to me, therefore, I purposely hesitated so long till the Duke, probably at a sign made to him by his wife, invited me himself to play. I then requested one of the servants to bring up my violin case, and I then began to play the piece I had proposed to myself without making the customary bows to the company. All these circumstances excited no doubt the attention of the company, for during the whole time of my performance the greatest stillness pervaded the apartment. When I had concluded the ducal pair and their guests applauded. Now also I first expressed my thanks by making a bow. Shortly afterwards the concert terminated, and the musicians retired. If our having constituted ourselves part of the company had furnished matter of surprise, this was still more increased when they saw that we stopped there also to supper, and during the supper were treated with great attention by the ducal hosts. The circumstance to which we doubtless owed this distinction — one so unheard-of and repugnant to all English notions of that day — was the fact that the Duchess had known us while yet living in her paternal house, and had there witnessed the friendly reception which, at the time when we lived at Gotha, we had frequently met with at the court of Meiningen. The Duke of *Sussex*, to whom I had brought a letter of recommendation from the Duke of *Cambridge*, then regent of Hanover, received me also with great distinction and conversed with me a good deal. During a conversation we had upon the subject of English national songs, the Duke even sent for his guitar and sang to me some English and Irish national songs, which afterwards suggested to me the idea of working up some of the most popular of these as a pot-pourri for my instrument, and of introducing the same at my concert.* When the company broke up, which was not till long after midnight, we returned home greatly pleased with the result of our daring and with the victory we had gained over the prejudices of London society.

Among those who solicited me to play solo at their concerts was Sir *George Smart*, one of the directors of the Philharmonic Society. During the season he gave a succession of subscription concerts which he called "sacred concerts," in which nevertheless a great deal of the music was "worldly" also. I played at two of them, in return for which Sir George undertook the arrangements for my benefit-concert — a by no means light task even for a native well versed in the matter, and which if I had undertaken in person would perhaps have occupied six weeks of my time, which I could employ in a much more advantageous manner. My concert took place on the 18th. June, and was one of the most brillant and well attended of the whole season. Almost every person to whom we had brought letters of recommendation — and among them also the Dukes of *Sussex* and *Clarence* — had taken either boxes or reserved seats, and several of those wealthy personages had forwarded considerable sums for them.

A great number of the subscribers to the Philharmonic Society also retained their seats, and as the lowest price for a ticket was half a guinea, and the room held nearly a thousand people, the receipts were very considerable. I derived a great additional advantage from the circumstance, that the expenses which otherwise in London are enormously high, were greatly reduced on this occasion by the refusal of several of the members of the orchestra to receive any gratuity, from a friendly feeling towards me, and from the agreement previously entered into by me with the Philharmonic Society, that the use of the rooms should cost me nothing. On the other hand,

---

* This is the Op. 59, the second of my works written in London.

however, I had to pay all the singers, and I yet well remember that I was obliged to pay Mrs. *Salmon*, the then most popular female vocalist in London, and without whose presence my concert would have been considered not sufficiently attractive, the sum of thirty pounds sterling for a single song; and she made it a further condition of agreement, that she should not sing until towards the end of the concert, as she had first to sing at a concert in the city, six miles of. I must here mention also a singular custom which prevailed at all concerts in London at that time, which now, however, like many other strange practices of that period, has been discontinued. Namely, it was required that the party giving the concert should provide the auditory with refreshments during the pause between the first and second parts of the concert. These were accordingly supplied at a buffet in an adjoining room, and one was obliged to agree beforehand with the confectioner upon the sum for their purveyance, which at my concert was undertaken for ten pounds sterling. If the company consisted for the most part of persons of rank and fashion, with whom it was not usual to take any refreshments, the confectioner used to make a good thing of it, but if it was a very numerous and mixed company, and the heat very great, he might frequently be a loser. But he never did a better stroke of business than at my concert.

This took place on the very day that Queen *Charlotte* of England made her entry into London on her return from Italy, to make her defence before Parliament against the charge of infidelity brought against her by her husband. All London was divided into two parties, the larger of which, composed of the middle and lower classes, was on the side of the Queen. The town was in the greatest commotion, and it was a very fortunate thing for me that I had already disposed of the whole of the tickets for my concert, as otherwise by this unfavourable circumstance I might have incurred a very great loss. The bills announcing my concert, posted at the corners of the streets, were quickly pasted over and covered with large placards in which in the name of the people a general illumination of the town was called for to celebrate the day; and *Johanning* brought me word that the populace threatened to smash the windows in every house, where this call was not complied with. As at that time the police force as well as the few military were not sufficiently numerous to protect the royal palaces from the threatened excesses of the populace, the partisans of the king, who were wholly unable to repress the tumult, were compelled to abide the worst, and contented themselves with making the best use of the short notice given by having their windows nailed up with boards, in order to save their costly mirrors and furniture. In this manner during the whole of the day the sound of the carpenter's hammer was everywhere heard, particularly in Portland Place, close adjoining where many of the nobility resided, and these preparations of defence were subjects of great derision and amusement to the young vagabonds of the street. While we were rehearsing at home the pieces to be performed in the evening, the people poured in crowds through the streets to meet the Queen upon her entry. As this took place in the direction of the city, it became perfectly quiet towards evening at the West-end. We found therefore, as we drove at half-past eight o'clock to the concert-rooms, the streets almost less thronged than usual, and met with no obstacle on our way. But we remarked everywhere active preparations for the illumination, in order that the sovereign will of the people might be immediately complied with. My wife, who was somewhat nervous respecting her first public appearance with the new harp, was in great trepidation as to what might occur from this excitement of the populace, and I was greatly afraid that the agitation in which I saw her would be prejudicial both to her play and to her health. I therefore endeavoured to soothe her by argument and persuasion, in which I happily succeeded. The concert-room filled by degrees with a numerous auditory and the concert began. I am able to give here the entire programme, as Sir *G. Smart* upon my last visit to London (in the year 1852) made me a present of a copy of that which was handed at the time to the audience upon their entry into the rooms. It runs as follows:

NEW ARGYLL ROOMS.
MR. SPOHR'S CONCERT.
Thursday, June 18th. 1820.

PART I.

Grand Sinfonia (M. S.)	Spohr.
Air, Mr. T. Welch, "Revenge, revenge, Timotheus cries"	Haendel.
Grand Duetto (M. S.), Harp and Violin, Mad. Spohr and Mr. Spohr	Spohr.
Aria, Miss Goodall, "Una voce al cor mi parla." Clarinet obligato, Mr. Willman	Pær.
Sestetto for Pianoforte, two Violins, Viola, Violincello and Contrabasso, Messrs.: Ries, Watts, Wagstaff, R. Ashley, Lindley and Dragonetti.	Ries.
Irish Melodies (M. S.), with Variations for the Violin, Mr. Spohr (composed expressly for this occasion)	Spohr.

PART II.

Nonotto for Violin, Viola, Violincello, Contrabasso, Flute, Oboe, Clarinet, Horn and Bassoon, Messrs. Spohr, Lindley, Dragonetti, Ireland, Griesbach, Willman, Arnull and Holmes	Spohr.
Scena, Mrs. Salmon "Fellon, la pena avrai"	Rossini.
Rondo for the Violin, Mr. Spohr	Spohr.
Aria, Mr. Vaughan "Rendi'l sereno"	Haendel.
Overture	Spohr.

* * *

Leader of the Band . . Mr. Spohr.
At the Pianoforte . . . Sir George Smart.

The new symphony, though already known to the orchestra, was again carefully rehearsed through with them, and was executed in a masterly manner, and it met with a more lively applause, if possible, than on its first performance. While the air that followed was being sung I tuned my wife's harp for her in the adjoining room and spoke some words of encouragement to her. I then led her into the concert-room and we took our places to begin the duet. Silent expectation pervaded the whole auditory, and our first tones were eagerly awaited, when suddenly a fearful noise was heard in the street, which was immediately followed by a volley of paving stones against the unilluminated windows of the adjoining room. Terrified at the noise of the breaking glass of the windows and chandeliers, the ladies sprang up from their seats, and a scene of indescribable confusion and alarm ensued. In order to prevent a second, volly of missiles, the gas lights in the adjoining apartment were speedily lighted, and we were not a little gratified to find that the mob after giving another uproarious cheer at the success of their demonstration went on their way, and thus by degrees the previous quiet was restored. But it was some time before the public resumed their places in the room and became so far tranquillized that we could at length begin. I was not a little fearful that the fright and the long pause would make my wife still more nervous and I listened therefore to her first accords in the greatest anxiety; but when I heard these resound with their usual power I became immediately tranquillized, and gave my attention wholly to the unity and ensemble of our play. This, which in Germany had always pleased so much, did not fail to make its effect upon an English audience also; the applause, indeed, increased with every theme of the duet, and at its conclusion seemed as though it never would cease. As we retired highly gratified with this success, we neither of us thought that it was the *last time*, that *Dorette* would play on the harp. But of that hereafter!

As regards the other items of the programme in which I took part, I was particularly pleased with the good reception which the nonette met with. I had already played it with the same artists at one of the Philharmonic concerts, and was invited on many sides to repeat it at my concert. The accuracy of our *ensemble* was this time more complete, and therefore it could fail in its effect. The Irish melodies were generally well received. Thus, in spite of the disturbing intermezzo, the concert terminated to the general satisfaction of all. The interval after the first part and the promenade in the adjoining saloon were this time entirely prevented by the damage which it had sustained; the confectioner told me that, having had no demand for his refreshments, he was the ten pound in pocket, although he had had some things smashed on the buffet by the volley of stones. When at length, exceedingly fatigued, we got into our carriage, we were not able to drive straight home, as the mob in the neighbourhood of Portland Place still had it all their own way. The coachman was therefore obliged to take all manner of circuitous turnings, and it was past one in the morning when we at length drove up to our own door. With the exception of our floor we found the whole house lit up, and the landlady was awaiting our return in the greatest anxiety, in order to light up our windows also. And indeed it was high time; for the mob were heard approaching. But as in obedience to their sovereign will they found the whole of Charlotte-street brilliantly illuminated, they passed on without committing any excesses. But it was not safe to extinguish the lights, and not until the lapse of several hours, when the town had become quite quiet, did we at length get the rest we so much needed.

* * *

Now comes a sorrowful period in my life, on which I now still think with grief. My wife felt so ill from the effects of the great exertions she had made in acquiring the mastery of the new harp and the alternate impressions upon her nervous system on the evening of the concert, that I was greatly afraid she was about to have a third attack of nervous fever.

It was therefore high time to come to some firm resolve as regarded her future well-being. Already after her second attack in Darmstadt, when she had become fully restored to health, I had endeavoured to persuade her to abandon her nerve-destroying instrument, but when I saw how much this proposition distressed her, I again immediately relinquished it. She was too much heart and soul the artiste, and had acquired too great a love for the instrument to which she owed so many triumphs, to be able to give it up readily; and it had always been a source of happiness to her to think that she could assist with her talent towards the maintenance of our family. But now, that she was but too convinced that her physical powers were not sufficient to conquer the new instrument, and a return to the old one would not satisfy her after having made herself intimately acquainted with the advantages of the new one in tone and mechanism, it became much easier for me to win her over to my way of thinking, particularly when I represented to her that as the artiste she could still be known, and in future appear at my concerts as pianiste, for which she had all the necessary qualifications. This tranquillized her very much, although she was obliged to admit to herself, that she would never be able to achieve upon the pianoforte the same success as on the harp, upon which in Germany at least she had not her equal. I moreover promised her, that in order to give her performances the charm of novelty, I would write some brilliant concert themes, and as it was very important for me to try my hand also at pianoforte compositions, I immediately set to work and finished before leaving London the first subject of the piano-quintet Op. 52. In order to remove the harp wholly from her sight, I sent it to Mr. *Erard*. When I informed him that my wife was compelled to abandon the harp entirely on account of the weak state of her health, he took it back very willingly, and refused a compensation for the use made of it up to that time. In a most gallant manner he said, the instrument had now acquired a real value, from having been played upon by so celebrated an artiste, and that too at her last public performance.

I now again took daily walks into the country with my wife and had soon the pleasure of seeing that she was gradually recovering her strength. The thought that she would soon see her children again contributed no doubt in a very great measure towards this improvement. I also longed to be home again with my family, and immediately the last Philharmonic concert was over, I made preparations for leaving.

I must here by way of appendix speak of the musical institution of Mr. *Logier*, which I visited several times with great interest, and respecting which I sent the following report to the Leipsic Musical Journal of August 1820: "Mr. *Logier*, a German by birth, but resident for the last fifteen years in England, gives instruction in pianoforte-play and in harmony upon a method of his own invention, in which he permits all the children, frequently as many as thirty or forty, to play at the same time. For this purpose he has written three volumes of studies, which are all grounded upon perfectly simple themes, and progress by degrees to the most difficult ones. While beginners play the theme, the more advanced pupils practise themselves at the same time in more or less difficult variations: one might imagine that from this manner of proceeding great confusion must ensue, out of which the teacher would be able to distinguish very little; but as the children who play these studies, sit near each other, one hears, according to whichever part of the room one may be in, either one or the other of the studies very distinctly. The teacher also frequently makes half of the pupils, at times all but one, cease playing, in order to ascertain their progress individually. In the last lessons he makes use of his chiroplast, a machine by means of which the children get accustomed to a good position of the arms and hands, and which so soon as they have progressed so far as to know the notes and keys, is removed first from one hand and then from the other, and then for the first time they put their fingers to the keys and learn to play scales; but all this, in the respective studies, with all the children at once, and always in the strictest time. When they have then progressed to a new lesson they do not of course succeed in bringing out more than a few notes of each bar, in the quick movement which they hear being played near or around them; but they soon overcome more and more of them, and in a shorter time than might well be believed, the new lesson is played as well as the previous one. But what is most remarkable in Mr. *Logier's* method of teaching is, that, with the very first lessons in pianoforte playing he teaches his pupils harmony at the same time. How he does this, I do not know; and that is his secret, for which each of the teachers in England who give instruction on his system pay him one hundred guineas. The results of this method with his pupils are nevertheless wonderful; for children between the ages of seven and ten years solve the most difficult problems. I wrote down on the board a triad, and denoted the key in which they were to modulate it: one of the littlest girls immediately ran to the board, and after very little reflection wrote first the bass, and then the upper notes. I frequently repeated this test, and indeed with the addition of all manners of difficulties: I extended it to the most divergent keys in which enharmonic changes were required, yet they never became embarrassed. If one could not succeed, another immediately came forward, whose bass perhaps was corrected by a third; and for everything they did they were obliged to assign the reason to the teacher. At length I wrote upon the table a simple treble — the first that came into my head — and told each of them to put the other three voices to it, each upon her own slate. At the same time I said to them that the solution of the theme which the teacher and I should consider the best, I would inscribe in my musical album as a souvenir of their performance. All were now full of life and activity, and in a few minutes one of the littlest of the girls, who had already distinguished herself by her play and in working out the first problems, brought me her slate to inspect, but in her haste she had omitted an octave in the third bar between the bass and one of the middle voices. No sooner had I pointed it out to her, than blushing and with tears in her eyes she took back the slate and rapidly corrected her error. As in her performance the bass was indisputably the best of all, the teacher wrote it in my album, and I subjoin it here with diplomatic accuracy.

The resolutions of the other children were more or less good, but all of them correct, and mostly written out in four different keys. Each also played her own immediately without any embarrassment on the pianoforte and without "fault," &c.

Upon my announcing our approaching departure to my old *Johanning,* tears came into the eyes of the kind and affectionate old man. He had become so fond of us that he would have even refused all remuneration for the services he had rendered us, and positively objected to take the sum I had reserved for him. But upon my insisting on his taking it he complied, on the condition that I would not refuse him a favour he wished to ask of me. I asked him what it was, and he did not keep me long in suspense, but stammered out in an embarrassed manner the request that I and my wife would do him the honour to take our dinner, the day before our departure, at his house. When we consented thereto without hesitation, his whole countenance immediately brightened up, and he could not find words to express sufficiently his gratitude. On the appointed day he made his appearance dressed as I had never yet seen him, in a full-dress suit of his deceased master's, with hair powdered, and in white silk stockings, and at our door stood a hackney carriage for four persons, which was to take us to his country house, and in which a musician whom he had also invited, and whose acquaintance we had already made, and who was the most intimate friend of his late master, was already seated. When we had got in, *Johanning* refused to take the fourth seat, saying that it would be unbecoming of him to do so, although I pointed out to him that he was now no longer my servant, but for this day my host and entertainer. But he was not to be persuaded, and took his usual place by the side of the coachman. On the way there our companion related to us many particulars highly creditable to *Johanning* — how he had shewn the most ardent attachment and fidelity to his master, and after his death had applied the greater part of the money he had left him, to the erection of a memorial to his master in Westminster Abbey, so that we felt penetrated with the highest respect for our recent servant. Upon our arrival he opened the carriage door and led us into his house. The property consisted of a small house with a small garden attached, and everywhere the greatest neatness and cleanliness. He led the way up one flight of stairs to his reception room, and did not fail to show us immediately the bell-pull near the mantle-piece, to which he forthwith gave a tug, although he kept no servant whom he could summon with it, since he and his wife were their own servants. We then took a turn through the little garden and then entered the parlour, where the table was laid for three persons. *Johanning* again refused to take a seat near us at table, and this time for the cogent reason that we should then have had no one to wait upon us. Upon this he brought up the dinner and as master of the house waited upon his guests, during which occupation his whole countenance wore an expression of the greatest pleasure. The dinner was exceedingly well dressed and served up on an elegant china dinner-service which had belonged to his master, and the excellent Rhenish wine which he placed before us was no doubt derived also from the same source. The dessert, strawberries and cherries, was the produce of his little garden, and this he did not fail to announce to his guests. — When dinner was over he led the way once more to his drawing-room, where we found Mrs. *Johanning*, who till then had been engaged in the kitchen in dressing and sending up the dinner, in full Sunday attire. There at length, though only after repeated pressing, the worthy old couple allowed themselves to be persuaded to take seats at the table, on which coffee had already been placed. *Johanning* was now in the height of happiness, and interpreted with no little satisfaction to his wife the praises which we had expressed and still reiterated of the admirable manner in which we had been entertained. Towards evening the coach again drove up to the door to take us back to town. But *Johanning* could not be deterred from resuming his old place by the side of the coachman, to accompany us home, and open the carriage door. In fact, even on the next morning he presented himself again, in order to be of assistance at our departure. At the coach-office we found also several friends and acquaintance waiting to bid us farewell.

* * *

We returned again by way of Dover and Calais, in order to take our own carriage which we had left at Lille. Our passage across this time was a very calm one and the weather fine, so that not any of the passengers were sea-sick. Between Calais and Lille the diligence stopped at a so charming place to dine that even now, after so long a time, I recollect it with a feeling of pleasure. It was at the small town of Cassel, which is situated upon a high isolated conical hill that rises in the midst of an extensive plain. The weather being fine, dinner had been laid for the travellers in the garden of the inn under a bower of vines, and during the repast, from this pleasant, cool situation we enjoyed an extensive view over the beautiful country round. In Lille we again spent some pleasant days in the society of the *Vogel* family and other of our friends there, and then without longer stay set out in our own carriage upon our further journey.

As a natural consequence of the painful ordeal of grief through which my parents had passed on our account, and after the first long separation from our children, our reception this time in Gandersheim was beyond measure one of heartfelt joy, and after our protracted exertions and fatigue we now indeed felt once more happy and freed from care in the calm repose of the country. This was just the time for me to set myself to new labours, and I there first completed the quintet for pianoforte, flute, clarinet, horn and double-bass which I had begun in London, and in which I proposed that my wife should make her appearance in the world of art as a pianiste on our projected winter tour. Indeed, it was high time to occupy her in its artistic study; for as she now felt quite re-established in health, she had the greatest desire to resume her harp. With the assistance of the new quintet, however, and supported by the medical counsel of my father, I soon succeeded in dissuading her from it. She therefore devoted her attention to the pianoforte with the greatest zeal, and in a short time had the gratification of finding she had reacquired her former technical skill upon that instrument. After the lapse of a few weeks she succeeded therefore in executing the new and difficult concert-piece to her and my satisfaction.

About this time we had a visit from two musical Hamburg friends, Messrs. *Fritz Schwenke* and *Wilhelm Grund*, the latter of whom brought his younger brother *Edward* with him, who was already a good violinist, to become my pupil. With the assistance of these three I now gave our musical friends of Gandersheim a quartet-party such as they had never heard before nor have since. In order to have my new quintet heard upon this occasion also, I quickly rewrote the accompaniment of the four wind-instruments, for a stringed-quartet, and in this shape was highly pleased with its effect, as also with the brilliant play of my wife. From the great success this had met with, she felt much encouraged in her new studies and consoled in some measure for her relinquishment of the harp. To provide her still with new materials for practice, I rewrote also two former harp-compositions for the piano, a pot-pourri and a rondo with violin, which appeared later as Op. 50 and 51. We practised these together also with the greatest care, and they were destined for performance at private parties on our next winter tour. After the departure of the Hamburg visitors I commenced the instruction of my new pupil. By his talent and amiability he soon won the esteem of the whole *Spohr* family, from the old grandfather down to little *Theresa*, whom he always called in pure Hamburg dialect: "Du säute Deren." As he played well on the piano, he undertook the musical instruction of *Emilia* and *Ida*, and young as he was, he knew how to keep them assiduous to their studies. Himself as violinist he soon made so much progress, that I practised him in and played with him the three extremely difficult violin-duets which I wrote in Switzerland (Op. 39) and for which I had never yet been able to meet with a fellow-player. By the accurate, pure and spirited execution of this almost always four-voiced duets we made a great sensation, and musical amateurs from the whole country round came to hear us play them. We played one of them also with great success at a concert in Hildesheim, given there by the director of music *Bischoff*, the same who undertook the Frankenhaus musical festivals. Towards autumn, just as I had begun to compose a new violin concerto (the 9th. D-minor. Op. 55, published by *André* of Offenbach) for the winter journey, I received an invitation from music-director *Rose* in Quedlinburg to conduct a musical festival which he was about to hold there. I very gladly accepted it, and made all haste to complete my concerto so as to be able to perform it there for the first time. While practising it I received great assistance from

Edward Grund, who was able to accompany through the score on the piano, an assistance, which I had never before experienced.

The musical festival took place on the 13th. and 14th. October 1820, and went off to the full satisfaction of the originator and the numerous auditory. Upon my proposition, *Schneider's* "Last Judgement" was given on the first day, at which the composer himself was present. On the second day, among other things my London symphony was performed, and, as well as my new violin concerto, was received with great approbation. I met in Quedlinburg many of my former friends and acquaintances from Sondershausen, Gotha, Leipzig, Magdeburg, Halberstadt and Brunswick, and passed several delightful days with them. After our return from this pleasant excursion, upon which my parents and *Edward Grund,* as well as my wife, had accompained me, it became full time to set out upon our winter tour, the terminus of which was to be Paris. A new parting from the children, my parents, and the pleasant society of Gandersheim, was therefore necessary; and *Edward Grund* returned to Hamburg with the intention of coming again in the spring to prosecute his studies under my guidance.

We took Frankfort, Heidelberg, Carlsruhe and Strasburg on our way to Paris, and gave concerts in all those towns. In Frankfort, where we lived in the house of my friend *Speyer*, we still found a lively remembrance of our artistic talents; our concert in the salon of the "*Weidenbusch*" was crowded to overflowing, although the room could easily accommodate eight hundred persons. My new violin concerto, excellently accompanied, made a great sensation; Councillor *André* himself, who previously had always some fault to find with my compositions, seemed quite satisfied with my new work; for he repeatedly requested me, after the rehearsal even, to let him have the publishing of it. Although I declined this most positively, as I was bound by a promise to my then publisher *Peters* of Leipsic, to let him have all my new manuscripts, yet in the evening at the concert *André* again pressed me, and so pertinaciously, that to get rid of him, and to prepare quietly for my solo-play, I at last called out to him "Yes." This precipitancy however cost me dear, for although I immediately informed *Peters* of all the circumstances, in order to exculpate himself with him, I was compelled to endure many bitter reproaches for my excessive pliancy towards Mr. *André*. The new piano quintet with wind-instrument accompaniment, which was now also performed, made likewise a great sensation, and *Dorette's* purity of piano-forte play, of which until then the friends of music in Frankfort had known nothing, was greeted with the loudest applause. I was more particularly pleased with this result, as of all others it was calculated to console my wife for the abandonment of her harp.

Of the other towns between Frankfort and Paris, and of the concerts given there I have forgotten everything; I must however advert to the acquaintance I made of Councillor *Thibaut* at Heidelberg on this occasion. That celebrated jurist conducted a choral society that he had instituted; but excluding all modern church music, he permitted *ancient* Italian music only to be sung, of which he had made a rich and rare collection. Until then I knew nothing more of this music than what I had heard in the Sixtine chapel at Rome, and was therefore very thankful to the Councillor for the permission he gave me to be present at the rehearsals of his society, at which I became better acquainted with several of those old works, which were carefully practised by them. *Thibaut's* opinion that this music *alone* represented the true ecclesiastical style, and surpassed all that had ever been written since, I cannot coincide with, for to me *Mozart's* requiem, incomplete as it passed from the hands of that master, who died during its composition, is alone worth more than all I ever heard of earlier church music; nevertheless, the simple-grandiose style of those works made then a **great** impression on me, and I begged permission to study their scores through. After some hesitation my wish was granted in such wise that **I was** permitted to visit *Thibaut's* music-room at particular hours, and to go through the works on the piano, but was not permitted to take any home with me. I took daily advantage of this favour, and by that means made myself intimately acquainted with the vocal method and harmonic sequence of the old masters. While so engaged I was seized with the desire of trying for once an ecclesiastic piece *alla Capella* for several voices, and in the following summer I carried out my idea at Gandersheim with the composition of the mass for ten voices, Op. 54. I certainly did not strive to imitate the simple treble movements of the old masters; but on the contrary I did a good deal towards carrying out the rich modulation of the later Mozart method.

Respecting our stay in Paris I published at the time "Four letters to a Friend" in the Leipsic Musical Journal of 1821, which I here append.

FIRST LETTER.

Paris, December 15. 1820.

I trust, my dear friend, that you will give me credit for writing to you so soon on the eighth day after our arrival, at a time when so many novelties crowd upon my notice, that I find it difficult to collect my thoughts. But for my own sake I must not permit the materials to grow upon me too much, otherwise I shall be wholly unable to deal with them in their due order.

With a beating heart I drove through the Barrière of Paris. The thought, that I should at length have the pleasure of making the personal acquaintance of the artists whose works had inspired me in my early childhood, excited the emotion which I then felt. In fancy I reverted to the days of my boyhood, in which *Cherubini* was my idol, whose works I had had an earlier opportunity of becoming acquainted with in Brunswick, at the then permanent French theatre there, than even the works of *Mozart*; I vividly recollected the evening when the "Deux Journées" was performed for the first time — how, intoxicated with delight and the powerful impression that work had made upon me, I asked on that very evening to have the score given to me, and sat over it the whole night; and that it was that opera chiefly that gave me the first impulse to composition. The author, and many other men whose works had had the most decided influence on my development as a composer and violinist, I was now soon to behold.

We had therefore scarcely got under cover, when I made it my first business to pay a visit to those artists. I was received by all in a friendly manner, and relations of friendship soon sprang up between me and several of them.

I was told of *Cherubini*, that he was at first very reserved toward strangers, repulsive even; I did not find him so. He received me, without any letter of introduction, in the most friendly manner, and invited me to repeat my visit as often as I pleased.

On the evening of our arrival *Kreutzer* took us to the grand opera, where a ballet of his, with pretty characteristic music: "Le carnaval de Venise," was performed. It is observable in the singers and dancers of the grand opera, that they have been accustomed to move in a more spacious place; in this one, where the space is much more confined as compared with the opera house that has been abandoned, they appear in a much too sharp relief. Several grand operas, those of *Gluck's* for instance, can no longer be represented at all, there being not even the necessary room for the whole orchestra. For this reason every one looks forward with hope for the early completion of the new opera house; but actively as they are working upon it, that will not be ready before the middle of next summer. Before the ballet the opera: "Le Devin du village," the words and music by *Rousseau*, was given. Is it a subject for praise or blame, that the French, nothwithstanding the many excellent things with which their operatic repertoire has been enriched during the last twenty years, still give the oldest things of all? And is it indeed a proof of an advanced cultivated taste for art, when one sees them give as enthusiastic a reception (if not more so) to the oldest operas of *Grétry* with their poverty of harmony and incorrectness, as to the master pieces of *Cherubini* and *Méhul?* I think not! How long have not the operas of *Hiller* and *Dittersdorf* and others of those days, disappeared from our repertoire, although these are far to be preferred for their real musical worth to the greater part of *Grétry's*. But on the other hand it is certainly very discouraging, that with us the new only, however poor and defective, finds a ready reception, and many excellent things of older date are set aside for them and forgotten. Nevertheless it must be said to the honour of the taste for art of the Germans, that *Mozart's* operas at least are the exception, and for the last thirty years have constantly been pro-produced in all the theatres of Germany, which is a proof that the German people are at length impressed with the inimitable perfection of those master-pieces, and are not to be deceived on this head, however extensively the sweet musical poison may spread which flows in upon us so profusely from beyond the Alps.

The orchestra of the grand opera, as compared with the other orchestras, reckons among its members the most celebrated and distinguished artistes, but in *ensemble* is said to be behind the Italian opera. I cannot yet judge how far that may be correct, as I have only heard the latter as yet. In *Kreutzer's* ballet, which was played by the orchestra with the greatest precision, I was greatly pleased with a hautboy solo, which was executed in a masterly manner by Mr. *Voigt*. This artist has succeeded in giving to his instrument a perfect uniformity of tone and intonation throughout the whole range from C to the high F, an accomplishment which almost all hautboy players have failed in attaining. His execution is moreover full of grace and good taste.

For some days past I have been less edified at the grand opera than I was the first time. "Les mystères d'Isis" was performed. Too well indeed are justified the complaints of the admirers of *Mozart* of the disfigurement of the beautiful

"Zauberflöte" in this piece of workmanship, which the French themselves re-christened on its appearance "Les Misères d'ici"! One must blush that it should have been Germans, who so sinned against the immortal master. Everything but the overture has been meddled with; all else has been thrown into confusion, been changed and mutilated. The opera begins with the concluding chorus of the Zauberflöte; then comes the march in Titus, and then in succession some fragmentary piece from other operas of *Mozart,* and even a little bit of a symphony of *Haydn*; then between these recitatives of Mr. *Lachnitz'* own manufacture. But worse than all this is, that the transposers have applied a serious text to many cheerful and even comic passages of the Zauberflöte, by which the music of those passages becomes a parody of the text and of the situation. In this manner, for instance, Papagena sings the characteristic air of the Moor: "Alles fühlt der Liebe Freuden," &c.; and the pretty terzet of the three boys: "Seid uns zum zweitenmal willkommen," &c., is sung by the three ladies. Of the duet: "Bei Männern, welche Liebe fühlen," &c., a terzet has been made, and so on. Worse than all, however, they have taken the liberty of making alterations in the score: for example, in the air: "In diesen heil'gen Hallen," at the words: "So wandelt er an Freundes Hand," the imitating bass

is entirely left out, which is here indispensably necessary, not alone to the harmony, but because it expresses the act of wandering in so characteristic a manner, and the bass sound the *B* only a few times instead. You may therefore readily imagine how insipid and meagre this passage now sounds, which in Germany is so frequently admired. Moreover, in the terzet of the three females, where *Mozart* strengthens and supports the third voice with the violins only, the transposers have added both violoncello and double-bass; so that at these tender passages, which are for three voices only, the bass lies in three different octaves, which to a cultivated ear is unbearable. Similar offences are of frequent occurrence. We must nevertheless do the French the justice to say, that they have always highly disapproved of this vandalic mutilation of a great master-piece (the extent of which from their ignorance of the original is yet not known to them); but how is it, that the „*Mystères*" have nevertheless kept their place undisturbed in the repertoire for the last eighteen or twenty years? — and here where the public moreover, as I see every day, rule so despotically in the theatre, and manage to have verything their own way! —

To me, as a German, the performance was not satisfactory. Even the overture was not executed so well as it should have been by so excellent a union of first-rate musicians. It was taken too quick, and still more hurried at the close, so that the violins instead of playing semiquavers could only play quavers. The singers of the grand opera, whose great merits may perhaps lie in declamatory song, are little qualified to render the soft airs of the Zauberflöte in a satisfactory manner. They sing them with a blunt roughness that deprives them of all tenderness. The getting-up in scenery, dresses and dancing is respectable, but not so handsome as I had expected. — Yesterday we went for the first time to the grand opera, and saw "Clari," a grand ballet in three acts, the music by *Kreutzer*. Little as I like ballets, and little, in my opinion as pantomime merits the aid of the resources of art, as these are lavished on it here, I nevertheless do not deny that the Parisian ballet may sometimes afford agreeable amusement, until one becomes wearied with the monotony of the mimic movements, and of the yet greater sameness of the dances. But with all the perfection with which it is given here, pantomime, from the poverty of its signs, which always require a printed explanation of their meaning, is, as compared to recitative drama, a mere outline by the side of a finished drawing.

However it may be embellished with golden ornament and decorated surroundings, as is the ballet here by magnificence of costume and decorations, it gives the outline only, and the life is wanting. In the same manner I may compare the drama to the opera — as a drawing by the side of the painting. From song, the poem receives its first colouring, and by it only, and the powerful aid of harmony, does it succeed in giving expression to the indefinable and merely imagined emotions of the soul which language must be content alone to hint at. The music to "Clari" is a great success, and in the second and third act especially the effect is most captivating. It facilitates greatly the comprehension of the subject by a correct delineation of the passions, and contains a treasury of pretty melodies which one regrets do not form part of an opera. Mademoiselle *Bigottini* played the chief character, and evinced a deep study of mime and action in her play. That in very impassioned situations she carried the expression of her features to the borders of grimace, may perhaps be imputed to the circumstance that hitherto she has always appeared in a spacious place, where on account of the distance it was requisite to give strong play to the features. Perhaps as a German this is my fancy only, for the applause was never more tumultuous than when (to my feeling) she overstepped the bounds of the beautiful and graceful.

Before the ballet, the one-act opera "Le rossignol" was given; from which *Weigl* took the subject of his German opera of "Nachtigall und Rabe." The music of the French opera is of no account, and interested me only through the masterly execution of a flauto-solo by Mr. Tulou. It is impossible to hear a finer tone than that Mr. Tulou draws from his instrument. Since I heard him, it appears to me no longer so inappropriate, when our poets compare the pleasing sound of a fine voice to the tones of a flute.

SECOND LETTER.

Paris, December 31. 1820.

Since the despatch of my first letter, a fortnight has elapsed, replete with enjoyment, and since then we have both seen and heard much that is beautiful; but for the present I must content myself with writing to you upon that which most nearly concerns my art. I have now made my appearance before musicians and dilettanti, connoisseurs and a lay public, as violinist and composer, first at Mr. *Baudiot's,* primo violoncellist of the royal orchestra, on the day after at *Kreutzer's,* and since then at three private parties. At the soirées of the two first the company consisted almost wholly of musicians; at *Kreutzer's,* in particular, almost all the first composers and violinists of Paris were present. I gave several of my quartets and quintets, and on the second day my nonet. The composers present expressed themselves to me in very laudatory terms upon the composition, and the violinists upon my play. Of the latter, *Viotti,* both the *Kreutzers, Baillot, Lafont, Habeneck, Fontaine, Guerin,* and several others whose names are not so well known in Germany, were present; and you may imagine that it was then highly necessary that I should collect my faculties, to do credit to my countrymen. The wind-instrument parts in my nonet were played by the five artists of whose masterly execution of *Reicha's* quintets you will have so frequently read in accounts from Paris. I had the pleasure of hearing them play two of those quintets, but shall reserve to myself all detailed observations thereon till I shall have heard some more of them. At the request of all the musicians present my nonet was played again the same evening; and if the readiness with which the assistant players read *à prima vista* that difficult piece of music had surprised me, I was still more gratified, upon its repetition, by the manner in which they now entered into the spirit of the composition and re-executed it.

The young pianist *Herz,* of whom you have also doubtless read in the Parisian musical miscellanies, played twice on that evening, at first his own variations on the theme from the "Schweizerfamilie," and then *Moscheles*' well-known variations on Alexander's march. The extraordinary execution of this young man is the astonishment of everybody; but with him, as with all the young artists here whom I have yet heard, it seems to me that his technical cultivation is in advance of that of his mind; otherwise, in a company composed of artists only, he would surely have given something different and more intellectual than the break-neck tricks of art he exhibited. But it is very singular, how all here, young and old, strive only to shine by mechanical execution, and individuals in whom perhaps the germ of something better lies, devote whole years and every energy to the study and practice of one single piece of music, frequently of the most worthless kind, in order to create a sensation with it before the public. That the mind remains torpid under such circumstances and that such people never become much better than musical automatons may be readily imagined.

Hence one seldom or never hears in the musical réunions here an earnest, well-digested piece of music, such as a quartet or quintet of our great masters; every one produces his show-piece; you hear nothing but *airs variés, rondos favoris, nocturnes,* and the like trifles, and from the singers romances and little duets; and however incorrect and insipid all this may be, it never fails to produce an effect, if it is executed right smoothly and sweetly. Poor in such pretty trifles, with my earnest German music I am ill at ease in such musical parties, and feel frequently like a man who speaks to people who do not understand his language; for when the praise of any such auditors extends even sometimes from my play to the composition itself, I cannot feel gratified by it, since immediately afterwards he bestows the same admiration upon the most trifling things. One blushes to be praised by such connoisseurs. It is just the same at the theatres: the masses, the leaders of the fashion here, know not positively how to distinguish the worst from the best; they hear *"Le

Jugement de Midas" with the same rapture that they hear *"Les deux Journées"* or *"Joseph."* It requires no long residence here, to adopt the frequently expressed opinion, that the French are not a musical nation.

The artists themselves here are of this opinion, and frequently reply, when I speak of Germany in this respect: "Yes, music is loved and understood there, but not here." In this manner may be explained how good music wedded to a wretched theatrical piece, falls to the ground, and wretched music united to a good *pièce de théâtre*, may be highly successful.

This has deprived me of all desire to write for any of the theatres here, as I had previously much wished to do; for apart from the fact that I should have to begin *de novo*, like a young composer — since, with the exception of some of my violin pieces, they know little or nothing of my compositions — and further that I should have to work my way through a thousand cabals, which would rise up against me as a foreigner with fearful violence before I could get my work performed, so that at the end I should find, although I might have written good music, its success would be uncertain, as that depends, as I have said, almost wholly on the theatrical piece. This may be seen from the notices in the journals here upon recent operas, in which whole columns are devoted to a critique of the text, and the music is dismissed with a passing notice of a few words only.

Were it not so lucrative to write for the theatres in Paris, there would have been long since no good composer willing to do so. But from the considerable gain which a successful opera brings in during one's whole life-time, new works are produced almost every day; authors and composers turn their mind constantly to the creation of new effects, but do not neglect at the same time, to ply the public for months together in the journals, and provide the necessary number of paid *claqueurs* in the pit on the evening of the performance, in order to ensure a brilliant reception for their work and thereby an ultimate rich harvest from its frequent repetition. If only half as much were to be gained by an opera in Germany, we should soon be equally rich in good composers for the theatre as we now are in instrumental composers, and we should have no further need to introduce foreign pieces upon our stage, for the most part unworthy of the artistic culture of Germans.

After a residence of now three weeks it may be well imagined that we have repeatedly visited all the theatres. I am the more pleased at this as the circle of my acquaintance has become larger, and my engagements both for the morning and evening have so much increased that for the next fortnight we shall be able to devote but few evenings to the theatre.

Of the *Théâtre français*, the Odéon, and the four lesser theatres, I shall say nothing; as in a musical point of view they offer nothing worthy of notice. In the two first they give nothing but *entr'actes*, and in the four others almost nothing else but vaudevilles. That this last kind of theatrical pieces, which, thanks to Apollo and the muses, has hitherto been transplanted into no other country, is so much liked here that four theatres give almost nothing else, is the most striking proof that the French are not musical; for the sacred art cannot be more abused anywhere than in these kind of songs, which are neither sung nor spoken, but rattled out in intervals, and which are in most striking anomaly with the melodies, and the accompanying harmony. All Frenchmen of taste are agreed that the vaudeville, which formerly was given in one theatre only, has by its increase deteriorated more and more the taste for true music, and therefore had a prejudicial effect upon art here. We have been to each of these theatres once, to hear the celebrated comedians *Brunet, Pothier* and *Perlet*, but are not likely to go a second time, for the enjoyment one derives from the wit and inexhaustible humour of those performers is too dearly purchased by hearing such wretched music. I was particularly struck by the skill with which the orchestra in those theatres follow the singers, who do not in the least adhere to the time, or the notes. But this is, also, their chief merit, for in other respects they are but middling musicians.

We have been frequently to the Italian opera, and much enjoyed ourselves there. Last evening we saw "Don Juan" there, at last, after it had been frequently announced. The house was again. as upon the previous performances, filled to overflowing, and hundreds of people could find no room, even half an hour before the curtain drew up. I was disposed to believe that the Parisians had at length understood the classical beauty of this work, and that they flocked always in greater numbers to enjoy it; but I soon relinquished that opinion when I saw that the finest parts of the opera — the first duet, the quartet, the grand septet, and several other things — passed off without making any impression upon them, and two subjects only received a storm of applause, which was given rather to the singers than to the composer.

These two subjects, which were each respectively encored, were the duet between Don Juan and Zerline: "Reich mir die Hand mein Leben" etc., and the air of Don Juan: "Treibt der Champagner" etc.; the first, because Signor *Garcia*, not having depth of voice sufficient, transposes it to B flat, and the last even a whole tone higher, to *C*. Madame *Fodor-Mainville*, who well knew that the song-pieces of Zerlina would please the Parisians more than all the rest of the opera, chose very wisely that part, and the result shewed that she had calculated rightly. What would she care, were the characters of the opera wholly transposed, so long as she meets with a storm of applause. The real connoisseur can only consent to this when he dismisses from his mind that she personates the role of a peasant girl, and when he wholly sets aside the true intention of the subject represented; for she decorates the simple songs of her part with a number of high-flown embellishments which, splendidly though she may execute them, are here wholly out of place; first because they do not at all belong to *Mozart's* music, and secondly, because they are wholly incompatible with the character. With deduction of this, it certainly affords an unusual enjoyment to hear this part, which in Germany is usually played by a third-rate singer, impersonated by a first-rate one, and so distinguished a vocalist. Signor *Garcia*, as Don Juan, uses also too much ornamentation. Where this is only moderately admissable, he comes out with a *fioritura* a yard long; and these are most out of place in the serenade, where the supposed mandoline accompaniment forbids the most simple ornament. Nevertheless he gives full latitude in it to his fancy, and in order to do this more conveniently, he takes the tempo very slow. On the other hand, however, he sings his song incomparably "Treibt der Champagner" etc., and I acknowledge that I never heard that air so well sung. The pliability of the Italian tongue is of great use to him in this, and instead of losing his breath in it, as is usual with our German singers, his vocal power increases to the end.

The other parts are sung more or less well, but none of them badly, and one must gratefully acknowledge that each does his best to do honour to the work. One may also be very satisfied with the performance, when one loses sight of the claims one is justified in making upon so celebrated a combination of artists. But to a German it soon becomes very evident that these singers, who execute Italian music only, and that of *Rossini* especially, in the highest perfection, cannot give the music of *Mozart* with the same excellence; the difference of style is far too great. The effeminate, sweet execution which accords so well with the former, obliterates too much the energetic character which distinguishes Don Juan above all other of *Mozart's* operas.

The orchestra, which the Parisians always pronounce the first in the world, made some mistakes. Twice for instance the wind instruments were very obviously at fault, and they wavered several times so much, that the conductor was obliged to beat the time for them. I became confirmed but the more strongly in my opinion, that a theatrical orchestra, however excellent it may be, on account of the great distance of the extreme ends, should not be conducted otherwise than by a continual beating of the time, and, that to mark the time constantly by motions of the body, and the violin, like Mr. *Grasset* does, is of no use. In other respects this orchestra is justly famed for the discretion with which it accompanies the singer, and in that might serve as a model for the other Parisian as well as many German orchestras.

The choruses are also excellent, and the effect particularly powerful and grand at the concluding allegro of the first finale. But why here, as well as almost everywhere else, is this allegro taken so unreasonably quick? Do then the conductors wholly forget, that by so doing they decrease instead of increasing the power, and that the triplet movement of the violins which must first give life and motion to the whole, cannot be brought out clearly and forcibly in a movement of such exaggerated rapidity, and instead of hearing the living whole, it becomes a mere skeleton sketch without fillings in?!

When one hears so beautiful a piece of music lose its effect by incorrectness of time, one wishes again that the marking of the tempi was finally and universally established either on *Mälzel's* or *Weber's* method, or still better upon both at the same time. But then of course orchestral conductors must follow them conscientiously, and not as now, follow their own fancy merely.

THIRD LETTER.

Paris, January 12. 1821.

With a mind greatly relieved, I write to announce to you, my dear friend, that I have made my public début and with success. It is always a hazardous undertaking for a foreign violinist to make a public appearance in Paris, as the Parisians are possessed with the notion that they have the finest violinists in the world, and consider it almost in the light of arrogant presumption when a foreign considers he has talent sufficient to challenge a comparison with them.

I may therefore well be a little proud of the brilliant reception I met with the day before yesterday, and the more so that, with the exception of a dozen persons, the auditory was personally unknown to me, and there were none among them who had been admitted with free-tickets in purchase of their service as *claqueurs*. But I had prepared myself very carefully for the occasion, and was properly supported by the careful accompaniment of Mr. *Habeneck*. I was, however, not in the least nervous, which is sometimes the case with me when I appear for the first time in a strange country, and which occurred to me the year before in London. The reason why I did not feel so in this instance, was doubtless, that here I had already played before all the most distinguished musicians, previous to my appearing in public; but in London eight days only after our arrival, without having been previously heard by any person, I was constrained to appear at the philharmonic concert.

Before I enter into any details of the concert, I must first relate how I came to give it. It is at all times a tedious business to make arrangements for a concert in any town, but in Paris, which is so extensive, where so many theatres are daily open, where there is so much competition and so many obstacles to overcome, it is indeed a Herculean task. I think also that this is the reason why so many artists who come to Paris, decline giving a public concert, which, besides being attended with the enormous expense of nearly 3000 francs, is always an undertaking of great risk. If these matters have been extremely unpleasant to me in other places, you may readily imagine how I feared to attempt them here. In order to get over the difficulty, I bethought myself of making a proposition to the directors of the grand opera, to divide with me the expenses and the receipts of an evening entertainment of which the first half should consist of a concert and the second of a ballet. Contrary to the expectation of all those to whom I had spoken on the subject, this proposition was acceded to.

The consent of the minister was however so long delayed, that the concert could not be announced till three days before it took place, and although the house was well filled, yet I ascribe to this delay that it was not so crowded as I had expected so novel and, from its novelty, so attractive an arrangement would have been for the Parisians. The half which came to my share, after deduction of the expenses, was therefore, as you may imagine, not very considerable: but as I had not calculated upon making much pecuniary gain in Paris, I do not regret this arrangement at all, as it saved me an immense deal of trouble, and yet gave me an opportunity of making my appearance in public. Of my own compositions I gave: the overture to "Alruna," the newest violin concerto, and the potpourri on the duet from "Don Juan." Between these a cavatine of *Rossini's* was sung by Mademoiselle *Cinte*, and a duet, also of the same master, by Messrs. *Bordogni* and *Levasseur*. At the rehearsal the overture was repeated three times, and in the evening therefore, although it did not go off quite so well as the last time at the rehearsal, the public nevertheless could not refuse their applause of its execution. In the concerto, as well as in the potpourri, some of the wind instruments failed twice, from a negligence in observing the pauses, which seems somewhat usual with the French, but fortunately it was not much disparaged by it. The satisfaction of the audience was unmistakably expressed by loud applause and cries of Bravo! To-day, however, the criticism of the majority of the journals is not so favourable. I must solve this riddle for you. Previous to every first appearance in public, whether of a foreigner or a native, these gentlemen of the press are accustomed to receive a visit from him, to solicit a favourable judgment, and to present them most obsequiously with a few free admission tickets. Foreign artists, to escape these unpleasant visits, sometimes forward their solicitations in writing only, and the free admissions at the same time; or, as is of frequent occurrence, induce some family to whom they have brought letters of introduction, to invite the gentlemen of the press to dinner, when a more convenient opportunity is offered to give them to understand what is desirable to have said of them both before and after the concert. This may perhaps occur now and then in Germany; but I do not think, that newspaper critics can be anywhere so venal as here. I have been told that the first artists of the *Théatre français*, Mlle. *Mars*. and even *Talma*, pay annually considerable sums to the journals, in order to keep those gentlemen constantly in good humour, and that the latter, whenever they wish to extricate themselves from any pecuniary embarrassment, find no method so sure as to attack some esteemed artist until he submits to a tribute of money. How the opinions of a press that are so purchasable, are at all respected, I cannot understand. Suffice however to say, I did not pay any of these supplicatory visits, for I considered them unworthy of a German artist, and thought that the worst that could happen would be, that the journalists would not take any notice at all of my concert. But as these have each a free pass to every performance at the grand opera, I found I was mistaken. They all speak of it; some with unqualified praise, but the majority with a *But*, by which the praise is more than sufficiently diminished. In all these notices, however, French vanity speaks with the utmost self-assurance. They all begin by extolling their own artists, and their artistic culture, above all other nations; they think that the country that produced Messrs. *Baillot, Lafont* and *Habeneck*, need envy no other its violinists; and whenever the play of a foreigner has been received here with enthusiasm, it is nothing more than a proof of the great hospitality which the French in particular shew towards foreigners. Apart from this vanity the notices are very contradictory: The "Quotidienne" says, for instance: "Mr. *Spohr* aborde, avec une incroyable audace, les plus grandes difficultés, et l'on ne sait ce qui étonne le plus, ou son audace ou la sureté avec laquelle il exécute ces difficultés." In the "Journal des Débats," on the other hand: "Le concert exécuté par Mr. *Spohr* n'est point surchargé de difficultés," etc. These gentlemen differ also in opinion respecting the merits or demerits of my compositions. The majority think them good, but without saying why; but "Le Courier des Spectacles," which altogether speaks most disparagingly of me, says: "C'est une espèce de pacotille d'harmonie et d'enharmonie germaniques que Mr. *Spohr* apporte, en contrebande, de je ne sais quelle contrée d'Allemagne." But *Rossini* is his man, of whom he says further on: "Cet Orphée moderne a défrayé de chant le concert de Mr. *Spohr*, et il lui suffit pour cela de prêter une petite aria et un petit duo bouffo." But as a violinist I found more grace in his eyes; he says for instance: "Mr. *Spohr* comme exécutant est un homme de mérite; il a deux qualités rares et précieuses, la pureté et la justesse," but then winds up his phrase like a true Frenchman: "s'il reste quelque temps à Paris, il pourra perfectionner son goût et retourner ensuite former celui des bons Allemands." If the good man only knew what the "bons Allemands" think of the musical taste of the French?!

This ridiculous vanity in the Parisians is shewn also in their conversation. When one or other of their musicians plays anything, they immediately ask: "Well, can you boast of anything like that in Germany?" Or when they introduce to you one of their distinguished artists, they do not call him the first in Paris, but at once the first in the world, although no nation knows less what other countries possess, than they do, in their — for their vanity's sake most fortunate — ignorance.

You are doubtless astonished that I have as yet said nothing of the music of the royal chapel; but I delayed doing so intentionally, until I had first heard some of *Cherubini's* masses. *Lesueur* and *Cherubini*, the two directors of the music of the royal chapel, assume the duties of their office every three months alternately; our arrival took place during the time of *Lesueur's* directorship, and *Cherubini's* did not begin till the first of January. But the musical directors of the royal chapel do not conduct the music themselves, and preside only in their court uniform at the head of the vocal personnel, without taking any active part in the performance. The director *de facto* is *Plantade;* *Kreutzer* leading player of the first violin, and *Baillot* of the second. The orchestra is composed of the first artists in Paris, the chorus is powerful and good. Every mass is rehearsed once or twice, and under *Plantade's* sure and spirited direction, every thing goes exceedingly well.

Although previously prepared by Mr. *Sievers'* account, I was very far from expecting to hear music here of the style we call church-music in Germany; yet I was greatly taken by surprise by the brilliant theatrical style of a mass by *Plantade*, which I heard on my first visit to the chapel on the 17th of last month. There is not the least trace of the ecclesiastical style, not a vestige of the canonical management of the voices, and still less of a fugue. But apart from this, there were very pretty ideas, and much good instrumentation, which would be quite in place in a comic opera. The concluding allegro, probably upon the words: *Dona nobis pacem* (for I am not certain, since the French pronounce Latin in a manner very unintelligible to a German ear) was so completely in the style of the finale to an opera (like those usually with three or four times increased tempo) that at the end, forgetting completely where I was, I expected to see the curtain fall, and to hear the public applaud.

At midnight, on the 24th December, we heard a so-called "*Messe de minuit*" of *Lesueur's* composition. First of all we were obliged to endure a great trial of our patience, in which during two somewhat tedious hours, from ten to twelve o'clock, we heard nothing but psalms, sung off in the most monotonous manner, and interrupted at intervals with barbarous peals of organ-play. At length, at midnight, the mass began. Again the same frivolous theatrical style as in that of *Plantade,* but which at the solemn midnight hour was still more insufferable. But what most surprised me, particularly from *Lesueur*, who is reputed here a first-rate harmonist, and was educated, if I am not mistaken, for a teacher of harmony at the *Conservatoire*, there was not even a four-part management of the voices! Though at times it may be effective in an opera, when writing only a two-part vocal distribution, to let the soprani go in octaves with the tenors, and the alti with the bass, partly with a view to facilitate the execution of the generally bad theatrical choruses, and partly to obtain by that means more material power; yet to me it seems quite barbarous to introduce this in the church, and I should therefore like to know what Mr. *Lesueur*, who must certainly be an artist of reflective powers, means by it. In the place of the offertory, variations by *Nadermann* for the harp, horn and violoncello were thrust in, executed by the composer and Mrs. *Dauprat* and *Baudiot*. You who know, that in Germany a serious symphony even appeared to me too mundane at this part, may therefore readily imagine what an unpleasant impression these frivolous, French variations on the harp must have made upon me in a mass at midnight; and yet I saw the people present in earnest prayer. How is it possible for them to feel a religious sentiment with such trivial music! This must be either a matter of no importance to them, or they know how to close their ears effectually; otherwise, like myself, they would of a certainty be reminded of the ballet at the grand opera, in which those three instruments are heard in a like manner in the most voluptuous dances. Although the harp in ancient times was the favorite instrument of a pious king, it should for all that be banished from the church, because it is wholly unfit for the severe style which is the only one suitable for that edifice.

But will you believe it, when I assure you that even the worthy master *Cherubini* himself, has allowed himself to be led away by this bad example, and his masses exhibit in many places a theatrical style. It is true that he makes amends for it in those places with superior music, full of effect;

but who can enjoy it, if he cannot wholly forget the place in which he hears it?

It would be less regrettable that *Cherubini* also should deviate from the true ecclesiastical style, if in some individual parts he did not shew in what a dignified manner he can move in it. Several separate subjects in his masses — particularly the scientifically conducted fugues, and above all his *Pater noster* up to the profane conclusion — afford the grandest proofs of this. But when one has once overcome the inclination to feel annoyed at this frequent, extremely digressive style, one feels then the highest enjoyment of art. By richness of invention, well-chosen, and frequently quite novel sequences of harmony, and a sagacious use of the material resources of art, directed by the experience of many years, he knows how to produce such powerful effects, that, carried away by them in spite of oneself, one soon forgets all pedantic cavil to give oneself wholly up to one's feelings, and to enjoyment. What would not this man have contributed to art, if instead of writing for Frenchmen, he had always written for Germans! —

FOURTH LETTER.

Paris, January 30. 1821.

The two months which I had allotted to our stay in Paris are drawing to a close. As I do not know whether circumstances may even permit us to come here again, we are exerting ourselves to find all the remarkable things we have not yet seen, and make daily excursions in Paris and into its environs. In order to devote my time wholly to this, I have given up the idea I had conceived of giving another soirée before our departure, and for which I had already made some arrangements. The fortnight which I should have been obliged to devote solely to that object, I can now therefore pass more pleasantly, and in greater freedom. I gave up with much more repugnance my project to give a second public concert, since, from the reception given to the first, I had good ground to expect a successful result. But during this month there was not a day to be found favorable for such a purpose; for on a week day the administration will not give up the theatre, as there is either a grand or an Italian opera, and of the three yet remaining Sundays, the first was too near, the second, as the anniversary of the death of Louis XVI., not to be had, and the third, already pre-engaged by Mr. *Lafont* for a concert. To extend our stay over the middle of next month, we have no desire, for we are heartily tired of the noisy life and ceaseless night-disturbance here, and ardently long for a quiet place of residence.

On the other hand I have latterly played more frequently at private parties, and seen with pleasure that my compositions, upon every repetition, have been received with greater enthusiasm, especially by musicians. This has been particularly the case with a new quintet for pianoforte, flute, clarinet, horn and bassoon, which I have written for my wife, and in which, since by the advice of the physician, she has abandoned the harp, she has appeared several times. The chief object of my coming here, to make myself personally known to the most distinguished artists here, and to become more nearly acquainted with them, I have thus fully effected; and I cannot speak sufficiently in praise of the sympathy and kindness which the greater part of them have evinced towards me. They repeatedly endeavoured to persuade me to make a longer stay, and should I feel disposed to give a second concert, they would not only take all the trouble of the arrangements for it off my hands, but promised to get together for me the best orchestra in Paris, without the cost to me of a single sou. Although I am not likely to avail myself of this offer, yet it was very gratifying to me.

Another no less important object of my coming here has also been achieved; I have had opportunities of hearing the most celebrated violinists of, and at present in Paris. *Baillot* gave a soirée at his house for me, at my request; I heard *Lafont* at his own concert; and the younger *Kreutzer* and *Habeneck* at morning concerts which were arranged expressly for the purpose. Should you wish to know which of these four Violinists has best pleased me, then without hesitation, in point of execution, I say, *Lafont*. In his play he combines beauty of tone, the greatest purity, power, and grace; and he would be a perfect violinist, if, with these qualifications, he possessed depth of feeling, and had not accustomed himself to the habit peculiar to the French school, of laying too much stress upon the last note of a phrase. But feeling, without which a man can neither conceive nor execute a good adagio, appears with him, as with almost all Frenchmen, to be wholly wanting; for although he dresses up his slow movements with many elegant and pretty ornaments, yet he still remains somewhat cold The adagio appears altogether to be considered here, both by artists and the public, as the least important part of a concerto, and is only retained perhaps because it separates both the quick subjects and increases their effect.

To this indifference for it — as indeed the general insensibility of the French for everything that works upon the feelings — I ascribe also, that my adagio and the manner in which I played, made less impression here than the brilliant allegro subjects. Accustomed to the special applause which my manner of playing it had received from Germans, Italians, Dutch, and English, I at first felt hurt to see it thought so little of by the French. But since I have observed how seldom their artists give them an earnest adagio, and how little their taste for it is awakened, I became pacified on that subject. The practice of giving emphasis to the last note of a period, by an increased pressure and a rapid upward stroke of the bow, even when that note falls on a part where the time is bad, is more or less common to all French violinists, but with none so prominent as *Lafont*. To me it is incomprehensible how this unnatural accentuation has arisen, which sounds exactly as though a speaker endeavoured to intonate the short final syllable of a word with particular force. If when executing a musical piece the cantabile of the human voice had always been kept in view as model (which in my opinion should be done by every instrumentalist) such errors would never have become confirmed habits. But the Parisians are so accustomed to this unnatural custom, that a foreigner who does not play in the same bizzarre manner, appears to them much too plain, or, as Mr. *Sievers* expresses it, "much too straightforward."

That *Lafont's* excellence restricts itself always to but a few pieces at once, and that he practises the same concerto by the year together before he plays it in public, is well known. Since I have heard the perfect execution which he attains by this means, I certainly will not cavil with this application of all his powers to the one object; but I could not imitate him, and cannot even understand how one can bring one's-self to practise the same piece of music for four or five hours daily, but still less how it is to be done without eventually losing every vestige of real art, in such a mechanical mode of proceeding.

Baillot is, in the technical scope of his play, almost as perfect, and his diversity of manner, shews that he is so, without resorting to the same desperate means. Besides his own compositions, he plays almost all those of ancient and modern times. On one and the same evening he gave us a quintet of *Bocherini*, a quartet of *Haydn*, and three of his own compositions — a concerto, an *air varié*, and a rondo. He played all these things with the most perfect purity, and with the expression which is peculiar to his manner. His expression, nevertheless, seemed to me more artificial than natural, and indeed his whole execution, from the too salient evidence of the means by which he gives that expression, has the appearance of mannerism. His bow-stroke is skilful, and rich in shades of expression, but not so free as *Lafont's*, and therefore his tone is not so beautiful as that of the latter, and the mechancali process of the up and down stroke of the bow is too audible. His compositions are distinguished above almost all those of any other Parisian violinist by their correctness; neither can they be denied a certain originality; but being somewhat artificial, mannered, and out of date in style, the hearer remains cold and without a sense of emotion. You know that he frequently plays and takes great pleasure in *Boccherini's* quintets. I was desirous of hearing him in these quintets, with about a dozen of which I am acquainted, in order to see whether from the manner in which he executes them he could succeed in making one forget the poverty of the compositions. But well as they were given by him, the frequent childishness of the melodies, and the poverty of the harmonies (almost always three-voiced only) were no less unpleasing to me, than in all those I had heard before. One can hardly understand how a cultivated artist like *Baillot*, to whom our treasures in compositions of this kind are known, can bring himself to play those quintets still, whose worth consists only in the regard had to the period and circumstances under which they were written. But that they are here listened to with as much pleasure as a quintet of *Mozart*, is another proof that Parisians cannot distinguish the good from the bad, and are at least half a century behind in art.

I heard *Habeneck* play two *airs variés* of his composition. He is a brilliant violinist and plays much with great rapidity and ease. His tone and his bow-stroke are somewhat coarse.

Kreutzer junior, the brother and pupil of the elder, played to me a new, very brilliant and graceful trio of his brother's composition. The manner in which he executed it reminded me somewhat of the style of the elder one, and satisfied me that they are the purest players of all the Parisian violinists. Young *Kreutzer* is wanting in physical power, he is somewhat ill, and dare not play sometimes for months together. His tone therefore is weak, but in other respects his play is pure, spirited and full of expression.

Two days ago I heard two more quite new quintets of *Reicha*, which he wrote for the morning-concerts of the five previously named artists. They were played at a rehearsal, which appears to me to have been given solely for the purpose of fishing for more subscribers to the morning-concerts, among the numerous persons who were invited. At least a list of them was handed round. It is sad to see what means artists here are obliged to resort to, in order to procure support for their undertakings. While the Parisians press eagerly forward to every sensual enjoyment, they must be almost dragged to intellectual ones. — I found the composition of these two new quintets, like those I had previously heard at *Kreutzer's*, rich in interesting sequences of harmony, correct throughout in the management of the voices, and full of effect in the use made of the tone and character of the different wind-instruments, but on the other hand, frequently defective in the form. Mr. *Reicha* is not economical enough of his ideas, and at the very commencement of his pieces he frequently gives from four to five themes, each of which concludes in the tonic. Were he less rich, he would be richer. His periods also are frequently badly connected and sound as though he had written one yesterday and the other to-day. Yet the minuets and scherzi, as short pieces, are less open to this objection, and some of them are real master-pieces in form and contents. A German soundness of science and capacity are the greatest ornaments of this master. The execution in the rapid subjects was again wonderfully correct, but somewhat less so in the slow ones.

I do not think I have yet spoken to you of the *Feydeau*. We have been less frequently to that theatre than to the other operatic theatres, because it so happened that on those evenings when we were at liberty pieces were generally performed that did not much interest us. Yet we were present at the first representation of *Méhul's* "Joseph," which, after a long repose was again put on the stage. The public however, did not seem very grateful for this to the directors of the theatre, for they gave it but a cold reception. In support of my assertion that the French take an interest only in the piece, and know little how to appreciate the excellence of the music, I may adduce, that the tirades in the dialogue were far more applauded than the song parts. The singers succeeded in obtaining applause only when, in the superabundance of an artificial feeling, instead of singing, they began to sob. At the pieces of the opera — for instance, at the first chorus of the brothers — there was not a hand stirred. Many of the tempi were taken quite different from those in Germany, but not to the advantage of the music; for instance, the fine morning-hymn of the Israelites, behind the scenes, was taken so quick, that it lost all its solemnity. A screaming violin, also, that supported the soprani was far too prematurely loud. The orchestra played well, and was particularly remarkable for a delicate *piano*.

Moscheles has been here a month. He makes a great sensation with his extremely brilliant play, and wins the admiration both of artists and dilettanti, the former by his execution of his richly intellectual compositions, and the latter by his free fantasias, in which, as far as his Germanism permits him, he accommodates himself to the Parisian taste. The brothers *Bohrer* have also returned to-day from a tour in the provinces, but will remain here a few days only, and then leave on a new tour viâ Munich to Vienna. I regret that I shall not have an opportunity of hearing these artists, whom I have not met for ten years. They wanted to persuade me to accompany them from here upon a tour in the southern provinces, where they assure me some money is to be made. But I have not the least inclination to go. The bad orchestras in the provincial towns, the bad taste and the unpleasant negociations to lessen the amount to be given up to the theatre and the poor of the towns, would make a journey of the kind too disagreeable to me. In a few days we shall return to Germany by way of Nancy and Strasbourg, and therefore shall soon greet you again in dear Fatherland.

Till then farewell!

* * *

To these letters regarding my sojourn in Paris, I have yet to add some few things from recollection. From the frequent opportunities I had of playing before *Cherubini* at private parties, I conceived a very ardent desire to have all my quartets and quintets so far as I thought them worthy of it, heard by that by me highly esteemed master, and to introduce them by degrees to his notice, in order to ask his opinion of them. But in this I succeeded with very few only, for when *Cherubini* had heard the first quartet (it was Nr. 1 of the Op. 45 written at Frankfort), and I was on the point of producing a second, he protested against it, and said: "Your music, and indeed the form and style of this kind of music, is yet so foreign to me, that I cannot find myself immediately at home with it, nor follow it properly; I would therefore much prefer that you repeated the quartet you have just played!" I was very much astonished at this remark, and did not understand it until I afterwards ascertained that *Cherubini* was quite unacquainted with the German masterpieces of this kind of *Mozart* and *Bethoven* — and at the utmost had once heard a quartet by *Haydn* at *Baillot's* soirées. As the other persons present coincided with *Cherubini's* wish, I consented the more readily, as in the first execution of it, some things had not gone altogether well. He now spoke very favourably of my composition, praised its form, its thematic working out, the rich change in the harmonies, and particularly the *fugato* in the last subject. But as there were still many things not quite clear to him in the music, he begged me to repeat it a second time, when we should next meet. I hoped he would think nothing more about it, and therefore at the next music party brought forward another quartet. Before I could begin, however, *Cherubini* renewed his request, and I was therefore obliged to play the same quartet a third time. The same thing occurred also with Nr. 2 of Op. 45, excepting that he spoke of it with more decisive praise, and said of the adagio: "It is the finest I ever heard." He was equally pleased with my pianoforte quintet with the concerted accompaniment of wind instruments, and I was frequently obliged to play it on that account. The first time my wife played the piano part; but when *Moscheles* subsequently requested permission to study it and to play it once, she had not the courage to play it any more in Paris, after him. He remained therefore in possession, and entered more and more into the spirit of the composition. He executed the two allegro subjects especially with far more energy and style, which certainly greatly increased their effect. As the wind instruments of *Reicha's* quintet were excellent, I never recollect to have heard that quintet so perfectly rendered as then, although I have heard it played in more recent days by many celebrated pianoforte virtuosi. From the continual repetition of my quartets in Paris I could find no opportunity of giving even one of my two first quintets for stringed instruments which had been some time written. Nevertheless I found for them a very sympathetic audience at Strasbourg, on my return journy, to which the taste for quartet-music has more readily penetrated from its contiguity to Germany. The quintet in *G* major, with the half melancholy half merry finale, became soon an especial favorite with the friends of music there, and at their request formed the finale of every quartet-party. In Carlsruhe, where on a former visit I had already played quartets frequently, particularly in the house of that lover of art Mr. *von Eichthal*, my stay this time was very much saddened by finding the friend of my youth *Feska* dangerously ill: he shortly afterwards succumbed to his incurable malady.

* * *

Returned to Gandersheim, I resumed again, immediately, the pleasant active life of the previous summer. *Edward Grund* soon arrived also, and devoted himself with his usual zeal both to his own improvement and to the instruction of my children. I myself first began with the composition of the already mentioned ten-voiced vocal mass, but

I was soon obliged to give it up for a short time. I received a letter from my old friend *Hermstedt*, in which he invited me on the part of the directors of the baths of Alexisbad in the Harz, to give a concert in the course of the approaching season. He offered at the same time to make all the necessary arrangements beforehand, so that I should not require to stay there longer than a few days. He also urgently pressed me to write a new clarinet concerto for him, and promised if he received it sufficiently early, to play it for the first time at the Alexisbad concert. As I liked to write for *Hermstedt*, who at that time was without doubt the first of all living clarinet virtuosi, I consented to his proposal, and set to work immediately. After despatching to him the new concerto *F* minor (the third for clarinet), I wrote for myself and wife another pot-pourri concerted for violin and pianoforte on two themes from the "Opferfest" — published afterwards as Op. 56, for which I worked out anew a former composition for clarinet with orchestral accompaniment which I had written in 1812 for *Hermstedt*, for the celebration of Napoleon's birthday, in Erfurt. I considered it one of my most successful pieces, and wished by this new elaboration of it, to make it more generally known. It may be readily understood that in this transfer from the clarinet and orchestra to the violin and pianoforte, very considerable modifications were requisite, and that I could adhere chiefly only to the form and modulations of the previous composition. By the time this piece of music had been studied by us in the usual manner, with the greatest care, the day fixed upon for our departure for Alexisbad arrived. Of this excursion I have now but very faint reminiscences. I neither know what we played at the concert, nor how the new clarinet concerto pleased, and the less so, that since that time I have not heard it again; for it has remained altogether in *Hermstedt's* hands, and has never been published. But I recollect very distinctly a natural phenomenon by which our concert was disturbed and for some time interrupted, as in London by the smashing of the windows. Just as the music was about to begin, a storm, which had threatened since noon, broke out with such violence, that what with the rolling of the thunder and the noise of the rain that poured down in torrents, nothing could have been heard. In the over-crowded concert-room, which was suffocatingly hot, the closely packed auditory were compelled to await the passing over of the storm, and the concert could not be commenced until the air of the room had been renewed by the opening of the doors and windows. Owing to this the concert did not terminate till complete nightfall. The confusion and perplexity which ensued among the departing audience now first reached their climax; for it was found that the otherwise very modest rivulet which runs through the valley of Alexisbad had become so swollen, and had torn up and flooded the roads to such an extent, that the numerous company that had come in from the neighbourhood of the town found it impossible to return home in the darkness of night. All therefore first rushed to the dining-room of the baths, but there no provision had been made for such an influx of guests. As soon as the regular visitors of the baths had retired to their apartments previous to sitting down to dinner, the strangers seized upon their seats at the table, and upon the eatables also, so that when the former returned they were obliged to content themselves with what they could lay hold of. Upon this very naturally a good deel of ill-feeling was excited, and the host had enough to do and a hard time of it to pacify and keep the people in bounds. Now, furthermore, it was found that to pass the night there were neither rooms nor beds sufficient for their accommodation, and a great number of the strangers were *nolens volens* obliged to lie down indiscriminately beside each other upon a shakedown of straw. Many did it good humouredly, but others with ill-suppressed curses. For the unconcerned spectator it was indeed a highly comical and amusing scene.

During the same summer, I received an similar invitation to go to Pyrmont and give a concert there. I acquiesced, and proceeded thither accompanied by my wife and my pupil

Edward Grund, who conducted the orchestra and very much facilitated my solo-playing by practising the accompaniment beforehand, which alone enabled me to play my own compositions. *Grund* had in truth become a first-rate artist, and began now to make musical tours with much success; which led to his appointment as director of the court-orchestra at Meiningen, which office he now still (1853) fills, respected by his prince and by the members of the orchestra, and zealously exerting his energies to the advantage of art. As upon his leaving Gandersheim, in the autumn of 1821, the musical instruction of my daughters completely ceased, and as they gave evidence of vocal powers that appeared worthy of a further artistic cultivation, I determined to remove to Dresden with my family, in order to give the children the advantage of the instruction of a then celebrated teacher of vocal music of the name of *Miksch* in that city. To *Emilia* I had indeed, myself already begun to give instruction in singing, but soon found that I had neither the necessary perseverance and patience, and that it drew my attention too much from my work of composition. Besides this, also, I determined as soon as my family had become somewhat settled in Dresden, to proceed alone upon some short artistic tours in the neighbourhood. I wrote therefore to my former pupil *Moritz Hauptmann* in Dresden, and requested him to treat with Mr. *Miksch* or my behalf, and so soon as he should agree, to hire apartments for me; shortly after which I received a reply informing me that all my wishes had been carefully complied with.

My mass for ten voices had been meanwhile completed, and I longed very much to hear it. As on my journey to Dresden I contemplated giving a concert in Leipzic, and on that account should be obliged to make a longer stay there, I bethought myself of getting it sung during the time I was there by the grand choral-society of that town, with the Director of which I was acquainted. I wrote to him therefore to inquire if he felt disposed to have the work practised beforehand, and as he replied in the affirmative, I sent the score to him to have the voice-parts immediately written out.

The parting from Gandersheim was this time a very sad one, as the children also, to whose society their grandfather and grandmother had become so much accustomed, were to part from them, and I was obliged to promise to return the next summer, even though for a short visit only.

On arriving in Leipzic, one of my first visits was to the Director of the choral-society, to ascertain something about my mass. But what I learned was not very satisfactory. The rehearsals it is true had been commenced; but the work had been found so enormously difficult, and was so imperfectly understood, that the director refused decidedly to let me hear it. At my urgent request, however, a trial was made, which went very badly, and as I did not nearly hear the effect which I had pictured to myself during the inspiration of the work, I concluded that I had produced a complete failure. After hearing it a few more times, I resolved to make some alterations in it, in order to facilitate its execution, and shortly after, the mass was published by *Peters* as Op. 54. A long time afterwards, when I had almost forgotten it, some parts of it were sung to me by the Berlin choral-academy under *Zelter's* direction. These had been so well studied, were intonated so clearly, and had so imposing an effect from the combination of so many voices, that I now became fully convinced that the work could be performed, and conceived the desire to have it studied by my choral-society in Cassel. This proved successful, as I did not lose my patience and the singers were indefatigable, and the entire mass, without any omissions, was performed in November 1827 on Saint Cecilia's day. The experience I had acquired during these rehearsals taught me, however, to avoid a too great abundance of modulations and difficult chords in succession.

Arrived in Dresden, we were conducted by *Hauptmann* to the lodgings he had hired for us, which were pleasantly situated in a quiet part of the town. Both my eldest girls immediately began their singing-lessons with Mr. *Miksch* and I then went in search of my former acquaintances among the artists and amateurs of music, and, foremost of all, of the orchestra director *Carl Maria von Weber*. He received me in a very cordial manner, and by degrees introduced me into all the musical circles, where I not only heard much good music, but had the opportunity of playing my own chamber-music. As the musicians who accompanied me evinced great interest in my quartet-play, this induced me, with their assistance to give quartet parties every week at my house, to which I invited the most ardent lovers of music in the town. At these I brought forward, as I could not succeed in doing in Paris, all the quartets and quintets in succession which I had written up to that time, and as I soon got to the end of them, and they met with great approbation from all hearers, I was encouraged to write some new ones. In a short time, I finished two (the two first of Op. 58), and I took such interest in this work, as well as in the whole artistic life of Dresden, that I at once gave up my contemplated musical tour, and deferred it to the latter end of the winter.

Meanwhile *Carl Maria von Weber* had succeeded in obtaining the permission to have his opera of "Der Freischütz" studied in Dresden, after it had met with such brilliant success in Vienna and Berlin; and the private rehearsals were already begun. As up to that time I had not entertained a very high opinion of *Weber's* talent for composition, it may be readily imagined I was not a little desirous of becoming acquainted with that opera, in order to ascertain thoroughly by what it had achieved such an enthusiastic admiration in the two capitals of Germany. My interest in it was increased the more from my having worked also a few years before, when at Frankfort on the Maine, upon the same materials, from *Appel's* book of apparitions, for an opera; and only abandoned the composition upon accidentally hearing that *Weber* was already engaged upon it. The nearer acquaintance with the opera, certainly did not solve for me the riddle of its enormous success; and I could alone account for it by *Weber's* peculiar gift and capacity for writing for the understanding of the mass. As I very well knew that this gift had been denied me by nature, it is difficult for me to explain how an unconquerable impulse should have led me nevertheless, to attempt dramatic composition anew. But so it was! Scarcely had I arrived home, than I took from my trunk, a half-forgotten work which I had begun in Paris. On a tedious rainy day which in that muddy city renders it impossible to go out of doors, I asked my landlady to lend me a book to read. She brought me an old, well-read romance: "La Veuve de Malabar." I found its interesting matter would well permit of being adapted to an opera, and I purchased it of her for a few sous, in order to make trial of it. While in Paris, and during the journey home I turned over in my mind the most favourable form for the composition of the opera, and began immediately after my return to Gandersheim to make the cast of a scene. In those hours when I did not feel disposed to work on the composition of the mass, I progressed with it, and by the time I removed with my family to Dresden, I had nearly completed it. I now reconsidered and worked over anew this sketch with renewed zeal, decided in the most precise manner everything that should take place in each scene, and then looked out for a poet who would feel disposed to write the opera according to this plan. Such a person I found in Mr. *Edward Gehe,* who readily entered into my ideas. In this manner originated the text of the opera "Jessonda." I was just on the point of beginning its composition, when an event took place that took off my attention from it again for some time.

One morning, in the beginning of December, *Carl Maria von Weber,* called upon me, and informed me that he had just received an invitation to Cassel, with the offer of the appointment of conductor of the orchestra at the newly-built court theatre there, but had decided upon declining it, as he was fully satisfied with his present position. Should he, however, **find** me disposed to apply for that post, he would in his reply to the letter, direct attention to me, and say that I was at present living in Dresden. As shortly before I had heard from a member of the Cassel orchestra who passed through Gandersheim much of the magnificence of the court theatre there and of the love of art of the elector *William* II. who had just entered upon the government, I could not doubt but that I should find there an important and pleasant sphere of action. I therefore accepted *Weber's* offer with many thanks, and before the lapse of a week, as a result of his reply, I received a letter from Mr. *Feige*, director-general of the Cassel court theatre, in which he offered me on the part of the elector the appointment of master of the court orchestra, and I was requested to send in my terms of acceptance by return of post. After I had consulted with *Weber* and my wife, I demanded: 1) the appointment for life, by rescript, at a salary of 2000 Thalers; 2) a leave of absence of from 6 to 8 weeks, every year; and 3) the assurance that the artistic direction of the opera should be made over to me exclusively. The whole of these stipulations were agreed to, but in return it was required of me that I should enter upon my post at the latest on the commencement of the new year. Overjoyed as we were at this new appointment, particularly *Dorette*, as she was thereby certain that she would be no more separated from her children for a long time, yet we were not altogether satisfied at having to leave our present residence so soon, where *Emilia* and *Ida* were making such progress, particularly in singing. We had besides taken our Dresden lodgings up to Easter, and a removal in the middle of winter was altogether very unpleasant. I therefore proposed that I should leave, to assume my place at Cassel, but that my wife and the children should remain in Dresden till the spring. Painful as was to her the separation from me for so long a time, she was compelled to admit the obvious convenience of my proposition. As the new year was now approaching, I therefore made the necessary preparations for my departure, and urged *Gehe* to work upon the matter for the second and third act of Jessonda, with all possible diligence, while I took the first act, which was ready, with me to Cassel.

Meanwhile another new and startling offer was made to me. Count *Salisch*, my old patron in Gotha, wrote word to me that the duchess had been informed I was now living in private at Dresden, and she was therefore desirous to know whether I might not be disposed to resume my old engagement, which, since the recent death of *Andreas Romberg*, was again vacant? Count *Salisch* added furthermore that they would be enabled to grant me a considerable increase of my former salary. Had I not already accepted the offer from Cassel, I might possibly have given this one the preference, in order to afford my wife the pleasure of a reunion with her mother and family by a return to her native town. But the choice was thus not permitted to me, and I might consider this rather in the light of a fortunate circumstance, as my sphere of action in Gotha would have been a very circumscribed one, in comparison with that in Cassel. In a few years also I should have again been left without a home, for the duke, and his successor also, prince *Frederick*, the last heir, died soon after each-other, and the state was divided among the other Saxon duchies. The orchestra was then pensioned off, and as I could not have endured to live in complete idleness, I should have soon removed again to some other place.

The parting from my wife and children, although for a short time only, was nevertheless a very sad one. *Dorette*, who wept bitterly, could alone be somewhat comforted by my promise to write every week and inform her of everything that I was doing. In Gotha, when on passing through I paid a visit to my mother-in-law, I was urgently pressed by her and the other relatives of my wife, as also by the members of the orchestra, to settle there once more. The duchess, also, to whom it was requisite I should pay a visit, as she had always evinced so much interest and kindness towards me, resorted to every means to make me give up Cassel, and offered to induce her brother the elector of Hesse to release me from my engagement. But as, since I had left Gotha, and looked about me in the world, the sphere of action in that place seemed to me too humble and restricted, I withstood every solicitation and made a speedy departure.

I had scarcely arrived in Cassel (New Year's Day 1822), than I was summoned to an interview with the elector, who received me with great kindness, and said many flattering things to me. Among other subjects he expressed the hope to see his opera become by my exertions one of the most celebrated of Germany, and requested me to make such propositions as were best calculated to effect that object. In order to do that I requested a fortnight's time, so that I might first make myself well acquainted with the means and materials at hand. After I had been present at a few rehearsals and performances, I then assumed my new post with the direction of *Winter's* "Opferfest." As the previous director of music, *Benzon*, had from all accounts, been so much wanting in authority, that the singers and the orchestra did not hesitate to oppose his regulations, which indeed led to his dismissal, I considered it immediately necessary to somewhat tighten the reins of discipline. I therefore became very strict at the rehearsals of the "Opferfest," but did not find the least disposition to resist either in the singers, or in the orchestra; and already in the first opera which I directed, succeeded in producing a better ensemble than they had hitherto been accustomed to. This was also generally aknowledged, and immediately procured for me the confidence of the elector, as also of the whole theatrical personnel. As I already found some excellent voices among the singers, viz. the first tenor *Gerstäcker* and the prima donna demoiselle *Dietrich,* and ascertained that *Feige* the director of the theatre was negotiating for the engagement of several other eminent artists, I limited for the present the proposals which I now sent in to the mere increase and improvement of the personnel of the chorus and orchestra. The latter consisted in part of civilian musicians, and partly of musicians belonging to the band of the body-guard, among whom were several of great excellence. The elector had granted to the latter as well as to the civilian musicians a rescript of engagement for life, so that I could no longer carry out my notion of constituting the orchestra solely of civilian musicians, in order to avoid any collision between the military and the orchestral duties of the non-civilians. I hoped at least, however, to get rid of the objectionable regulations which obliged the military musicians to appear in full uniform, which upon my first visit to the theatre was a great eye-sore to me. But neither did I succeed in this, for upon my representing it to the elector he replied, "It is contrary to military etiquette for a soldier to appear before me otherwise than in full uniform;" and when I made answer that the close-fitting uniform made the orchestral duties more difficult, and that the high epaulettes in particular made it quite impossible for the violinists to hold their instrument in the proper way, he proposed to give the musicians a particular and convenient uniform without epaulettes, for the orchestral service, rather than give up his whim. He rejected also my then suggested proposal to give the civilian-musicians the same kind of uniform; and in this manner this party-coloured orchestra remained unchanged to the astonishment of all foreigners. until the year 1832, when the present elector became co-regent in the government.

But my propositions for the increase and improvement of the orchestra were all adopted, and I received instructions to engage some more good violinists, and some first-rate solo-players for the leading wind instruments. By this means the opportunity was afforded me of bringing my brother near to me once more, who, after the expiration of his engagement in Vienna had met with an engagement in the Berlin court orchestra. I was equally successful with my former pupil and friend *Hauptmann*, and both received a rescript of engagement for life. Some excellent musicians were soon found also for the wind instruments, and by this increase and by diligent study and exercise, the orchestra became one of the best in

Germany, and has so remained, in spite of all the personal changes until now (1853).

But I must revert to the year 1822. My accession to office was celebrated by the whole theatrical company, by a grand dinner, at which the two heads of the theatrical administration, the intendant Mr. *von Manger*, director of the police, and director-general *Feige* presided. Songs, speeches and toasts were sung and made in my honour, and I felt myself quite at home in a circle where I was met on every side with so much friendliness, and indeed in so hearty a manner. As the Elector, who in the first years of his rule was very generous, had made Messrs. *von Manger* and *Feige* grants of money for special performances for the relief of native and travelling musicians, this gave rise to brilliant and interesting soirées at both their houses. These meetings were enlivened by genius and wit, and there prevailed thereat a joviality which though somewhat free was yet decorous. I at first therefore frequented them with pleasure; but towards the time when I expected my family I gradually withdrew from them, partly because I was obliged to confess to myself that my wife would not quite approve of this circle and partly because I was fearful of endangering my official authority by a too companionable intercourse with the singers.

A few days after my arrival in Cassel I was presented to the Electress and her daughters, the Princesses *Caroline* and *Marie*, and was invited to their evening parties. At one of these I was requested to play some of my quartets, which I expressly practised beforehand with the most distinguished members of the the court-orchestra. Messrs. *Wiele*, solo violinist, *Barnbeck*, first violinist, and *Hasemann*, first violincellist (my former quartetist in Frankfort, who had been engaged at Cassel shortly before). These music parties, which were much spoken of, were probably the reason why the Elector, who, separated from his wife, never joined her evening circle, gave me the order to give a court-concert, in order to afford an opportunity for himself and the Countess *Reichenbach* to hear me play. This concert, for which I enlisted the services of all the talent among the singers and court-orchestra, was given in the grand saloon of the palace, before a brilliant company (in which of course the Electress did not appear, as the Countess *Reichenbach* occupied her place), and as it was the first at the new court, it made a great sensation. It was, however, the only one for a long time, as the Elector and the Countess took but little interest in concert music.

By the wish of the orchestra I assumed also the direction of the concerts which they gave in the new town-hall saloon, and appeared also at one of them as solo player. In the first years their receipts were divided, as they had previously been, among the members of the orchestra; but later, upon my proposition, they were appropriated to a relief-fund for the widows and the families of deceased members of the orchestra, and managed by a committee according to rules and regulations devised for that purpose. This relief fund, which from that period was supplied from the receipts from the concerts given every winter by the court orchestra and those from the performance of an oratorio on Good Fridays, is still in existence (1853), and in the course of years has alleviated the distress of many widows and orphans of the members of the orchestra. But for several years past the concerts have been no more given in the town-hall, but in the court theatre, from the time the former Elector became patron of the institution, who, as little as the present Elector, could make up his mind to be present at a concert given anywhere else than in the theatre.

* * *

(Resumed in April 1858 after a pause of five years.)

(In this continuation, of the Journal, written in *Spohr's* seventy-fifth year, the manuscript would no longer permit of being printed *so verbally* as previously, and here and there, to avoid too much prolixity, it was necessary to make *omissions*. Some *gaps*, nevertheless, which required filling up have been so far completed only as the citation of *Spohr's own words* in letters written to absent friends, would permit of, — so that the reader may rely upon the subject matter as faithfully given and that *only Spohr himself speaks, without any additions from the pen of others*, up to the mournful period (June 1858) when his biographical notes, which reach to the year 1838, break off altogether.)

Shortly after my arrival in Cassel, I was invited by the countess *Hessenstein* to a music-party. I there met several dilettanti of the town, who all sang, though in their own very bad style only. As nevertheless some of them had the gift of good voices, it suggested of me the idea of directing my exertions on that side also, and beginning by the institution of a choral society. I therefore formed an acquaintance with some of the singers, communicated my plan to them, and we immediately arranged to meet on an early day in order to consult further upon the steps necessary to be taken. As result of this meeting a code of regulations was draw up, and as early as the 22nd March following an invitation was sent round to the dilettanti of Cassel, signed by myself, Mr. *von Steuber*, and secretary *Knyrim*, to join the society we were about to establish under the name of the "Society of St. Cecilia," in order, "after the example of the majority of the larger towns of Germany, to strive here also towards the same noble aim, to awaken and cultivate a pure and correct taste for music of an exalted and earnest character." As the enterprise met with a cordial welcome, the society was soon formed, and upon its opening began first with the study of *Mozart's* incomparable *Ave Verum*, then with *Haydn's* Hymns of Thanks, and *Mozart's* first mass, followed by a *Salve Regina* by *Hauptmann*, a charmingly beautiful composition in the real, pious ecclesiastical style. Meanwhile the number of members had increased to more than fifty, and such satisfactory progress was made in the weekly rehearsals, that already in the first year of its institution the society performed several times in the catholic church accompanied by the organ, during divine service, masses by *Hauptmann* and others.

In the theatre also, after I had got to know the singers and orchestra more intimately, my sphere of action began to extend itself. The first quite new work studied under my direction was the opera "Zemira and Azor," which I had written at Frankfort, and which was first performed on the 24th March. A young, talented singer, Miss *Canzi*, who was just then on a professional visit to Cassel, sang the part of Zemira, and *Gerstäcker*, the then much admired first tenor of our stage, the part of Azor. As the other characters of the opera were also well represented, it could not fail to be as well received here as at Frankfort, so that not only was it repeated during *Canzi's* stay, a few days afterwards, but also immediately studied by her successor, Miss *Roland*, and given several times during the course of the year with great applause. But far more pleasure than from the enthusiastic approbation of the public, did I receive from the circumstance that the opera pleased me, who had not heard it for two years, and I was a still more severe judge of my later productions. I was also now more than ever convinced, that this, like many of my compositions required to be given in strict accordance with the spirit of the work to please the non-connoisseur as well; and that my music, if negligently played, can readily be so spoiled, that the connoisseur himself would be at a loss to understand it. Meanwhile, in the beginning of March 1822 my family arrived under the protection of my brother *Ferdinand*, who had fetched them from Dresden on his way here from Berlin, and we removed together to the house I had hired in the Bellevue. Once more settled down in the domestic circle I immediately began to compose the new opera "Jessonda," and finished it in December of the same year. [In a letter written to *Speyer* of Frankfort on 26th January 1823, he says: "I have been latterly so much engaged upon a new opera that I have somewhat neglected everything else. It is now ready, and I am right glad to have completed so important a work. If I expect more from this opera than from the earlier ones, it is because of my greater experience, and the inspiration I felt in the study of almost every 'number' of the successfully written libretto. In order to devote myself to the work in my hours of inspiration only, I have allowed myself also more time with this than with all the former ones."] Some "numbers" from it — the overture, an air of Jessonda's, and the well-known duet between Amazili und Nadori — were performed the very same winter at the subscription concerts, and my daughter *Emilia* gained much applause in them. The entire opera was first represented upon our stage on the birthday of the Elector, the 28th July, in the following summer, and was received with general acclamation. [In a letter of the 2nd August 1823, appears, further: "You wish to hear from me something respecting the first representation of 'Jessonda;' it is a subject scarcely becoming me to write upon, for without wishing to do so, I must nevertheless speak in praise of it. The effect was great! It is the fashion here, upon birthdays to receive the court only with applause, and then the opera is listened to without any *loud* demonstration of approbation. It should also have been so now; but already before the end of the first act a storm of applause burst forth, and etiquette was forgotten for the rest of the evening. The performance was excellent. *Gerstäcker*, Miss *Roland*, *Hauser* were grand. Miss *Braun* was endurable at least, and better than in other characters. The chorus and orchestra, scenery, dances, spectacle combats, storm, decorations, costume, every thing, was excellent. . . . This work has made me very happy, and I have reason to hope that the opera will please much in other places."]

From the windows of our house on the Bellevue we had a very fine view across the meadows into the valley, which is enlivened by the Leipzic high-road, and the beauty of the country induced us to take frequent walks in the charming environs of Cassel. In these walks we were mostly attracted by the numerous villas situated in gardens, outside the Wilhelmshöhe, and also of the Cologne gate; and as we began to like this part very much, we soon felt the wish, also, to have such a house with garden as we had already once rented in Gotha, that we might call our own property. When therefore in our rambles any one of these particularly took our fancy. I often made enquiries whether the owner was disposed to sell it, but was frequently answered in the negative, until at length a small country-house outside the Cologne gate, close to the town and not far from the theatre, in a quiet neighbourhood surrounded on all sides by gardens, was offered to me to purchase. As the price asked for it did not exceed the amount of my small savings placed with the firm of *William Speyer* of Frankfort, I concluded the purchase of it at once, and already in the autumn we moved into the newly-acquired property and had the pleasure of gathering forthwith a good harvest of fruit and vegetables. The only thing I missed in the new house was a spacious music room. I therefore had a partition wall removed that separated two rooms on the first floor, and by that means gained a sufficiently roomy saloon for a quartet party, which, however, had the defect in an acoustic point of view, of being too low; for which reason I proposed to myself at a later period to erect a building with a music room.

Our pretty quiet country-house incited me anew to fresh compositions, and so I first wrote a third quartet to the two already begun in Dresden, which were published by *Peters* of Leipzic as Op. 58. In order to have this quartet heard and the former ones, I established here also a quartet circle, at which, in turn with some other families who were lovers of music, we gave three quartets every week, and concluded the evenings with a frugal supper. At first the quartet consisted of myself, Mr. *Wiele,* solo violinist, and subsequently concert-master of our court orchestra, of my brother *Ferdinand,* who took the viol, and of our excellent violincellist *Hasemann.* But as by degrees, both in the orchestra, and in this small circle, death made some vacancies, others were obliged to be substituted in their place, and then some time was always required until we obtained once more the old, customary ensemble again. In 1831 my brother was first snatched from us, then *Wiele,* and at last *Hasemann;* but their places were again filled by new members of our court orchestra, so that the quartet parties, which only took place in the winter months, never ceased entirely, and I myself up to quite recently (1858) played two quartets in each of them.

After I had completed the third quartet of Op. 58, a fancy seized me to carry out an idea I had long conceived, and of which, if I am not mistaken, *Andrew Romberg*, when we played a quartet together for the last time before his death, first spoke of, viz. to try my hand at a double quartet. The circumstance that *Romberg* had entertained the idea for several years without ever attempting it, incited me to it yet more, and I imagined to myself the manner in which he had also comprehended it, and how two quartet parties sitting close to each other, should be made to play *one* piece of music, and keep in reserve the eight-voice play for the chief-parts of the composition only. According to this idea, I also wrote my first double quartet (*B minor*), began the theme of the first allegro with both quartets *unisono*, and *forte*, in order to impress it well upon the hearers, and then carried it concerted through both quartets in turn. Of the families who belonged to the quartet circle, the marshal of the court *von der Malsburg* had the most spacious place, for which reason I waited until the turn came to him to give the quartet party, at which I then with the assistance of my best pupils and of a second violin-cellist from the orchestra, gave the new double quartet to our circle, to hear. I was greatly pleased to find that its effect was far greater than that of simple quartets and quintets, and as this kind of chamber music excited also great sensation abroad*, as was proved by its frequent performance, I expected nothing less than that the composers of that day would soon imitate it and make it general. But this was as little the case, as with some other extensions of the forms of art, which I

---

* The "Vienna Allgemeinen musikalischen Anzeiger," of the 14th March, said among other things, in announcing the publication by *Peters* [Op. 65] of this work: "To waste words in praising this double quartet, which all unite in admiring, would be carying coals to Newcastle."

have tried in later years, as for instance in the symphony for two orchestras: "Irdisches und Göttliches im Menschenleben," (The earthly and heavenly in human life, Op. 121) in the historical symphony (Op. 116), and the four-handed piano-forte accompaniment to some tenor songs. One single young composer only, of Lubeck, of the name of *Pape*, who was afterwards appointed violincellist in the orchestra of the theatre at Bremen, once sent me a double quartet in manuscript. He had great talent for composition, but found no opportunity of making his things known, and like so many young Germans, became desponding for want of the recognition of his talent. This has never been published, and thus my four double quartets remain the only ones of their kind. An octet for stringed instruments by *Mendelssohn-Bartholdy* belongs to quite another kind of art, in which the two quartets do not concert and interchange in double choir, with each other, but all eight instruments work together. This kind, although not so interesting as the double quartets, has been imitated; for the violincellist *Schuberth* of St. Petersburg published one of the kind at his brother's, the music-publisher's in Hamburg, which has been played by us in Cassel several times, and been well received.

At this time I was engaged besides on various other compositions: two pot-pourris on themes from "Jessonda" (Op. 64 and 66, at *Peter's* in Leipzic), one for violin, the other for violin and violincello, both of which I played in the course of the winter in our subscription concerts. I further composed a hymn to St. Cecilia, written by Miss *von Calenberg* for the festival of the 22nd November, which consisted of chorus with a brilliant soprano solo, the latter very well executed upon the occasion by my eldest daughter *Emilia*.*

For the celebration of this day, which our choral society did this year for the first time, a company of about 120 persons assembled, mostly friends of the members of the society,

---

* The manuscript remained unpublished for many years, and was only recently published bei *Luckhardt* in Cassel as Op. 97.

in the Austrian saloon, which had been handsomely decorated for the occasion, and ornamented with a life-size picture of St. Cecilia. The festival began with the hymn to St. Cecilia, after which a member delivered a discourse upon the musical art, and with the most flattering expression of the thanks and acknowledgements of the society, presented me with a valuable gift, consisting of two large bronze candelabra executed by the subsequently so celebrated sculptor *Henschel*, and ornamented with scenes from my three operas performed here. This was followed by a "Lord's Prayer" by *Feska*, the *Salve regina* by *Hauptmann*, and during the supper, some songs for male voices were sung. In the following year *Hauptmann* composed another hymn written Miss *von Calenberg* in celebration of the name-day of our holy patroness, and as this, together with my composition, met with the same general approbation, both these pieces of music were executed in turn upon all the subsequent celebratimes of the festival. The voluntary contributions which were collected upon these occasions were applied only to charitable purposes, and the celebration of the day although sometimes interrupted by some disturbances, continued to be observed up to a late period, sometimes on a more limited and at others on a more extensive scale.

In the following year (1824) I received an invitation from Councillor *Küstner*, who was then director of the Leipzic theatre, to bring out my opera of "Jessonda" upon that stage. [A letter of the 14th February furnishes an account of its successful performance there on the 9th of that month: "Upon entering the orchestra I was received with general acclamation, the overture was called for again with a loud and continued *da capo*. Every 'number' was received with lively applause, and four of them called for again, of which one was a chorus, the first of the 2nd act. The greatest, and really stormy enthusiasm, was created by the duet between Amazili and Nadori. After the conclusion of the first act a speaker stood up in a box on the first tier, and addressed me in a speech in which he charactesised me as a *true master* of *German art*, and called upon the audience to give me a "three times three"! This actually took place with a flourish of trumpets and kettle-drums in a tutti such as I thought would bring down the walls of the theatre. At the conclusion of the opera the same scene occurred, and the house rang with cries of "*da capo* Jessonda!" The day after the performance Councillor *Küstner* sent me double the amount of the honorarium agreed upon, and when upon my departure from the inn I was about to pay my bill, I found that it had been already settled. ... *Peters*, the publisher of the selections from it for pianoforte, declared to me also, that after *such a success* of the opera, the honorarium I had fixed was too small, and that I must now permit him to fix one for it."] On the 14th June of the same year, the opera was also produced at Frankfort, for the first time, and after that on the stage of all the principal theatres of Germany.

Some time afterwards I received the command from the Elector to write a new opera to celebrate the marriage of his daughter the Princess *Marie* with the Duke of Saxe-Meiningen, which was to take place in the spring of 1825. The subject I had before proposed in Vienna to *Theodore Körner* to arrange for me, *Musäus's* tale of the "Rübezahl," now came into my mind, and I therefore applied to Mr. *Edward Gehe* in Dresden, who had written the libretto of "Jessonda" so much to my satisfaction. But as I could not send to him a clear outline of the scenes for the opera, not being myself as yet well decided respecting the working-up of the materials, his fancy could not assist him in the matter, and he sent me a libretto that did not all come up with my ideas, and to which I did not at all feel myself inclined to compose. I now called to mind my former kettle-drummer in the Frankfort orchestra, the already-mentioned *George Döring*, who was at the same time a literary man, and who since then had made himself known by several successful novels. I therefore addressed myself to him, and explained my views respecting the working-up of the "Rübezahl," particularly pointing out to him, that as I intended this to be a grand opera, it would not be necessary to write it in rhyming verse. In *Gehe's* "Rübezahl" there were many things both shallow and inappropriate, and which appeared to me as caused by the shackles imposed upon the author by the rhyme, and this *Döring*, by my express wish, was to avoid altogether. Although this has been greatly objected to, I am nevetherless of opinion that the want of the rhyme in my opera "Der Berggeist," although it does not fulfill all that could be desired, is the least to be blamed for it. Although *Döring's* libretto was neither altogether to my mind, yet there was no time to be lost, and less so, since this was not the only work the elector had requested me to prepare for the celebration of the marriage. I had besides to compose a grand march with introduction of the melody of the old German ballad: "Und als der Grossvater die Grossmutter nahm," together with a torchight-dance for fifty-three trumpeters, and two pair of kettledrummers (for these were the numbers to be found in the music bands of the army of the Elector of Hesse); and as for the sake of the modulation I was obliged to take various tones of the trumpets, and the trumpeters of the bands not being very musical, I was obliged to practise them also beforehand in this torch-light-dance.

At the end of the year, nevertheless, I was ready with all these compositions, and could now proceed to the study of the "Berg-Geist." Our first tenor *Gerstäcker*, who had been ill for some time past, had meanwhile become worse, and his malady had taken so sad a turn, that all likelihood of his being able to sing was out of the question, and we were now without a first tenor. The Elector therefore gave orders to invite some foreign singer to perform for a series of nights in his place, and we were so successful as to engage for several weeks the services of the tenorist *Cornet* of Hamburg, who was then in great repute, together with his betrothed, Miss *Kiel* of Sondershausen, who undertook the first soprano part in the new opera. Scarcely, however, had I begun the study of the work by our own theatrical company, than I received from

Spontini an invitation that very much surprised me, viz. to proceed to Berlin, to direct the first representation there of the opera of "Jessonda," fixed for the 4th of February, and to preside myself at the two last grand rehearsals. *Spontini*, who must often have seen himself reproached in the Berlin newspapers, for giving nothing but his own operas, and witholding other meritorious works from that stage, might have come to the idea of meeting that reproach in the most signal manner by inviting the composer of "Jessonda." But in reality he did not seem to trouble himself much in furthering the representation of the opera; for as soon as, having obtained leave of absence, I arrived at Berlin, and waited upon *Spontini*, he received me in a very friendly manner, it is true, but informed me that the preparatory-rehearsals even had not yet been begun, and that he had sent me the invitation without the previous knowledge of the intendant of the royal theatre, Count *Brühl*. I now first sought to soften the sensitiveness of the latter on the score of such a neglect, and in order not to be obliged to return home without having effected anything, I then consulted with him on all that was necessary to expedite the representation of the opera.

In the preparatory rehearsals which now took place, I had the satisfaction of finding that the principal parts were in good hands: *Bader* and *Blume* as Nadori and Tristan, and Mdmes. *Schulze* and *Seidler* as Jessonda and Amazili, were excellent singers; the part of Dandau also was well filled by Mr. *Krause*, and that of Lopez, which had at first been given to a comic singer, by which the serious character of the opera would have been damaged, was taken by the baritone *Devrient*, after I had agreed to make some alterations in the recitatives. The opera could thus have been soon placed on the repertory, when *Bader* suddenly fell ill, and after his convalesence Mrs. *Seidler*, being seized with a hoarseness occasioned some obstruction. As the term of my leave of absence was nearly at an end, I made application for an extension of it. But the Elector had felt himself aggrieved by the obstacles thrown in my way by *Spontini* and the Berlin intendance, and he allowed me but a few days more, after the expiration of which I was to return, whether the opera was brought out or not. Fortunately, Mdme. *Seidler* got better; I could now therefore direct in person the first representation of "Jessonda" in Berlin, and be witness to its very favourable reception. Immediately after, I left, and travelled three whole nights without resting, in order to regain the time lost.

The two singers from Hamburg had arrived in the meantime, and had already performed with great applause; I could therefore begin the stage rehearsals of the "Berg-Geist" at once. But between whiles I received furthermore the elector's order to arrange choruses for the prologue to the opera, in which were to be introduced some popular Thuringian melodies. To effect this I applied to my pupil *Grund*, concertmaster at Meiningen, who procured for me the desired melodies, which I then made use of in the work as well as they would admit of it.

On the 23th March 1825, the marriage took place in the palace of Bellevue. On the procession of the new-married pair and their suite from the dining-hall to the white saloon, the orchestra played my march, which had a good effect, and at the part where the "Grossvater-Lied" was introduced was very pretty. The Elector, and the Duke (who was decidedly more musical than his father-in-law) both congratulated me much upon the grand march, which, at their request, was played a second time. The reception of the married couple at the festive representation on the following evening in the theatre, was a very brilliant and noisy one; for I ordered the fifty-three trumpeters and the two pair of kettle-drummers whom I had placed up in the gallery to join in with the acclamations and vivats of the audience! The festive-prologue written by counsellor *Niemeyer* followed; then my new opera "Der Berg-Geist," which in truth was received by the thronged and brilliantly lighted house with as much boisterous applause as "Jessonda," but which neither pleased me so much, nor was so popular on other stages as the latter. The Elector, who was very satisfied with all I had written for the occasion, sent for me the next-day, thanked me, and presented me with a very handsome snuff-box, upon the lid of which, though somewhat unsuitable for a musician, was a very artistic chasing representing a combat of cavalry, set and framed under glass. But — and that was the best part of it — it was filled with Friedrich's-d'or, and therefore a handsome and princely gift.

A few months afterwards Councillor *Küstner* sent for my new opera to Leipzic, and in September the first representation of it on that stage took place. [A letter of the 18th September speaks of it in the following manner: "The day before yesterday "Der Berg-Geist" was launched here with the greatest success ... The *mise en scene* was more brilliant than was ever known before in Leipzic, and some of the scenes were more beautiful than any I had ever yet seen. The scene-painter *Gropius* is in a fair way to become the first in the world; neither in Italy, Paris nor London have I ever seen anything so charming as the closing-scene of the second act. ... The reception the opera met with, was the most flattering I had ever yet experienced. ... The performance may be said to have been a very successful one. With the exception of one error in the overture, and one obstinate rock which would not come up out of the earth, nothing went wrong. On the stage, almost all did better than in Cassel, particularly the Berg-Geist *(Köckert)* and Oscar *(Vetter)*. ... The orchestra, although far inferior to ours, was unusually good."]

In the summer of 1825 an aimable young man, *Frederick Curschman* of Berlin, came to Cassel to perfect himself under my guidance as a musician. Although he had begun the study of jurisprudence at Göttingen, he thought nevertheless of giving up the law, and had already tried his hand with success at various kinds of literature, particularly in songs, which he sung with a pleasing baritone voice, and thereby introduced himself into our musical circle. As his musical education was still imperfect, I advised him to apply first to *Hauptmann*, who at my request had undertaken to instruct my violin pupils in the theory of music, and shown great skill in that capacity. *Curschmann* also immediately joined our society of St. Cecilia, and became a very valuable member of it, as he not only sang the bass soli very well at sight, but frequently took the pianoforte accompaniment, and did the duty of a librarian with great zeal. Together with some of our best dilettanti he formed also an opera circle, in which for the first time were produced several of his compositions which afterwards became such favorites, and parts of his little opera "Die Todten, oder Abdul und Erinnieh," which was brought out at a later period upon the stage here. He thus in many ways enlivened the culture of art in our town, and soon became the favorite of the musical world.

In the same year Councillor *Rochlitz*, the editor of the Leipzic Musical Journal, offered me the text of an Oratorio: "Die letzten Dinge," to compose for; which I received with great pleasure, as my previous attempt in that style of art, "Das jüngste Gericht," the oratorio performed at Erfurt, by no means pleased me any longer, and therefore I had not once been disposed to perform a single "number" of it at the meetings of our society. I now began with new studies of counter-point, and of the ecclestiastic style, and set zealously to work on the composition, in which I followed the prescriptions of the author which he had forwarded to me with the text, in respect to its treatment, and which I not only strictly adhered to, but found of assistance to me. The first part of the oratorio was thus soon ready, and as early as the end of November I could give it with the members of our choral society, at a concert in behalf of the sufferers from the fire that had occurred shortly before at Seesen; although it is true, with pianoforte accompaniment only. On that occasion, I observed with great pleasure, that it made a deep impression upon the assistants, as well as upon all the auditory, and this observation was of the more importance to me, as it convinced me that I had found the proper style for this kind of work. I had in particular striven to be very simple, religious, and true in expression, and carefully to avoid all artistic trickery, all bombast and every thing of difficult execution. With increased zest I now proceded to compose the second part, so that the whole work was finished by the following Good Friday (1826) and then first performed complete in the Lutheran church. [A letter of the 26th March speaks of it in the following manner: "Yesterday was a great day of festival for the lovers of music here; for never yet had so solemn a musical performance as my oratorio taken place in Cassel. It was in the evening, and the church was lighted up. My son-in-law *Wolff*, who had been long in Rome, proposed to illuminate the church as at Rome on Good Friday, with lights disposed overhead in the form of a cross, and carried out his idea. A cross fourteen feet long, covered with silver-foil, and hung with six hundred glass lamps, was suspended overhead in the middle of the church, and diffused so bright a light that one could everywhere clearly read the text-books. The musicians and singers, nearly two hundred in number, were placed in the gallery of the church, arranged in rows one above the other, and for the most part unseen by the auditory, which, amounting to nearly two thousand persons, observed a solemn stillness. My two daughters, Messrs. *Wild*, *Albert* and *Föppel*, together with an amateur, sang the soli, and the performance was faultless. The effect was, I must myself say, extraordinary. Never did I before experience such satisfaction from the performance of one of my greater works! I had always had to lament either an imperfect execution, an unsuccessful effect, or something else. This time it was quite different. The work, also, is simple and easy, and yet not less comprehensive in contents, than the others.] The visibly deep impression that the oratorio made upon the public may also have been yet further assisted by the solemn grandeur of the illuminated cross-which harmonized greatly with the religious sentiment inspired by the day. The elector only was not pleased with the selection of the Lutheran church and its "catholic illumination." as he called the cross, and he ordered that the orchestra should give their future Good Friday concerts in the court and garrison church, lit up with chandeliers to be furnished from the electoral household lighting department.

Shortly afterwards I received an invitation from my London friend *Ferdinand Ries*, who had returned to Germany, and was then living in the neighbourhood of Godesberg on the Rhine, to direct personally my new oratorio at the Rhenish musical festival at Düsseldorf, the arrangements for which had been confided to him. Although the Rhenish musical festival was held at Whitsuntide, and therefore at a time when our theatrical vacation had not yet begun, and I therefore required to obtain an express permission to do so, I nevertheless succeeded in obtaining it immediately, for the Elector felt himself flattered when his director of music was invited to important musical performances, and thereby acquired honour and fame.

While therefore I prepared to set out with my whole family, except *Ida* (who, in the meanwhile, had married Professor *Wolff*,) four of the most ardent lovers of music here, Mr. *Curschmann*, the referendary *Charles Pfeiffer*, Mrs. *von der Malsburg* and her friend Miss *von Heister*, made up their minds to join us, and like us to travel by post, in order to be able to put up at dinner-time, and at night at the same places. Favoured by the finest weather, we set out on our journey on the 9th May 1826, and as the carriages always kept close together, we exchanged places in them sometimes, always took our meals together, and our pleasant and spirited conversation was not at all interrupted, so that I never recollect having made a more agreeable journey.

On the third day we were met three miles from Düsseldorf by the festival committee and the family of the State-Councillor *von Sybel*, at whose house I and the members of my family were to stop; and scarcely had we arrived at Düsseldorf, than we were welcomed by the choral-society with a serenade. At the first general rehearsal, which was held on the following morning, I had the satisfaction of finding that my oratorio had been carefully and correctly studied by the different societies, and was sung with an enthusiastic feeling for the work. I could not feel so content with the orchestra, which had been gathered together from different places, and in which dilettanti assisted, and among others, my friend *Thomae* from Cleves, among the wind instruments. It was therefore a difficult matter to bring all the instruments to the same pitch, and it could only be effected by great patience and frequent repetitions. In the afternoon of the same day, the rehearsal of the performances for the second day was held, which *Ries* conducted. At it were given a new symphony by *Ries* (manuscript *D* major), a Sanctus and a Credo from a mass by *Frederick Schneider*, the jubilee overture of *Carl Maria von Weber*, and lastly, a selection of the finest "numbers" from *Handel's* "Messiah." As Miss *Reinigen* of Crefeld, the solo singer, was taken suddenly ill, my daughter *Emilia* was obliged to take the soprano part also in the vocal performances. But so diligently did she study it, that already at the very first rehearsal she went through the business right well, and by her aid all derangement of the festival was obviated. But so much the greater was *Ries's* difficulty with the wind instruments in his symphony. He nevertheless displayed in the matter great patience, and dealt very leniently with the awkwardness of the dilettanti. On the following day were held two more rehearsals of the performances for the first and second day of Whitsuntide (the 14th and 15th May), which then, after such careful rehearsals passed off without a fault. My oratorio was received with such enthusiasm by those who played and by the auditory, that on the evening of the very first day, the prolongation of the festival was mooted in order to repeat once more "Die letzten Dinge" for the benefit of the Greeks. This was publicly announced on the second day of the performances, and the majority of the strangers present stopped in order to be present at its repetition. Thus my work had the honour conferred upon it of a second performance, of which I might well be proud, as since then so far as I know of, such a thing has never happened to any work given at the Rhenish musical festivals. In the musical journals, also, there appeared several very favourable notices of my oratorio, and I therefore hastened to publish selections from it for the pianoforte. But the edition I issued was soon sold off, and a second was therefore published afterwards by *Simrock* of Bonn, who also brought out the song parts with it, by which the performances of the work in almost all the towns of Germany, Holland and Switzerland was very much facilitated. I could therefore be very content with the reception of this oratorio, and frequently as it was performed and spoken of, no voice was ever heard raised in condemnation of it.

In the course of this year I wrote besides a second quintet (*B* flat minor, Op. 69, published by *Peters*) and three quartets (Op. 74, also by *Peters*). But I now longed to begin a greater work, and particularly an opera, although the "Berg-Geist" acquired no extensive popularity, since, after the representations in Cassel and Leipzic, it was only given at Prague, where it met several times with a brilliant reception. As *Curschmann* at the same time entertained a similar desire, he had requested his fellow-traveller and friend, *Charles Pfeiffer*, who at that time had begun to make himself a name as a poet, to work up a novel of *Tieck's*, "Pietro von Abano" as an opera text. He may however have felt himself not yet quite sufficiently advanced in his musical culture, and therefore when *Pfeiffer* had completed the first act of the libretto, he abandoned his project of attempting so soon a grand opera. He now offered me the composition of Pietro, and as the novel, as well as the manner in which it had been worked up, pleased me greatly, I soon came to an arrangement with both gentlemen respecting it, and in February 1827, set to work very assiduously upon it, and completed it in August of the same year. The opera occasioned me anxiety at first, on account of the immediate succession of two scenes — a funeral, and the pranks of a band of merry students — so strikingly dissimilar and incongruous as to render their proximity unpleasant: neither did I as all like the speaking part of the bishop, without any singing. But as this part was taken by *Seydelmann*, who was then engaged at our theatre from pure interest he took in the work, and was performed in a very dignified manner, I became more satisfied with it, and had the gratification of finding that it made a deep impression upon the performers, the orchestra, and my musical friends who were permitted to assist at the rehearsals. On its first representation, on the 13th October 1827, it was also received by the public with a similar enthusiasm to "Jessonda," and I had therefore reason to hope that like it also, it would soon obtain popularity beyond Cassel. But when at the request of the directors of some other theatres I forwarded the book to them, I soon found that not only did the catholic towns disapprove of the introduction of the bishop and the ecclesiastical forms on the stage, but the intendants of theatres in protestant towns, also, and among others, Count *Brühl* in Berlin, who rejected the opera, because they had some scruples about the contents. At that time it is true, many of the later operas and plays, which since then have hardened the public against all objectionable matter, had not become the fashion of the day. But *Meyerbeer*, who now wanted to hear the opera with all these circumstances of form, expressed himself in regard to it in the following manner in a letter of the 4. March 1828: "I cannot conclude my letter without thanking you for the pleasure that the perusal of the score of your master-piece "Pietro von Abano," which Mr. *Schlesinger* lent to me, has afforded me, and I am happy to be able to say, that in particular the first act, the first finale (although only furnished by the poet with two personages), the scene between Antonio and the half-lifeless Cecilia in the second act, and the ingenious manner in which the stringed instruments, half *con sordini*, half *senza sordini*, shadow forth the dialogue between the living Antonio and the spirit-like Cecilia; the imposing finale of the second act; and besides these, numerous other features of splendid dramatic intention, excellent declamation, novel, picturesque instrumentation and harmony, have truly charmed me, and excited in me the most ardent desire to be present at a performance of your master-piece."

In the year 1828, I wrote my second double-quartet, and endeavoured to bring it nearer to my first idea of the double choral style, than the first: in this I succeeded to my own satisfaction. I played it for the first time publicly in one of our winter-concerts of December, with great applause, and it soon found the same appreciation and publicity in other places as the previous one. Shortly afterwards I received an invitation to conduct my oratorio "Die letzten Dinge" at a musical festival that was to take place at Halberstadt on the 4th June 1828, and I set out this time accompanied only by my wife and my youngest daughter *Theresa*, as shortly before, my daughter *Emilia* had married a manufacturer of the name of *Zahn*, and could leave her domestic concerns as little as *Ida*.

My oratorio was excellently performed by the different choral-societies that had been invited for that purpose, as they were all enthusiastic admirers of it, and gave it the preference over all other works then performed.

At the second concert I played my new concertino in *A* major (Op. 79, published by *Schlesinger*), and I think that, upon the same occasion, also, my just finished third symphony in *C* minor (Op. 78, also published by *Schlesinger*) was then performed for the first time. One circumstance, the remembrance of which is still impressed upon my memory, and which relates to my daughter *Theresa*, then nine years old, I must yet relate. I took the child with me to all the rehearsals, as she would always attend those at Düsseldorf, and I augured from that, a great love for music. In Halberstadt *Theresa* expressed especial pleasure in the concluding "number" of the oratorio, and as that was a fugue on the words: "His is the kingdom, the power, and glory." I furthermore concluded that she had not only a strong sentiment for music generally, but also for its graver forms, and I even imparted to *Dorette* the pleasure I felt at the happy disposition of our child. But when I questioned *Theresa* more closely respecting her preference for the fugue, I was informed to my great surprise and to my shame, "that she only liked the piece of music in question better than all the rest, because she knew, that, as at Dusseldorf, the rehearsal would soon be over, and that then we should *go home to dinner!*" — Shortly afterwards I received from the parties who got up this musical festival a permanent, and more gratifying cause to remember the same; for they sent me, as a mark of their gratitude, a costly table-clock, ornamented with appropriate emblems, and bearing on the pedestale an inscription, with the date.

In the course of the year I wrote three more violin-quartets, which were published by *Schlesinger* as Op. 82, after which, as I was not very successful with my operas upon other stages, I turned once more to church music, and in the spring of 1829, wrote my "Lord's prayer," on the text of *Mahlmann*. The effect which this work produced at its first performance, although only with pianoforte accompaniment, on the festival of St. Cecilia the same year, was greatly increased, when a few months afterwards it was given at one of our winter-concerts with full orchestral accompaniment. It was not only received here in Cassel upon every repetition up to more recent times, with great approbation, but it soon found much approval in other places also.

On the 4th June 1829, another musical festival took place at Nordhausen, to which I was also invited. Of the first day's performance I have nevertheless, now no clear recollection; but on the second day I played with *Müller* of Brunswick, with *Wiele* of this place, and with *Maurer* of Hannover, a concertante for four violins, of the composition of the latter. For myself, I chose to play the fourth, on the occasion, as my Stradivari-violin had a particularly good tone on the *G* string, and as we had practised together that celebrated piece of music very assiduously, the applause was quite extraordinary. My new clarinet-concerto in *E flat*, which I had written for *Hermstedt* for this musical festival, met with no less approbation, but it is no longer in my possession, neither do I now know whether it is still in existence. During our stay in Nordhausen, we lived in the house of a Mr. *Fleck*, a merchant, whose wife was a very amiable hostess. One day at dinner, *Edward Grund* my former pupil, was prompted to propose a toast to her, in doing which he introduced the observation that she "was anything but a Fleck* in human society, but much rather to be called a gleam of light." I also remember still with pleasure the beautiful weather that favoured the dinner which the people of Nordhausen gave to their guests upon a neighbouring hill which commanded a view of the town. The collation was spread upon the greensward, and as good wine was by no means wanting, the company soon became very merry, and returned to town in the best possible humour.

In August 1829, I wrote a solo-quartet in *E major* (Op. 83, published by *Schlesinger*). But my desire to try my fortune once more with an opera gave me no rest, and I therefore persuaded my friend *Charles Pfeiffer* to work up for me the subject of a Spanish novel by *Washington Irving*, that seemed to me very attractive, and in every respect adapted for an opera. But as *Pfeiffer's* name could not be mentioned in the playbills, as in the electorate of Hesse it is not considered becoming for a servant of the state to occupy himself with poetical works together with his official duties, the indetectable name of *Schmidt* was chosen instead of his; just as when "Pietro" was brought out the author's name was not mentioned, as *Feige*, then the director of the theatre, did not like to be responsible to the Elector and the public for permitting a fictitious name proposed by me to be placed upon the playbill. — In October 1829, I, therefore, with my usual zeal, with

---

*) Fleck, in the German language, signifies, a spot, stain, or blemish.

every new work, set about the composition of the opera of the "Alchymist," completed it in April of the following year, and immediately distributed the parts, in order to perform it on the 28th July, the birthday of the Elector. It pleased here in Cassel quite as much as my previous operas, but out of Hesse was represented at Prague only, though with great approbation;* while the selections made from it for the pianoforte, arranged by my brother *Ferdinand*, found a more widespread publicity.

In June 1830 *Paganini* came to Cassel and gave two concerts in the theatre, which I heard with great interest. His left hand, and his constantly pure intonation were to me astonishing. But in his compositions, and his execution I found a strange mixture of the highly genial and childishly tasteless, by which one felt alternately charmed and disappointed, so that the impression left as a whole was, after frequent hearing, by no means satisfactory to me. As his visit took place just on Whitsunday, I took him the next day to Wilhelmshöhe, where he dined with me, and was very lively, indeed somewhat extravagantly so.

A few months afterwards the revolution of July broke out in France, and as a general excitement had extended itself to Germany also, symptoms of discontent with the public authorities showed themselves also here in Cassel. Just previously, the Elector had gone to Vienna, accompanied by the Countess

---

*) In the Vienna "Musicalischer Anzeiger" of the 23rd January 1834 is the following notice respecting it: "All who have had the opportunity of hearing and judging for themselves, know and feel that the esteemed maestro, in all his dramatic compositions, with the exception of the single, purely genial "Faust," introduces his hearers less into the wondrous realm of fancy, than he leads them like a true friend, by pleasant meandering paths through the charming and balmy groves of harmony. This work also, breathes the same calm, reflective spirit that speaks to the heart, the same pure taste, the same style, as noble as it is elegant, the same constancy, unity and well-sustained interior connection, that so particularly characterizes all the works of this perhaps most substantial of all living composers, and which distinguish also no less this musical creation."

Reichenbach, with the object, as it was believed, of effecting at the Austrian court the elevation of that personage to the dignity of a princess. He had afterwards repaired to Carlsbad, and from there came all manner of strange reports about his serious illness, resulting from some personal conflicts with the Countess *Reichenbach*, on account of which, his physician Mr. *Heräus*, proceeded to Carlsbad, but not having been admitted to an audience, returned to Cassel. A deputation from the members of the privy council was hereupon sent to Carlsbad; was received several times by the elector, and brought back intelligence that he would shortly return to his capital. Before this took place however, on the evening of the 6th September, disturbancees broke out. I was at the moment with my wife at the theatre, where *Raupach's* comedy "Der Zeitgeist" was being performed, and I remarked on a sudden, that messengers had been sent to the officers who were present, informing then that "the alarm" had been sounded in the town, and upon this they all immediately left. This created so much sensation in the house, that the rest of the audience thought that nothing less than a great fire had broken out in the town, and they also left the house in the midst of the performance. Fearing for the safety of our own and our children's dwellings, we went out with the rest, and were at length informed that the excited people had riotously attacked several bakers' shops, and committed depredation in the houses of the owners, because, notwithstanding the fall that had taken place in the price of corn, they had raised the price of bread. In order to prevent further excesses on the part of the populace, a number of the citizens had, with the consent of the ministry, taken up arms, and the military occupied not only the electoral palace, but the Königstrasse and the Friederichsplatz, so that the people leaving the theatre could not pass through the closed streets. We were therefore compelled to make a circuit to reach our house and when arrived there, dared not retire to rest at the usual hour, as the commotion that prevailed in the town was still very great.

The Elector did not return till the 12th September, but at first unaccompanied by the Countess *Reichenbach*, and with the greatest privacy. He immediately proceeded to Wilhelmshöhe, whither, a few days after, the magistracy with chief-burgomaster *Schomburg* at their head, followed him, to express their pleasure at his convalescence and return; as also to petition him to assemble the estates, which had not been done since 1815, and to advise with them upon the alleviation of many existing grievances. The magistracy was nevertheless not admitted to an audience till the following morning in the electoral palace at Cassel, during which, half the town had collected on the Friedrichsplatz, in order to ascertain immediately whether the result of the deputation was successful, and if such should be the case the master-cooper *Herbold*, had agreed to make it known to the people by waving a white handkerchief from the window of the chamber of audience. When therefore the deputation in solemn procession from the Ober-Neustädter town-hall, approached the palace, and had crossed its threshold, all eyes were directed to the windows of the audience-chamber, and the decision was anxiously awaited.

The Elector, to whose ears doubtless many disquieting reports had come, and who could place no dependance on his troops (many of whom, as at a latter period was shown, desired a constitution) for the protection of his palace and the successful suppression of the revolution, gave, to the universal joy of the people a satisfactory reply. Scarcely had the waving of the white handkerchief announced this to the populace, than the assembled thousands upon the Friedrichsplatz rent the air with deafening cheers of Long live the Elector! upon which he shewed himself for a moment at one of the windows, and acknowledged them with several bows. In the evening the town was spontaneously illuminated, and at the theatre, instead of the previously announced piece of the "Ahnfrau" the "Barber of Seville" was chosen, and the public in their delight at the appearance of the Elector and his son before the beginning of the opera, greeted him with tumultuous cheers, and struck up the "Hail to the elector Wilhelm." This was followed on the 19th of September by the promised summoning of the ancient estates of Hesse, consisting of deputies from the nobles, the towns, the universities and the peasanty, who assembled on the 16th October, and immediately promulgated a satisfactory report to the people. On the following day the opening of the assembly of the states was celebrated by the performance of divine service in the great church, and by command of the government by a solemn choral hymn sung by the society of St. Cecilia accompanied by the court orchestra. For this occasion I selected the last "number" of my cantata composed in Vienna, "Die Befreiung Deutschlands" (The emancipation of Germany), with its solo-quartet, and the concluding fugue: "Lasset uns den Dankgesang erheben" (Let us raise the the song of thanks), a four-voice choral piece which was alternately sung, with the congregation, and the Halleluja from *Händel's Messiah.*"

The propositions brought forward by the estates, after several weeks' discussion between the electoral commissaries and the deputies, were with various additions and modifications, admitted as basis of the new constitution of the state as well as for the propositions made by the Elector respecting a fixed amount for a civil list, and division of the whole of the state revenues, which besides had been chiefly accumulated from the sale of the men taken into the pay of the English to fight against the revolted North-American colonies during the time of the Elector Friedrich II. The 9th January 1831 was the day fixed for the promulgation of the new constitution, and on the evening of the day before, the Electress came back with her daughter *Caroline* from Fulda, where she had been residing for some time past, in order to be present at this joyful event. The elector received her upon his arrival at her residence in the Belle-vue palace, and I received order from the officer of the lord marshal of the court, to give the reconciled couple a serenade with the court orchestra. After I had held the rehearsal in the course of the afternoon for that purpose, I proceeded with the orchestra in exceedingly cold weather to the Belle-vue palace, and having ascertained the apartment in which the court was assembled we drew up outside and played as well as the extremely unfavourable weather would permit. Towards the end of the music the princely pair shewed themselves, the Elector embraced his wife at the window, and the inhabitants of Cassel, who in spite of the cold had collected in crowds, broke out into a loud cheer of joy. The next morning the public announcement of the new constitution was made, and the oaths were taken with due solemnity on the part of the civic-guard publicly upon the Königsplatz, on that of the military on the Friedrichsplatz, and by all the authorities, the court officials and the orchestra in their proper localities. In the evening the town was illuminated, and at the theatre, brilliantly lighted up, "Jessonda" was given as festive opera for the occasion, preceded by a play written for the occasion by counsellor *Niemeyer*. In the latter was introduced at the same time a hymn composed for it by me, "Hesse's song of joy on the establishment of its constitution;" and at the conclusion, the well-known and previously mentioned melody, which, with appropriate words, was sung also by the audience, after which the latter greeted the electoral family assembled in the state box with a storm of cheers. Everybody now looked forward to a happy future; but unfortunately the Countess *Reichenbach*, with her brother Mr. *Ortlepp*, returned the day after to Wilhelmshöhe. This had no sooner become known in Cassel, as also that the elector had visited her there, than the disturbances immediately broke out afresh. Citizens and peasantry gathered in crowds before the palace at Wilhelmshöhe, and threatened aloud to drive the countess out by force, until it was at length ascertained that she had left for Hanau, and a public announcement was placarded in Cassel: "that the *cause* for the disturbance had been removed." But a few weeks afterwards the Elector followed her, as it was thought to take up his residence altogether at Hanau.

Meanwhile at my house the construction of an additional

building which had been begun the previous summer from a plan drawn by my son-in-law *Wolff* was completed. By this, in addition to somewhat more house-room, I obtained more particularly a music room such as we had long felt the want of for our quartet parties, which although closely adjoining the house itself, had nevertheless a higher roof, in order to give it the desired height. In its decoration also, the chief endeavour was to obtain a favourable acoustic arrangement, so as to dispense with all drapery over the windows and doors, which is so obstructive of sound. On the 2nd February 1831, we consecrated the newly-acquired space with the celebration of our "Silver Wedding"; at which my parents from Gandersheim were come to assist, and had brought with them as a present a porcelain vase richly ornamented with silver, upon which, besides the names of the donors, was engraved the inscription: "May the silver of to-day be one day gold!" This fete, properly speaking was got up by my children, in conjunction with our musical friends, and was opened by the torch-light dance from my "Faustus" executed by the guests, with appropriate words to the choral parts. This was followed by a succession of "Tableaux vivants," in which the chief incidents of my life were ingeniously represented. Among many other poems both of comic and serious import, which were recited at table, my friend *Pfeiffer* had also contributed a composition with the view, that all the persons present should appear in the costume of the characters in my operas, and that *K. Pfeiffer* himself should recite the poem. This poem gave me great pleasure at the time, and its recital, with all its allusions, excited general merriment, and no one would have dreamed that its youthful author would be snatched in a few months by death from our circle. Early in the morning of the 31st July, while bathing in the river Fulda, he was struck with apoplexy, and his beautiful and diversified labours in literature were suddenly arrested for ever. For his obsequies I composed a solemn dirge for several voices, and subsequently, when the civil guard of this place had a monumental memorial erected over his early grave, upon its consecration the chorus from "The last things," "Selig sind die Todten," was sung by the St. Cecilia society with the assistance also of its female members, a circumstance which upon no previous occasion of the kind had ever taken place in Cassel. Dr. *B. W. Pfeiffer*, the father of the deceased, who previously had been known to me only in his official capacity as chief advocate of the court of appeal, visited me upon the occasion to thank me for my attention, and in this manner I first became personally intimate with him, to whom I was at a later period to be more nearly allied as son-in-law.

Unhappily that was the last family rejoicing which my brother *Ferdinand* lived to see. He shortly after fell so seriously ill that the physicians immediately pronounced him irrecoverable, and I was present a few days afterwards when he breathed his last. As his widow, in spite of all her solicitations, received no pension from the bureau of intendance, and was therefore reduced to the small income paid to her from the relief-fund which I had instituted a few years before, I set aside for her subsistence a yearly allowance, with the aid of which she was enabled to give a good education to both her children and to allow her son *Ludwig*, my godson, to prepare himself for his collegiate studies. After some years of diligent study, with a view of going to the university of Marburg, the young fellow returned to his earlier expressed desire to devote himself entirely to music. Upon a closer examination, however, this did not seem to me advisable, as it was now too late for him to acquire the necessary thorough musical education, and by my advice he adhered to his chosen profession of the law, passed a brilliant examination in 1847, and entered into the official service of the electorate of Hesse.

In the month of April in pursuance of the new constitution, the first assembly of the estates upon the basis of the new election law was summoned, and held its sittings in a saloon of the Belle-vue palace. *Schomburg*, the burgomaster of the capital, was unanimously chosen as its president, and the government did not dare oppose his nomination. As the sittings were public, this awakened immediately an active political vitality in the town, and the debates were followed up to the conclusion of the session with great interest by all classes. Professor *Sylvester Jordan*, the deputy from the Marburg university, soon distinguished himself by his eloquence, and he almost always succeeded in carrying through his liberal motions in the assembly.

In order to extend these liberal sentiments among the inhabitants of Cassel, some men well known for their liberal opinions considered it requisite to form a political club, under the name of the "reading museum," and I willingly joined my exertions to theirs. At this place every afternoon during the session, the various subjects which had been discussed in the chamber were made known. The sittings of the deputies were often very stormy ones, though the chairman reprimanded the non-members every time they applauded a speaker, and threatened to have all disturbers turned out by the civic guard, yet the daily visitors at the sitting did not much care about it and still endeavoured to influence the voting. But the administration of public affairs suffered considerable detriment from the circumstance that the Elector had quitted his palace at Cassel since March, and taken up his residence permanently, at Hanau. As the assembled estates had failed in all their repeated efforts to persuade him to return to Cassel, they resolved towards the end of August, in conjunction with the town council of Cassel, to send a deputation to Hanau, with the proposition that the Elector should either return without delay to the capital or adopt means for the undisturbed administration of affairs. The deputy from Rinteln, *Wiederhold*, president of the high court of judicature, was one of the deputation, and he succeeded in inducing the Elector to take his son as co-regent with him in the government, and to transfer the administration of affairs to him exclusively so long as he himself remained away from Cassel. Thus the young Prince, after a long residence at Fulda, returned to Cassel as co-regent, together with the Countess *Schaumburg,* with whose morganatic marriage with his son the Elector now expressed himself reconciled. The Prince delivered to the estates a deed of agreement concerning the solemn maintenance of the constitutional laws, and was at first received at Cassel with satisfaction, particularly as he nominated the mediator, *Wiederhold,* minister of justice. But as it was soon observed that the Electress, on account of her refusal to acknowledge the Countess *Schaumburg* as her daughter-in-law, experienced many annoyances and affronts, considerable disapprobation was displayed in the town, and all classes generally sided with the amiable Electress, who by her kind sentiments and mild manners had for long years acquired the love and respect of the people of Hesse. As for me, I had, however, to congratulate myself on being in favour with the Prince at that time; and he requested me to make arrangements for giving him some court concerts at the palace of Wilhelmshöhe. Upon his returning shortly to the town he even requested me in a very courteous letter, to afford him and the Countess the pleasure of hearing some of my quartets, and to arrange for that purpose a quartet party at the palace. It would seem, however, to have been a somewhat tedious affair for them, for I never received a second invitation.

In the autumn 1831 I finished my "Violin-Schule" (course of instruction for the violin) a work which I had undertaken at the solicitation of many persons, and on which I was engaged for more than a twelvemonth, having always begun between-whiles some other compositions which had more attraction for me.*

---

* It was published by *Haslinger,* in Vienna, and the "Wiener Theater-Zeitung," conducted by *Ad. Bäuerle,* speaks of it in the following manner: A fit companion to *Hummel's* 'Clavier-Schule' (pianoforte school): for in the same way that that opens a new department of education in pianoforte play, this embraces the whole art and science of violin play, and lays down clear principles for an art which hitherto has been taught more by oral precepts, or, at the utmost, by small fragmentary pamphlets.

I afterwards wrote three quartets, which were published as Op. 84, by *André* of Offenbach, and later for the St. Cecilia society three psalms of *Moses Mendelsohn's* translation for two four-voice chorals and four solo-voices, which were published by *Simrock* of Bonn [Op. 85], and had an extensive circulation.

In the summer of 1832 I was ordered by my physician to proceed to the well-known warm sulphur baths of Nenndorf, to cure a stiffness in one of my knees, and which I had contracted the preceeding winter from a cold caught while skating. My wife, who accompanied me, had taken with her

---

It required the penetrating, searching mind of a *Spohr,* who surpasses in complete scientific culture the authors of every existing school, to condense in systematic order so important a branch of art, which has been two centuries in acquiring shape; so that the *violin,* so prominent in all music, may be cultivated upon sure and proper principles, and its study carried out with certain success. How well the great maestro *Spohr* goes to work to effect this we shall shew in a subsequent clearer exposition of the contents; for he has not only copiously treated the scientific musical culture of the pupil by the clear outspoken method of the instruction in the explanatory text, assisted by the excellent and appropriate pieces which he supplies for practice, but also, in the mechanical part of the instruction, in which the mechanism of the human body is so beautifully and appositely shewn in all its bearings on the mechanical structure of the instrument. The excellent preface to the work presents rules of conduct both for the instructors and parents of pupils for the obviation of a host of evils which have hitherto arisen from false and erroneous modes of proceeding, from the circumstance that few lovers of music, and few teachers of music even, are sufficiently acquainted with these arcana of the art. Well and clearly does he enumerate the means of encouragement by which the industry of the pupil may be incited. How generous is the invitation of the *famed master to the students of the violin,* that they should impart to him their experience in the progress of their studies of his code of instruction for violin-play, for the further extension of his own knowledge! In this the *great earnestness* of the true artist for the attainment of the one great object is made conspicuously evident." . . . . The notice concludes with the following words: "The world-famed master, *Spohr,* has by this *excellent work alone* ensured an undying celebrity, and thereby added but a new and beautiful leaf to the laurel wreathe that encircles his brows."

among other books, a volume of the poems of my friend *Pfeiffer*, which were not published till after his decease; and as I had long wished to set something from it to music in memory of him, I chose one of them: "Die Weihe der Töne," which pleased me very much, and appeared to me particularly well suited for the composition of a cantata. But when I was about to begin the work, I found that the text of this style of poem did not lend itself altogether well to it; and I felt much more disposed to represent the subject matter of the poem in an instrumental-composition; in this manner originated my fourth symphony, under the title: "Die Weihe der Töne." [In a letter to *Speyer* of the 9th October 1832, this is adverted to in the following words: Although I have now no duties to perform at the theatre,[*] and have had leisure sufficient for composition, I have nevertheless been but little disposed latterly, to set to work. From the great interest which I took and still constantly take in the political regeneration of Germany, the recent retrograde steps have too much annoyed me to permit of my giving myself calmly to any work of deep study. Nevertheless I have again lately completed a grand instrumental composition, and that is a fourth symphony, but which differs greatly in form from the previous ones. It is a musical composition inspired by a poem of *Karl Pfeiffer's*: "Die Weihe der Töne," which must be printed, and distributed in the music room, or recited aloud before it is performed. In the very first part, I had for task, the construction of a harmonious whole from the sounds of nature. This, as indeed the whole work, was a difficult, but a highly attractive problem," &c.]

My musical friends in Hannover, and friend *Hausmann* at the head of them, had no sooner become informed of my presence in Nenndorf, than they apprised me of their intention to pay me a visit, and to bring their instruments with them, so that I had an opportunity of giving the lovers of music

---

[*] The court theatre was closed at this time.

then in Nenndorf a music-party, at which I played my recently written quartet. Meanwhile my cure was successfully completed, and I was relieved of my lameness of the knee, chiefly by a powerful but very painful douche upon the suffering part. Returned to Cassel. I first of all finished my new symphony, and let my friends hear it at a rehearsal, and subsequently at a subscription concert. I still recollect with pleasure the great effect it produced upon all who heard it. It was afterwards given with great applause at the Gewandhaus concert in Leipzic, and *Rochlitz* wrote a very animated notice of the work in his Musical Journal. None of my symphonies can boast of having achieved so wide a circulation in almost all the towns of Germany; it is still a favorite work, and in most permanent concerts is played at least once every year.

In April 1832, by order of the Prince, the court theatre was closed "for an indefinite period," all the singers and comedians, with the exception of those who had contracts of engagement for a longer period, having previously received due notice of dismissal. Two singers only, messieurs *Föppel* and *Rosner* (whose wife was the *prima donna*) could not be comprised in this decision. Together with the orchestra, I was also summoned to attend; all who had no rescript from the elector received notice of dismissal, and we others were asked whether we were disposed to resign our places for an indemnification to be agreed upon with each individual separately. I, who had first to give my answer to this proposal on the part of the administration, immediately declared that I was not disposed to agree to it, but would abide by my engagement, and, should it become necessary, would maintain my right before the proper tribunal. The other musicians also at once pronounced their adhesion to my declaration, and we thus lost one hautboy player only, whom I had at an early period engaged at Prague by the authority of the elector, to make up the complement of the orchestra, and who upon his joining, had unfortunately neglected to have his rescript made out. The first bassoonist, who was in a similar predicament, succeeded nevertheless in maintaining his place, being enabled to produce a letter from me in which I had engaged him in the name and by the authority of the elector, that the letter would guarantee his engagement until the rescript was prepared; by this circumstance he was saved to the orchestra. We others were then not called forward any more, and all remained upon the old footing.

In the autumn of 1832, my brother *William* wrote to me from Brunswick to apprize me that in the ensuing November would be the "goldene Hochzeit" (the golden wedding) of our parents; and he proposed to me that all their children should meet in Gandersheim, to congratulate our parents, and present them with a musical-clock. That it would be a source of still greater pleasure to my parents, if I combined a musical entertainment with the festival, I could readily imagine, and I therefore urged *William Wolff,* the brother of my son-in-law, to write a poem for me, to set to music, at the performance of which my wife and I with the piano and violin should represent the orchestra, my three daughters take the solo parts, and my brothers with their wives, and my sons-in-law sing the chorus. So soon as I had received the words in the form which I had suggested, I immediately went to work, wrote a cheerful polonaise (in the execution of which I gave my wife and self the opportunity of shewing our skill as virtuosi on our respective instruments); this I followed up with a general chorus, after which I brought in the three soli of my daughters, who at the conclusion sang a trio; and then lastly I added a general chorus finale. While I was practising this festal cantata with my wife and children, I sent to my brothers their chorus parts also, for the same purpose, and we all met at Gandersheim a few days before the fête-day, which was on the 26th November. As our parents could not accommodate all of us with bed-rooms, I hired for myself and my numerous company, the whole accommodation of an inn, and then consulted with my brothers and sons-in-law as to the best and most effective manner of celebrating the day. *Wolff* suggested above all things to hire the handsomest and largest room in the whole town; to decorate it with festoons of evergreens and artifical flowers; to display there our presents, and give our cantata before our parents and the families of our friends. We were not long in finding a room, for there was but *one* at all suitable in the whole place, and that moreover scarcely large enough to hold all the invited guests. From the neighbouring wood we procured in abundance the necessary branches and evergreen for the decorations, and were then all employed for several days together in making the festoons and in preparing garlands of paper-flowers, as also with drawing and painting transparencies. When we would get tired of all this work, I began the rehearsals of the cantata, and could not but admire the industry of the fair sex among us, who had practised their husbands so well in the tenor and bass parts of the chorus, although they were almost utterly unmusical (though gifted with good voices), that their performances were creditable enough to hear. In this manner the time passed very quickly till the festival, and we then had the gratification of seeing our parents deeply moved by our entertainment, and our presents greatly admired by our Gandersheim friends. Besides a musical-clock, which in particular was an object of great attraction, the presents consisted of a very handsome and convenient foot-stool embroidered for my father by his Brunswick daughter-in-law, and in numerous specimens of work executed for my mother by the Cassel ladies. The banquet, which was in part brought from my parents' house and part furnished from a restaurant, was a very profuse one, at which the wines and liquors brought by us brothers met no less with great approval, so that the festival of the *Spohr* family went off very satisfactorily, and was long a topic of conversation in Gandersheim. The general interest exhibited on the occasion by the townspeople and those of the neighbourhood was very gratifying, and this among other things was exhibited by the contributions sent to my mother to entertain the numerous guests, for she received a complete houseful of provisions, in the shape of game, pies, pastry, flour, eggs, fruit &c. This gave the whole affair a complete patriarchal character; and every body did his or her utmost to evince their friendship for the worthy and venerable pair, and their respect for the man, who for so many years had stood by them as the faithful physician with help and with advice, and who, wherever he could, had always relieved the necessities of the poor.

After my return I received the command of the Prince to give a succession of concerts during the winter, in place of the theatrical performances, which had been suspended since the spring. These concerts were to take place every Sunday for the benefit of the treasury of the theatre, and the singers who remained with us were to be employed therein. The public, however, greatly displeased at this, and that the receipts from the concerts were thus to be diverted from the relief fund for the widows of the members of the orchestra, came to the determination not to subscribe to them, and thus the receipts were almost null. Few of the concerts only, and that in which the "Weihe der Töne" was first given, were well attended, but in the others the house looked very dreary and empty. Meanwhile it would seem that the Prince and the Countess *Schaumburg*, had found the winter tediously long with a closed theatre; for towards the spring I received orders to proceed to Meiningen to engage for the months of March, April, and May, a company of travelling performers who were there at that time, under the direction of *Bethmann* from Berlin. As I expressed the wish to take my wife with me, the Prince ordered his master of the horse, *von der Malsburg*, to furnish me with a convenient court carriage from the electoral stables, and we proceeded to Meiningen with post horses. But there were other obstacles to be overcome on this mission, besides the negotiations with *Bethmann*. The latter, for instance, had accepted an engagement for the whole summer from the court of Meiningen, and it was necessary to prevail upon the duke to part with the services of the company earlier than he had intended. To this, however, the duchess notwithstanding her differences with her brother, on account of his quarrel with the mother, rendered me her assistance. Shortly after my return, *Bethmann* and his company arrived, and for the re-opening of the new theatre gave the "Freischütz," with much applause. Miss *Meisselbach* pleased especially by her performance of Agatha. The former director of the theatre, *Feige*, and I were then appointed in superintendance over Mr. *Bethmann*, with instructions to place at his disposal, the three singers whose engagements were yet unexpired, the orchestra, and the whole of the company of the scene-painters and workmen of the theatre, the extensive wardrobe, decorations, &c. We now worked out together the order of the repertory, *Feige* and *Bethmann* for the plays and I for the operas, and were soon enabled to represent once more all the operas that were previously performed on our stage. At this time I wrote my third double quartet [E *minor*] and another concertante for two violins, which were soon after published by *Simrock* in Bonn as Op. 87 and 88.

In June of the same year another grand musical festival took place at Halberstadt, which was undertaken by the minister *Augustin* and his son, as the sixth musical festival of the Elbe, to direct which concert-master *Frederick Schneider* of Dessau and myself were invited. It differed chiefly from the previous ones in the erection of an enormous tent, or rather of a large booth constructed of planks, upon the square in front of the cathedral, for the refreshment and social entertainment of the visitors, as well as of the auditory and assistant artists, and in which all strangers could assemble at any hour of the day. The musical performances took place on three successive days, and began with *Händel's* oratorio of "Samson" under *Schneider's* direction. The next morning the objects most worthy of notice in Halberstadt were visited, particularly the collections of paintings belonging to the Canon *von Spiegel* and Dr. *Lucanus*. It was intended to have given a concert at the theatre, but as it was not sufficiently spacious to hold the numerous auditory, a second concert was given simultaneously in the large room of the "Golden Angel," and the non-resident virtuosi and singers were divided equally to perform at both places. The tickets which were distributed admitted to the rehearsals also, so that each person could hear one of the concerts at the morning rehearsal, and the other at the evening performance; and one single piece of music only was given at *both* concerts, which was the favorite duet from "Jessonda" between Amazili and Nadori, sung by Mrs. *Schmidt* and Mr. *Mantius*, because neither party would permit this piece to be taken from it by the other. — I conducted at the concert given in the room at the "Golden Angel," and played my new concertante in *H minor* with concert-master *Müller* from Brunswick. On the third day the last concert took place in the forenoon, and under my direction, upon which occasion I found upon my conductor's desk a present of a red velvet coverlet bearing an inscription embroidered in silver. At this concert were performed *Mozart's* symphony in *C major*, and that of *Beethoven* in *C minor*; my Lord's prayer and a *Te Deum* by *Schneider*, and I had the satisfaction of observing that at this musical festival my three compositions met with the most general applause. At noon a grand banquet in the large tent terminated the festival, at which the proceeding were of a very noisy character.

We were obliged to devote the remainder of the vacation to a journey to Marienbad in Bohemia, where it was hoped my wife, who constantly suffered from nervous debility, would regain some strength from bathing and drinking the waters, as well as from the enjoyment of the fresh air from the mountains. Among the visitors at the baths we met *Raupach* of Berlin, with whom I took frequent long walks, during which he related to me many things relating to his approaching theatrical labours. He was at that time full of a new drama which he was going to write immediately upon his return home, in which he intended to lash the ill-natured and hypocrites, and the scene of which he had laid in China. But he probably never completed it, or perhaps the ill-natured ones of Berlin found means to prevent its representation, for so far as I know, no piece of the kind from the pen of *Raupach* was ever made public. The society of music at Marienbad, whose director was a linen manufacturer in the neighbourhood, had much pleased and surprised me with a very successful performance of *Cherubini's* overture to "Medea," with which, by way of serenade, he had greeted my arrival, and for which I the more readily complied with his wish to write a walz for them *à la Strauss*, to which also my inclinatien to try every sort of composition, had long predisposed me. At first, when I had practised their orchestra in it, the walz pleased me very well; but afterwards I found it wanting in that freshness and originality which distinguish most of the walzes of *Strauss* and *Lanner*. Nevertheless, by the desire of my publisher *Haslinger* of Vienna, he brought it out as Op. 89, not only in the original form as an instrumental piece, but also arranged for two and four hands.

On my return to Cassel I next wrote six four-voice songs for men's voices, which *Schuberth* of Hamburgh published as Op. 90, and began my fourth quintet in *A minor*, finished in February of the following year, and which *Simrock* of Bonn published as Op 91.

On the 5th April 1834, my children and friends took me by surprise with an unsually grand fete in celebration of my fiftieth birthday. For that very evening I had announced an opera and could not at all understand, why the intendance had suddenly countermanded it, but this had been solicited by my folks unknown to me. My wife and I now availed ourselves of the evening thus left at our disposal to accept an invitation to my son-in-law *Zahn's* and we were both not a little surprised to find the apartments brilliantly lighted up with candelabra, and ornamented with ingenious transparencies and flowers, with my bust crowned with a wreath, and a brilliant company assembled to celebrate the day with music (a cantata composed by *Hauptmann*) and with speeches.

This was unhappily the last festivity of the kind that my good wife lived to see. Our stay at Marienbad had not given her any permanent relief, and as her sufferings returned once more with the commencement of the winter, it became necessary for her to resume the attempt at cure in the next vacation. This time we met at Marienbad the brothers *Bohrer*, and after I had renewed my former acquaintance with these talented artists, we had frequent quartet parties together, in which we also prevailed upon the old linen-weaver, who was a good violin player, to join us. These music-parties enlivened my wife as well, who benefited so much by the waters that we returned to Cassel with the mostly lively hope of her ultimate recovery. But soon afterwards her condition again became worse, and I now felt but little disposed to proceed with my new oratorio which I had begun in April. Already the year before, on our return journey through Leipzic, Councillor *Rochlitz* had offered me an oratorio of the passion written by him: "Des Heilands letzte Stunden" [the last moments of the Saviour] to set to music. Although it had already been once set to music, under the title "The end of the just," by *Schicht*, I nevertheless took it with pleasure, as he assured me that although the previous composition had been played and with some applause, yet it had not produced sufficient effect; for which reason he had again remodelled the text and had made it more suitable to the object proposed. As, however, I became informed that he had proposed this new text to *Mendelssohn* also for composition, before proceeding with the work I first wrote of the latter, requesting him to inform me whether he had the intention of composing the oratorio? As he replied in the negative, and informed me that he himself intended to put a text together from scripture ("Paulus"), I began my work in the spring of 1834, which was subsequently interrupted by our journey to the baths. As I nevertheless remarked that my wife, notwithstanding her suffering condition, interested herself as much in my present work as she had done in my previous ones, I soon forgot every thing in the inspiration with which I devoted myself to it. Although upon my return home from the rehearsals at the theatre *Dorette* received me always with sad looks and anxious observations respecting her health, she nevertheless evinced again so great an interest in the progress of my work, and listened with such lively attention to that which when ready I rehearsed at the St. Cecilia society, that again I always resumed the continuation of the work with new courage. Frequently nevertheless she would interrupt me with the melancholy question: "What will become of our *Theresa*, should I sink under my illness?" — for her anxiety for *Theresa* had at that time become her fixed idea — and when I made reply to her: "A happy wife, as our other children have become," a radiant smile overspread her face, for she had also doubtless remarked, that *Theresa*, in spite of her youth, had already many aspirants for her favour, and she herself received with no displeasure the attentions of a member of our St. Cecilia society. In this manner I got to the end of the first part of my oratorio, and my wife had the pleasure of seeing the interest and enthusiasm with which it was sung by the society; but after that her strength quickly declined and she was obliged to take to her bed. When I saw the thoughtful expression of face of our physician and family friend Dr. *Bauer*, I called in also the most reputed physician of our town, Dr. *Harnier*, to consult with him. But he also shook his head and could give me little hope to save her. As my daughters *Emilia* and *Theresa* took upon them the closest care of their mother, I was enabled to comply with *Dorette's* wish to continue my work during the day upon the completion of the oratorio, in which she greatly interested herself, but was obliged to watch by her bed at night in turn with *Emilia*. I had scarcely got to the third "number" of the second part, when her malady assumed the form of a nervous fever, which carried her off, and to the present day I think with bitter sadness of the moment when I pressed the last kiss upon her forehead.

My son-in-law *Wolff* took upon himself all the mournful

preparations for the funeral, for which in my despair I was wholly incompetent, and by that means I was enabled to leave the town for a week with my youngest daughter, who was quite beside herself for grief at the death of her mother, and who moreover had passed the last day by the side of her sister *Ida*, who was likewise ill. I hired apartments at an inn at Wilhelmshöhe, and we strove to regain the necessary self-possession by long and fatiguing wanderings in the neighbouring bare and wintry woods. When we were at length obliged to return into town we felt the solitude of our house but the more intensely. It was therefore long before I could find resolution sufficient to continue the score upon which I had inscribed a memorandum of the day of my wife's decease, the 20th November; until at length the disposition to work returned, and I finished the oratorio by the end of the winter. On Good Friday 1835 I gave an entire performance of it. The thought that my wife did not live to witness the completion and performance of the oratorio diminished greatly the satisfaction I experienced at this most successful of my works, and I did not attain a full conception of its effect until in its later performances. An opportunity for a repetition of the oratorio presented itself the same summer on Whitsunday, on which day the Prince, contrary to custom, had granted us permission to give a concert in the church. The theatrical vacation coming soon after this, I was obliged to seize the opportunity, and comply with the advice of my physician to proceed to a sea-bathing place, and I selected for the purpose Zandford, a newly-established and as yet not much frequented watering-place about 3 miles[*] from Haarlem. Besides *Theresa*, my sister-in-law, *Minchen Scheidler*, who for some years since the death of my mother-in-law had resided with us, and who during our former journeys was accustomed to visit her brother professor *Charles Scheidler* at Jena, accompanied me on this journey, and both were exceedingly pleased with it. We de-

---

[*] English.

scended the Rhine to Dusseldorf, were I had projected staying for a few days, as *Mendelssohn*, who had accepted the situation of director of music in the new theatre built by *Immermann*, now lived there. The wife of Councillor *von Sybel*, at whose house I lived during the musical festival, had heard of our intention to make a short stay in Dusseldorf, and urged me to take up my lodging in her house, which I did the more readily as I had heard that *Immermann* was a visitor in her house and generally spent his evenings there.

I took my violin with me, and my last works also, among which a second recently finished concertino, *E major*, Op. 92, published by *Breitkopf* and *Härtel* of Leipzic. We first went to Frankfort, stopped there one day only at *Speyer's* house, and then continued our journey from Bieberich by the steamboat. At Dusseldorf we were received at the house of Mrs. *von Sybel* in a very friendly manner, and already on the first evening had the pleasure of making *Immermann's* acquaintance, who to the special delight of my sister-in-law read to her his charming "Tulifäntchen." Of *Mendelssohn*, who was not there, I heard, that he also was one of the friends of the house, but never appeared there on those evenings when *Immermann* came, because with him, who devoted his whole attention to the spectacle only, he had disagreed about the opera.

The next morning, when I paid a visit to *Mendelssohn* and met his sister there, he played to me the first "numbers" of his oratorio "Paulus," with which I was not altogether quite pleased because it was too much in the style of *Händel*. He and his sister, on the other hand, appeared greatly pleased with my concertino in *E major*, in which there occurred a characteristic *staccato* in one long stroke, by way of novelty, such as he had never before heard by any other violinist. Accompanying me then in a very clever manner from the score, he could not hear this *staccato* often enough, and repeatedly requested me to begin with it again, saying the while to his sister: "See, this is the famous *Sporish staccato*, which no violinist can play like him!" Thence I went to see *Immermann*, who proposed to me to pay a visit to *Grabbe*, who at that time, at *Immermann's* invitation, was staying at Dusseldorf, and I thus on the same day made the acquaintance of that strange being. When, upon my entering his lodging, the little fellow set eyes upon a giant like me, he drew back timidly into a corner of the room, and the first words he spoke to me were: "It would be an easy matter for you to throw me out of that window." I replied: "Yes, I certainly could, but I am not come here with that intention." This comical scene over, *Immermann* then first introduced me to the foolish yet interesting creature.

In the house of our hospitable hostess we passed some pleasant days alternately in *Mendelssohn's* and *Immermann's* society, and then resumed our journey on board the Dutch steamer to Cleves, where I was desirous of visiting my old friend *Thomae* for a few days. We found him a widower also; for he, too, had recently lost his wife. The nut-tree in his garden, of which we had set the nut in 1818 with such solemnity during our stay with his family, was in full leaf and flourishing amazingly. *Thomae's* children, who were now all grown up, and of whom the eldest son had now taken his father's place as notary, were all in good health, but he himself seemed low-spirited and ill. Our visit nevertheless afforded him great pleasure, and upon our departure he presented *Theresa*, as god-daughter of his deceased wife, with a gold watch, and entreated us to visit him again on our return. In this manner, after quitting the steamboat at Rotterdam, we arrived safely at Zandford, by way of the Hague, Amsterdam and Haarlem. When we had hired apartments at the bath-house and looked out of our windows upon the sea for the first time, my sister-in law uttered the ominous words: "Here I could wish to remain for ever!" After I had arranged with the physician of the bathing-etablishment, who came from Haarlem daily to visit the bathers, respecting the terms for his attendance during my bathing cure, and had immediately begun to bathe, I soon went into the sea with real pleasure, and took great delight in swimming about in it. Our fellow inmates of the bath-house and guests at the dinner-table were some puritan families from Elberfeld and Barmen, whose religious notions I had soon sufficient opportunity to learn by their conversation at table, but which by no means inspired me with a wish to make their nearer acquaintance. After dinner we used to take our walks in the wood, which, beginning immediately behind the downs, extended almost as far as Haarlem, and in this manner we passed the fine weather with which we were favoured in the summer of 1835, very happily in our retirement. This was, however, soon to be interrupted by an unexpected artistic enjoyment; for the lovers of music of Amsterdam, who had been informed of my presence in Zandford, invited me and my fellow travellers to a concert which they had arranged in my honour. We proceeded therefore by omnibus to Haarlem, and thence by the canal boat to Amsterdam, where we alighted at the house of Mr. *Tenkate*, a former acquaintance of mine. In his company we went to the concert given in the concert room of *Felix Meritis*, at which several of my compositions were given; first one of my symphonies, then the duet from "Jessonda." sung by Mr. *de Vruecht* of Haarlem and the prima donna of the German theatre; after which Mr. *Tours* of Rotterdam played a violin-concerto of mine, and Mr. *Vruecht* terminated the concert with some songs. After we had supped at the house of our host, and were on the point of going to bed, a serenade was given me, which we listened to from the balcony of the house.

My sister-in-law, who during the concert had complained of a head-ache, now probably caught cold, for despite my warning she would stand out also in the chill night air on the balcony to hear the serenade; and upon our return to Zandford, upon consulting the bath-physician next morning, he found that a cutaneous eruption had made its appearance in the night, which, however, he did not consider dangerous. The vacation meanwhile was drawing to a close, and the physician was of opinion that after the invalid had kept her bed for a few days, we should soon be enabled to set out upon our return journey. But on the evening of the same day, while I was sitting at the bed-side of my sister-in-law, as the sun was going down, and speaking with her of our return home, she requested in a tone of anxious and nervous agitation to be allowed to get up, and while exerting my utmost strength to prevent her from rising, she fell back suddenly upon the pillows, and losing all consciousness, breathed her last. Both *Theresa* and I, seized with alarm, called for assistance, upon which a young man, a medical student whose apartment was contiguous to ours, came in with all his instruments and immediately proceeded to open a vein. But it was without success. No blood would flow, the surgeon pronounced her dead and was now using every effort to bring *Theresa* to her senses, who had fainted away with fright. Thus was sadly realised the ominous desire of my sister-in-law: "Here I could wish to remain for ever!" What we felt as we followed her a few days afterwards to her last resting-place, and how sadly this scene resuscitated the mournful recollection of that we had witnessed the year before in Cassel, I need not attempt to describe.

We now proceeded with all possible speed on our return journey, and at the landing-place of the steam-boat near Cleves met our friend *Thomae*, who, when he learned our new loss, persisted no further in his desire that we should again stay a few days at his house. As my leave of absence was moreover expired, we continued our journey to Cassel without further delay. But I there felt the lonesomeness of our home yet more keenly, deprived of the one whom we had left behind, and I therefore began to experience the want of a partner through life who would also take an interest in my musical labours. The meetings of our society of St. Cecilia were near at hand, where at our weekly rehearsals the opportunity might present itself to me to make unperceived such observations as would perhaps enable me to select a lady in whom I might hope to find a solace for the remainder of my life, and one fitted to restore to me my lost happiness. I there bethought me especially of the sister of my deceased friend *Karl Pfeiffer*, whose serious tone of mind and warm interest for high-class music I had observed during her constant punctual attendance for several years at the concerts of the society, and who, moreover, as I knew through her brother, had a particular predilection for my music. Besides this, in my almost daily walks on the Cologne Alley, which took me past the garden of Chief Councillor *Pfeiffer* of the court of appeal, I had for a long time past the opportunity of witnessing at a distance the happy and unpretentious manner of life of the family. As at that time (September 1835) the electoral troops were concentrated for the autumn manœuvres, and had formed a camp in the neighbourhood of the castle of Wilhelmsthal, whither the Casselers now resorted as their chief promenade, I bethought me of making a party thither, and through my daughter *Theresa* requested the parents *Pfeiffer* to permit both their daughters to accompany us.

During this little excursion, I had the opportunity in the course of conversation to become acquainted with the high and varied intellectual culture of the two sisters, and so I became fully confirmed in my resolve to sue for the hand of the eldest sister, *Marianne,* whose knowledge of music and skill in pianoforte play I had already observed, when she sometimes gave her assistance in accompaniment at the concerts of the St. Cecilia society. As I had not the courage to propose for her by word of mouth, there being more than twenty years difference in our ages, I put the question to her in writing, and added, in excuse for my courtship, the assurance that I was yet perfectly free from the usual infirmities of age. I now awaited the answer with the most anxious expectancy. To my great joy it proved one of assent, upon which I hastened to her parents, and in due form asked her in marriage. They wished every happiness to our union, and we now daily learned to know each other better. As at my age there was not much time be lost, I urged that the wedding should take place immediately after the new year, which after some opposition from the relations and the bride, was consented to. Our wedding was fixed for the 3nd of January 1836, and I asked my parents to become witness to my new happiness. Yet, on the appointed day our wedding nearly failed to take place, for the required permission of the co-regent Prince had not yet been received, notwithstanding all the exertions of my friend Mr. *von der Malsburg*, whose office it was, as marshal of the court, to have it made out.

My father-in-law, who in former years had given private readings in public law to the Prince, and then did not stand very high in his favour, had totally lost it since, as a member of the first parliament (from 1831 to 1832), he had effected by his able and convincing report to the assembled states a great diminution of the disproportionate amount of the military expenditure. The Prince bore this doubtless in mind, and therefore delayed granting his permission for the marriage of his daughter. Neither did we receive this until my bride had signed a bond, which was expressly required of her, whereby she waived all claim to a future pension. As I, in case of my death, was enabled to provide for my wife by other means, we consented to this requisition; and in this manner our wedding did yet take place on the day which had been appointed. The nearest relatives of the family of my parents-in-law, to the number of three and thirty, together with my own parents, my daughters and their husbands, were assembled on the occasion. The marriage ceremony, at the request of my bride, was performed by her favorite preacher *Asbrand*, whom she knew personally and highly esteemed.

I now lived again in my former and accustomed domestic manner and felt unspeakably happy with my wife! As we frequently played together, I became more and more acquainted with her high sentiment for the noble in the science of music, and from her great ability for reading at sight, was enabled in a short time to play with her not only all that I had previously written for the violin with pianoforte accompaniment, but many new things in that style of art, and which I had not previously known, were suggested to me by her. This inspired me with a great desire to try something for once in duets especially written for pianoforte and violin. The first I wrote for ourselves was the duet in *G minor* (Op. 95 published by *Breitkopf* of Leipzic). Thus engaged I frequently observed with great pleasure the lively interest she took in my works, in the same manner as my departed wife had afforded me so much happiness and stimulated my labours. When I had written out a passage, upon playing it with her I could immediately hear its full effect, which interested and made us both equally happy. Besides the above I composed at this period six songs for a counter tenor voice, published by *Simrock* of Bonn as Op. 94.

When the summer and the season of vacation drew nigh, we resolved upon a journey to visit our respective relatives. But as there was no railway at that time, we were obliged as formerly to travel with post horses, and proceeded by way of Eisenach to Gotha, where we visited a step-sister of my late wife, who had married a tradesman of the Name of *Hildt* of that place. We found them in their flower-garden, spent a pleasant evening with them, and left the next day for Erfurt. As the musical amateurs of that place had heard of our coming beforehand, we were immediately received at the hotel of "The Roman Emperor" by a deputation, who invited us in a most flattering address to the festive entertainments which had been prepared for us. At the banquet which was given on the first day, I was welcomed in a poem composed for the occasion, after which my health was drunk with an enthusiasm which afforded great gratification to my wife and daughter. In the evening we drove to the "Steiger," the favorite place of resort of the citizens of Erfurt; but as it shortly afterwards began to rain, we could not much enjoy the beautifully laid out gardens, and were compelled to take refuge in the saloon itself. Fortunately they had taken care to provide a good pianoforte and I could therefore let the company hear my new duet for violin and piano, and also my concertino in *E sharp*, both of which I played with my wife. After that, *Theresa* sang some of my newest songs, and by some of the ladies and gentlemen of Erfurt my bass duet from "Faust" and several songs were sung. This improvisated musical party appeared to please the company greatly, and thus, despite the rain, we returned to town very satisfied with our day's pleasure. Early on the following morning we were taken by surprise with a serenade performed in our honour by the military-band drawn up on the square in front of the hotel. It began with the well-known sounds of one of my symphonies, which was followed by several other pieces, and lastly by the first finale from "Zemira and Azor." We then went to see objects of note in the town, particularly the fine cathedral, upon entering which we were greeted by the pealing notes of the celebrated organ, and afterwards, the introduction to the "Last moments of the Saviour," as also several other melodies, chiefly from my earlier oratorios, were executed in a very impressive manner. After we had partaken of a magnificent repast at the house of Major *von Rommel*, whose wife was a cousin of Mrs. *Spohr's*, we drove to the theatre, where preparations had been made for a grand concert, at which, with a brilliantly lighted house, the "Weihe der Töne" and my "Lord's Prayer" were performed in a very satisfactory manner.

The next morning we continued our journey to Leipzic, and there again attended several interesting musical parties, which my old friends *Rochlitz* and *Weiss*, as also the distinguished pianiste Mrs. *Vogt*, gave at their houses in our honour, and where I played some of my more recent quartets, which were as yet unknown to the Leipzickers, particularly the *Quatuor brillant* in *A major*, which I had composed in the previous autumn (Op. 93, published by *Haslinger* of Vienna). In Dresden, at the hotel of the "Stadt Gotha," we met the family *Kleinwächter* of Prague, father, son and daughter — as also my friend *Adolph Hesse*, the celebrated organist of Breslau, whom I had personally known since 1828, when he first visited me in Cassel, and who entertained a great friendship for me. With him we proceeded on a preproposed tour through Saxon Switzerland, and performed the first distance, to the entrance of the Uttewalder Ravine, in the carriage, which, when we became tired of climbing the steep heights which offered the chief points of view, always took us again and carried us conveniently from one magnificent rocky aspect to the other. We had nevertheless some long and fatiguing pedestrian trips, for instance that of the ascent of the great Winterberg, when the heat was very oppressive. From Hirniskretschen, the limit of our journey, we descended the Elbe to Schandau, partook of a pleasant dinner there, during which we rallied each other mutually upon our fatigue, which we endeavoured as much as possible to conceal from the visitors at the baths, who sat with us at table, and which gave rise to many comical incidents.

In Dresden we went to a very interesting quartet party at the house of the court musician *Franz*, a former pupil of mine, for which occasion it was festively decorated with wreaths and flowers. We there met the three directors of orchestra *Reissiger*, *Morlachi* and *Rastrelli*, and I played one of my double quartets and my newest concertino. As we purposed leaving Dresden the next morning it was now necessary to take leave of our amiable fellow travellers *Kleinwächter* and *Hesse*, in whose society we had passed so many pleasant hours, and who during the time of our being together, had really heaped upon us every demonstration of affection and attention. They parted from us with tears in their eyes, and we continued our journey through Leipzic and Halle to Brunswick, where we were desirous of visiting my brothers *William* and *Augustus*, and at the same time of assisting at the musical festival which was then about to be held there. This took place in the Ægydian church, and opened with *Händel's* "Messiah." Although that noble work was long since well known to us from previous performances of it, we were nevertheless again truly charmed by the grandeur of the choruses, the powerful cast, and *Mozart's* instrumentation. On the two following days mixed concerts of vocal and instrumental music were given; but the pieces performed being for the most part operatic music, they appeared to us not altogether suited for the church. At all the grand dinners which took place daily at noon under the large tent that had been erected on the wall promenade, the hilarity was generally somewhat tumultuous; and one scene that occurred on the last day was of a very comical nature.

Mantius, the tenor singer of Berlin, who had already sung some songs with great applause, was at last requested to sing the favorite one of "Fair Annie."* This song has an apparent termination, which is followed by a yet more brilliant finale. It so happened that the auditory always broke out into a loud applause before *Mantius* had got to the end. After this had occurred to his great annoyance at some verses, he at the following verse mounted upon a bench, and at last even got upon the table, in order at length to obtain a complete hearing for the brilliant point of the song, but again his efforts were fruitless! The apparent termination was always too irresistible, and although *Mantius* previous to the last verse again implored his hearers both earnestly and piteously to restrain their applause until he had really come to the end, one of them nevertheless allowed himself to be carried away by his feelings and to shout bravo at the wrong time, and that was quite sufficient for the rest to join in. The expression of despair with which, though overwhelmed with applause, the singer now jumped down from the table, was indescribably ludicrous.

Upon our leaving Brunswick we were pressingly invited by Councillor *Lüder*, who had also been present at the musical festival, to spend a few days with him at his country seat

---

* "Schön Hannchen."

at Catlenburg, upon our way back; and this formed a worthy termination to this interesting journey.

On our return to Cassel I found a letter from my former pupil *Gercke*, director of music at Paderborn, in which we were invited to the millenium jubilee of St. *Liborius*, which was to take place there on the 21st July. The celebration of this festival was to commence on the first day with church solemnities, and on the second with the production of my oratorio: "Des Heilands letzte Stunden" (The last moments of the Saviour). As my holidays were not quite expired, we quickly made up our minds, and in a few days again took our seats in the travelling carriage, in which this time my sister-in-law *Caroline Pfeiffer* filled the fourth place. We slept at Lichtenau and set out from there so early the next morning, that we arrived at Paderborn before eight o'clock, but we found nevertheless the town so full, that we could not be accommodated at either of the two hotels there. The host of the second hotel seemed however to regret his inability to accommodate us, and hired for us a couple of rooms in a private house opposite. But we could there procure two beds only, so that he was obliged to arrange a sleeping place for me and my wife for the night in the hotel, and that indeed in a room occupied by a hair-dresser during the day in the pursuance of his calling, and for the sale of his wares. We had scarcely entered our unseemly apartment than we received a visit from the dilettanti of the town, and from the artists who had come to take part in the musical performances. We were then conducted to the house of one of their friends, where the best places were given to us at the windows, to see with more convenience the brilliant procession which accompanied the relics of St. *Liborius* in their golden shrine, to the cathedral. When the immense crowd of the population had somewhat dispersed we also proceeded to the cathedral, where we admired the richly decorated and beautiful structure, and heard *Carl Maria von Weber's* mass in *D major*, the too worldly style of which however did not altogether please us. On the following evening my oratorio was performed in the church of the Jesuits, brilliantly lighted up, whither we were accompanied and a passage made for us through the thronged aisle up to the front places assigned to us on cushioned seats close to those of the bishop of Paderborn, chief president *Vincke* and the commandant of the town. I remarked with pleasure that here also a great enthusiasm was felt for my oratorio; *Gercke* directed exceedingly well, the choruses had been well studied, and among the solo-singers, who were for the most part dilettanti, the well-known concert singer Mrs. *Johanna Schmidt* particularly distinguished herself in the part of Mary. Scarcely had we retired to rest after this busy day, than we heard a torch-light serenade under our windows, consisting of instrumental music and four-part songs. When on the repeated loud calls on my name I went to the window with the intention of returning thanks, I found in front of it so high a pile of pasteboard boxes belonging to my co-occupant of the room as to impede my efforts to open it, and I was therefore compelled to convey my deferred oral thanks in a written shape the next morning previous to our leaving.

In this manner we returned to Cassel from this excursion also very gratified, after which, inspired with improved health and in very happy domestic circumstances, I began a new period of industrious composition. Already on the return journey from Dresden I had constantly thought of a new composition, and sketched out the programme of it. This was another sonate for me and my wife, which was afterwards published as a duet for piano and violin "Nachklänge einer Reise nach Dresden und in die sächsische Schweiz" (Reminiscences of a journey to Dresden and through Saxon Switzerland) Op. 96, by *Simrock* of Bonn and dedicated to our amiable fellow travellers of Prague and Breslau. In the first theme I endeavoured to describe the love of travel, and in the second the journey itself, by introducing the winding of the postillions' horns, customary in Saxony and the neighbouring part of Prussia, as the dominant in the scherzo, played by the violin upon the G string in a horn-like manner as chief theme, worked out with striking modulations on the pianoforte, and then I depicted in the trio a fanciful dreaming-like sentiment, such as one so willingly yet unconsciously gives onesself up to in the carriage! The subsequent adagio represents a scene in the catholic royal-chapel at Dresden, which begins with an organ-prelude on the pianoforte alone; after which the violin plays the intonations of the priest before the altar, which are followed by the responses of the chorister-boys in the same tones and modulations as they are given in catholic churches and that of Dresden. This is followed by a air for *castrato*, in which the violinist has to imitate the tone and that style of singing. The last theme of all describes in a rondo the journey through Saxon Switzerland, in which it endeavours so recal the recollection of the grand beauties of nature and to represent the merry strains of the Bohemian music, which one hears resound from almost every rocky glen; to effect all which in so compressed a limit could of course be but imperfectly realised.

In the course of the year 1836 I wrote also a number of songs, six of which, in one book, were published by *Breitkopf & Härtel* as Op. 101, and among the rest "Sangeslust" (The love of song) given in *Breitkopf & Härtel's* musical album, with four-handed accompaniment; furthermore a Psalm for chorus and soli with orchestral accompaniment, and a fantasia in the shape of an overture to *Raupach's* mythical tragedy "Die Tochter der Luft" ("The Daughter of the Air") which was shortly afterwards performed at one of our subscription concerts. But as in this shape it did not altogether please me, I afterwards worked it up as the first theme of my fifth symphony, which I composed for the "*concerts spirituels*" at Vienna and which was shortly afterwards published by *Haslinger* as Op. 102.* In the beginning of the following

---

* Its first performance in Vienna produced there a great sensation, as several gratifying reports, accompanied by a costly silver cup with suitable inscription, testify. The Vienna Musical Journal said in a very

year. (1837) I wrote my third duet for pianoforte and violin in *E major*, which was afterwards published by *Paul* of Dresden as Op. 112.

About this same time I made earnest preparations to carry out an idea which had long occupied my thought, namely to give a musical festival, for which Cassel seemed to me in many respects exceedingly well adapted. My plan of this was as follows, on Whitsunday afternoon to give *Mendelssohn's* oratorio of "Paulus" (St. Paul) in the church of St. Martin; on Whitmonday evening, with the church lighted up, to perform my symphony "Die Weihe der Töne" and my oratorio of "Die letzten Dinge;" an Whittuesday in the forenoon, at the theatre, a concert of foreign and native singers and virtuosi, and on the same evening, as was usual on the second festival day, a new opera.

The invitations abroad, the assembling of the musicians, and the rehearsal of the oratorios by the choral-society had already begun, when to my application to the Prince

---

enthusiastic review, among other things: It is again a work, that speaks its own master's praise in elegant language; a pure whole, a thing apart of itself, all of one casting. The introduction, andante *C sharp*, breathes a cheerful repose which gradually assumes an impassioned character and prepares the hearer for the transition to the allegro, *C minor*, which, replete with treasures of harmony bears in itself the germ of an imposing effect. . . . . The second theme, Larghetto, *A major*, is a conglomerate of deep feeling, warm fantasy, and of song replete with sentiment etc.; in this again each note speaks to the heart with irresistible force. . . . . The scherzo, *C sharp*, opens with a bold freshness of appeal to life and cheerfulness, the sharp rhythms, the unceasing and restess competition of the wind and stringed instruments, the impetuous bursts of tonic power as opposed to the soft clear flowing cantilene of the alternative, — and, all these effected in a manner so original and striking as to defy expression in words. . . . . . . For the *presto* finale, the poet of sound appears to have husbanded as much as possible the sum total of his creative powers. . . . . Not one of the numberless beauties were lost upon the hearers, each theme in succession received the merited tribute to his mastery; and indeed the richly fantastic scherzo electrified all so unanimously, that a *da capo* was imperatively called for." . . . .

for permission I received the following authoritative dicision from his private secretary: "The days of performance must be changed, as the evening of Whitsunday could not be granted without disturbing those who had prepared themselves to receive the holy sacrament on that evening; neither could any concert be allowed on Whitmonday (on account of the church service and the opera); nor could any scaffolding be erected in the large church for the chorus, as it would be unbecoming in the locality of the burial vault of the electoral family. His highness must await other proposals, before he could graciously condescend to grant his permission."

To this I replied that a musical festival in Cassel could alone prove successful, and the risk of the very considerable expense could alone be safely incurred if it were permitted, as at other places, and as is the custom at the musical festivals on the lower Rhine, to take place in the Whitsuntide holidays, when a great number of strangers would flock to the town and the lovers of music of the neighbouring places would not be prevented by business from attending. That if Whitsunday evening could not be granted, no other two succeeding evenings of that time could be found for performances in the church. As, furthermore, no other appropriate place was to be found in Cassel, than the large church, and that the erection of seats therein could not be allowed, I found myself compelled to abandon totally the projected musical festival.

Unpleasant to all parties as was this complete failure of the plan, I was compelled to abide by it, despite the somewhat considerable expense I had already incurred, and of which I could reimburse myself but a very small part only by the re-sale of the procured song-parts to the choral society. As meanwhile, however, we had industriously practised *Mendelssohn's* oratorio, and become more and more delighted with it, I proposed to give it on Whitsunday at the concert which had been permitted for the benefit of the relief fund; but this was refused also by the Prince, so that we were obliged to content ourselves with gratifying the lovers of music with two private performances of the oratorio upon the pianoforte at the society of St. Cecilia.

In the summer of 1837 I received an invitation to go to Prague to direct the performance of my opera "Der Berg-Geist" (The Spirit of the Mountain) and for that purpose I thought of proceeding thither at the commencement of the holidays. But as the permission had not been received at the treasury of the theatre on the evening before, I addressed myself to the Prince between the acts of the opera, and enquired of him, Whether he had any orders for me to execute upon the journey. In the somewhat indistinct answer I received from him I understood, it is true, something about my permission not having been made out; but as I had no time to lose, I found myself under the necessity of setting out without it at 4 o'clock the next morning. Seeing *Feige*, the director of the theatre, walking in the neighbourhood of my house at that early hour, I thought he might have been sent to ascertain whether I really had the boldness to set out on my journey without the written permission. On the first day's journey indeed, I was not without some uneasiness lest a mounted messenger might be sent after us to order our return. I therefore hastened as much as possible at every post-station the putting-to of fresh horses, and we thus crossed the frontier without molestation. After a journey of six days we at length reached Prague, where *Marianne* and *Theresa* were greatly struck by the beauty of the city and had moreover the gratification to learn from the theatre bills placarded at the corners of the streets, that my opera Jessonda was to be given that evening, in which a foreign singer was to make her debut. That the opera was a great favorite here was evident from the fact that immediately after the performance of the overture, the public encored it. The "Blumenduet" (flower duet) and the duet "Schönes Mädchen" (lovely maiden) were also encored. But I was very much annoyed at several omissions, for which however the director of the Prague orchestra was not to blame, being omissions which were customary in Vienna, from whence the score had been supplied. The principal singers were very good, so that a favourable result was also to be anticipated for the "Berg-Geist."

On the following morning I was taken by suprise by a visit from a zealous lover of music, Dr. *Hutzelmann*, who had been informed that I was fond of swimming, and had for that reason come to take me to the military school of natation on the Moldau; the officer attached to that establishment, who accompanied me, soon remarked that I was a practised swimmer, and proposed a swimming excursion outside the school, in which he ordered me to be accompanied by two soldiers in a boat. They took my clothes with them, and after I had swum for about half an hour with the stream, they assisted me into the boat, in which I dressed myself while the soldiers rowed us back to the town. While I was swimming near the boat, our conversation turned more and more upon my compositions, with which the musical instructor in swimming was almost as well acquainted as myself. He proposed to me a similar enjoyment every day in the Moldau, and next morning found him already waiting for me with his boat near the swimming-school. Meanwhile the rehearsals of the "Berg-Geist" went on exceedingly well. The director of the orchestra had very carefully managed the private rehearsals, and studied everything so well, that in two performances which I myself conducted the opera was eminently successful. Upon my entering the orchestra I was not only received by the public in the most enthusiastic manner, but loudly called for each time at the conclusion of the opera. The singers who supported the chief characters were madame *Podhorski* as Alma, Messrs. *Pöck* and *Emminger*, as Berg-Geist and Oskar, who sang and performed exceedingly well, and the opera maintained its place in the repertory of Prague theatre for a long time. We remained a few days longer in Prague, and I played at several private parties not only quartets but also my sonatas and solo-music with my wife's accompaniment, who likewise played some quite new composition of *Kittl* and *Kleinwächter* for four hands, in which she displayed great ability and quickness in reading at sight. The *Kleinwächter* family made several excursions with us into the beautiful environs of Prague, by which means we became intimately acquainted with all the attractions of that fine city. At length however we were obliged to tear ourselves away from these enjoyments and resumed our journey. Now also came the most fatiguing part of our tour, that to Vienna, in which we suffered exceedingly from the heat and dust, as also from the dirty and wretched accommodation of the inns where we passed the night. On the fourth day we arrived half dead at Vienna and put up at the "Erzherzog Carl" hotel. After I had called upon my former friends, we passed some very pleasant days there, for which we had to thank my Cassel friends *von Steuber*, the ambassador from the Elector of Hesse, the Baron *von Lannoy*, and particularly my Viennese publisher, *Haslinger*. The latter took us every evening to some new gardens, where *Strauss* and *Lanner* gave their concerts, and where we supped exceedingly well *à la carte* at the little tables spread for the entertainment of the guests. Sometimes, also, we went to the theatre, to see the real Viennese popular farces, but my female companions were not sufficiently acquainted with the Viennese dialect, to relish them thoroughly.

After the lapse of a fortnight, in which we participated in all the amusements of Vienna, we took leave of our kind friends and resumed our journey towards the beautifully situated Salzburg, which is one of the finest possible, particularly the first half, the way across the lake to the Ischl baths. In Salzburg, which as the birth-place of *Mozart* was to me sacred ground, we first of all visited his widow, the present wife of Privy Councillor *von Nissen*, who was very pleased at our calling upon her, and in whose house we made the acquaintance of her two sons. In the excursions we made into the neighbourhood in one of the customary light, one-horse vehicles of the country, we were most pleased at the celebrated Gollinger waterfall, and with a sliding trip through the rock-salt-works at Hallein, which was something quite new for my female fellow travellers. From Salzburg we now went on to Munich, where I learned to my great surprise, that the Prince of Hesse had just arrived there. As it was now necessary for me to apologise to him for my departure from Cassel, I addressed myself for that purpose to the Marshal of the court, *von der Malsburg*, and at the same time informed him that I had been requested by the intendant of the Munich theatre to conduct there the performance of my opera "Jessonda," but for which I would first request the Prince's permission. On the following morning the Prince sent word to me that it would be very agreeable to him that I should direct the opera, and in that case he would prolong his stay to hear it. Adorned with a hat lent to me by Mr. *von der Malsburg* and a little bit cut off from the ribbon of his order, I repaired the next day to the appointed audience, and was received by the Prince with the following words: "Why, you disappeared from Cassel all at once." To which I replied: "I thought I had taken my leave in the form prescribed," and as he said nothing further on the subject, the matter was so far settled for this time. But the contemplated representation of "Jessonda" did not take place during my presence in Munich, as the king expected some days after a visit from the Prince, and had deferred the opera till then, and in the meantime my leave of absence had expired. We therefore left Munich before. On our way back we paid a visit to my uncle Professor *Adolphus Hencke* in Erlangen, where we made the acquaintance of the present Councillor *Rudolph Wagner* of Göttingen, and returned to Cassel before the Prince arrived.

Shortly afterwards, I received a letter from *Hermstedt*, wherein, by request of the Princess von Sondershausen, he commissioned me to write some soprano songs for her with pianoforte and clarinet accompaniment. As this task was much to my liking, I composed in the course of a few weeks six songs of this kind (Op. 103, published by *Breitkopf & Härtel* of Leipzic) which by the express desire of the Princess I dedicated to her, and for which I received from her the present of a very costly ring.

I began the year 1838 with the composition of the "Vaterunser" [Lord's Prayer] of *Klopstock* (Op. 104, *Breitkopf & Härtel*, Leipzic) which I wrote with a double chorus for men's voices; at first only for pianoforte accompaniment, and afterwards instrumentated for orchestra, as it was intended to be performed at the singing festival for the benefit of the *Mozart* institution at Frankfort, where though I was obliged to decline directing in person, it was first performed on the 29th July, and having been well studied, produced, according to the reports from there, a very solemn and imposing effect.

In the succeeding months I again composed several songs for soprani or tenori, which appeared as Op. 105, at *Hellmuth's* in Halle.

Meanwhile the first public performance of "Paulus" took place at last on Good Friday in the garrison-church, and we were looking forward with pleasure to its repetition on Whitsunday, when our good *Theresa* fell suddenly ill of a malignant nervous fever, which in a short time brought her blooming life to a close. On the Tuesday before Ascension Day we had, chiefly at *Theresa's* own wish, made a pleasant excursion to Wilhelmshöhe; there she first complained of indisposition, and on our return home she was immediately obliged to take to her bed. As Dr. *Ludwig Pfeiffer*, our then attendant physician and second brother of my wife, was just then absent from Cassel, we called in once more her uncle, Dr. *Harnier*, who although no alarming symptoms as yet shewed themselves, visited the patient several times daily, until after the lapse of a week, to our great terror he pronounced her complaint to be nervous fever. This now constantly increased in vehemence, and as in her fits of delirium she spoke continually of a journey we had contemplated to Carlsbad, the idea of which had greatly pleased her, I promised her that she should go thither as soon as she recovered. This greatly soothed her, but nevertheless did not diminish the fever, and on Whitsunday morning the blooming maiden of nineteen succumbed to the fearful malady. The loss of the talented amiable girl plunged us in such misery that we looked forward with earnest longing to the approaching theatrical vacation, in order to leave immediately the mournful surroundings of our home, and seek far away from Cassel some respite from the constant remembrance of our anguish.

After we had been delayed another eight days in Cassel by the reiterated retarding of my leave of absence, we were enabled to set out for Carlsbad on the 23nd June, accompanied by my mother-in-law, to whom the use of the waters had also been recommended, which was exceedingly welcome to me, particularly on account of my wife, who had taken very much to heart the loss of our *Theresa*. No sooner were we arrived in Carlsbad than we met with *Hesse* of Breslau, and in our walks to the springs soon made the acquaintance of other warm lovers of music, with whom on dull days, when the weather would permit of no excursions together to the charming environs, we made up small music parties at our lodgings. As a young lady from Breslau, Miss *Ottilia Schubert,* sang most charmingly, my wife practised her in my new songs with clarinet accompaniment, at which a first-rate clarinet player, Mr. *Seemann* from Hannover, took the clarinet part; in this manner our hearers became acquainted with a new style of songs which they had not known before, and which interested them exceedingly. Somewhat later, *De Beriot* also arrived with his sister-in-law *Pauline Garcia*, in Carlsbad, and the concert which he gave at the theatre afforded us very great enjoyment. He played with great purity, brilliancy and execution, but his compositions did not altogether please us, and Miss *Garcia*, afterwards the so-celebrated Mrs. *Viardot-Garcia,* sang with a voice of great compass, though not exactly a very fine one, and with great artistic skill. She especially delighted her hearers with the execution of her Spanish romances and ballads, in which she accompanied herself very well on the pianoforte.

[Here, unfortunately, *Spohr's* own narrative of his life closes for ever! — To the subsequent encouragements of his relatives to resume it he used to reply: "I take no pleasure in writing now; and there are sufficient materials for the continuance of the Biography at any time, in the diaries and papers of my wife." — Hereupon, this latter, mindful of this express indication of her husband's, resolved to place notes, journals, and letters of every kind, and even memoranda jotted down for her sole private use and edification, at the disposal of those members of the family who undertook by means of extracts, without any pretence to literary skill — in simple, unadorned truthfulness, after *Spohr's* own example — to carry out the history of his life to the end.]

* * *

After a beneficial use of the waters, *Spohr* left Carlsbad, and on his way back stopped at Leipzic, where some musical parties quickly got up by the families of his acquaintance enabled him to pass some very agreeable days, and at which he played his favorite quartet in *A minor*, with his newest concertino, to the great delight of his hearers. Upon this occasion, it was a source of great pleasure to him to make the long desired acquaintance of *Robert Schumann*, who though in other respects exceedingly quiet and reserved, yet evinced his admiration of *Spohr* with great warmth, and gratified him by the performance of several of his interesting fantasias.

Mendelssohn was at the time unfortunately absent, and in his next letter to *Spohr* expressed his great regret thereat; and requested him at the same time to send him his last symphony (No. 5, *C minor*), as it was intended to perform it at the opening of the approaching season in the first concert of the Leipzic Gewandhaus. While expressing his thanks for it beforehand, he says at the same time, in reference to a song of *Spohr's* with which he had just previously become acquainted: "As I am now on the subject of thanks, I must thank you many times and with all my heart for the beautiful song in *F sharp* with clarinet accompaniment, the "Zwiegesang," which pleases me exceedingly and has so completely charmed me with its prettyness, that I both sing and play it every day. It is not on account of any one particular feature that I admire it, but for its perfectly natural sweetness as a whole, and which from beginning to end flows so lightly and gratefully to the feelings. How often have I sung it with my sisters, and each time with renewed pleasure! And for that I must now also thank you. . . . ."

The first work with which *Spohr* occupied himself after his return to Cassel, was a fourth quartet for stringed instruments *(G minor)*, which was published by *Paul* of Dresden as Op. 106, both in its original form and as arranged by *Spohr* himself for the pianoforte for four hands. — About the same time he received the very unusual order to make arrangements for a concert at court, which after frequent and long deliberations, at length took place on the 19th. September at the palace of Wilhelmshöhe. The instrumental pieces were performed by the members of the electoral chapel, but the vocal subjects were at *Spohr's* recommendation confided to *Firnhaber*, a distinguished dilettant professor from Hildesheim, who himself had a court appointment, and had been for some years tutor to Baron *Scholley*, stepson to the Prince. With a very fine high tenor voice, he combined a good musical education, and a lively sentiment for art, and *Spohr's* compositions, with the manifold beauties of which he had made himself more and more acquainted during his residence in Cassel, soon inspired him with real enthusiasm. As *Spohr* also took as much pleasure in his society as in his charming style of singing, he was a constant assistant at all music parties, and his presence in Cassel suggested to *Spohr* many of his most pleasing and favorite songs, of which were: the book of songs from Op. 101 to 105; the duet for soprano and tenor Op. 107, (both published by *Simrock*) and *Franz Dingelstedt's* "Mitternacht" (midnight), which song was published by itself by *Paul* of Dresden. Respecting the last, the author of the words, who had then an appointment at the gymnasium of Fulda, wrote to *Spohr* at a subsequent period, expressing the greatest satisfaction: "Yesterday evening I heard your song 'Mitternacht' sung, and still deeply impressed by it, I hasten to thank you, and to express both my delight and my pride therein. I will not say that you have entered into the spirit of *my words* — for what are they after all? No, it is you who have caught the long, low, solemn whisperings of midnight. For the first time I regret that I am not sufficiently acquainted with music to understand and express the enthusiasm of the initiated in matters of change of tempi, tone &c.; in your art I am a naturalist merely, but I enjoy this production of it yet more deeply and intimately than they all; for I feel as a poet in the matter! — Not a word more now of common-place praise and song of thanksgiving! You have afforded me an hour of delight, and stirred within me emotions such as alas! I can feel here but seldom: a reward for my aspirations, an incentive to future efforts! You, I am sure, understand me!" . . . ,

In October 1838 *Spohr*, following the example set by many of the larger towns of Germany, succeeded at length in carrying out his reiterated proposition to give a concert at the theatre in aid of the funds for the erection of the testimonial to the memory of Mozart. The first part of the concert comprised among other things *Mozart's* symphony in *D minor*; and in the second, tableaux vivants, with appropriate music, from *Mozart's* operas, in which at the conclusion, the last chorus of the requiem resounded, and the bust of *Mozart*, placed in the foreground of the stage, was crowned by genii with wreaths of laurel. — A similar festival took place the following spring in aid of the fund for the memorial to *Beethoven*, but with this difference, that the programme contained besides the choicest selection from the works of that honoured maestro, a composition of *Spohr's* also, his most recent concertino: "Sonst und Jetzt," which he had performed for the first time shortly before at one of the regular winter concerts, and upon this occasion reproduced at the express desire of the Prince. The success upon both occasions was extremely great.

At the commencement of the same year, several other remarkable concerts took place, and among others, *Ole Bull* performed twice in the theatre, to overflowing houses, notwithstanding the increased prices of admission, and filled the public with astonishment and admiration of his play. *Spohr* himself took the warmest interest in the wonderful play of his colleague in art, and gave a musical party at his own house in his honour, in which he first played one of his own quartets, but in the following he resigned the first place to *Ole Bull*, and even took the second violin. His opinion respecting *Ole Bull's* play may here be given in his own words, when writing to his friend *Speyer* upon the subject: "*Ole Bull* has lately given two concerts at the theatre and greatly charmed the public. His many-toned strokes and the accurate certainty of the left hand are remarkable, but like *Paganini*, he sacrifices too much to the tricks of the art. His tone on the weak strings is bad, and he can only use the *A* and *D* string on the lower part and *pianissimo*. This gives to his play a great monotony when he cannot bring in his tricks of art. We found this in two of *Mozart's* quartets, which he played at my house. On the other hand, he plays with much feeling, but not with a cultivated taste." With every acknowledgment made by *Spohr* of the extraordinary performances of *Ole Bull*, certain features of charlatanism, so foreign to his own *simple* nature, did not escape him, and he frequently related at a subsequent period with a good-natured smile to his own friends, and to others, how *Ole Bull* at a passage which offered him an opportunity of shining in one of his incomparable *pp*, kept his bow hovering over the strings for several seconds, so that the public who listened in breathless silence for the last sound of his constantly decreasing tones, might believe they still continued dying away in *ppp*.

About this time also, the representation of a small opera: "Der Matrose," in the composition of which *Spohr* had assisted, was frequently repeated. The text, adopted from the French, was written by the admired comedian *Birnbaum*, and at his wish set to music by four composers of this place, *Spohr*, *Hauptmann*, *Baldewein* (director of music), and the song-writer and teacher of music *Grenzebach*, collectively. Besides the overture, *Spohr* had undertaken the song of a home-returning mariner, together with the finale and all these "numbers," and the whole operetta met with lively approbation from the public. Unfortunately *Spohr*, at a later period, was no longer in possession of these, as they remained in the hands of Mr. *Birnbaum*, for whose benefit the first representation of the opera was intended. The highly characteristic mariner's song only appeared some time afterwards, arranged by himself with four-handed accompaniment for the pianoforte, and was published by *Paul* of Dresden.

In April 1839 *Spohr* received a pressing invitation from England to direct the performance of his oratorio "Des Heiland's letzte Stunden" at the grand musical festival which was to take place in September at Norwich. After he had succeeded in obtaining the requisite leave of absence from the Prince, the customary tour during the summer holidays was this time limited to a shorter excursion, in which he made visits to his relatives and friends. He next proceeded to Holzminden — where *Spohr's* younger brothers *Augustus* and *Charles* resided with their families, the former, as a fiscal assessor, and the latter a law official of the duchy of Brunswick. Thence he went on to Gandersheim to visit his venerable parents, and lastly to Catlenburg, to Councillor *Lüder*. As a matter of course on this journey he was not without his violin, and wherever *Spohr* came he found grateful hearers, who considered themselves superlatively happy in listening to his play. More than any of the other pieces that he executed, his newest, charming composition, a Spanish rondo for pianoforte and violin, afforded them delight; this soon became one of the most favorite pieces of music in Cassel also, and remained so up to a very recent period. At a later period, when it was published by *Mechetti* in Vienna as Op. 111, there appeared simultaneously a pianoforte arrangement of it for four hands by *Czerny*, which was certainly most welcome to all who had not the advantage of hearing the original composition executed by a distinguished violinist.

Returned to Cassel, *Spohr* finished his "Historical Symphony in the style and taste of four different periods" which he had begun before he set out on his journey. (Theme the first: The period of *Bach-Händel*, 1720. Adagio: *Haydn-Mozart* 1780. Scherzo: *Beethoven* period 1810. Finale: The most modern period 1840) a work, which afforded him not only during its creation, but also upon the occasions of its closely following performances in Cassel, the greatest satisfaction. Abroad also, and first in London, where he sold it to the Philharmonic Society for the term of one year, and subsequently in Germany, where he was permitted to make it known after the lapse of that period, it met with the most lively reception. Many voices were, however, raised in blame, and of these that of *Schumann*, in his musical journal, was the severest in tone. On the other hand Baron *Lannoy*, in Vienna, reported that the work had been received with great favour: *Mendelssohn* sent in a most flattering account of its reception at Leipzic; and many letters full of praise arrived from England.

In the beginning of September *Spohr* set out upon the journey to England, accompanied by his wife and his friend Mrs. *von Malsburg*, with whom he had been many years acquainted.*

After an exceedingly rough passage, which delayed his arrival in London by six hours, *Spohr* was very agreeably surprised in the midst of the confusion incidental to such circumstances, on being addressed by a gentleman, a stranger to him, exhibiting an order from the custom-house authorities, to deliver *Spohr's* luggage without examination, and who then took

---

* As *Spohr* himself always considered this English musical festival (the Norwich festival) and the flattering reception given to him and his works in that country, as the most brilliant period in his active life, its description may reasonably find a place here in a somewhat more detailed form.

him and his female fellow-travellers speedily and safely to land in a boat, where a coach was in waiting to take him to the hospitable house of professor *Edward Taylor*. In the amiable family-circle of that gentleman and surrounded by the genuine English usages and comforts which had so many charms for the guests, they soon found themselves at home, and a few days sufficed to lay the foundation of a life-long friendship. As their farther journey permitted but a short stay in London, it was necessary to make the best use of the time to see the objects most worthy of notice in the metropolis, which filled the travellers with wonder and admiration. The visit to Westminster Abbey made a deep impression upon all, and this was expressed in the letters they sent home:* "The very entry into this majestic structure, which is certainly the finest of all the objects of note in London, makes an impression so deep and solemn upon the mind, that we could scarcely repress our emotion; and in reality one seems to move no longer among things of this world. The tones of a splendid organ may have contributed to this feeling, — for divine service was just being performed, — and this was followed by sacred psalmody sung in double chorus so pure, so sweet and executed with such feeling, that they seemed like the voices of angels from the realms of bliss. We had neither of us ever heard any thing like it before. Now again the notes of the organ pealed forth, and we distinguished harmonies of *Spohr's*, and soon recognised the touching sounds of his mass for ten voices; and then the grand overture to "Des Heilands letzten Stunden" was splendidly performed by the celebrated organist *Turle*. . . ."

But the time pressed for the departure to Norwich, where

---

* The extracts given here and subsequently from the letters of *Spohr's* relatives, may find their excuse in the circumstance that he himself had neither leisure nor inclination to write letters during this journey, but was greatly pleased when his female companions wrote home frequently (which of course was always in harmony with his own sentiments), — and he seldom allowed such a letter to leave without having expressed his full concurrence with the contents.

professor *Taylor*,* the chief director of the whole musical festival had already made the necessary preliminary rehearsals of *Spohr's* oratorio, and now received the travellers to accompany them to the mayor of Norwich. On the following morning the mayor took his guests to hear divine service in the cathedral, which is of immense size and considered one of the finest in England. In a letter upon the subject *Spohr's* relative thus expresses herself: Of *such* a celebration of divine service, though it lasted nearly three hours, one is not readily weary; the heavenly music with which it is interspersed in various ways, I cannot describe, and it is performed with a purity and finish such as made great impression also on *Spohr* himself. The congregation did not sing at all, but always followed in their hymnbooks and prayer-books, the text of which (all taken from the Bible) I certainly could understand better than the *sermon*. The choir robed in white, with their tender tones, made an irresistible impression; words, music, and execution, all were in such perfect unison, that I could scarcely imagine a finer worship of the deity in heaven itself. When at the conclusion we passed through the spacious nave of the magnificent building with the whole congregation, the masses of people arranged themselves on either side to permit our passage, and looked at *Spohr* as something wonderful; many also, requested to be introduced to *Spohr*, and our kind mayor, who accompanied us and conducted *Spohr*, was quite happy, and proud of the whole scene. His daughter *Mary*, a charming

---

* As a member of the committee he had conducted the correspondence with *Spohr* relative to his coming, concerning which the following remarks appeared in the "Spectator": "It is highly to the credit of the great master, that to the question what compensation he required for the time and exertions required of him during the journey, and for direction of the oratorio, he simply replied: 'The committee will doubtless have no objection to pay my travelling-expenses?' We are glad to learn that the modesty of this reply and *Spohr's* coming to England without any further negotiation on the matter with the committee, was duly recognised by the latter, who thereupon came to the resolution to present Mr. *Spohr* with a sum of 100 guineas over and above the account of his expenses.

maiden of fifteen, is also enthusiastically fond of music and particularly of *Spohr's;* she plays herself very nicely on the piano, and when her father informed us that it would make her exceedingly happy to play a few notes with *Spohr*, he accompanied her in one of his favorite sonatas of *Mozart*..."

If *Spohr* had understood the English language, the impression made upon him by the divine service would perhaps have been greatly disturbed by the circumstance that the sermon preached upon the occasion was in a great measure levelled against his oratorio. Already before his arrival in Norwich, several persons of the puritanical party had raised their voices against its performance, and endeavoured in every way both in print and in the pulpit to shew that it was profane and sinful to make so sacred a subject as the sufferings and death of Christ, a theme for music. It thus so happened that on the Sunday morning on which *Spohr* visited the cathedral a zealous clergyman considered it his duty to hurl a crushing discourse against his oratorio: The "*Calvary,*" as it is rendered in English, and at the conclusion implored his hearers not to surrender their souls for one day's pleasure, but to stop away from its performance. The "Monthly Chronicle" further observes on the subject: "We now see the fanatical zealot in the pulpit, and sitting right opposite to him the *great composer*, with ears happily deaf to the *English* tongue; but with a demeanour so becoming, with a look so full of pure good will, and with so much humility and mildness in the features, that his countenance alone spoke to the heart like a good sermon. Without intending it, we make a comparison, and cannot for a moment doubt in which of the two dwelt the *spirit* of religion, which denoted the true christian!"

On the day after the performance of the oratorio the same journal says: "This day was to decide the fate of the oratorio "*Calvary,*" and had the decision been unfavourable the fame of Norwich was for ever departed. The public mind was therefore on the greatest stretch, for many persons feared the powerful influence of an adverse clergy. But a better spirit, a sentiment of right feeling triumphed, and hours before the opening of the doors the matter was decided. From far and near the auditory flocked in thousands, evincing a powerful feeling of excitement, and an enthusiasm which increased continually during the performance; and beyond all expectation, a complete triumph was achieved. It may justly be said of this oratorio, that a heavenly inspiration breathes throughout; more than any other work of modern times it is one sprung from the genial source of a warm heart, and cannot be heard with a tearless eye. . . . ." — The bishop of Norwich, who in accordance with his religious bias belonged also to the party of the opponents of the oratorio, and was therefore on a footing of reserve with the mayor, was nevertheless desirous to make the personal acquaintance of his celebrated guest, and sent him repeated notes of invitation to dine with him; as these however were written in English, they of necessity were handed to the mayor as interpreter of their contents, who each time transmitted to him in the name of *Spohr* a reply excusing his inability to accept it. At length it was proposed that he should be introduced to the bishop at one of the concerts, and to this the mayor assented on the condition that *Spohr* should promise him to meet the bishop half way only, and not move a step farther towards him, when he rose from his distant seat to approach *Spohr*.

This adherence to the stiff formality of English ceremony, which was a special and prominent feature in the grandiose arrangements of the mayor, was frequently the source of a variety of ludicrous scenes and discussions. Thus it was that *Spohr*, on the first day that he had gone to the rehearsal of his oratorio, sent thence in haste home to his female fellow travellers, who had remained behind, two gentlemen, strangers, with the invitation that they also should proceed thither, to share in the impressive sight which the magnificent St. Andrew's Hall had presented to him immediately upon entering it. As may readily be imagined the ladies acceded to the invitation, and accepted unhesitatingly the attendance of the "gentlemen as yet unintroduced to them in the house," by which they excited the astonishment of every one there, even to the very domestics; but they had the satisfaction of witnessing themselves, upon arriving at the hall, the enthusiastic reception with which the whole assembly greeted *Spohr* upon his entering the orchestra. Of this the "Monthly Review" speaks as follows: "I would have wished all the world had heard the thunders of applause, the very storm of greetings with which *Spohr* was received by the whole orchestra, down to the very boys of the choir. This reception of the great man, which drew tears of emotion from the eyes of his wife, must also have deeply moved him." On the following evening the first concert was to take place, and *Spohr* was to perform in it his concertino "Sonst und Jetzt" ("Then and Now"); but as there were some difficult passages for the drum in it, he had requested the attendance of the young drummer-boy at his residence in the forenoon, in order to give him personally the necessary instructions concerning his part. When the neat little fellow made his appearance, it was however found that he understand no language but English, and in this predicament he was obliged to have recourse to the assistance of the mayor's amiable little daughter, who then, although astonished at all the unusual doings in her father's house, willingly endeavoured to explain in English to the strange boy the remarks made by *Spohr* in the French language, with many scientific expressions which were quite unintelligible to herself; but which at length she effected with a result so accordant with *Spohr's* wishes, that for years afterwards he always recalled to mind with real pleasure the ludicrous but interesting scenes of that charming effort at intercommunication.

In the evening on which the first of the six monster-concerts took place in the spacious hall filled with nearly 3000 persons and 500 assistants, a symphony of *Haydn* and several song pieces were first given, among which also, the duet from Jessonda: "Schönes Mädchen": but then as the "Times" expressed it, "all eyes were turned with expectancy owards the orchestra in order to greet *Spohr* upon his appearance with an enthusiastic applause. . . . ." "A deep silence of suspense and expectancy reigned at the commencement of his concertino, which he has called "Sonst und Jetzt," in order to express the opposite character of the themes which therein denote the different style of the more ancient and modern compositions." The opinion upon *Spohr's* play then follows in terms of the highest praise, and concludes with the words: "His instrument speaks as eloquently to the heart as the finest melody. The accomplished mastery of his bow as of his fingers, is yet surpassed by the wonderful power of his *mens divinior*. The concertino, after a short but beautiful prelude, begins with a charming minuet of the old school, adorned with a whole wealth of harmonies, which seem to flow of themselves from *Spohr's* pen; then follows a Turkish allegro, replete with fancy and overflowing with the brilliant lustre of modern execution."

A letter written home and others describe the succeeding concerts: "The first sacred concert on Wednesday morning was wonderful; it lasted from half-past 12 to 4 clock, and comprised in the first part many fine old things of *Purcell*, *Palästrina* and others; and in the second and third parts the magnificent oratorio of *Händel*: "Israel in Egypt;" in which the choruses were executed with immense power, and the soli by the English church-singers in the most perfect manner. *Spohr* was inexpressibly delighted with it, and said, "English church-singers only are capable of rendering *Händel's* sublime music in all its grandeur." A peculiar custom which pleases me greatly is, that every time a chorus expresses the praise of God, or in any way adverts to God or Christ, the whole mass of people rise from their seats, and listen to it *standing*. — The order of the musical pieces in the evening concert was very much the same as in the previous one. It began with *Mozart's* symphony in *E flat major*, which was followed by twenty other different subjects, among which were some pieces from operas by *Mozart* and *Weber*, and *Spohr's* terzet from "Zemira and Azor," which is never omitted at any English musical festival. *Spohr* played with his former pupil *Blagrove* his charming concertante in a surpassingly fine manner, and the effect was if possible greater than yesterday. Our hospitable host, who is exceedingly assiduous in his attentions, and accompanies *Spohr* every time on going and returning, seems also extremely happy to be near him, and to joy in his high repute. To-day is, in the opinion of everybody, the grand and most important day, on which *Spohr's* oratorio is to be given. You all know that music, and how grand it is, but no one who was not present, can picture to himself what it was *here*, heard in such a place, faultlessly executed by such a mass, and listened to with such religious attention and enthusiasm. At and after the first part one remarked several exclamations of delight and wonder, but at the second a solemn emotion seemed to reign throughout the whole auditory, and more and more eyes became suffused with tears; not the women only, but strong men were deeply moved And such an effect I consider as the highest and purest praise. They were happy moments for me also when afterwards crowds of gentlemen and ladies who did not like to intrude upon *Spohr*, came to me, to congratulate me, and assured me with much emotion, that this was the most sublime and beautiful thing that was ever composed, with many other similar expressions. The third part, which *Spohr* listened to with us with the greatest delight, comprised the requiem of *Mozart* and other pieces of sacred-music by *Mozart* and *Bach*. . . ."

The public papers gave a detailed account of the deep impression made by *Spohr's* oratorio, and among others the "Norwich Mercury" said: "The beautiful hall was crowded, nevertheless, even before the commencement, a breathless silence pevailed; a solemn religious sentiment reigned throughout the assembly. The inspired composer raised his staff — the staff descended — and mournful tones, low and faintly heard like distant wailings felt upon the ear, and made a powerful impression on the feelings: the brilliant hall seemed as though changed to a solemn temple — and every worldly thought was in an instant dissipated. — The overture reveals the character of the whole; the succeeding introductory chorus of the most agreeable softness and purity seems to foreshadow a peace momentarily witheld from us by a characteristic sentiment of sadness. The ensuing recitative of St. John relates the treason of Judas, and this is immediately followed in striking contrast by the aria of the betrayer, in which the disorder of the mind induced by the reproofs of conscience is expressed with great power and truth by the accompaniment. Now begins the part of Mary, with a charming air accompanied by the female chorus, and which, replete with tenderest devotion, appeals to our inmost feelings. In a difficult but very expressive recitative St. John prepares us for the entry of St. Peter, who has denied his master, and in the air sung by him, replete with intensity of expression, the composer in good taste and with correct judgment expresses the distinction between the reproving conscience of the erring apostle and the preceding hopeless agony of spirit in the betrayer. In the succeeding chorus reigns a simple majesty, a confidant reliance upon the justice of God, the expression of which is eminently successful. — In the scene which follows, in which the judgment hall is opened to us and Christ denounced before Caiphas, the inspiration of the composer has reached its culminating point: the manifold contending passions — the fiendish excitement of the populace, the humble resignation in the sorrow of the disciples, the exalted resignation of the saviour — all these are brought by him with such painful truthfulness of expression before the mind, that we feel it impossible to approach in music nearer to reality and truth than *Spohr* has succeeded in doing in his treatment of this pre-eminently tragic moment of the Redeemer's life.

The second part begins with an introductory funeral march, and a striking chorus of the disciples expressive of their sympathy with and lamentations for the fate of their master. The ensuing chorus of the priests and people, who wildly and savagely taunt the redeemer upon the cross, is in our opinion almost the most powerful and wonderful passage in the whole work. The moving recitative of John and Mary is, moreover, intense in its effect, and their aria full of melody and grace, close upon which follows the gem of the whole oratorio, the unsurpassable terzet for two soprani and an alto, "Jesus, himmlische Liebe" (Jesus, heavenly love), with its sweetly soothing harmonies. This terzet is a master-piece of the purest finish; *Spohr* himself never wrote any thing more beautiful. The solemn earnestness of the chorus: "Allgütiger Gott," with the canonic entrata at the words: "In seiner Todesnoth," is indeed in conception and form the most original. In masterly recitatives John prepares us for the concluding scene, and after the last words of Jesus: "It is fulfilled," the low sound of distant thunder is heard, which continues as though warningly during the fine and truly pious quartet. And now the orchestra seems to burst all bounds, and to contend in one wild storm, which the powerful hand of the composer can alone direct and allay. We have already heard many musical representations of storm and tempest, but as yet nothing at all like this; and we think that this immense effect is derived from *Spohr's* seizing the powerful phenomena of nature more in their general grandeur than in their detail. We are struck with awe at the overpowering effect itself and with wonder at the mind that could so apply and direct all the resources of art. A recitative with splendid modulations leads to the short choral passage of the disciples, in which the divinity of the Redeemer is proclaimed, simply, firmly and powerfully. The final chorus, a prayer of the disciples full of sorrow and hopeful faith, is simple, melodious and elevated; a poetical outpouring in music, which must excite the sympathy of every human being who has a trusting belief in a future life. — When the last accord died away in its tragic grandeur, we looked around us — not a breath was to be heard, deep silence everywhere — all were impressed with feelings more powerful than they could express. It was a moment of holy reverential exstacy — no noisy outburst of rapture, — the impression was too overpowering for earthly utterance, — but it was a lasting one, and will assuredly never be forgotten."

The English newspapers spoke also respecting *Spohr's* manner of conducting, and the "Spectator" said on the subject: "It is truly delightful, wonderful in precision and firmness of tact, and at the same time accompanied by motions plainly indicative of the effect proposed." And again: "We see in *Spohr*, a man who has a clear comprehension of his object, and knows his work as thoroughly in all its details as in the whole. At the rehearsal, whenever a note was missed, he sang it, in whatever harmony it might chance to be, and in doing so his voice was very melodious."

The letter previously referred to says further, in reference to the following days, under the date of September 20th: "Yesterday, before the commencement of the evening concert, a deputation from the committee waited upon *Spohr* with the request to play his concertino once more; this, however, he decidedly begged to be excused compliance with, and the more so, as he had already agreed to direct in person the overture to and air from "Faust," with which the second part of the concert began. Immediately he entered the orchestra for that purpose, he was again greeted with loud and long continued applause, in which doubtless the audience expressed, besides, their sense of admiration of his oratorio, which, according to English custom, could not be applauded at the time of performance. To-day *Händel's* splendid "Messiah" was given for finale, which here also never fails to make its constant impression. And now at length the grand festival has terminated with all its pleasures and magnificences! It indeed required an inspired and corporeal strength of frame such as *Spohr* fortunately possesses, to hear in the short space of so few days the ordeal of six concerts of four and a half hours' duration each, besides rehearsals and daily dinner parties, with unimpaired freshness of spirit — not to speak of all the visits paid him and the strangest requests from far and near, with which he complied as far as he could. The last day with its scenes of leavetaking, was also a very trying one to the feelings, and cost me I must confess, many tears. — The parting from all the kind people who, although we were strangers to them, had received us with such great heartiness, was very painful. When next I see you I will relate many wonderful instances of the amiability of these Englishmen, and of their admiration of *Spohr*, which even extended itself to me. But the estimation in which *Spohr* is held here in England, and the manner in which this is evinced on all sides is almost incredible". . . .

After so brilliant a success of *Spohr's* oratorio, and after he had himself witnessed, as the "Spectator" expresses it — "How the orchestra and singers competed to shew him that England was the country of all others best fitted for the performance of his oratorio," nothing could be more agreeable to him than the proposal made to him during his stay, to compose especially a new oratorio for the next Norwich musical festival, which would take place in 1842.

Scarcely was he returned to Cassel than professor *Taylor* sent him the English text of "The fall of Babylon," of his composition, the text of which, though much to *Spohr's* liking, it was necessary first to have translated into German, as he had not confidence sufficient in his knowledge of the English language to undertake the composition from the original text. Though the translation did not so completely succeed in a truthful rendering of the expressions and rhythm of the English text, as that this could subsequently be adapted to the composition without much alteration, it nevertheless sufficed so well for the desired object that *Spohr* could proceed at once upon a work which so greatly interested him. Filled with real inspiration for the task, he devoted thereto every leisure hour that remained to him from his numerous professional duties, nor did he rest until he had completed the whole and satisfied himself with its performance on the pianoforte at the St. Cecilia festival of 1840, that he had fully succeeded in it. In pursuance of an understanding with the Norwich committee a public performance of it with full orchestra was to take place in Cassel on the ensuing Good Friday of 1841 and a second at Easter 1842, but with these exceptions the work was to remain unused and in abeyance until the Norwich festival in the autumn of the latter year, and then first be made public simultaneously in England and Germany in both languages. —

But to return to the year 1840, which *Spohr* entered upon with great activity in the preparatory studies for the representation of the opera "The Lovers' Duel," which till then had never been performed in Cassel; for the principal characters of which he had just then found suitable performers. The first representation took place for the benefit of the relief fund, and with a very full house brought unusually good receipts, which however unfortunately were extracted from the treasury of the theatre on the following night in the most incomprehensible manner, and despite the well-secured locality in which the money was deposited. But a very small amount could then be collected to replace this loss to the relief fund, a circumstance which greatly marred the satisfaction *Spohr* had derived from the success of his opera, which had met with a most gratifying reception from the public.

About this time *Spohr* received an invitation from Aix-la-Chapelle to direct the musical festival of the district of the Lower Rhine, which was to be held there; on which occasion a very pressing solicitation for his leave of absence was addressed to the Prince on the part of the committee. This memorial had the desired effect; for shortly afterwards the Prince sent for *Spohr*, and tendered him of his own accord in the most friendly manner the leave of absence he had not yet solicited.

As every obstacle was now smoothed away, *Spohr* set out upon his journey at the end of May, and was not only received upon his arrival in Aix-la-Chapelle with serenades of welcome, but also on his putting up for each night at Frankfort and Cologne on his journey through. In the splendidly furnished house of the notary *Pascal*, in which Mr. and Mrs. *Spohr* found a most hospitable reception, the succeeding days devoted to the necessary rehearsals passed quickly and agreeably. On Whitsunday, in the theatre, which had been converted into a music saloon, *Händel's* "Judas Maccabeus" was performed, of which some epistolary notices spoke as fellows: "When *Spohr* entered the orchestra to conduct the oratorio he was received with enthusiastic applause; we had the best places in the first row reserved for us, exactly opposite to where the very prettily arranged mass of five hundred and forty-seven co-operators, brilliantly illuminated, presented a very charming coup d'œil. The music, which had already greatly pleased us by its splendid effect in the rehearsals, was now naturally heard to yet greater advantage. The solo singers — Mrs. *Fischer-Achten*, *Albertazzi* and *Müller*, Mr. *de Vrucht* from Amsterdam and Mr. *Fischer* — good as they were on the whole, did not make upon us the same impression of *finished* excellence as did the choruses, which completely charmed us." In the second concert also, in which besides *Spohr's* "Lord's Prayer," the overture to "Medea," the *A major* symphony of *Beethoven*, and *Mozart's Davidde penitente*, were performed, *Spohr* upon every entry and exit was greeted with unbounded applause, and at the termination a wreath of laurel was presented to him by two young ladies. In the third concert, of a mixed character, Mrs. *Fischer-Achten*, and *Albertazzi*, with the celebrated *Staudigl* of Vienna, were respectively heard and excited general admiration. The singing of all three, was each in its kind what may be termed of the most perfect finish. As worthy finale to the whole, the repetition of the last magnificent chorus from *Spohr's* "Lord's Prayer" followed, which again drew from the audience the most enthusiastic bursts of applause. . . . ."

As on the following forenoon the brothers *Müller* of Brunswick gave a quartet concert in the "Redoutensaal," *Spohr* delayed his departure, at their urgent entreaty, in order to play his third double quartet with them, which was again also rewarded with its usual rapturous ovation. In this manner was this grand festival brought to a successful termination, and the general satisfaction which it had elicited was but little detracted from by the reproving voice of Mr. A. *Schindler*, whose *cartes de visites* made him known as *"ami de Beethoven,"* and who in previous musical festivals had begun to distinguish himself by his disputes with *Mendelssohn* respecting his slow tempi in the conducting of works of *Beethoven's*, and now also in a similar manner found fault with *Spohr* for his manner of conducting the *A major* symphony. This — with the exception of the general disapprobation that it elicited — had no further result than that *Spohr*, at the urgent and reiterated desire of the committee, replied to *Schindler* in a short but decisive letter, but which, couched in *Spohr's* usual mild language, did not disturb the personal understanding of either during the festival.

After a few week's return only, to Cassel, and during the theatrical vacation, *Spohr* set out upon another journey and proceeded first to Gandersheim, where all his brothers with their families were assembled, to pay a last visit to their mother, who was dangerously ill, and who, in spite of her suffering condition, felt extreme pleasure in seeing them round her. Although she had not left her room for several weeks, and had therefore been unable to go up stairs to the upper story of the house, yet when she heard that *Spohr* was going to play something with his wife in the music-room there, she requested to be assisted to get up there, "to hear her loved son for the last time, and in fancy to dream away in listening to his tones;" and upon that occasion, seated in the midst of her children, listened to him with joyful emotion and interest. As on the days immediately ensuing a visible improvement in her condition seemed to have taken place *Spohr*, in full hopes of greeting his mother once more upon his return, continued his journey to Lübeck with a mind more at rest. But alas! his hopes were not realised, for before he returned to Gandersheim he received the lamentable announcement of her death!

From Lübeck *Spohr* proceeded to Hamburg, where he

arrived just in time to undertake the direction of his opera "Jessonda." The performance of the opera, in which Mrs. *Walker* as Jessonda, and Mr. *Reichel* as Dandau, especially distinguished themselves, was in every respect a great success, and there were immense applause and loud demonstrations in honour of *Spohr*. As it took place immediately after the close of the performances of the Italian operas, the "Hamburger Zeitung" gave a comparative notice in its next issue of these two different kinds of musical entertainment. It began with the words: "On Saturday the whole song-loving company of Italian operatic performers departed in high spirits; on Sunday, *Spohr* the German master took the director's chair in the town theatre to conduct his splendid "Jessonda" in person. With the *former*, abundance of noise, merriment, and somewhat of dissension, to-do, and submissive politeness — but *here*, calm, noble dignity, honest thanks, becoming demeanour, and permanent merit &c." Further on it adds: "The lovers of music in Hamburg celebrated on Sunday a real musical festival in the theatre; they were not only enabled to express aloud their recognition of the German master, but they had the opportunity also of drawing a comparison between 'Jessonda' and 'Lucretia Borgia.' In 'Jessonda' all is tender yearning, and sweet hope, the golden age of fond first love: in "Lucretia Borgia" Hyena-like cunning in the poison-envenomed breast; nothing of love's purity, loves grosser passion alone; and in the same relative characteristic proportion is the poesy of the music." No one experienced more delight at this new triumph of *Spohr* than his enthusiastic admirer *Julius Schuberth*, the well-known music publisher, under whose hospitable roof *Spohr* and his travelling companions spent most agreeably the four days of their stay in Hamburgh, which their kind host strove by every possible means, to render a series of festive pleasures and of distinguishing attentions. Among others a brilliant musical party was got up in which *Spohr* performed some of his quartetts, and was greatly charmed with Miss *Unna's* beautiful execution in his quintet for the pianoforte.

Upon this occasion *Schuberth* expressed so great a wish to publish some similar grander pianoforte pieces of *Spohr's* composition, that the latter was induced to write shortly after his return from Hamburg, his first trio for pianoforte, violin and violincello, and therewith at the same time fulfilled a wish that had been for years reiterated by Mrs. *de Malsburg*, the distinguished dilettante pianiste, to whom he then dedicated the work. This first trio by *Spohr* (Op. 119) was welcomed with great satisfaction by the musical world, and numerous journals far and near expressed their delight and thanks upon its appearance. The "Leipzic New Musical Journal" speaks of it in the following terms: "Although the great master has never written any thing of this kind until now, he nevertheless moves in this new *genre* with true artistic consciousness of power, and with genial freedom. The trio is one of the finest productions of the genius of *Spohr*, in which together with the greatest possible finish in form, a profusion of beauties of the first class, and master strokes of genius stand out in prominent relief. As the gem of the whole the scherzo and its trio must be mentioned. Here, as though at the stroke of the magician's wand, a fairy island of the blessed rises to the imagination, — we are environed as though by a garden of wonders, a blooming oasis of sound full of the deep glowing splendour of oriental colouring! .... It is moreover exceedingly remarkable how *Spohr* here understood the way to unite two elements which are otherwise strangers and indeed usually antagonistic to each other: the *humoristic* and the *impassioned, elegiacally tender* element of *feeling*. ....."

At the commencement of the year 1841 *Spohr* wrote a fantasia for pianoforte and violin on themes from his opera "Der Alchymist" (The Alchymist), the charming melodies of which were especially favourable to such a reconstruction (Op. 117, Vienna, published by *Mechetti*); an English psalm for soli, with chorus and organ accompaniment (Op. 122, published by *Simrock* of Bonn); and a song,

"Schill," for men's voices, with accompaniment of military music, written for the inauguration of *Schill's* asylum for invalids at Brunswick, and which was next publicly given by the Casseler glee society at a concert for charitable purposes, and met with such general approbation that *Spohr* conceived the idea of sending it to Frankfort and therewith fulfil his promise of a contribution to the "Collection of small compositions to the *Mozart* institution." Upon the same occasion he replied to a question which had been put to him concerning a qualified candidate to the first stipend paid by that institution, by recommending *Jean Bott* of Cassel, although but 14 years of age, and wrote of him in the following terms: "*Bott* is a virtuose on the violin and pianoforte and even now displays so remarkable a talent for composition, that I anticipate for him a brilliant future. He has been a pupil of mine on the violin for the last six months, and I never yet had one so clever. *Hauptmann* (his instructor in composition) says the same of him." Supported by such distinguished recommendations the young musician, after the works which he had sent in had been submitted to the test, received the desired stipend for one year, followed up his studies under *Spohr* and *Hauptmann* with great zeal, and while yet a boy received an appointment in the Cassel "Hofkapelle."

As *Spohr* had proposed to himself to pass the theatrical vacation this time in a trip to Switzerland, he determined upon going thither by the way of Stuttgard and Hechingen, in order to make the personal acquaintance of the reigning Prince of Hohenzollern-Hechingen, who at various times had written to him, and shown himself to be an enthusiastic lover of music by expressing his admiration of *Spohr's* "Weihe der Töne" in terms of great praise.

As *Spohr's* intended visit at Hechingen was known beforehand he was welcomed there upon his arrival in the most heartfelt manner. What took place during their stay here was thus described in a letter written home: "On the very first evening Kapellmeister *Täglichsbeck* and Court-Councillor *Schil-*

ling came to fetch us from Stuttgard, to drive us about the town, and for the purpose, as they said, of showing us the new concert-hall. But on our arrival there, to our surprise we found a numerous company assembled, and we were received by the Prince in the most gracious and friendly manner. After a short conversation, he led *Spohr* to an elevated platform, upon which the whole orchestra were assembled, and in front the *head Pastor*, *Reiners* (who was also contrebassist in the orchestra), who then adressed *Spohr* in a solemn and very impressive speech of welcome, at the conclusion of which the hall resounded with such an outburst of enthusiastic greetings, accompanied by music, that one might have thought it was filled with thousands of spectators. After this the Prince seated himself near *Spohr*, and to our great surprise and pleasure his splendid fifth symphony (*C minor*) fell upon the ear, and was performed throughout with the greatest finish and inspiration. During its performance the Prince evinced feelings of delight such as we had never yet witnessed, he could scarcely control himself; held *Spohr* constantly by the arm or hand, and not only whispered to him his admiration at every passage, but frequently gave expression to his feelings aloud. ...

When the Prince had ascertained whether *Spohr* would sup or not in the dining-room below, he gave orders for a place to be reserved for him next to *Spohr*, although, as sovereign Prince, he had never yet partaken of a meal in a tavern. This supper was most remarkable and amusing: besides the Prince, who sat between me and *Spohr*, and was very lively, the whole *beau monde* of Hechingen was assembled to see *Spohr*, and each ordered supper according to his own fancy. Gentlemen of the chamber, clergymen, councillors, and their wives, mingled *pêle mêle*, did and said a thousand humorous things, and evinced an extraordinary musical enthusiasm. *Spohr* also was greatly pleased to have made the acquaintance of this happy, music-mad little spot of Germany. Music, particularly that of *Spohr*, is everything here, and ladies and gentlemen know his symphonies and quartets in a manner such as very few in Cassel know them. If at eleven o'clock at night we had not risen to depart, in spite of the Prince, he would not have done so, for he is quite in love with *Spohr*. On the following morning before eight o'clock some one knocked again at our door, and his serene highness entered to enquire how we had slept in Hechingen. He then took us into the palace gardens and into the very pretty little palace itself, where we were to rehearse our trio for the music party that had been agreed upon for the evening. When we had played through the first part, he availed himself of the short pause to fetch his wife also, that she might share his pleasure, and thus we were saved the already arranged formalities of a court presentation. . . . We were invited to dinner at *Täglichsbeck's*; but scarcely was the dinner over, than the Prince came again with two court carriages, in which the whole company drove to the charming country palace "Lindig," the beautiful view round which filled us all, and *Spohr* especially, with the greatest delight. . . ." Of the evening court-party that followed, the same letter says: "In a vaulted saloon built especially for musical performances a double quartet was first played by *Spohr* in a manner quite wonderful, then the Prince sang several songs with much expression, and at last came our trio. The company, consisting mostly of officials and of but few musicians, was in raptures of delight, and gave evidence in their remarks of much musical intelligence. At last supper was served up at small separate tables each accommodating four persons; at the chief table *Spohr* was shewn to a seat next to the Princess, who evinced great amiability and kindness towards him, while the Prince in the best of spirits was my neighbour.

Our departure was fixed for the following morning, but the Prince declaring that he could not yet part with *Spohr*, expressed the intention of accompanying him one post, and then of dining with us once more, and "not to appear egotistical, to enjoy the pleasure alone," invited a whole party, who were to accompany us in his carriage. Two gentlemen were sent on in our carriage, to order a dinner for sixteen persons at the small town of Balingen three leagues distant. . . . During the dinner, which consisted of a great number of excellent dishes, and at which also the champaign, brought from the Prince's cellars, was not wanting, the conversation was extremely lively and seasoned with many witty sallies, but always intermingled with the prominent sentiment of that musical enthusiasm, in which the Prince is really imbued to a singular degree.

At length however the long-deferred parting moment arrived! The cheerful voice grew silent, and a mournful stillness came over all; the Prince was quite beside himself; he embraced *Spohr* repeatedly, and when we had at length taken our seats in the carriage, he was once more surrounded by the company, and the Prince declared in the name of all that these days which had brought such happiness to Hechingen should be commemorated the following year by a festival."

Carrying with him the most agreable recollections of the time they had passed there, *Spohr* and his wife now resumed their journey to Switzerland, the chief object of which was to enjoy the beauties of nature; but they were also enabled to combine therewith a visit to the musical festival which was about to take place at Lucerne. Although *Spohr* had declined the invitation which he had received at Cassel to direct at the festival, it afforded him nevertheless much pleasure to be present at it among the auditory. On the first day his oratorio: "Des Heilands letzte Stunden," was performed in the fine church of St. Xavier, in which the solo parts were sustained chiefly by dilettanti, with the exception of that of Mary, by Mrs. *Stockhausen*, who had already acquired great celebrity in it at the Norwich festival, and all of whom sang "with truly angelic voices." The choruses also, were excellent, and the orchestra only did not quite satisfy *Spohr's* artistic expectations. The oratorio excited here also general enthusiasm, but the travellers missed here "the deep devotion, the christian-like comprehension and pious mental resignation," which they had remarked in the English auditory of the year before. The oratorio was followed by a brilliant festal overture by *Lindpaintner* and another oratorio, the "Christi Himmelfahrt" (the Ascension), by *Neukomm*, at which the composer was also present, and was greatly gratified by *Spohr's* approbation, who praised the choruses and the fugues. In the second concert, which was a miscellaneous one, the songs sung by Mrs. *Stockhausen* (mother of the recently celebrated baritone) were the points of attraction; but two distinguished dilletanti, doctor *Ziegler* and his sister, from Winterthur, were likewise much applauded in the duet from "Jessonda."

On the return journey from Switzerland, *Spohr* stopped for a few days in Frankfort, in order to be present at the performance of *Gluck's* "Iphigenia in Aulis." The chief characters, Iphigenia and Agamemnon were ably represented by Miss *Capitän* and Mr. *Pischek*, and it afforded the more pleasure to *Spohr* to hear the noble simplicity of this fine music rendered in a satisfactory manner, as his repeated endeavours to introduce an opera of *Gluck* into the repertory of the Cassel theatre had been always unsuccessful, and he could not hope for any better success for the future.

Scarcely was *Spohr* returned to Cassel than he began with great zeal a new work, the plan of which he had conceived upon the journey, while in view of the magnificent Swiss mountains and lakes. When once more seated with his wife in the carriage, on his return from the Lucern musical festival, he told her with the greatest joy, that, inspired and refreshed with all the beautiful and pleasing impressions made upon him by nature and art combined, — he felt the strongest impulse to write a truly grand orchestral work, and if possible in some new and more extended form of the symphony. On the half-sportive reply which she made to him: "If the simple symphony does not give sufficient scope to your creative faculty, then write a double symphony for two orchestras, in the style of the double quartet," he seized the suggestion immediately with much warmth and thereupon sank into a deep reverie, as though he were already beginning the composition, but soon after, added: that, exceedingly attractive as the problem was, it could only be successfully carried out if made subservient to the expression of a determinate idea — and that two orchestras should have given to them respectively the expression of a meaning and sentiment in strong contrast with each other. After long reflection and study; and after successive rejection of many self-proposed formulæ, he at length, as though by inspiration, seized the idea: to represent the two principles of good and evil in the human heart by the two orchestras, and to give the name to the double symphony of "Irdisches und Göttliches im Menschenleben" (the earthly and the divine in the life of man). The first subject should be called "Kinderwelt" (the world of childhood); the second "Zeit der Leidenschaften" (the age of the passions); the third "Endlicher Sieg des Göttlichen" (the final victory of the divine principle); besides which a special explanatory motto was to be given to each theme. After this manner the plan was conceived with a heart overflowing with pleasure, and then carried out with real enthusiasm. As regards the opinion respecting the degree of success with which he achieved the performance of so extremely difficult a task — that was of course a matter to be left entirely to the individuality of the hearers; but in the first performance of the work in Cassel under his own direction and in the spirit of its composer, it excited the greatest admiration in an attentively listening auditory; for while connoisseurs acknowledged the excellence of the music, apart from its special motive or subject, the feelings of the uniniated were in a high degree moved and satisfied. Such is the report of it contained in one letter out of many written at that time: "Last evening *Spohr's* new double symphony for two orchestras took place; the larger and more numerously filled orchestra represented the evil principle, the small one, consisting only of eleven solo instruments represented on the contrary the principle of good. In the subject "The world of childhood" the latter orchestra maintains the superiority in a marked and especial manner; sweet, innocent melodies bring back to us in the most enchanting manner the joys of childhood — its pretty sports, and wiles seem to rise before our vision, and we feel ourselves wholly wrapped in the bright dreams of the past; but the tones of the great orchestra remind us sorrowfully of the reality, and of the struggles of an earthly life scarcely yet begun. This subject, although gaiety is the prominent characteristic, yet speaks to us with a peculiar purity and tenderness of sentiment; and of a surety only a soul as pure and loving as that of our *Spohr* could so depict in tones the tenderness of the world of childhood.

The second subject: "The victory of the passions," begins with a very beautiful soft duet between hautboy and clarinet (depicting the first awakening of love), then soon the two orchestras mingle, as it were, wildly and stormily, a true picture of the human heart in the contests of this life; now here now there, the small orchestra is carried away with it, but even then it does not wholly cease to intervene as the good genius with moving and at times warning tones of tenderness. This subject, which is very rich in ideas and harmonies, appeared most to carry away the mass of the public, but the deepest impression made upon every sensitive heart was that made by the third theme: "Eventual victory of the divine principle." In this, the warning voice of the small orchestra becomes continually more impressive, the earthly passions for the most part become gradually subdued, one almost seems to feel how their force is broken, and then again at frequent intervals they seem to rally, until the solemn moment, in which after a general pause both orchestras at length, in solemn unison of accords announce the victory achieved by the good genius in all its power. From that point nothing but pious, pleasing sounds, as though from the realms of bliss, are heard, now alternately and now from both orchestras in unison, leading as it were the strangely-moved feelings of the auditory to the soft consolatory finale."

Notices of a similar character — sometimes estimating

the work from a purely human, at others from an artistic point of view were received from all sides after the appearance of the symphony, published as Op. 121, by *Schuberth* of Hamburgh; and then it soon became extensively circulated in the larger towns of Germany and England. This sufficed to afford *Spohr* the personal satisfaction, that in whichever way his intentions were considered, they were upon the whole rightly understood and estimated.

In November of the same year the Cassel musical world was thrown into a state of joyful excitement by the arrival of *Lisst*, who had gained the most enthusiastic applause in two concerts, which he gave in the theatre. Previous to his appearance in public, the more restricted circle of the lovers of music, had been greatly gratified by hearing him execute *Spohr's* quintet for the pianoforte at a music party given by *Spohr* for his entertainment, at which he played also several of his own compositions in an insurpassibly masterly style. *Spohr* took the liveliest interest in the performances of his colleague in art, but he paid him the tribute of his highest admiration for his wonderful playing *at sight;* and in after years, as a proof of *Lisst's* eminent talent in this respect also, he would cheerfully relate, how at a private soirée at Mrs. *von der Malsburg's*, accompanied by *Spohr* on the violin, *Lisst* played his "Reisesonata" and his only just then published fantasia from the "Alchymist," which was therefore *wholly unknown* to *Lisst*, but which to the great astonishment of all the auditory he played at sight with the most perfect finish.

On the 5th. December of this year the fiftieth anniversary of the death of *Mozart* was everywhere solemnized by the lovers of music; but as no public festival could be held in Cassel, *Spohr* got up a private performance of the society of St. Cecilia for the benefit of the poor, which was of a most solemn and impressive character. In the centre of the saloon the bust of *Mozart*, crowned with a laurel wreath, surmounted an altar hung with black drapery; on one side of the altar was assembled the numerous auditory, and on the other the singers in deep mourning. The *"Ave verum"* of *Mozart* was first sung; then a short oration *in memoriam* followed, and the conclusion was formed by the swan-song of the departed master, his immortal requiem.

In the beginning of the year 1842, *Spohr* composed six four part-songs, for soprano, alto, tenor and bass (Op. 120, published by *Appel* in Cassel), then his second trio for pianoforte, violin and violincello, which in the course of the year was followed by a third. These were published by *J. Schuberth* as Op. 123 and 124.

As during the winter *Spohr* had felt returning symptoms of his former liver-complaint, he availed himself this time of the summer vacation to go to Carlsbad, to drink the waters; but on the journey thither, at the pressing invitation of Mr. *von Holleben*, an acquaintance of his youth, and now, grandmaster of the hunt at Rudolstadt, he paid him a visit. In the amiable family circle of his early friend the hours passed quickly and pleasantly in the retrospect of their youthful associations, and in the interchange of narratives and incidents of their later life; but amid all these, music was not wanting; and to hear it each time, an increased number of the lovers of music were invited. At these parties *Spohr* willingly played several of his newest compositions, and more especially afforded universal pleasure with the two trios, in which his wife took the pianoforte part. Upon these occasions he had more especially an enthusiastic auditress in the Princess von Bückeburg, who then resided in Rudolstadt, and who was very desirous of giving a fête at her own house in honour *Spohr*, had not Mrs. *von Holleben*, as she afterwards related with much triumph, following the example of the mayor of Norwich (whose comical proceeding towards the bishop of that place *Spohr* had previously narrated with much humour), declined in the name of her guests, although without previously enquiring of them, every invitation that they received.

During the succeeding month's stay in Carlsbad, *Spohr*

followed up most conscientiously the prescribed use of the baths and waters, and, besides the enjoined morning walks of several hours' duration, he after dinner made more distant excursions into the beautiful and by him already previously so much admired environs. Between whiles, however, he managed to devote many hours to the study and practice of his noble art, playing assiduously with his wife, and charming the circle of his more immediate acquaintance with his play. He was forbidden, while taking the waters, to indulge even in a slight degree his constant impulse to the composition of something new; nevertheless during this time he composed a song: "Tears," by *Chamisso*, which afterwards appeared in the "Album of Song" of *Rudolf Hirsch* (published by *Bösenberg* of Leipzic).

On his return to Cassel, *Spohr* was painfully moved by the intelligence of the approaching departure of his friend *Hauptmann*, who had accepted the proffered appointment of Cantor at the *Thomas School* in Leipzic. However heartily he might have rejoiced to see *Hauptmann* exchange his place in the court orchestra of Cassel for one so much more befitting and worthy of him, yet for the moment the sentiment of sorrow was the prominent feeling, he that would thenceforth be bereft of the society and intercourse of a man, who through a period of twenty years had stood so near to him both as friend and as colleague in art. As *Hauptmann* was an active and highly esteemed member of the St. Cecilia society, upon *Spohr's* proposition, a farewell festival in his honour was given, at which the musical part of the entertainment consisted chiefly of *Hauptmann's* compositions. But as *Spohr* was desirous of contributing at least one musical piece having especial reference to the occasion, he made choice of the pretty cantata composed by him for the "Golden Wedding" of his parents, which, with altogether new and appropriate words, inspired all hearers with the more interest as *Spohr* took upon himself the violin obligato part that formed the accompaniment to the pianoforte.

Towards the end of the year *Spohr* wrote a "concert overture in the serious style" (Op. 121, at *Siegel's*, in Leipzic), which was performed at the first of the Casseler subscription concerts, and shortly afterwards at the Gewandhaus concert in Leipzic, and at both places produced the earnest and grandiose effect which the composer had in view. He next, at the repeated solicitations of publisher and friends, tried his hand at a species of composition which he had never till then tried, a sonata for the *pianoforte alone*, which after having accomplished to his satisfaction, he resolved to dedicate to his friend *Mendelssohn*. The latter having been made acquainted with it, wrote to him immediately and accompanied the expression of his thanks "for the high and distinguishing honour" with the following words: "If I could but express to you, how deeply I feel what it is to be thus able to call one of your works one's own particular property, and how my heart joys not alone in the distinction conferred, but equally in your friendly thought of me, and your constant desire for my welfare. A thousand thanks to you for it, dear Mr. Kapellmeister, and rest assured that to the best of my ability I will endeavour to make my now obstinate fingers bring out the beauties of the sonata properly. But that is again only a pleasure that I shall be doing myself, and I should so like to render you one in return for it," &c. The "obstinate fingers" must nevertheless have soon succumbed to the will of the master, for when upon a subsequent visit to Leipzic, *Spohr* had the gratification of hearing him play the sonata, it was everything he could have wished, and he recognised in such an execution the ideal which when composing it his fancy had conceived. Shortly afterwards, when it was brought out by *Mechetti* of Vienna, as Op. 125, and thereby became more widely known, *Spohr* received many gratifying notices of it from all sides. But he was especially taken by surprise on the receipt of a letter from Hungary, enthusiastic in admiration of the sonata, from the to him wholly unknown director of the choir, *Seyler*, of the Cathedral of Gran, in which he says among other things:

"Times innumerable, in the hours when my duties permit me some relaxation, do I charm myself at the piano with that sonata you dedicated to Mr. *Mendelssohn-Bartholdy*. Carried away by the magic of its tones I now take up the pen, in behalf of all pianists of feeling who may not always have the opportunity to be enchanted by your greater musical productions, to render you the warmest thanks for this beautiful work.... I would moreover earnestly entreat you to let me know whether we pianists may encourage the hope of having such another composition, with which with two hands alone, we may discourse with the spirit of the world-famed German hero of musical science?" &c. Although this and many other similar testimonies might have fully removed *Spohr's* former doubts as to whether he could contribute anything sufficiently satisfactory as a composer for the pianoforte, yet as may be readily imagined it was more in his interest to give his sole attention to the violin as concerted with pianoforte music; and his next works were six duets for pianoforte and violin (Op. 127), but which he could not finish and send in to his publisher *Julius Schuberth* of Hamburgh, who awaited them with much impatience, till after the lapse of several months, as just at that time he was more than usually occupied in perfecting his orchestra in the study of several larger works. He first of all wished to give *Bach's* "Passion" on the coming Good Friday, and although, with the same intention he had previously rehearsed it several times with all the musical strength he could enlist in Cassel, yet years had since then elapsed; and it cost him a very great exertion of his patience and perseverance to bring his orchestra and singers up to such a pitch of excellence as to ensure the public performance of that extremely difficult music in a creditable and worthy manner.

After *Spohr* had toiled for long months in practising the choruses and the long-wished-for day of performance was drawing nearer and nearer, the required permission of the Prince was suddenly refused, without any reason being assigned for it; and it was not until a second application had been sent in, accompanied (to meet all eventualities) by a certificate of the clergyman, that he considered "the music selected for performance perfectly fitted for the church and for the day," that the desired permission was granted; and that to the great satisfaction of *Spohr* and every lover of music in Cassel, it could be performed on the day appointed. But these obstacles repeatedly thrown in the way of its production were very nearly the cause of *Spohr's* total departure from Cassel, for at that very time he again received from Prague a very advantageous offer of appointment there, respecting which he wrote as follows to his friend *Hauptmann*: "I am so weary of all the vexations I meet with here that even at my time of life I could almost make up my mind to leave this place, were not my wife so much attached to her family, and that she would be unhappy away from her friends. The opportunity now presents itself in an offer from the states of Bohemia of the post of director of the Prague conservatory of music vacant by the death of *Dionys Weber*, as an indemnifaction for the salary I should throw up here. Such a field for exertion and a residence in musical Prague would suit me well. But under the circumstances adverted to above I must of course decline it. . . ." In *Hauptmann's* very explicit reply to this he says among other things: "By *Spohr's* leaving under the pressure of such existing circumstances, Cassel will become a desert as regards music," but he nevertheless advises him to leave it without hesitation, and "will not yet relinquish the thought to see him move away from good, beautiful but *oppressed* Cassel, to majestic Prague."

But as *Spohr* in the meanwhile had come to a decision, and of his own impulse allowed his kindly consideration for his wife and her parents to prevail with him, their daily intercourse having become with him also a pleasurable habit, he wrote back in his reply the following few but characteristic words: "The interest and sympathy, which breathes throughout your kind letter was most gratifying to me also in regard to the Prague business. But I had already made up my mind in the interim, and I am glad that my answer declining the offer had been sent to Prague, before my father-in-law knew anything about it, or with tears in his eyes could have to thank me for my decision. . . ." — In this manner *Spohr* remained in Cassel, to which he had become attached as to a second home, and he continued to discharge his duties with his customary zeal.

He now again gave his attention to the study of a difficult work: "The flying Dutchman" of *Richard Wagner*, which *Spohr* proposed to himself to bring out as a festival opera for Whitmonday, having heard much in its praise from Dresden, and upon perusal of the libretto, which had been sent to him, had found the subject so satisfactory in every respect, that he pronounced it a little master-piece, and regretted, "not to have met with a similar and as good a one to set to music, ten years before." When at the rehearsals he had become more closely acquainted with the opera, he wrote to *Lüder* respecting it, and invited him to the approaching performance in Cassel: "This work, although somewhat approaching the new-romantic music *à la Berlioz,* and although it has given me immense work on account of its extreme difficulty, interests me nevertheless in the highest degree, for it is written apparently with true inspiration — and unlike so much of the modern opera music, does not display in every bar the striving after effect, or effort to please. There is a great deal of the fanciful therein; a noble conception throughout, it is well written for the singer; enormously difficult it is true, and somewhat overcharged in the instrumentation, but full of new effects, and will assuredly, when it once comes to be performed in the greater space of a theatre be thoroughly clear and intelligible. The theatre rehearsals begin at the end of this week, and I am exceedingly desirous to see how the fantastic subject and the still more fantastic music will come off *en scène*. I think I am so far correct in my judgment, when I consider *Wagner* as the most gifted of all our *dramatic* composers of the present time. In this work at least his aspirations are noble, and that pleases me at a time when all depends upon creating a sensation, or in effecting the merest ear-tickling," &c. Notwithstanding the apparent almost insurmountable difficulties, *Spohr* succeeded in giving one performance, which left nothing to be desired, and the work was most favourably received by the public. In full satisfaction to the author he felt impelled to write to *Wagner* to make him acquainted with it; upon which the latter in the fulness of his joy replied: "My very esteemed sir and master, I was really obliged to recover myself somewhat from the joy — from the rapture I may say — which your extremely kind letter afforded me, before I could undertake to write, and express to you the gratitude of my heart. . . . In order to enable you to understand the extraordinary emotion your intelligence produced in me, I must first calmly explain what were my expectations in regard to the success of this opera. From the unusually great difficulties which it presented I could expect but little from it, however good the musical and dramatic strength with which it might be put upon the stage, unless there was a man at their head who, endowed with peculiar energetic capacity and goodwill, would espouse my interests with predilection and in the face of every obstacle. That you, my highly-esteemed master, possessed beyond all others the qualifications for so energetic a direction, I well knew, — but whether you would consider my work sufficiently worthy of your attention to take so decided an interest in it, that was certainly the very natural doubt that made me despair more and more, the nearer the day of its announced performance approached; so that I confess I had not the courage to go to Cassel, to become personally a witness to my shame and to the realisation of all my fears. But I now see indeed that a lucky star has risen over me, since I have gained the sympathy of a man from whom an indulgent notice only would have been sufficient fame for me: — but to see him take the most decisive and crowning measures in my behalf, is a piece of good fortune which assuredly distinguishes me above many, and which really for the first time fills me with a sentiment of pride, such as hitherto no applause of the public could have awakened in me" &c. With equal gratitude and kindliness *Wagner* acknowledged the correctness of the omissions made by *Spohr* in the opera, in the which he "recognised but further proof of the true interest he had evinced for him," and this he reiterated in all his subsequent letters with the warmest expressions of attachment and esteem.

With the commencement of the theatrical vacation, *Spohr* made preparations for the journey to London, where he hoped to receive satisfaction for the disappointment of the refusal of leave absence in the previous autumn, to proceed to Norwich to conduct the much-talked-of performance of his oratorio, "The fall of Babylon." For months previously the committee had applied to that effect through the embassy at Cassel, to the Prince, but had met with a summary refusal, upon which *Spohr* received several letters from England, expressing how much they felt aggrieved by it, and lord *Aberdeen* especially, who had authorised the application to the Prince through the medium of the English embassy. Upon this the committee met in Norwich and sent a deputation to London to the duke of Cambridge, who expressed himself willing to write personally to the Prince in the most pressing terms. But without avail; after a lapse of two months his application was refused also, and both he and the whole royal family were not a little hurt by it. In Norwich, meanwhile, it was thought that every means had not yet been exhausted, and to *Spohr's* extreme surprise he suddenly received an enormous petition signed by a considerable number of the inhabitants of Norwich, beseeching the Prince in the interests of that city to allow *Spohr* to direct his oratorio there. Although he himself had now little hope of a favourable issue to this prayer, he was nevertheless greatly moved by the receipt of so imposing a document, and awaited a reply with the greatest anxiety. This however did not come; but the Hessian minister for foreign affairs, *von Steuber*, wrote the following letter to the wife of Mr. *von der Malsburg*, grand marshall of the court, by whom the petition had been presented: "I have to announce to your Excellency that I delivered the petition in question, and urged personally all the circumstances detailed therein, but as you yourself feared, there is no hope of a successful result" &c. —

Although *Spohr* could not personally share in the triumph which this new oratorio achieved for him in England, he nevertheless received almost daily detailed epistolary accounts of the success of the festival, and at length also a whole box full of newspapers of every shade of politics, which seemed almost to vie with each other in expressions of admiration of his work. Of these, some few of the most conspicuous and characteristic in style of comment may here be cited: "The Times" says among other things: "The gem of the festival was *Spohr's* oratorio. The text is written with especial regard to the nature and the character of an oratorio, and the subject which *Spohr* has illustrated by the exercise of his talent is especially favourable to its exhibition. Three nations are represented: the captive Hebrews, the luxurious Babylonians and the Persians in their pride of conquest: these furnish materials for the most varied musical treatment by the composer, of which he has availed himself in the most admirable manner, and thoroughly understood how to adhere throughout the music to the identity and nationality of the different nations. His peculiar genius for the invention of beautiful melodies, and his power to enrich these with appropriate harmonies is also preminently conspicuous in this splendid work." After a detailed analysis of the separate "numbers" it is further said: "The general opinion of the oratorio is this: It is a master piece of art, worthy to rank with "Die letzten Dingen" and "Des Heilands letzten Stunden." Emphatic as this praise may be, it is nevertheless just. Though from the same hand, the work is nevertheless essentially different from these. The former excite feelings of deep devotion and christian piety, in the latter we distinguish the character of the deity more in its majesty and omnipotence; Jehovah displays himself to us in acts of power by dooming the ungodly to punishment. The work fulfils all the conditions of a true oratorio, and its performance was a triumph of English art. One thing only was deeply and generally deplored, that *Spohr* was prevented from being present at this triumph." In the Morning Chronicle, after similar enthusiastic expressions of opinion, follows: "In a word, the music is characterised by the whole power and peculiarity of *Spohr's* genius, and we may boldly assert that it is the grandest work written since the days of *Händel*." — The immense crowd that pressed forward to the hall to witness the performance is adverted to by all the papers, and the Morning Herald especially, speaks of it thus: "Although to hear *Spohr's* oratorio an unusually numerous auditory was to be expected, yet no one could have formed an idea of what actually occurred. From an early hour in the morning carriages arrived in numbers, filled with the rank and beauty of the county. . . . The whole interior of the building was immediately filled; where a resting-place could be found for one foot only, fool-hardy individuals were to be seen located in the most dangerous situations, and every one seemed determined to endure the greatest inconvenience rather than forego the pleasure of hearing *Spohr's* oratorio. Many persons clambered up to the roof, and from thence in at the window, but numbers were compelled to remain outside, and content themselves with looking down from their dizzy height upon the crowds below. This is no exaggeration, but strictly true; and that such a degree of interest should have been evinced for a new musical work, is certainly an event that stands alone in the history of music," &c. While *Spohr* found at home a cheering distraction in these gratifying accounts, his admirers and frienads in England were considering how to make him some compensation for his loss, and before the close of the year he received an invitation to London during his next vacation, to conduct his oratorio.

Upon *Spohr's* arrival in London in June 1843, Professor *Taylor,* who had conducted his oratorio at Norwich, in his stead, and who had discharged that difficult task most creditably, had so far made all the preliminary preparations that after a few rehearsals, its performance could take place at the Hanover Square Rooms to his full satisfaction. The public also gave vent to their enthusiasm, with the most reiterated and demonstrative applause, and at the conclusion greeted him with three cheers. Nevertheless all those who had been present at the festival in the fine St. Andrew's Hall at Norwich, were not by any means satisfied that *Spohr* had not been permitted to hear his work under equally favourable circumstances, in all its grandeur, and he received the invitation to direct a second grander performance, which the Sacred Harmonic Society were desirous of giving with their chorus of five hundred voices in the large concert-room of Exeter Hall. But as he had proposed to himself to devote the yet remaining week's leave of absence to a journey to Wales, of the scenery of which he had heard so much spoken in praise, and as the time moreover appeared to him much too short for a careful study of his oratorio, he returned an answer declining the invitation. Upon subsequent pressing solicitation, nevertheless, and repeated conferences, he at length yielded, and it was then agreed that the requisite rehearsals should be made during *Spohr's* absence, so that he would have nothing more to do than to take upon himself the direction of the performance, and meanwhile he could proceed undisturbed upon his projected journey. Highly necessary to him, also, was such a refreshing change of scene after the almost overwhelming fatigues of the musical entertainments and dinner-parties of the preceding weeks, at the greater part of which he himself took an active share in the performances. At the last concert of the Philharmonic Society, in which he directed the performance of several of his compositions: "Die Weihe der Töne," the overture to the "Alchymist," and the flower duet from "Jessonda," but first himself executed his concertino in *E major* upon the violin, he was, as recorded by the "Spectator" — "welcomed like a Prince, the whole company rising spontaneously from their seats to salute him" . . . . and when he had concluded his artistic and indescribably charming play, the irrepressible outbursts of delight shewed how completely he had touched the heart-strings of his auditory. At the end of the concert the directors conveyed to him moreover the wishes of the queen, that he would play once more in an extra-concert to be given for that purpose. As he could not well refuse this, the concert took place a week afterwards, and comprised in its compendious programme among other things a symphony of Mozart, the ninth symphony of *Beethoven*, with the choruses, and three of *Spohr's* compositions: concertino in *A major*, the overture to "Macbeth," and Tristan's air in "Jessonda," in which *Staudigl* was twice encored.

Respecting the further circumstances of the concert a letter written home contains the following: "The extra-concert of yesterday was a very brilliant success, and afforded us high enjoyment. The appearance there of the Queen was an event of which all the newspapers and everybody also spoke beforehand with much interest; as since her coronation she had never yet appeared at one. When she entered the room, dressed in a plain black robe, but wearing a good many diamonds, the public clapped their hands and rose from their seats, upon which the soli and chorus sang "God save the Queen" with great effect. During the entre-acte, the Queen sent for *Spohr* to the adjoining apartment, where she discoursed with him for some time in a very flattering manner, and advised him during his further journey in England to travel *incognito*, otherwise in every town he would be annoyed and intruded upon in the same manner as in London. Prince Albert and the King of the Belgians entered also into conversation with him, and he was much edified by their remarks. Several persons whom we knew, who sat near the Queen, laid great stress upon the circumstance that upon *Spohr's* appearance in the orchestra, she and her husband bowed very profoundly, and clapped their hands very warmly," &c. At further music parties he experienced great pleasure in hearing his trios, quartets, airs and duets from his operas, and songs, executed with the most perfect finish, and was always much delighted with the wonderfully pure execution of the favorite English glees. Upon these occasions he was not at all disturbed by the enormous quantity of musical pieces which were brought forward, for with his inexhaustible nerve and power of endurance he was fortunately enabled to compete with the English.

As a curiosity of the kind the following programme may be adduced, of a musical festival got up by Mr. *Alsager*, then co-editor of the Times, in honour of *Spohr*:

Queen Square Select Society.
Musical Festival in Honour of the arrival of Spohr in London.
Sunday July 2, 1843.
Act. 1.

Double Quartet No. 1	Spohr.
Quintet-Pianoforte, Flute, Clarinet, Horn and Bassoon	Spohr.
Double Quartet No. 2	Spohr.
Nonetto	Spohr.

Déjeuner à la fourchette.

Act. 2.

Quintet	Spohr.
Ottetto	Spohr.
Double Quartet No. 3	Spohr.

To commence at 2 o'clock — Déjeuneur at 5 —
Second act to commence at 7.

This festival, which was in every respect successful, and got up with princely magnificence, must have been the more gratifying to *Spohr*, when he saw how the company, consisting of fifty persons, listened until late in the evening with admirable perseverance and wrapped attention to his tones, without evincing the least sign of weariness. When gratified beyond measure by a festive testimonial so unusual, he felt called upon to express his very great thanks to Mr. *Alsager,* he found to his great surprise on the following day among the mass of letters which he constantly received, one also from him expressing his heartfelt thanks, which concluded as follows: "May you enjoy all the happiness that can result from the consciousness that you are a benefactor to the world and communicate happiness to others in a circle still increasing and never ending."

Upon their pleasure trip on the 12th July *Spohr* and his wife were accompanied by Professor *Taylor*, in whom they found both a well-informed and amiable guide and companion. They visited Winchester, Portsmouth, Southampton, Bath, Bristol and Wales. With the natural beauties of the latter *Spohr* was so much charmed that in many parts he considered them to surpass Switzerland, and all that he had ever seen. On the return journey to London, he was loud in his expressions of admiration of the beauties of Cheltenham, and of the fine university of Oxford. Though in accordance with the advice of the Queen he had thought to make this little journey *incognito*, nevertheless his arrival soon became known in each town, and the composer of "Die letzten Dinge," the pianoforte arrangement of which he found in almost every house, was received by every one after his own manner, with the highest honours, upon which occasions many incidents occurred that either greatly amused or moved him. Meanwhile, in London, every possible exertion had been made, and upon his return, *Spohr* found that his oratorio had been studied with such faultless precision, that as he wrote word in a letter home "at the grand rehearsal he was really much moved both with its excellent execution, and the conviction that such a number of persons totally stranger to him, and for the most part engaged in business (who in London have indeed but little leisure time) should have devoted their evenings to a late hour, during his absence of eight days, to the study of this difficult work, from pure love of it, and to afford him an agreeable surprise."

The performance itself is then thus described: "Imagine a gigantic hall with places for 3000 persons, crammed full, head above head; in a balcony apart, as the bill expresses it

'Madame *Spohr* and Friends' looking down upon the scene. Opposite the magnificent and stupendous organ and on all sides around it, an orchestra and choir of singers numbering five hundred persons, grouped in the most charming manner; in that orchestra *Spohr* enters, and at the same moment the whole public and orchestra rise from their seats, all waving handkerchiefs and hats and shouting long and loudly altogether "Bravo, Hurrah!" But no sooner did *Spohr* lift his *baton* than all sat down, and a deep silence of anxious attention reigned. Then resounded through the spacious hall the first moving accords of the overture, like music from another sphere. The whole performance proceeded now grandly and as though with one impulsive inspiration in all. A solemn thrilling emotion pervaded us, and at many powerful passages, such as "Er regiert auf ewig (he rules for ever) Hallelujah!" — "Du nur allein bist Gott" &c. (Thou, and Thou only art God), — then it was as though all mankind had assembled to praise God with the purest harmony. But doubly wonderful at such outbursts of powerful grandeur is the ever-recurring entry at the right moment of the tenderest shades of expression. . . . Three airs and the grand chorus of the Persians were encored with vehement acclamation. At the conclusion the people, at a loss to find a new and further way of expressing their rapture, demonstrated it more prominently by mounting at once upon the benches. When at length *Spohr* had made his way through the mass of those who pressed forward to shake hands with and congratulate him as he passed on to the door of the hall, I observed with astonishment that the whole company remained behind, and whispered to each other, which induced me to think something important was still to take place; when after a time the noise broke out anew and *Spohr* was again vehemently called for. Upon this two gentlemen led him back once more, and having informed him that the public much wished him to address a few words to them, he at length determined to do so, and made a short speech in G e r m a n, which although they did not understand, was very gratefully received by the assembly. Hereupon the President stepped forward, and having delivered a long address to *Spohr* in English, which was repeatedly interrupted by applause and cries of "Hear! hear!" he presented to him in the name of the company a large silver salver with a beautifully engraved inscription commemorative of the evening festival," &c. — This solemn concluding scene crowned all that *Spohr* had yet experienced, and the sad moment of parting from hospitable England now approached. *Spohr* himself was painfully moved by it, although the earnest solicitations of every kind which poured in upon him, gave him little time for calm reflection. Daily from various quarters did he receive the blank sheets of albums with the request for some souvenir from his own hand, many of which yet awaited their execution and kept him occupied at his writing-table up to the time of his departure. After he had satisfied these last requests even, and at length embarked on board the steamer, he good humouredly remarked to the crowd of friends and admirers who had collected to bid him farewell: "There is now indeed scarcely a lover of music in England who has not my autograph," — the steamer was hailed from the shore, and on looking in that direction he saw a boat rowing fast towards them, and shortly, several gentlemen came on board, bearing numerous albums that had arrived too late, with the entreaty that *Spohr* would write something in each during the journey down to Gravesend, whither they would accompany him with that view! Actually also, did *Spohr* comply, and writing, he left the shores of England, and so made the parting moments somewhat less painful to him!

Early in the month of October 1843, a meeting of the Philological Society was to take place in Cassel, and the generally expressed wish to honour the same with some musical performances was the more natural, from the means necessary thereto being more especially at command there. Upon *Spohr's* recommendation the president of the society and Gymnasial-Director *Weber* proposed the performance of "Antigone" at the theatre, with *Mendelssohn's* choruses; and *Spohr* expressed himself ready to comply with the wishes of the magistracy to give a performance of his oratorio: "Der Fall Babylons" in the church, for the benefit of the poor of the city. As, however, the permission of the Prince could not be obtained for both, the foreign guests were obliged to content themselves with a private performance of "Antigone" in the spacious hall where they held their sittings, upon which occasion Councillor *Niemeyer* read the tragedy, and the choruses were sung with accompaniment of two pianofortes by the singers of the men's choral society under *Spohr's* direction. In this manner all went off very effectingly, and the strangers were so well content that they not only expressed their most heartfelt thanks to *Spohr* for his exertions, but at their next sitting, (at which he assisted with much interest) unanimously voted also a letter of thanks to *Mendelssohn*. *Spohr* himself was also so much pleased with the spirited and truly original music "that he now exceedingly desired to hear it also with full orchestral treatment. But as under the present overruling circumstances in Cassel this was not to be achieved, he shortly afterwards gave a repetition of the reading of the tragedy in the same manner, for a charitable purpose, but in a more spacious building, by which means a wider circle of the lovers of music were enabled for the first time to become acquainted with the interesting work.

About this time *Spohr* began to turn his mind seriously to the composition of another opera, which probably arose from the frequency with which the libretto of operas were sent to him. But as none of them satisfied him, and as upon a closer examination, either the treatment of the subject or the form of the musical pieces did not suit him, he conceived the idea of writing with the assistance of his wife the text of a libretto, and chose for subject the once favorite drama of Kotzebue: "The Crusaders," which seemed to him particularly adapted to the object he had this time in view, namely, an entire deviation from the customary form, as well as from the style, of his own previous opera music; in composing the whole throughout as a musical drama, without unnecessary repetitions of the text and ornamentations, and with a constantly progressing development in the treatment. As soon as the libretto was completed, he set to work with great spirit, and in a short time completed the first act, which he immediately arranged for the pianoforte, and had performed in his house by a select number of the best dilettanti, in order to convince himself of the success of his work, before he proceeded further with it. When he became satisfied how·clearly and intelligibly, even without the aid of scenic representations, the lifelike expression of his music depicted the different characters and situations, andh ow powerfully both singers and auditory were impressed by it, he proceeded with confidence with the next act, and finished that also, all but the instrumentation, before the commencement of the theatrical vacation.

As object of his customary summer journey *Spohr* had selected Paris, in order to shew his wife the grandeur of that brilliant capital, and to visit at the same time the international exhibition of industry, which, as the first of its kind, had so greatly excited public attention, that strangers from every quarter of the globe flocked to it to behold the endless treasures in every department of manufacturing industry, and to admire the products of art. With the daily concourse of the visitors it was however almost impossible to obtain an undisturbed and attentive view; it was therefore matter of no small self-congratulation for *Spohr* and his wife to receive a ticket of admission procured by especial favour upon a day that had been set apart for the King's visit to the exhibition, when exhibitors only were permitted to be present. By this means they were also furnished with the rare opportunity of seeing the venerable *Louis Philippe,* accompanied by his wife, his sister *Adelaide,* and the then still very youthful Duke de

Montpensier, pass close before them, and to hear distinctly the King's remarks upon the various manufactures displayed.

At a season of the year so unfavourable for musical performances of any consequence, *Spohr* could scarcely hope to enjoy that gratification, but there, in a foreign land he had the unhoped-for satisfaction of an enjoyment he had vainly endeavoured to obtain at home, that namely of assisting at a performance of "Antigone" with *Mendelssohn's* choruses, which on that evening had been given for the thirty-second time in succession at the Odéon theatre to constantly crowded houses, and *Spohr* was deeply impressed with the excellence of the music and of the scenic arrangements.

But although the best musicians were for the most part absent from Paris, he nevertheless passed some very pleasant hours in the society of Mr. *Habenec* (director of the conservatory), *Panseron*, *Halevy*, *Auber*, *Berlioz*, *Adam*, &c. On the part of the conservatory it was also greatly wished to shew him some mark of attention, although under the circumstances some difficulty was experienced in doing so, as appears from a notice in a Parisian journal, in the following words: "Mais que faire pour prouver à l'auteur de 'Faust' et de 'Jessonda' que la France sait apprécier dignement ses belles compositions et leur auteur? Une idée vient soudain à un ami de Mr. *Habenec*: 'L'époque des magnifiques concerts du Conservatoire est passée! dit-il; eh bien! écrivons partout, réunissons une partie de nos artistes, et essayons de tresser une petite couronne à *Spohr*, en exécutant devant lui un de ses plus beaux morceaux.' Le projet est approuvé, on n'avait que quelques jours pour le mettre en œuvre. Des circulaires sont adressées à vingt, trente lieues de Paris. Des hommes d'un talent supérieur, qui n'auraient pas quitté leur *dolce far niente* à prix d'argent, se hâtent d'accourir, et la Société des Concerts, à l'exception de deux de ses membres qui sont maintenant en Italie, se trouve réunie à Paris comme un seul homme. La salle du Conservatoire est ouverte, tous les exécutants s'y rendent, et *Spohr* y est amené comme spectateur unique; c'est pour lui seul que soixante-dix-huit musiciens sont là, c'est aux pieds de sa gloire qu'ils viennent se prosterner, et lui font entendre son chef-d'œuvre symphonique: 'La création de la Musique' ('Weihe der Töne')."

Upon *Spohr's* entry into the room he was greeted with loud applause, and addressed in a speech by Mr. *Habenec*, who invited him to direct his symphony in person, as at the next winter concerts, the society intended to perform it, and it would therefore be of the utmost value to all, to be initiated by the personal direction of the composer himself into its mode of performance. In reality, also, many indications and repetitions were necessary upon the occasion, until every thing, went satisfactorily; but *Beethoven's* pastoral symphony, which followed, and had been frequently played, was executed with that masterly precision for which that orchestra was so celebrated.

On the following day *Spohr* set out on his return to Cassel, which he again left after the lapse of a few weeks, to comply with an invitation from his native town of Brunswick, where they had long desired to give a grand musical festival in his honour, and had therefore made arrangements to have a performance of his oratorio the "Fall of Babylon," at the end of September.

On his way thither he received a foretaste of the Brunswick festivities, at Seesen, where he slept the first night, and where he had passed the first years of his childhood; the inhabitants of that place having been thereby induced to believe that it was really his birth-place. He was greatly surprised at being welcomed immediately upon his arival here with a kind and most hearty address and ushered with much ceremony into the handsomely decorated grand room of the hotel, where he found disposed in a wide semicircle, symmetrically arranged, a selection from all the musical talent of the young folks of Seesen, with the members of the choral society of that place; who, besides singing several songs, executed a chorus from "Die letzten Dingen" and a pleasing poem composed especially for the occasion, addressed to *Spohr*, and arranged for four voices.

Brunswick was no less demonstrative in celebrating the presence of its illustrious guest, and detailed notices of an impromptu festival given to *Spohr* are furnished by several letters, in which the brilliant external display, as well as the expressive and appropriately arranged musical entertainment, appealed with equal force and charm to the heart and mind. A cantata set to music by *Methfessel* for female voices and chorus, "Welcome to *Spohr*," was first sung, with a soft accompaniment of wind instruments placed out of sight in the background, and executed by them in the most finished manner. But scarcely had the guest so honoured time to express his thanks at the conclusion of this pretty song, when quite unexpectedly, and in striking contrast with it, a powerful chorus of male voices from the opposite side of the hall began a second "festive song to *Spohr*," which prepared the minds of all for the enjoyment of the subsequent more exhilarating festivities.

On the following day *Spohr* directed the performance of his oratorio: "The fall of Babylon," in the Ægydian church, which was here also executed with great spirit, and was well received. The circumstance that its performance took place in the same church in which more than 60 years before he was baptised as an infant greatly increased the interest of the day, and gave occasion to several other poetic effusions.

A grand concert of a mixed kind concluded the festivities of the day; the first part of which comprised the overture to "King Lear" by *Berlioz*, directed by Kapellmeister *Müller*, airs from "Oberon" and "Jessonda" an adagio for violin by *Spohr*, executed by concert-director *Müller*, and *Maurer's* concertante for four violins (played by *Müller, Zimmermann, C. Müller jun.* and *Jean Bott* of Cassel); the second part consisted of *Spohr's* fifth symphony, *C minor*. Thus ended this pleasing festival, the heartfelt pleasure at which was alone saddened to *Spohr* by thoughts of his beloved father, who, up to the few months preceeding his death in Brunswick had passed the last years of his life in Seesen, but who, after watching for years at a distance the career of his son with pleasurable pride, could now no longer be a witness of the high esteem and honour shewn to him by his native town.

At the end of the year *Spohr* received an invitation to a grand musical festival at New-York — the first from that side of the Ocean, to the direction of which he had been unanimously selected at a general meeting of the society of music of that city, "as the first of all living composers and directors of music." There were to be two performances of sacred and two of secular music, and above all his oratorio of the "Fall of Babylon" — "the fame of which had spread from England to the new world," was to take precedence. Although such a proposal might have had great attractions for *Spohr*, and have yet more incited his constant love of travel; and although in New York he would have moreover the pleasure of seeing again his daughter *Emily*, who with her husband and child had emigrated there some years before, yet he soon made up his mind to decline it, as a residence there of the few weeks only which the duties of his place would have perhaps permitted, would scarcely have compensated for the fatigues of a long voyage.

On New Year's Day 1845, *Spohr's* new opera, "The Crusaders," was performed for the first time; and not only upon the first night, but upon the quickly succeeding further performances, it met with an unexampled brilliant reception for Cassel. *Spohr*, who had looked forward with particularly anxious expectation to the success of this work, was much gratified at this result, and wrote to his friend *Hesse* as follows: "That my opera should have made so deep and lasting an impression upon the public, the lesser number of which only consisted of musically educated persons, I ascribe to the truthful character of my music, which aims only at representing the situation perfectly, and discards all the flimsy parade of modern opera-music, such as florid instrumental soli and noisy effects.* And I was furthermore exceedingly pleased

---

* To similar observations in a letter to *Hauptmann* he adds: "I could not make up my mind to write *one* unnecessary note for the sake of brilliancy."

that the singers, who did not find in their parts anything of that which usually gains for them the applause of the crowd, evinced nevertheless at every rehearsal a greater interest in it, and a zeal to study such a I never before observed in them. But the result shews also, that this style of song, which is so convenient for every one, and affords the opportunity of displaying the best tones, and the degree of feeling and expression which each is capable of, is a very grateful one; for never were our singers so applauded, and after the second performance they were all called for together on the stage." The newspapers having circulated a great deal in praise of the new opera, and it having become more extensively known by the pianoforte arrangement which was shortly afterwards published by *J. Schuberth*, it was soon announced for performance at other theatres in Germany, viz. at Berlin, Dresden, Brunswick and Detmold; but in other (catholic) cities, like Munich, Vienna &c., objection was taken to the libretto, which had been asked for examination, and therefore the performance was abstained from.

As *Spohr* was invited to direct personally the first performance of his "Crusaders" at Berlin, he was desirous that this should take place during his theatrical vacation; and although he was apprised from there that it was the most unfavourable season of the year for it, as the chief characters of his opera could not be satisfactorily represented till after the return of the absent principal singers, he nevertheless though it more advisable to do without their assistance, than by a longer delay to make the possibility of his coming a matter of uncertainty.

At the beginning of the holidays he therefore set out on the journey, but first to Oldenburg, to direct a grand concert there, the receipts from which were destined for the institution of a pension fund for the members of the orchestra there.

The programme had been previously cast by *A. Pott*, the resident director, his former pupil and enthusiastic admirer, and consisted wholly of *Spohr's* compositions, viz.

concert overture in the serious style; latest violin concerts in *E minor*, executed by the composer; duett from "Jessonda" sung by Mrs. *Schmidt* of Bremen and Mr. **; clarinet concerto, played by Mr. *Köhn*, member of the ducal orchestra; grand symphony in *C minor* (No. 5); the "Lord's Prayer," for solo, chorus, and orchestra.

Upon *Spohr's* arrival he found the whole of the musical pieces (the last two of which he himself directed) so well practised under *Pott's* direction, that at the rehearsal he was greatly pleased by it. At the public performance, also, every thing went off so well, that Mrs. *Spohr* expresses herself in a letter home as follows: "We felt as though we had been suddenly transported to England. The music, the finished execution, the spacious, densely filled, and splendidly acoustic building, the enthusiastic applause and admiration — all were in truth *grandly English*. And all this was doubly surprising and gratifying when one thinks that this took place in a small town with a population of only 12,000. Orchestra and singers, three hundred persons in all, worked together with wonderful harmony. Every piece of music was excellent, but the impression made by the 'Lord's Prayer' was *quite indescribable,* and the words in which *Pott* shortly before expressed himself to *Spohr*, after a rehearsal of it: 'Happy is the man who can pray with such intense devotion; peace must indeed dwell in his soul,' presented themselves here in their full import to my mind. *Spohr*, also, was of my opinion that he had never heard the piece so well played, for even in the finest shades of the expression there was nothing more to be desired. The whole platform from which *Spohr* led the orchestra, and the steps leading to it, were strewn with the finest roses; the whole front of the orchestra was decorated with wreaths; and beneath his bust, crowned with laurel, were the words *'Louis Spohr'* in gigantic letters, composed of roses and laurel artistically interwoven. While the assembly were listening with the deepest attention to the splendid tones, it was little imagined by any one how every enjoyment was embittered to *Spohr*, by a sudden seizure with cramp in the stomach, which soon became so intense, as he himself afterwards related, that when conducting the symphony and the 'Lord's Prayer' he had great difficultly in keeping himself erect. After the concert we were to have assisted at another *fête*, given by the minister *von Beaulieu* at his house, in honour of *Spohr;* but under the circumstances this became impossible, and we hastened home with all speed, where, having arrived, *Spohr* went immediately to bed, and was obliged to resort to sedatives; but the cramp would not yield to them, and the doctor who was called in, vainly endeavoured to afford him relief, so that the pain became intense. At this very moment when *Spohr* lay in such a sad condition of suffering that he expected every moment would be his last, a singular and striking contrast was presented to his position, by a monster torch-light procession followed by a large concourse of the inhabitants of Oldenburg, which halted under our windows, and began a grand serenade with the overture and several choruses from 'Jessonda,' performed by all the native and foreign musicians then in Oldenburg, together with three choral societies. Many other pieces were to have been performed, but by *Spohr's* wish, *Pott* availed himself of the opportunity when a loud cheer was raised by the crowd, to address them in his name from the window in a speech of thanks, which, although improvised, was as well put together and delivered as though he had long previously studied it. But when he acquainted them with *Spohr's* illness also, a general depression spread immediately through all present, and the previously so joyous assembled serenaders, withdrew in silent sadness. In our house, meanwhile, all was remarkably lively: the hostess, Mrs. *Oppermann*, wife of the Councillor *Oppermann* of the high court of appeal, was entertaining two carriage-loads of guests who had come to the concert, together with all her acquaintance, who had assembled below to be enabled to hear the serenade music better. In strange contrast with these intervened the various attendances to the necessities of our patient, the messages to the apothecary, my agony of mind — in fact, it was a situation singular indeed of its kind.

"At midnight the physician came again, wrote some new prescriptions, and gave fresh instructions, but all in vain; the attacks of the cramp lasted till near 3 o'clock, when they became at length less violent, and by degrees entirely ceased. But as the doctor was of opinion this morning that the motion of the carriage might be prejudicial to the invalid, we have deferred our departure, and the more so, as we could be nowhere better off than here, where we receive the kindest attention and care from the whole household, and everything that the heart can wish is at our service. To-day, *Spohr* received from the Grand-duke a splendid diamond ring as a 'souvenir of Oldenburg,' which greatly surprised and pleased him. The Grand-duke had intended to place the ring himself on his finger at the dinner to which he had invited him, but this also was defeated by the illness that overtook him," &c.

Spohr having determined by the advice of the physician to proceed as soon as possible direct from Oldenburg to the baths of Carlsbad, and devote the remainder of his vacation to the re-establishment of his health by drinking the waters, he thought he should no longer be able to fulfill his promises — to direct his "Jessonda" at Bremen, and the first performance of the "Crusaders" at Berlin — wherefore with a heavy heart he sent off letters announcing his inability to proceed to those places.

Meanwhile, however, the remarkable efficacy of the Carlsbad waters, which he had already several times experienced, evinced itself again upon him in so satisfactory a manner, that in the very first week of his stay the idea suggested itself to him, to remain for the present but a fortnight only in Carlsbad, and defer following up the cure of its waters to the following summer, so that his so unwillingly abandoned purpose of proceeding to Berlin might yet be carried out. In this hope he continued the course of baths with such unwearied perseverance and unswerving confidence that he was enabled to reach Berlin in sufficient time to assume personally the direction of his "Crusaders."

At the first grand rehearsal, in which he was introduced by *Meyerbeer* and Councillor *Küstner* to the assembled company of the theatre, he became convinced that his work had been studied with particular pleasure and predilection, and the song parts, although not filled by stars of the first magnitude, were nevertheless impersonated, as regarded the chief and secondary characters, in a thoroughly satisfactory manner. On the evening of the performance he was received upon his appearance with the greatest enthusiasm by the public, and loudly called for after every act. On the following night the opera was repeated with the same brilliant success. The public papers contained also the most favourable notices of each, and the "Vossische Zeitung" especially gave an article from the pen of *Rellstab* to this effect: "We have to speak of an event in art that will occupy one of the most prominent and honourable places in the history of our stage — the first performance of *Louis Spohr's* new opera, "The Crusaders." The merits of the master have already made themselves so prominently conspicuous, and the worth of that which we possess in him is so fully acknowledged, that it is not necessary even to speak of the character of his music nor of its effects upon the development of art in the present day . . . . What we had to expect as a whole, every body knew who knows the artistic direction of *Spohr's* genius — and who does not know it? That we should hear a work that might be ranked with the noblest of the kind to which the composer has adhered throughout his whole life, was to be expected. But we must frankly confess, we had not dared to hope for so much freshness, so many instances of fiery power, as the now more than sexagenarian master actually gives us! Throughout the whole, he is the same we have long known; but in many circumstances of the detail he presents us with numerous gifts of new and finished excellence — and also of frequent brilliancy. His muse has never addressed herself to the crowd: she never sought to seduce by coquettish and alluring advances; her language, her movements have been alone animated by a noble spiritual inspiration, and sought to win the heart by purity and dignity. We had at first intended to indicate the most prominently beautiful passages, which we consider it just to particularise; but we soon found them so numerous, that we were compelled to content ourselves with a selection. In the first act we recall to mind the singular freshness of Baldwin's greeting; Emma's devout song: "Dass ich die Braut des Himmels bin," the effective and ominous mingling of the tolling of the funeral bell in the discourse with the porteress; the first strong physiognomic delineations of the abbess Celestina, in the words: "Ich kenne Dein Geschlecht — Dein Schicksal führt Dich her;" we remember some features that designate the same character and its impassioned ebullition, as: the soft transition of the orchestra after the words: "Ihr sollt das Mädchen lieben;" and the subsequent words: "Gerichtet hat ihn Gott! — die Mutter weint, — die Tochter büsst, — dem Todten sei verziehen;" which are of the deepest and most impressive effect from their musical treatment. — The march of the Saracens in this act is also of most original colouring, and recurs again in the third act, where it is connected with that which has gone before, and is handled in so startling and beautiful a manner in the orchestra, that the public expressed their delight at the return to it there by a general outburst of applause. — If we cite fewer passages in the subsequent acts, it is not that these were poorer, but not to weary the reader's patience with the enumeration of individual parts; and indeed the power of the music increases with the interest of the subject treated. The recognition scene between Balduin and Emma, Balduin's threat at its conclusion, and the whole finale of the second act, form striking moments, which always ensure the admiration of the hearer. In the third act, the duet between Balduin and Bruno is a fine master-piece of music, and the conclusion, the despair of Balduin, replete with energetic force, and instrumented in a truly powerful manner. The battle chorus of the Turks, from its prominent difference of colouring, excited the enthusiasm of the auditory, who followed the conformity of the opera well sustained throughout from that part to the end, with the most lively interest. . . . . . . We must also acknowledge the zeal of all the performers . . . . But no less are thanks and honour due to the public! They have this time shewn themselves fully sensible of their office of judge and reward-giver, and gave that unremitting attention to the work throughout which is most expressive of the admiration and interest it awakened. Scarcely any fine passage passed unnoticed by more or less warm demonstrations. . . . The day thus terminated in a triumph for long years of meritorious services, and in a day of honour for this particular work, which bears witness to the wealth in artistic riches possessed by the composer, and in what sure keeping and governance they are in the hands of our highly esteemed master;" &c. — Passing over other similar notices, a criticism (signed H. T.) may be adverted to here, for its strikingly harsh contrast with the former; overflowing with dissatisfaction and every kind of reproach of this opera, and which although not among the other papers now before us, is still remembered by the family as one that greatly surprised them by its contents. In cases of this kind *Spohr* always laughed at the angry zeal of his friends, affirming that every one had a right to express his personal opinion freely, but at the same time with the remark: "When a piece of music is really good, no reviling critic can take from it an atom of its merit!" —

Though the brilliant success of this opera, which *Spohr* had written under circumstances of particular predilection, constituted the most important moment of his eight days' visit to Berlin, he passed the previous and subsequent days in the most agreeable manner in the amiable family circle of Professor *Wichmann*. But not alone in the hospitable reception accorded him and his wife, which afforded them all the delights of a charming domesticity, did *Spohr* experience the highest gratification; for from other quarters also marks of attention were shown him yet more demonstrative of the honour in which his genius was held.

Especially gratifying as were to him the attentions of his colleagues in art, *Meyerbeer, Taubert, Hub. Riess,* and others, he was not insensible to the tribute of acknowledgment paid to him by the King; and the honour of an invitation to the royal table was yet more enhanced in worth to him, from its being communicated to him at the King's request in a personal visit from the celebrated *Alexander v. Humboldt*. Of this royal dinner party, at which, besides *Humboldt, Tiek, v. Savigny,* and other personages of note were present, who emulated with each other in pleasing and intellectual conversation with the King and Queen, *Spohr* always spoke with much pleasure in later years. More especially, however, he would recur to the following amusing incident:

Between the King and *Spohr*, who was seated opposite to him, rose an ornamental centre-piece of considerable height, in the shape of a costly flower-vase, which whenever the King was desirous of addressing his conversation to *Spohr*, greatly interfered and prevented him from seeing his face. Upon each occasion, the King was obliged to stoop in order to look round the inconveniently intervening object, until growing impatient, after having made several signs to the servants to remove it, which they appeared not to have understood, the King seized it with his own hand, and removing the obtrusive ornament procured for himself an unimpeded view across the table to *Spohr*. — On the last evening, while the *Wichmann* family and their guests were seated in the illuminated garden saloon in friendly chat, they were greatly surprised by the sudden entry from the obscurity of the garden of several dark figures, which were followed by a constantly increasing number, until the whole of the members of the royal orchestra, with *Meyerbeer* and *Taubert* at their head, assembled, upon which the senior member presented *Spohr* with a beautifully executed golden laurel-wreath, while *Meyerber*, in a speech of much feeling, thanked him "for all the grand and beautiful things which in his enthusiastic love of true German art he had hitherto created, and especially for this his excellent work, "The Crusaders," &c. This discourse upon the evening of his taking leave, spoken with warmth and sincerity by such a man, could not fail to make a deep impression upon *Spohr* and every person present, and it was followed by a silence the most profound; until professor *Wichmann*, who was the first to recover his self-possession, approached *Meyerbeer*, and to the just praises conveyed in his excellent speech, replied with much humour in the words: "Positively, *Demosthenes* was a mere stump orator in comparison to you!" at which the cheerful tone of the company was magically restored, and *Spohr* then returned thanks in a concise yet feeling manner. Besides this handsome present from the royal Berlin orchestra, he took back with him to Cassel another souvenir of his stay there, viz. his own bust executed by professor *Wichmann*, which on account of its speaking resemblance and artistic excellence has always been greatly admired both by connoisseurs and the general public.

Scarcely had *Spohr* returned to Cassel than he was again upon the move, and this time to Bonn, where on the 11th. of August the inauguration of the monument to *Beethoven* was to be celebrated. To the invitation that had been sent to him many weeks before, to conduct a portion of the musical performance upon the occasion, he had at first, it is true, replied declining it, as a special leave of absence would have been necessary for him to proceed thither, and after having already applied for one the year before to direct the Brunswick musical festival, he did not like to make a similar application so soon. It was however shortly announced to him in a second letter, that the committee of the festival having been informed that the

Prince was then staying at Cologne for a few days, they had despatched a deputation thither to invite him and the Countess *Schaumburg* to the approaching ceremony in her native town of Bonn, and to solicit at the same a leave of absence for *Spohr*, which had been graciously granted. As no further obstacle now intervened, *Spohr* lost no time in proceeding thither, to lend his personal assistance at the grand festival, which had drawn together from far and near the musical youth of Germany, to do honour to the great master whose memorial was to be inaugurated.

Of the festivities preceding and subsequent to the uncovering of the statue — the launching of the steam-boat "*Ludwig van Beethoven*," the excursion to Nonnenwerth, the grand procession, the pyrotechnic display, illumination, banquet and ball — all these things have been so frequently described verbally and in writing by many who were present at the festival, that we will here only concisely advert to its musical features.

In the first grand concert *Beethoven's* mass in *D major* and the ninth symphony were performed under *Spohr's* direction, and as the published accounts of the festival express it, "both these works, which present very great difficulties, were performed with the most finished execution, so that this concert alone, combined with the sight of the hall in which it took place, was well worth the journey to Bonn." On the following day, *Beethoven's* grand mass in *C major* was performed at the celebration of divine service in the minster church, and upon the uncovering of the statue a festive cantata by *Breitenstein* was performed under his direction. At the second grand concert in the hall *Spohr*, by the desire of *Lisst*, again directed a part, while the services of the latter, as an active member of the committee, being continually required in various departments, with the exception of his performance of *Beethoven's* pianoforte concerto in *E major*, he confined himself to the direction of the *C minor* symphony and some "numbers" of the Fidelio. The third, so-called musicians' concert, was subjected of a necessity to many changes of the fourteen pieces of which its programme consisted, as, besides the Princes who were already arrived, the King and Queen of Prussia, the Queen of England with her consort, and other exalted personages were expected at the solemnities of the inauguration of the statue, and *Lisst* did not like to begin his festive cantata before their arrival. But it became at length necessary to make a beginning, and scarcely was the first "number" of *Lisst's* cantata concluded, than the royal personages made their appearance, and the assembled company saluted them with the national-hymn: "Heil Dir im Siegerkranz;" after which *Lisst* had the whole cantata repeated; upon the conclusion of which it was left to the two Queens to make the selection of the next musical-pieces which were to be performed in their presence. It was thus, that not only the pieces of the programme were changed from their announced order of succession, but several of the pieces were necessarily wholly omitted on account of the delay that had thus occurred; and the musical part of the festival was brought to a termination in a somewhat unsatisfactory manner, and without a real and proper conclusion in the opinion of a majority of the auditory. A chosen few, however, among whom was *Spohr*, received an invitation to the grand court concert, given by the King of Prussia in honour of his exalted guests at his palace of the Brühl, in the neighbourhood. *Meyerbeer* directed, and the programme consisted, with the exception of some pianoforte-pieces performed by *Lisst*, of song-pieces only, sung by the most eminent vocalists, Messrs. *Mantius*, *Pischeck* and *Staudigl*, with Mdmes. *Lind*, *Garcia* and *Tuczek*.

After a summer so busily occupied, and in which *Spohr* was deprived of all leisure for composing, the impulse to write something new was awakened but the more strongly upon his return to Cassel, and several instrumental compositions followed each other in quick succession, to which style of art, since the termination of his opera, his whole mind again more especially addressed itself. About this period he wrote his 15th. violin-concerto (*E minor*, Op. 128, published by *Schuberth*), which he first played at the subscription-concerts in Cassel, and in July 1845 at the previously mentioned musical festival at Oldenburg, and then in commemoration of that event dedicated it to *Poll* the music director of that place. This was followed by the sixth quintet for stringed instruments *(E minor* Op. 129, published by *Breitkopf & Härtel)*; and in the course of the winter by a quintet for pianoforte, two violins, viola and violincello, in *D minor* (Op. 130, published by *Schuberth*); the 30th. quartet for stringed instruments (Op. 132, published by *Breitkopf)*; and a quartet concert to for two violins, viola and violincello, with orchestra — the latter of which was played at the next subscription concerts, and by the addition of the rich instrumental accompaniment proved especially adapted as a simple quartet for performance at a concert in a spacious building. Before it had appeared in print (Op. 130, at *Schuberth's*), it was sent for from London and Vienna, and especially asked for at Leipzic, at which place the directors of the Gewandhaus concerts were always extremely desirous of being able to announce in their programme a new composition in manuscript by *Spohr*. Such upon this occasion was also the sentiment of *M. Hauptmann* in a letter to *Spohr*: "Everything coming from you, old or new, always finds the most favourable reception here: one can easily judge from the applause whether a thing merely pleases, or whether it makes a deep pleasurable impression, and that is always the case with your things. Either song or instrumental music of yours is always listened to with real predilection, the concert-loving public finds itself then in an atmosphere that suits it; and in this manner also the quartet concerto (with the execution of which I was not altogether satisfied) met with a very warm approval. To my mind it is perfectly *Spohrisch*, i. e. as masterly, as it is replete with feeling: the great difficulties attending such an undertaking are not in the least perceptible when listening to it, and as in your double quartets, the greatest clearness is always apparent in the most scientific combinations, which cannot always be said of other compositions that overstep the limits of the ordinary;

that is, what the initiated understand and consider as high art, but which the mere hearer of feeling finds pleasing and which put him in good humour," &c. The correspondence upon these subjects was chiefly conducted by *Mendelssohn*, who also made the proposition to introduce the third act of the Crusaders as a whole, in one of the concerts there, and afterwards announced to *Spohr*, who was of opinion that *this* opera in particular was not very suited to the purpose, his entire satisfaction: "The first time I saw your work in Berlin, the third act appeared to me the most spirited, and finest in the whole opera, and I was convinced that it would be very effective in a concert. You seemed to doubt it, and therefore I am the more pleased that yesterday's performance of it made so great an impression, which, to judge from the attention of the auditory, the applause and their observations, appears to me very evident... The chorus was about two hundred strong, and the hymn in *H major*, the chorus for male voices in *C major*, and then the scene in the convent, sounded wonderfully fine. A thousand hearty thanks for this enjoyment, and for all the many beautiful things for which we are indebted to you. . . . Unfortunately I was not able so to manage that the direction of this concert would fall to me; but it went so well under *Gade*, and he had made himself so well acquainted with the whole work, that even you would scarcely have desired more," &c.

In striking contrast with these friendly words of acknowledgement from so competent a judge, a circumstance occurred about the same time, which from being considered by *Spohr* himself as the only one of the kind throughout his long musical career, may not be undeserving of special mention here. Though the opera of the Crusaders had been sent by special request to Dresden for performance there, upwards of a twelvemonth, it had never yet been put upon the stage; and during that time the directors *Reissiger* and *Wagner*, as also the celebrated tenor *Tichatscheck*, for whose splendid voice the part of Balduin seemed almost purposely written, had repeatedly expressed by letter their pleasure with the work, and their regret at the constantly recurring delays, which deprived them of all hope of *Spohr's* proceeding there to direct it — when suddenly, to his great astonishment, the score, not a little worn and defaced, was sent back from Dresden, without honorarium, and even without the libretto, to which *Spohr* had with much trouble appended many remarks and directions in writing; accompanied only with a letter from the manager, Mr. *von Lüttichau*, the very unsatisfactory contents of which may be inferred from the following accidentally preserved copy of *Spohr's* reply:

"Your Excellency's letter of the 15th. inst. has very much surprised me. I never could have believed, after my long, and I think I may say honourable, career as a musician, that I should have lived to experience the indignity to have the score of one of my works — not sent in as the first essay of a beginner for examination and trial, but *ordered* by previous application — sent back to me in such a manner. What you are pleased to assign by way of explanation or excuse for so strange a proceeding, I cannot possibly accept; for it was no fault of mine that the opera was not brought out at the appointed time, and both soon enough and frequently enough had I drawn attention to the circumstance that I could obtain no leave of absence out of my vacation time. How the opera, which is known by nobody in Dresden, should now have lost the charm of novelty I can as little understand, as that the contents of the opera, which were already known to you when you ordered it, should now all at once be found objectionable, while here and in Berlin, it has not met with the least objection in its present form, nor formerly, when performed in the shape of a play throughout Germany. Had your excellency felt any anxiety lest the opera would not remunerate for the time given to its study, and the expenses it might entail, you could assuredly have found some relief for your doubts in the many numerously attended performances which have already taken place here, in Berlin, Brunswick, &c. It is difficult for me also to conceive how the work of an old experienced composer should be rejected by a theatre which does not disdain the rapid works of beginners and dilettanti such as .... and .... The insult that has been offered to me is therefore wholly inexplicable, and I must console myself with the reflexion, *that it is the only one of the kind offered to me during my long career as a composer*, and I congratulate myself that I am not under a theatrical directorship which so little understands how to respect the feelings of a veteran artist," &c. To this a reply was received from the vice-manager, *K. Winkler,* who at the request of Mr. *von Lüttichau,* expressed his regret that the return of his score, which had become necessary, should have so much offended *Spohr,* assuring him furthermore, that the chief reason for it was the words and subject of the opera, during the ecclesiastical excitement.

But that *Spohr's* view of the matter was not much changed by this attempt at exculpation is evident from a letter he wrote to *Richard Wagner,* in which he opens his whole mind to him, and having first expressed his disappointment that *Wagner's* opera "Tannhäuser," which he had proposed to the Prince to have performed in celebration of his birth day, had not received the official sanction, he avails himself of the opportunity to detail fully to him the incomprehensible conduct of the Dresden theatrical directorship. *Wagner,* who then first was made acquainted with all the particulars, gave expression to his anger thereat, in so plainspoken a manner, that the publication of his letter, highly interesting as it is, would perhaps be unadvisable. After the prospect of a meeting with *Wagner* in Dresden had been dispelled in so vexatious a manner, *Spohr* proposed to him a *rendez-vous* at Leipzic, where he intended making a stay of a few days on his contemptated journey with his wife to Carlsbad. As *Wagner* seized the idea with much pleasure, the long desired personal acquaintance was at length made with the greatest mutual satisfaction, and letters addressed to the family at home speak among other things of this meeting, and other interesting circumstances that occurred during their stay there:

"We are passing our time here most delightfully, and enjoying a very feast of the finest music. On the very first evening we had a music party at *Hauptmann's*, where trios by *Mendelssohn* and *Spohr*, in which each master took part, were played; and the company, consisting chiefly of connoisseurs in art, were highly delighted indeed. On the following day a very charming dinner-party was given at *Wagner's* suggestion, who has himself no means of entertaining friends at Leipzic, by his brother-in-law, Professor *Brockhaus*, in honour of *Spohr*. We there made the acquaintance of his sister and several others of his relatives, all of them most intellectual creatures, and enjoyed ourselves greatly. Besides the members of the family, *Heinrich Laube*, the author, and his very learned wife, were present, who gave a yet more lively impress to the conversation. We were most pleased with *Wagner*, who seems every time more and more amiable, and whose intellectual culture on every variety of subject is really wonderful. Among other things he gave expression to his sentiments on political matters with a warmth and depth of interest that quite surprised us, and pleased us of course the more from the great liberality of feeling he displayed. We passed the evening most delightfully at *Mendelssohn's*, who did his utmost to entertain and please *Spohr*. This family has for me something very idealistic about them, they present a combination of inward and external features, and withal so much beautiful domestic happiness, that one seldom sees the like of in actual life. In their establishment and whole manner of living there is so much unassuming modesty amid all the obvious luxury and wealth around them, that one cannot but feel at one's ease. And to me most gratifying is his unmistakable attachment to and esteem for *Spohr*. He himself played a most extremely difficult and highly characteristic composition of his own, called 'Siebenzehn ernste Variationen' (seventeen serious variations), with immense effect; then followed two of *Spohr's* quartets — among them the newest (the 30th.) — on which occasion *Mendelssohn* and *Wagner* read from the score with countenances expressive of their delight. Besides these, the wife of doctor *Frege* sang some of *Spohr's* songs, which *Mendelssohn* accompanied beautifully; and in this manner the hours passed rapidly and delightfully with alternate music and lively conversation, till midnight drew on unobserved, and at length gave impressive warning to break up. *Wagner,* who was obliged to return to Dresden the following day, came to take leave of us, which both to us and to him was a sad moment. But after he had left, he was frequently the subject of our conversation, for he left us the words of a new opera which he had written (Lohengrin) to read, and which is exceedingly original and interesting. . . . Yesterday at the dinner-table we made another agreeable acquaintance, that of the poet *Robert Prutz,* who being seated exactly opposite to us, introduced himself, sustained a very lively conversation, and appeared quite charmed at meeting with *Spohr.* After dinner a performance was arranged in the church by the pupils of the Thomas School, where, without any accompaniment *Spohr's* psalm with double choir, 'Aus der Tiefe' (out of the deep) and his favorite motet by *Bach:* 'Ich lasse Dich nicht' (I will not leave thee) were sung. . . . Last evening an extra concert was given for *Spohr* in the well-known Gewandhaus, which, under *Mendelssohn's* direction, was in every respect a brilliant entertainment. The programme consisted wholly of *Spohr's* compositions, of which we had not been apprized before hand, and which was on purpose to take us by surprise. It comprised: 1stly. The overture to Faust; 2dly. An air from Jessonda sung by the prima donna, Mrs. *Meyer;* 3dly. Grand violin concerto played to *Spohr's* complete satisfaction by the wonderful boy *Joachim;* 4thly. Songs with clarinet accompaniment, by the wife of doctor *Frege, Mendelssohn,* and a firstrate clarinetist, so wonderfully executed that it went to the very heart; 5thly. 'Weihe der Töne,' which for years has been a bright-shining star with the Leipzic orchestra. At the request of *Mendelssohn, Spohr,* although he would rather have remained a hearer only, took the direction of the two last subjects, on which occasion he was greeted by the orchestra and the auditory, which consisted of about two hundred select guests, with a storm of applause, as he had also been saluted with upon his entrance. The whole was a grand elevating festival, and for *Spohr* a deeply-felt gratification. *Mendelssohn* was extremely amiable, and the whole evening as though intensely happy, which proved how foreign to his mind is every feeling of jealousy. This evening the last music party will meet at *Vogt's*, where *Mendelssohn* proposes to himself an especial pleasure, not only in taking part in *Spohr's* first trio as pianist, but as *viol* in his splendid third double quartet."

In this manner up to the last moment was *Mendelssohn's* thoughtful and kind attention evinced to *Spohr*, and upon his departure on the following morning, when the numerous friends who had accompanied us to the railway-station had taken leave of him, he was, as the further accounts of the journey express it, "the last of all, who, as the train at first proceeded slowly, ran for a considerable distance by the side of the carriage, until he could no longer keep up with it, and his kindly beaming eyes were the last that left their expression on the minds of the travellers from Leipzic," little anticipating indeed that it was to be their last meeting on this side of the grave!

Scarcely had *Spohr* arrived in Carlsbad, than he received a pressing invitation from the Landgrave of *Fürstenberg*, president of the society of music of Vienna, to direct there two grand performances of his renowned oratorio, "The Fall of Babylon," upon the occasion of a festival at which 1000 singers would assist. But as this was to take place in November, and it would be necessary to ask for another "extraordinary" leave of absence to comply with the invitation, this was applied for through the Austrian embassy. But notwithstanding the signature of *"Metternich"* gave its imposing weight to the application, the Prince refused compliance, and thus not only was *Spohr* prevented going, but the performance of his oratorio was necessarily deferred to a more favourable opportunity.

Among the various incidents which this time occurred in agreeable relief and interruption to the daily routine prescribed for taking the baths, was first a concert given by the violinist *Ernst,* of which a letter speaks as follows: "The concert of so celebrated a virtuoso was quite an event for Carlsbad, and afforded us much pleasure. Besides the song scene of *Spohr*, he played several of his own things, some of which were very beautiful, curious compositions replete with all manner of difficulties and wonderful artistic resorts for display, and which he executed with great precision and ease; but alhough he played *Spohr's* concerts with much care and great expression, yet we have not only heard it played by *Spohr* himself, but by his talented pupil *Jean Bott,* much more correctly. The overcrowded house presented a curious spectacle, for not only was the space allotted to the spectators, but the whole stage also, occupied by the public, which sat round disposed in a large semicircle," &c. But amusing scenes of another kind also occurred at Carlsbad. One day a good-natured invalid visitor of the baths took it into his head to give a little treat to the fifteen young serving-women attached to the baths, at which several hundred spectators were present; and above all, *Spohr,* with his characteristic good humour, took great pleasure at the sight of the assembled girls, dressed in their uniform (white gowns, green spencers, and pink aprons), each with a fresh-gathered rose in her hair, seated at a long table, and looking around on all the spectators with eyes beaming with pleasure as they partook of their treat of coffee and cake. At another time, by a similar but anonymous kind-hearted individual a parcel was sent to *Spohr* containing two enormous herrings, remarkable samples of their species, with the laconic inscription appended to them: "I love *Spohr's* music! The great German *Spohr* will not despise the accompanying quite fresh herrings, a very rare, but permitted dish here. Carlsbad June 6." Though *Spohr* had always been used to receive a great variety of presents, and frequently of the strangest kind, as tokens of esteem and admiration, yet he had never before received one of so surprising and comical a kind, at which, with *Ernst*, who happened to be present at the moment he received them, he laughed very heartily, and then without much speculation or care as to who the anonymous donor might be, ate with much relish the delicious fish, as a change from the scant prescriptive supper permitted to the bath patients. As the greatest moderation not only in physical but mental exertions and enjoyments formed part of the bathing cure, *Spohr*, as a conscientious patient, had at first considered it a duty to refrain from every musical excitement, particularly from that of composing, until the impulse became so strong within him that he thought it more prejudicial to suppress by force than to give some form to the vivid ideas that floated across his fancy; and thus with unforced readiness flowed from his pen the last part yet wanting to complete the fourth pianoforte trio which he had already begun in Cassel; and it being as it were the bubbling and overflow of the gaiety of his spirits, he was accustomed to call it by way of souvenir of the benefit he derived from the bubbling springs of Carlsbad, "*Der Sprudelsatz*" (The bubble piece). As however there was no good player on the violincello in Carlsbad, he thought he should be obliged to wait till his return to Cassel for a thorough performance of the trio; but during a short stay at Meiningen on his return journey, *Edward Grund*, the already frequently mentioned music director, with incredible diligence took all the requisite measures for getting up a quartet party on the same evening in his house, where *Spohr* had the unexpected opportunity of hearing his trio, with the aid of his wife and the distinguished violincellist *Metzner*, for the first time, which afforded also no little delight to the company present. As it also soon became a favorite piece with the musical circles of Cassel, *Spohr* kept it by him for a long time in manuscript, before he sent it to his publisher, *Schuberth*, who looked forward with truly restless impatience to the appearance of this trio of *Spohr's* in order to make it public. (Op. 135.)

In the beginning of the year 1847 the day drew near at length, the celebration of which had for weeks beforehand set the natives of Cassel on the tip-toe of pleasurable expectation, that, namely, of his twenty-fifth year's jubilee as director at the court theatre of Cassel. The lively interest taken far and near in this festival evinced itself in so many demonstrations of attachment and esteem towards the individual thus honoured, that a published account of them written by Dr. *Frederick Oetker*, the proceeds of which were devoted to charitable purposes, formed a complete pamphlet, for a short extract from which we have alone room here:

"Early on the morning of the 20th. January, the recipient of the day's honours was awakened from his slumbers by a serenade played by his pupils *Jean Bott* and *A. Malibran*, who, assisted by musicians of the court orchestra, performed his second double quartet. This was followed by a long successsion of congratulatory visits from relatives, friends, pupils, and admirers of all classes and from every quarter, who came to express their wishes for his health and happiness. From the society of St. Cecilia there came a well selected deputation, composed of representatives of soprani, alti, tenori and bass, in whose name the secretary *Knyrim*, the only remaining original member, expressed in hearty words their grateful acknowledgement of the many services rendered to art, and to the society in particular, by the honoured jubilant. These were succeeded by the postmaster-general *Nebelthau*, as member of the council of state, who presented *Spohr* a congratulatory address in writing from the chief magistrate of Cassel, and then the music director from Göttingen, Mr. *Wehner*, delivered a wreath of laurel from that place, accompanied with a congratulatory poem, and with a diploma nonimating *Spohr* an honorary member of the singing association of Göttingen. Accompanied with a most obliging letter the King of Prussia sent to him the order of the red eagle, third class, and the Prince, who had some years before already conferred upon him the Hessian order of the lion, forwarded to him upon this occasion a further mark of distinction, nominating him music director-general, with grant of official character at court. The rescript of this patent was personally handed to *Spohr* by the chamberlain *von Heeringen*, who the previous year had been nominated intendant-general of the court theatre, in order at the same time to express both his good wishes and the high esteem he felt for *Spohr* as a man and as an artist, which he moreover proved upon this occasion by the splendid festal performances he had ordered at the theatre in celebration of this day. This consisted in a musical-dramatic production "of scenically connected music-pieces from the operas of *Spohr*," the tickets of admission to which, besides those to the extra standing places, had been issued many days before, so that the house was actually crammed. When *Spohr* made his appearance in the box in the first tier, which had been appropriated to him and his family, he was received with the most tumultuous demonstrations of joy, with which the strains of his overture to the opera of "Alruna" soon mingled. This was followed by a tableau from "Zemira and Azor," representing the union of the lovers. After the conclusion of this tableau, as also after each of the following scenes from *Spohr's* operas: "Zemira", "Zweikampf," "Jessonda," "Berggeist," "Pietro von Abano," "Alchymist," and "Kreuzfahrer," the fairy with her golden magic wand came upon the stage and introduced the succeeding scene each time with appropriate verses. After each piece of music the outburst of applause was repeated, and at its conclusion redoubled in energy, to be again resumed with equal perseverance as in succession the two overtures to the "Mountain Sprite" and to "Faust" were executed with remarkable precision under the direction of *Bochmann* the military band-master. Then followed an appropriately conceived festal-play called "Die Huldigung" (The Homage). The scene represented a handsome park ornamented with statues, vases and garlands; in the back ground a modest dwelling, but richly decorated with garlands of flowers: *The house, in which Spohr was born*, in Brunswick. Gardeners and maidens are busied in decorating the garden; to their question as to the purpose and occasion of the festival the steward informs them, telling them the name of the honoured jubilant, and in citing his works speaks also of 'Die letzten Dinge' and 'Der Fall Babylons.'

"All now set up a shout of joy, and from every part of the house rang the enthusiastic cheers of the excited assembly. Upon this the orchestra struck up the polonaise in "Faust," while the committee of the fete waited on *Spohr* to conduct him to a throne of flowers, where he was again greeted with a poetical address, and a crown of laurel placed upon his head "as Apollo's favoured son," amid the joyful vivats of the public. After the fete at the theatre was over, and he proceeded to partake of a family supper at the house of his son-in-law *Wolff*, he received late in the evening a brilliant serenade from the members of the lyrical association, who had assembled before the house by the light of numerous coloured lamps. The singing being concluded they then sent up a deputation to present the diploma of an honorary member of the society to the jubilant. Thus terminated this eventful day, but not the festivities; for the following day brought further congratulatory addresses in prosa and verse with honours of every kind, among which the presentation of the freedom of the city from the chief magistrate of Cassel, and as also worthy of mention, the gift of a costly silver vase from the joint members of the orchestra and theatrical company, presented by the committee of the festival."

On the twenty-second of January another grand fete took place, given as a surprise to their friend and master by the members of the quartet circle, so frequently adverted to. After *Spohr* had been conducted with great ceremony into the presence of the company, composed of about seventy persons, a congratulatory poem composed by Dr. *Oetker* was read.

The musical part of the fete which now followed consisted of *Spohr's* third double quartet, executed under the direction of his pupil *Jean Bott*; of two of his incomparable songs with clarinet accompaniment, sung by a distinguished dilettante; and the pianoforte quintet with wind-instrument accompaniment. After the conclusion of these extremely successful performances, all adjourned in the best spirits to the supper-room, where, seasoned with toasts both of earnest and mirthful import, the happy evening was brought to a close in an appropriate manner.

The account of this jubilee published shortly after by *Fr. Oetker* gave occasion at the same time to *Spohr* for the commencement of his autobiography. The author of that pamphlet having at the same time expressed the intention of following it up with a detailed account of his life, requested *Spohr* to furnish him first with the necessary notes; but he himself, while making the necessary sketch of it, took so much pleasure in recalling the varied events of each year as they presented themselves to his memory, that he conceived the idea of preferring to undertake its full detail himself.* With a lively interest he now immediately set himself to this work, which nevertheless proceeded but slowly, when the impulse for musical composition assumed again its mastery. He then first wrote six *pièces de salon* for violin and pianoforte, distinguished by the titles: *Barcarole, Scherzo, Sarabande, Siciliano, Air varié* and *Mazurka*, collected in one volume as Op. 135, published by *J. Schuberth;* these were followed by his fourth double quartet, and some months later, at the express wish of the Philharmonic Society of London, by the eighth symphony *(G minor)*, which appeared at Leipzic as Op. 137 *(Peters)*, in score and arranged for four hands for the pianoforte.

---

* From this somewhat accidental origin of *Spohr's* autobiography it may be readily inferred, that it contains nothing more than a faithful picture of his eventful life, interesting to the majority of those who take a warm interest in his musical compositions; and that it was not his intention in any manner to have it considered in the light of a contribution to the history of art, nor as a critical opinion of the works of his colleagues in art, which has been here and there erroneously expected from this biography.

Subsequently also, *Spohr's* activity was unusually taxed at the theatre, as he was required for the approaching Whitsuntide holidays to prepare not only the usual opera but also (an exceptional case) a grand concert, in which among other things his double symphony and his first concertante were executed by himself and his pupil *Jean Bott*. For Whitmonday a new opera, "Arria," by *Hugo Stähle*, had been selected, which as the maiden-work of a young composer who had grown up amid them had greatly awakened the interest of all lovers of music in Cassel. Already when a boy the young musician had exhibited such prominent talent, that *Spohr* was induced, at the wish of his father, Major *Stähle* of Cassel, to take him as a pupil in composition. With constantly increasing interest he now watched the progress of his talented pupil, who, already a good pianist, soon tried his hand at greater pianoforte-compositions, among which a quartet in *A major* (Op. 1, published by *Schuberth*) is especially remarkable as a success. Encouraged by this, he then, though not yet one and twenty years of age, ventured under *Spohr's* guidance upon the composition of music to the opera above named, written by his friend *Jac. Hofmeister*, and that so fully satisfied *Spohr*, that upon his pressing recommendation its performance was determined upon and soon put in process of execution. Though *Spohr* experienced real satisfaction at the highly favourable reception this opera met with from the public, and looked forward hopefully to a brilliant future for the young composer, this first triumph was unhappily his last; for after the lapse of a year, he was seized with an inflammatory fever, which arrested his career of promise by an early death!

After *Spohr* had several times deferred his last visit to England to direct according to invitation the performance of some of his works, he at length resolved in the summer of 1847, to yield once more to the reiterated invitations he had received, and to direct the three grand concerts, in which the Sacred Harmonic Society proposed to give the whole of his sacred pieces — oratorios, psalms, &c. At the commencement of the theatrical vacation he therefore set out, accompanied on the journey to England by his wife and sister-in-law, and this time by way of the interesting cities of Brussel and Ghent to Ostend, where he proposed to embark. A letter written home adverts as follows to their stay in Ghent: "On our way we had been informed that upon the very day of our arrival a grand singing festival was to take place, of the united Flemish and German lyrical societies; but as we did not arrive here before 7 o'clock in the evening, some time after the chief part of the concert had begun, we thought to avail ourselves of the fine summer evening to take a walk through the town, which we found large and handsome beyond our expectation. Scarcely however had we proceeded above a hundred yards when *Spohr* was recognised by some gentlemen, who hastened towards him with the greatest surprise, and compelled us almost by foce to go with them and hear the second part of the concert, the first part being just finished. In this manner we were all three hurried into a fine building, the 'Palais de Justice' and stood suddenly in the immense hall filled with several thousand persons, when at the same moment one of the gentlemen who brought us in, a member of the committee of the festival, with a loud voice called out: 'Messieurs, le grand compositeur *Spohr* vient d'arriver dans notre ville, le voici!' At this announcement the whole assembly rose from their seats, and clapping their hands cried: 'Vive *Spohr*, le grand *Spohr!*' and a perfect shower of flowers in the shape of bouquets large and small were showered upon him from all sides. It was long before the tumultuous applause ceased; meanwhile seats were yielded to us in the best places, and there we sat somewhat out of countenance in our dusty travelling costume in the midst of handsomely dressed ladies. But the whole scene, from its very unexpectedness, had someting extremely original and almost overpowering about it. We then heard, with the rest, the second part of the concert, in which the different lyrical associations sung in part with, and partly without, orchestral accompaniment. They all met with the most lively applause, which their execution in reality also deserved.

"It lasted until past 9 o'clock, and then a crowd of persons pressed forward to salute *Spohr* and to speak to him, so that it was late enough before we got home to supper, and retired to rest. But this was again to be of short duration, for between 11 and 12 o'clock we heard all manner of noises and preparations for a grand serenade, which the Ghent society 'Des Mélomanes' had resolved upon giving to *Spohr*. *Nolens volens* he was obliged to get out of bed and dress anew not only in acknowledgement of the fine music and tremendous vivats of the assembled crowd, but also to receive a deputation, which at the solemn midnight hour announced to him his nomination as honorary member of the society," &c.

Upon *Spohr's* arrival in London he and his travelling companions were again hospitably received in the friendly family of Professor *Taylor,* and for them now began in every respect a period of great enjoyment. The oratorio performances in Exeter-Hall appointed for every Friday, went off with their usual finished perfection; but the programme that had been previously determined upon had suffered from the alteration, that in place of the "Calvary," which it was feared would here also excite objection on the part of the clergy, a second performance of the "Fall of Babylon" was announced; while in the third concert, as it had been previously determined, "Die letzten Dinge," the "Lord's Prayer," and *Spohr's* recently composed 84th. Psalm after *Milton's* metrical translation, were given. The enthusiasm at all the three concerts, which was scarcely susceptible of increase on all that had previously been shewn, was evinced this time more particularly by rapturous encores of a great number of choruses and solo pieces. The intervening days were passed in a no less satisfactory manner, in which all emulated in affording some enjoyment, or in testifying their respect for *Spohr* in various ways. In varied and constant interchange, invitations, festivities, promenades and railway excursions succeeded each other, one of which extended as far as 70 English miles, to the celebrated university city of Cambridge, with its grand and peculiar style of architecture; and another to the city of Ely, remarkable for its situation upon a beautiful and fruitful hill rising from the midst of a low moorland, and yet more for its beautiful cathedral, considered one of the finest specimens of Gothic architecture in England. In this, as a remains of its former splendour, the finest ecclesiastical psalmody is still chanted during divine service by sixteen singers especially maintained for that purpose, and seldom in that solitary place could perhaps be found hearers so devoutly attentive and edified as were *Spohr* and his travelling companions.

In pleasant reunions with the *Horsley*, *Benedict* and *Taylor* families, his most intimately known friends, *Spohr* especially passed many happy hours, in whose circles allied so intimately to art and artists, fine music was a never-failing enjoyment, and in which frequently, to the delight of his hearers, *Spohr* contributed his personal aid. The more decidedly however, did he decline every request to perform in public, and in one exceptional instance only consented to assist at a concert given in his honour by the *Beethoven* quartet society. The programme of this concert, which displayed the heading "Homage to *Spohr*," comprised however on this occasion nothing of *Beethoven*, and three compositions of *Spohr* only, selected from different periods of his life, viz: 1st. A quartet *(G minor)*, a production of his early youth; 2dly. A duet composed about 20 years later, played by *Joachim* and *Sainton* in a masterly manner, and 3rdly. The third double quartet *(E minor)*, in which *Spohr* took the first violin part, and by his play and by the whole composition, the first "number" of which alone had kindled the admiration of the public, drew down a very storm of applause. The newspapers adverted in terms of the highest praise to the selection of the three compositions and to their separate beauties. Upon this occasion, respecting the duets the "Times" said as follows: "These duets for two violins belong to the greatest productions of *Spohr's* richly inventive genius.

Out of seemingly small materials the great composer has achieved harmonic effects scarcely inferior in richness and fullness to the quartet. The duet in *E flat* is positively overflowing with beauties of melody and counterpoint, a perfect masterpiece." ... And added further on: "The double quartet in *E minor* is one of *Spohr's* most surpassingly rich compositions. ... Every separate theme bears the stamp of genius, and is worked out with a perfection of finish that displays the highest degree of intelligence." ... "If *Spohr* had never written anything else, his fame would have been established by this work alone, as one of the greatest composers in the world." ... "*Spohr* plays now but seldom in public, but both musicians, and the general public alike, eagerly seize the rare opportunity of hearing the greatest violinist of the present day. His style is a pattern of purity and taste. ... He not alone produces difficulties of every kind, and handles them with the ease of mere play toys, — but in his execution displays moreover the full energy and inspiration of youth." ...

The end of the vacation was now rapidly drawing near, and with it once more the hour of parting; and on the last days of his sojourn so manifold were the demands made upon his time and attention that all his habitual calm self possession was taxed to the utmost. With heart and mind impressed with happy and elevating reminiscences he returned to his native country, where with his accustomed cheerfulness and zeal he was soon re-engaged in the performance of the duties of his post.

In the beginning of November he was plunged into grief by the sudden intelligence of the death of his friend *Mendelssohn*, deeply lamenting whose loss both as a man and a musician, he expressed himself as follows in a letter to *M. Hauptmann*: "What might *Mendelssohn* in the full maturity of his genius not have written, had fate permitted him a longer life! For his delicate frame the mental exertion was too great and therefore destructive! His loss to art is much to be lamented, for he was the most gifted of then living composers, and his efforts in art were of the noblest!" — His next thought was to institute a festival *in memoriam* of the too early departed one, but as he received for answer to his proposal to that effect, from the intendant of the court theatre, that: "the proposed festival in memory of the deceased could not be permitted at the concerts of the court theatre, as it did not find approval in the highest quarters," he determined to give it on a smaller scale at a private concert in celebration of the 25th. anniversary of the St. Cecilia society on the 22nd. November, and upon the occasion to inaugurate the fete with a poem composed for the occasion with a chorus from *Mendelssohn's* "Paulus." But after everything had been arranged for the best and the grand rehearsal been held, intelligence was suddenly received of the dangerous illness of the Elector Wilhelm II., who resided in Frankfort, which was followed by that of his death, and the order for a general mourning throughout the Electorate and a desistance from every kind of music on the following days. Hereupon, after a delay of a month, the performance of the projected festival was again about to take place, and *Spohr* had once more fixed the day for it, when death once more intervened — this time afflicting his own family with a very painful loss. On the 18th. December *Spohr's* mother-in-law was seized with illness, and after a few days' suffering was snatched from the disconsolate family to which she had been bound by ties of the tenderest affection. The Christmas holidays, which had usually been with them a period of happy festivity, were now changed to days of gloom and mourning, and the more so from the circumstance that Mr. *Pfeiffer* (father) was laid on a sick-bed by the unexpected blow, and the happy reunion in the paternal house, where *Spohr* always felt so happy, and so well knew how to make others so, seemed to be interrupted for a long time, if not for ever! The subsequent weeks passed amid cares and anxieties, and not until his father-in-law's convalescence could *Spohr* think of celebrating the long-prepared-for festival.

The programme was so arranged, that it presented in chronological order twelve music pieces of *Bach*, *Händel*, *Haydn*, *Mozart*, *Beethoven*, *Hauptmann*, *Mendelssohn* and *Spohr*, as specimens of the style of each of those masters, to whose works the St. Cecilia society during its existence of twenty-five years had especially devoted its efforts. After the last song piece but one: "Wir preisen selig die" &c., from "Paulus," a poem was recited, entitled: Feeling of sorrow upon the early death of *Felix Mendelssohn-Bartholdy*.

This was followed by the presentation of a double breast-pin set with diamonds, accompanied with a poetical address to *Spohr* — the subject represented by the pin being a violin, and bass-clef. A "Hymn to *Spohr*," composed by *H. Stähle*, was then sung; and in conclusion, at the banquet which followed, a discourse was delivered relative to the origin and services of the society for the prosperity of which the speaker himself (Mr. *Weinrich*), in the triple character of singer, librarian, and treasurer, had laboured with unwearied zeal for many years.

In 1848, shortly after the outbreak of the disturbances in France, *Spohr*, somewhat under the influence of ideas of liberty, &c., composed his sextet for two violins, two viols and two violincellos (Op. 140, published by *C. Luckhardt* of Cassel), on making entry of which in the list of his compositions, he appended the words: "Written in March and April, at the time of the glorious revolution of the peoples for the liberty, unity and grandeur of Germany." And this composition, so rich in freshness of melodies, in genuine ætherial harmony, that scarcely any other of *Spohr's* works surpasses it, furnishes an eloquent testimony to the state of his feelings and his aspirations, which, soaring above the storms of the present, speak only of peace, hope and concord, as in spirit he beheld them spring out of the momentary struggles. Satisfied as *Spohr* might feel with this composition — the first since the dawning of the new æra upon Germany — he nevertheless for some time wholly abandoned all further composition, feeling, as he complained in a letter to his friend *Hauptmann*, that "the excitement of politics and the constant reading of the newspapers incapacitated him from giving his attention to any serious and quiet study."

On the 6th. August a grand popular festival took place in Cassel, which kept the whole of the inhabitants in a state of joyous mobility for the day. It commenced early in the morning, with the public recognition of the imperial administrator by the garrison assembled upon the "Forst." This was followed by the consecration and presentation of colours to the newly-formed corps of body-guards, combined with a grand church service in the presence of the Electoral family upon the Bowling-green in the Karlsaue, and in the afternoon there was a people's festival, in which the whole population of Cassel — a mixed troop of all classes — flocked to the Aue, either as participators in, or spectators of, the popular games, the dancing and the music. Towards evening, to the surprise of everybody the Elector, in plain black dress-coat, was seen threading his way among the joyous crowd, with looks expressive of the cheerful interest with which he acknowledged the cheers of the people who thronged every part of the park. The festivities of the day were terminated by a concert under *Spohr's* direction, executed by the singers and members of the choral societies of Cassel in front of the orangery, at which also the Elector appeared, and after a lengthened conversation with *Spohr*, asked him expressly for the song "Was ist des Deutschen Vaterland."

In June 1849 *Spohr* set out for Carlsbad, and stopped on his way thither a few days at Leipzic, where in the circle of his musical friends, he again passed many happy hours devoted to his noble art. On the first evening, at the house of his friend Mr. *Vogt*, two of his latest and as yet unpublished compositions — the fourth double quartet *(G minor)* and the but recently finished 31st. quartet *(C major)* — both of which were subsequently published by *C. Luckhardt* in Cassel as Op. 136 and 141. The double quartet was received more especially with such warm admiration, that *Spohr* gratified the wish expressed by several of his auditors to repeat it once more on the following day at the conservatory before a large circle, among whom were the teachers and pupils of that institution. On the last evening, his old friend *Moscheles* prepared for him a brilliant fête, and embellished the musical part of it by his own masterly performance of *Spohr's* first trio, and his pianoforte quintet with wind instruments, after which the strains of a choral song, "Honour to *Spohr*," were suddenly heard from the garden in front of the house, and some of his four-part songs, some of *Mendelssohn's* and some of *Hauptmann's*, were executed in a most effective manner.

The now ensuing stay in Carlsbad, extending to several weeks, was upon this occasion particularly pleasant in many respects. In the intercourse with several distinguished men well known for their public activity, *Spohr* took great pleasure. Among these especially were *Hansemann* of Berlin and *Simson* of Königsberg, to the latter of whom, from the thorough community of sentiment in their mutual political creed, he was especially attracted. As both men evinced at the same time a warm love of music, they, together with their families were soon admitted into the small circle of the elect who had the *entrée* to the musical performances of *Spohr* and his wife. With these and other charming families the afternoons were then passed in excursions on all sides into the beautiful environs, in which *Spohr*, although long since well acquainted with every spot, always experienced a new delight and one equally shared by his wife.

From his stay in Carlsbad *Spohr* also experienced the most desirable benefit to his health, resulting in so complete and permanent a relief to the liver complaint which had recurred at previous frequent intervals, that, grateful as he felt for the pleasant and health-restoring time he had passed there, he had now no further necessity to resort to the wonderful efficacity of its waters.

Strengthened and refreshed in body and mind, he returned to Cassel, and shortly afterwards began the composition of his fifth pianoforte trio *(C minor,* Op. 141, published by *Schuberth* in Hamburg); which was followed by three duets for two soprani, published by *Peters* of Leipzic, which for their sweetly expressive melodies and their ease of performance, like those which had previously appeared from the pen of *Mendelssohn*, soon became favorite pieces in musical circles.

Towards the end of the year 1849 *Spohr* was afflicted by a heavy sorrow, in the sudden illness that befell his wife the day after Christmas Day, and which increased so much in severity as to imperil her life at the entry of the new year. At length, however, her good and unimpaired constitution, aided by the most unremitting care, overcame her malady, and *Spohr* hailed once more with delight the day when she could again resume her accustomed seat by his side at the dinner-table. But on the next day (January 22) an untoward accident befell himself. While on his usual daily way to the theatre rehearsal, a sharp unexpected frost having set in during the night, he slipped, and fell with such violence as to inflict a very severe blow on his head, from the consequence of which the unremitting care of his experienced medicial attendant Dr. *Harnier* did not re-establish him till after the lapse of several weeks. Shortly after his recovery, he wrote his ninth symphony, "Die Jahreszeiten" (The Seasons), the plan of which had much occupied his mind during his illness, and as he himself complained, "regularly haunted him during the long sleepless and feverish nights." He gave in so far a new form to it, that he divided it into two grand themes, with the designations: Part I.: Winter, transition to spring, spring. Part II.: Summer, transition to autumn, autumn. Although *Spohr* wrote the symphony in the dull cold days of winter, the result nevertheless was just the least characteristic of his *winterly* intentions. While in the *spring* theme every note rings joyous with the glad awaking of nature, — in that of *summer*, the sultry heat is expressed in tones the effect of which is such, that the astonished hearer positively seems to *feel* it — and lastly the *autumn*, with its exhilarating music of the chase, and the masterly interwoven Rheinweinlied (vintage song of the Rhine) — can scarcely fail in inspiring the hearer with the most lively enthusiasm.

About this time *Spohr*, with every lover of music in Cassel, experienced great pleasure from the visit of a young female artiste nearly related to him. This was *Rosalie Spohr*, the second daughter of his brother *William*. From early childhood she had evinced a passionate love of music, and subsequently devoted herself with unwearying zeal to the study of the harp. Although at first it was not the wish of her parents that their daughter should perform in public, yet when they had subsequently become convinced of her real artistic talent, they could no longer oppose her ardent wishes, and at the age of 22 she proceeded, accompanied by her father, upon her first musical tour. After she had given proof of her abilities in several public performances at Hamburg and Leipzic, she visited Cassel, where she played several times in private circles, and at one concert at the theatre under the direction of *Spohr*, on which occasion she not only earned the warmest approbation of a delighted auditory but a yet more gratifying reward in the commendatory words of her highly-esteemed uncle. The young musician subsequently achieved many a brilliant triumph in her further visits to the larger cities of Germany and Holland; but her promising artistic career was shortly brought to an unexpectedly early termination, first by deaths in her immediate family circle, and afterwards by her marriage with count *Xavier Sauerma*.

During the summer vacation, in order at length to pay his long-promised visit to Breslau, *Spohr* proceeded thither by way of Leipzic in the hope of hearing *Schumann's* new opera of "Genoveva;" but to his great regret, upon his arrival there, he was informed of the delays that had intervened to defer its performance, and was obliged to content himself with attending several rehearsals, but which, on account of the frequently interrupting repetitions, could naturally afford him but a very imperfect conception of the whole work. Although by no means an admirer of the compositions of *Schumann* so far known to him, in which he had frequently found a want of euphony and melodious breadth of harmonies, he formed a very favourable opinion of the opera, and it especially pleased him to observe that the same method of treatment which he had resorted to in the composition of the "Crusader" had been followed, in that *Schumann* did not permit the unnatural interruption of the action by a wearisome and constant repetition of words. It was no less interesting to *Spohr* to become acquainted with some of his larger pianoforte compositions, the desired opportunity for which was afforded him at the musical parties given to him, at which Mrs. *Clara Schumann* played a trio and pianoforte-concerto of her husband's with the most finished excellence, with which exception all the rest were compositions of *Spohr's*, among which the sextet he wrote during the March revolution: and at an extra-concert at the Gewandhaus his newest symphony, "The seasons," was performed to the great delight of all who heard it.

The remainder of his stay in Breslau, which was there expressively designated as a "fortnight-long *Spohr* festival," was a continuous round of entertainments, musical soirées, &c. The "Neue Oder-Zeitung" describes *Spohr's* advent as "an event, that had set all the educated classes of the town in commotion," and further adds: "Everybody crowds forward to see the German master — all are anxious to say that they have at least had the satisfaction of a personal meeting. There is a peculiar gratification in standing opposite to the man who, though his eye rests upon us with the coldness of the stranger, has been long known to us in spirit as one of our best and dearest friends — whose works have recalled to us the golden dreams of our youth, and whose noble creations purify our souls. All in Germany who love music and who play, recognise the master to whom as musicians they are indebted for a great part of their culture, for many elevating feelings, many hours of happiness. Is it then to be wondered at that every one crowds around the master — that all are ready to acquit part of that debt to him by loud and honourable acknowledgements?"

His festive reception, which commenced at the very railway station, was followed in the evening by a grand serenade and procession by torch-light, for which all the musical and choral societies of Breslau had met to execute the choicest pieces of music, chiefly selected from *Spohr's* operas, and which at intervals they gave singly, or executed in combination and *en masse*. At the grand concert that took place under his own direction at the spacious and handsome Aula, his own compositions alone were given: Overture to and air from *"Faust,"* the third symphony, with the "Lord's Prayer;" and the "Breslauer Zeitung" designates it as "a musical festival singular in its kind in the city of Breslau, for that *Spohr* at the present time was the *only* one who had so much distinguished himself in very kind of composition, that the church, the concert room, and the theatre, could equally boast of his works; and that such a performance by such united powers (singing academy, theatrical orchestra, society of musicians, &c.) had never yet taken place there." At the different banquets that were given to *Spohr*, his music in various ways formed part of the entertainment, and the songs that were written in his honour for the occasion had been adapted to appropriate melodies of his, which greatly increased their effect and frequently took the company by surprise.

At the express wish of the friends of music of Breslau, he determined to assist personally at a concert given in the smaller saloon of the Aula, before a great number of musical amateurs who had been invited; in his sextet and third double quartet, of which the "Breslauer Zeitung" speaks with much enthusiasm, and after dwelling upon the generally acknowledged specialities of his play, says further: "that the master at his *present age* still possesses all those specialities; that he plays with the fire and energy of a young man, and throws off the greatest difficulties with a power and boldness that are astonishing — that it is a thing quite *unusual* and was never seen there before."

On the part of the directors of the theatre the happy selection of *Spohr's* opera "Zemire und Azor" was made in his honour, which, with its charming melodies, never fails to make the most pleasing impression on the public on the first time of hearing; and with its music so truly appropriate to its subject, opens to us as it were the bright world of fairy land, which although more than ever fading away from the materialistic age in which we live, yet idealised by such sweet sounds, can never lose its fascination for the mind. This effect was produced on this occasion in Breslau also, as demonstrated by the brilliant reception with which it was welcomed, and the generally expressed wish for its speedy repetition under *Spohr's* direction, who then also experienced great pleasure in those two fine performances of his work. — He was no less gratified by the organ concert given him by his friend *Hesse* in the fine church of St. Bernard, in which he exhibited his great mastery of that grand instrument in every possible manner. Devoted admirer and adherent of *Spohr* as he was, he was still loathe to part from him, when after a fortnight passed in Breslau he departed with the purpose of making an excursion in the Riesengebirge with his wife. As a guide intimate with the localities *Hesse* accompanied them, and was not a little gratified in witnessing the feelings of delight with which *Spohr* was impressed by the natural beauties of his Silesian fatherland. Neither was music, loved music forgotten, for it was not only the subject of daily discourse, but in the Riesengebirge itself the powerful serenades of the music chorists of Warmbrunn and Hirschberg greeted their master, *Spohr*. — The return journey to Cassel was made *viâ* Berlin, where *Spohr* found an invitation from the conservatory, which, although but thinly composed in summer, performed nevertheless a part of his oratorio "Calvary" and his psalms with double chorus in a brilliant manner, by way of compensation both to themselves and him for his inability to comply with the invitation they had given him almost every winter to come and either personally direct or hear his oratorio.

Meanwhile the political state of Germany, and more particularly of Hesse greatly grieved *Spohr*, and as the best consolation he abandoned himself to his musical studies, the zest for which did not leave him even in this time of trouble and sorrow. In the course of the months of October and November he composed his seventh quintet for stringed instruments *(G minor,* Op. 144, published by *Peters)*, and three songs from "One thousand and one days in the East," by *Bodenstedt* (also published by *Peters)*.

It was in the summer of this year that *Spohr* experienced the malice and chicanery of the court. He had intended to start the first day of his vacation for a tour in Switzerland and upper Italy. He accordingly sent in his request to the Elector, which he considered a mere pro-formâ matter. To *Spohr's* great surprise the answer was in the negative — no leave of absence would be granted. Hereupon *Spohr* set off without leave. He passed through the *Via Mala*, over the Splügen to Milan and Venice, and returned over the St. Gotthard pass to Lucern, and so back to Cassel, where he arrived before the vacation had expired. After a short repose he availed himself of the remaining time to pay a long-promised visit to *Wehner* the director of the orchestra at Göttingen, who, conjointly with all the lovers of music at that place, used every exertion to do honour and afford gratification to their esteemed guest. A serenade given by the members of the choral society on the first evening of his arrival was followed on the next morning by a musical greeting performed by the band of the regiment lying at Nordheim in the immediate neighbourhood. At a grand concert given at the Aula *Spohr* directed in person his symphony "Die Weihe der Töne," which was followed by his potpourri on themes from Jessonda, performed by one of his most distinguished pupils, *Auguste Kömpel,* who when a boy had awakened the warmest interest on the part of *Spohr* by his remarkable talent, and after having studied under him for several years with the greatest success, was first appointed a member of the court orchestra at Cassel and subsequently Kammermusicus and member of the royal orchestra at Hanover.* As finale to the concert *Mendelssohn's* music to Athalia, combined with a melodramatic poem, was executed by the members of the Göttingen choral society; and thus *Spohr*, who had been present at its grand rehearsal with the greatest interest, had the much desired opportunity of becoming acquainted with the only one of the grander lyrical compositions of *Mendelssohn* which he had not yet heard. On the following day there was also some excellent music.

Wehner had made arrangements for quartet music at his own house, and previous to a large dinner party, which he gave as a mark of respect to *Spohr*, some exceedingly fine music was performed with the most finished excellence, and to the delight of all present *Spohr* himself took part in his own sextet. The dinner was seasoned by a succession of appropriate toasts and piquante speeches, the chief subjects of which were music and politics, and lastly also "*Spohr's* bold stroke" — the journey without leave — was drank amid the clang of classes and the enthusiastic cheers of the company, who highly approved of the spirit he had shown. But the "bold stroke" was, as may be imagined, considered with much less approbation in Cassel, and a few weeks after *Spohr's* return he was officially required by the general-intendant to explain and justify "his absence from Cassel without leave." His explanation was considered unsatisfactory, and he was condemned to pay a fine of 550 thaler (82 *l.* 10 *s.*). He went to law; but the end of it was that he paid the money, which was handed over to the pension fund instituted by him.

*   *   *

---

* To him, as a true representative of the *Spohr* school was the preference given over all the competitors who bid in emulation of each other and at very high prices for the highly coveted Stradivari violin of his honoured master; and which became his property one year after the decease of the latter.

It was in the midst of these troubles that he wrote a series of six *pieces de salon* for violin and piano and the 32nd. violin quartet (Op. 145 and 146; Leipzig, *Peters*).

In the beginning of the year 1852 *Spohr* received a visit from the director of the Italian opera in London, Mr. *Gye*, who proposed to him to direct there his opera of "Faust" during his summer vacation, and for that purpose to write a connecting recitative instead of the dialogue in the original, by which means alone the urgent wish of the Queen for the performance of the opera on the Italian stage could be gratified. As *Spohr* at first considered that such a change would be impossible in many of the scenes, he felt compelled to decline the proposal; but they were not so easily to be pacified in London by so unexpected an answer, and after receiving several further pressing letters upon the subject, *Spohr* set himself to work, and, contrary to his own expectation, with such satisfactory results, that after its completion he expressed himself upon the subject in a letter of the 21st. May to *Hauptmann* in the following words: "You have no doubt already heard that at the express wish of the Queen of England and of Prince Albert I have remodelled my opera "Faust" for the grand opera. This work has afforded me great pleasure, and agreeably engaged me for a period of three months, in which I have been as it were transported completely back to the happy days of my youth in Vienna. At first, with the assistance of my wife, I had to alter the dialogue scenes in such a manner as to adapt them to composition. In doing this I have endeavoured to impart more interest to them than they previously possessed, and to make elision of those things which from the first had displeased me at many performances I had seen of this opera. I think and hope that I have succeeded in both. I had then to replace myself as it were in the same mood, and style in which I wrote Faust, and I hope that I have succeeded in this also, and that no one will observe a difference of style between the old and the new. The opera consists now of three acts; the second concludes with the wedding scene, and the third begins with a new entr'acte, which depicts with reminiscences from the trio of the torch-dance and the witches' music the night of debauch passed by Faust, and then passes into a grand recitative by Mephistopheles, to which his air in *E major* is connected. After the disappearance of the witches a recitative by Faust follows, blended with intonations of former and later conception, and hereupon a shorter one between him and *Wagner*, which is succeeded by the concluding finale. My curiosity is now intense to hear the opera in its new form! Should nothing come of the journey to London, I hope to hear it soon at Weimar, as *Lisst* has asked for it in its new form for the court theatre there." — The new recitatives thus reached London so early, that weeks before *Spohr's* arrival there the study of the parts could be commenced; but at the first rehearsal he remarked that the in every other respect so greatly distinguished Italian singers, were not all he could have desired in their comprehension of this to them wholly foreign style of music, for which reason he immediately ordered daily thorough rehearsals under his own direction, in which he soon had the satisfaction of seeing that the whole of the singers entered more and more into the conception and spirit of his musical intentions, and submitted with the greatest willingness to his every nod, until every thing went so faultlessly that after the four last grand rehearsals which took place, and the lapse of three weeks, it was possible to give a perfect public performance.

To avoid all seeming reiteration of the numerous musical events and marks of respect, that in the interim were shewn to *Spohr* on this visit, it will suffice to mention one agreeable surprise only of which *Spohr* used to speak with delight in after years. This was the magnificent performance of his oratorio "Calvary" (des Heilands letzte Stunden) at Exeter Hall, under the excellent conducting of *Costa;* and which, performed by greater masses of assistants than at the memorable Norwich festival (700 singers and musicians), completely overpowered *Spohr* himself, as well as the enthusiastically delighted public; in so much, that he was obliged to agree in the remark of his friends, that the effect in many parts, especially that of the powerfully imposing choruses, was more immense than the composer himself had even conceived.

On Sundays, on which days, according to English custom, the theatres are closed, there are no concerts, and even all private music is hushed, *Spohr* gladly availed himself of the invitations he received to make excursions far away from the gigantic town, to recruit his energies somewhat in the fresh air, from the daily musical fatigue and excitement. Sometimes it was to Clapham and Kensington, on a visit to the *Sillem* and *Horsley* families; sometimes farther by railway to Sir *George Smart's* pleasant country-house at Chertsey, which *Spohr* always called "the little paradise;" or to Professor *Owen's* in Richmond-park; from which he always returned requickened in mind and body to the wear and tear of London life. *Owen's* charming residence and his amiable manners were always subjects of agreeable recollection to *Spohr*, and he would often relate how the celebrated naturalist, in his kindly unassuming manner, would come out to welcome him on a hot summer's day, clad in a light summer jacket and a broad-brimmed straw hat, but in honour of "his welcome renowned guest," decorated with the Prussian order "pour le mérite," and then till late in the evening devise every possible means of affording him pleasure and entertainment.

Meanwhile the rehearsals of Faust had prospered so well, that on the 15th. July the first public performance took place under *Spohr's* direction, and a letter written home refers to it in the following manner:

"The opera went off incomparably well, and made a wonderfully powerful effect upon everybody. Indeed to us also it appeared in quite a new light — everything was so grand, so splendid! The new additional themes blend charmingly with the whole, and present singularly fine effects. Decorations, scenery, all are new, exceedingly brilliant and got up at great expense: orchestra, singers, and chorus, did their best, so that the Londoners say, that they have not seen so splendid an operatic performance for many years; and it was received throughout also with the most enthusiastic applause. That the foreign (almost all Italian) singers would have sung this German music with so much zest and pleasure, we could scarcely have believed possible. Those who most distinguished themselves were Mrs. *Castellan* (Kunigunda), *Ronconi* (Faust), *Formes* (Mephistopheles), and *Tamberlik* (Hugo). The latter charmed every body, for he has a splendid tenor voice with immense power, and he executed the beautiful air, accompanied by a magnificent chorus of forty male voices, with such fire and irresistible power that a *da capo* was called for by general acclamation. And *Formes* also, in his song in *A major*, which had greatly gained by the newly composed exceedingly beautiful introduction and recitative scene. . . . . The whole house was in ecstacy, and in the intervals between the acts, and at the end, *Spohr* was warmly congratulated by a host of friends and admirers." With similar success and with yet more perfect execution, the second and third performance of Faust, under *Spohr's* direction, took place within a few days; after which he once more left England, accompanied to the place of embarcation by numerous lovers of music, who up to the last moment projected the most inviting plans for the next summer.

Agreeably impressed with the successful issue of his journey, he returned to Germany, picturing to himself the happy hours in which, as was his custom, he should again relate amid the expectant circle at home the interesting incidents of his visit. But this time the pleasure of once more meeting the members of his family was but too soon overshadowed, and *Spohr* beheld with much alarm the suffering constitution of his father-in-law, whose declining bodily strength had for some time past excited the utmost anxiety; but which assumed appearances so threatening during the last few weeks, that the anxious members of his family, despite their tender care and hopefulness, could no longer deceive themselves as to the near approach of his dissolution. With sorrowing hearts they beheld with every day the nearer approach of the long-dreaded moment; till on the 4th. October 1852, the loved and honoured parent breathed his last. This sad event cast an enduring shadow over *Spohr's* life, for with his wife he not only lamented the loss of the beloved father, but mourned thenceforth that of the truthful friend whose feelings and sentiments had been so congenial with his own.

* * *

In the autumn of 1852 the duties of *Spohr's* office were unexpectedly much alleviated by the nomination of a second director; an appointment which indeed, with his great activity and as yet unimpaired powers, he had never contemplated as a thing to be desired; but which was nevertheless the more agreeable to him from the circumstance that the newly-created appointment was given to his favorite pupil, concert-master *Jean Bott*, in order to secure his rejection of the post of musical director at Hanover, which had been offered to him under very favourable circumstances. By this means the Cassel court orchestra was saved the loss of so distinguished a member, and his services were fully secured. *Spohr* consented also very willingly to the requisitions of the managers of the theatre to abandon to the direction of the new co-director the operas proposed, and suggested but few modifications in this arrangement. By this means *Bott* assumed the direction of a number of light operas, chiefly French and Italian, but undertook as heretofore to lead as first violin in the orchestra under *Spohr's* direction in all grand German operas, which were reserved to the latter. The repertory of the new and zealous co-director soon received an interesting addition, for in the beginning of the year 1853 *Shakspeare's* "Midsummernight's Dream," with *Mendelssohn's* music, was performed on the Cassel stage for the first time; on which occasion *Spohr* expressed himself in the following words in a letter to *Hauptmann:* "The most charming music that I know of *Mendelssohn* is indeed his music to the "Midsummernight's Dream," which has at length been performed here also, and right well. *Bott* practised the orchestra in the music most assiduously, and for me it was a great enjoyment to be enabled for once to listen as auditor to the performance of good music." In regard to *Spohr's* own labours the same letter then speaks further: "We are now studying 'Tannhäuser,' (which the Elector has at length permitted), and we shall give that opera for the first time on Whitmonday. It will be put on the stage with the greatest care and both decorations and costumes will be rich. There is much that is new and beautiful in the opera, but much also that is most distressing to the ear. For the violins and basses it is more difficult than anything I ever yet met with," &c.

After the first performances of this difficult work had passed off in the most successful manner, *Spohr* wrote again respecting it to his friend *Hauptmann:* "'Tannhäuser' was performed last night for the third time, and again to a full house. The opera has gained many admirers, by reason of its earnestness and its subject-matter, and when I compare it with others produced of late years, I am also of their way of thinking. With much of what was at first very disagreeable to me I have become familiarised from frequent hearing; but the want of rhythm, and the frequent absence of rounded periods is still to me very objectionable. The manner in which it is performed here is really very fine, and in few places in Germany can be heard with such precision. In the enormously difficult 'ensembles' of the singers in the second act, not one single note was omitted last night. But with all that, in several parts these assume a shape which make a downright horrifying music, particularly just before the part previous to where Elizabeth throws herself upon the singers who rush upon Tannhäuser. — What faces would *Haydn* and *Mozart* make, were they obliged to hear the stunning noise that is now given to us for music! — The choruses of pilgrims (but which are here supported by clarinets and bassoons *p*.) were intonated so purely last night, that I became somewhat reconciled for the first time to their unnatural modulations. It is astonishing what the human ear will by degrees become accustomed to!" &c.

Although, as may be inferred from the above remarks, *Spohr*, with his preminent sentiment for harmony and beautiful, regular forms in music, could not readily reconcile himself to the tonic creations of more modern times, which so frequently deviate from them, he nevertheless took a lively interest in them, and was so anxious to become acquainted with *Wagner's* newest opera "Lohengrin," that while awaiting the as yet witheld permission of the Elector for a full theatrical performance, he determined upon giving some scenes from it at the ensuing winter concerts, and wrote to *Hauptmann* on the subject as follows: "If you wish to afford us a pleasure by sending something for our winter concerts, let me ask of you the music to 'Lohengrin.' I was in correspondence with *Wagner* this summer, and he knows that I am exerting myself to put that opera upon the stage here, also. He will therefore have no objection to a performance of some scenes beforehand. I shall write to inform him of it also upon a fitting occasion, but I do not like to renew the correspondence on the subject, without being empowered to ask at the same time for the score for our theatre, which will not be before next summer, for the birthday of the Elector." This expectation was nevertheless not realised, for the Elector's permission was neither granted for the day appointed, nor upon a subsequent reiterated solicitation; and in this manner *Spohr* was never enabled to hear this opera, which both in Cassel and other places he had repeatedly striven to do.

With the approach of the vacation of the summer 1853 *Spohr* made preparation once more (for the sixth and last time) for the journey to England, whence in the month of January he had received, (and as chance would have it upon the same day) two letters of invitation from two wholly different parties. One, from the theatre-director *Gye*, contained a recapitulation of the plan formed in the previous summer, of bringing out an Italian translation of *Spohr's* "Jessonda" during the approaching season; the other, from Dr. *Wylde*, the director of the recently instituted New Philharmonic Society, contained a pressing invitation to *Spohr*, to undertake the direction of the grand concerts which the society contemplated giving during the summer months. The latter attractive invitation was the one that decided his yet wavering resolution, since it was of the greatest interest to him to procure a hearing for his grander orchestral compositions, which would there be performed with all that power which was already known to him, before a public who, like all the performers, understood so thoroughly the spirit of his music.

Scarcely had he arrived in London than an agreeable musical surprise awaited him, for on his first visit to Dr. *Wylde* he was pressed by him to proceed immediately to a morning concert then about to take place, and arrived there just in time to hear an excellent performance of his nonett, and at the conclusion was warmly greeted by the audience, to whom the announcement of the presence of the composer was both an agreeable and sudden surprise. Under similar circumstances he was present the next evening at the last Philharmonic concert in the Hanover Square Rooms, where he was greatly gratified by the very successful performance of his historical symphony, which was enthusiastically applauded. A few days afterwards the first of the concerts of the New Philharmonic Society took place under his personal direction, of which mention is made as follows in a letter written home: "Last evening *Spohr* consummated the first of his great achievements; the direction of the fine New Philharmonic concerts in Exeter-Hall, where he was again received with the same enthusiasm as formerly, and which was manifested throughout the whole performance. We found our exalted expectations of this gigantic orchestra, wholly composed of musicians of high standing, fully realised, and the impression made by the immense mass in the spacious and densely crowded hall was truly grand and imposing. Even the ninth symphony of *Beethoven*, abnormal as are many things therein, and especially the last subject, with the 'song to pleasure,' executed in the finished manner it was, afforded a real enjoyment. *Spohr's* 'Overture in the severe style' opened the concert, and had a grand effect; as also that of 'Jessonda,' which was even encored. This was followed by the tenor song in 'Jessonda,' splendidly sung by *Th. Formes*, and received with tumultuous applause," &c.

Not less interesting also was the programme of the last concert directed by *Spohr;* it comprised besides his own compositions — a quartet concerto, a double symphony, and the overture to the "Mountain Sprite," — the *D major* symphony of *Beethoven*, the overture to "Fidelio," the duet for two pianofortes of *Mendelssohn* and *Moscheles* (executed by Miss *Claus* and Miss *Goddard*), and some other pieces. The performance of the whole of the pieces of music was all that could be desired, and in regard to the fine effect of *Spohr's* symphony, a letter specially remarks: "The double symphony seemed as though it had been written expressly for such orchestral powers and for this place. The lesser orchestra was, in accordance with several trials made at the rehearsal, placed high up above, and apart; and sometimes between the powerful and imposing masses of tone of the larger orchestra it sounded really like music from another sphere."

The chief object of *Spohr's* journey to London was thus once more fully achieved: but on the other hand the projected performance of "Jessonda" during the same time, met with numerous unexpected obstacles. In order to allow *Spohr* the number of rehearsals he considered necessary for the study of the work, another opera, also a newly studied one, "Benvenuto Cellini," by *Berlioz*, was selected for performance during the intervening opera nights; and as is the custom, was to be repeated several times without further rehearsal. But upon the very first night of its performance, it met with a very unfavourable reception from the public, and *Spohr* himself, interested as he felt to hear this much-talked-of music, respecting which opinions were so conflicting, was not much edified thereby, as appears from a letter written to his friend Mr. *Lüder*: "In the opera of *Berlioz*, which I heard in London this summer, there are some fine things, but scarcely has one begun to feel interested in it, than there comes a something so bizarre and harsh, that all the pleasure one has felt is destroyed. I have a special hatred of this eternal speculating upon extraordinary instrumental effects, for his opera contains without doubt many really happy conceptions both melodic and dramatic, and these are always marred by them. This it was also that displeased the London public, which was at first very favourable disposed towards him, and received him upon his entering the orchestra with loud applause; but as the opera proceeded their dissatisfaction increased, until at length, upon its conclusion, the audience broke out into one general storm of hisses and whistling; a circumstance never known to have occured before at the Italian opera in London in presence of the Queen! — It is with *Berlioz* as with all the other coryphées of the music of the future; they do not abandon themselves to their natural feelings in their work, but speculate on things which have never yet been. That is the reason why these gifted musicians seldom write anything that is enjoyable, particularly for people who in the last century grew up in the knowledge of *Haydn, Mozart* and *Beethoven*," &c. With so explicit an opinion as that pronounced by the London public, the theatrical direction did not dare risk a second performance of the opera, and other operas were obliged to be substituted, which required also several rehearsals, and "Jessonda," which was as yet only in the first stage of study, was still farther postponed. This, nevertheless, was no great source of uneasiness to *Spohr*, and the time thus gained was agreeably occupied by him in other musical enjoyments.

On this visit indeed *Spohr* and his wife found a home replete with every domestic comfort in the house of Dr. *A. Farre,* who emulated with his kind lady in his attentions towards them, and kindly devoted every hour that his professional engagements permitted to the entertainment of his guests; in this manner a warm friendship was soon established between the two families, and the weeks passed under his roof were ever recalled by *Spohr* as among the most pleasing of his recollections. As Dr. *Farre* and several of his medical colleague were very musical and good singers, they had formed themselves, in conjunction with some other families devoted to the art, into a musical circle, in which music of a high class was zealously cultivated, and that of *Spohr* was more especially the favorite. In a soirée of this kind he had one evening the agreeable surprise to hear his oratorio "Die letzten Dinge" performed by eight and twenty dilettanti with faultless precision, a production which, in rare contrast with the habitual English taste for massive instrumentation, appealed to the feelings in the most pleasing manner by the *perfect purity* and intensity of its expression. At a brilliant musical soirée given by Dr. *Farre* himself, in compliment to his guests, a succession of pieces selected from *Spohr's* different operas was also given in the most efficient manner, and was subject of no small surprise and gratification both to him and the assembled company.

Meanwhile, the rehearsals of "Jessonda" had slowly proceeded, it is true, but there had arisen so many causes for a delay in its production, that before this could take place, the period of his vacation expired, and *Spohr* was obliged to leave London for Germany; but in doing so he had the satisfaction of leaving his opera in charge of a worthy representative, Mr. *Costa*, under whose direction, a fortnight afterwards, it was performed several times with the most brilliant success.

Upon his landing at Calais *Spohr* was warmly received by the amateurs of music of that town, who had become apprised of the day of his arrival, and he was invited by them to a grand entertainment given in his honour. Its chief feature was a luxurious banquet, but of which also an agreeable musical surprise formed a part; for at the conclusion of the dinner the pleasing notes of *Spohr's C minor* quartet were heard in the adjoining apartment, which was followed by the execution of several other pieces, and continued up to the departure of the delighted guests at a late hour. This day, so unexpectedly passed in Calais in the midst of musical and festive enjoyments, was a subject of special gratification to *Spohr*, as he had least of all expected, here, upon the soil of France, to have met with such proofs of esteem and so much admiration for his music.

On the return journey he was much occupied with an idea which he had conceived in England of a new grand composition for the pianoforte with instrumental accompaniment, and which upon his arrival home he forthwith began with zest and spirit. Thus was produced — in the seventieth year of *Spohr's* age — one of his finest masterpieces, the septet for pianoforte, two stringed and four wind instruments, replete with the freshness of youthful thought in every part, with a *larghetto* which has scarcely its equal in bewitching harmony and beauty of modulations. While yet in manuscript it was publicly performed at the next subscription concert, on which occasion both the composition and the excellence of the execution met with the most favourable reception and acknowledgement. The pianoforte part, which was as grateful as it was difficult, was taken by *J. Bott*, and the audience testified yet more warmly their just appreciation of his execution from his having displayed also on the same evening his brilliant talent as violin player in *Spohr's* 15th. violin concerto. By the desire of the lovers of music of Cassel, a repetition of the new septet was given at the next concert; after which, while yet in manuscript, it was performed at one of the quartet soirées in Leipzic, and the fullest justice done to the pianoforte part by the truly artistic execution of *Moscheles*, and received there by the public with the most gratifying applause.

For the next summer vacation (1854) *Spohr* had contemplated another journey to Switzerland; and so great this time was his desire to pass once more the most pleasant summer month in the undisturbed enjoyment of the beauties of nature, that the numerous invitations he had received to the musical festivals in England and Holland were powerless to induce him to relinquish his long previously projected plan. As he was on the eve of departing, he received by telegraph a farther pressing entreaty from his grand-daughter *Antonia Wolff* at Ratisbonne, who had there married a collegiate professor, a Mr. *Schmitz,* and who besought him to go by way of the old imperial city, where a visit from him had long been anxiously desired by all lovers of music, and to pass a few days with his grand-children and great-grand-children. Attractive as was this invitation, *Spohr* with regret felt compelled to decline it, his holidays being so strictly limited; and no railroad existing at that time to Ratisbonne, it would have led him too far out of his projected route. — After a short sojourn at Marburg, Heidelberg, and Baden-Baden — so famed for the beauty of their respective environs — he proceeded to the south of Switzerland, and especially enjoyed the voyage by steamboat upon the magnificent lakes. After a few days' stay at Lausanne, Geneva, and Vevay, further excursions were then made into the more easily accessible neighbourhood, where all around smiled in summer's rich attire, while beyond the lake rose in majestic contrast the lofty chain of the Alps, with its snow-capped summits.

Leaving the lake of Geneva the travellers continued their journey to Freiburg and Bern, at both which places quite unexpectedly calls were made upon the interest they took in music. At Freiburg, as soon as they had alighted at the hotel, *Spohr* was invited to join the other strangers present in a subscription towards the honorarium which it was there customary to tender to the organist of the church of St. Nicholas, for the performance of a piece of music upon its so much celebrated organ. At the appointed hour, just as the shades of evening closed around, the small party assembled, and solemnly pealed the tones of the mighty organ through the spacious and empty aisles of the stately church, producing their wonted powerful effect upon *Spohr*. The organist, either not aware of the high musical authority before whom he was playing, or thinking to impose on him like the other strangers present by the exhibition of his wonderful artistic skill, struck up suddenly in the most inappropriate manner sundry things from modern operas, and then concluded with such a thundering peal on the instrument that the first exalted impression was wholly obliterated and *Spohr* could not forbear the undisguised expression of his disapproval of such a profanation of the grand fabric of sounds, which, with its inscription: "*In majorem gloriam dei,*" seemed rather to him in a more exalted degree worthy alone to intonate the praises of God.

Scarcely arrived in Bern, *Spohr* was surprised to see notices stuck up at the corners of the streets announcing two concerts of sacred music in which his oratorio "Die letzten Dinge" formed the chief feature of each, though preceded on the first evening by a cantata by *Sebastian Bach*, and on the second by four of *Marcello's* Psalms. The first concert had already taken place the evening before, but as a great number of hearers as well as performers had come in from the neighbouring towns to the second concert, Mr. *Edele,* the director of the "Society of Ancient Classical Music" at Bern, had made arrangements to give a repetition of the oratorio on the next evening, so that at this second performance of it *Spohr* was enabled to hear it executed with the greater precision. As the news of *Spohr's* presence soon spread through the church, the opportunity was seized of giving the composer of the work which had just been performed with such devout inspiration, a public mark of the great esteem in which he was held in Bern; and in the later part of the evening he was suddenly greeted by a quickly improvised serenade, and addressed in several animated speeches. On the following morning *Spohr* left Bern, and after spending several pleasant days with his female fellow-travellers in the Bernese Oberland and on the shores of the Vierwaldstädter Lake, he continued his journey across the Lake of Constance to Bavaria and its capital,

Munich, where the much-talked-of grand exhibition of industry had just been opened. Though the one week spent there may have been found scarcely sufficient to see all the treasure of art and manufacture which had been collected partly for permanent and partly for a short exhibition only, the travellers do not appear to have thought a longer stay desirable, for they soon experienced also the prejudicial influence of the bodily and mental over-exertion, which, combined with the still more injurious climatic influences which during that disastrous summer carried off so many of the visitors to that then over-crowded city. Under such circumstances nothing could be more desirable than a visit to Alexandersbad, where Dr. *Theodor Pfeiffer*, a near relative, and proprietor of the cold-water-cure establishment, had long kindly invited them. A short stay in that place, with its healthful mountain air, sufficed to restore their depressed animal spirits, and *Spohr* gladly joined in all the social parties in their excursions to the romantic environs, and shared in all the cheerful parties of the company at the baths, which in kindly social spirit lived as one family. All this, together with the whole arrangements and rules of life, which were simple and in accordance with nature, were so much to *Spohr's* taste, that from that time he always considered Alexandersbad as the beau-ideal of an invigorating summer residence, and after another visit there he firmly maintained that opinion for the rest of his life.

Spohr commenced the following year (1855) with the composition of six four-voice part-songs for soprano, alto, tenor and bass, which were soon after excellently sung at a private concert of the St. Cecilia society with double vocal support, under his own conducting, and aided by his own powerful bass. They made an unusual sensation among the lovers of music present, above all one entitled "Man's Consolation" (the words by *von Müller von der Werra*), which went home to all hearts.

In the spring of the same year, *Spohr* obeyed an invitation from the king of Hanover to direct his double symphony, and several other of his compositions, at a grand concert. Upon his arrival at the railway terminus he was met by music-director *Wehner*, at the head of a numerous body of musicians and friends of the art, and in the evening at the hotel he was saluted with two serenades, by the military band, and the members of the choral society. On the subject of the pleasant days he passed in Hanover upon that occasion both in a musical and festive point of view, *Spohr* wrote to his friend *Hauptmann*: "I enjoyed myself much on my little excursion to Hanover. I played a quartet at the King's, and it seemed to me that his musical culture went so far as to like that kind of music. At a morning concert got up by the chapel royal to let me hear two of my compositions which they had very carefully practised, I played also my quartet *(E minor)*. The compositions adverted to were the 7th. violin concerto, executed in a very masterly manner by *Joachim*; and the first double quartet, of which *Kömpel* played the first violin in the first, and *Joachim* in that of the second quartet. This also, was played in the most finished manner. On the second day the chapel royal gave a first rehearsal of my symphony, "The Terrestial and Divine in human Life," which was followed by a grand dinner, which lasted five hours, and during which the speeches, songs and toasts were numerous and varied. Although much exhausted I was obliged to go to a musical party in the evening given by my old friend *Hausmann*, where I played two of my quartets, and as on the previous evening, did not get to bed till two o'clock. On the third day there was a grand rehearsal in the forenoon, and in the evening the concert for the benefit of the poor, for which the King had sent me the invitation to come to Hanover. I conducted the first half, consisting of the overture and duett from 'Jessonda' and my symphony. All these, executed in a masterly manner, particularly the double symphony, which I never heard better played, not even in London. The small orchestra led by *Joachim* was composed of the élite of the chapel royal and was very conveniently placed on the stage, so that it was advantageously separated from the large one. The latter was composed of twenty violins, six viols, five violincellos and five counter-basses. It contrasted well therefore by its imposing power, in the sonorous and not too spacious theatre, with the solo orchestra upon the stage. The effect was very satisfactory. But in fact the orchestra is a very superior one, particularly in the stringed instruments. The harmony comprises certainly several distinguished virtuosi, but in ensemble, it is neither so even in tone, nor so pure in intonation as ours. The second part of the concert was conducted by *Fischer;* it consisted of the overture to "Euryanthe," *Beethoven's* violin concerto (with new, superfluously long, very difficult and ungrateful, cadences by *Joachim*), and some 'numbers' of 'Lohengrin.' The concert was crowded and must have brought in a round sum to the poor-box. — On the morning before I left a deputation from the chapel royal presented me with a leader's bâton more rich and tasteful in design than anything of the kind I ever saw. As I afterwards learned, it was made by order of the king, to be presented to me by the chapel royal. It consists of a beautifully grooved ivory staff with a golden handle richly set with coloured stones, with a similar gold ornamentation at the top, ending in a knob set likewise with small stones. The whole thing is extremely tasteful, and has upon the handle in raised letters: 'The Royal Hanoverian Chapel to Music-director-general Dr. *Spohr*, March 31st. 1855.' The Elector, who sent for the work of art to inspect it, expressed himself, as I am told, upon returning it, with very unreserved dissatisfaction that the inscription did not express 'Director-general of Music to the Elector,' and said, "who will know hereafter whose director general of music he was!"* &c.

---

* The leader's bâton here described with such evident satisfaction, formed a worthy companion to a scarcely less costly and tasteful one that *Spohr* had been presented with by his faithful pupil *F. Böhme* of Holland. He was always very proud of such appropriate and artistically executed presents, and it was always his custom to take them out of their respective cases with his own hands, and to replace them after use with equal care.

The first impression experienced by *Spohr* on his return from Hanover, was also an agreeable one, for he found at home a telegraphic message that had arrived during his absence, to the following effect: "Inspruck, March 27th. 1855, 10 m. p. 10 at night. One hundred and fifty dilettanti of Inspruck, who have just performed the music of "Jessonda" with rapturous applause, send to the master their heartfelt greetings." The letters which subsequently arrived from Inspruck informed him in a more detailed manner, "that the opera had been three times performed there in the national theatre to crowded houses, for the benefit of the fund for the relief of the poor, and in a manner surpassing all expectation, by musical and vocal dilettanti;" and expressed at the same time "the hope that the friends of music in that place would have the gratification of greeting the honoured and veteran composer in their own mountains in the course of the year, and hear again that classic opera under his own personal direction."

That hope however was not realised, for the journey contemplated this year was in the opposite direction, towards the north; first to Hamburg, where *Spohr* had not been since the great fire in 1842, and was therefore greatly interested to see the magnificent manner in which it had been rebuilt. Fully satisfied in that expectation, he had at the same time the pleasure of seeing again several much-loved friends (among whom the family of the *Grunds*), and to hear many successful musical performances, both in private and public circles. — Being so near to the sister town Lubeck, to which his wife was still fondly attached, and for whose kind-hearted inhabitants he himself, since his visit in the year 1840, had a predilection, it was natural that both should much desire to make a trip thither, upon the railway which had since then been opened to connect the two towns. Although it is true that during the fifteen years which had elapsed, many former friends had gone to their last rest, yet the venerable old instructor was still living, and met his former lady pupil and her renowned husband with the same warmth of heart.

Verging upon eighty years of age, he had recently retired from professional life, but the institution he had so long successfully directed flourished still, conducted in the same spirit by his worthy son Dr. *Adam Meier;* and *Spohr* and his wife, deeply moved by his touching kindness, took up their abode beneath the hospitable roof that was so endeared to them by past recollections. — As the interests of music were also well represented by Kapellmeister *Hermann,* a former pupil and a warm partizan of *Spohr*, the days passed agreeably in social intercourse with old friends and new acquaintances.

In the course of the year 1855 *Spohr* wrote his 33rd. violin quartet (Op. 152, published by *Siegel* of Leipzic) and three grand duets for two violins (Op. 148, 150 and 153, published by *Peters* of Leipzic) which last he dedicated to the brothers *Alfred* and *Henry Holmes* of London. Neither could he have commended his work to better hands to ensure a performance and publicity worthy of them, for although those young artists never had the advantage of his personal instruction, yet by dint of a diligent study of his ,,Violin School," they had become so penetrated with the spirit of his composition and his style of play, that *Spohr* during his last stay in England had been exceedingly gratified to hear his older violin duets executed by the two talented youths in a really masterly manner; and when a few years afterwards, upon an artistic tour on the continent, they visited Cassel, they caused, as *Spohr* himself remarks in a letter: "everywhere the greatest sensation by their splendid play, and especially excited admiration by the highly finished and surprising performance of his duets and concertantes."

In the spring of 1856 *Spohr* received a letter from a former pupil, the director of music *Kiel*, of Detmold; where upon, at the desire of his Prince, he proposed to *Spohr* the composition of some songs for a baritone voice, with pianoforte and violin accompaniment. Although doubtful at first that such a combination would be suited to a deep male voice, he nevertheless interested himself in the trial, and in a short time he wrote a collection of six songs of the required kind, with which he himself felt highly satisfied. He then gave a hearing of them in manuscript to his musical friends in his own house, in which he himself took the violin part, which had proved of a somewhat difficult nature, and gave the voice part to *Heinrich Osthoff*, an ex-concert-singer, who for some years past had been settled in Cassel as a teacher of music, and who from his particularly excellent and expressive execution of all *Spohr's* song pieces, sacred and otherwise, was a welcome guest in all musical circles. In Detmold also, the new songs dedicated to the Prince were very favorably received, and the Prince, as his director of music informed *Spohr*, sang them every day with increased satisfaction. When *Spohr* shortly afterwards forwarded the first printed presentation copy (published by *Luckhardt* of Cassel, Op. 154) to the musical prince, the latter in an autograph letter of thanks thus expressed himself: "that the great pleasure the fine songs already gave him would be yet increased when he should have the opportunity of singing them with *Spohr's* own accompaniment." The obliging letter was at the same time accompanied by a valuable souvenir, in the shape of a shirt-pin with the appropriately selected emblems of an oak-leaf in green gold, with an acorn of pearl set in gold, presented to *Spohr* as an honourable acknowledgement "of his true *German* worth as musician and as man."

The first weeks of the summer vacation were passed by *Spohr* in a very pleasant and recreative journey to Dresden, Saxon Switzerland and Prague; after which, having reposed a short time in his own beautiful flower-garden, he undertook a journey into the Harz, at the solicitation of an enthusiastic musical friend, the jurisconsult *Haushalter* of Wernigerode.

The increased leisure time gained by *Spohr* in consequence of the appointment of his new colleague he now devoted to composition, for which, despite his advanced age, the impulse and love had not yet diminished. Though his musical ideas may no longer have flowed so copiously, and assumed as readily the form he wished, as in former years, and though he himself at times expressed doubts as to whether his later works would take equal rank with his earlier compositions, yet he frequently received an enthusiastic recognition of the merit of his newest compositions from quite unexpected quarters, which always gave him fresh courage to continue his musical creations.

Spohr now determined to write another quartet (his 34th.), upon terminating which he immediately opened the winter series of his still continued quartet circle with it. Although this new composition was considered extremely fresh and charming by both co-operators and auditory, yet he himself was so little satisfied with it, that after repeated alteration, which were rejected as soon as made, he laid aside the whole quartet as a failure; nor did he write another until a whole twelvemonth had elapsed: this differed in every respect from the former, and he substituted it for it under the same number. Upon its first performance at the quartet meeting this piece of music pleased him right well; but shortly afterwards it seemed to him to require many improvements, and as these did not turn out to his satisfaction, sorrowfully, but resigned to the consciousness that he could no longer carry out in a satisfactory manner the ideas which floated before his fancy, he associated the new 34th. quartet with that which he had previously rejected, and expressed the wish to his wife that neither should at any time be made public.

He came to a similar decision in respect to a symphony which he had composed shortly before, which was performed once only in the presence of a few only of his most intimate musical friends, at a rehearsal by the court orchestra of Cassel. Notwithstanding the numerous beauties and novelties in thought which it contains, to him nevertheless it did not appear worthy of being placed in the fine catalogue of his earlier written symphonies, and in this manner by himself was this — his tenth — symphony condemned, not to destruction it is true, but to eternal concealment.

In the summer of 1857 *Spohr* availed himself of the vacation to go to Holland, his former visit there being still borne by him in pleasing recollection, he had therefore long been desirous of proceeding thither with his wife to shew her that country, as yet unvisited by her, and remarkable for so many peculiarities. Little as he had calculated upon any musical enjoyments there at such a season of the year, his pleasure was great to hear on the very first evening at *Verhulst's*, in Rotterdam, in a numerous circle of musicians and lovers of music, several quartets both of his own and of *Verhulst's* composition, upon which occasion the violinist *Tours*, whose acquaintance he had formerly made, proved himself a great virtuoso, as first violin. The director of music *Böhm*, of Dortrecht, who had shown from his youth a strong attachment to the honoured master, exhibited it anew by the unwearying attention with which he strove to alleviate all the cares and difficulties of travel in a foreign country, and took them wholly upon himself. Willingly following the arrangements of the excellent "travelling marshall," as *Spohr* was wont playfully to call him, the travellers were now enabled to see the many remarkable objects in the chief cities of Holland in a comparatively much shorter time, after which a further journey was undertaken from Amsterdam to that part of North Holland lying beyond the Y. The singular topographical feature of the whole country, the meadows intersected by innumerable canals and lakes, meadows covered with grazing cattle, the hundreds of gaily painted windmills, the cheerful blue sky, and the easy travelling upon the smoothly paved highroads, more like the parquetted floors of an apartment — in short, the whole delightful journey, with its interesting final objects, the celebrated places Saardam and Broek, presented a succession of charming pictures that surpassed all expectation and put *Spohr* in particular in the most cheerful possible mood.

Their kind "marshall" *Böhm* accompanied the travellers on their return as far back as Utrecht, but placed them there in good hands, under the hospitable roof of one of *Spohr's* grateful pupils, the director of music *Kufferath*, with whom they passed some exceedingly pleasant days. As the country round Utrecht abounds with handsome country-seats and parks, these furnished occasion for frequent delightful walks with the family of their host; and the musical entertainments given to *Spohr* — a quickly arranged organ-concert got up by *Nieuwenhuisen*, the organist of the cathedral, and a grand serenade by torch-light in the evening — made the memory of those days worthy of being associated with the pleasing reminiscences of his former visit.

On the return-journey *Spohr* stopped a day at Cologne, where *Hiller*, the director of music, quickly improvised a brilliant dinner-party in his honour, and afterwards gratified him with the performance of some highly interesting musical pieces in his own house. *Hiller* himself played with great spirit a recently composed sonata for the pianoforte of extreme difficulty of execution, some numbers of the comic opera composed by him called: "Jest, cunning and revenge," which was received with universal satisfaction, and by *Spohr* in particular with lively applause. This was succeeded later in the evening by a musical surprise; the celebrated Cologne choral society, wholly composed of male voices, had assembled in all silence in the hotel, and at the door of their honoured guest sang their finest songs in the most masterly manner, which, together with a spirited address, spoken by professor *Bischof*, afforded him very great pleasure.

Gratified in every respect with his journey, *Spohr* returned to Cassel, where, reinvigorated and refreshed, he devoted himself with his usual zeal and interest to the materially lightened labours of his office, shared now with his young and active colleague.

Meanwhile, at that time was heard here and there the report that it was contemplated to pension him off; but when he was apprised of this by a friend, and it was put to him whether he would not rather anticipate such an intention by proposing himself to retire upon his pension, he replied with decision, that: his duty and inclination impelled him alike to remain in the performance of his official engagements so long as he could fulfil them satisfactorily. Thus things remained on the old footing, until on the 14th. November, both contrary to his wish and expectation, he received the following rescript from the Elector:

"In pursuance of our most gracious will and pleasure, we have granted to the director-general of music and court Kapellmeister at our court-theatre, Dr. *Louis Spohr*, by reason of his advanced years, permission to retire into private life, and have been further pleased to grant him a yearly pension of 1500 Thalers from our court treasury from the date of the month next ensuing. The department of our lord high marshall of the palace will make the further dispositions to that effect. Cassel, November 12, 1857. *Friedrich Wilhelm.*"

Painfully affected as *Spohr* was upon the receipt of this, he with his usual good sense soon overcame the shock of the first impression and contemplated the matter on its brighter side; in which sense he then gave expression to his sentiments in his letters to distant friends, and among others, in replying shortly afterwards to the director of music *Bott* respecting other affairs, he wrote as follows; "You do not appear to have yet learned that the Elector, without my solicitation, has placed me in retirement, and although the terms of my engagement specified that my salary should be paid so long as I lived, he has pensioned me off on 1500 Thalers per annum. It has nevertheless appeared in all the newspapers, together with the account of the festive form in which I directed for the last time the opera of Jessonda at the theatre. At first it gave me very great pain, for I felt still perfectly competent to conduct the few operas which latterly fell to my share. But I soon learned to estimate my present freedom at its real value, and now feel very glad that whenever I choose I can get away by rail whithersoever my fancy takes me! I have submitted also to the deduction from my salary, having been informed that I should not be able to compel the payment of the full salary without a new law-suit, and because it was repulsive to my feelings to take the whole amount without performing any service for it, and I can live very well with three-fourths of it by means of my savings!"

Thus terminated *Spohr's* personal co-operation at opera and concert. But that he still cherished as warm an interest in the latter his letters to distant friends attest, and in this spirit he wrote on December 22nd. to Mr. *Lüder*: "Since we were at your house, we have had here the second subscription concert! It was the first concert that took place in Cassel without my co-operation, and at which I was present from beginning to end as an auditor. It consisted of carefully rehearsed music: the two finales from "Zemire and Azor" and "Euryanthe;" of instrumental music *Mozart's C major* symphony with the fugue (called Jupiter); of concert things *Beethoven's* violin concerto with *Joachim's* cadences, and a concert piece by *Moscheles* for two pianofortes, called *Hommage à Händel*, very correctly and effectively played by Messrs. *Reiss* and *Tirendell*. The concert opened with the overture to "Rosamunda" by *Schubert*, one of his youthful works, but which is very pleasing, and was quite new to me. *Reiss* has again achieved great praise both by his arrangement and by his careful rehearsal and study of the music." In the same letter he farther says: "We have also had again two quartet parties, and I am happy to say, that I am still all right at the violin, only I must always prepare myself a few days before, which was not necessary some years ago!*"

---

* These quartet evenings in the society of a few of the families of his most intimate friends, were always a source of great pleasure to *Spohr*. Every year, on the approach of winter, he took early steps for their re-arrangement, and generally opened the series in his own house. Painful as it was to him whenever the death of one of the members of the circle caused a vacancy therein, the loss of his two oldest and most faithful friends, chief director *von Schmerfeld* and Lord marshall *von der Malsburg*, who had died in the two previous years, was long and deeply deplored by him.

The at this time still powerful impulse to compose, on the one hand, and the dread of being no longer capable of producing anything good and new on the other, gave rise to many painful struggles in the mind of *Spohr*, — till one morning he entered his wife's apartment, and with a cheerful countenance announced to her that he had found the right way to get out of the difficulty. He had resolved upon writing a requiem, and had already conceived some fine ideas for it; he had the greatest hopes that he would be able to complete it, and produce a worthy conclusion to his numerous works. In happy and inspired mood he now immediately went to work; and in a few days wrote the first subjects, but this pleasure, like that which he had shortly before boasted of in his quartet play, was soon dissipated. On the second day after Christmas Day, while on his wonted way to the reading room of the museum in the evening twilight he had the misfortune to fall over the stone steps at the entrance, and to break his left arm. Beyond all expectation, nevertheless, the fractured limb was happily healing fast, and when, after a lapse of several months, with anxious fear of the result, he once more took up his violin, to draw the first tones from it, the trial seemed quite satisfactory. But after several days' practice, followed up with great perseverance, he nevertheless became convinced to his great sorrow that his arm would never recover its lost strength and elasticity; upon which, as in this also he could no longer satisfy himself, deprived of another of the most precious elements of his existence, with a grieving heart he laid by his beloved violin!

Meanwhile, notwithstanding, many wished-for opportunities presented themselves elsewhere to *Spohr*, to keep alive his interest in musical enjoyments and to cheer him with the performance of his greater works. Scarcely was he recovered from the fracture of his arm, than he accepted an invitation to Magdeburg, to hear the performance of his oratorio, "Des Heilands letzte Stunden," which was to take place there on Good Friday. With this performance he expressed himself highly pleased, in a letter to Mr. *Lüders*: "Orchestra, choruses, and solo-singers were alike excellently practised in their respective parts, and the effect, in the church of St. Ulrich, which is so favorably constructed for sound, was indeed heavenly. The solo-voices, for the most part belonging to the *Seebach* choral society, were particularly fine, harmonious and powerful dilettante singers, and led by their director *Mühling* they were so penetrated with the true spirit of the composition, that I was quite taken by surprise, and delighted!

The accompaniment also of the solo instruments in the grand air of Mary in the second part was very fine; for *Grimm* the harpist had been sent for from Berlin, and the other solo instruments — violin, violincello and horn — were played by members of the present orchestra of the Magdeburg theatre, who are, as luck would have it, virtuosi."

In a similar letter of the 6th. April to *Hauptmann*, in speaking of his further contemplated plans of journey, he says: "Whether all these excursions will be carried into effect, is not yet decided; but for the rest of my life my artistic enjoyments are limited to them; for I am now perfectly convinced, that I cannot accomplish any great work more. I regret to say, that my last attempt of the kind failed, and my requiem remains a fragment; nevertheless, as the subject as far as the *Lacrimosa dies illa*, at which I stuck fast, pleases me well, and seems to have much that is new and ingenious in it, I shall not destroy it, as I should like to take it up again, and will make another attempt to complete it."

This attempt, to which with much perseverance he devoted half a day, proved however a failure, and brought him finally to the avowed painful determination to relinquish composition entirely; as he did not feel capable of putting his musical ideas into a distinct shape. At the conclusion of the letter adverted to, he says further: "I thank you heartily for your kind wishes upon my birth-day! Notwithstanding my present low spirits on account of my artistic impotency, I nevertheless passed it agreeably enough. That may have arisen from my happily performed journey." Scarcely three weeks afterwards, *Spohr*, again full of pleasurable anticipation, set out anew, and this time to Bremen, where the director of music *Engel* purposed to open his recently established choral society with the public performance of *Spohr's* oratorio, "The Fall of Babylon," a great undertaking, but so worthily executed that *Spohr* himself was greatly surprised and deeply moved.

For the beginning of July *Spohr* had been invited to Prague, where the half-centennial anniversary of the Conservatory of that city was to be celebrated by three grand musical performances — among which was his opera "Jessonda." The celebration of divine service in the cathedral on the first morning was followed in the evening by a grand concert in the theatre. It began with a new Symphony by *Kittl*, the director of the conservatory, which, like the other *Pièces d'Ensemble*, was performed by the pupils of the institution; while the solo-pieces were executed by foreign resident musicians who had received their education there; among these, the celebrated violinists *Dreyschock* and *Laub*. "On the second evening," in the words of the "Tagesboten aus Böhmen," "not only in honour of the great musician present, but in order to give every true lover of art a right festive evening, the 'Jessonda' of *Dr. Louis Spohr* was selected, and Prague had this time the satisfaction of seeing the inspired and still vigorous veteran conduct the performance of his work himself .... As *Spohr* took his place at the conductor's desk, which was hung with wreaths of laurel and ornamented with a crown of the same, he was received by the densely crowded house, which comprised all the leading artists and lovers of music of Prague, with long and enthusiastic applause. At every moment of interest, of which the fascinating "Jessonda," (the not yet surpassed model of German lyrical opera) is one uninterrupted beautiful chain, the most gratifying acclamations were first directed to the master, and then to the singers. After the second act, the venerable poet of sweet sounds was vehemently called forward upon the stage, as also after the last act, when another crown of laurel was thrown to him..... The conducting of the honoured master *Spohr* is still marked by unimpaired vigour, and attention to every detail; his stroke of the baton has its usual characteristic stamp" &c. The *concert spirituel*, which had been arranged for the third evening, as the finale to the musical part of the festival, comprised as chief subject, the ninth Symphony of *Beethoven*; but at the grand dinner given on the following day, a series of select musical pieces was performed, and the opportunity seized, both by loud calls for the repetition of the overture to "Jessonda," and every possible mode of demonstration, to honour *Spohr*, the Nestor of the numerously congregated musicians, as the king of the feast. Not less however than by all these demonstrations was he gratified by the kind anticipation of his wishes with the invitation to visit the country-house in the neighbourhood of Prague which had been hallowed by *Mozart's* lengthened residence; to which the present proprietor Herr *Popelka* himself accompanied him, to shew him the room, which *Spohr* also looked upon as sacred ground, where *Mozart* had composed his "Don Juan."

Spohr was less fortunate upon his return journey in realising a long-cherished and ardent wish. He had for several years vainly endeavoured to hear upon a foreign stage *Mozart's* opera "Idomeneo," which he had never been able to give a performance of in Cassel, and which was known to him only in the pianoforte selection. With this object also, already in the beginning of the summer, apart from and independent of his subsequently promised visit to Prague, he had projected a journey to Dresden, for the reason, as he then expressed in a letter to his friend *Lüder* — "that with the constantly increasing dearth in the repertory of modern operas, an as yet unheard opera of *Mozart* was too important an event, and for him an artistic necessity too great, that he should not joyfully undertake even a much longer journey to hear it." Long previously he had written on the subject to his friend the director of music *Reissiger*, and at length thought to see his hope realized in Dresden, either before or after the Prague musical festival.

Unfortunately, however, owing to the absence of the chief singers of the opera, it could not be carried out, and so, consoling himself meanwhile till the autumn, he took the road to Alexandersbad, where during a pleasant sojourn of a week, he reposed from the exertion of the previous journey in the enjoyment of the quiet relaxation he so much desired.

Greatly gratified, and visibly refreshed as *Spohr* again returned from this pleasant excursion to Alexandersbad, yet from that period he exhibited a constantly increasing low-spirited and thoughtful mood, which was so opposite to his former manner. To his wife, who vainly tried every means to cheer him, he would then reply after a protracted and earnest silence, that he was weary of life, as he could no longer be doing; that he had enjoyed to exhaustion all that mortal life could given, and lived to see a more widely spread recognition and love for his music than he even could have hoped for, — that now he ardently wished for death, before the infirmities of old age completely prostrated him. Nevertheless he always felt cheerfully moved again by invitations to new journeys, and musical enjoyments, of which several presented themselves in the autumn. In September namely, the journey to Wiesbaden to the musical festival of the Middle-Rhine, and in October to Leipsic, to the performance of his own and other works which particularly interested him, at the Gewandhaus concert, at the conservatory and at the church, — on which occasions he at both places followed the musical performances with persevering interest and pleasure, and received with lively satisfaction the various ovations of which he was the object. Although upon this journey to Leipsic, and lastly also to Dresden, he found no opportunity to realise his *most ardent expectation* to hear the "Idomeneo," he nevertheless was somewhat compensated for the disappointment by the kindness of the Frankfort theatrical Intendant, who on his previously expressed wish, announced *Cherubini's* opera of "Medea" for the evening of his arrival there, on his way through to Wiesbaden, and thus afforded him the high enjoyment of hearing that classically beautiful music.

As with the decrease in the length of the days and with the gloom of winter, the sleeplessness and nervous excitement which had affected him so prejudicially at Leipsic also, increased during the long nights, and from that time slowly but obviously augmented; leaving as their result a still greater debility and uneasiness during the day; his cheerfulness abandoned him entirely. — Shortly after his visit to Leipsic, where the orchestral pieces under the excellent direction of *Rietz* gave him especial pleasure, he wrote among other things to *Hauptmann* . . . . "I cannot express to you how this time all the music I heard in Leipsic pleased me. . . . From the devotional sentiment which your motette raised in me on Sunday, I envy you not a little the energy with which you still continue to work, while with me it is all over with composing and with violin play! Yesterday I received from *Zellner*, the musical critic at Vienna, the intelligence that one of my oratorios is to be performed there, and he invited me on the part of the originators of the design, to come and direct it myself. For several years the Austrian society had contemplated giving my 'Fall of Babylon' as a musical festival in the Imperial Riding School; but then, even with the aid of *Metternich*, I could not get permission to go there. Now, when I could get away, as I am an invalid, and the journey too far and fatiguing, I am obliged to renounce it. I shall therefore decline the invitation and content myself with shorter journeys in the fine season of the year. But on such occasions, struggles with my inclinations and low spirits always follow! and so one is induced to envy the lot of several who were personally known to me. who of late died suddenly. . . ." Impressed with similar painful thoughts and not without many inward struggles, *Spohr* wrote the letter to decline the invitation that he received at that time to Königsberg, to the centenary *Händel* Festival, where he had been chosen to direct the magnificent "Messiah" and one of his own works; and where it was intended to pay to him, as sole worthy representative of the great *Händel*, all the homage and honours which could not be rendered to *Händel* personally, in all the overflowing fulness of their warmth."*

As *Spohr* for many years had been considered by the whole musical world as the highest authority in everything that pertained to his art, a day seldom passed without bringing applications or requests of some kind, frequently from the most distant localities, which his ever-ready disposition to oblige never permitted him to leave unnoticed, but to which, now although with a heavy heart, he was more and more compelled to waive replying. One application nevertheless may here be mentioned, which, coming at a particularly favourable moment, rekindled his zest to make a last essay at composition, and which in reality also was his last! For many years he had been repeatedly solicited in the most irresistible words by Mr. *Chr. Schad*, the publisher of the Almanack of the German Muses, to write a few little songs for it, and *Spohr* had each time the satisfaction to learn that those willingly bestowed little contributions were received with a more than usual approbation. In the autumn of 1857, when with considerable timidity he had endeavoured to satisfy Mr *Schad's* urgent wish for a composition for the words of the old ballad of *Walter von der Vogelweide*, "the silent nightingale," he received a very poetical letter of thanks expressing the writers "admiration of the musical sentiment and depth of feeling with which the beautiful ballad had been rendered by the composer," and that "it is a great satisfaction for a German heart that two masters of his nation, although separated by an interval of six hundred years, should have exhibited the rich treasures

---

* To the many marks of honour which *Spohr* still received in the latter years of his life must be added also his nomination to the honorary membership of the "Musical Society," which had just previously been instituted in London. Upon the occasion of his presentation with this diploma, an enumeration of the various diplomas which he had already been presented with gave an amount of *Thirty-eight*, among which was one from New York, from Buenos-Ayres, St. Petersburg, and Stockholm, with two from Rome and two from Holland.

of their inmost feelings, in so noble, so simple and so harmonious a form of words and tone," &c. Now at length, in October 1858, six months after having laid aside his incompleted requiem as his last composition, he received another letter, beginning with the words: "Your silent nightingale which built her harmonious nest in the thick verdure of last year's Almanack of the Muses, has met with the loudest approbation of the German nation for the very eloquence of that silence. And who better than the loved great master *Spohr* would know how to utter sounds more replete with the soul's harmony, — who know how to move more deeply and purely a German heart! No wonder is it that I again knock at your door to-day. I come in the name of, and at the request of, more than eighty of the best hearts and heads in Germany, who have chosen me as their standard-bearer for a noble patriotic object.... I lay before you three of the most beautiful of *Göthe's* songs for your unrestricted choice, and resign myself to the pleasing hope of seeing one or the other enveloped in a melodious garb by your master-hand." And, indeed, already on the following morning his wife heard with joyful emotion the sound of the long-silent keys of the pianoforte, in his room, and his still pleasing voice as he sang in accompaniment. A few hours afterwards he came also with a look of pleasure to fetch her, to sing to her forthwith the new music he had composed to *Goethe's* "Herz, mein Herz, was soll das geben," having already completed it as regarded the chief thing; though the rhythm and conclusion not being yet to his fancy, would require a longer time to finish. When however, his wife, greatly pleased with the lively, pretty melody, could not refrain from making the observation that it had a very striking resemblance to *Beethoven's* composition to the same words, he assured her that he had no knowledge of it, or at least no recollection of it at all, but expressed the wish to have it procured, in order to satisfy himself of the resemblance. — With his own song he was now tolerably satisfied, and said, with truth also, that it would have a very good effect, if those who sung it did not *spoil it by too slow a Tempo*, as was so frequently the case with his compositions, a remark which is in so far characteristic, as *Spohr*, so often as he heard his works performed abroad, or not under his own immediate direction, always felt annoyed by the time being taken frequently *too slow*, but scarcely ever complained of one taken *too fast*. When at length the new song was studied under his superintendance by his niece *Emma Spohr*, who, gifted with a fine voice, always sung songs of the kind in the family-circle, he sang to her himself with the most lively emotion, and with almost breathless rapidity, the three closely following strophes, without interlude, to encourage her to a similar execution. But a few weeks afterwards, when he again caught sight of the manuscript, he said, with a sorrowful expression of face, that the song was worthless, and regretted that he had sent it for publication in the Almanack of the Muses!

As evidence of his restless impulse to be usefully active, one instance may here be adduced:

When, after breaking his arm, he was compelled to give up violin playing himself, he thought also that he could no longer give satisfaction as a *Teacher* of his instrument; he had dismissed his last violin pupils, young persons without pecuniary means whom he instructed from a humane feeling and zeal for the art. — But now, in December 1858, he again resumed his labours as a beneficent instructor, and expressed himself to *Hauptmann* upon the subject in the following words: "In order still to be somewhat actively engaged in the cause of art, I have commenced giving pianoforte lessons gratis to a young lady who wishes to qualify herself for a teacher of that instrument. But when it is requisite to play anything to my pupil, I am of course obliged to call my wife or sister-in-law to my assistance."

In this manner, the this time especially dreaded winter, — his last — had come! On New Year's morning 1859, after a sleepless and restless night passed in a state of painful nervous excitement, he received in earnest silence the wishes of the season from his family and friends, — but still looked forward with hope to a "fine spring and summer," which he contemplated passing happily once more, partly at home among his favorite flowers, and partly in little journeys. For such journeys, which his friends always designated as "little triumphal excursions," the most alluring invitations had again long been received from all sides, but of these of course he could only accept those which were to places most easily accessible. When upon such occasions with an effusion of grateful satisfaction he gave utterance to his feelings in the words: "It often seems to me as though all the world thought only of conferring upon me a very feast of pleasure before I die," it was unfortunately always followed by the sad addition: "but no one knows how miserable I feel, and no one can relieve me of my sufferings." — With almost morbid impatience he now looked forward to the next spring, when he had proposed to himself, at the special request of *John J. Bott*, who was now appointed director of music at the court orchestra of Meiningen, to proceed thither, to direct the concert which was then to be given for the benefit of the widow's relief fund. The few hours occupied by the journey on the newly-opened Werra railway were easy and comfortable to him, and upon his reception at the terminus of Meiningen *Spohr* was particularly gratified at meeting once more both his favorite pupils *Grund* and *Bott*, who greeted their honoured master with expressions of the heartiest welcome, and who the next day were unwearied in showing their grateful attachment to him in every possible manner. Immediately on the first evening, as a further festive welcome, a grand serenade by torch-light was given to him, in which under *Bott's* conducting (in the *Spohr* style), male choral and four-part-songs interchanged alternately with the music of the full orchestra; and at the close, at the moment when the cheers of the assembled crowds were loudest, the whole living mass was suddenly illumined by the coloured fires of a brilliant sun, which disclosed also to view, as though by magic, the fine parks opposite the house. At the rehearsal for the concert on the following evening, *Spohr* found all the musical pieces so carefully studied and in accordance with all his intentions, that he could look forward with pleasing certainty to its performance on the next evening, and the more so, as the two directors of music, *Grund* and *Bott*, felt an especial pleasure in resuming their former places under the direction of their master, as co-operating violinists in the orchestra, and in thus giving him the most powerful support.

The "Meininger Tageblatt" makes mention of the concert in the following terms: "Upon the stage, between branches of palm and laurel, was placed a collossal bust of *Spohr*. The conductor's desk had been decorated by female hands with ingenious devices and garlands of flowers. The house, filled to overflowing, awaited in breathless suspense the appearance of the famed old master. 'He comes!' .... was whispered through the spacious house, and a thousand-tongued welcome of joy greeted the honoured man. In a few minutes afterwards he had lifted the conductor's baton — a solemn silence immediately ensued; and in a few moments the first notes of the symphony "Die Weihe der Töne" resounded. The eyes of all were directed to the Nestor of the science of music, who brought to our mind the Olympian Jove — *omnia supercilio moventis*. All the orchestral assistants felt the importance of the moment, and lent their most efficient aid. The same calm which everywhere breathes through the works of this musician was seen also in his conducting. Not the least fraction of a beat was thrown away — in all and everywhere, were seen the director of orchestra and the musicians, as a grand impersonated whole, achieving in every part a fresh triumph. The honoured poet of sweet sounds directed besides his grand symphony, five other of his works, and with so steady a hand, that the crowded house was filled with admiration." ... This part of the concert in which *Spohr* wielded for *the last time* the conductor's baton, comprised among the rest, his concertante in *H minor*, which was executed by director of music *Bott* and concert-master

Müller in a masterly manner, and gave him great pleasure. In appropriate choice followed the overture to the "Mountain Sprite," with which thirty-four years before he had opened the festive celebration of the marriage of the ducal pair. As upon that occasion the exalted couple listened with pleasure to the tones of the master, and exhibited a warm interest not only by their presence at the rehearsal and performance, but by the most marked attentions; and the duke, who many years previously had presented *Spohr* with the cross of knighthood of the order of the house of Saxe-Ernest, changed it upon this occasion for the grand cross of the order. — The last evening in Meiningen was further celebrated in honour of *Spohr* by a grand masonic fête, which afforded him no less gratification; as also a hearty written testimony of thanks addressed to him by the intendant of the court orchestra, Mr. *von Liliencron*, from which, as it refers to *Spohr's last appearance as conductor*, we may here cite some words, which will perpetuate the memory of that day: "The house filled to the very utmost, — the enthusiastic acclamations, — the flowers and wreaths, testified to you yesterday, how fascinated we all were by your tones, how deeply moved at the sight of the loved and highly honoured master. If the recollection of that delightful evening will remain indelibly impressed upon all who were present, so will the benign purpose of that concert impress the recollection of your appearance among us; for in future years, when it shall be read what was presented on the 12th. April 1859 to the widows and orphans by the court orchestra of Meiningen, it will be said: that was the day on which *Spohr*, the master, wielded the conductor's baton in our midst."

A second journey undertaken shortly after by *Spohr*, was to the pleasant little princely residence of Detmold, where he was again welcomed by a grateful pupil, the director of music *Kiel*, and its art-loving prince, in a similar manner as in Meiningen, with two successive days of festivities in his honour. The proffered direction of a grand concert solely embracing his own compositions he had firmly declined, and as auditor could therefore give himself up more completely to the enjoyment of his own excellently performed music, two numbers of which in particular afforded him exceeding pleasure; the performance namely by his former pupils *Kiel* and concertmaster *Bargheer*, who together executed his *A minor* concertante, and the symphony "Die Jahreszeiten" — a favorite and prominent point of excellence with the court orchestra of Detmold — and which he had especially chosen by a previously communicated request.

Returned once more to Cassel after a week happily passed in the midst of the enjoyment of art and nature, *Spohr* unhappily could no longer conceal from himself, that even these short journeys were now followed by many painful results, in the shape of a yet more increased nervous restlessness at night — yet his spirit soon yearned again for diversity and change of place, and especially towards his favorite Alexandersbad, where he confidently hoped a longer stay in the fine air of that locality would again induce an improvement in his health, and particulary restore his sleep at night. Strengthened in this belief by the opinion of his ever-sympathising and watchful medical attendant Dr. Ad. *Harnier*, he set out for Alexandersbad, where he remained some weeks. His health improved, and he passed better nights. But on his return he visited Würzburg, and was present at the performance of his "Letzte Dinge;" and this, and his reception, and the leave-taking, made such an impression on him, that it went far to neutralize the improvement in his health that had taken place at Alexandersbad.

His pleasure at hearing good music remained with him to the last, for which reason he never missed a concert, and even frequently went to the theatre, where above all things the music so dear to his heart — the operas of *Mozart* — ever filled him anew with the fresh transports of a youthful joy. — At home he passed the greater part of the day in reading, but no longer as formerly in that of political journals and instructive scientific works, which had excited and absorbed his interest, — he now delighted rather in entertaining moral works, simple novels that appealed to the heart, and the like, which for the time distracted his attention from his suffering condition. — At frequent intervals he would request his wife to play something to him, and herein he would shew a preference for the pianoforte music of *Bach* and *Mendelssohn*, yet without withdrawing his interest from the productions of more modern composers.

A pleasing diversion in the uniform sameness of his everyday life, was afforded to him in the first days of October by a visit to the princess *Anna*, wife of prince *Frederick*, the heir apparent to the Hessian throne, at the express invitation of that princess, during a residence of some days at Cassel in the Bellevue palace. Upon his return he related with feelings of pleasure the amiable anticipatory attentions of the princess, who, in consideration of *Spohr*'s greater convenience, had descended with her husband and child, prince *Wilhelm*, then five years old, to an apartment on the ground-floor, where he was received, and where after a lengthened pleasing conversation with the princely pair, she, at the conclusion, besought him with the most winning kindliness of manner, to write a few lines by way of souvenir in her album. In satisfaction of this request, on the 7th. October, he wrote, though indeed with a weak and tremulous hand, yet with his usual readiness, a particularly requested passage of the well-known duett in "Jessonda," in the costly album that had been forwarded to his house.

On Sunday the 16th. October, a change, at first scarcely observable, evinced itself in his condition: an expression of calm contentment such as not had been seen for a long time, settled on his features; in spite of the preceding restless night, of the obvious continual bodily sufferings and increasing debility no more complainings were heard to fall from his lips; yet he was more than usually silent. and though he replied in a kind tone to every inquiry adressed to him, it was as short as possible. In the afternoon, on rising from the dinner-table, he stood for a long time at the open door of the house, musing as he gazed upon the rich autumnal beauties of his flower-garden, — but upon the proposition of his wife to take his coffee outside under the bower, he replied, that he wished to take it that day in his room, and that she with her sister would play something to him. This of course was with pleasure immediately complied with. After he had listened to some symphonies arranged for four hands, — apparently as though half-lost in a dream, yet as might be inferred from many remarks that fell from him, with much attention, he requested further by way of conclusion, his newest quintet (Op. 144, *G-minor*) with the piano-forte arrangement of which for four hands he had but shortly before become acquainted; to this also he listened with full interest and obvious satisfaction. After the last theme he inquired: "How long ago may it be that I wrote that?" and when his wife, who could not immediately remember the year, replied it might be perhaps three or four years ago, — he said with a sigh: "Then *there* I did still succeed in effecting it! and now I can no longer do so!" With these words he rose from his chair, to prepare for his customary evening walk to the reading rooms, which, despite all his weakness and some admonitions from his wife, he nevertheless slowly, and supported by her, still persevered in. But feeling exceedingly anxious at home respecting him, she despatched a devotedly attached servant to see after him, much earlier than he had been ordered to bring him back: upon which, in a condition of extreme debility, he immediately permitted himself to be led home, and shortly after his frugal supper to be put to bed. After the usual parting evening kiss, he said to his wife: "he hoped from being so tired he should at length have a *good night's rest*," — and thereupon sank into a soft slumber from which he did not awake till the next morning and then with a cheerful mien. He had found the much-desired repose, he felt no longer any bodily suffering, the serene expression of his countenance betokened it from that moment to his last breath! To rise he refused; neither would he take breakfast; but requested his wife to sit on the bed beside him; took her hand, and kissed it tenderly, with an affectionate expression in his kindly beaming eyes that spoke to her more eloquently than could a thousand words. Shortly afterwards his attentive physician arrived, and immediately perceived that a higher power had granted to him the long-desired rest. His family was already prepared for the approaching heart-rending separation. His children and nephews, near and distant friends, hastened to his couch, all desirous to look as long as possible on his loved and honoured face, each glad to snatch one look more from his truthful loving eyes! In this manner he lay, surrounded by all that were most dear to him in life, in calm repose; from day to day with decreasing consciousness of existence; in spirit mayhap, already appertaining to a higher world, — until the evening of the 22nd. Oct. (1859), when at half-past ten his weary eyes closed for ever! — —

The pious tones which once with a holy inspiration had gushed from the pure fount of his soul — tones to which he had himself listened in silent devotion but a few weeks before, — resounded now in mourning over his grave; and sad and sorrowful, though at the same time sweetly consolatory, still echo far and wide to the hearts of all:

"Blessed are the dead, v die in the Lord, now and for ever. They repose from their labours, and their works follow them!"

Finis.

Music and Books published by Travis & Emery Music Bookshop:
Anon.: Hymnarium Sarisburiense, cum Rubricis et Notis Musicis.
Agricola, Johann Friedrich from Tosi: Anleitung zur Singkunst.
Bach, C.P.E.: edited W. Emery: Nekrolog or Obituary Notice of J.S. Bach.
Bateson, Naomi Judith: Alcock of Salisbury
Bathe, William: A Briefe Introduction to the Skill of Song
Bax, Arnold: Symphony #5, Arranged for Piano Four Hands by Walter Emery
Burney, Charles: The Present State of Music in France and Italy
Burney, Charles: The Present State of Music in Germany, The Netherlands …
Burney, Charles: An Account of the Musical Performances ... Handel
Burney, Karl: Nachricht von Georg Friedrich Handel's Lebensumstanden.
Burns, Robert: The Caledonian Musical Museum ..The Best Scotch Songs. (1810)
Cobbett, W.W.: Cobbett's Cyclopedic Survey of Chamber Music. (2 vols.)
Corrette, Michel: Le Maitre de Clavecin
Crimp, Bryan: Dear Mr. Rosenthal … Dear Mr. Gaisberg …
Crimp, Bryan: Solo: The Biography of Solomon
d'Indy, Vincent: Beethoven: Biographie Critique
d'Indy, Vincent: Beethoven: A Critical Biography
d'Indy, Vincent: César Franck (in French)
Fischhof, Joseph: Versuch einer Geschichte des Clavierbaues. (Faksimile 1853).
Frescobaldi, Girolamo: D'Arie Musicali per Cantarsi. Primo & Secondo Libro.
Geminiani, Francesco: The Art of Playing the Violin.
Handel; Purcell; Boyce; Geene et al: Calliope or English Harmony: Volume First.
Häuser: Musikalisches Lexikon. 2 vols in one.
Hawkins, John: A General History of the Science and Practice of Music (5 vols.)
Herbert-Caesari, Edgar: The Science and Sensations of Vocal Tone
Herbert-Caesari, Edgar: Vocal Truth
Hopkins and Rimboult: The Organ. Its History and Construction.
Hunt, John: - see separate list of discographies at the end of these titles
Isaacs, Lewis: Hänsel and Gretel. A Guide to Humperdinck's Opera.
Isaacs, Lewis: Königskinder (Royal Children) A Guide to Humperdinck's Opera.
Kastner: Manuel Général de Musique Militaire
Lacassagne, M. l'Abbé Joseph : Traité Général des élémens du Chant.
Lascelles (née Catley), Anne: The Life of Miss Anne Catley.
Mainwaring, John: Memoirs of the Life of the Late George Frederic Handel
Malcolm, Alexander: A Treaty of Music: Speculative, Practical and Historical
Marx, Adolph Bernhard: Die Kunst des Gesanges, Theoretisch-Practisch
May, Florence: The Life of Brahms
May, Florence: The Girlhood Of Clara Schumann: Clara Wieck And Her Time.
Mellers, Wilfrid: Angels of the Night: Popular Female Singers of Our Time
Mellers, Wilfrid: Bach and the Dance of God
Mellers, Wilfrid: Beethoven and the Voice of God
Mellers, Wilfrid: Caliban Reborn - Renewal in Twentieth Century Music

Music and Books published by Travis & Emery Music Bookshop:
Mellers, Wilfrid: Darker Shade of Pale, A Backdrop to Bob Dylan
Mellers, Wilfrid: François Couperin and the French Classical Tradition
Mellers, Wilfrid: Harmonious Meeting
Mellers, Wilfrid: Le Jardin Retrouvé, The Music of Frederic Mompou
Mellers, Wilfrid: Music and Society, England and the European Tradition
Mellers, Wilfrid: Music in a New Found Land: … … American Music
Mellers, Wilfrid: Romanticism and the Twentieth Century (from 1800)
Mellers, Wilfrid: The Masks of Orpheus: …… the Story of European Music.
Mellers, Wilfrid: The Sonata Principle (from c. 1750)
Mellers, Wilfrid: Vaughan Williams and the Vision of Albion
Panchianio, Cattuffio: Rutzvanscad Il Giovine
Pearce, Charles: Sims Reeves, Fifty Years of Music in England.
Playford, John: An Introduction to the Skill of Musick.
Purcell, Henry et al: Harmonia Sacra … The First Book, (1726)
Purcell, Henry et al: Harmonia Sacra … Book II (1726)
Quantz, Johann: Versuch einer Anweisung die Flöte trave rsiere zu spielen.
Rameau, Jean-Philippe: Code de Musique Pratique, ou Methodes.
Rastall, Richard: The Notation of Western Music.
Rimbault, Edward: The Pianoforte, Its Origins, Progress, and Construction.
Rousseau, Jean Jacques: Dictionnaire de Musique
Rubinstein, Anton : Guide to the proper use of the Pianoforte Pedals.
Sainsbury, John S.: Dictionary of Musicians. (1825). 2 vols.
Serré de Rieux, Jean de : Les dons des Enfans de Latone
Simpson, Christopher: A Compendium of Practical Musick in Five Parts
Spohr, Louis: Autobiography
Spohr, Louis: Grand Violin School
Tans'ur, William: A New Musical Grammar; or The Harmonical Spectator
Terry, Charles Sanford: Bach's Chorals – Parts 1, 2 and 3.
Terry, Charles Sanford: John Christian Bach
Terry, Charles Sanford: J.S. Bach's Original Hymn-Tunes for Congregational Use.
Terry, Charles Sanford: Four-Part Chorals of J.S. Bach. (German & English)
Terry, Charles Sanford: Joh. Seb. Bach, Cantata Texts, Sacred and Secular.
Terry, Charles Sanford: The Origins of the Family of Bach Musicians.
Tosi, Pierfrancesco: Opinioni de' Cantori Antichi, e Moderni
Tosi, Pierfrancesco: Observations on the Florid Song.
Van der Straeten, Edmund: History of the Violoncello, The Viol da Gamba …
Van der Straeten, Edmund: History of the Violin, Its Ancestors… (2 vols.)
Walther, J. G. [Waltern]: Musicalisches Lexikon [Musikalisches Lexicon]
Zwirn, Gerald: Stranded Stories From The Operas

Travis & Emery Music Bookshop
17 Cecil Court, London, WC2N 4EZ, United Kingdom.
Tel. (+44) 20 7240 2129

© Travis & Emery 2010

Discographies by Travis & Emery:
Discographies by John Hunt.

1987: 978-1-906857-14-1: From Adam to Webern: the Recordings of von Karajan.
1991: 978-0-951026-83-0: 3 Italian Conductors and 7 Viennese Sopranos: 10 Discographies: Arturo Toscanini, Guido Cantelli, Carlo Maria Giulini, Elisabeth Schwarzkopf, Irmgard Seefried, Elisabeth Gruemmer, Sena Jurinac, Hilde Gueden, Lisa Della Casa, Rita Streich.
1992: 978-0-951026-85-4: Mid-Century Conductors and More Viennese Singers: 10 Discographies: Karl Boehm, Victor De Sabata, Hans Knappertsbusch, Tullio Serafin, Clemens Krauss, Anton Dermota, Leonie Rysanek, Eberhard Waechter, Maria Reining, Erich Kunz.
1993: 978-0-951026-87-8: More 20th Century Conductors: 7 Discographies: Eugen Jochum, Ferenc Fricsay, Carl Schuricht, Felix Weingartner, Josef Krips, Otto Klemperer, Erich Kleiber.
1994: 978-0-951026-88-5: Giants of the Keyboard: 6 Discographies: Wilhelm Kempff, Walter Gieseking, Edwin Fischer, Clara Haskil, Wilhelm Backhaus, Artur Schnabel.
1994: 978-0-951026-89-2: Six Wagnerian Sopranos: 6 Discographies: Frieda Leider, Kirsten Flagstad, Astrid Varnay, Martha Moedl, Birgit Nilsson, Gwyneth Jones.
1995: 978-0-952582-70-0: Musical Knights: 6 Discographies: Henry Wood, Thomas Beecham, Adrian Boult, John Barbirolli, Reginald Goodall, Malcolm Sargent.
1995: 978-0-952582-71-7: A Notable Quartet: 4 Discographies: Gundula Janowitz, Christa Ludwig, Nicolai Gedda, Dietrich Fischer-Dieskau.
1996: 978-0-952582-75-5: Leopold Stokowski (1882-1977): Discography and Concert Register
1996: 978-0-952582-76-2: Makers of the Philharmonia: 11 Discographies: Alceo Galliera, Walter Susskind, Paul Kletzki, Nicolai Malko, Issay Dobrowen, Lovro Von Matacic, Efrem Kurtz, Otto Ackermann, Anatole Fistoulari, George Weldon, Robert Irving.
1996: 978-0-952582-72-4: The Post-War German Tradition: 5 Discographies: Rudolf Kempe, Joseph Keilberth, Wolfgang Sawallisch, Rafael Kubelik, Andre Cluytens.
1996: 978-0-952582-73-1: Teachers and Pupils: 7 Discographies: Elisabeth Schwarzkopf, Maria Ivoguen, Maria Cebotari, Meta Seinemeyer, Ljuba Welitsch, Rita Streich, Erna Berger.
1996: 978-0-952582-75-5: Leopold Stokowski: Discography and Concert Listing.
1996: 978-0-952582-76-2: Makers of the Philharmonia: 11 Discographies Alceo Galliera, Walter Susskind, Paul Kletzki, Nicolai Malko, Issay Dobrowen, Lovro Von Matacic, Efrem Kurtz, Otto Ackermann, Anatole Fistoulari, George Weldon, Robert Irving.
1996: 978-0-952582-77-9: Tenors in a Lyric Tradition: 3 Discographies: Peter Anders, Walther Ludwig, Fritz Wunderlich.
1997: 978-0-952582-78-6: The Lyric Baritone: 5 Discographies: Hans Reinmar, Gerhard Huesch, Josef Metternich, Hermann Uhde, Eberhard Waechter.
1997: 978-0-952582-79-3: Hungarians in Exile: 3 Discographies: Fritz Reiner, Antal Dorati, George Szell.
1997: 978-1-901395-00-6: The Art of the Diva: 3 Discographies: Claudia Muzio, Maria Callas, Magda Olivero.
1997: 978-1-901395-01-3: Metropolitan Sopranos: 4 Discographies: Rosa Ponselle, Eleanor Steber, Zinka Milanov, Leontyne Price.
1997: 978-1-901395-02-0: Back From The Shadows: 4 Discographies: Willem Mengelberg, Dimitri Mitropoulos, Hermann Abendroth, Eduard Van Beinum.
1997: 978-1-901395-03-7: More Musical Knights: 4 Discographies: Hamilton Harty, Charles Mackerras, Simon Rattle, John Pritchard.
1998: 978-1-901395-95-2: More Giants of the Keyboard: 5 Discographies: Claudio Arrau, Gyorgy Cziffra, Vladimir Horowitz, Dinu Lipatti, Artur Rubinstein.

1998: 978-1-901395-94-5: Conductors On The Yellow Label: 8 Discographies: Fritz Lehmann, Ferdinand Leitner, Ferenc Fricsay, Eugen Jochum, Leopold Ludwig, Artur Rother, Franz Konwitschny, Igor Markevitch.

1998: 978-1-901395-96-9: Mezzo and Contraltos: 5 Discographies: Janet Baker, Margarete Klose, Kathleen Ferrier, Giulietta Simionato, Elisabeth Hoengen.

1999: 978-1-901395-97-6: The Furtwaengler Sound Sixth Edition: Discography and Concert Listing.

1999: 978-1-901395-98-3: The Great Dictators: 3 Discographies: Evgeny Mravinsky, Artur Rodzinski, Sergiu Celibidache.

1999: 978-1-901395-99-0: Sviatoslav Richter: Pianist of the Century: Discography.

2000: 978-1-901395-04-4: Philharmonic Autocrat 1: Discography of: Herbert Von Karajan [Third Edition].

2000: 978-1-901395-05-1: Wiener Philharmoniker 1 - Vienna Philharmonic and Vienna State Opera Orchestras: Discography Part 1 1905-1954.

2000: 978-1-901395-06-8: Wiener Philharmoniker 2 - Vienna Philharmonic and Vienna State Opera Orchestras: Discography Part 2 1954-1989.

2001: 978-1-901395-07-5: Gramophone Stalwarts: 3 Separate Discographies: Bruno Walter, Erich Leinsdorf, Georg Solti.

2001: 978-1-901395-08-2: Singers of the Third Reich: 5 Discographies: Helge Roswaenge, Tiana Lemnitz, Franz Voelker, Maria Mueller, Max Lorenz.

2001: 978-1-901395-09-9: Philharmonic Autocrat 2: Concert Register of Herbert Von Karajan Second Edition.

2002: 978-1-901395-10-5: Sächsische Staatskapelle Dresden: Complete Discography.

2002: 978-1-901395-11-2: Carlo Maria Giulini: Discography and Concert Register.

2002: 978-1-901395-12-9: Pianists For The Connoisseur: 6 Discographies: Arturo Benedetti Michelangeli, Alfred Cortot, Alexis Weissenberg, Clifford Curzon, Solomon, Elly Ney.

2003: 978-1-901395-14-3: Singers on the Yellow Label: 7 Discographies: Maria Stader, Elfriede Troetschel, Annelies Kupper, Wolfgang Windgassen, Ernst Haefliger, Josef Greindl, Kim Borg.

2003: 978-1-901395-15-0: A Gallic Trio: 3 Discographies: Charles Muench, Paul Paray, Pierre Monteux.

2004: 978-1-901395-16-7: Antal Dorati 1906-1988: Discography and Concert Register.

2004: 978-1-901395-17-4: Columbia 33CX Label Discography.

2004: 978-1-901395-18-1: Great Violinists: 3 Discographies: David Oistrakh, Wolfgang Schneiderhan, Arthur Grumiaux.

2006: 978-1-901395-19-8: Leopold Stokowski: Second Edition of the Discography.

2006: 978-1-901395-20-4: Wagner Im Festspielhaus: Discography of the Bayreuth Festival.

2006: 978-1-901395-21-1: Her Master's Voice: Concert Register and Discography of Dame Elisabeth Schwarzkopf [Third Edition].

2007: 978-1-901395-22-8: Hans Knappertsbusch: Kna: Concert Register and Discography of Hans Knappertsbusch, 1888-1965. Second Edition.

2008: 978-1-901395-23-5: Philips Minigroove: Second Extended Version of the European Discography.

2009: 978-1-901395-24-2: American Classics: The Discographies of Leonard Bernstein and Eugene Ormandy.

2010: 978-1-901395-25-9: Dirigenten der DDR: Conductors of the German Democratic Republic

Discography by Stephen J. Pettitt, edited by John Hunt:

1987: 978-1-906857-16-5: Philharmonia Orchestra: Complete Discography 1945-1987

Available from: Travis & Emery at 17 Cecil Court, London, UK. (+44) 20 7 240 2129. email on sales@travis-and-emery.com .

© Travis & Emery 2010

www.ingramcontent.com/pod-product-compliance
Lightning Source LLC
Chambersburg PA
CBHW082017300426
44117CB00015B/2261